Harden's

LONDON restaurants 2023

SURVEY DRIVEN REVIEWS OF 1.7K RESTAURANTS

Take your dining to the next level

Enjoy benefits at the UK's Best Restaurants

Join today at hardens.com

© Harden's Limited 2022

ISBN 978-1-9160761-4-3

British Library Cataloguing-in-Publication data: a catalogue record for this book is available from the British Library.

Printed in the UK by CPI Books

Assistant editors: Bruce Millar, Antonia Russell

Harden's Limited
Missionworks, 41 Iffley Road, London W6 0PB

Would restaurateurs (and PRs) please address communications to 'Editorial' at the above address, or ideally by email to: editorial@hardens.com

The contents of this book are believed correct at the time of printing. Nevertheless, the publisher can accept no responsibility for errors or changes in or omissions from the details given.

No part of this publication may be reproduced or transmitted in any form or by any means, electronically or mechanically, including photocopying, recording or any information storage or retrieval system, without prior permission in writing from the publisher.

CONTENTS

Ratings & prices

How this guide is written

Survey results
Most mentioned 11
Nominations 12
Highest ratings 14
Best by cuisine 16

The restaurant scene 18

Openings and closures 20

Directory 24

Area overviews 262

Maps 298
1 – London overview
2 – West End overview
3 – Mayfair & St James's
4 – West Soho
5 – East Soho, Chinatown & Covent Garden
6 – Knightsbridge, Chelsea & South Kensington
7 – Notting Hill & Bayswater
8 – Hammersmith & Chiswick
9 – Hampstead, Camden Town & Islington
10 – The City
11 – South London (& Fulham)
12 – Docklands
13 – Shoreditch & Hoxton
14 – East End

RATINGS & PRICES

Ratings

Our rating system does not tell you – as most guides do – that expensive restaurants are often better than cheap ones! What we do is compare each restaurant's performance – as judged by the average ratings awarded by reporters in the survey – with other similarly-priced restaurants. This approach has the advantage that it helps you find – whatever your budget for any particular meal – where you will get the best 'bang for your buck'.

The following qualities are assessed:

F — Food
S — Service
A — Ambience

The rating indicates that, ***in comparison with other restaurants in the same price-bracket**,* performance is…

5 — Exceptional
4 — Very good
3 — Good
2 — Average
1 — Poor

Prices

The price shown for each restaurant is the cost for one (1) person of an average three-course dinner with half a bottle of house wine and coffee, any cover charge, service and VAT. Lunch is often cheaper. With BYO restaurants, we have assumed that two people share a £7 bottle of off-licence wine.

Map reference *– shown immediately after the telephone number.*

Full postcodes *– for non-group restaurants, the first entry in the 'small print' at the end of each listing, so you can set your sat-nav.*

Website, Instagram *– shown in the small print, where applicable.*

Last orders time *– listed after the website (if applicable); Sunday may be up to 90 minutes earlier.*

Opening hours *– unless otherwise stated, restaurants are open for lunch and dinner seven days a week.*

Credit and debit cards *– unless otherwise stated, Mastercard, Visa, Amex and Maestro are accepted.*

Dress *– where appropriate, the management's preferences concerning patrons' dress are given.*

Sustainability *– if a restaurant or group has a star rating from the Sustainable Restaurants Association, this is shown.*

HOW THIS GUIDE IS WRITTEN

Celebrating our 32nd year!
This guide is based on our annual poll of what 'ordinary' diners-out think of London's restaurants. The first such survey was in 1991 with a few over 100 people taking part. This year, the total number of reporters in our combined London/UK survey, conducted mainly online, numbered 3,500, and, between them, they contributed 30,000 individual reports. Last year, some aspects of the guide needed amendment in order to allow for the effects of the Covid pandemic: for example, presenting two years of openings in a single edition. As far as possible this year, the format and content have been arranged on the same basis as all previous years, on the presumption and hope that where we are now is the long-anticipated 'new normal'.

How intelligent is AI?
At a time when the credibility of online reviews and influencer posts are under ongoing scrutiny, there is an ever-greater need for trusted sources such as the Harden's annual national diners' poll. In particular, the active curation by humans that we provide. For – while obviously folks can attempt to stuff the Harden's ballot too – our high degree of editorial oversight, plus our historical data about both the restaurants and those commenting, makes it much harder to cheat. In this way Harden's can socially source restaurant feedback, but – vitally – curate it carefully. It is this careful curation that provides extra 'value-added' for diners.

How we determine the ratings
In general, ratings are arrived at statistically. We create a ranking akin to football leagues, with the most expensive restaurants in the top league and the cheaper ones in lower ones. Any restaurant's ranking *within its own particular league* determines its ratings.

How we write the reviews
The tone of each review and the ratings are guided by the ranking of the restaurant concerned, derived as described above. At the margin, we may also pay regard to the balance of positive votes (such as for 'favourite restaurant') against negative ones (such as for 'most overpriced'). To explain why an entry has been rated as it has, we extract snippets from user comments ("enclosed in double quotes"). On well-known restaurants, we receive several hundred reports, and a short summary cannot do individual justice to all of them. What we seek to do – *without any regard to our own personal opinions* – is to illustrate key themes in the collective feedback.

How do we find our reporters?
Anyone can take part. Register now at www.hardens.com if you have not already done so! In fact, we find that once people have taken part, they often continue to do so.

Emerging from two years in which the pandemic kept them closed for long periods and caused untold disruption, restaurants barely had time to take a breath before they were hit by a whirlwind of price rises and staffing issues that threaten to be even more damaging.

Soaring energy costs, sky-rocketing food inflation, combined with a dearth of people ready, willing, or able to take up the tens of thousands of vacancies, has seen many restaurants reluctantly forced to reduce opening hours or mothball sites as well as rethink menus.

Just as they demonstrated incredible creativity, resilience, and innovation to keep serving us (when permitted) through Covid, our favourite places for eating out are, for the most part, putting those attributes to good use again. Even more hearteningly, many have spotted that we've really hit the perfect nexus between what's good for business and the planet.

How can diners spot those restaurants that are taking action to tackle climate change while simultaneously protect their profits?

With energy prices up as much as 400% and the UK experiencing record temperatures (another tangible reminder of the climate crisis), more restaurants are switching to induction hobs, providing a cleaner, more efficient cooking process as well as a cooler kitchen.

Shorter menus, featuring whole, local and seasonal ingredients, many with more veg-based dishes are becoming the norm, as chefs and restaurants look to reduce their food costs and minimise waste, while also taking account of smaller kitchen teams. The scarcity of vegetable oil, caused by the war in Ukraine means you're likely to notice some restaurants eschewing the deep frier – creating a third additional beneficiary – your health.

The real mark of a restaurant that's taking real steps to serve up meals designed to help you use the power of your appetite wisely is one boasting Food Made Good stars – awarded to those that complete the Sustainable Restaurant Association's Rating and that reach the requisite scores. From January 2022, the Green Claims Code has provided us all with a citizens' charter to challenge spurious sustainability claims. A valid rating from the SRA, is the best way for a restaurant to demonstrate that it's not just talking the sustainability talk.

Knowing what sustainable food really looks and tastes like doesn't come naturally to all. Throughout 2023, encouraged by the SRA, many restaurants will be highlighting their One Planet Plate – as part of the continuing campaign to point out the most sustainable dishes on the menu so you can vote with your fork for a better food future.

Look out for those restaurants serving a One Planet Plate, (www.oneplanetplate.org) and search in the guide for those with an SRA Food Made Good Sustainability Rating, either One, Two or Three Stars, achieved by proving they are taking action on these ten key things:

- Support Global Farmers
- Value Natural Resources
- Treat People Fairly
- Feed Children Well
- Celebrate Local
- Source Fish Responsibly
- Serve More Veg & Better Meat
- Reduce Reuse Recycle
- Waste no Food
- Support the Community

www.foodmadegood.org
Twitter: @the_SRA
Instagram: @foodmadegood

www.oneplanetplate.org
@oneplanetplateglobal

HOW THIS GUIDE IS WRITTEN

Consequently, many people who complete the survey have done so before. With high repeat-participation, the end-result is really more the product of a very large and ever-evolving panel, or jury, than a random 'poll'.

Wouldn't a random sample be better?
That's a theoretical question, as there is no obvious way, still less a cost-efficient one, to identify a random sample of the guests at each of, say, 5,000 establishments across the UK, and get them to take part in any sort of survey. People steeped in statistical market research tend be most keen on this idea. Other folks accept that having someone stand with a clipboard at Oxford Circus asking random people their opinion on Le Gavroche is unlikely to glean useful data.

Do people ever try to stuff the ballot?
Of course they do! Sometimes with the aid of social media agencies. Many rogue entries are weeded out every year. But stuffing the ballot is not as trivial a task as some people seem to think: the survey results throw up clear natural voting patterns against which unfair 'campaigns' tend to stand out.

Aren't inspections the best way to run a guide?
This could be called the 'traditional' model of restaurant reviewing; and chefs seem particularly prone to tout this form of recognition as the one form of criticism that they will respect. And, doubtless the inspection model has its strengths. But a prime weakness is that it is so expensive it precludes too many visits. Take its most famous exponent: Michelin. The tyre man has not historically claimed to visit each entry listed in its guide annually. Even once! But cost alone is not the only reason to query the inspection model. Another vital issue: who are its inspectors? Often catering professionals, whose tastes may be at odds with the natural customer base. On any entry of note, however, Harden's typically has somewhere between dozens and hundreds of reports annually from the folks who keep the restaurant in business. We believe that such feedback, carefully analysed, is far more revealing and accurate than an occasional 'professional' inspection.

TAKE YOUR DINING TO THE NEXT LEVEL

Love good food?
Join the club!

hardens.com

SURVEY MOST MENTIONED

These are the restaurants which were most frequently mentioned by reporters. (Last year's position is given in brackets.) An asterisk* indicates the first appearance in the list of a recently opened restaurant.

1	J Sheekey (4)
2	Scott's (2)
3	Chez Bruce (3)
4	The Wolseley (6)
5	Core by Clare Smyth (1)
6	Clos Maggiore (17)
7	The River Café (7)
8=	The Delaunay (31)
8=	Brasserie Zédel (9)
10	Le Gavroche (5)

11	Noble Rot (11)
12=	A Wong (12)
12=	Andrew Edmunds (26)
14	Gymkhana (16)
15	Bocca di Lupo (18)
16	La Trompette (8)
17	The Five Fields (19)
18	The Ivy (28)
19	Bentley's (22)
20=	The Ritz (25)

20=	Noble Rot Soho (-)
22	The Cinnamon Club (10)
23	La Poule au Pot (27)
24	Medlar (20)
25	Trinity (33)
26	Gordon Ramsay (29)
27	Murano (36)
28	Pied à Terre (21)
29	Hélène Darroze, The Connaught Hotel (39)
30	Sams Riverside (14)

31=	Gauthier Soho (12)
31=	Wiltons (-)
31=	Elystan Street (24)
34=	Sabor (-)
34=	Lorne (-)
36	Kiln (-)
37=	Galvin La Chapelle (23)
37=	Mere (32)
39=	St John Smithfield (-)
39=	Parsons (-)

SURVEY NOMINATIONS

Top gastronomic experience

1. Core by Clare Smyth (1)
2. Chez Bruce (3)
3. The Five Fields (5)
4. Le Gavroche (2)
5. Frog by Adam Handling (-)
6. La Trompette (4)
7. The Ritz (-)
8. The Ledbury (-)
9. The Anglesea Arms (-)
10. Medlar (-)

Favourite

1. Chez Bruce (1)
2. The Wolseley (4)
3. The River Café (6)
4. Core by Clare Smyth (3)
5. Le Gavroche (-)
6. Frog by Adam Handling (-)
7. The Delaunay (-)
8. La Trompette (2)
9. Pied à Terre (-)
10. Sams Riverside (-)

Best for business

1. The Wolseley (1)
2. The Delaunay (3)
3. Hawksmoor (2)
4. Coq d'Argent (9)
5. Scott's (6)
6. The Ivy (-)
7. Wiltons (-)
8. Cabotte (-)
9. Goodman (-)
10. The Dining Room, The Goring Hotel (8)

Best for romance

1. Clos Maggiore (1)
2. La Poule au Pot (2)
3. Andrew Edmunds (3)
4. The Ritz (9)
5. Sessions Arts Club (-)
6. Chez Bruce (10)
7. Core by Clare Smyth (-)
8. Scott's (-)
9. Le Gavroche (4)
10. The Five Fields (6)

RANKED BY THE NUMBER OF REPORTERS' VOTES

Best breakfast/brunch

1. The Wolseley (1)
2. Dishoom (2)
3. Côte (3)
4. The Delaunay (4)
5. Granger & Co (5)
6. The Ivy Cafés, Grills & Brasseries (9)
7. Caravan (7)
8. Megan's (6)
9. Fischer's (-)
10. The Breakfast Club (8)

Best bar/pub food

1. Harwood Arms (1)
2. Canton Arms (4)
3. The Anchor & Hope (2)
4. The Anglesea Arms (10)
5. The Wigmore, The Langham (-)
6. The Red Lion & Sun (7)
7. Bull & Last (3)
8. The Eagle (5)
9. The Camberwell Arms (-)
10. The Cadogan Arms (-)

Most disappointing cooking

1. Oxo Tower (Restaurant) (1)
2. The Ivy (-)
3. Gordon Ramsay (2)
4. Holborn Dining Room (-)
5. Rick Stein (8)
6. German Gymnasium (-)
7. Scott's (-)
8. Hélène Darroze, The Connaught Hotel (5)
9. Gauthier Soho (-)
10. Murano (-)

Most overpriced restaurant

1. The River Café (1)
2. Sexy Fish (2)
3. Hélène Darroze, The Connaught Hotel (9)
4. Oxo Tower (Restaurant) (6)
5. Gordon Ramsay (5)
6. Hakkasan (-)
7. Nusr-Et Steakhouse (-)
8. Hawksmoor (-)
9. Sushisamba (-)
10. Scott's (-)

SURVEY HIGHEST RATINGS

FOOD

SERVICE

£130+

1	Evelyn's Table	1	Endo at The Rotunda
2	Endo at The Rotunda	2	Core by Clare Smyth
3	Core by Clare Smyth	3	Pied à Terre
4	Maru	4	The Ledbury
5	Estiatorio Milos	5	The Five Fields

£100–£129

1	SOLA	1	LPM
2	LPM	2	Ekstedt at The Yard
3	A Wong	3	The Ritz
4	Nobu, Como Met'	4	Chez Bruce
5	Dinings	5	Hide Ground

£75–99

1	Cornerstone	1	Sale e Pepe
2	Benares	2	Noizé
3	Lyle's	3	Charlie's at Brown's
4	Amaya	4	Margot
5	Myrtle	5	Villa Di Geggiano

£55–£74

1	A Wong	1	Behind
2	Jin Kichi	2	The Sea, The Sea
3	Behind	3	Hereford Road
4	Sabor	4	Babur
5	The Sea, The Sea	5	Bombay Palace

£54 or less

1	Dastaan	1	The Wet Fish Café
2	Kiln	2	Sumi
3	Supawan	3	Black Dog Beer House
4	Farang	4	Yard Sale Pizza
5	Lahore Kebab House	5	Paradise Hampstead

AMBIENCE

1. Pied à Terre
2. Endo at The Rotunda
3. The Ledbury
4. Da Terra
5. Core by Clare Smyth

1. The Ritz
2. Petersham Nurseries
3. The Chiltern Firehouse
4. Zuma
5. Ekstedt at The Yard

1. Rules
2. Sale e Pepe
3. Sams Riverside
4. Cambio de Tercio
5. Clos Maggiore

1. Circolo Popolare
2. Sessions Arts Club
3. La Poule au Pot
4. The Sea, The Sea
5. Oslo Court

1. Mercato Metropolitano
2. Ciao Bella
3. Bar Italia
4. Brasserie Zédel
5. Smokestak

OVERALL

1. Endo at The Rotunda
2. Core by Clare Smyth
3. Pied à Terre
4. Da Terra
5. The Ledbury

1. The Ritz
2. LPM
3. Ekstedt at The Yard
4. Chez Bruce
5. Kol

1. Sale e Pepe
2. Benares
3. Charlie's at Brown's
4. Cornerstone
5. Sams Riverside

1. The Sea, The Sea
2. Behind
3. Sabor
4. The Anglesea Arms
5. Sessions Arts Club

1. Supawan
2. Black Dog Beer House
3. Ciao Bella
4. Potli
5. Kiln

SURVEY BEST BY CUISINE

These are the restaurants which received the best average food ratings (excluding establishments with a small or notably local following).

Where the most common types of cuisine are concerned, we present the results in two price-brackets. For less common cuisines, we list the top three, regardless of price.

For further information about restaurants which are particularly notable for their food, see the area overviews starting on page 262.

British, Modern

£75 and over
1. Evelyn's Table
2. Core by Clare Smyth
3. The Five Fields
4. Da Terra
5. Kitchen Table

Under £75
1. Behind
2. The Plimsoll
3. The Camberwell Arms
4. The Anglesea Arms
5. The Jones Family

French

£75 and over
1. LPM
2. Pied à Terre
3. Club Gascon
4. Bibendum
5. Sollip

Under £75
1. Les 2 Garcons
2. Casse-Croute
3. Le Vacherin
4. Oslo Court
5. Blanchette

Italian/Mediterranean

£75 and over
1. Theo Randall
2. Luca
3. Caractère
4. Murano
5. Norma

Under £75
1. Manteca
2. Popolo
3. Vasco & Piero's
4. Bocca di Lupo
5. Anima e Cuore

Indian & Pakistani

£75 and over
1. Amaya
2. BiBi
3. Gymkhana
4. Tamarind
5. Kahani

Under £75
1. Grand Trunk Road
2. Dastaan
3. Babur
4. Trishna
5. Lahore Kebab House

Chinese

£75 and over
1. A Wong
2. Imperial Treasure
3. Min Jiang
4. Hunan
5. Yauatcha

Under £75
1. Barshu
2. Silk Road
3. Mandarin Kitchen
4. Four Seasons
5. Singapore Garden

Japanese

£75 and over
1. Endo at The Rotunda
2. Maru
3. Nobu, Metropolitan Hotel
4. Dinings
5. Umu

Under £75
1. Jin Kichi
2. Sushi Atelier
3. Tsunami
4. Chisou
5. Sticks'n'Sushi

British, Traditional
1. The Ritz
2. Quality Chop House
3. The Game Bird

Vegetarian
1. The Gate
2. Mallow
3. Farmacy

Burgers, etc
1. The Plimsoll
2. Bleecker Burger
3. MEATLiquor

Pizza
1. 50 Kalò di Ciro Salvo
2. Yard Sale Pizza
3. Homeslice

Fish & Chips
1. Olympus Fish
2. Toff's
3. Nautilus

Thai
1. Kiln
2. Supawan
3. Farang

Steaks & Grills
1. Quality Chop House
2. City Social
3. Lurra

Fish & Seafood
1. Estiatorio Milos
2. Cornerstone
3. Behind

Fusion
1. Da Terra
2. Sollip
3. Tsunami

Spanish
1. Sabor
2. Cambio de Tercio
3. Barrafina

THE RESTAURANT SCENE

Muted post-Covid bounce-back

For the London restaurant scene, there has been no 'twang back' to high growth, post pandemic. Instead the outlook has been tame – but not disastrous – with net growth towards the bottom of the range considered normal since 2000.

There are 136 newcomers this year: the lowest level of openings since the 2012 edition (launched in calendar 2011). This figure is boosted by nine (9) restaurants that re-opened, having been marked as 'Temporarily Closed'. It falls right at the bottom of the range of 134-200 noted in all but two of the last twenty years.

Closures stand at 85. This is not a high level and suggests that the challenge faced by the restaurant scene is not yet (for all the awful headlines) a lack of custom.

Net growth (Openings minus Closures) was 51: an indifferent level by the yardstick of the last 31 years. It was well out of the range of the 100+ new openings recorded in 2014-2018, which now feels like a golden era.

Brexit is particularly hitting hospitality

Immediately post-pandemic, restaurateurs and their backers seemed to be betting that the 'new normal' would look fairly like the old one. That view is currently being revised down to the low end of that historic norm.

The Covid-induced shift to WFH looks ever-less like a brief passing phase. Lower office occupancy explains why more licensed premises in the City of London have closed than anywhere else in the country, with the number of such locations down by 14% since 2020.

Another headwind, of course, is the war in Ukraine and rising costs. That's certainly contributed to rising menu prices (see below), but the extent to which it's already causing folks to cut back on eating out is harder to discern.

And then, of course, there's the ongoing recruitment crisis in hospitality and Brexit's effects. Supporters of the vote's outcome are apt to point to staff shortages in hospitality across Europe (in France, for example). They explain the ongoing dire inability to recruit in London restaurants as a broader Covid-related labour market shift that's disadvantaged hospitality in all countries.

But, as recent Oxford University research shows, UK hospitality is notably hard-hit by Brexit, because Europeans have historically made up such a big chunk of its workforce.

When this guide began, before 1993's Maastricht Treaty, restaurateurs often bemoaned their inability to expand due to poor supply of good staff. Now this limitation is back with a vengeance. The consequences so far do not include better employment conditions for anyone, but do look set to add up to a less lively restaurant scene.

On the rise: the Middle East

After Modern British (26) openings, Italian cuisine was this year's favourite (with 18 debuts), beating Japanese cuisine, which was last year's runner up, into third place (with 9 openings). This year's most promising rising star cuisines were Middle Eastern (accounting for 8 openings).

In terms of location, Central London was unusually dominant, accounting for 57 arrivals. In the 'burbs, East London led the way (with 25 openings) just beating South London (with 23). West London registered a poor year (16), only just exceeding North London's rate of opening (15).

Dorothy… did you remember your wallet?

Was it just a dream? It seems like only a few ticks since a dinner costing over £100 per head was a talking point. Now, for anything that might pass as 'haute cuisine', a mere 'ton' per head seems suspiciously cheap. The situation all feels a little bewildering. How did we get here?

A perusal of the Harden's archive shows that it was the post-Brexit, 2017 edition (published in autumn 2016) in which we first introduced a £100+ top price band at the front of the book. At that time, there were 37 such entries, of which just one had a formula price over £150 per head.

Fast forward five years, and £100+ is – in this edition – for the first time the delimiter merely of our second highest price category. Our highest band is now set at £130+.

Now, there are 154 entries in the guide above the £100 level. And in a neat symmetry with the figures above, there are 37 restaurants with a formula price over £150 per head.

In fact there are 17 entries now over £200 per head and six above £250! It feels like everything is speeding up.

That's because it is! But London's ever-more pricey restaurant scene is not just a factor of price inflation as caused by staff shortages and rising food costs. It is also driven by the arrival in recent years of a higher proportion of openings focused at the very top end.

Restaurant price inflation

The average price of dinner for one at establishments listed in this guide is £69.28 (c.f. £64.14 last year). Prices have risen by an annualised rate of 8.1% in the past year. Having led inflation in recent times, this rate was slightly below CPI growth of 10.1% for the 12 months to July 2022. However, given how quickly prices are rising, this disparity is most probably just a reflection of the time lag between our research effort and publication. The rise is most marked amongst pricey restaurants (over £100 per head). In this group, the annualised growth is again higher than for restaurants generally, at 11.7% (up from 8.8%).

OPENINGS & CLOSURES

The listings below relate to the period from Autumn 2021 to Autumn 2022. Most restaurants marked as "Temporarily closed" last year went on to close permanently. Where they have reopened, this is listed below as a (re) Opening. Only branches of small groups in the listings below contribute to the grand total figures.

† marked last year as temporarily closed.
* temporarily closed as we to go to press.

Openings (136)
Acme Fire Cult
Akub
Alex Dilling Café Royal
L'Amorosa †
Andina Spitalfields (E1)
Apricity
Aragawa
Artisans of Sardinia
Attimi
The Audley
The Aubrey
Le Bab (SW9, SW11)
Balady (EC1)
Bacchanalia
The Barbary Next Door
Belvedere
Björn Frantzén at Harrods
Black Bear Burger (EC1, E14)
The Black Lamb
Boiler & Co
Bone Daddies (SW15)
Bossa
Bottle & Rye
La Brasseria (W11)
Bubala Soho (W1)
Bund †
Caia
The Campaner
Cantinetta Antinori
Caravan (E14)
Caravel
Cedric Grolet, The Berkeley
Cher Thai
Chick 'n' Sours (E8) †
Chotto Matte (W1)
Chucs (NW8)
Cicchetti Knightsbridge (SW3)
Cycene
Dai Chi
Danclair's
Dear Grace
Les 2 Garcons
Dipna Anand
Dragon Castle †
Ela & Dhani
Elis
Emilia's Crafted Pasta (E14)
Facing Heaven
Fatto Pizza & Beer KX (N1)
Firebird
Flat Iron, The Cut (SE1)
Forza Win
400 Rabbits (SE17)
Galvin Bar & Grill
Gazette (SW17, EC4)
Giulia
Goddard & Gibbs
Gopal's of Soho †
Granger & Co (W1)
Gunpowder Soho (W1)
Gura Gura
Hawksmoor (E14)
Haz (WC2)
Hithe & Seek
Holy Carrot
Isibani
Itaku
The Ivy in the Park (E14)
Jeru
Joia
The Jones Family Affair
Kanada-Ya (W1)
Kasa & Kin
Kerridge's Fish & Chips
Kilig
Koya Ko (E8)
Koyn

OPENINGS & CLOSURES

The Libertine
Lina Stores *(W1, EC4)*
Lino's
Lisboeta
Long Chim
The Lore of the Land †
M Restaurant *(E14)*
Maddox Tavern
Magenta
Manna †
Maria G's
Marugame Udon *(W1, SE10, E14)*
Masalchi
The Meat & Wine Co
Mayfair
MEATliquor *(WC1, SW4)*
Mildreds *(WC2)*
Miro Mayfair
Miscusi *(WC2, N1)*
Miznon London
Nessa
Noci
El Norte
Off the Hook
Other Naughty Piglet †
Ottolenghi *(SW1)*
Parrillan *(SE1)*
Pastan
Patty and Bun *(W11, W12, SW11)*
Le Petit Beefbar
The Pig's Head
Plaza Khao Gaeng
Popeyes
Porte Noire
Postbox
The Princess Royal
RAI
Rambutan
The Residency
Restaurant 1890
Restaurant St Barts
Revolve
Richoux *(W1)*
Riding House *(WC1)*
Riviera
Rock & Rose *(W4)*
Roji
Roti King *(SW8)*
The Rushmere
Sagar *(SW1)*
Salt Yard *(W12, SE1)*
Saltie Girl
Santa Maria *(N1)*
Sarap Filipino Bistro
The Seafood Bar
Shoryu Ramen *(W8)*
Sichuan Fry
Simpsons in the Strand †
Socca
Soffice London
Sparrow Italia
Speedboat Bar
St Martin's House
Stem & Glory
Straker's
Street Burger *(EC1)*
SUDU
The Tamil Prince
Tapas Brindisa *(SW11)*
Taqueria *(EC1)*
Taro *(SW1, N3, E£17)*
temper Shoreditch
The Tent
Three Uncles *(SW9)*
Tofu Vegan *(NW11)*
28-50 Oxford Circus *(W1)*
Vinoteca Borough *(SE1)*
Yard Sale Pizza *(SE4)*
Zephyr
Zia Lucia *(N16)*

OPENINGS & CLOSURES

Closures (85)

Acre
Adams Café
Albertine
L'Artigiano
Bando Belly
Baozi Inn (WC2)
Bertie Blossoms
The Betterment
Boisdale of Bishopsgate
Bone Daddies (W8)
Boxcar Bar & Kitchen
Burger & Lobster (EC1)
Casacosta
Casita Andina (W1)
Ceviche Old St (EC1)
Chick 'n' Sours (E1, W1)
Chicken Shop & Dirty Burger (SW19)
The Clock N8
Colette (SW10, SW19)
Comptoir Gascon
Il Convivio
Corner Room
Darjeeling Express
Davies and Brook
Dip & Flip (SW11, SW19)
Dirty Burger (SW8, E1)
Dynamo (SW17)
Epic Pies
Firebrand (EC1R)
Flat Three
Flor
Gallipoli (N1)
The Gate (NW8)
The Good Plot
The Greenhouse
Hankies (SW1, W2)
Haz (EC3)
Hot May Pot Pot
Hot Stone (W1)
Kazan (Café) (SW1)
Kiraku
The Laughing Heart
Liv
M Bar & Grill Twickenham
Madame Pigg
Malabar
Malabar Junction
Mama's Jerk
Mãos
Michael Nadra (W4)
Molly's Café
Momo
Morso (NW10)
Nordic Bakery (W1)
The Oak SW11 (SW11)
On The Bab (EC1)
Ottolenghi (EC1)
Party Store Pizza (SW4)
Pastaio (W12)
Patri Ealing (W5)
Patty and Bun (W11, EC3, E2)
Peg
The Phoenix
Pino
Pizza Pilgrims (W1)
RAW (W1)
Relais de Venise (W1)
Roux at the Landau*
Sake No Hana
Salon Brixton
Shampers
Shoryu Ramen (WC1)
Showaken
Sidechick
Sri Suwoon
St Clair
Stockwell Continental
Sushi Tetsu
Sushiology by Atari-Ya (W1)
Talad
Taro (EC4)
Terroirs (SE22)
Tomahawk Steakhouse
Turul Project
28-50 (WC2)
Vinoteca (W1)
The White Onion
Wright Brothers (EC2)
Yming

DIRECTORY

Comments in "double quotation marks" were made by reporters.

A Cena TW1 — £60 — 3 3 3
418 Richmond Road   020 8288 0108   1–4A

A "wonderful, smart, family-run Italian with imaginative cooking" ("not pizza and pasta!") that's an "ideal neighbourhood restaurant" for those living near St Margaret's – "we've eaten here every three weeks since moving to the area almost a year ago, and there's a constantly changing menu with high-quality presentation and service". Top Tip – "the set-price lunch/early evening dinner is particularly good value". / TW1 2EB; www.acena.co.uk; @acenarestaurant; Tue-Sat 10 pm, Sun 2 pm; closed Tue-Thu L closed Sun D, closed Mon; booking max 6 may apply.

A Wong SW1 — £112 — 5 5 3
70 Wilton Rd   020 7828 8931   2–4B

"A next-level culinary adventure" – Andrew Wong's "unique interpretation" of his native cuisine "makes you rethink everything you thought you knew about Chinese cooking" and has elevated his relatively humble-looking establishment, near Victoria station, to a place of foodie pilgrimage. Run for decades by his parents (when it was called Kym's), the premises have been transformed over the last 10 years by their LSE-graduate son, to become Michelin's highest-rated Chinese restaurant outside China; and, "put very simply, there is no better Chinese restaurant in London". (A move to a new site has been mooted over the years, with no final announcement as yet). The "exquisite" dishes display an "unexpected degree of artistry" – in particular "the Five Movements tasting menu is absolutely incredible": "ruinously expensive but bizarrely feeling like exceptional value". ("The grated foie gras with pork and wind-dried sausage was a full-on work of genius; as was the crab claw with tomato and wasabi, which truly looked nothing like the description, but was so moreish it's untrue"). Somewhat more affordably, "the innovative Dim Sum is simply outstanding… if you can get in" ("the second star makes it even harder for long-time fans to book"). "And prices are up, up and away…but still it's worth it for such astonishing food". / SW1V 1DE; www.awong.co.uk; @awongSW1; Tue-Sat 10.30 pm; closed Sun & Mon; credit card required to book.

The Abingdon W8 — £67 — 3 3 3
54 Abingdon Rd   020 7937 3339   6–2A

"A cut above the normal pub" – with its "stylish mix of bar area and secluded, more intimate booths", this smart venue on a Kensington backstreet has entertained well-heeled locals with a menu of elevated gastropub fare for a quarter of a century. / W8 6AP; www.theabingdon.co.uk; @theabingdon; Mon-Sat 10 pm, Sun 9 pm.

Acme Fire Cult E8 NEW — £41
The Bootyard, Abbot Street   no tel   14–1A

Vegetables are centre-stage at Andrew Clarke and Daniel Watkins's vibey Dalston BBQ, which – with its mostly outdoor set-up in a former car park, live-fire cooking, impressively bearded chef, and extensive microbrewery beer selection (40FT Brewery's Steve Ryan is a partner) – reads like a checklist of East London clichés. It opened in April 2022 too late to generate feedback in our annual diners' poll, but all the newspaper press critics are impressed, with The Evening Standard's Jimi Famurewa declaring: "It has the spirit, soul and craft of a serious restaurant, coupled with a vibrant, veg-heavy menu that feels like pyromaniacal Ottolenghi." / E8 3DP; www.acmefirecult.com/acme-at-40ft-brewery; @acmefirecult; Wed-Sat 9.30 pm, Sun 4 pm; closed Wed L closed Sun D, closed Mon & Tue.

Addie's Thai Café SW5 — £40 — 3 2 2
121 Earl's Court Rd   020 7259 2620   6–2A

This "deservedly busy" Thai canteen has been an Earl's Court staple since the late 1990s, serving a cheap and tasty menu which is "all good, from the prawn crackers to som tum". / SW5 9RL; www.addiesthai.co.uk; @addiesthai.co.uk; Mon-Sun 10 pm; closed Mon & Tue, Sun L; no Amex.

Afghan Kitchen N1 £33 3 2 2
35 Islington Grn   020 7359 8019   9–3D
This enduring little café on Islington Green has thrived for three decades on its "amazing" cheap curries (if certainly not its basic interior). / N1 8DU; @afghankitchenldn; Tue-Sat 11 pm; closed Sun & Mon; cash only; no booking.

Aglio e Olio SW10 £49 3 2 2
194 Fulham Rd   020 7351 0070   6–3B
This "family-run bustling Italian with a loyal clientele" near Chelsea & Westminster hospital is "the locals' favourite – I could eat here once a week". The food (especially the pasta) is "well above average" ("bring a hearty appetite as portions are generous") and prices "reasonable", but it does get "very hectic" to the point of being "too noisy in the evenings". / SW10 9PN; www.aglioeolio.co.uk; Mon-Sun 11 pm.

Akira at Japan House W8 £86 3 3 2
101-111 Kensington High Street   020 3971 4646   6–1A
"A revelation!" – the "pricey-but-good" first-floor restaurant (or better still "the private tatami mat dining room") at Kensington's Japan House cultural centre serves "food close to what you eat in Japan" alongside an extensive sake menu, and "everything is beautifully presented". "Quite apart from the food, the entire experience in the building and the Japanese welcome make a visit worthwhile". / W8 5SA; www.japanhouselondon.uk; @japanhouseldn; Tue-Sat 11 pm; closed Sun & Mon.

Akoko W1 £147 4 4 4
21 Berners Street   020 7323 0593   5–1A
"An incredibly special dining experience, like nowhere else in London" – Aji Akokomi has achieved something "totally unique, supremely atmospheric and slick" at his Fitzrovian homage to West Africa. The warm bronzed interior is all urban sophistication, but channels an earthy African energy with its impeccably chosen (and, for the most part, specially commissioned) décor and tableware. The open kitchen was on our visit predominantly staffed by Europeans and Asians, but they deliver "an exquisite and well thought-out" extended tasting menu, mixing Nigerian, Ghanaian and Senegalese culinary influences, and with an "on-point wine pairing" option. Head chef, Theo Clench (who won it a Michelin star) moved on in March 2022 just prior to our annual diners' poll – no public appointment of a successor has been made as yet. / W1W 3LJ; akoko.co.uk; @akokorestaurant; Tue-Sat 11 pm; closed Tue-Fri L, closed Sun & Mon.

Akub W8 NEW
27 Uxbridge Street   no tel   7–2B
Fadi Kattan crowd-funded nearly £1m to open this Palestinian newcomer in Notting Hill which – originally slated to debut in 2021 – is set to open in the second half of 2022. He opened his first restaurant (Fawda) in Bethlehem in 2016. Here, the focus will be specialities from that city as well as Jerusalem, Jericho, Gaza and Nablus, and the website promises 'hot bright salads of the Gaza coastline, deep stews from the rolling hills of Ramallah and foraged akub will feature alongside the locally sourced British ingredients'. / W8 7TQ; www.akub-restaurant.com; @akub.london; closed Mon-Sat & Sun.

Al Duca SW1 £63 3 2 2
4-5 Duke of York St   020 7839 3090   3–3D
This "conveniently placed old favourite", on a St James's corner, serves "above-average Italian" including "particularly good fish cooking", backed up by an "intriguing wine list with some unusual choices". Nobody would accuse it of much in the way of pizzazz, but even those who say it's "middle of the road and time for a revamp" still rate it well all-round. / SW1Y 6LA; www.alduca-restaurant.co.uk; @al_duca; Mon-Sun 11 pm; closed Sun.

Al Mare,
Jumeirah Carlton Tower Hotel SW1 £98 3|3|3
Cadogan Pl   020 7858 7250   6–1D
"I was very sad to see the Rib Room go…" – this luxurious new Italian is a sequel to the age-old traditional British venture that sat (in a slightly different position) within the hotel for 60 years. And like its predecessor, it is certainly *"expensive"*. But while one or two reports write it off as being *"disappointing all-round"*, the majority are more upbeat. It is a *"beautiful and well spaced room"* with views of the leafy square, and most diners feel that Marco Calenzo's cooking, which puts an emphasis on seafood, is *"thankfully very good"* or even *"exceptional"*. Top Tip – interesting option of a 45-minute business lunch. / SW1 9PY; www.jumeirah.com/en/stay/london/the-carlton-tower; @jumeirahgroup; Mon & Tue 10.30 pm, Wed-Sat 10 pm, Sun 3.30 pm; closed Sun D.

Alain Ducasse at The Dorchester W1 £224 2|3|2
53 Park Lane   020 7629 8866   3–3A
"It was a lovely meal, no doubt… but it was nothing particularly memorable… far from mind-blowing… certainly not worth 3 Michelin stars… really quite overpriced": this has too often been the story of this Mayfair dining room, fêted from its 2010 debut by Michelin on the strength of carrying the name of arguably France's most famous chef. To be fair, this luxurious chamber does also have its fans, for whom executive chef Jean-Philippe Blondet's menu is *"simply the pinnacle of modern French cooking"* (with a wine list to match); and *"a real treat, from the moment you are greeted at the entrance to the last second as you leave"*. But this year, as every year, it is concerning just how many reports say *"it's just not up there with the best…"*; *"…nice but very unremarkable"*. / W1K 1QA; www.alainducasse-dorchester.com; @alainducasseatthedorchester; closed Mon-Sat & Sun; Jacket required.

Alex Dilling Café Royal W1 NEW
Café Royal, 68 Regent Street   020 7406 3333   4–2C
Since it closed its iconic Café Royal Grill Room, this super-swanky five star by Piccadilly Circus has lacked a flagship restaurant. … till now, that is, when – in early September 2022 – they open this new 34-cover dining room, overseen by the eponymous former chef of Mayfair's now-defunct Greenhouse. The website promises a 'modern take on traditional French gastronomic cuisine' in a room 'overlooking the curvature of Regent Street'. / W1W 4DY; www.hotelcaferoyal.com/alexdilling; @hotelcaferoyal; Fri & Sat 8 pm, Sun 4 pm.

Alexandrie W8 £74 3|3|3
38C Kensington Church Street   020 7937 2244   6–1A
This *"impressive Kensington gem"* serves *"traditional Egyptian dishes with a sophisticated French influence"* – *"hopefully it will find more fans post-pandemic"*. Top Menu Tip – *"mehalabya (Egyptian milk pudding) is a delicious way to end the meal"*. / W8 4BX; @alexandrie_kensington; Wed-Sat 10 pm, Sun 9.30 pm; closed Wed-Fri L, closed Mon & Tue.

The Alfred Tennyson Pub Belgravia SW1 £75 2|2|3
10 Motcomb Street   020 7730 6074   6–1D
This smartly kitted-out pub with a *"nice outdoor terrace"* on a cobbled Belgravia street has a *"short, simple and well-executed menu"*, providing *"Sunday roast and fish 'n' chips of quality"*. / SW1X 8LA; thealfredtennyson.co.uk; @cubitthouse; Mon-Sat 10 pm, Sun 9.30 pm.

Ali Baba NW1 £32 3|2|2
32 Ivor Pl   020 7723 5805   2–1A
"A family Egyptian with unique character" – this unchanging venture (est 1970) occupies a room behind a takeaway, near the top of Baker Street. The affordable dishes are highly authentic, as is the no-frills vibe. Unlicensed so BYO. / NW1 6DA; alibabarestaurant.co.uk; @alibabarestaurantlondon; Mon-Sun 10 pm; cash only; booking online only.

Allegra E20 £63 3 3 3
The Stratford, 20-22 International Way   020 3973 0545   14–1D
With a chef (Patrick Powell) from the Chiltern Firehouse and an interior by the design team behind Copenhagen's Noma, this seventh-floor venue near Westfield Stratford is a "lovely slice of West End-type glamour in East London". "Great food and wine, nice outdoor terrace" complete a uniformly positive picture. / E20 1GQ; www.allegra-restaurant.com; @allegrarestaurant; Wed-Sat 10 pm; closed Wed & Thu L, closed Mon & Tue & Sun.

The Alma SE19 £67 3 3 4
95 Church Road   020 8768 1885   1–4D
"A step above normal pub grub": chef David Yorkiston's kitchen produces a high standard of cooking at this carefully modernised mid-Victorian pub on Crystal Palace's hip 'Triangle' – a "lovely building" with large windows, oodles of outdoor space, and a lively atmosphere. "It's a shame children under 10 can't go or we'd be there all the time!" / SE19 2TA; thealmapub.com; @TheAlmaCP; closed Mon-Sat & Sun; payment – credit card only; booking online only.

Aloo Tama SW1 £26 4 4 3
18 Greencoat Place   020 7834 9873   2–4C
"This cosy little restaurant behind Victoria station serves tasty home-style Nepalese cuisine". It's "well hidden, and surely dependent on word of mouth" – which makes it all the more impressive that it's "mostly full". "So book to avoid disappointment" – they're "welcoming and keen to help diners explore the non-standard menu choices". They also have a lunchtime food truck at the Merchant Square market in Paddington. / SW1S 1PG; www.alootama.com; @alootamaofficial; Tue-Sat 10 pm, Sun 9 pm; closed Tue-Sun L, closed Mon.

Alter E1 £34 4 3 2
15 Leman Street   no tel   10–2D
"An 'alter' I'm happy to worship at!" – Andy Goodwin brings an innovative approach to plant-based cuisine at this modern hotel dining room, near Aldgate East. To the odd sceptic, it's too "exhausting and suitable only for hardcore vegans" ("lack of any protein leaves sauces too soupy, and lots of pickles leads to vinegary flavours"), but for fans (the majority) it's "just incredible… tastes I've never experienced before… beautifully presented… a perfect balance of fresh vegetables served with creativity, flair and passion!" / E1 8EN; www.alterldn.com; @alter_ldn; Tue-Sat 10 pm; closed Tue, Sat L, closed Sun & Mon.

Amaya SW1 £89 5 3 4
Halkin Arcade, 19 Motcomb St   020 7823 1166   6–1D
"Exploding any lingering prejudices about Indian food" – this "innovative and beautiful" operation (created in 2004 by Ranjit Mathrani, Namita Panjabi and Camellia Panjabi, who own Chutney Mary et al) "remains a favourite premium destination" for "Indian cuisine at its finest, with a great open kitchen". "It is pricey, but the food is exceptional, while service is fast and friendly". / SW1X 8JT; www.amaya.biz; @amaya.ldn; Tue-Sat 10.30 pm, Sun 10 pm; closed Mon.

Amazonico W1 £95 3 3 4
10 Berkeley Square   020 7404 5000   3–3B
"It's the full experience – live music, vibe, décor, cocktails, food – that makes for a magical evening", according to fans of this forested Brazilian-Japanese fusion haunt, in the heart of swanky Mayfair. On the downside, prices for its sushi and luxurious grills are "absurd", but even those finding the venue "faintly ridiculous and definitely pretentious" say "the décor is worth the price of admission and I couldn't help enjoying the ride!"
/ W1W 6EF; amazonicorestaurant.com/london; @amazonicolondon; Mon-Sat 1 am, Sun midnight.

The American Bar SW1 £75 2 3 5
The Stafford, 16-18 Saint James's Place   020 7493 0111   3–4C
"A quick lunchtime drink can turn into several hours of cocktails and delightful bites" at this St James's institution: "a bar full of Americana and with staff who put on a great show of mixology". The Med-inspired brasserie menu is arguably "limited" but suits the venue, which is a "very buzzy" and "efficiently run" space. / SW1S 1NJ; thestaffordlondon.com/the-american-bar; @americanbarlon; Sun-Wed midnight, Thu-Sat 1 am; booking lunch only.

Amethyst W1 £193
6 Sackville Street   020 3034 3464   3–3D
Carlo Scotto, formerly of short-lived but excellent Xier (RIP), is the chef at this highly ambitious and heavily trailed Mayfair newcomer, which opened in May 2022 (too late for survey feedback) about nine months later than originally announced. It occupies a dramatic two-floor site near Green Park tube, where the main action surrounds a striking, zig-zag chef's table on the ground floor seating 20 around an amethyst and quartz centrepiece, in view of the open kitchen. The 12-course tasting menu (£150) incorporates Nordic, Japanese, French and Arabic influences and one early fan was The Times's Giles Coren, who – awarding it 27/30 – noted the meal's "delicacy and dedication to detail", with every dish "beloured intensively at the pass by Mr Scotto". In the 'Wine Cellar' basement seating 16, there's also the option of a six-course menu. / W1W 3DD; www.amethystdining.com; @amethystdining; Tue-Sat 11 pm.

L'Amorosa W6 £63 4 4 4
278 King St   020 8563 0300   8–2B
Ex-Zafferano head chef, Andy Needham's "fab and friendly neighbourhood Italian" near Ravenscourt Park station reopened in spring 2022 after a catalogue of disasters (pandemic, floods, dodgy construction upstairs...) – much to the relief of its many fans. There's "always well-prepared food and a warm reception". Top Menu Tips – "lovely risottos and the ragu". / W6 0SP; www.lamorosa.co.uk; @#lamorosa; Thu-Sat 9.30 pm; closed Thu-Sat L, closed Mon-Wed & Sun.

Ampéli W1 £119 3 4 3
18 Charlotte Street   020 3355 5370   2–1C
Influenced by the modern wine-focused restaurants of Athens – photographer Jenny Pagnoni's Fitzrovia two-year-old specialises in Greek and Eastern Mediterranean dishes (many seared in the Josper oven). Feedback remains limited but is upbeat: "delicious food, marvellous service and a beautiful venue". / W1W 2LZ; www.ampeli.london; @ampeli.london; Tue-Sat 10 pm; closed Sun & Mon; payment – credit card only.

Amrutha SW18 £31 4 5 2
326 Garratt Lane   020 8001 4628   11–2B
"Carefully prepared Indian-style vegan dishes" and "wonderfully friendly service" are behind the popularity of old school friends Arvin Suntaramoophy & Shyam Kotecha's Earlsfield crowd-pleaser. And the "as-much-as-you-can-eat ethos" and BYOB policy means it is "incredibly well-priced". Top Tip – if you're really hard up, they'll feed you in return for a couple of hours' work. / SW18 4EJ; www.amrutha.co.uk; @amruthauk; Tue-Sat 10 pm, Sun 9 pm; closed Tue-Fri L, closed Mon.

FSA

The Anchor & Hope SE1 £67 3|3|3
36 The Cut   020 7928 9898   10–4A
"Still serving hearty gastropub food in a chilled-out way" – this "long-time favourite" near the Old Vic remains one of London's top foodie boozers thanks to its "ever-changing menu" of "innovative dishes with a nod to nose-to-tail dining". Its performance has been less consistent in recent years, though ("some options matched the reputation for robust, powerful flavours, but others in my party reported basic errors that we wouldn't expect at these prices"). / SE1 8LP; www.anchorandhopepub.co.uk; @anchorhopecut; Wed-Sat 9 pm, Sun 3.30 pm; closed Wed-Fri L closed Sun D, closed Mon & Tue; no Amex; no booking.

Andanza SE1 £51 4|3|3
66 Weston Street   020 7967 1972   10–4C
"Spectacular if slightly cramped tapas restaurant" that occupies a former bookies' in Bermondsey. "Staff are keen to talk about the menu and any of the dishes are brilliant". / SE1 3QJ; www.andanza.co.uk; @andanza.se1; Mon-Sun 11 pm; booking online only.

Andina Spitalfields E1 NEW £48 2|1|3
60-62 Commercial Street   020 3141 6000   13–2C
Nowadays just in Spitalfields (with Soho, Shoreditch and Notting Hill branches opening and closing over the years), this Peruvian-inspired haunt received mixed reviews this year, linked with one or two incidents of "awful" service. Feedback on its Latino fare, which majors in ceviches and salads (but which is also accompanied by a selection of larger and mostly meaty 'classic dishes') is more consistent, though, and fans say it's "still a cracking place, even after relocating". / E1; www.cevichefamily.com/andina; @andinalondon; Mon & Tue, Sun 9.30 pm, Wed-Sat 10.30 pm.

Andrew Edmunds W1 £69 3|4|5
46 Lexington Street   020 7437 5708   4–2C
"The kind of place to bring your lover" – this "perfect", "sweet" townhouse is an "old-favourite", whose "cosy, panelled and candle-lit" setting is perennially nominated as one of London's most romantic. Despite its "Dickensian" charm, it has an "idiosyncratic", even "groovy" vibe, inspired by its long-term independent owner, whose shop dealing in antiquarian prints is next door (and pre-dates the restaurant, which opened in 1985, by about a decade). From a slightly "limited" menu, the "robust and honest" cuisine "isn't going to win any innovation awards, but is very well-executed and well-priced; and it moves with the times. "The real attraction is the superb wines at non-greedy prices" selected by Edmunds ("not as broad a list as Noble Rot but much more affordable"), which helps fuel its "decadent and sexy" appeal. Service can be "hard pressed" but is "so friendly". Top Tip – the basement has its plus points, but the best seats are on the ground floor. / W1W 0LP; www.andrewedmunds.com; @andrew.edmunds; Mon-Sun 10.30 pm; no Amex; booking max 10 may apply.

Angelina E8 £61 4|2|3
56 Dalston Lane   020 7241 1851   14–1A
Italian and Japanese cuisines are combined on multi-course 'kaiseki' (10-course) and 'omakase' (4-course) menus to intriguing effect at this ambitious haunt in Dalston. Its highly rated again by reporters this year, despite a couple of experiences where service went awry ("we received the same dish twice, which we did not refuse as it was enjoyable!") / E8 3AH; angelina.london; @angelina.dalston; Mon-Fri 10 pm, Sat 10.30 pm, Sun 3.30 pm; closed Mon-Fri L closed Sun D; no shorts.

FSA RATINGS: FROM **1** POOR — **5** EXCEPTIONAL

Angie's Little Food Shop W4 £48
114 Chiswick High Road 020 8994 3931 8–2A

This "rather sweet little café" in Chiswick from transplanted South African Angie Steele provides "very friendly and quick service for a light menu" of healthy-ish treats from breakfast to 5pm. / W4 1PU; www.angies.co.uk; @angieslondon; Tue-Fri 5 pm, Sat 10.30 pm; closed Tue-Fri D, closed Sun & Mon.

Angler, South Place Hotel EC2 £111
3 South Pl 020 3215 1260 13–2A

"Perfectly executed fish" from a "varied and delicate" menu adds to the elevation of this 7th-floor D&D London perch, at the top of a hotel near Broadgate, where the "nice verandah" comes into its own in the summer months. Cooking of this quality is rare in the City, and even non expense-accounters will seek it out. This year's most critical report? – "probably worth its Michelin star, but pricey and the chef didn't take any gambles". / EC2M 2AF; www.anglerrestaurant.com; @angler_restaurant; Tue-Sat 9.15 pm; closed Sun & Mon; may need 8+ to book.

The Anglesea Arms W6 £61
35 Wingate Rd 020 8749 1291 8–1B

"One of London's truly great gastropubs" – this characterful boozer occupies an attractive backstreet near Ravenscourt Park and has "friendly staff and a nice buzz". "The menu changes a lot but is always delicious", delivering "reliable unpretentious food at honest prices" that's of "more-than-pub quality", plus "a good selection of wines". / W6 OUR; www.angleseaarmspub.co.uk; @theangleseaarmsw6; Mon-Sat 11 pm, Sun 10.30 pm; closed Mon-Fri L; payment – credit card only; no booking.

Anglo EC1 £101
30 St Cross Street 020 7430 1503 10–1A

"A tiny spot with just over 20 covers and food to die for" – the focus is very much on the "very clever cooking at an affordable price point" at this "personal" Farringdon address, run by head chef Anthony Raffo and manager Marie Danzanvilliers. The food is "super-seasonal" ("sometimes foraged within a stone's throw of the restaurant"), "traditional techniques are revived with pickles and ferments" and the resulting dishes have "exceptional flavour combinations and contrasts". / EC1N 8UH; www.anglorestaurant.com; @anglorestaurant; Tue-Sat 8.30 pm; closed Tue-Thu L, closed Sun & Mon; booking max 6 may apply.

Anima e Cuore NW1 £62
129 Kentish Town Rd 07590 427171 9–2B

"Behind an unprepossessing facade, on an equally unprepossessing part of not-quite-Camden, not-quite-Kentish Town, lie gastronomic delights from Italy" conjured up in a tiny kitchen by Moroccan-Italian Mustapha Mouflih, a chef who "combines high-quality ingredients with imagination". "Even if the ambience is somewhat chaotic and basic, at best, the cooking is wonderful" ("the ravioli, malfatti, tortellini and so on are of a freshness and stuffed with flavours you would otherwise have to get on a plane to find"). / NW1 8PB; www.animaecuore.co.uk; Tue-Sat 11 pm, Sun & Mon 8 pm.

Anjanaas NW6 £33
57-59 Willesden Lane 020 7624 1713 1–1B

The "delicious southern Indian dishes" at this Kilburn Keralan have "a fine subtlety in their flavours". "It has the feel of an unpretentious family-run business, where their hearts are in the cooking and service". / NW6 7RL; www.anjanaas.com; Mon, Wed & Thu 10.30 pm, Fri & Sat 11 pm, Sun 10 pm; closed Tue.

F S A

Annie's W4 £60 3̲ 3̲ 4̲
162 Thames Rd   020 8994 9080   1–3A
A "great neighbourhood restaurant and brunch spot" – this cosy all-day operation in pretty Strand on the Green was the first from West London restaurateur Lorraine Angliss and has catered for 20 years to a local clientele looking for "reliable cooking" rather than gastronomic fireworks. (A branch in Barnes shut up shop a couple of years ago, blaming the closure of Hammersmith Bridge for reduced trade). / W4 3QS; www.anniesrestaurant.co.uk; @anniesrestaurant; Tue-Sat 10 pm, Sun 9 pm; closed Tue-Fri L, closed Mon.

The Anthologist EC2 £53 2̲ 2̲ 3̲
58 Gresham St   0845 468 0101   10–2C
A handy location, near the Guildhall, "buzzy" large interior and versatile menu of "decent (if unspectacular) food" mean it's worth remembering this "reliable option in the City", although it "can be incredibly busy". / EC2V 7BB; www.theanthologistbar.co.uk; @drakeandmorgan; Mon-Wed 11 pm, Thu & Fri midnight, Sun 5 pm; closed Sun D, closed Sat.

L'Antica Pizzeria da Michele £64 5̲ 3̲ 2̲
44 Old Compton Street, W1   020 7434 4563   5–2A
199 Baker Street, NW1   020 7935 6458   2–1A
The "outstanding pizzas" – "huge, delicious and authentically Neapolitan" – win top marks for the two London outposts of a Naples original dating back 150 years, which featured in Elizabeth Gilbert's global bestseller 'Eat Pray Love'. The toppings are "mostly traditional", with some "interesting combinations and extras". Don't be misled by the "plain exterior, which makes it look like all the cheap restaurants and snack places along Baker Street" – this branch and its Soho sibling are "very good indeed". / www.anticapizzeriadamichele.co.uk; anticapizzeriadamicheleuk.

Antillean SE1 £62 3̲ 2̲ 3̲
74 Blackfriars Rd   020 3011 4449   10–4A
"The lovely space that was Baltic (RIP)" – a former Georgian coachbuilding works south of Blackfriars Bridge – nowadays hosts chef-patron Michael Hanbury's yearling, which is billed as the capital's 'first pan-Caribbean restaurant'. The service has sometimes seemed "slightly confused", but the "original and very flavourful" food receives steady praise. / SE1; antillean.co.uk; @antilleanrestaurant; Tue-Sat 11 pm; closed Sun & Mon.

Applebee's Fish SE1 £74 3̲ 3̲ 3̲
5 Stoney St   020 7407 5777   10–4C
"Reliably good fish and seafood" make this straightforward operation "an attractive option at the edge of Borough Market". It's a flexible spot, which makes for an easy transition between indoor and al fresco eating. / SE1 9AA; www.applebeesfish.com; @applebeesfishlondon; Mon-Wed 10 pm, Thu-Sat 11.30 pm, Sun 6 pm; no Amex.

Apricity W1 NEW £84 2̲ 4̲ 3̲
68 Duke Street   020 8017 2780   3–2A
Former Tredwells chef, Chantelle Nicholson, has opened this Mayfair newcomer in April 2022, with a hyper-seasonal, low-waste ethos and prettily distressed, minimal décor. Initial reports in our diners' survey are mixed. All feedback suggests the (vegetable-heavy) menu "sounds so interesting", but what are "exceptional plant-based dishes" to some tastes arrive with "not a lot of flair or flavour" to others. (And press reviewers are also split: what is to The Guardian's Grace Dent "too good and truly delicious" to The Evening Standard's Jimi Famurewa "occasionally feels like it loses sight of fun and basic diner enjoyment"). / W1U 6JU; www.apricityrestaurant.com; @apricityrestaurant; Tue-Sat 9 pm; closed Sun & Mon.

FSA

Apulia EC1   £61   3 2 2
50 Long Lane   020 7600 8107   10–2B
"Ideal if you're visiting the Barbican" – this "reliable, genuine, family-run Italian" opposite Smithfield market is a "very friendly little place". The "great pizza and pasta" and "very good Italian wine list" are "fairly priced" and represent "good VFM", especially for the area. / EC1A 9EJ; www.apuliarestaurant.co.uk; @apuliarestaurant; Mon-Fri 10.30 pm, Sat 10.45 pm, Sun 10.15 pm.

aqua kyoto W1   £92   3 3 4
240 Regent St (entrance 30 Argyll St)   020 7478 0540   4–1A
With its outdoor rooftop terraces over central London near Regent Street, this Hong Kong-owned Japanese joint (a sibling of more famous Aqua Shard) makes a "romantic" location – "even a touch exotic" – to dine on "lovely food" which "looks as good as it tastes". "The rent must be pretty steep, presumably explaining why prices are very high too". / W1B 3BR; www.aqua-london.com; @aquakyotolondon; Sun-Thu 10 pm, Sat, Fri 10.15 pm.

Aqua Shard SE1   £112   2 2 3
Level 31, 31 St Thomas St   020 3011 1256   10–4C
Near the top of the Shard, on its 31st floor, there's no doubt this is a stunning venue, most recommended for a special date or the "amazing afternoon tea". No-one says its modern British menu is disappointing, but there is a feeling that it's "very expensive" and the cynical verdict is that "you don't go for the food, you go for the toilets, which give you an unparalleled widescreen view of London". / SE1 9RY; www.aquashard.co.uk; @aquashard; Mon-Sun 10.15 pm; closed Sat & Sun L.

Aquavit SW1   £97   2 3 2
St James's Market, 1 Carlton St   020 7024 9848   4–4D
The "outstanding Scandinavian" flavours created by Swedish chef Emma Bengtsson – a superstar in New York – are showcased in this stark, "very spacious" modern venue ("lots of "high-quality wood and granite") in the St James's Market development behind Piccadilly Circus. It's never reproduced the excitement in London that it enjoys in Manhattan. Even critics acknowledge "it could be so good", but some items seem "absurdly expensive" and the room itself can seem icy in its beauty. / SW1Y 4QQ; www.aquavitrestaurants.com; @aquavitlondon; Tue-Thu 9 pm, Fri & Sat 10 pm; closed Sun & Mon; cash only.

Arabica   £58   3 4 2
7 Lewis Cubitt Walk, N1   020 3747 4422   9–3C
3 Rochester Walk, SE1   020 3011 5151   10–4C
"Excellent" Middle Eastern food – "lots of very tasty dishes, with the veggie plates taking the crown" – wins solid ratings for this former festival stall that has moved steadily upmarket over two decades, and now has a glass-fronted flagship at Borough Market, a restaurant in King's Cross and an outlet in Selfridges' food hall. For regulars, its revised menu inspires mixed feelings ("an improvement" to some, "a step back" for others).
/ www.arabicalondon.com; arabicalondon.

Aragawa W1 NEW
38 Clarges St   020 7493 3807   3–4C
Esteemed Tokyo steakhouse, Aragawa (est 1967, and actually predated by its Kobe branch) is set to open in late 2022 on the Mayfair site that for over 20 years as Miyama (long RIP) was an exemplar of traditional Japanese cuisine. Tokyo diners may pay over £400 per head for the best cuts… and that's before you go wild with the list of Premiers Grands Crus on the wine list. / W1.

F S A

The Araki W1 £380 5 4 3
Unit 4 12 New Burlington St   020 7287 2481   4–3A
Matsuhiro Araki returned to the Far East in 2019 (he had moved to London while his daughter went to uni in the UK) and left this nine-seat Mayfair venue (for which he gained three Michelin stars) in the hands of his apprentice – UK-born Marty Lau – who has run it along similar lines ever since. Of course, it's a second-mortgage job, but the sushi omakase menu here is very seldom rated anything less than "outstanding", and why Michelin now chooses to ignore a restaurant which satisfies such a high proportion of customers at one of London's top price points is baffling. One quibble – "it's £300 a person, but you still have to leave after your 2-hour sitting".
/ W1S 3BH; the-araki.co.uk; @arakisart; Tue-Sat 9 pm; closed Tue-Sat L, closed Sun & Mon; no Amex; no shorts.

Arcade Food Hall WC1
103-105 New Oxford Street   020 7519 1202   5–1A
The food court in the landmark Centrepoint building by Tottenham Court Road station was relaunched by JKS Restaurants under a new, tightly curated format and with new outlets in early summer 2022, after two years of off-and-on trading during the pandemic. It now offers American, Middle Eastern, Indian, Nepali, Indonesian, Thai, Vietnamese, Japanese and Spanish food options, along with a jelly & ice cream bar and several booze outlets – with between them six negroni or five G&T options, among others. Everything is listed on one centralised menu, so you can mix and match without slogging around – and queuing up at – a succession of individual stalls. / WC1W 1DB; www.arcade-london.com; @arcadefoodhall; Tue-Sat 11 pm, Sun 5 pm; closed Sun D, closed Mon.

Ark Fish E18 £53 3 3 2
142 Hermon Hill   020 8989 5345   1–1D
With "fish fresh from Billingsgate" and enthusiastic family ownership, this substantial South Woodford chippy is a "good local standby", well worth a sit-down meal rather than take-away. / E18 1QH; www.arkfishrestaurant.co.uk; @ark_fish_restaurant; Tue-Thu 9.45 pm, Fri & Sat 10.15 pm, Sun 8.45 pm; closed Mon; no Amex; no booking.

Arros QD W1 £102 2 2 2
64 Eastcastle Street   020 3883 3525   3–1D
"Good food, but not great value" is a common verdict on this Spanish venture north of Oxford Street – the London outpost of chef Quique Dacosta, whose Alicante restaurant has three Michelin stars. It certainly looks impressive, with an open kitchen dominated by a six-metre woodfired stove, at which choice cuts of meat and fish are grilled alongside a dozen rice dishes cooked in the pan. But while it is praised for its "perfect paella", it is also often cited as diners' "most overpriced meal of the year".
/ W1W 8NQ; www.arrosqd.com; @arrosqd; Tue-Sat 11 pm, Sun 3 pm; closed Sun D, closed Mon.

Artisans of Sardinia SW15 NEW £65 3 4 3
16 Lacy Road   020 8785 9962   11–2B
Massimo Masili's Sardinian showcase is a "very welcome new addition to the SW15 dining scene" thanks to its "excellent food and extremely friendly service". It can, though, seem "too expensive for what it is" – "Putney location, Mayfair prices!" / SW15 1NL; www.artisansofsardinia.com; @artisansofsardinia_putney; Tue-Sat 10.30 pm; closed Sun & Mon.

FSA RATINGS: FROM 1 POOR — 5 EXCEPTIONAL

L'Artista NW11 £51 243
917 Finchley Rd 020 8731 7501 1–1B
"Delicious Italian favourites", "efficient service with a smile" and a "great family vibe" is the formula that makes this Golders Green institution so popular. "I remember bringing my girlfriends here when I was a teenager, so it's been serving pizza and pasta for a very long time!". "Don't worry about its location under the railway arches – the noise of the trains is drowned out by the noise of the customers". / NW11 7PE; www.lartistapizzeria.com; Mon-Sun midnight.

Artusi SE15 £51 433
161 Bellenden Rd 020 3302 8200 1–4D
This tiny, hip Peckham local "delivers great food" from a short but impeccably prepared Italian menu. They look after their neighbourhood clientele well, with "home delivery kits a lifesaver during lockdown". The name checks Pellegrino Artusi, 19th-century don of Italian cuisine. / SE15 4DH; www.artusi.co.uk; @artusipeckham; Tue-Thu 9.30 pm, Fri & Sat 10 pm, Sun 4 pm; closed Tue L closed Sun D, closed Mon.

Asakusa NW1 £39 432
265 Eversholt St 020 7388 8533 9–3C
This "lovely little Japanese restaurant" near Mornington Crescent tube has no airs and graces, but provides "great food and atmosphere", with a menu that covers most of the classics of the cuisine, from sushi and sashimi to yakitori grills, hotpots and noodle dishes. / NW1 1BA; asakusa.has.restaurant; Mon-Sat 11.30 pm; closed Mon-Sat L, closed Sun.

Assaggi W2 £75 343
39 Chepstow Pl 020 7792 5501 7–1B
"Excellent Italian food and very personable service" have made this unusual venue, on the first floor of a Notting Hill pub, a place of more-than-local interest for more than 25 years. Admittedly it no longer generates anything like the gigantic buzz it once did, but diehard fans say "it's comforting that it survived the pandemic and the food's even better post-lockdown". / W2 4TS; www.assaggi.co.uk; @Assagginottinghill; Tue-Sat 10 pm; closed Sun & Mon; no Amex.

The Atlas SW6 £52 323
16 Seagrave Rd 020 7385 9129 6–3A
This "fab gastropub" with a "great menu" of Mediterranean-inspired scoff may not be quite worth a detour – but is certainly "a strong recommendation if you're in the area", close to West Brompton tube station. In business in its current incarnation for almost 25 years, it now has an "excellent terrace garden", making it even more attractive for Sunday lunch or warm summer evenings. / SW6 1RX; www.theatlaspub.co.uk; @theatlaspub; Mon-Sun 9.30 pm; closed Mon-Thu L.

Attawa E8 £20 332
6 Kingsland High Street 020 7254 1236 14–1A
This Dalston two-year-old from MasterChef: The Professionals 2019 semi-finalist Arbinder Dugal is a "very solid representative of the by-now-not-quite-so-new wave of modern Indian restaurants – probably the best in this part of town". Named after the owners' home village in the Punjab, it serves a short menu of tasty north Indian dishes. / E8 2JP; attawa.co.uk; @attawadalston; Tue-Sun 10 pm; closed Tue-Sun L, closed Mon.

Attimi N10 NEW £48 333
The Broadway 020 8444 8777 1–1B
This new Italian in Muswell Hill has an "interesting selection of tasty and well-presented small plates", with a "focus on quality and taste". The chic modern interior makes for a "nice buzzy atmosphere", and locals are encouraged to use it as a wine bar – there are more than 100 bottles in stock, most of them Italian. / N10 3SH; @attimi_restaurants_london; Tue-Fri 10.30 pm, Sat & Sun 10 pm; closed Tue-Fri L, closed Mon.

F S A

The Aubrey SW1 NEW   £243   3 4 3
Mandarin Oriental, 66 Knightsbridge   020 7201 3899   6–1D
Billing itself somewhat misleadingly as an 'eccentric Japanese izakaya experience' (which would suggest it's down-to-earth… which it isn't), this luxurious space decked with Japanese prints is this Knightsbridge hotel's new incumbent for the basement space that was previously Bar Boulud (RIP). It is rated on limited feedback to date, but all of it enthusiastic. Top Tip – bargain set lunch menu featuring katsu sandos, plus cocktails. / SW1S 7LA; www.mandarinoriental.com/london/hyde-park/fine-dining/japanese-izakaya/the-aubrey; @mo_hydepark; Mon-Wed midnight, Thu-Sat 1 am; closed Sun.

The Audley W1 NEW
43 Mount Street   no tel   3–3A
The first London project for Artfarm – behind The Fife Arms in Braemar and Somerset's Roth Bar & Grill, and now owner of Soho's Groucho Club – this fine Victorian boozer (built in 1888) in Mayfair is set to relaunch in autumn 2022. Set over five floors, it will comprise a street-level pub, first-floor dining room ('The Mount Street Restaurant') and upper-floor event spaces, all showcasing artworks created by Hauser & Wirth's roster of artists. / W1W 3AH; theaudleypublichouse.com; @Audleypublichouse; Mon-Sun 11 pm.

Augustine Kitchen SW11   £58   4 4 3
63 Battersea Bridge Rd   020 7978 7085   6–4C
"Weekday set lunch is incredibly good value" and justifies the hop over to Franck Raymond's bistro, just south of Battersea Bridge, where the "excellent" Gallic food is inspired by the Alpine cuisine of his childhood, near Evian on Lake Geneva. / SW11 3AU; www.augustine-kitchen.co.uk; @augustinesw11; Tue-Sat 9 pm; closed Sun & Mon.

Aulis London W1   £188   4 4 4
16a St Anne's Court   020 3948 9665   4–1D
"Charlie Taylor and his small team are brilliant hosts, striking the perfect balance of informality and professionalism to draw you into the intimate dinner-party style mood" at this tiny chef's table experience in a Soho alleyway, whose menu is, in part, a showcase for owner Simon Rogan's famous L'Enclume. "Don't come expecting linen table cloths and flunkies: you are dining in an extended kitchen, so it only works if you want the food to be the star. And it's truly stellar" – "strong classic flavour combinations inspired by seasonal produce". One niggle repeated a couple of times this year: "numerous dishes seemed simply ready to plate" which can detract from the experience ("I was disappointed that all we really saw was the final touches to the preparation, it was fun, but I missed the opportunity to learn more about the food, as you can at some chef's tables"). For the most part, though, few doubt that a meal here is anything other than "stunning". Despite awarding L'Enclume three Michelin stars, the tyre men bizarrely award no stars here. / W1W 0BF; aulis.london; @aulissimonrogan; Tue-Sat 11.30 pm; closed Tue-Thu L, closed Sun & Mon; no Amex.

Authentique Epicerie & Bar NW5   £47   3 3 3
114-116 Fortess Road   020 3609 6602   9–2C
"Like a French tapas bar", this Tufnell Park showcase celebrates the wines (700) and beers (75) of the French-speaking world, with themed dinners highlighting produce from 12 regions in rotation. "As the name suggests, food is secondary – decent, but basically an accompaniment to the outstanding selection of reasonably priced wines". / NW5 5HL; authentique-epicerie.com; @authentiquelondon; Tue-Sat 11 pm, Sun 8 pm; closed Mon.

Avanti W4   £34   3 3 2
South Parade   020 8994 9444   8–1A
This Mediterranean fusion spot on the edge of Bedford Park in Chiswick combines "excellent pizzas and tapas". The gazebo adds to the Med effect in good weather. / W4 1LD; avantichiswick.com; Mon-Sun 10 pm.

Ave Mario WC2 £58 3|3|4
15 Henrietta Street   no tel   5–3C
"Totally bonkers" and "Insta heaven" – the latest maximalist, Central Casting interpretation of Italian restaurant culture from the French group Big Mamma (who hit paydirt with Gloria and Circolo Populare) opened in Covent Garden in summer 2021. Despite being massive (with 295 covers over two floors and two terraces), and its cheesily cheeky menu ('Lettuce Pray' salad, 'Chocolate al Porno') it's not inspired a huge number of reports. Perhaps this was due to the pasting it received from the press ("Nonna's gone to Iceland", said The Evening Standard's Jimi Famurewa) but our (quite limited) feedback includes no major complaints. / WC2W 8QG; www.bigmammagroup.com/en/trattorias/ave-mario; @bigmamma.uk; Sun-Wed 10.30 pm, Thu-Sat 10.45 pm.

L'Aventure NW8 £75 4|4|4
3 Blenheim Terrace   020 7624 6232   9–3A
"Run by the owner for 41 years and I have been a customer for over 35 years and the quality has never varied!" – Catherine Parisot's "brilliant longstanding favourite" in St John's Wood "never fails to delight": in particular its cute interior and pretty location make it a top choice for a date. Under the "able guidance" of la patronne, it provides classic 'cuisine bourgeoise': "you always know what you are going to get as the menu never changes, but the food is always good". / NW8 0EH; www.laventure.co.uk; Mon-Sat 11 pm; closed Sat L, closed Sun.

The Avenue SW1 £71 3|3|3
7-9 St James's Street   020 7321 2111   3–4D
This cavernous modern brasserie (owned by D&D London) was something of a 1990s icon, but – despite a convenient St James's location – goes somewhat unsung nowadays. On limited feedback, though, all reports are upbeat, saying it's "a good spot for a business lunch", or that "Jose and his team know how to lay on a good brunch". / SW1A 1EE; www.avenue-restaurant.co.uk; @avenuestjames; Tue-Sat 9.30 pm, Sun 5 pm; closed Sun D, closed Mon.

Aviary EC2 £101 2|3|4
10th Floor, 22-25 Finsbury Square   020 3873 4060   13–2A
This hotel rooftop bar-restaurant overlooking Finsbury Square is a "gorgeous spot for lunch – quiet and with good views". Glass igloos are installed for winter, so it's a year-round operation. The modern corporate brasserie cooking attracts little notice, either favourable or otherwise. / EC2E 1DX; aviarylondon.com; @aviaryldn; Mon-Sun midnight.

Awesome Thai SW13 £39 3|3|2
68 Church Rd   020 8563 7027   11–1A
This "great local Thai" in Barnes owes its enduring popularity to its efficient and "welcoming" family owners and its handy position in the centre of the more villagey bit of SW13 (directly opposite the Olympic Studios indie cinema). / SW13 0DQ; www.awesomethai.co.uk; Fri & Sat, Mon-Thu 10.30 pm, Sun 10 pm; closed Mon-Thu L.

BabaBoom SW11 £39 3|3|2
30 Battersea Rise   07809 903181   11–2C
A tight menu of "delicious" Middle Eastern-inspired street food, especially kebabs, is found at this Battersea Rise venue and its 2022 spin-off in Westfield Stratford. Founder Eve Bugler, an ultra-marathon runner and erstwhile director of Nando's, launched the business in 2015 with backing from senior industry figures including former boss David Niven, Mark Selby of Wahaca and Peter Borg-Neal of Oakman Inns. / SW11 1EE; www.bababoom.london; @bababoomlondon; Thu-Sat 11 pm, Sun-Wed 10 pm.

FSA

Babur SE23 — £57 — 5 5 3
119 Brockley Rise   020 8291 2400   1–4D
"The deft flavours of fine Indian dining" at this "Honor Oak stalwart" have induced discerning diners to "make the awkward trip" to SE23 for almost 40 years now. "The place maintains its standards" and has a credible claim on being "the best Indian in southeast London" thanks to its "exciting" dishes, "excellent" service and "elegant" interior. / SE23 1JP; www.babur.info; @baburrestaurant; Mon-Sun 11 pm; no shorts.

Bacchanalia W1 NEW
Berkeley Square   no tel   3–2B
Richard Caring has outlined plans for his most spectacular and decadent restaurant yet. This former Porsche garage in Berkeley Square will channel the atmosphere of Ancient Greece and Rome, alongside suitably Mediterranean-inspired cuisine and promises to make his glitzily glam Sexy Fish, a near-neighbour, look like a vicarage tea party. No opening date yet! / W1W 5AR; Tue-Sun 4 pm.

Bacco TW9 — £71 — 3 3 2
39-41 Kew Rd   020 8332 0348   1–4A
This "excellent local Italian" in the middle of Richmond offers "friendly service and attractive menu choices at reasonable prices". Pre-show options ensure that it's "good for the local theatres". / TW9 2NQ; www.bacco-restaurant.co.uk; Tue-Sat 10 pm; closed Sun & Mon; no shorts.

Bageriet WC2 — £20 — 4 2 2
24 Rose St   020 7240 0000   5–3C
"Fabulous Swedish cakes and good coffee" are the siren call to this tiny Scandi kafé in Covent Garden, if you can nab a seat – but "it's just so small you can't always get in". Top Tip – "the prinsesstårta is to die for". / WC2E 9EA; www.bageriet.co.uk; Tue-Fri 5.30 pm, Sat 6 pm; closed Tue-Sat D, closed Sun & Mon; no booking.

Bala Baya SE1 — £69 — 3 3 3
Old Union Yard Arches, 229 Union Street   020 8001 7015   10–4B
"The really tasty and innovative modern Israeli cuisine never fails to impress" at former Ottolenghi chef Eran Tibi's all-day venue in the "very hip setting" of a Southwark railway arch. "Every wine is from Israel – and ours were very good". / SE1 0LR; balabaya.co.uk; @bala_baya; Mon-Sat 11 pm, Sun 10 pm.

Balady — £31 — 4 2 1
750 Finchley Road, NW11   020 8458 2064   1–1B
39-41 Leather Lane, EC1   020 8458 2064   10–1A NEW
"Outstanding delicious falafels" – "some of the best in London" – are the star turn at this Jewish-Moroccan veggie spot in Temple Fortune. "Don't be put off by the strip lighting aesthetic, although there's possibly better ambience in the street outside". In the last couple of years the three Sabbo brothers have opened follow-ups in High Barnet (selling meat) and Clerkenwell's Leather Lane (and also in Lakewood, New Jersey!)

Balthazar WC2 — £85 — 1 2 3
4 - 6 Russell Street   020 3301 1155   5–3D
"An excellent simulacrum of a Parisian brasserie" – this big, prominently situated Covent Garden fixture, just off the Piazza (created by English-born New Yorker, Keith McNally, but nowadays part of Caprice Holdings) provides "good vibes for Sunday brunch or a meal around a show". But even fans feel "the main draw is the buzzy atmosphere, not the unexciting food" and – especially when it becomes "too busy for its own good" – this is, for its critics, "the worst kind of hell", with food that's "absolutely average and poor value for the price". / WC2B 5HZ; www.balthazarlondon.com; @balthazarldn; Mon-Sat 10.30 pm, Sun 9.30 pm.

FSA RATINGS: FROM 1 POOR — 5 EXCEPTIONAL

FSA

Bancone £56 4|4|3
10 Lower James Street, W1   020 3034 0820   4–3C
39 William IV Street, WC2   020 7240 8786   5–4C
"A perfect pre-theatre choice that's quick and classy" – these West End pasta-stops off Trafalgar Square and in Soho provide "excellent pasta, reasonable prices and a speedy turnaround". "Buzzy rather than comfortable (many tables only have stools), really keen nearly all Italian staff provide the (fairly) limited menu" – "fab fresh pasta" with "modern Italian flavours" that's "not complicated, but done with precision", all "at an amazing price". / www.bancone.co.uk.

Bang Bang Oriental NW9 £48 3|2|2
399 Edgware Road   no tel   1–1A
The "wonderful street-food vibes" justify a trip to Colindale to visit this enormous Oriental food court. "Quality varies greatly between the units", but if you make the right choices, you're bound to enjoy a "party for the mouth". / NW9 0AS; www.bangbangoriental.com; @bangbangoriental; Sun-Thu 9.30 pm, Fri & Sat 10 pm; no booking.

Banners N8 £57 2|3|3
21 Park Road   020 8348 2930   1–1C
With an all-day menu that bounces happily from the Caribbean and Mexico to the Isle of Man and Thailand, Juliette Banner has provided up-beat service in Crouch End for more than 30 years. "A Banners breakfast is the perfect cure for a hangover" – and you can also earn one with the "great cocktails". The "authentic American-style burgers" must have attracted Bob Dylan, the bard of Americana, whose 1993 visit is commemorated with a plaque – you can even book the table he sat at! / N8 8TE; www.bannersrestaurant.com; @BannersN8; Sun-Thu 9.30 pm, Fri & Sat 10.30 pm; no Amex.

Bao £38 3|4|4
31 Windmill St, W1   020 3011 1632   5–1A
53 Lexington St, W1   07769 627811   4–2C
4 Pancras Square, N1   no tel   9–3C
13 Stoney Street, SE1   020 3967 5407   10–4C
1 Redchurch Street, E2   no tel   13–1B
Netil Market, 13-23 Westgate Street, E8   no tel   14–2B
"The best-ever bao buns: so light and fluffy with absolutely delicious fillings" again win raves for this five-strong chain, backed by JKS Restaurants (which plans a Battersea opening later in 2022). "Worth queuing for, although happily they now take bookings". Top Menu Tips – "very good Taiwan-style spicy beef noodles"; "the warm bao with horlicks ice-cream is the most unusual!" / baolondon.com; bao_london.

Baozi Inn £36 3|2|2
24 Romilly Street, W1   020 7287 3266   5–3A
34-36 Southwark Street, SE1   020 8037 5875   10–4C
"Authentic and tasty dumplings" and other northern Chinese street-food classics make any of Wei Shao's small group "a great standby for a quick and fun meal". Some prefer to stay longer ("our family goes for a Sunday feast") with the biggest range of dishes at the 120-cover flagship near Borough Market. There are also branches in Chinatown, Soho, and the Market Halls in Victoria and Oxford Street. / baoziinn.com.

Bar des Prés W1 £116 3|4|4
16 Albemarle Street   020 3908 2000   3–3C
"Asia meets France" at this Mayfair yearling from French TV chef Cyril Lignac, named after his Paris restaurant in St Germain des Prés. "There's a large team of sushi chefs and the place has a lively, Parisian feel", with "French desserts, which are superb" – as they should be, given that Lignac trained as a pâtissier. It's no shock that the place is pricey, but fans say it's worth it: "absolutely top class, can't wait to return". / W1W 4HW; bardespres.com; @bardespres; Mon-Sat 11 pm, Sun 10 pm; no trainers.

FSA

Bar Douro SE1 £50 4 4 4
Arch 35b, 85b Southwark Bridge Rd   020 7378 0524   10–4B
"Really enjoyable Portuguese tapas" is served in this "lovely, light and airy space", tucked under a railway arch, near London Bridge. Founded by Max Graham, from the Churchills port dynasty, fans even say it's "reminiscent of early-years Barrafina". Top Tip – "the tiny clams". (Note: don't be put off by the queue outside – it may be for the pancake shop in front!). / SE1 0NQ; www.bardouro.co.uk; @bardouro; Tue-Sat 10 pm, Sun 9 pm; closed Tue-Thu L, closed Mon; booking max 4 may apply.

Bar Esteban N8 £62 3 3 3
29 Park Rd   020 8340 3090   1–1C
This "cosy and vibey" tapas bar has a strong local following in Crouch End, and celebrates its tenth anniversary this year. 'Esteban', its founder, is in fact Glasgow-born record producer Stephen Lironi, a long-time fan of Spanish cuisine; chef Pablo Rodriguez is from Barcelona, while manager Naroa Ortega is from Bilbao. / N8 8TE; www.baresteban.com; @bar__esteban; Mon, Fri, Tue-Thu 10 pm, Sat 11 pm, Sun 9.30 pm; closed Mon, Fri L; booking max 8 may apply.

Bar Italia W1 £37 2 4 5
22 Frith St   020 7437 4520   5–2A
"Irresistible for its history and authenticity" (as well as for "espresso and pastries") – this 24-hour coffee bar defines Soho as the hub of London nightlife, as it has done ever since 1949, when the Polledri family – still the owners – opened it to serve what was then a thriving local Italian community. It's "still skanky – but great" for those who appreciate post-war interiors. / W1D 4RF; www.baritaliasoho.co.uk; @baritaliasoho; Mon-Sun 5 am; no booking.

The Barbary WC2 £76 4 3 4
16 Neal's Yard   no tel   5–2C
"Everything's delicious beyond words", say fans of Layo and Zoe Paskin's "hugely fun" and stylish North African-inspired small-plates operation in Neal's Yard, younger sibling of the Palomar. With "excellent bar food at a counter", it makes the "best pre-theatre spot around". Top Tips – "the Jerusalem bagels and squid are stand-out items". / WC2H 9DP; www.thebarbary.co.uk; @barbarylondon; Tue-Sat 10 pm, Sun 9 pm; closed Tue, Wed L, closed Mon; no booking.

The Barbary Next Door WC2 NEW £45 4 2 2
16a Neal's Yard   awaiting tel   5–2C
On the minuscule Covent Garden site that was Jacob The Angel (RIP), this "cheek-by-jowl café" serves similar North African-inspired small plates to the neighbouring mothership. "The bill for the admittedly good food racks up", though, and some feel it's "not good enough value, considering you can hear your fellow diners chewing and you're fighting for elbow room". / WC2W 9DP; thebarbarynextdoor.co.uk; @thebarbarynextdoor; Wed-Sat 10 pm, Sun 4 pm; closed Wed L closed Sun D, closed Mon & Tue.

La Barca SE1 £83 3 3 3
80-81 Lower Marsh   020 7928 2226   10–4A
This "busy Italian", whose familiar ship has sailed behind Waterloo station for almost 50 years, has hosted countless pre- and post-theatre meals for audiences and cast from the Old Vic opposite. It's "unchanged for decades, but actually very appealing as a result". Though sometimes considered "expensive for what it is", fans say the cooking is "cracking". / SE1 7AB; www.labarca-ristorante.com; @labarca1976-gb; Mon-Sat 10.30 pm; closed Sat L, closed Sun; booking max 12 may apply.

FSA RATINGS: FROM 1 POOR — 5 EXCEPTIONAL

FSA

Barrafina £70 5 4 4
26-27 Dean Street, W1 020 7813 8016 4–1D
10 Adelaide St, WC2 020 7440 1456 5–4C
43 Drury Lane, WC2 020 7440 1456 5–2D
Coal Drops Yard, N1 0207 440 1486 9–3C
2 Dirty Lane, SE1 no tel 10–4C NEW

"Sights and smells of Spain sitting at the counter" provide "heaven on a stool" at the Hart Bros' faithful recreations of Barcelona's Cal Pep: still, after 15 years, one of the most-mentioned groups in our survey. The "extraordinary tapas is full of fresh ideas" – there's "always something new to try on the menu" (created by their chef/director Angel Zapata Martin) – and it "still deserves top marks, particularly the seafood" (which is the only option nowadays at the WC2 'Mariscos' outlet). A meal is "not cheap" mind you (in fact, even fans can find prices "crazy") but the overall verdict? "Worth the queue, and the bill!" (In July 2022, they added a new, fifth branch to the group, in SE1's Borough Yards developments).
/ www.barrafina.co.uk.

Barshu W1 £51 5 2 2
28 Frith St 020 7287 6688 5–3A

This "amazing Sichuan specialist" stands out from the competition with a "really interesting selection" of super-spicy options that are "a long, long way above and beyond the usual Chinatown fare". "The recently revamped menu is now even better than before" – "not the greatest ambience but my goodness the food is good" ("took a gourmet friend who declared that six of the seven dishes were exceptional… the seventh was just delicious!"). Top Tip – "if you have a dry wok dish and don't finish it, get a doggy bag".
/ W1D 5LF; www.barshurestaurant.co.uk; @barshurestaurant; Sun-Thu 10 pm, Fri & Sat 10.30 pm.

Base Face Pizza W6 £38 3 4 3
300 King Street 020 8617 1092 8–2B

Jazz music's loss was Hammersmith pizza-lovers' gain: professional bass-player Tim Thornton lost his living when live music was silenced under lockdown, so he turned to making "really delicious" pizzas. Now he has a "fantastic little pizza restaurant" on King Street that is "busy and full of locals" ("the best pizzas we've eaten in years – a real find!"). / W6; www.basefacepizza.com; @base.face.pizza; Tue-Sun 10 pm; closed Tue-Sun L, closed Mon.

Beast W1 £121 2 2 2
3 Chapel Pl 020 7495 1816 3–1B

A candle-lit temple to the atavistic delights of consuming quantities of ribeye steak and king crab that's "in fact very good, if grossly overpriced for what it is" ("£100 for a bit of crab!"). But spending big is arguably central to the 'Beast Experience' touted (tongue in cheek), on the website: 'the place will make an impression on your client or whomever, and everyone will remember the occasion'. / W1G 0BG; www.beastrestaurant.co.uk; @beast.restaurant; Mon-Sat 10.30 pm; closed Mon-Thu L, closed Sun; may need 7+ to book.

The Begging Bowl SE15 £54 4 4 3
168 Bellenden Rd 020 7635 2627 1–4D

After 10 years, this "lively" Peckham neighbourhood Thai remains a "consistently terrific place" that "delivers great food that's as good as you get in Bangkok, but with a twist". Co-owner Jane Alty, who makes regular trips to Thailand to research recipes and ingredients, discovered the cuisine while working in the kitchen at David Thompson's Nahm (long RIP). / SE15 4BW; www.thebeggingbowl.co.uk; @the-begging-bowl; Tue-Sat 10 pm, Sun 4 pm; closed Tue-Thu L closed Sun D, closed Mon; booking online only.

F S A

Behind E8 £72   5 5 4
20 Sidworth Street   no tel   14–2B

"Hackney's newest foodie hotspot doesn't disappoint" and "the passionate commitment of all involved shines through" at Andy Benyon's year-old 18-seater, near London Fields. "Very friendly chefs serve you personally" at a counter overlooking the kitchen "allowing a view of the preparation of each course (it's a bit like dining on the set of an episode of MasterChef: The Professionals)". The focus is on fish and seafood, and "a succession of elegantly prepared dishes bring complex flavours to some of the most sustainable species on the market", all adding up to a "superb" overall meal. Given its high quality, it's not an overpriced venue at all: "you get amazing value on top of an amazing experience!" / E8 3SD; www.behindrestaurant.co.uk; @behindrestaurant; Tue-Sat 11 pm; closed Sun & Mon; booking online only.

Bellamy's W1 £69   3 5 4
18-18a Bruton Pl   020 7491 2727   3–2B

"With its quietly thrumming ambience, well-spaced tables and unobtrusive service from staff used to looking after royalty", this "eternally discreet" brasserie hidden in a cute Mayfair mews is a long-established favourite for a blue-blooded, establishment crowd (and "perfect for doing business in"). Elegantly suited owner, Gavin Rankin, smoothly commands the space – "his team are wonderfully welcoming" and "all this is supported by classic French food, an excellent and keenly priced wine list, and a set lunch menu that's a bargain (ideal for when Finance put a cap on your entertaining budget)". Top Menu Tips – "Martinis, oysters and staples like steak tartare are prominent". / W1J 6LY; www.bellamysrestaurant.co.uk; @bellamysmayfair; Mon-Fri 10.30 pm, Sat 11.30 pm; closed Sat L, closed Sun; Jacket required.

Bellanger N1 £59   2 2 3
9 Islington Grn   020 7226 2555   9–3D

Created by Jeremy King and Christopher Corbin, this smart brasserie on Islington Green is long on Belle Époque-style charm, and – thanks to "a menu that suits most moods and a warm welcome" – has, for many locals, become "a go-to for most occasions, particularly family lunch and brunch". Its cuisine (with some emphasis on its selection of tartes flambées) has always tended to be "fine if not particularly distinguished" but the experience is enhanced by "decent, unrushed service". Now part of Minor International's Wolseley Hospitality Group following its April 2022 takeover of Corbin & King: "I fear for it under its new ownership" is a common worry among regulars. / N1 2XH; www.bellanger.co.uk; @bellanger_n1; Tue-Sat 10 pm, Sun 9 pm; closed Mon.

Belvedere W8 NEW
off Abbotsbury Rd in Holland Park   020 7602 1238   8–1D

One of London's most stunning and prettily located venues – this 17th-century former ballroom in Holland Park itself is scheduled to reopen in the latter half of 2022 under the ownership of Ilya Demichev and George Bukhov-Weinstein, the Russians behind Chelsea's Wild Tavern and surf-and-turf specialists Goodman and Burger & Lobster. The menu is expected to be Italian-led and there will be room for 120 diners on two floors – each with its own bar. The venue has had various high-profile tenants, including Marco Pierre White, but has often slipped into complacency based on its location – let's hope they break that mould. / W8 6LU; www.belvedererestaurant.co.uk; @the-belvedere-restaurant-holland-park; Mon-Sat 11 pm, Sun 3.30 pm; closed Sun D.

F S A

Benares W1 £95 4 4 4
12a Berkeley Square House, 020 7629 8886 3–3B

Sameer Taneja's "exceptional" cuisine continues to maintain the high standing of this well-known Berkeley Square destination. Despite the odd "unexciting" report, most accounts are of "fabulous" meals from "a menu that's very spice-led and refined-tasting". Located on the first floor, its modern design "doesn't feel too 'posh Mayfair' in ambience terms", with meals here said to be "well-paced" and "refreshing". / W1J 6BS; www.benaresrestaurant.co.uk; @benaresofficial; Tue-Sat 10.30 pm; closed Sun & Mon; no trainers.

Bentley's W1 £98 4 4 3
11-15 Swallow St 020 7734 4756 4–4B

"A classic for oyster lovers!" – acclaimed Irish chef, Richard Corrigan, continues to be a superb steward of this 106-year-old veteran (established in 1916), cutely tucked away in a side street near Piccadilly Circus, which he has rebuilt over the years into one of the Top 40 destinations in our annual diners' poll. "For outstanding oysters or fish, you can't go wrong", with tips including "cracking fruits de mer" and "simply delicious fish stew". His "fabulous" and "professional" staff help create a "lovely" atmosphere, although the top 'craic' in the ground-floor bar is often tipped over the grander but more sedate upstairs restaurant. (Another excellent option, particularly in summer, is the superb heated outdoor terrace). On the downside, the pricing is somewhat "prohibitive of a frequent visit", but fans say "despite the expense, a meal here is an all-round package that is predictable in a good way". Top Menu Tips – "oh-so-tasty options from the specials board" and "ask for more soda bread!!" / W1B 4DG; www.bentleys.org; @bentleysoysterbar; Mon-Sat 9.30 pm, Sun 8 pm; booking max 8 may apply.

Berber & Q £61 5 4 4
Arch 338 Acton Mews, E8 020 7923 0829 14–2A
Exmouth Market, EC1 020 7837 1726 10–1A

"Smoky perfection!" – Josh Katz's "yummy and very moreish" Middle East-inspired grills in a vibey Haggerston railway arch and on Exmouth Market have won a massive reputation since he launched his take on 'live-fire cooking' in 2015; and the "buzzy, intimate atmosphere" of both locations is also a big winner. Top Menu Tip – "the flatbreads, chicken and cauliflower shawarma are standouts".

Berenjak W1 £64 4 4 4
27 Romilly Street 020 3319 8120 5–2A

"I can't stress how addictive it is!" – Kian Samyani (backed by JKS Restaurants) channels his Iranian heritage at this "friendly" Soho charcoal grill (one of Dua Lipa's fave raves, apparently) to deliver "terrifically tasty kebabs grilled over the coals, with sourdough tandoori flat breads that are perfect for dunking in any of their truly moreish dips". And it's "fun to sit at the bar and watch the action", too. As of summer 2022, it's on the expansion trail, taking over the two-storey Borough Market site that was until recently Flor (RIP), to offer a wider menu incorporating larger dishes and an expanded wine list from the Eastern Med. / W1W 5AL; berenjaklondon.com; @berenjaklondon; Tue-Sat 10 pm; closed Tue-Fri L closed Sat D, closed Sun & Mon.

Bermondsey Larder SE1 £52 4 4 3
153-157 Tower Bridge Road 020 7378 6254 10–4D

With a "taster menu that's second to none", Robin and Sarah Gill's crack kitchen team have settled in well to their new home in a Bermondsey 'aparthotel'. They moved over from Clapham's The Dairy, which did not survive the pandemic, but a taste of the latter's "imaginative, skillful small-plate cooking" using carefully sourced seasonal ingredients is still available here. / SE1 3LW; www.thedairybermondsey.com; @bermondseylarder; Thu-Sat, Wed 10 pm, Sun 4 pm; closed Wed L closed Sun D, closed Mon & Tue.

FSA

The Berners Tavern W1 £100 2 2 5
10 Berners Street 020 7908 7979 3–1D
"Jason Atherton certainly knows how to tart up traditional British fare", according to fans of his "indulgent and delicious" cuisine within this "fabulous" space – a converted banking hall that's part of Marriott's glam, Ian Shrager-designed Edition hotel, north of Oxford Street. Ratings overall, though, are in middle territory, with harsher reports feeling it "rarely elevates above the level of a good gastropub". Top Menu Tip – "the mac 'n' cheese is simply the best". / W1T 3NP; @bernerstavern; Thu & Fri, Tue, Wed, Sat 9.45 pm; closed Tue, Wed, Sat L, closed Sun & Mon.

Best Mangal £48 4 4 2
619 Fulham Rd, SW6 020 7610 0009 6–4A
104 North End Rd, W14 020 7610 1050 8–2D
A wide range of Anatolian grilled meat including "superb lamb doner made in-house, fresh every day", earns consistent high praise for these "welcoming" and "good value" venues in Fulham and West Kensington. / www.bestmangal.com.

Bibendum SW3 £196 4 3 4
81 Fulham Rd 020 7589 1480 6–2C
With its "light-filled setting and high ceilings", this "beautiful and iconic dining room" (converted in 1987 by the late Sir Terence Conran) on the first floor of South Kensington's landmark Michelin Building makes an "impressive" choice for either a business meal or a date, and is "best seen at lunchtime". Over the five years since Claude Bosi took over the stoves, he has started to make the venue his own, and many reports this year are of a "stupendous culinary experience" thanks to his "incredible" and "inventive" cuisine, matched with "an amazing cellar" and provided by "attentive but not over-pompous staff". The caveat is an obvious one – a meal here comes "at a cost…" / SW3 6RD; www.claudebosi.com; @claudebosiatbibendum; Wed & Thu 9 pm, Fri & Sat 9.30 pm; closed Mon & Tue & Sun; booking max 12 may apply.

Bibendum Oyster Bar SW3 £85 4 3 4
Michelin House, 81 Fulham Road 020 7581 5817 6–2C
"If you fancy oysters or other seafood, head for the Michelin Building" – one of London's few venues that truly deserve the adjective 'iconic' – where the "cheaper" alternative to Claude Bosi's grand restaurant upstairs is his "classic oyster bar (nice wines too)" in the elegant foyer of the building, in which "you can sit, nibble on light fare and watch the world go by". / SW3 6RD; www.bibendum.co.uk; @claudebosiatbibendum; Wed & Thu 9 pm, Fri & Sat 9.30 pm; closed Mon & Tue & Sun; no booking.

BiBi W1 £93 5 5 4
42 North Audley Street 020 3780 7310 3–2A
"Absolute 'god tier level' from start to finish!" – JKS Restaurants have totally nailed it once again with this "novel" autumn 2021 newcomer, which inhabits the "tiny but convivial space" on the fringe of Mayfair that was formerly Truc Vert (RIP); and which has now become "a high-end homage to old-school curry houses, including flock wallpaper!". Chef Chet Sharma delivers "an amazing original riff on classic Indian flavours" with "a range of new and vibrant dishes" that are "truly memorable" and "an utter joy". Service is "impeccable and well informed" too and the press have utterly raved (Grace Dent called it "part genius and clearly part subversive"; Giles Coren awarded '11/10') – so, it's "a rare example of a restaurant where every broadsheet reviewer had got it exactly right!" / W1W 6ZR; www.bibirestaurants.com; @bibi_ldn; Tue-Sat 10 pm; closed Tue L, closed Sun & Mon.

FSA

Bibimbap Soho W1   £42   3 3 2
11 Greek St   020 7287 3434   5–2A
This Soho canteen is "one of the better Korean restaurants in town", serving "authentic" Korean fast food headed by the dish it takes its name from – hot rice with savoury toppings that you stir before eating. There's also a take-away option in the City. / W1D 4DJ; bibimbapsoho.co.uk; @bibimbapsoho; Sun-Fri 10 pm, Sat 10.30 pm; no Amex.

Bibo by Dani García EC2   £79   2 2 3
Mondrian Hotel, 45 Curtain Road   020 3146 4545   13–1B
Bibos in Madrid, Marbella, Cádiz and Doha have pre-dated this latest opening for celeb Andalusian chef Dani Garcia, within the newly opened Mondrian Shoreditch (on the site of Red Rooster, RIP). Perhaps because of the drubbings it's received from press reviewers, not very many reporters visited. One or two that did found it "all-round exceptional", but others were "fairly underwhelmed, first by the lengthy explanation of the tapas, and then by the pretty pedestrian-for-the-money food". / EC2; www.sbe.com/restaurants/bibo/shoreditch; @bibo_shoreditch; Sun-Wed 10.30 pm, Thu-Sat 11.30 pm.

Big Easy   £72   2 2 3
12 Maiden Ln, WC2   020 3728 4888   5–3D
332-334 King's Rd, SW3   020 7352 4071   6–3C
Crossrail Pl, E14   020 3841 8844   12–1C
"Big, bold and brassy, with lashings of tasty American food" – a meal in this BBQ and crabshack is "like having a holiday in the southern USA". And you don't have to battle through Heathrow to get there: a King's Road, Chelsea fixture for more than 30 years, it now has spin-offs in Covent Garden and Canary Wharf. "Our grandsons loved this place. We enjoyed it too, and the cocktails were nice". / www.bigeasy.co.uk.

Big Fernand SW7   £28   4 4 2
39 Thurloe Place   020 3031 8330   6–2C
London outpost (in South Ken's 'Little France') of a Paris-based chain, with over 50 branches in France and the Arab World – this 'Maison du Hamburgé' is "not to be missed" for its "great value and utterly delicious burgers" (e.g. "with raclette! who knew?"). / SW7 2HP; www.bigfernanduk.com; @bigfernand_uk; Sun-Thu 10.30 pm, Fri & Sat 11 pm.

Big Jo Bakery N7   £27   3 3 3
318-326 Hornsey Road   020 3915 6760   9–1D
From the same hipster-favourite stable as Primeur and Westerns Laundry, this eat-in artisan bakery between Finsbury Park and Holloway serves a small, simple menu from the blackboard as well as pâtisserie and brunchish fare from breakfast onwards. Feedback is relatively limited, but one Hornsey reporter feels it's "worth crossing north London for". / N7 7HE; www.bigjobakery.com; @bigjobakery; Thu-Sat 11 pm, Sun-Wed 4 pm; closed Sun-Wed D.

The Bird in Hand W14   £53   4 4 4
88 Masbro Road   020 7371 2721   8–1C
"Pizzas with an absolutely stunning crust – and excellent toppings as well" – win rave reviews for this pub conversion near Brook Green. It's a well-run operation, part of the Oak group of pizza-pubs, and everything on the menu is "fresh and well-sourced". / W14 0LR; www.thebirdinhandlondon.com; @thebirdw14; Tue-Sun 11 pm; closed Tue-Fri L, closed Mon; booking weekdays only.

F S A

Bistro Union SW4 £60   3 4 2
40 Abbeville Rd   020 7042 6400   11–2D
"Great to have in the locale" – Adam Byatt provides a "friendly neighbourhood spot" at this "good 'Abbeville village' location" with "lovely food, very nice service and a good atmosphere". It's not of the calibre of his main HQ though – "it's Trinity's little sister, but it's not clear that's reflected in the cooking". / SW4 9NG; www.bistrounion.co.uk; @bistrounionclapham; closed Mon-Sat & Sun; booking max 8 may apply.

Björn Frantzén at Harrods SW1 NEW
87-135 Brompton Road   no tel   6–1D
Harrods enticed Swedish superstar Björn Frantzén to open his first London outlet as the trump card in their beefed-up in-store hospitality offering, with a scheduled late-2022 launch date. His self-named Stockholm flagship is a regular on 'World's Best' lists and his Singapore offshoot Zén is not far behind, which indicates he's not bad at running multiple sites globally. We look forward to feedback. / SW1S 7XL; www.harrods.com; Mon-Sun 8.30 pm.

Black Bear Burger £46   4 3 2
11-13 Market Row, SW9   020 7737 3444   11–2D
Market Halls Canary Wharf, Canada Square, E14   no tel   12–1C NEW
Boxpark Shoreditch, 2-10 Bethnal Green Road, E1   no tel   13–2B
17 Exmouth Market, EC1   020 7837 1039   10–1A NEW
"The burgers are so juicy and tasty" – "just the right combination of taste and juiciness" – at this small group, which has continued to expand from its Shoreditch's Boxpark origins via a proper restaurant in Brixton Market Row to new branches in Market Halls Cargo at Canary Wharf and also the largest opening to date: a 45-seater in Exmouth Market (formerly a Dirty Burger). The brand only uses grass-fed, dry-aged British beef. / blackbearburger.com; black_bear_burger.

The Black Book W1 £53   3 4 4
23 Frith Street   020 7434 1724   5–2A
"A hidden gem in Soho" for œnophiles – this "lovely, intimate basement" has a "great selection of wines for the enthusiast", including "old, rare and super-interesting bottles", "from top producers and at affordable prices". Founded by master sommeliers Gearoid Daveney and Xavier Rousset as the premises for Trade, a private club for people working in hospitality, it remains at its best as an after-hours option. There's a "simple menu" of charcuterie, well-made cheese toasties and the like. Top Tip – "a dangerous joint to know about as it's open till 3am on weekends!" (1am midweek). / W1W 4RR; blackbooksoho.co.uk; @theblackbooksoho; Tue, Wed 1 am, Thu-Sat 3 am; closed Tue-Sat L, closed Sun & Mon.

Black Dog Beer House TW8 £54   4 4 3
17 Albany Road   020 8568 5688   1–3A
This "very well run" Brentford backstreet boozer was created five years ago out of the former Albany Arms by Pete Brew – clearly a victim of nominative determinism, he has even established an in-house nano-brewery, Fearless Nomad. Fans say, "the food is as good as it gets in a pub, and all the better for having a brilliant selection of cask and keg ales to choose from". / TW8 0NF; www.blackdogbeerhouse.co.uk; @blackdogbeerhouse; Mon, Wed-Sat 11 pm, Sun 10.30 pm; closed Tue.

The Black Lamb SW19 NEW £60
67 High Street   020 8947 8278   11–2B
Wimbledon's White Onion (RIP) has gone from the Village high street, to make way for the Gladwin family's 6th London opening in their Sussex-based business's field-to-fork empire, a 'countryside-luxe' take on British food, together with wines from the family's 'Nutbourne' vineyard. An early doors July 2022 review here by The Evening Standard's Jimi Famurewa echoed the mixed reports our survey sometimes throws up regarding the Gladwin chain: he accused it of being "afflicted by a kind of well-meaning mediocrity", delivering a "playful spin on… quintessentially British flavour combinations… devoid of the requisite skilled execution". / SW19 5EE; www.theblacksheep-restaurant.com; @theblacksheep_resto; Wed-Fri 10.30 pm, Tue 10 pm, Sat 11.30 pm, Sun 8.30 pm; closed Tue L, closed Mon.

Black Radish SW19 £81   4 5 3
28 Ridgway   020 8617 3960   11–2B
"The food is exceptional" from a monthly changing menu at this three-year-old independent in Wimbledon Village, owned by "talented young chef" Toby Cartwright, who is supported well by a "knowledgeable front of house team". Most of the restaurant's fan club are local, but they feel it deserves wider recognition. / SW19 4QW; www.blackradishsw19.com; @blackradishsw19; Wed-Sat 11.30 pm; closed Wed-Fri L, closed Mon & Tue & Sun.

Black Salt SW14 £49   5 3 2
505 - 507 Upper Richmond Road West   020 4548 3327   11–2A
"Oh, the lucky punters of East Sheen!" – this suburban yearling is "more convenient than Dastaan in Ewell" (its legendary elder sibling) but has become a similar must-visit for those serious about ticking off London's best Indians. Manish Sharma's "very classy" cooking is "some of the best ever" according to some reports, with "very subtle spicing and very good quality ingredients… amazing". "Bravo!" Top Menu Tips – the lamb chops and chilli garlic tiger prawns. / SW14 7DE; blacksaltsheen.com; @blacksaltsheen; Tue-Thu 10 pm, Fri & Sat 10.30 pm, Sun 9 pm; closed Tue-Fri L, closed Mon.

Blacklock £51   3 4 3
24 Great Windmill St, W1   020 3441 6996   4–3D
16a Bedford Street, WC2   020 303 4139   5–3C
28 Rivington Street, EC2   awaiting tel   13–1B
13 Philpot Lane, EC3   020 7998 7676   10–3D
"You can't really go wrong with the plates of meaty delicious chops" ("nothing delicate or subtle just full flavours doing the meat full justice") at these "no-frills but hearty" pit stops, which provide a "vibrant" and "excellent-value" option for an inexpensive meal out. "It's great to be able to choose how many chops you want to eat and the sides and sauces are the absolute best". "They deliver an impressively consistent performance", and "given that there is nowhere to hide when the food is this simple, it's hats off to the chefs here!" "Don't go for a quiet night", though, as they "can be rather rowdy". Top Tip – "the Monday night Butcher's Block offer is super value, especially when teamed up with £10 corkage to BYO". / theblacklock.com; blacklockchops.

Blanchette W1 £67   3 4 3
9 D'Arblay St   020 7439 8100   4–1C
"A real gem in the heart of Soho", this little slice of Belle Époque Paris serves small plates of "proper bistro food in a proper bistro setting" – "not fancy, but delicious". Founded by three French brothers and named after their mother, it celebrates its 10th anniversary this year. / W1F 8DS; www.blanchettesoho.co.uk; @blanchettelondon; Mon-Sat 11 pm; closed Sun.

FSA

Blandford Comptoir W1 £72 3|3|3
1 Blandford Street   020 7935 4626   2–1A
A visit to this "very focused" Marylebone wine bar from sommelier Xavier Rousset is "an exciting experience for wine lovers" – "the breadth and array of Rhône vintages allow for an exploration that's not possible anywhere else". The "small plates" of bistro food tick the boxes, but can seem "rather mundane" by comparison. / W1U 3DA; blandford-comptoir.co.uk; @blandfordcomptoir; Tue-Sat 11 pm; closed Sun & Mon; no Amex.

Bleecker Burger £28 4|2|2
205 Victoria St, SW1   no tel   2–4B
The Balcony, Westfield White City, W12   020 3582 2930   1–3B
Unit B Pavilion Building, Spitalfields Mkt, E1   07712 540501   13–2B
Bloomberg Arcade, Queen Victoria Street, EC4   awaiting tel   10–3C
"The best burgers in town" – "the juiciest, the most flavourful" – are a credible claim for this quartet in Spitalfields, Victoria, the City's Bloomberg Arcade and Westfield White City, the highest-rated of the non-mainstream burger chains in our survey this year. New Yorker Zan Kaufman named them after the Greenwich Village street where she ate the burger that inspired her to quit her job as a corporate lawyer and start flipping patties on the back of a London truck, 11 years ago. / www.bleecker.co.uk; bleeckerburger.

Bleeding Heart Bistro EC1 £63 3|3|4
Bleeding Heart Yard   0207 2428238   10–2A
"Overlooking the atmospheric and historic Bleeding Heart Yard", this "agreeable" if "slightly cramped", "old-school" bistro (with a splendid terrace in summer) is "well worth the venture outside the City perimeter" for finance-types, both for a "fun and not too formal" client lunch or a "so romantic" evening meal. "Dependable quality French-ish fare" completes the picture. / EC1N 8SJ; www.bleedingheart.co.uk; @bleedingheartyd; Mon-Fri 10.30 pm, Sat 10 pm; closed Sat L, closed Sun; booking max 12 may apply.

Blue Boar Pub SW1 £77 3|2|2
Conrad London St James, 22-28 Broadway   020 3301 1400   2–3C
This 'modern take on the British pub' with food by chef Sally Abé, formerly of the stellar Harwood Arms, is "part of the huge improvement of the City of Westminster's offering over the last few years". "The food is good, particularly the meat" – but calling it a 'pub' can feel like "a hopeless misnomer" ("it is a hotel restaurant with formal service – OK, no tablecloths – but waiters standing to attention") and at quiet times it can lack atmosphere. / SW1S 0BH; blueboarlondon.com; @blueboarpub; Mon-Sun 11 pm.

Bluebird SW3 £96 2|1|4
350 King's Road   020 7559 1000   6–3C
This stylish conversion of a landmark 1920s Chelsea car showroom from the D&D London stable certainly looks the part, but it continues to generate amazingly little feedback in our annual diners' poll beyond the occasional complaint along the lines of: "service was appalling and the food not much better". / SW3 5UU; www.bluebird-restaurant.co.uk; @bluebirdchelsea; Mon-Wed, Fri, Thu, Sat 10.30 pm, Sun 9.30 pm.

Bob Bob Ricard £86 2|4|5
1 Upper James Street, W1   020 3145 1000   4–2C
Level 8, 122 Leadenhall Street, EC3   020 3145 1000   10–2D
"Always fun with the 'Press for Champagne' button!" – Leonid Shutov's decadently boothed joint sets an extravagant tone, ideal "for special occasions" and also "taking the awkwardness out of any business lunch or dinner". It's "not a cheap option, though, so you have to like the guest…". The luxurious food, including a selection of caviar, is "fair" – "stick with the classics (such as beef Wellington to die for) to avoid disappointment". Fortunately, the wine is "not overpriced" thanks to a £50 mark-up limit which favours the top of the list. In late 2021, Shutov relaunched the glitzy

FSA RATINGS: FROM 1 POOR — 5 EXCEPTIONAL

offshoot in the City's Cheesegrater, changing its name from Bob Bob Cité to Bob Bob Ricard City. Early reports say it's "got a lot to live up to, but it turns out the vibe amongst the banks, bling and skyscrapers of the Square Mile really works!". More spinoffs are planned, as in late summer 2022, the brand announced it has VC backing for national and international expansion.(Note: Bob Bob Ricard has raised funds for Ukraine and changed the spelling of chicken Kyiv following the Russian invasion).

BOB's Lobster SE1 £59 3 4 2
Unit 71, St Thomas Street   020 7407 7099   10–4C
"Very good lobster backed up by good chips" and "fast service" win fans for this American-style joint near Borough Market, also with a bright red-and-white VW campervan offshoot that parks at various locations through the summer. But the bill can be "toppy". / SE1 3QX; www.bobslobster.com; @bobs_lobster; Tue-Fri 11 pm, Sat 9 pm; closed Tue-Thu L, closed Sun & Mon.

Bobo Social SE17 £67 3 3 3
23 Sayer Street   020 7636 9310   1–3C
One of the bright sparks near Elephant & Castle – this attractive haunt (with cocktail bar) majors in breakfast and brunch options, but also offers a small, eclectic selection of impactful bites (the Bobo Burger, truffle pasta, Thai curry, steak, fish 'n' chips…). We've rated it on limited feedback. / SE17 1FY; bobosocial.com; @bobosocial; Mon-Sun 11.30 pm; payment – credit card only.

Bocca di Lupo W1 £66 4 3 3
12 Archer St   020 7734 2223   4–3D
"Wildly popular for its diverse offering of small plates of terrific and original Italian regional cuisine": Jacob Kenedy's "relentlessly busy" ("cramped and noisy") West End venue is many reporters' first choice for a favourite London Italian. Aided by a convenient situation, just a short stroll from Piccadilly Circus and "well-located for the theatres" – it's become a regular feature in the list of Top-20 London restaurants in our annual diners' poll. The selection of carefully researched and sourced Italian 'tapas' are "reliably original and sometimes surprising"; and matched with a "hugely varied" Italian wine list. The food rating slipped a tad this year, though, due to gripes of some dishes "lacking their customary perfection" or "leaning towards being overpriced". "It's a fairly small, intimate venue with counter seating at the front, where you can watch the chefs cook, as well as some more relaxed and comfortable tables at the back" (most regulars feeling it's "best at the bar"). Top Tip – "superb negronis and stuffed olives and the risotto is always top notch". / W1D 7BB; www.boccadilupo.com; @bocca_di_lupo; Mon-Sat 11 pm, Sun 9.30 pm; booking max 10 may apply.

Bocconcino Restaurant W1 £107 2 2 2
19 Berkeley St   020 7499 4510   3–3C
"The glitz, the glamour, the bling" – this Mayfair outpost of Mikhail Gokhner's Moscow-based chain dishes up wood-fired pizza and Italian comfort food with mixed results: to critics it's extravagant pricing is far too OTT, but there is also the odd fan who "wanted to dislike it but was charmed". / W1J 8ED; www.bocconcinorestaurant.co.uk; @bocconcino_london; Mon-Sat 12.30 am, Sun 10.30 pm.

FSA

Boiler & Co SE1 NEW £52 5 4 3
5 Canvey Street   020 7928 1554   10–4B
"Imaginative Caribbean fine dining" is an unlikely find at any time – particularly considering the bland location of Anguilla-born Kerth Gumbs's Bankside newcomer, which opened in early 2022 amidst the anonymous glass-fronted offices behind Tate Modern. The Evening Standard's Jimi Famu thought his east Caribbean-inspired tasting menu to be "dumbfoundingly good… laser-honed… top end" cuisine, while one early reporter questions "is this a potential Michelin star at some stage". Definitely "worth trying". / SE1 9AN; boilerandco.com; @boilerandcompany; Tue-Thu 11 pm, Fri & Sat 1 am, Mon 5 pm, Sun 4 pm; closed Sun & Mon D.

Boisdale of Belgravia SW1 £85 2 2 3
15 Eccleston Street   020 7730 6922   2–4B
"With its excellent exterior cigar terrace, range of whiskies and food usually with a Scottish twist – there's always a fun evening" (often buoyed by live jazz too) at Ranald Macdonald's Scottish-themed Belgravia stalwart, a short walk from Victoria station. Eldest son of the 24th chief and captain of Clanranald, his wine-trade background is evident in a strong list, while the selection of steaks and venison reveal him as an early champion of British ingredients. Critics say the food is only "average", but for a red-blooded business meeting it's tailor made for the purpose. / SW1W 9LX; www.boisdale.co.uk/belgravia; @boisdale_uk; Mon-Fri 1 am, Sat midnight, Sun 4 pm; closed Mon, Sat L closed Sun D.

Boisdale of Canary Wharf E14 £69 3 2 4
Cabot Place   020 7715 5818   12–1C
"If you want a reliable weekend meal and some, mmmm, smooth funktastic jazz", this Canary Wharf member of Ranald Macdonald's Caledonian-themed group often comes recommended thanks to its "great live music entertainment", "good-value set menus" and "decent roasts". During the week, its menu of oysters, Scottish beef and other fairly traditional fare is nominated for an "excellent business lunch". / E14 4QT; www.boisdale.co.uk/canary-wharf; @boisdale_restaurants; Tue, Wed 11 pm, Fri & Sat 2 am, Thu midnight, Sun 4.30 pm; closed Mon.

Bombay Brasserie SW7 £88 3 3 3
Courtfield Road   020 7370 4040   6–2B
"Authentic flavours", "attractive surroundings" and "reasonable prices for what you get" win consistent solid ratings for this upmarket Indian veteran, now 40 years old and owned by the Taj Hotels group. / SW7 4QH; www.bombayb.co.uk; @bombaybrasseriesw7; closed Mon-Sat & Sun.

Bombay Bustle W1 £73 5 4 4
29 Maddox Street   020 7290 4470   3–2C
"Noisy and aptly named bustle" – this "well-executed and brilliant concept" (sibling to Jamavar) is inspired by the street food of Mumbai: a "deeply impressive range of dishes" and results are "mind-blowing" – with just "the right balance of spices and herbs. / W1W 2PA; www.bombaybustle.com; @bombaybustle; Mon-Sat 10.30 pm, Sun 9.30 pm.

Bombay Palace W2 £62 5 4 3
50 Connaught St   020 7723 8855   7–1D
"The name is very apt" for this "superb" and rather old-fashioned operation, "quietly tucked away behind Edgware Road". Now celebrating its 40th anniversary, it serves "consistently brilliant" and "authentic food, using traditional recipes", including an "imaginative selection of Indian street-food dishes". "It's not pretentious, and the service is good – never rushed. The makeover a couple of years back still looks attractive and helped modernise the venue". / W2 2AA; www.bombay-palace.co.uk; @bombaypalacelondon; Mon, Thu, Wed, Sun 9.30 pm, Fri & Sat 10.30 pm; closed Wed L, closed Tue.

FSA RATINGS: FROM 1 POOR — 5 EXCEPTIONAL

F S A

Bone Daddies £42 3|3|3
Nova, Victoria St, SW1   no tel   2–4B
30-31 Peter St, W1   020 7287 8581   4–2D
46-48 James St, W1   020 3019 7140   3–1A
24 Old Jamaica Road, SE16   020 7231 3211   10–4D
22 Putney High St, SW15   020 8246 4170   11–2B **NEW**
The Bower, 211 Old Street, EC1   020 3019 6300   13–1A
This ten-year-old rock 'n' roll ramen concept is in expansion mode at the moment, having pushed into the southwestern suburbs with openings in Richmond and Putney in recent years, followed by High Street Ken and the former Eurostar terminal at Waterloo station in 2022. They "still do a very fine bowl of tonkotsu", and the classic rock soundtrack stays the same.
/ www.bonedaddies.com; bonedaddies.

Bonoo NW2 £57 3|3|3
675 Finchley Road   020 7794 8899   1–1B
A wide variety of unusual and tasty small plates is on the menu at this family-run Indian in Child's Hill, which scores consistently high ratings for its delicious cooking. / NW2 2JP; www.bonoo.co.uk; @bonoo.indian.tapas; Mon-Sun 10.30 pm; closed Mon-Sun L.

**Booking Office 1869,
St Pancras Renaissance Hotel NW1** £83 3|3|5
Euston Road   020 7841 3566   9–3C
During the pandemic, this fine space was given a lavish makeover and relaunched in late 2021, complete with eight 8-metre tall palm trees, striking pendant lights (made up of 267 brass leaves each), and a 22-metre long bar. The all-day menu created by chef Patrick Powell is a succession of luxurious bites (there's a raw bar, salads, fish finger sarnie, steak…), making this "an excellent place for a good-quality and fairly priced bar-type meal" as you make the most of the extensive cocktail menu. In summer months, the hotel also runs a substantial roof garden along the same theme. / NW1 2AR; www.booking-office.co.uk; @bookingoffice; Tue-Thu midnight, Fri & Sat 1 am, Mon 11 pm; closed Mon D, closed Sun.

Books for Cooks W11 £23 3|4|4
4 Blenheim Crescent   020 7221 1992   7–1A
"A hidden find" in Notting Hill's famous cookbook shop, where staff knock up a set lunch following recipes from one of the books in stock. ("Where can you have a 3-course lunch for £7?". "Not sure if I want too many people to know about this place – absurdly cheap no-choice menu, but one of the best meals I had all year. Can still taste it now. Please don't go!"). / W11 1NN; www.booksforcooks.com; @booksforcookslondon; Tue-Sat 6 pm; closed Sun & Mon.

Boqueria £51 3|3|2
192 Acre Ln, SW2   020 7733 4408   11–2D
278 Queenstown Road, SW8   020 7498 8427   11–1C
"Bright modern tapas with some old favourites" are on the menu at this "stylish" pair south of the river, named after the food market in Barcelona. "Consistently good cooking" and "reasonable prices" are the plus points, although they may "lack the extra zing of the very best places".
/ www.boqueriatapas.com; boqueria_london.

Il Bordello E1 £57 3|2|3
Metropolitan Wharf, 70 Wapping Wall   020 7481 9950   12–1A
"If you want a family Italian restaurant look no further", say fans of this trattoria and pizza favourite of two decades standing at the foot of a Wapping warehouse conversion: "supported by locals and always busy".
/ E1E 3SS; www.ilbordello.com; @ilbordellorestaurant; Mon-Sat 11 pm, Sun 10.30 pm; closed Mon L.

FSA

Il Borro W1 £128 3 3 3
15 Berkeley Street   020 3988 7717   3–3C
The jury is still out on this ultra-high-end Italian following its lockdown-delayed 2021 opening in the Mayfair premises formerly occupied by Nobu Berkeley (RIP). It's a "lovely space" with a "great fit-out", and "the fish is fantastic" – so "all the ingredients are there and it could become really good once it has shaken down". On the debit side, it's "ridiculously overpriced" (which it needs to be to cover the rent, a local record). Owned by the Ferragamo fashion family, it's named after their Tuscan estate, whose produce and wine are on the menu. / W1W 8DY; ilborrotuscanbistro.co.uk; @tuscanbistrolondon; Mon-Wed midnight, Thu-Sat 1 am, Sun 07.

Bossa W1 NEW
3 Vere Street   awaiting tel   3–1B
Launching beneath the Brazilian consulate in Marylebone in a former branch of Maroush – this late 2022 debut represents part of the ever-more thriving Latino scene in the capital. Brazilian chef Alberto Landgraf is of German and Japanese heritage and, back in the day, started working in hospitality in London (for Gordon Ramsay and Tom Aikens) to fund his studies as a physics graduate. Back home and bitten by the hospitality bug, he later went on to found Epice (in São Paolo) and Oteque (in Rio, and on the World's 50 Best list) before now returning to the capital promising 'contemporary Brazilian food and a very strong wine and cocktail list'. / W1W 0DG; Mon-Sun midnight.

Bottle & Rye SW9 NEW
Ground Floor, 404-406 Market Row   no tel   11–2D
From Robin and Sarah Gill, this July 2022 newcomer in Brixton's Market Row is a little (28 covers) all-day venture, which invokes Parisian café culture as its inspiration. As the name hints, it's as much about drinking as it is about eating, with an imaginative small menu served alongside a list of ever-changing funky wines and cocktails. / SW9 8LD; www.bottleandrye.com; @bottleandrye; Mon-Wed 10 pm, Thu-Sat 10.30 pm.

Boudin Blanc W1 £87 3 3 4
5 Trebeck St   020 7499 3292   3–4B
"Unquestionably French", this "fun and atmospheric bistro" is a "long-term favourite" in Mayfair's cute Shepherd Market. Top Tip – "arrive early – the brilliant specials are very popular and can run out". / W1J 7LT; www.boudinblanc.co.uk; @leboudinblanc; Tue-Sat 10.30 pm; closed Sat L, closed Sun & Mon.

Boulevard WC2 £57 2 3 3
40 Wellington St   020 7240 2992   5–3D
This "old-fashioned" Gallic brasserie has served "wonderfully consistent French fayre" "right in the middle of Covent Garden" for more than 30 years. It's "great fun with very decent food for the price given the area", with a "cheap, cheerful and reliable" prix-fixe menu for pre- or post-theatre dining. / WC2E 7BD; www.boulevardbrasserie.co.uk; @boulevardbrasseriewc2; Mon & Tue, Sun 10 pm, Wed-Sat 11 pm.

The Boundary E2 £69
2-4 Boundary Street   020 7729 1051   13–1B
In May 2022 (too late for any survey feedback), this Shoreditch design hotel reopened its ground-floor bar/restaurant (fka The Albion Café) as an all-day brasserie. The 100-seat space, whose original hard-edged design was overseen by the late Sir Terence Conran, has been modified and somewhat cosied up (no longer with its own street entrance). Chef Robin Freeman also looks after the hotel's glam-looking refurbished rooftop bar and restaurant, while what was once Tatra in the basement is nowadays an event space. The rooftop looks set to become the place to be here. / E2 7DD; boundary.london; @boundaryldn; Mon-Sun 11 pm.

FSA RATINGS: FROM 1 POOR — 5 EXCEPTIONAL

Boxcar Baker & Deli W1 — £10 — 3 3 3
7a Wyndham Place   020 3006 7000   2–1A
"Great coffee and an always-buzzy vibe" make it worth remembering this attractive, all-day Marylebone deli/café, which serves a mix of patisserie, cakes, soups, salads and sarnies from breakfast onwards. / W1W 1PN; boxcar.co.uk; @boxcarbaker; Mon-Sun 5 pm; closed Mon-Sun D.

Brackenbury Wine Rooms W6 — £55 — 2 3 3
111-115 Hammersmith Grove   020 3696 8240   8–1C
A *"fantastic wine list"*, including *"interesting wines by the glass"*, is the strong suit at this Hammersmith hub, where verdicts on the *"bistro cooking"* range from *"dependable, with good ingredients"* to *"OK but rather boring"*. Breakfast gets a thumbs-up – *"fab baps"* and *"they remember how you like your coffee."* / W6 0NQ; winerooms.london/brackenbury; @wine_rooms; Mon-Sat 11 pm, Sun 4 pm; closed Sun D.

Bradley's NW3 — £66 — 2 2 2
25 Winchester Rd   020 7722 3457   9–2A
Simon Bradley has been cooking for well over 30 years at this stalwart venue, in a backstreet near Swiss Cottage tube station, whose smart interior is judged somewhere between *"gloomy"* and *"pleasant"*. The *"mostly good"* (if occasionally *"erratic"*) European cuisine and *"nicely priced wine list"* mean it's *"well above the norm for the area"*, making it particularly *"useful for a pre-Hampstead Theatre meal"*. / NW3 3NR; www.bradleysnw3.co.uk; @bradleysnw3; Wed-Sat, Tue 9 pm, Sun 2.30 pm; closed Tue L closed Sun D, closed Mon.

La Brasseria — £86 — 3 3 3
42 Marylebone High Street, W1   020 7486 3753   2–1A
290 Westbourne Grove, W11   020 7052 3564   7–2B **NEW**
"The quality and consistency of the dishes is first-class and service excellent" at the original location of this Italian duo ('La Brasseria Milanese'), which opened in Marylebone in May 2018. A second all-day offshoot opened in Notting Hill in autumn 2021. It's inspired little commentary as yet, but Tom Parker Bowles in The Daily Mail praised its *"handsome"* styling and a menu of *"old-fashioned crowd pleasers and greatest hits"*.
/ https://www.labrasseria.com.

Brasserie Blanc — £62 — 2 2 2
119 Chancery Lane, WC2   020 7405 0290   2–2D
Goldhurst House, Parr's Way, W6   020 8237 5566   8–2C
9 Belvedere Rd, SE1   020 7202 8470   2–3D
60 Threadneedle St, EC2   020 7710 9440   10–2C
"A perfect location opposite the National Theatre and Festival Hall and good pre-theatre set-menu" win particular nominations for the SE1 branch of this well-known national group. Even some fans *"wish there were more adventurous choices on the menu"*, but they still recommend the *"French-influenced"* brasserie cooking as *"better quality than many rivals even if it is very much chain fare"*. The overall verdict, though, is that it's *"just OK, especially bearing in mind the prestigious name under which they trade"*.
/ www.brasserieblanc.com.

Brasserie of Light W1 — £77 — 2 2 5
400 Oxford Street   020 3940 9600   3–1A
"Fabulous décor" is the main talking point at Richard Caring's brasserie for shoppers on the first floor of Selfridges, which is dominated by Damien Hirst's 24ft tall crystal-encrusted Pegasus (Caring has become the artist's leading British collector in recent years). The place is also *"great for people-watching & a buzzy atmosphere – I love it"*. And the food? *"OK, but nothing to shout about"*. / W1W 1AB; www.brasserie-of-light.co.uk; @brasserieoflight; Mon-Sat midnight, Sun 11 pm.

FSA

Brasserie Zédel W1 £49 １４５
20 Sherwood St   020 7734 4888   4–3C

"A unique feature in London's dining scene" – this "incredible subterranean cathedral of Art Deco glamour and French classic cuisine" was created 10 years ago by Corbin & King in homage to the brasseries of Paris. It occupies a "vast" and "absolutely stunning Art Deco basement" (Grade I listed with "gilding, marble columns and red velvet seating") and "what is so outstanding is to find a restaurant of this quality just a stone's throw from Piccadilly Circus". To be clear, the lengthy menu of brasserie staples "won't surprise you" – the catering has always been "OK" at best, and the food score this year was beyond humdrum. But next to the "white tablecloths and terrific old-world atmosphere and buzz"; plus "formally attired" service that's "efficient and charming"; then "the food is almost beside the point" and the availability of "some extremely cheap menus" underpins its "eyebrow-raisingly good value (so you can forgive it a lot)". With the management changes within The Wolseley Hospitality Group just prior to our annual diners' poll, many reporters feel "it's sad to see the founders no longer involved" and continue to worry – "will its distinctive qualities be lost?" Top Tip – "try to go later in the evening when the band is playing for an authentic French vibe. Also pop into the Bar Americain for a pre- or post-dinner cocktail." / W1F 7ED; www.brasseriezedel.com; @brasseriezedel; Mon-Sat 11 pm, Sun 10 pm.

Brat E1 £87 ４３３
First Floor, 4 Redchurch Street   no tel   13–1B

"Sensational" cooking over an open fire in the corner of the room has won the highest culinary esteem (including from the Harden's London Restaurant Awards) for Tomos Parry's "unassuming" Shoreditch venue, which sits in a "functional and slightly industrial", first-floor dining room above 'Smoking Goat'. In particular, "the signature turbot is a must-try" ('Brat' is another name for turbot) and has become a checklist item for London foodie fashionistas. Its food rating slipped this year from the highest heights on a few reports of "great but slightly inconsistent" meals. For most of its many fans, though, a meal here is still "always wonderful". Top Menu Tips – aside from the turbot: "still superb bread and anchovy…", "soused mackerel in a piquant broth was divine…", "smoked potatoes are my Death Row dish…" / E1 6JJ; www.bratrestaurant.com; @bratrestaurant; Mon-Sun 9.45 pm.

Brat at Climpson's Arch E8 £94 ４３３
Climpson's Arch, 374 Helmsley Place   020 7254 7199   14–2B

A "too-cool-for-school railway arch" and covered courtyard ("a great fun place on a sunny day") provides the "quirky" setting for Tomos Parry's "funky hang-out" in London Fields (a pandemic pop-up in 2020 that turned permanent). Staff are "casual but super-knowledgeable" and deliver "simple food cooked over fire" that's often "fabulous" ("that turbot… Wow!"). But, while most reporters have found it "hard to pick fault the few times we have visited", others feel it's "interesting and trendy, but at a hell of a price for a glorified pop-up" or say "I really wanted to like it but came away underwhelmed by the food and the plastic tent (prefer the original)". / E8 3SB; bratrestaurant.com/climpsons-arch; @bratrestaurant; Wed-Sat 10 pm, Sun 9 pm; closed Wed-Fri L, closed Mon & Tue; payment – credit card only.

Bravi Ragazzi SW16 £48 ４２２
2a Sunnyhill Road   020 8769 4966   11–2D

This ten-year-old pizzeria has a loyal following for its "exceptional" sourdough base and toppings. Neapolitan-born co-founder Andrea Asciuti has also launched a modernised take on his home city's cooking with 081 Pizzeria at Peckham Levels. / SW16 2UH; www.braviragazzipizzeria.co.uk; @braviragazzipizzeria; Mon-Thu 10.30 pm, Fri & Sat 11 pm, Sun 10 pm; closed Mon-Thu L.

Brawn E2 — £76
49 Columbia Road 020 7729 5692 14–2A

This former icon of East End gastronomy is starting to look like a handy stop-off point near Columbia Road flower market, but not much more. The odd fan still hails its Med-inspired food and funky wine list as "exceptional all-round", but – as Ed Wilson and his team have diverted effort to Sargasso in Margate – interest seems to be on the wane here (and, given the surprising paucity of reports, we've left it un-rated this year). / E2 7RG; www.brawn.co; @brawn49; Tue-Sat, Mon 10.30 pm; closed Mon L, closed Sun.

Bread Street Kitchen EC4 — £82   2 3 3
10 Bread Street 020 3030 4050 10–2B

"As Gordon Ramsay chain restaurants go, the food is dependable enough" at this generously spaced modern brasserie, in a big mall next to St Paul's (but even those who agree it's "absolutely fine" may also consider it "very poor value"). "Despite being in EC4, the restaurant has a decent vibe", and it's tipped both for a business lunch and its "generous Sunday lunch". / EC4M 9AJ; www.gordonramsayrestaurants.com/bread-street-kitchen; @breadstkitchen; Mon-Wed midnight, Thu-Sat 1 am, Sun 10 pm.

Breakfast Club — £42   3 3 3
Branches throughout London

These "quirky, popular and lively venues" (nine in London; four more out of town) serve "British and American comfort foods" in "good portions" – think pancakes, full English fry-ups, French toast, plus cocktails later in the day. It's all "deeply unhealthy – but soooo delicious with good-quality ingredients". Top Tip – "benefits for over-65s" (in the shape of half-price dishes). / www.thebreakfastclubcafes.com; thebrekkyclub.

Briciole W1 — £64   3 3 2
20 Homer St 020 7723 0040 7–1D

"Real country-style cooking" can be found at this "good-value neighbourhood deli/trat" near Edgware Road station, serving "the sort of dishes you would find in many a small-town restaurant in Italy". Originally it was a spin-off from Latium (RIP) in Fitzrovia, which closed in 2018 after 14 years. Top Menu Tip – "black bean and pork stew, polenta, bitter turnip tops and perfectly stewed borlotti beans". / W1H 4NA; www.briciole.co.uk; @briciolerestaurant; Mon-Sat 10.30 pm, Sun 10.15 pm.

Brick Lane Beigel Bake E1 — £9   4 2 1
159 Brick Ln 020 7729 0616 13–1C

"Unmatched in London", this remnant of the East End Jewish community is "always busy, and you can see why". Every week it produces up to 20,000 beigels (note the traditional European spelling), available 24/7 stuffed with "good portions of salt beef", lox, pickled herring and more. "A dire location, but I can't help going back on a regular basis, as I've done for nearly four decades". / E1 6SB; www.beigelbake.co.uk; @beigel_bake; Mon-Sun midnight; cash only; no booking.

Brigadiers EC2 — £71   5 4 4
Bloomberg Arcade, Queen Victoria Street 020 3319 8140 10–3C

"One of the sheer tastiest places to eat in town" – JKS Restaurants' highly popular outpost in Bloomberg Arcade continues to inspire raves for its "delicious and different" Indian cuisine (very much "not your traditional curry house"). The large interior, with its many bars and TV screens, is more divisive: it's "awesome" for its core clientele, but "the ambience screams 'City Boys' (especially when there's sport on)". Top Menu Tip – "Indo-Chinese chilli paneer lettuce cups… so many tastes at the same time!" / EC2E; brigadierslondon.com; @brigadiersldn; Mon-Sat 10.45 pm; closed Sun.

FSA

Bright E8 — £84 — 4 4 3
Netil House, 1 Westgate Street   020 3095 9407   14–2B

"No name on outside" bespeaks the confidence of this hipster favourite in London Fields (from the same stable as P Franco and the recently defunct Peg) – a high-ceilinged, sparse space that lives up to its title (but can become "very noisy"). In the group's trademark style, it serves "a short menu of good small plates and selection of low-intervention wines, including by the glass". / E8 3RL; www.brightrestaurant.co.uk; @bright_restaurant; Wed & Thu 11.30 pm, Fri-Sun midnight; closed Wed & Thu L, closed Mon & Tue.

The Bright Courtyard W1 — £84 — 3 2 2
43-45 Baker St   020 7486 6998   2–1A

"Good food", including dim sum, makes this modern Chinese an "always dependable" option in Marylebone, although the setting – an office block near Portman Square – isn't an attraction in itself. / W1U 8EW; www.lifefashiongroup.com; @BrightCourtyard; Mon-Sat 10.30 pm, Sun 9.30 pm.

Brinkley's SW10 — £69 — 2 2 3
47 Hollywood Rd   020 7351 1683   6–3B

The flagship of John Brinkley's wine-focused southwest London group attracts a well-heeled Chelsea set out for a good time. "You really shouldn't expect great food, let alone good value at this address" – but there's plenty of fun to be had here, and at spin-offs in Wandsworth Bridge Road and overlooking Wandsworth Common. / SW10 9HX; www.brinkleys.com; Mon-Sun 11 pm.

Brinkley's Kitchen SW17 — £65 — 2 2 3
35 Bellevue Rd   020 8672 5888   11–2C

This "always busy neighbourhood favourite" overlooking Wandsworth Common ticks the boxes as a "very handy local", with John Brinkley's trademark "keenly priced wine list" and "competent modern British food". / SW17 7EF; www.brinkleys.com; @brinkleyskitchen; Tue-Sat 11 pm, Sun 4 pm; closed Tue-Fri L closed Sun D, closed Mon.

The Broadcaster W12 — £61 — 3 3 3
101 Wood Lane   020 4549 7420   1–2B

Near the entrance to the former TV Centre (and Westfield's John Lewis), this striking-looking modern pub opened in October 2021, followed the following summer by its good-looking 'Aerial Roof Top' bar. It's not dissimilar to King's Cross's well-known Lighterman (same owners) and well-rated for its food – a contemporary brasserie menu that makes something of a feature of its selection of flatbreads. / W12 7FA; www.thebroadcaster.co.uk; @thebroadcasterlondon; Tue-Fri 11.30 pm, Sat 12.30 am, Sun 7 pm; closed Mon.

Brook House SW6 — £68 — 3 3 3
65 New King's Road   020 7371 5283   11–1B

Overlooking Eel Brook Common in Fulham, this "great (although rather pricey for a pub)" rustic-chic Fulham gastroboozer offers "fast service from attentive staff", and is the follow-up from former royal equerry Mark Dwyer and his partner Eamonn Manson, who sold their local trio the Sands End (Prince Harry's occasional watering hole), Cross Keys and Brown Cow for a reported £10m six years ago. / SW6 4SG; brookhousefulham.com; @brookhousefulham; Tue-Thu 11 pm, Fri & Sat midnight, Sun 5 pm; closed Tue L closed Sun D, closed Mon; payment – credit card only.

Brookmill SE8 — £47 — 3 3 3
65 Cranbrook Road   020 8333 0899   1–4D

The food is "always good" at this gentrified Victorian pub on a corner site near St John's station in Deptford, part of a well-run quartet of indie gastropubs in southeast London. It has a garden as well as smartly kitted-out guest rooms. / SE8 4EJ; www.thebrookmill.co.uk; @brookmillse8; Mon & Tue 11 pm; closed Mon & Tue L, closed Wed-Sat & Sun.

F S A

The Brown Dog SW13 £58 **3 2 3**
28 Cross Street   020 8392 2200   11–1A
"Tucked away among the terraces of Barnes's cute 'Little Chelsea'", this "longstanding food pub" is these days rather more gastro than boozer, and attracts "local ladies who lunch with its tasty cooking". "Dogs, kids and menfolk are equally welcome" – the latter two more in evidence at the weekend. / SW13 0AP; www.thebrowndog.co.uk; @browndogbarnes; closed Mon-Sat & Sun.

Brown's Hotel,
The Drawing Room W1 £84 **3 4 4**
Albemarle St   020 7493 6020   3–3C
The "quiet and stylish" wooden-panelled Drawing Room has changed little since this Mayfair hotel was built in 1837, and makes a "lovely setting" for afternoon teas that have been enjoyed by Queen Victoria and Agatha Christie, among a roll-call of the great and the good of the past two centuries. Despite the pedigree, fans feel it's "not as stilted and pompous as some famous places", and offers a "much better and friendlier tea, with delicious homemade-style cakes and scones". / W1S 4BP; www.roccofortehotels.com/hotels-and-resorts/brown-s-hotel/dining/the-drawing-room; @Browns_Hotel; Mon-Sun 9 pm; no shorts.

Brunswick House Café SW8 £66 **3 2 5**
30 Wandsworth Rd   020 7720 2926   11–1D
You "dine under chandeliers" in the "unique ambience" of a Georgian mansion at Vauxhall Cross which doubles as an architectural salvage emporium and restaurant with "an ever-developing, innovative menu". Chef Jackson Boxer has "turned things up a notch – the food is really very interesting again after a little dip in form over recent years" – while "the atmosphere remains fantastic: louche at lunchtime, party vibes in the evening". / SW8 2LG; www.brunswickhouse.london; @brunswick_house; Wed-Sat, Tue 09.45 pm, Sun 5 pm; closed Tue L closed Sun D, closed Mon.

Trattoria Brutto EC1 £49 **3 4 5**
35-37 Greenhill Rents   no tel   10–1A
"Very cool… very Tuscan… great negronis… it's like going on a mini-break!" – Russell Norman's "dark and sexily down-to-earth" newcomer is "a fun riff on a Florentine trattoria theme (steak Florentine stars on the menu) from the founder of the late-lamented Polpo, and a very worthwhile addition to the Smithfield area". He's achieved "a superb homage" – it's "skilfully run with its own distinct personality", staff are "charming" and if it's "true that it's noisy, it's good noise: the sound of people enjoying themselves!". Practically nobody has a bad word to say about the "delightfully non-standard Italian food" either: "rustic dishes that are generally simple and well-executed". "I rarely return this many times, in such a short space of time, but this place has it all!" Top Menu Tip – "anchovy with sourdough is the perfect simple starter". / EC1E 6BN; msha.ke/brutto; @bru.tto; Tue-Sat 10.30 pm; closed Sun & Mon.

Bubala £40 **4 4 3**
15 Poland Street, W1   no tel   4–1C **NEW**
65 Commercial Street, E1   020 7392 2111   13–2C
"Prepare to be blown away by the flavours at this tiny spot in Spitalfields" – its "absolutely brilliant vegetarian and vegan", Middle Eastern-inspired dishes "truly sing", delivering "a taste explosion" such that "carnivores will not miss the meat" ("the charred oyster mushroom skewers are stunning… thinking about the labneh, hummus and laffa bread makes me salivate!"). Having opened it in 2019, Marc Summers launched a 50-cover sibling in Soho in July 2022 on the former site of Vasco & Piero's Pavilion (see also), complete with open kitchen and counter-style dining. The chef is rising star Helen Graham.

F S A

The Bull N6 £63 3|3|3
13 North Hill   020 8341 0510   9–1B
A big outside terrace adds further to the appeal of this attractive old Highgate pub, well-rated for its "reliable food and great beer". / N6 4AB; thebullhighgate.co.uk; @bullhighgate; Mon-Sat 10 pm; closed Sun.

Bull & Last NW5 £74 3|3|3
168 Highgate Rd   020 7267 3641   9–1B
"Near the edge of Hampstead Heath", this mega-popular gastroboozer "lives up to the hype" and has "retained its pubby feel in spite of a major renovation", which added six bedrooms. At busy times it can be a bit "rowdy", but "the place balances great food with a pub atmosphere which adds to the flavour, and the staff are always 'on it'". / NW5 1QS; www.thebullandlast.co.uk; @thebullandlast; Mon-Thu 11 pm, Sat midnight, Sun 10.30 pm; closed Sat D, closed Fri.

Bun House WC2 £17 4|3|3
26-27 Lisle Street   020 8019 9888   5–3A
"Top egg yolk buns" are a big draw at China-born architect Z He and chef Alex Peffly's well-known Chinatown pit stop, which provides an "excellent bustling ambience and wonderful heart-filling food". / WC2W 7BD; bun.house; @8unhouse; closed Mon-Sat & Sun; payment – credit card only; no booking.

Bund N2 £37 3|3|3
4-5 Cheapside, Fortis Green   020 8365 2643   1–1B
This Pan-Asian two-year-old between Muswell Hill and East Finchley makes a "really great neighbourhood" spot, with its contemporary take on hit oriental dishes from Singapore via China to Korea and Japan. / N2 9HP; bundrestaurant.co.uk; @bundrestaurant; Tue-Sun 10 pm; closed Tue-Sun L, closed Mon.

Burger & Beyond E1 £50 4|3|2
147 Shoreditch High Street   020 3848 8860   13–1B
A "cool spot" in Shoreditch that's the permanent home of a former truck selling some of the "best burgers in London" – "flavoursome, with great ingredients", most notably Yorkshire-bred beef which is dry-aged in Himalayan salt fridges. They also do chicken burgers, funky sides and boozy milkshakes. Spin-offs have opened in Soho and Borough Market, with delivery kitchens in Camden, Vauxhall and Acton. / E1 6JE; burgerandbeyond.co.uk; @burgerandbeyond; Mon-Thu 10 pm, Fri & Sat 11 pm, Sun 9.30 pm.

Burger & Lobster £72 3|3|3
Harvey Nichols, Knightsbridge, SW1   020 7235 5000   6–1D **NEW**
26 Binney Street, W1   020 3637 5972   3–2A
29 Clarges Street, W1   020 7409 1699   3–4B
36 Dean Street, W1   020 7432 4800   5–2A
6 Little Portland Street, W1   020 7907 7760   3–1C
18 Hertsmere Road, E14   020 3637 6709   12–1C
52 Threadneedle Street, EC2   020 7256 9755   10–2C
Bow Bells Hs, 1 Bread St, EC4   020 7248 1789   10–2B
"Does what it says on the tin", with "no delay making choices". This "simple, good and easy" surf-and-turf chain has grown to nine sites in the capital in 11 years – most with "sufficient space to eat and talk" (rare enough in fast-food joints). The formula is working around the world, too, with openings from New York to the Genting Highlands in Malaysia. "Love the way they give you plastic sheets to cover yourself from flying bits of lobster!" / www.burgerandlobster.com.

F S A

Busaba £48   3 2 2
Branches throughout London
This "cheap 'n' cheerful" Thai-fusion group (founded in 1999) with its mix of pad thais, curries and other spicy bites maintains a decent fan base and achieved very steady ratings this year. Creator Alan Yau of Wagamama and Hakkasan fame has long since departed and the business has had a bumpy ride, settling down to nine London branches and offshoots in Oxford and Cardiff. / www.busaba.com; busabaeathai.

Bustronome WC2 £132   2 3 4
40b Victoria Embankment   020 3744 5554   5–4D
"A gourmet meal on a sightseeing bus in London" – might sound hellish but is surprisingly well-reviewed, including by some locals: "the food was tasty and it was a great experience!" / WC2W 6PB; @bustronomelondon; Mon-Sun 10 pm.

Butlers Wharf Chop House SE1 £82   2 2 3
36e Shad Thames   020 7403 3403   10–4D
"A great place for meat, nicely served" – this modern version of the traditional British chophouse is a business-friendly destination close to the City, from the D&D London stable. Its main attraction is a comfortable dining terrace above the river, with spectacular views of Tower Bridge. The restaurant was created by Sir Terence Conran as part of his 'Gastrodome' complex on the South Bank of the Thames, and has flown somewhat under the radar for many years now. / SE1 2YE; www.chophouse-restaurant.co.uk; @butlerswharfchophouse; Mon-Fri 10 pm, Sat 4 pm, Sun 9 pm; closed Sun L closed Sat D.

Buvette W11 £67   2 2 3
9 Blenheim Crescent   020 7229 8398   7–1A
"Really loved discovering Buvette in Paris so was excited to see them opening in London… but while the food was good, the interior lacks the heart of its Paris neighbour" – this cute 'gastrothèque' in Notting Hill is part of an NYC-based group and hasn't made too many waves since it opened in 2020. The extensive drinks offering is a lot longer than its menu of brunch-friendly fare (Les Croques, Salades, Les Oeufs Vapeur) alongside one or two slightly more substantial options (e.g. Steak Tartare or Salmon Rillettes). / W11 1NN; ilovebuvette.com/eat-drink-london-location; @buvettelondon; Mon-Thu 10 pm, Fri midnight, Sat 11 pm, Sun 9 pm.

Byron £45   3 3 3
Branches throughout London
Back from the brink? After a tumultuous couple of years, a CVA, sale, the closure of over half its branches, and new CEO, ratings have steadied at this well-known burger chain. It may only be "standard burger fayre", but most reports say it "ticks so many boxes". / www.byronhamburgers.com.

C&R Café W1 £35   3 2 2
3-4 Rupert Court   020 7434 1128   4–3D
"Cheap 'n' cheerful" Malaysian-Chinese diner on the edge of Chinatown that's built a strong fan-base over 25 years for its "excellent food that does not break the bank", combining classic regional dishes with more unusual family recipes. Top Tip – "exceptional Singapore laksa". / W1D 6DY; www.cnrcaferestaurant.com; @cnr.cafe.restaurant; Tue-Thu, Sun 10 pm, Fri & Sat 11 pm; closed Mon.

F S A

Cabotte EC2 £77 3 5 4
48 Gresham St 020 7600 1616 10–2C

"Flying slightly under the radar", this "superior City venue" is "a lovely find, right in the heart of the the Square Mile where it can be hard to encounter a good meal" ("clients are always pleased to visit it!"). "The front of house team are so charming" and deliver "precise and tasty" Gallic cuisine. The major attraction here, though, is the "comprehensive wine list" – "one of the best wine selections in London: it's hard to find a better selection of Burgundy, but the other region lists are well represented", with "many rewards to be found, both on pricing and rare gems". / EC2E 7AY; www.cabotte.co.uk; @cabotte_; Mon-Fri 10 pm; closed Sat & Sun.

The Cadogan Arms SW3 £69 2 2 3
298 King's Road 020 3148 2630 6–3C

Since it was "gussied up" last year, this "beautiful and comfortable" old Chelsea pub (built in 1838) hasn't made waves, despite a PR push and a laundry list of influential backers (including the owners of JKS Restaurants and Kitchen Table's James Knappett). Its slick gastropub fare can be "excellent", but is not reliably so; service sometimes strikes an "entitled" note; and it can appear "sad to see an institutional Chelsea boozer become a self-conscious eatery". / SW3 5UG; thecadoganarms.london; @cadoganarmspublichouse; Mon-Thu 10 pm, Fri & Sat 10.30 pm, Sun 6 pm; closed Sun D.

Cafe Cecilia E8 £57 2 2 3
Canal Place, 32 Andrews Road 0203 478 6726 14–2B

By the canal in Hackney, this August 2021 newcomer arrived with high expectations thanks to the CV of chef Max Rocha and was quickly blessed by The Guardian's Grace Dent, who felt that despite it's "homespun edge", it was "only just getting started on its path to being one of London most serious restaurants". Our feedback was more cautious: split between finding it "a really nice, friendly new favourite" and "not living up to the hype". / E8 4RL; www.cafececilia.com; @cafececilialondon; Wed & Thu, Sun 3 pm, Fri & Sat 8.30 pm; closed Mon & Tue.

Café Deco WC1 £53 3 2 2
43 Store Street 020 8091 2108 2–1C

"It can feel a little uncomfortable" and "canteen-like", but this converted greasy spoon in Bloomsbury (nowadays a 'bar, restaurant and wine shop') belies its looks by serving "imaginative seasonal cooking from a constantly changing menu reflecting the availability of ingredients". The involvement of chef Anna Tobias (who's worked with a host of star chefs) and the hip 40 Maltby Street team hasn't harmed its PR – our feedback is positive, but not quite at the level of raves from the likes of Grace Dent and Tom Parker Bowles. / WC1W 7DB; www.cafe-deco.co.uk; @cafe_deco_bloomsbury; Tue-Sat 9.30 pm; closed Sun & Mon; no Amex.

Café du Marché EC1 £59 3 4 5
22 Charterhouse Sq 020 7608 1609 10–1B

A "charming" old-style Gallic brasserie (est. 1986), with a "genuine French ambience, in an interesting setting tucked away on the edge of the City" near Smithfield Market. Its classic cuisine remains well-rated, and live jazz in the evenings adds to a special appeal that many find "romantic". / EC1M 6DX; www.cafedumarche.co.uk; @cafedumarche; Tue-Fri 10 pm, Sat 9.30 pm; closed Sat L, closed Sun & Mon.

FSA

Café in the Crypt,
St Martin in the Fields WC2   £34   2 2 4
Duncannon St   020 7766 1158   2–2C

Tucked away in the crypt beneath St Martin-in-the-Fields, this "handy" self-service cafeteria occupies a "fantastic space which always feels welcoming" and its no-frills soups, salads and hot plates are just the job for a "quick bite and coffee/glass of wine" when you visit the National Gallery across the road. / WC2N 4JJ; stmartin-in-the-fields.org/cafe-in-the-crypt; @stmartininthefields; Mon & Tue, Sun 5 pm, Thu-Sat 7.30 pm, Wed 3 pm; closed Sun-Wed D; no Amex; may need 5+ to book.

Café Kitsuné at Pantechnicon SW1   £20   3 3 4
19 Motcomb Street   020 7034 5425   6–1D

For a posh cup of coffee, the chichi, Japanese-inflected patisserie at the foot of this monumental Belgravia landmark (with mezzanine and foyer seating) has a number of fans – grab a brew, take the weight of your feet and nibble on a double-baked matcha croissant or lunchtime sando. / SW1S 8LB; www.pantechnicon.com; @_pantechnicon; Mon-Sun 7 pm; booking max 12 may apply.

Cafe Murano   £74   2 2 2
33 St James's St, SW1   020 3371 5559   3–3C
36 Tavistock St, WC2   020 3371 5559   5–3D
Pastificio, 34 Tavistock Street, WC2   020 3535 7884   5–3D
184 Bermondsey Street, SE1   020 3985 1545   10–4D

"A good choice for a light meal in the centre of own, with a broad menu of uncomplicated dishes to suit most people", and offering "a delicious and authentic taste of Italy" – that's how their large army of followers see Angela Hartnett's "buzzy" and "unpretentious" cafés, proclaiming them "a decent effort all in all". Major complaints are few, but ratings overall end up middling due to gripes of "tired" décor; or culinary results that are "OK but nothing special". Top Menu Tip – "the arancini are always worth a go". / www.cafemurano.co.uk; cafemurano.

Café Spice Namaste E16   £69   5 4 4
1-2 Lower Dock Walk, Royal Dock   020 7488 9242   12–1D

"New venue, same great flavours and hospitality" – Cyrus and Parvin Todiwala score a major thumbs up for their new "Indian paradise", which, in early 2022, relocated from their age-old location (on the grungy fringes of the City), to this "new site in a fabulous spot on the Royal Docks, and right on the River Thames too, giving you amazing views back up the river past City Airport to Canary Wharf" (nearest DLR, Gallions Reach). The menu is in a new format too – focused more on small plates and designed for sharing – and delivers "Indian dishes often with a Portuguese twist that are excellent". A "genuine welcome" is also part of the attraction, and – having been greeted – a well-stocked cocktail bar is another new addition that will help you recover from the schlep to get there... / E16 2GT; www.cafespice.co.uk; @cafespicenamasteldn; Tue-Sat 10 pm; closed Tue L, closed Sun & Mon.

Caffè Caldesi W1   £73   3 2 2
118 Marylebone Ln   020 7487 0754   2–1A

"Wonderful pasta prepared on site" is the highlight at Tuscany-born chef Giancarlo Caldesi and wife Katie's long-running Marylebone headquarters (they also have a country venue in Bray and a cookery school). Fans reckon it's "always a treat to dine here – it's traditional Italian with attentive and authentic service". / W1U 2QF; www.caldesi.com; @caldesiinmarylebone; Mon-Sat 10.30 pm, Sun 4.30 pm; closed Sun D.

Caia W10 NEW
46 Golborne Road   07927 328076   7–1A
Opened in summer 2022 (too late for our annual diners' poll), this 60-seat Portobello 'Wine bar, music venue and open-fire restaurant' is founded by locals Rishabh Vir and Tim Lang; its features include a seasonally changing menu cooked on a custom-made grill in the open kitchen and a 12-seater wine room. / W10 5PR; caia.london; @caia.london; Tue-Thu midnight, Fri & Sat 1 am; closed Tue-Fri L, closed Sun & Mon.

Cakes and Bubbles W1 £71   343
Hotel Cafe Royal, 70 Regent Street   020 7406 3310   4–4C
"Extraordinary" and "visually stunning" – the desserts and cakes at this café on a prime site in Regent Street come sprinkled with Adrià family magic (patron Albert is the brother of Catalan genius Ferran Adrià, and worked as pastry chef at his world-beating restaurant El Bulli, RIP). However, even those who feel "the desserts are really exceptional" can also note that "they don't really deserve the price tags". Still, "once at least you should give it a try, especially with all London's Christmas lights aglow". / W1W 4DY; www.cakesandbubbles.co.uk; @cakesandbubbleslondon; Mon-Sun 10 pm.

Calici NW3 £51   322
29 Belsize Lane   020 7435 9888   9–2A
This three-year-old neighbourhood Italian wins solid ratings for its modern cuisine and is a bright spark in Belsize Park's fairly dim culinary constellation. / NW3 5AS; @calici_restaurant; Tue-Thu, Sun 11 pm, Fri & Sat 11.30 pm; closed Tue-Thu L, closed Mon.

The Camberwell Arms SE5 £61   444
65 Camberwell Church St   020 7358 4364   1–3C
"Feeling like a piece of hip Shoreditch dropped onto a random patch of Camberwell" – this "thriving" fixture is one of London's best-performing gastropubs in our annual diners' poll. "It's always busy and buzzing and deservedly popular, with friendly and efficient service even when it's super-busy." "Its innovative food, with a focus on sharing, is definitely not playing it safe" and "when it rocks, it really does: big umami blasts of good flavours, realised without fuss". Top Menu Tip – "Sunday lunch with the whole family is a real treat… the shared big joints are wonderful". / SE5 8TR; www.thecamberwellarms.co.uk; @thecamberwellarms; Wed-Sat, Tue 11 pm, Sun 5 pm; closed Tue L closed Sun D, closed Mon; payment – credit card only.

Cambio de Tercio SW5 £81   544
161-163 Old Brompton Rd   020 7244 8970   6–2B
"Spanish food is all the rage now but this place has been thriving for years", say fans of Abel Lusa's "fun" but relatively unsung Hispanic in the Old Brompton Road, founded in 1995. "If you're into great Spanish food, this is possibly the best in London" – and it has a "terrific Spanish-only wine list". "Food, wine and service are simply first class", and "they never let you down". / SW5 0LJ; www.cambiodetercio.co.uk; @cambiodetercio; Tue-Sat 11.30 pm, Sun & Mon 11 pm.

Camino £63   232
3 Varnishers Yd, Regent Quarter, N1   020 7841 7330   9–3C
2 Curtain Road, EC2   020 3948 5003   13–2B
15 Mincing Ln, EC3   020 7841 7335   10–3D
"Reasonable enough tapas, with all the standard dishes" help make this long-running Hispanic trio into "decent" value and also quite "fun" options. The original and best-known branch is "tucked away incredibly close to King's Cross station, which makes it very handy for a meet-up" (with Shoreditch and Monument also useful addresses). / www.camino.uk.com.

The Campaner SW1 NEW
1 Garrison Close, Chelsea Barracks   no tel   6–3D
In the rarefied quarters of the Candy Brothers' plutocratic Chelsea Barracks development, this autumn 2022 newcomer aims to be the first permanent occupant of the purpose-built space that has previously hosted two Ollie Dabbous pop-ups: The Chelsea Barracks Kitchen and Hideaway. José Parrado of Barcelona's ventures Martinez and Bar Canete is behind the project, whose name means bell ringer in Spanish. / SW1S 8BP; thecampaner.com; @thecampanerchelsea; Mon-Thu midnight, Fri & Sat 12.30 am.

Cantinetta Antinori SW1 NEW
4 Harriet Street   no tel   6–1D
A new spin-off from a famous Florence-based international group (founded in the 1950s, whose HQ is the 15th-century Palazzo Antinori) – this Autumn 2022 newcomer is the brand's first UK venture. It occupies a three-storey site just off Sloane Street, from which it will offer all-day dining featuring Tuscan food and wine in a fairly old-school vein. The opening sounds like it's a project of serious intent, as evidenced by their 10-year lease. Cantinetta Antinori also has outlets in Zurich, Moscow, Vienna and Monaco. / SW1S 9JR; cantinetta-antinori.com/en.

Canto Corvino E1   £77   2 2 3
21 Artillery Lane   020 7655 0390   13–2B
By Spitalfieds, this modern Italian makes a feature of fairly straightforward dishes – pasta is a speciality as are grills from the Josper oven. Feedback this year was up-and-down, with some resistance to their current pricing.
/ E1 7HA; www.cantocorvino.co.uk; @cantocorvino; Mon-Sat 9 pm; closed Sat L, closed Sun.

Canton Arms SW8   £52   3 3 4
177 South Lambeth Rd   020 7582 8710   11–1D
"Simply the best food you'll find in a proper boozer" – this sibling to SE1's Anchor & Hope narrowly beats its relation these days in votes as London's top gastropub (and is a respectable No. 2 on the list). "This isn't a restaurant masquerading as a pub, but the real thing, with atmosphere to match and a great selection of proper beers". "Decent, hearty gastropub fare with a European accent" is served from a "seasonal menu" delivering "big flavours"; and there's also "an interesting wine list, where natural wines are highlighted to avoid surprises". "If the service is a bit idiosyncratic, that's all part of the fun". / SW8 1XP; www.cantonarms.com; @thecantonarms; Tue-Sat 9.45 pm, Sun 3.45 pm; closed Tue, Wed L closed Sun D, closed Mon; no Amex; no booking.

Caractère W11   £111   4 5 4
209 Westbourne Park Road   020 8181 3850   7–1B
"Bringing the expertise and professionalism of Le Gavroche to a more local setting" – Emily Roux (daughter of Michel) and her husband Diego Ferrari's (former head chef at Le Gavroche) Notting Hill four-year-old has become one of London's more notable destinations. It's "an excellent combination of gastronomic dining in a relaxed and civilised interior with just the right balance of buzziness" that provides "understated luxury, but without an eye-watering price tag". The French/Italian menu "changes regularly to show off seasonal ingredients" – "slightly quirkily presented" and with "thoroughly enjoyable" results. And the experience is buoyed by "excellent attention to detail from arrival to departure" from its "skilled and friendly" staff. *Top Tip* – "divine" lunch menu, which is "brilliant value". / W11 1EA; www.caractererestaurant.com; @caractererestaurant; Mon-Sat 9 pm; closed Sun.

FSA

Caraffini SW1 £75 3 4 3
61-63 Lower Sloane St   020 7259 0235   6–2D
"Just part of Chelsea's culinary 'furniture'!" – this *"always friendly Italian stalwart"* (est 1994), south of Sloane Square, is an *"old favourite"* for a dedicated silver-haired following, who've patronised it for many years. *"The same friendly faces (albeit sometimes masked! in the Covid months)"* provide *"courteous and amiable service"* of *"reliable, traditional dishes"* (*"certainly not cheap but good quality"*). / SW1W 8DH; www.caraffini.co.uk; @caraffinirestaurant; Mon-Sat 10.30 pm; closed Sun.

Caravaggio EC3 £62 2 3 2
107-112 Leadenhall St   020 7626 6206   10–2D
"Somehow still relevant as a City lunch spot", this *"reliable"* Italian in a converted banking hall is *"really a canteen for senior people at Lloyd's – but done in an excellent manner"*, with *"well-executed fare, quickly delivered"*. The late, great Luciano Pavarotti declared it open in 1996. / EC3A 4DP; www.caravaggiorestaurant.co.uk; @caravaggio_ldn; Mon-Fri 10 pm; closed Sat & Sun.

Caravan £59 2 2 2
Yalding House, 152 Great Portland Street, W1   020 3963 8500   2–1B
1 Granary Sq, N1   020 7101 7661   9–3C
Metal Box Factory, Great Guildford St, SE1   020 7101 1190   10–4B
Unit 2, Reuters Plaza, E14   020 3725 7600   12–1C **NEW**
11-13 Exmouth Mkt, EC1   020 7833 8115   10–1A
Bloomberg Arcade, Queen Victoria St EC4   020 3957 5555   10–3C
"Delicious shakshuka with maxing smoky flavours" is typical of the *"colourful and flavoursome"* brunch-friendly dishes at this *"very buzzy if not loud"* chain, known for its *"top coffee"* (which they roast themselves), and whose best-known sites are the Exmouth Market original and large Granary Square branch. Recently, they also added an opening in Canary Wharf and a brew bar at their Caledonian Road roastery (not listed), with further 'measured expansion' planned. For the most part, they are still mostly seen as a *"reliable"* choice for an *"interesting and healthy"* breakfast: *"not everything is a hit but for a casual lunch I am pretty happy"*. Top Tip – *"when the sun is shining, it's worth waiting for an outside table"* in N1.
/ www.caravanonexmouth.co.uk.

Caravel N1 **NEW** £48 3 3 4
172 Shepherdess Walk   020 7251 1155   14–2A
A real *"find and well worth visiting"* – this converted barge moored on the Regent's Canal near Angel has a tight modern Franco-Italian menu from Lorcan Spiteri, who trained under Jeremy Lee at Quo Vadis. With the Studio Kitchen next door, it is the first venture from Lorcan and his brother Fin, who were born to the job – dad is restaurateur John Spiteri (St John, Quo Vadis, Sessions Arts Club), mother Melanie Arnold co-founded Rochelle Canteen.
/ N1 7ED; thestudiokitchen.co.uk/the-boat; @caravel_restaurant; Thu-Sat 10.30 pm; closed Thu-Sat L, closed Mon-Wed & Sun.

Carmel NW6 £81 5 4 4
Lonsdale Road   020 3848 2090   1–2B
"A great addition to Queen's Park" – this October 2021 newcomer from the team behind East London hipster favourite, Berber & Q, gives them another hit on the other side of town. *"Everything about this place is spot-on"*: from the charming staff, to the *"excellent atmosphere"*, to the *"delicious and inventive Israeli-style cooking"*… *"it was one of those meals that I did not want to end"*. Quibbles? – *"some might dislike the lack of tables with much privacy, or the trendy wine list full of options you have never heard of!"*
/ NW6 6RR; www.carmelrestaurant.co.uk; @carmelrestaurantldn; Tue-Sat 11 pm; closed Sun & Mon; payment – credit card only.

Carousel W1 £71 4|3|2
19-23 Charlotte Street 020 7487 5564 3–1C
Relocated from Marylebone to this new Fitzrovia site, sprawling across three knocked-together Georgian townhouses: "a great place where an amazing array of constantly changing residencies by superstar chefs from all corners of the globe, make it a unique place to be entertained", and one that's typically "good value" too. On the downside, the "acoustics of the new venue are underwhelming" for some reporters. (The rating is for the visiting chef programme – no-one really mentions their new permanent in-situ wine bar operation). / W1W 1RL; www.carousel-london.com; @Carousel_LDN; Tue-Sat midnight; closed Sun & Mon.

The Carpenter's Arms W6 £57 3|3|3
91 Black Lion Ln 020 8741 8386 8–2B
Cutely tucked away near Hammersmith's gracious St Peter's Square, this independent Victorian boozer is a superior local whose inviting menu is more 'gastro' than it is 'pub' (although it serves a fairly traditional Sunday lunch). The "delightful garden" makes it a special treat for a meal in the summer. / W6 9BG; www.carpentersarmsw6.co.uk; @thecarpentersarmsw6; Thu-Sat 9.30 pm, Wed 21.30 pm, Sun 6.30 pm; closed Mon & Tue; payment – credit card only.

Casa do Frango £56 4|2|3
32 Southwark Street, SE1 020 3972 2323 10–4C
3 King John Court, EC2 020 7654 3020 13–1B
"Nando's eat your heart out", say fans of the "real" Portuguese peri-peri grilled chicken "and very tasty sides" at this "fun if busy, busy, busy" (to the point of being "overwhelming") duo near Borough Market and Shoreditch (of which the former is by far the most commented-on). It's backed by MJMK (who also run Kol, Lisbetoa et al) and a first central London branch seating 200 is set to open in 2022 in Mayfair's Heddon Street. / www.casadofrango.co.uk; casadofrango_london.

Casa Fofó E8 £75 5|4|3
158 Sandringham Road 020 8062 2489 14–1B
"Not prioritising form over substance" – Adolfo de Cecco's well-reputed three-year-old is "fairly un-smart for a foodie hotspot" but "cosy and romantic", especially in the "covered back garden, which is gorgeous as the sun sets (a very 'London' setting)". "Outstanding food is brilliantly and passionately served" from an "eclectic tasting menu" ("and they've lightened up since Grace Dent accused them of being too serious a couple of years ago!") / E8 2HS; www.casafofolondon.co.uk; @casafofolondon; Wed-Sun 9.30 pm; closed Wed-Fri L, closed Mon & Tue; no Amex.

Casa Pastór & Plaza Pastór N1 £73 3|2|2
Coal Drops Yard 020 7018 3335 9–3C
"Noisy!…but great margaritas" and some "very tasty" bites are the draw at the Hart Bros' Mexico City-style street food specialist in Coal Drops Yard. On the debit side, it can be "hard to feel truly relaxed in this mammoth space". See also El Pastor. / N1N 4AB; www.tacoselpastor.co.uk; @tacos_el_pastor; Tue-Sat 11 pm, Sun 8 pm; closed Tue-Thu L, closed Mon.

Casa Tua WC1 £48 4|2|3
106 Cromer Street 020 7833 1483 9–4C
"The beef ragu is an absolute delight" – just one highlight among this "amazing fresh pasta" and other "beautiful" dishes at this "lovely neighbourhood spot in the backstreets of King's Cross": a simple corner café that's "a decent-value find in the area". / WC1W 8BZ; www.casatuacamden.com/kings-cross; @casatualondon; Mon-Sun 10 pm.

F S A

Casse-Croute SE1 £69 4 4 4
109 Bermondsey St   020 7407 2140   10–4D
"La vraie chose! A French restaurant staffed by French cooking staff and waiters who speak French amongst themselves" – "cramped, noisy, but still brilliant". With its "excellent" menu of Gallic classics, chalked up daily, you'd be happy to find this bistro in Bordeaux or Briançon – let alone Bermondsey. It's "great fun and great food" – a "cosy place where one can happily while away a whole evening". / SE1 3XB; www.cassecroute.co.uk; @cassecroute109; Mon-Sat 11 pm, Sun 5 pm; closed Sun D.

Cavita W1 £97
55 Wigmore Street   020 3928 1000   3–1A
Originally slated for late 2019 (and following a pop-up at the Dorchester's glam rooftop), Adriana Cavita's May 2022 debut was worth waiting for by all accounts, although it arrived too late for our annual diners' poll. Occupying two dining spaces (one with views of the open kitchen), it is decked out in earthy tones and with a mass of hanging plants; while the menu incorporates a 'raw' seafood selection and street-food dishes, but with larger sharing plates as the main event. According to an early review by The Evening Standard's Jimi Famurewa it's "a scintillating, fully-formed reminder of exactly how it should be done" delivering a "knockout combination of abuela-level domestic generosity and top-tier chef's technique" that's "absolutely stormingly good". / W1W 1PU; www.cavitarestaurant.com; @cavita.restaurante; Tue-Sun 10.30 pm; closed Tue-Sun L, closed Mon.

Cay Tre £45 3 3 2
42-43 Dean St, W1   020 7317 9118   5–2A
301 Old St, EC1   020 7729 8662   13–1B
Some of the "tastiest Vietnamese food in town" is found at this pair in Hoxton and Soho from Hieu Trung Biu, a pioneer of pho and other southeast Asian specialties in the capital over two decades. Popularity means they can be "deafeningly loud". / www.caytrerestaurant.co.uk; caytrerestaurant.

Cecconi's £87 2 2 4
19-21 Old Compton Street, W1   020 7734 5656   5–2A
5a Burlington Gdns, W1   020 7434 1500   4–4A
58-60 Redchurch Street, E2   020 3841 7755   13–1C
The Ned, 27 Poultry, EC2   020 3828 2000   10–2C
"The original location is by far the best" – "almost Continental in feel, and opposite the back entrance of the Royal Academy in Burlington Arcade": "a regular haunt" for Mayfair types where "a seat at the bar is the best possible place in the world". "Always buzzy and with exceptional Bellinis, it's best for breakfast or brunch". On the downside, "the high prices of the food reflect the area and locale". Its simpler spin-offs (most notably pizza joints in Soho and Shoreditch) capture a fragment of this "fun and upmarket" style. / cecconis.co.uk; cecconislondon.

Cedric Grolet at The Berkeley SW1 NEW £90 3 4 4
The Berkeley, Wilton Place   020 7107 8866   6–1D
"OMG so good and so spectacular!" – Paris pâtissier par excellence Cédric Grolet opened his first permanent London showcase in this Knightsbridge 5-star in early 2022, and its 'kitchen table' is a place to ogle, then eat – "good-looking French chefs work in front of you" to create trompe-l'oeil fruit and flowers "made for Insta and for foodies". "Loved my experience here, expensive but so worth it". (The price shown is for the 'Gouter' 5-piece menu with tea, but the bookable counter described about is £135 per head; or take out from about £5 per item). / SW1S 8RL; www.the-berkeley.co.uk; @the_berkeley; Mon-Sun 7 pm.

FSA RATINGS: FROM 1 POOR — 5 EXCEPTIONAL

F S A

Cent Anni SW19 £58 3|2|2
33 High Street   020 3971 9781   11–2B
This "really consistent performer" serving "straightforward Italian classics" – "not haute cuisine" – is "a great place to go with the family", making it a "solid addition to the Wimbledon Village scene". Top Tip – "50% discount on wine on Wednesdays is a major attraction". / SW19 5BY; centanni.co.uk; Mon-Sat 11 pm, Sun 10.30 pm.

Cepages W2 £56 4|3|4
69 Westbourne Park Road   020 3602 8890   7–1B
"Sharing plates of classic French dishes" help make this Gallic bistro deep in Westbourne Park "perfect for a casual dinner with friends". "It can be crazy busy but has a lovely buzz". / W2 5QH; www.cepages.co.uk; Mon-Sat 11 pm, Sun 10 pm; closed Mon-Fri L.

Ceru £41 3|2|2
7-9 Bute St, SW7   020 3195 3001   6–2C
13 Queensway, W2   020 7221 2535   7–2C
"Delicious food from the Levant, served with charm" has earned an enthusiastic following for Barry and Patricia Hilton's "interesting Middle Eastern" bistros: particularly the original, tucked away in South Kensington's 'Little France' in a quirky modernised unit with a Scandi-meets-North-Africa vibe. A thumbs-up too for its newer, year-old Queensway branch. / www.cerurestaurants.com; ceruLondon.

Ceviche Soho W1 £72 3|2|3
17 Frith St   020 7292 2040   5–2A
This "buzzy and fun Peruvian with super-fresh ceviche and a range of interesting small plates" has become a "Soho staple" since it was launched in 2012. Reviews were more mixed this year, however. To fans, it's "hard to fault", with "a menu that's as vibrant and enjoyable as ever". To critics, "overhyped" – "perfectly nice, but not matching expectations" and "nothing special". / W1D 4RG; cevichelondon.com; @cevicheuk; Wed & Thu, Sat, Fri 8.30 pm, Sun 5 pm.

Chakra W8 £44 3|2|3
33c Holland Street   020 7229 2115   6–1A
The cute location is a highlight of this "hidden gem", obscurely tucked away in a plush Kensington backstreet, where the Indian food is "solid and great value for money". (It's actually part of a chain of four, but there's scant feedback on its siblings in Little Venice, Barnes and Kingston). / W8 4LX; www.chakralondon.com; @chakralondon; Tue-Thu 10 pm, Fri & Sat 10.30 pm, Sun 9 pm; closed Mon.

Chameleon NW1 £60 3|3|4
One Marylebone, 1 Marylebone Road   020 7186 2444   9–4B
Feedback is limited but full of praise for chef Elior Balbul's Tel Avivian sharing-style cuisine at this dramatic venue, which shares Grade I listed Holy Trinity Church (designed by Sir John Soane) with event space 'One Marylebone'. In summer there's a garden terrace ('God's Garden') and in winter the option to eat in a set of greenhouses. / NW1 4AQ; chameleon.london; @chameleonlondon; Tue-Sat 11.30 pm; closed Tue-Fri L, closed Sun & Mon; Jacket required.

Champor-Champor SE1 £54 4|3|3
62 Weston St   020 7403 4600   10–4C
"Hidden away behind London Bridge", this "cute", eclectically decorated stalwart no longer attracts the outsized following it did many years ago, but continues to attract fans from across town for its interesting Thai-Malay cuisine. / SE1 3QJ; www.champor-champor.com; @champorchamporldn; Mon-Sat 10 pm, Sun 9.30 pm.

Charlie's at Brown's W1 £93 4 5 5
Brown's Hotel, Albemarle Street   020 7493 6020   3–3C

"Jesus has worked another miracle" at this Mayfair landmark: the Jesus in question being Jesus Adorno, former maître d' of Le Caprice, who joined in September 2021. It was an inspired appointment, and with his "quite exceptional" team he has helped further raise the game of this "beautiful" Mayfair dining room, where Adam Byatt (of Trinity) and his head chef Matthew Stirling have, since 2019, been brought on board to provide a "lovely" seasonal British menu of upscale brasserie fare. Despite its "well-spaced" tables and fine wood panelling, the venue has never in recent decades fully capitalised on its virtues as one of London's better traditional hotel dining spaces. That time is now! / W1W 4BP; @browns_hotel; Mon-Sun 10 pm.

Chateau W4 £35 3 4 2
213 Chiswick High Road   020 8742 2344   8–2A

Now celebrating its tenth anniversary, this Middle Eastern venture on Chiswick's main drag has gradually expanded its scope over the years from offering daytime "lovely loose-leaf tea and good coffee with a great selection of cakes". "At night, it transforms into a Lebanese / Eastern Med restaurant, serving a pretty traditional menu with fresh tasty dishes and Lebanese wines to hand". / W4 2DW; chateau-chiswick.com; @chateau_chiswick; Mon-Sat 10 pm, Sun 7 pm.

Che Cosa N19 £32 3 3 2
653 Holloway Road   020 7018 7077   9–1C

"Two minutes' walk from Archway tube", this "tiny Italian" comes recommended for its homemade pasta and specials" and "delicious Italian sourdough pizza", all delivered by "polite and considerate staff". Top Menu Tip – "the olives Ascolana appetiser – fried breadcrumbed green olives stuffed with minced meat". / N19 5SE; www.checosa.co.uk; @checosa.restaurant; Sun-Thu 11.30 pm, Fri & Sat 12.30 am.

The Cheese Barge W2 £52 2 3 3
Sheldon Square   07862 001418   7–1C

"Bonkers idea", but "great fun" – Matthew Carver's custom-designed, double-decker barge moored in Paddington Basin serves a "good cheese-based menu" that celebrates cheeses made in Britain and Ireland. "It makes for a jolly experience on a sunny day, but" – although true turophiles might disagree – can seem something of "a one trick pony". Stablemates include the world's first cheese conveyor belt, in Seven Dials. / W2 6HY; www.thecheesebar.com/paddington; @thecheesebarldn; Tue-Sun 2 pm; closed Tue-Sun D, closed Mon.

Chelsea Cellar SW10 £51 3 4 4
9 Park Walk   020 7351 4933   6–3B

This "treasured Chelsea local, tucked away in a cosy basement off the Fulham Road 'beach'", inspires a devoted following from its regulars, looking after them with "classy and delicious" Italian dishes and an impressive wine list. Tourists and casual passers-by are unlikely even to notice the all-but-hidden entrance, adding to the clubbish appeal. / SW10 0AJ; www.thechelseacellar.co.uk; @thechelseacellar; Tue-Sat midnight; closed Tue-Sat L, closed Sun & Mon.

Cher Thai SW4 NEW £31 4 4 3
22 North Street   020 3583 3702   11–1D

"A new arrival in Clapham that's making a really good name for themselves" as a "neighbourhood gem". This small venture – the work of a husband-and-wife team – launched just before the February 2020 lockdown, and is finally winning recognition for its "really excellent Thai food: perhaps nothing ground-breaking, but the classics are prepared as well as I can remember having them in London in recent years". / SW4 0HB; www.cherthailondon.co.uk; @cherthailondon; Tue, Thu, Wed 10.30 pm, Fri & Sat 11 pm, Sun 10 pm; closed Mon.

FSA

Chez Antoinette £43   3 4 3
The Caxton, 22 Palmer Street, SW1   020 3990 5377   2–4C
Unit 30 The Market Building, WC2   020 7240 9072   5–3D

"Invitingly tucked away off Victoria Street", "it feels like stepping into Paris" at this "good little bistro", where "helpful staff" deliver "a short but interesting" all-day menu of "simple but delicious fare" at "good value prices" ("excellent saucisson, and good bavette steak, duck leg… a very good tarte Tatin and reasonably priced house wine!"). Only fleeting mentions for the branch cutely located in the tourist hell of Covent Garden on the lower ground level of the market itself, but all good.

Chez Bruce SW17 £100   5 4 3
2 Bellevue Rd   020 8672 0114   11–2C

"The very definition of a neighbourhood star" – Bruce Poole's "unpretentious, yet ever-reliable" south London icon, on Wandsworth Common, is – for the 17th year running – Londoners' No. 1 favourite in our annual diners' poll. For its legions of fans it's "the lodestar as to 'how to do it well' without making people feel ripped off" – "a proper grown-up restaurant, yet without being staid or stuffy". Matt Christmas's "unfussy" but "cleverly crafted" cuisine is "consistently superb" ("imaginative and expertly executed, with nothing just for show/colour, and with all constituents perfectly balanced"). "Engaging staff are knowledgeable without being intimidating" and if you're a wine connoisseur you'll be delighted by the "comprehensive and well-selected wine list" (although, "if you just want the house white then they won't be at all sniffy"). "The modest dining room is bright, with no background muzak, and always pleasantly buzzy and busy". A few reports do note the odd "Covid blip" or staffing issues, but (practically) all accounts say it's now "back to its best". "Year after year, this is one of the places I feel a sense of homecoming, gradually developing rituals around different reasons to justify a trip. Wonderfully comforting, satisfying and delightful all round!" ("If I were on Desert Island Discs, this would be my luxury item!") Top Tip – "the £57.50 3-course lunch menu is some of the best value in town". / SW17 7EG; www.chezbruce.co.uk; @chez.bruce; Tue-Thu 9.15 pm, Fri & Sat 9.30 pm, Sun 9 pm; closed Mon.

Chez Elles E1 £62   3 3 3
45 Brick Ln   020 7247 9699   13–2C

This "reliably good Gallic bistro" stands out from the crowd in Brick Lane, perhaps the last address you'd expect to find something "so French" in London. / E1 6PU; www.chezellesbistroquet.co.uk; @chezellesbistro; Tue-Sat 11.30 pm; closed Tue-Sat L, closed Sun & Mon.

Chicama SW10 £77   3 3 3
383 King's Road   020 3874 2000   6–3C

"Super-fresh fish", "inventive, well-cooked seafood dishes with a Peruvian slant" and a "great atmosphere" (boosted by "the best pisco sours") are the key ingredients of this King's Road "crowd-pleaser" – the younger stablemate of Pachamama in Marylebone – which can be "so warm you think you are somewhere tropical". Any gripes? – "just wish they'd turn the music down!" / SW10 0LP; www.chicamalondon.com; @chicamalondon; Mon-Fri 11 pm, Sat & Sun 4 pm; closed Sat & Sun D.

Chick 'n' Sours £41   4 3 3
1 Earlham Street, WC2   020 3198 4814   5–2B
22 Assembly Passage, E1   no tel   13–2D
390 Kingsland Rd, E8   020 3620 8728   14–2A

"So good – I'm still daydreaming about it", say fans of "the most delicious fried chicken burgers" served up alongside sour cocktails and local beers at this former pop-up with branches in Haggerston and Covent Garden, and an evening-only take-away outlet in Whitechapel (Fri/Sat/Sun). Top Menu Tip – "best is the K-Pop burger with spicy Korean-style coleslaw. Yom!" / www.chicknsours.co.uk; chicknsours.

FSA

The Chiltern Firehouse W1 £109 2️⃣2️⃣5️⃣
1 Chiltern St 020 7073 7676 2–1A

"Blindingly expensive, but unforgettable" – "you're paying for the experience not the food" at this sexy and enduringly fashionable Marylebone operation, which "everyone knows is about the 'scene' and rubbernecking the clientele". When it comes to its long, luxe-brasserie menu (burrata, oysters, steak, tuna tartare, pizza…), results are "OK, but not worth the cash, unless you are as super-rich as the rest of its customers". Top Tip – "go for breakfast, to get a sense of the ambience". / W1U 7PA; www.chilternfirehouse.com; Mon-Sun 10 pm; closed Mon-Sun L.

China Tang, Dorchester Hotel W1 £101 2️⃣3️⃣3️⃣
53 Park Ln 020 7319 7088 3–3A

The late Sir David Tang's take on 1930s Shanghai in the basement of this famous hotel divides opinion: some praise its "sublime food" including "wonderful Peking duck" (with the option of caviar) and other luxurious dishes to share (such as suckling pig or abalone) for £200-£300; others complain of "crazy prices" for "average meals" that are "no better than the standard Cantonese". On the plus side, the more affordable dim sum selection is available in the evening as well at lunchtime, and plenty of guests have a good time (to the point one reporter found it "rowdy"). Top Tip – plan on a cocktail in the superbly atmospheric bar. / W1K 1QA; www.chinatanglondon.co.uk; @chinatanglondon; Mon-Sun 11 pm; closed Mon-Wed L.

La Chingada SE8 £15 4️⃣3️⃣2️⃣
206 Lower Road 020 7237 7448 12–2B

"Simple dishes are well-realised" at this basic Mexican, which has moved from its previous site (a take-away with a few seats at the counter) to this (marginally grander) former caff nearby in Surrey Quays. / SE8 5DJ; lachingada.co.uk; @lachingadalondon; closed Mon-Sat & Sun.

Chishuru SW9 £49 3️⃣3️⃣2️⃣
Unit 9 Market Row 07960 002150 11–2D

"Wow! Wasn't sure what to expect of the African food, but it was mind-blowing" – Adejoke Bakara's "bold and beautiful" dishes win many converts to her "simple, warm and inviting" two-year-old in Brixton, where she channels her Nigerian heritage into contemporary West African cooking washed down with cocktails and funky wines. But does it risk over-exposure? A couple of diners this year judged it "overpriced for food that's good but not exceptional". / SW9 8LB; www.chishuru.com; @chishuru; Fri-Sun, Tue-Thu 10.30 pm; closed Tue-Thu L, closed Mon; payment – credit card only; booking online only.

Chisou £70 3️⃣2️⃣2️⃣
22-23 Woodstock Street, W1 020 7629 3931 4–1A
31 Beauchamp Pl, SW3 020 3155 0005 6–1D

"High-quality sushi – the fish is super-fresh" and "very good tempura" are the highlights at this classic Japanese duo in Mayfair and Knightsbridge. A meal here is "certainly not cheap but it is fantastic": "there are one or two London restaurants that do better Japanese and sushi. But not at these prices". Top Tip – "ask for sea urchins in season". / www.chisourestaurant.com.

Chook Chook SW15 £55 4️⃣3️⃣3️⃣
137 Lower Richmond Road 020 8789 3100 11–1B

"Generous portions of super-delicious food" – "the sort you would expect to find in India rather than Britain" – has won local acclaim for this three-year-old on the edge of Putney, with a luxury train theme linking cuisines from across the subcontinent. / SW15 1EZ; chookchook.uk; @chookchooklondon_; Mon-Thu 10.30 pm, Fri & Sat 11 pm, Sun 10 pm; closed Mon-Fri L.

F S A

Chotto Matte £70 4 4 4
11-13 Frith St, W1 020 7042 7171 5–2A
26 Paddington Street, W1 020 7058 4444 2–1A **NEW**
"Love the spin on the Peruvian x Japanese dishes" – Kurt Zdesar's Nikkei concept fueled by its 'Tokyo to Lima' cocktail menu is growing like topsy, expanding from its Soho home (undergoing 'an exciting restyle' as of summer 2022) to Marylebone Village in January 2022, with forthcoming debuts in Doha, Riyadh and San Francisco as part of a plan to expand to 20 sites globally in the next 5 years. The vibe is as energetic as its expansion plans: *"too noisy for the seniors in our group, but all the youngsters loved it!"* / chotto-matte.com; chottomatteldn.

Chourangi W1 £46 4 3 3
3 Old Quebec Street 020 3582 2710 2–2A
An *"inventive menu"* inspired by the melding of Indian, Chinese and British cuisines in historic Calcutta makes this Marble Arch yearling *"a great addition to the area"*. Named after a central district of the city, it was founded by chef-patron Anjan Chatterjee and Indian airline entrepreneur Aditya Ghosh. / W1W 7DL; chourangi.co.uk; @chourangildn; Tue-Sat 10.30 pm, Sun 10 pm; closed Mon.

Chriskitch N10 £44 3 3 3
7a Tetherdown 020 8411 0051 1–1C
"No menu and it's whatever is made on the day – I love it!". Australian chef Chris Honor's all-day neighbourhood café in Muswell Hill serves *"Ottolenghi-style food"* to a high standard. / N10 1ND; www.chriskitch.com; @chriskitchfood; Sat-Mon 5 pm, Tue-Fri 6 pm; closed Sat-Mon & Tue-Fri D; may need 3+ to book.

Christopher's WC2 £94 2 2 3
18 Wellington St 020 7240 4222 5–3D
This veteran American-style surf 'n' turf restaurant occupies a stunning Covent Garden mansion but for most of its long history (three decades) has been a missed culinary opportunity. So, *"go to see the room, but don't expect much of the formulaic food"*, which often elicited criticism this year (*"like an expensive McDonalds"*). *"One day someone will take this astonishing space with its magical stone spiral staircase and open a great destination"*.
/ WC2E 7DD; www.christophersgrill.com; @christopherswc2; Tue-Thu midnight, Fri & Sat 1.30 am, Sun 5 pm; closed Sun D, closed Mon; may need 6+ to book.

Chucs £94 2 2 3
25 Eccleston Street, SW1 020 3827 3000 2–4B
65 Lower Sloane Street, SW1 020 3827 2999 6–2D
31 Dover St, W1 020 3763 2013 3–3C
97 Old Brompton Road, SW7 020 8037 4525 6–2B
226 Westbourne Grove, W11 020 7243 9136 7–1B
3 Circus Road, NW8 020 4537 6277 9–3A **NEW**
"A throwback to old-school dining" – this wittingly old-fashioned chain (created in the last 10 years) channels an imagined La Dolce Vita lifestyle into its *"enjoyable if slightly stuffy"* mix of chic Italian cafés and restaurants (if you are of a certain age, think 1980s Tatler). They look *"pretty"* and are *"attractive in their own way"*: *"not bad if a bit overpriced"*. That's the kind view anyway: harsher critics say they *"could do better"* and *"don't deserve a revisit"*. But they must be doing something right, as in July 2021 they opened in St John's Wood. / www.chucsrestaurants.com; chucsrestaurants.

FSA

Chuku's N15 £40 4 4 3
274 High Road   no tel   1–1D
Emeka and Ifeyinwa Frederick's vibey three-year-old in Seven Sisters (motto, 'Chop, chat, chill') has won a big name for its quirky Nigerian tapas (e.g. jollof quinoa, moi moi, honey suya prawns), fab soundtrack and upbeat service. Whether its recommendation by Diane Abbott is a plus or a minus is hard to call… / N15 5AJ; www.chukuslondon.co.uk; @chukusldn; Tue-Sat 10.30 pm, Sun 8.30 pm; closed Tue-Fri L, closed Mon; payment – credit card only; booking online only.

Church Road SW13 £62 3 4 3
94 Church Road   020 8748 0393   11–1A
"High quality reflects the Phil Howard influence" at the Elystan Street chef's relaxed operation on his home turf in Barnes, launched in 2019 with business partner Rebecca Mascarenhas, on the site of their previous, less ambitious offering, Sonny's (RIP). It's "a cosy yet elegant" use of the space, with food "better than at your average local, and with a very good wine list". / SW13 0DQ; www.churchroadsw13.co.uk; @churchroadsw13; Wed, Sat 10 pm, Thu & Fri 10.30 pm, Sun 3 pm; closed Wed L closed Sun D, closed Mon & Tue.

Churchill Arms W8 3 2 3
119 Kensington Church St   020 7792 1246   7–2B
This "neighbourhood landmark" on Kensington Church Street was built in 1750 and has won renown in recent decades, both for its lavish floral displays (which earned it recognition from the Chelsea Flower Show) and also for the "excellent, cheap 'n' cheerful Thai" that operates in its pretty and quirky dining annex, all "at a great price-point for the area". Long-term customers say "it's not as good as it once was, but still a reliable stalwart". / W8 7LN; www.churchillarmskensington.co.uk; @churchillarmsw8; Mon-Sat 11 pm, Sun 10.30 pm.

Chutney Mary SW1 £90 4 3 4
73 St James's Street   020 7629 6688   3–4D
A trip to the "wonderful, fun cocktail bar" makes a brilliant introduction to this "spacious, elegant and bustling" operation, whose "marvellous décor truly gives it character". The original venture of Ranjit & Namita Mathrani, plus the latter's sister, Camellia Panjabi (who also now own Amaya, Veeraswamy and Masala Zone), it moved several years ago from SW10 to this swanky St James's address. The "sophisticated Indian cooking" has "superb spicing" with plenty of "depth and complexity" and "wonderful" flavours, and amongst London's posh Indians it remains one of the best known. / SW1S 1PH; www.chutneymary.com; @chutneymary.london; Sun-Wed 9.30 pm, Thu-Sat 10 pm; closed Mon L.

Chutneys NW1 £25 3 3 2
124 Drummond St   020 7388 0604   9–4C
"Still offering great value" for "fresh and really tasty food", this canteen is one of the stalwarts of the 'Little India' enclave behind Euston station, where Indian students gathered to eat from the 1950s. The daily vegetarian buffet lunch is a steal at under £10, while the meat and fish options on the main menu are not much more expensive. / NW1 2PA; www.chutneyseuston.uk; @chutneysnw1; Mon-Sat 11 pm, Sun 10 pm; no Amex; may need 5+ to book.

Ciao Bella WC1 £54 3 4 5
86-90 Lamb's Conduit St   020 7242 4119   2–1D
"Not completely cheap but extremely cheerful" – this "absolutely classic Italian restaurant" has wowed Bloomsbury for 40 years with "all your favourite dishes – pasta, antipasti, arancini, panna cotta". "Everything is just right" and there's "always a great atmosphere, good fun and friendly service". It's "perfect for groups and families, but not so much for intimate dinners" – although nobody told Boris Johnson, who wooed his paramour Jennifer Arcuri here over chips and red wine. / WC1N 3LZ; www.ciaobellarestaurant.co.uk; @ciaobella_london; Mon-Sat 10.45 pm, Sun 10.30 pm.

FSA RATINGS: FROM 1 POOR — 5 EXCEPTIONAL

F S A

Cibo W14 £60 4 4 3
3 Russell Gdns 020 7371 6271 8–1D
"Spankingly good Italian food" is found at this long-established modern venue in an "isolated location" behind Holland Park, whose "posh locals know a good thing when they see it". There are plenty of "unusual options on the menu", with an emphasis on "original and well-prepared fish dishes". / W14 8EZ; www.ciborestaurant.net; Mon-Sat 9.45 pm; closed Mon-Sat L, closed Sun.

Cigalon WC2 £51 3 3 3
115 Chancery Lane 020 7242 8373 2–2D
The sun-drenched flavours of Provence – both food and wine – are brought into focus at this Chancery Lane outpost of Pascal Aussignac's Club Gascon group, which occupies an engaging glass-ceilinged room, originally built as an auction house. The downstairs cocktail bar, Baranis, also boasts the UK's only indoor petanque pitch. The worst comment? "OK but not inspiring". / WC2A 1PP; www.cigalon.co.uk; @cigalon_london; Tue-Fri 9 pm; closed Mon, Sat & Sun.

Cin Cin W1 £39 3 4 4
21a Foley St 020 7436 0921 2–1B
This "lovely neighbourhood Italian" in Fitzrovia opened in April 2021 as a spin-off from a successful Brighton duo, and has made a "great transition to London" on an eye-catching corner site (formerly Bonnie Gull, RIP). The food is "delicious", although "portions are lady-sized rather than man-sized". The business was founded ten years ago when Italian-Australian lawyer David Toscano bought an old Fiat van to participate in a Brighton street-food festival. / W1; www.cincin.co.uk/london; @cincinuk; Wed-Sat 11.30 pm; closed Mon & Tue & Sun; no shorts.

Cincinnati Chilibomb EC2 £23 3 4 2
26 Curtain Road 07910 010210 13–2B
"US-style dive bar" in Shoreditch "serving what may well be the finest bar-meal/hangover-cure in London – beef chili in a hollowed-out brioche bun, topped with cheese and your choice of chili sauce in varying levels of insanity". Tim Brice, aka 'Captain Chili', took over the former site of Rok (RIP) to open his little corner of Americana in February 2021. Apparently the Cincinatti chilibomb was developed by Greek immigrants who adapted Tex-Mex chili con carne in the 1920s. / EC2E 3NY; www.cincinnatichilibomb.co.uk; @cincinnatichilibomb; Tue-Sat 11 pm; closed Sun & Mon.

Cinder NW3 £68 2 2 2
66 Belsize Lane 020 7435 8048 9–2A
This "tiny" Belsize Park two-year-old from chef Jake Finn (ex-La Petite Maison and The Ritz) is a "buzzy neighbourhood spot", where most of the food has been 'kissed by flames' on the Josper grill. But while it's undoubtedly a boon "in an area of drought for decent restaurants", opinions divide on its performance: to fans it provides an "excellently judged, seasonally changing menu"; to sceptics, it's "somewhat underwhelming and a bit expensive". / NW3 5BJ; www.cinderrestaurant.co.uk; @cinder_london; Tue-Sat 10.30 pm, Sun 10 pm; closed Mon; payment – credit card only.

Cinnamon Bazaar WC2 £56 4 4 4
28 Maiden Lane 020 7395 1400 5–4D
The "gorgeous food, with amazing flavours and presentation" at this Covent Garden café matches the high standards Vivek Singh sets at his grander Cinnamon restaurants, some of the best-known Indian kitchens in London. It's a useful destination pre-theatre. / WC2W 7NA; www.cinnamon-bazaar.com; @cinnamonbazaar_official; Mon-Sun 11 pm.

FSA

The Cinnamon Club SW1 £75 4 3 4
Old Westminster Library, Great Smith St   020 7222 2555   2–4C
"The atmospheric book-lined walls of Westminster's former public library are a highlight" and add *"a lot of character"* to Vivek Singh's famous venue a short stroll from the Palace of Westminster: one of the Top 40 most-mentioned restaurants in our annual diners' poll and the best-known top Indian destination. *"It's worth a visit just for the bar!"* – where an evening often commences – but the prime attraction is *"clever", "high-end"* nouvelle Indian food *"that's truly different"* and with *"very delicate spicing"*. *"The huge area can make service a challenge"* but generally staff cope well.
/ SW1P 3BU; www.cinnamonclub.com; @thecinnamoncollection; Mon-Sat 11 pm; closed Sun; no trainers; booking max 14 may apply.

Cinnamon Kitchen £60 3 3 3
4 Arches Lane, SW11   020 3955 5480   11–1C
9 Devonshire Sq, EC2   020 7626 5000   10–2D
"Big flavoured, modern Indian dishes" from an *"interesting and different menu"* win praise for Vivek Singh's high quality duo: *"a more affordable introduction to the Cinnamon Club's cuisine"*. The newer SW11 branch, *"with service around an open kitchen in a lively railway arch"* near Battersea Power Station is jollier than its longer-established City sibling, where *"the décor is quite boring and service a tad patchy"* (although the latter is also *"pretty decent value in an area that has limited options for a weekend lunch"*). / www.cinnamon-kitchen.com; cinnamonrestaurants.

Cinquecento £48 2 2 3
1 Cale Street, SW3   020 7351 9331   6–2C
233 Portobello Road, W11   no tel   7–2B
Opinions diverge on this Neapolitan duo, whose year-old Portobello branch already eclipses the small, tucked-away Chelsea original in terms of feedback. Fans hail their *"excellent pizzas and other dishes"*, while others find them *"surprisingly average"* and *"inexplicably popular"*.

Circolo Popolare W1 £57 3 3 5
40-41 Rathbone Square   no tel   5–1A
"A fun place to go with mates" – the Big Mamma Group's *"vibey"* Fitzrovian has won renown as a ready-made party scene. The outsized portions of simple Italian fodder from a monthly changing menu are arguably *"utterly bonkers"* and deliver an affordable occasion, although one or two critics feel it's *"losing some of its originality"* and providing too many *"unmemorable"* dishes nowadays. / W1W 1HX; @bigmamma.uk; Mon-Sat 10.30 pm, Sun 10 pm.

Citro N6 £52 4 3 2
15A Swain's Lane   07840 917586   9–1B
This *"fabulous local Italian"* in Highgate ticks all the boxes, with *"home-made pasta and great accompaniments"* plus *"fresh and original pizzas"*, delivered with the *"personal family touch"* that generates an *"excellent vibe"*. / N6 6QX; www.eatcitro.com; @citro_restaurant; Tue-Sat 10 pm, Sun 3 pm; closed Tue, Wed L closed Sun D, closed Mon.

City Barge W4 £68 2 2 3
27 Strand-on-the-Green   020 8994 2148   1–3A
An *"absolutely wonderful little pub"* at Strand-on-the-Green, Chiswick, whose *"riverside location and snug dining room"* make any meal *"a lovely experience from start to finish"*. A couple of reporters feel that the food *"is not as good as it was pre-lockdown"*, but in general it's acknowledged as a *"good standby"*. / W4 3PH; www.citybargechiswick.com; @CityBargeW4; Mon-Thu 11 pm, Fri & Sat midnight, Sun 10.30 pm.

City Social EC2 — £107 — 3 3 4
Tower 42 25 Old Broad St   020 7877 7703   10–2C

"Jason Atherton's City branch is still guaranteed to wow guests – from the plush elevator to the stunning views, everything screams impressive" at this 24th-floor venue in Tower 42 (fka the NatWest Tower). The food is "tasty" – if "not the most adventurous" (i.e. plenty of steaks) – "but staking out a view in one of the deep booths, glass in hand, and watching the city spread out for miles is a pretty spectacular way to spend an evening". / EC2N 1HQ; www.citysociallondon.com; @citysocial_t42; Tue-Sat 9.30 pm; closed Sat L, closed Sun & Mon; booking max 4 may apply.

The Clarence Tavern N16 — £61 — 3 4 3
102 Stoke Newington Church Street   020 8712 1188   1–1C

The food is "a comforting delight – never lacking in flavour" at this Stoke Newington boozer, for two years part of the Anchor & Hope group and with former Great Queen Street (RIP) chef Harry Kaufman at the helm. "There's the kind of consistency emerging that one would expect of the team – which is pleasing to see in a bit of town with no shortage of choice, but often very little of consistent note". Grade II-listed, the Clarence was known as the Daniel Defoe under its previous ownership before reverting to its original name. / N16 0LA; www.clarencetavern.com; @theclarencetavern; Tue-Sat 11 pm, Sun 5 pm; closed Tue L closed Sun D, closed Mon; payment – credit card only.

Clarette W1 — £89 — 3 3 3
44 Blandford St   020 3019 7750   3–1A

Converted from a Tudorbethan pub in Marylebone (complete with black and white exterior and leaded-glass windows), this three-floor wine bar and restaurant is part-owned by a scion of the French dynasty behind Château Margaux, explaining the extensive list of vintages from the estate on the French-centric list, many available by the glass. The better-than-incidental French/Italian cooking is also well-rated. / W1W 7HS; www.clarettelondon.com; @clarettelondon; Tue-Fri 11 pm, Sat midnight; closed Tue-Thu L, closed Sun & Mon.

Claridges Foyer & Reading Room W1 — £109 — 3 4 4
49 Brook Street   020 7107 8886   3–2B

"The epitome of Best of British" – "nobody does afternoon tea like Claridges": "it's a casually elegant delight from start to finish". "Everyone is made to feel like a VIP and the food is good without being intimidating" ("awesome cakes and a great range of sandwiches"). Top Tip – when you finish your tea, "don't forget the jewel that is the tiny Champagne bar". / W1W 4HW; www.claridges.co.uk; @claridgeshotel; Mon-Sun 10 pm.

Clarke's W8 — £95 — 4 4 3
124 Kensington Church Street   020 7221 9225   7–2B

"Sally Clarke remains very present" at her "sophisticated" and "welcoming" Kensington HQ, which she established in 1984 at the bleeding edge of a trend to a more seasonal, ingredient-led style of dining that's nowadays become an accepted norm. Consequently, for some fans, this has been "a 'go-to' for decades" owing to its "consistently superb cuisine", creating dishes "with fantastic attention to detail" that "are imaginative without seeming 'tricked up'". The décor has always divided opinions here: "quite formal" for some tastes, but to others "romantic" and "perfect for a relaxed evening with grown-up conversation". Ratings slipped a little this year across the board, though, as even those hailing it as "excellent" may note that "prices seem to have jumped here even more than most post-Covid". / W8 4BH; www.sallyclarke.com; @sallyclarkeltd; Tue-Sat 10 pm; closed Sun & Mon; booking max 8 may apply.

The Clerk & Well EC1 £51

156 Clerkenwell Road   0207 837 8548   10–1A

"Recently revamped" with eight 'boutique guestrooms', this handsome Clerkenwell establishment is one of the oldest public houses in central London. There are too few reports for a rating as yet, but it looks promising and "the Sunday roast sharing board is pretty impressive". / EC1E 5DU; www.clerkandwell.co.uk; @theclerkandwellpub; Mon-Sun 11 pm.

The Clifton NW8 £67   3 4 4

96 Clifton Hill   020 7625 5010   9–3A

"You never tire of the Clifton", a rather grand St John's Wood pub serving "delicious" food from a "perfect menu – not too much, not too little". There's "great service" too, led by the trio who relaunched the pub five years ago, having saved it from developers. The Clifton also has a bit of louche history: originally a hunting lodge, it was used by 'Bertie', the future King Edward VII, for assignations with his mistress Lillie Langtry. / NW8 0JT; www.thecliftonnw8.com; @thecliftonnw8; Mon-Sat 10 pm, Sun 9 pm.

Clipstone W1 £85   4 3 2

5 Clipstone Street   020 7637 0871   2–1B

"Rocking something reminiscent of an upscale NYC-style neighbourhood vibe (a real triumph in the context of central London)" – Will Lander and Daniel Morgenthau's "unpretentious, relaxed and happy" corner site in Fitzrovia "keeps up very high standards": "the menu is always original", service is "charming", there's an "interesting wine list" and a "noisy buzzy atmosphere". It can be slightly "erratic" though, and arguably "in being rather cramped, it needs to get off the fence and either up the party mood, or space the tables and quieten down a little". / W1W 6BB; www.clipstonerestaurant.co.uk; @clipstonerestaurant; Tue-Sat 9.45 pm, Sun 8.45; closed Mon.

Clos Maggiore WC2 £95   3 3 5

33 King St   020 7379 9696   5–3C

"Get lucky and score a table in the conservatory and you've landed the most romantic rendezvous in town!" at this "lovely" oasis in bustling Covent Garden – for many years now, reporters' No. 1 choice "for celebrating anniversaries, engagements, weddings, etc…". The "beautiful glazed dining room is hung with blossom and has both a roof that opens in warm weather and a cosy fire for cold days". And not everyone feels that all is lost if you don't nab one of these prime seats ("everyone raves about the garden room but there is a small dining room upstairs that we love too!"). Though it has never been a prime foodie destination, the kitchen typically wins acclaim for its "accomplished modern European cuisine", which is backed up by "the longest wine list ever seen" (although pricing of some vintages gave cause for complaint this year). There continues to be a school of thought that its food is "sadly not as good as it was pre-lockdown" or that "staff changes have made it seem less welcoming". But ratings recovered well here this year after a dive last year, and on most of the very many reports we receive: "you always feel special here!" / WC2E 8JD; www.closmaggiore.com; @clos_maggiore; Wed-Sun 10 pm; closed Mon & Tue; no shorts.

The Clove Club EC1 £206   4 4 3

Shoreditch Town Hall, 380 Old St   020 7729 6496   13–1B

"In the unlikely, understated but pleasant environs of Shoreditch Town Hall", this iconic modern venue – a UK flag-bearer on the World's 50 Best – is approaching its 10th year and, for the most part, "still knocking the ball out of the park". With its "calm, unpretentious room table setting" and "cool open-kitchen approach", it delivers "imaginative and precise cooking with a wide range of tastes and textures" that fans say is "the best of the best", and bolstered by novel wine and drink pairings. (Michelin, never exactly ahead of the curve, awarded it two stars in 2022). "Professional, attentive and caring service" plays its part and there's been "outstanding attention to detail since reopening post Covid". The whacking bill continues to be an issue here, though. Even many fans find it "disturbingly pricey" – although they note "you get what you pay for" – but others feel the value just doesn't stack up: "third visit probably now our last… at over £600 for two, it's now just toooooo expensive". / EC1V 9LT; www.thecloveclub.com; @thecloveclub; Mon-Sat 11 pm; closed Mon L, closed Sun.

Club Gascon EC1 £137 4 3 3
57 West Smithfield 020 7600 6144 10–2B

"Reliably great after all these years" – Pascal Aussignac and Vincent Labeyrie's renowned institution near Smithfield Market occupies a stylishly converted former Lyons Tea House and continues to mine southwest France for its culinary inspiration: notably "very inventive presentations of foie gras" paired with "a different range of wines that one sees in most other restaurants, given its regional emphasis". / EC1A 9DS; www.clubgascon.com; @ClubGascon; Tue-Sat 9.30 pm; closed Tue-Sat L, closed Sun & Mon; no shorts.

The Coach EC1 £65 2 3 3
26-28 Ray Street 020 3954 1595 10–1A

The attractively converted garden room and beautiful upstairs dining room are highlights at this fine old pub (dating from 1790) in Clerkenwell. It hit foodie fame a couple of years ago under well-known chef, Henry Harris: since then the verdict on its gastroboozer fare has been: "variable, but still capable of hitting some top notes". / EC1E 3DJ; www.thecoachclerkenwell.co.uk; @thecoachlondon; Mon-Sat 9 pm, Sun 4 pm; closed Sun D.

Coal Office N1 £83 4 3 4
2 Bagley Walk 020 3848 6085 9–3C

"Amazing, and amazing fun… one of my best meals of the year and I wasn't expecting it at all!" – this "tightly packed" space from chef Assaf Granit and the Tom Dixon studio has a "wonderful location" next to the latter's HQ: which is adjacent to Granary Square and Coal Drops Yard. Deceptively simple in style, "it's great to take guests here and watch their faces as they realise this isn't just another noisy cocktail joint but a seriously good restaurant". The menu of "Middle Eastern food with a modern twist" delivers "dish after dish of mind-blowing flavours" – "original and fabulous… if in tiny portions". "It's tight on space, so get ready to snuggle up", or "sit outside on a sunny day, which is the perfect way to spend a couple of hours". "Only problem? Getting a booking!" / N1N 4PQ; coaloffice.com; @coaloffice; Mon-Wed, Sat & Sun, Thu & Fri 11 pm; closed Mon-Wed L.

Coal Rooms SE15 £71 4 3 3
11a Station Way 020 7635 6699 1–4D

"Extra points on ambience for the Victorian toilets" at the 19th-century booking hall and goods rooms of Peckham Rye station, now transformed into an all-day café and evening restaurant. It serves a "limited" but "delicious" menu of modern European dishes and fans say results are "always spot-on". / SE15 4RX; www.coalroomspeckham.com; @coalrooms; Wed-Sat 11 pm, Sun 6 pm; closed Sun D, closed Mon & Tue; payment – credit card only.

The Coal Shed SE1 £77 3 3 3
One Tower Bridge 020 3384 7272 10–4D

"A restaurant of choice when you go to the nearby Bridge Theatre" – this five-year-old sibling to a Brighton original provides "a good welcome", plus "very good steaks" and a "short but acceptable" menu of other options. "If it were not a little pricey for what it offers, I would be even more enthusiastic!" / SE1 2SE; www.coalshed-restaurant.co.uk; @thecoalshed; Tue-Sat 11 pm, Sun 8 pm; closed Tue, Wed L, closed Mon.

F S A

CoCoRo W1 — £39 — 4|3|2
31 Marylebone Ln 020 7935 2931 3–1A
"Don't let the décor fool you: the traditional sushi and other dishes here are really good and good value!", according to fans of this "cheap 'n' cheerful" small chain, whose most commented on outlets are the "really-Japanese-in-feel" Marylebone original and more deli-style Highgate spin-off (Bloomsbury and Bayswater inspire little feedback). / W1U 2NH; cocororestaurant.co.uk; @cocorolondon; Mon-Sun 10.30 pm.

Cocotte — £54 — 3|4|3
271 New King's Road, SW6 020 7610 9544 11–1A
11 Harrington Road, SW7 020 7589 1051 6–2C
95 Westbourne Grove, W2 020 3220 0076 7–1B
8 Hoxton Square, N1 020 7033 4277 13–1B
79 Salusbury Road, NW6 020 7625 6606 1–2B
"Delicious roast chicken, with sides such as potato purée and root veggies" – as well, of course, as fries and salads – have won a growing fanclub for Romain Bourrillon's upbeat French-rotisserie chain, whose most popular branches in our annual diners' poll are in Bayswater, Queen's Park and Parsons's Green. / www.mycocotte.uk; cocotte_rotisserie.

Colbert SW1 — £63 — 2|3|3
51 Sloane Sq 020 7730 2804 6–2D
"A top location on a corner of Sloane Square" helps define this "Parisian-like café/brasserie", which is decorated "with minute attention to detail in the quintessential Corbin & King style". It's "always crowded and noisy", but doesn't inspire affection the way its siblings do; and it's nominated much more as a convenient rendezvous than as a destination in itself. "All the Gallic classics are there on the menu", and while the food is "reliable" enough, definitely don't expect fireworks. "Very efficient and friendly service" this year though. Top Tip – "good range of breakfast menus". / SW1W 8AX; www.colbertchelsea.com; @ColbertChelsea; Tue-Sat 10.30 pm, Sun & Mon 10 pm.

La Collina NW1 — £74 — 3|2|3
17 Princess Rd 020 7483 0192 9–3B
This "friendly and cosy" independent Italian with a "good garden space" has established a comfortable niche for itself in Primrose Hill over the past dozen years. It's run by Patrick Oberto and his partner Diana Rinaldo, who took over the site in 2011. / NW1 8JR; www.lacollinarestaurant.co.uk; @lacollinaprimrosehill; Tue, Sun 9.15 pm, Wed-Sat 9.45 pm; closed Tue-Fri L, closed Mon; booking max 8 may apply.

The Collins Room SW1 — £131 — 3|3|4
The Berkeley Hotel, Wilton Place 020 7107 8866 6–1D
Pimp your Insta in fine style with a trip to this pretty chamber and its fashionista afternoon 'Prêt-à-Portea', whose exquisitely crafted cakes are regularly re-shaped to mirror the fashions of different designers. From April 2022 it is 'couture cakes inspired by designers from Saint Laurent to Schiaparelli': 'Schiaparelli's couture golden mini dress combines caramel sponge, dark Valrhona chocolate and hazelnut praline, all topped with a shimmering, chocolate oversized collar', apparently. Not one if you're counting the pennies of course, but something genuinely different and deftly realised for those with money to burn. / SW1X 7RL; www.the-berkeley.co.uk/restaurants-bars/collins-room; @the_berkeley; Mon-Sun 10.30 pm.

F S A

Le Colombier SW3 £92 2 4 4
145 Dovehouse Street   020 7351 1155   6–2C
"You could be in Paris… except the staff are nicer" at Didier Garnier's stalwart "absolute old favourite" in a quiet Chelsea backstreet. For its silver-haired Francophile following, it ticks all the boxes for "a proper French restaurant", serving ultra-classic bistro fare ("the menu changes rarely"), "wonderful desserts" and a "fabulous Gallic wine list at very reasonable prices". More sceptical reporters feel it's "delightful", but that "it's a pity they don't put a bit more effort into the cuisine". They are drowned out, though, by the proportion who feel that "for a very relaxing meal, there's nowhere better". Top Tip – "try and get a table under the awning". / SW3 6LB; www.le-colombier-restaurant.co.uk; Tue-Sat 10.30 pm; closed Sun & Mon.

Colonel Saab WC1
Holborn Hall, 193-197 High Holborn   020 3004 0004   5–1D
Will this late 2021 newcomer finally make a go of this marvellous site in Holborn's former Town Hall, that's so far seen off Shanghai Blues, Burger and Lobster, and most recently Gezellig (RIP)? Dubbed a 'Curry Catastrophe' by the Evening Standard's David Ellis, our feedback is a little more upbeat, but too limited for a safe rating. / WC1W; www.colonelsaab.co.uk; @colonelsaab; Mon-Sat 10.30 pm, Sun 8 pm.

Colony Grill Room, Beaumont Hotel W1 £107 3 4 4
8 Balderton Street, Brown Hart Gardens   020 7499 9499   3–2A
Within a luxurious Art Deco hotel near Selfridges, this swish venue (majorly refurbished in 2021) has the "proper spacing", "low level of noise" and "expert management" that's ideal for a business meal ("particularly if you book a booth"). The menu aims to recreate that of 'a New York-style grill room with a timeless selection of transatlantic favourites, salads, crustacea and steaks', and by and large it succeeds. Top Tip – "afternoon tea like you're in a Wodehouse novel". / W1W 6TF; www.colonygrillroom.com; @thecolonygrillroom; Mon-Sat 9.30 pm, Sun 2.30 pm; closed Sun D.

Le Comptoir Robuchon W1 £132 3 4 3
6 Clarges Street   020 8076 0570   3–4C
With its marble bar and banquette seating, this gracious venue (which opened in late 2019) near Shepherd Market is the London flagship for the late Joel Robuchon's global luxury restaurant chain (Robuchon International). It inspires curiously little feedback for its luxurious, rather safe, modern French cuisine ('Le Burger', £36; 'La Sole Meunière', £59), but all reports are uniformly upbeat. Top Tip – "good-value fixed lunch menu with generous courses". / W1W 8AE; www.robuchonlondon.co.uk; @lecomptoirrobuchon; Tue-Sat 11 pm; closed Tue, Sat L, closed Sun & Mon.

The Connaught Grill W1 £154
Carlos Place   020 7107 8852   3–3B
Bearing no resemblance to the 'Connaught Grill' in operation from 1955-2000 (nowadays, the space occupied by Hélène Darroze), this relative newcomer opened in early 2020, closed for much of the pandemic, then re-emerged in April 2022 (too late for much feedback in our annual diners' poll). Occupying a newly converted area within the hotel, the sleek interior – with much bespoke woodwork – is a world away from the 'period piece' style of its former namesake. Likewise the menu, overseen by NYC chef Jean-Georges Vongerichten and much of it produced from the rotisserie and a wood-burning grill. Where, in its former incarnation, you might have enjoyed Consommé 'Prince of Wales', followed by Médaillons de Cailles 'Belle Epoque', now you can have Heirloom Tomato Salad followed by grilled Japanese Sirloin Black Beef. / W1W 2AL; www.the-connaught.co.uk/restaurants-bars/the-connaught-grill; @theconnaught; Wed-Sat 10.15 pm, Sun 4.30 pm; closed Wed-Sat L closed Sun D, closed Mon & Tue.

FSA RATINGS: FROM 1 POOR — 5 EXCEPTIONAL

Coppa Club £53 2 3 4
29 Brewhouse Lane, SW15   020 3937 5354   11–2B
Three Quays Walk, Lower Thames St, EC3   020 7993 3827   10–3D
"An ideal location next to the Thames" is a plus for both London outposts of this national chain, which have "superb" situations near Tower Bridge and Putney Bridge and outside terraces with cute outside 'igloos'. In ethos, they resemble hotel brasseries… just without the attendant hotel: staff are "accommodating" and even if the food is not exciting it's dependable and relatively affordable.

Copper & Ink SE3 £86 4 3 3
5 Lee Road   020 3941 9337   1–4D
"Why go into central London to eat?" – this "neighbourhood restaurant punches well above its location" in Blackheath, with "former Masterchef finalist Tony Rodd continuing to produce fine value for money": "his tasting menu which changes each month is always where the most fun is to be had, churning out some very special plates of food reflecting the seasons". Partner Becky Cummings runs the front of house and "they have put together a really special local restaurant with a fine drinks list to match". / SE3 9RQ; www.copperandink.com; @copperandink; Wed-Sat 11.30 pm; closed Mon & Tue & Sun.

Copper Chimney W12 £41 3 3 3
Southern Terrace, Westfield London   020 8059 4439   1–3B
With 15 restaurants in five Indian cities, this long-established Indian chain (est 1972 in Mumbai) chose Westfield (near the main entrance) for its first UK branch, which opened a couple of years ago. We still don't get a huge volume of reports, but all are upbeat, especially from those with kids in tow: "authentic, fairly priced, and with something for the whole family to enjoy". / W12 7GA; www.copperchimney.uk; @copperchimney_uk; Sun-Thu 10 pm, Fri & Sat 10.30 pm.

Coq d'Argent EC2 £96 2 2 3
1 Poultry   020 7395 5000   10–2C
"The great location" atop No 1 Poultry, "in the heart of the City", makes this D&D London venue "perfect for entertaining out-of-town business guests" (who might recognise it from the James Bond sequence in the opening ceremony of the London Olympics). It's "slick and efficient", too, which helps for scheduling "a time-critical business lunch". On the debit side, "staff sometimes get overwhelmed by the number of diners", and "the nosh is upmarket but predictable" – "glad I wasn't paying for it!". / EC2R 8EJ; www.coqdargent.co.uk; @coqdargent; Mon-Sat midnight; closed Sun; booking max 10 may apply.

Coqfighter W1 £30 4 3 2
75 Beak Street   020 7734 4001   4–2C
Fried chicken specialists who have elevated the fast-food classic to delectable and "moreish" culinary heights – this Soho outfit was founded by a trio of transplanted Melburnians who missed one of their home city's prime nibbles. They also have outlets in King's Cross, Finsbury Park and the Boxparks in Shoreditch and Croydon, as well as delivery kitchens in Brockley and Balham. / W1W 9SS; www.coqfighter.com; @coqfighteruk; Sun-Thu 10 pm, Fri & Sat 11 pm.

Cora Pearl WC2 £69 3 3 4
30 Henrietta Street   020 7324 7722   5–3C
"Romantic but with a buzz", this Covent Garden crowd-pleaser excels for its "consistent mixture of ambience, service and quality food". Not surprisingly "a pre-theatre favourite", it offers "no real gastronomic experiences" but superior comfort food, such as the "delicious and imaginative mini ham-and-cheese toastie starter portions: to die for!". Like its older sister Kitty Flsher's in Shepherd Market, it's named after a courtesan who, in times gone by, frequented the area. / WC2W 8NA; www.corapearl.co.uk; @corapearlcg; Tue-Sat 10 pm, Sun 3.30 pm; closed Sun D, closed Mon.

FSA

CORD EC4
85 Fleet Street   020 3143 6365   10–2A

The Paris-based Cordon Bleu culinary institute (est 1895) has one of the grander names in gastronomy to trade under, and opened a restaurant in the Lutyens-designed former Reuters building in Fleet Street in summer 2022, with former Plaza Athénée and Folie chef Christophe Marleix running the kitchen. One early visitor, Giles Coren of The Times, found it a "time machine", with classical cooking and "four chefs in vertiginous toques" – "how much you enjoy it will depend on what you think of the direction restauration has taken since Le Cordon Bleu was the sine qua non (1973?)". There's also a daytime café for anybody who wants to nosey around inside. / EC4E 1AE; www.cordrestaurant.co.uk; @cordrestaurant; Mon-Fri 11 pm; closed Sat & Sun.

Core by Clare Smyth W11   £226   5 5 4
92 Kensington Park Rd   020 3937 5086   7–2B

"The best restaurant in London" – Clare Symth's "supreme" Notting Hill five-year-old once again topped our diners' poll as the capital's No.1 gastronomic experience: "a real triumph". And yet, while "it's a special place, the experience is not over-wrought": "it deftly straddles that line between fine dining but not being stuffy". "Clare and head chef Jonny Bone run a great kitchen", but they achieve "the finest cooking without it being up-your-arse mucked around, just with the beautiful presentation of seasonal ingredients" all "served with flair and precision in a fine dining room". "The friendly and very efficient front of house team is led by Rob Rose. And when it comes to wine we always rely on sommelier Gareth's recommendations. He has never let us down yet and works within a sensible budget". "Clare and Jonny always greet you: in fact, everyone says hi and has time to chat. Save up your money and spend it here!" / W11 2PN; www.corebyclaresmyth.com; @corebyclaresmyth; Thu-Sat 2.15 pm; closed Thu-Sat D, closed Mon-Wed & Sun.

Cork & Bottle WC2   £58   2 4 4
44-46 Cranbourn St   020 7734 7807   5–3B

"Hidden right next to the horrors of Leicester Square!", this 50-year-old wine cellar rates highly for its "really special ambience" and "knowledgeable and helpful" service. Will Clayton still runs the place on the lines laid down by founder Don Hewitson, although "the food offering has improved over time – not gourmet, but always a good pairing for the wine". This year will see the millionth serving of the famous cheese & ham pie that is always on the menu. / WC2H 7AN; www.thecorkandbottle.co.uk; @thecorkandbottle; Mon-Sat 11.30 pm; closed Sun; no booking D.

Cornerstone E9   £92   5 5 4
3 Prince Edward Road   020 8986 3922   14–1C

"Unbelievably good food…", "so clever…", "each dish was perfection…", "the best fish dishes I've eaten…", "mind blowing!" – Tom Brown inspires superlatives with the "small yet superbly composed" creations as his "truly innovative seafood destination". "The décor is industrial as you would expect in trendy Hackney Wick" and you can "sit at the counter and watch the chefs at work". Service that's "highly professional without being stuffy or offhand" completes an "unfailingly amazing" formula that's currently one of the strongest all-round performances in town. Top Menu Tip – "signature crab crumpet is changed for winter by adding a rarebit on top". / E9 5LX; cornerstonehackney.com; @cornerstonehackney; Wed-Sat, Tue 9 pm; closed Tue L, closed Sun & Mon.

FSA

Corrigan's Mayfair W1 £118 3 4 3
28 Upper Grosvenor St   020 7499 9943   3–3A
Richard Corrigan's Mayfair HQ, just off Park Lane, aims to 'champion all game that is coastal and wild, furred and feathered' and the result is a selection of fairly traditional British dishes, infused "with the occasional Irish flavour" ("top-quality venison" and "perfectly cooked fish" inspired particular mention this year). In style, it's quite a "formal" space, although "service is efficient and not too stuffy for the type of establishment" (and "if the great man himself makes an appearance, prepare to be entertained!"). One much-repeated complaint this year, though: it's becoming "heart-stoppingly expensive". / W1K 7EH; www.corrigansmayfair.com; @corrigans_mayfair; Tue-Sat midnight; closed Sun & Mon; booking max 12 may apply.

Côte £59 2 2 2
Branches throughout London
*"Nothing to set the heart racing, but decent, plain food, friendly staff and reasonable prices" all continue to carve out a surprisingly massive fanclub for this middle-of-the-road bistro chain as a "tolerable and relatively reliable fall back". It's particularly liked for breakfast ("something for everyone"), pre-theatre, or a family meal ("unfussy" and "you know what you are getting"). Few reports are wild with enthusiasm though – even some fans fear their feedback reads "almost as if I am damning it with faint praise". And sagging ratings support those who feel it's now really coming "off the boil" (indeed, struggling to simmer), in particular when it comes to ambience.
/ www.cote.co.uk; cote_brasserie.*

The Cow W2 £77 3 2 3
89 Westbourne Park Rd   020 7221 0021   7–1B
Almost 30 years on, Tom Conran's Irish-themed gastropub is "still ace" – "all chaos and noise; with happy, if haphazard service; plus excellent prawns by the half-pint, and outstanding fish soup (of sonorous depth, with generous chunks of fish and a whopping kick of chilli and love)" – and of course "a fine pint of Guinness". Top Tip – "downstairs is where the atmosphere is", not the cramped first-floor dining room. / W2 5QH; thecowlondon.com; @thecowlondon; Mon-Sat 11 pm, Sun 11 pm; booking online only.

Coya £114 3 3 3
118 Piccadilly, W1   020 7042 7118   3–4B
Angel Court, 31-33 Throgmorton St, EC2   020 7042 7118   10–2C
Resident DJs are intrinsic to the vibey style of Arjun Waney's "very opulent" Peruvians, which since their launch ten years ago now feature Paris, Monaco and Mykonos on their list of locations alongside those in Mayfair and near the Bank of England. The "exciting" Latino cuisine is "beautifully presented" and contributes to an "amazing overall experience". The crowd is "a bit flash" for some tastes, but you can always "ignore the bankers and the Gulf trust fund babies and focus on the plate". / www.coyarestaurant.com; coyamayfair.

The Crabtree W6 £52 3 3 4
Rainville Road   020 7385 3929   11–1A
A "wonderful location" on Fulham's Thames-side pedestrian path, with Craven Cottage and the River Café a few minutes' walk in either direction, is the strong suit of this spacious gastropub, which has a "quality food and drink offering". In milder weather there's a "fabulous asado grill in the garden, with a great range of vegan and vegetarian options". The atmosphere swings from tranquil midweek to rammed on sunny weekends and match days. / W6 9HA; www.thecrabtree6.co.uk; @thecrabtreew6; Mon-Sat 11 pm, Sun 10.30 pm.

FSA

Crate Brewery and Pizzeria E9 £36   3|2|3
7, The White Building, Queens Yard   020 8533 3331   14–1C
Just across the canal from the Olympic Park – and with a large waterside terrace – this warehouse microbrewery (nice brews!) in 'The White Building' has just the right mix of grunge and hipster vibe to inspire a trip to Hackney Wick. Decent pizza too… but be prepared for a wait at busy times.
/ E9 5EN; www.cratebrewery.com; @cratebrewery; Sun-Thu 11 pm, Fri & Sat 1 am; payment – credit card only.

Crocker's Folly NW8 £55   4|3|4
23-24 Aberdeen Pl   020 7289 9898   9–4A
"Classic up-market Lebanese food" and "a good choice of Lebanese wines" from the Maroush group can be enjoyed in the unlikely surroundings of this lavish late-Victorian gin palace – a 'folly' constructed in the mistaken expectation that a railway terminus would be built nearby (the site turned out to be Marylebone). "The front bar is a reconstruction of the original pub, and is great for a pre-dinner drink". Top Tip – "avoid Lord's cricket days, when it gets busy with rowdy fans". / NW8 8JR;
www.maroush.com/restaurant/crockers-folly; @maroush; Mon-Sun midnight.

The Crooked Well SE5 £69   3|3|3
16 Grove Ln   020 7252 7798   1–3C
"One of the very finest gastropubs in South London", this handsome Camberwell tavern is a "really solid and enjoyable local", and is run by landlord Hector Skinner, who set it up with three pals a dozen years ago. "If it was in Clapham it would be very famous and utterly heaving". Top Menu Tip – "the sharing roast chicken and the rabbit pie are the best mains".
/ SE5 8SY; www.thecrookedwell.com; @thecrookedwell; closed Mon-Sat & Sun; payment – credit card only; booking max 6 may apply.

The Crossing SW13 £73   3|2|3
73 White Hart Ln   020 8392 1617   11–1A
An "ambitious newcomer" in Barnes, where veteran hospitality operator Christian Arden has transformed a former pub (fka The Tree House) to the tune of £400k, with chef Anthony Demetre (of Arbutus and Wild Honey) consulting on the menu. "The food is really good, fully deserving of its recent rave review in the Telegraph from William Sitwell!" / SW13;
www.thecrossing-barnes.co.uk; @thecrossingbarnes; Mon-Sun 11 pm.

The Crystal Moon Lounge,
Corinthia Hotel London SW1 £104   3|4|4
Whitehall Place   020 7321 3150   2–3C
The "fabulous afternoon tea" in the lounge of this luxury hotel off Trafalgar Square makes for a "really special way to celebrate a birthday". "Impeccable service" and "inventive" cakes and pastries are a match for the plush surroundings. / SW1A 2BD; www.corinthia.com/en/hotels/london/dining/afternoon-tea; @corinthialondon; Mon-Sun midnight.

Cubé W1 £130   4|4|2
4 Blenheim Street   020 7165 9506   3–2B
A short walk from Oxford Circus, this five-year-old izakaya is well-worth discovering. "Like with many Japanese restaurants the food rather than the ambience is the reason to visit: the sushi is exquisite, the chef is extremely accommodating and the experience is consistently good". / W1W 1LB;
www.cubemayfair.com; @cubemayfairuk; Mon-Sat 11 pm, Sun 10 pm.

FSA RATINGS: FROM **1** POOR — **5** EXCEPTIONAL

The Culpeper E1 £58 333
40 Commercial St   020 7247 5371   13–2C

This "upscale gastropub" in Spitalfields is a "beautifully refurbished" old boozer, now incorporating bedrooms and a roof garden. The "industrial chic" first-floor dining room may have a "simple menu, but the dishes are far from simple, packed full of flavour and balanced superbly – fine-dining food at gastroboozer prices". / E1 6LP; www.theculpeper.com; @theculpeper; Mon-Thu midnight, Fri & Sat 1 am, Sun 6 pm; closed Sun D.

Cut W1 £132 333
45 Park Ln   020 7493 4545   3–4A

"Puck never disappoints" according to fans of Wolfgang P's first European outpost across the road from The Dorchester's main entrance, who say its "amazing cocktails" and wide selection of prime cuts from both UK farms and also farther afield (including USDA steaks, Australian wagyu, and Japanese Pure A5 Wagyu) are ideal business entertaining fodder; and also well-suited "for a chilled evening" generally. Even some fans note that "it's very pricey" or that "you may have to make your own atmosphere", but the harsh critiques of some former surveys were absent this year. / W1K 1PN; www.dorchestercollection.com/en/london/45-park-lane/restaurants-bars/cut-45-park-lane; @45parklane; Mon-Sun 10.30 pm.

Cycene E2 NEW
9 Chance Street   awaiting tel   13–1C

The renowned Māos (RIP) has gone at James and Christie Brown's hipster retail happening in Shoreditch – 'The Blue Mountain School' – to be replaced by this late 2022 newcomer. A bigger (and more conventional) two-floor operation is promised, overseen by Theo Clench, who till recently was the executive chef at Fitzrovia's funky West African, Akoko and here we're told to expect a menu reflecting east Asia and Australasia. One course will be dedicated to bread alone, apparently, and guests will eat part of their meal behind the pass. / E2 7JB; Mon-Sun midnight.

Cyprus Mangal SW1 £57 322
45 Warwick Way   020 7828 5940   2–4B

"The smell of the ocakbasi barbecue transports you to the eastern Med" at this good-value Turkish-Cypriot grill near Victoria station in Pimlico. It has satisfied appetites for nearly two decades with "flavourful and plentiful lamb dishes, plus piquant salads and salty rice to set them off". / SW1V 1QS; www.cyprusmangal.co.uk; @cyprusmangal; Mon-Sun 11 pm.

Da Mario SW7 £49 233
15 Gloucester Rd   020 7584 9078   6–1B

Family-owned Italian near the Albert Hall that's "a good option for getting away from the chains". Open for five decades, it was apparently a favourite lunch haunt of Princess Diana, who would bring Princes Wills and Harry for pizza. / SW7 4PP; www.damario.co.uk; @Da-Mario-Kensington; Mon-Sun 11.30 pm.

Da Mario WC2 £71 232
63 Endell St   020 7240 3632   5–1C

"Narrow, buzzy and full of black-and-white photos of Sophia Loren, Audrey Hepburn and Marcello Mastroianni in their heyday" – this longstanding Covent Garden stalwart "is like a trattoria from one's dreams of holidays in Tuscany or Rome". "Andrea, the entertaining owner, loves a good chat with guests while they enjoy delicious Italian dishes just like mamma used to make. All ages have a great time". / WC2H 9AJ; www.da-mario.co.uk; @da_mario_covent_garden; Tue-Sat 11 pm, Sun 9 pm; closed Mon; no shorts.

Da Terra, Town Hall Hotel E2 £223 5 4 4
8 Patriot Square   020 7062 2052   14–2B

"Just blow-your-mind amazing!" – Rafael Cagali's "thought-provoking tasting menu extravaganzas" continue to affirm the status of this "wonderful dining room in Bethnal Green's old town hall" (previously The Typing Room and Viajante) as one of London's foremost culinary destinations. "Brazilian influences that you're unlikely to experience anywhere else" are "what really lift Da Terra from a splendid fine dining tasting experience to a really memorable and unique one". "Tastes and textures are sublime" and "presentation is consistently gorgeous (like works of art), with a charming and compelling degree of theatre". "With its open kitchen, many dishes are served by the chefs" and service is "highly professional and interactive". / E2 9NF; www.daterra.co.uk; @daterrarestaurant; Wed-Sat 8 pm; closed Wed & Thu L, closed Mon & Tue & Sun; booking online only.

Daddy Bao SW17 £36 4 3 3
113 Mitcham Road   020 3601 3232   11–2C

Taiwanese steamed buns with tasty fillings are the stars at the Tooting branch of Frank Leung's highly rated Bao family trio ('Mr' in Peckham, 'Master' in Westfield Shepherd's Bush), named in honour of his father, Joe, who retired after a lifetime in restaurants five years ago. / SW17 9PE; www.daddybao.com; @daddybao; Tue-Thu, Sun 09.45 pm, Fri & Sat 10.45 pm; closed Tue-Fri L, closed Mon.

Daddy Donkey EC1 £14 4 3 2
100 Leather Ln   07950 448448   10–2A

"Still The Daddy!… I was glad to return to the office and find it was still trading!" – "Leather Lane Market may not be the most relaxing venue for al fresco dining" but this busy takeaway draws fans with its "great burritos, plus a wide variety of toppings". / EC1N 7TE; www.daddydonkey.co.uk; @daddydonkeyburritos; Mon-Sun 5.30 pm.

Daffodil Mulligan EC1 £75 3 4 3
70-74 City Road   020 7404 3000   13–1A

"Simple food and amazing produce served with a smile" is the premise at this Irish restaurant just south of Silicon Roundabout, backed by a team including chef Richard Corrigan, éminence grise of Irish gastronomy in London, and run by his son Richie. The beef is from Peter Hannan in Northern Ireland, and downstairs in the basement there's an outpost of Gibney's, a famous pub in Malahide near Dublin. / EC1E 2BJ; www.daffodilmulligan.com; @daffodilmulligan; Wed-Fri, Tue, Sat 10 pm, Sun 5 pm; closed Tue L closed Sun D, closed Mon.

Dai Chi W1 NEW £16
16a D'Arblay Street   awaiting tel   4–1C

Angelina founders, Joshua Owens-Baigler and Amar Takhar, have overhauled the Soho bar they launched as Golden Gai last year, and reopened it in November 2021 as this 'kushikatsu' (deep-fried skewers coated in Panko crumbs) specialist, here served omakase style. Despite full-on raves from many press critics, including The Guardian's Grace Dent ("delightfully odd", but with "some of the most fantastic cooking in London"), it inspired curiously little feedback in our annual diners' poll – more reports please! / W1W; www.daichi.london; @daichi.london; Mon-Thu 11.30 pm, Fri & Sat midnight; closed Mon-Fri L, closed Sun.

F S A

Dalloway Terrace, Bloomsbury Hotel WC1 £80 2 3 4
16-22 Great Russell St   020 7347 1221   2–1C

The "beautiful terrace" with its "attentive staff" at this very central hotel makes for an oasis of calm close to busy Oxford Street. Named in reference to Virginia Woolf, the queen bee of the Bloomsbury set, it has a "fun atmosphere", and the heating and retractable roof make it ideal for afternoon tea throughout the year. / WC1B 3NN; www.dallowayterrace.com; @dallowayterrace; Mon-Sun 11 pm.

La Dame de Pic EC3 £143 4 4 3
10 Trinity Square   020 7297 3799   10–3D

"As good as the London three star Michelin-rated restaurants", say advocates for this august dining room, in a plush five-star near the Tower of London (which already holds two of the tyre man's gongs). Run from afar by Anne-Sophie Pic (Michelin's most decorated female chef, and owner of Maison Pic south of Lyon), it flies a little under the radar in terms of its local profile, but is perennially hailed in reports for its "exquisite cuisine and exemplary, un-clichéd service". Even those boosting it, though, note its heart-stopping bills, and it was more often judged as "overpriced" this year. / EC3E 4AJ; ladamedepiclondon.co.uk; @ladamedepiclondon; Wed-Sat 9 pm; closed Wed & Thu L, closed Mon & Tue & Sun; no shorts.

Danclair's SW9 NEW £42
67-68 Granville Arcade, Coldharbour Lane   020 7733 9800   11–2D

A colourful, small new space in Brixton's Granville Arcade (Brixton Village as it's called nowadays) created in mid 2021 by Brian Danclair who also runs nearby 'Fish Wings & Tings' (now over a decade old). It's still off-radar in our survey, but both The Sunday Times's Marina O'Loughlin ("a restaurant on the verge of a party" with a "bass-heavy soundtrack and hectic colour scheme probably detectable from space") and The Evening Standard's Jimi Famurewa ("None of what is on offer… seeks to reinvent the wheel… yet, there is something quietly radical about its forceful sincerity") have raved in recent times. / SW9 3PR; danclairskitchen.co.uk; @danclairskitchen; Wed-Sat 11 pm; closed Wed-Sat L, closed Mon & Tue & Sun.

Daphne's SW3 £89 2 2 3
112 Draycott Ave   020 7589 4257   6–2C

"A real favourite" of the Chelsea set since the 1960s, when it was launched by Daphne Rye, Richard Burton's agent (but most famous for its 1990s association with Princess Di) this smart Italian still has its cheerleaders, who insist that "it never fails" – "the best just get better". Others beg to differ, saying it's "sad to see such an establishment going downhill", or damning it with faint praise as "pleasant enough if rather undistinguished". These days it's part of Richard Caring's Caprice group, and feeds shoppers from nearby Brompton Cross. / SW3 3AE; www.daphnes-restaurant.co.uk; @Daphneslondon; Mon-Sat 11 pm, Sun 10.30 pm.

Daquise SW7 £58 2 2 3
20 Thurloe St   020 7589 6117   6–2C

"Time has stood still" at this "old-fashioned and sedate" Polish institution by South Ken tube, since it opened in 1947: a "lovely, happy place that is utterly confident in what it does and sees no need to mess about with its authentic, filling and homely Polish cooking". ("It's perhaps a curious choice for romance, but my Polish wife loves it!") / SW7 2LT; www.daquise.co.uk; @daquise_london; Tue-Sun 11 pm; closed Mon; no Amex.

FSA RATINGS: FROM 1 POOR — 5 EXCEPTIONAL

Darby's SW11 — £82 — 3 3 4
3 Viaduct Gardens Road, Embassy Gardens   020 7537 3111   11–1D

"It's in an odd area (unless you are the US Ambassador to the UK!)", but Robin Gill's "big, grand and stylish" two-year-old is "well worth the hike". "Sitting in the shadow of the imposing US Embassy" at Nine Elms, its "very polished" interior is "part oyster bar, part secluded booths" and feels "reminiscent of the grand steakhouses of NYC". "If you like oysters and Guinness, or even if you don't", it's "a great spot to waste an afternoon", serving "boldly flavoured" food: "great meat and fresh, beautifully cooked fish". But "while it's good, even so the pricing feels a little punchy".
/ SW11 7AY; www.darbys-london.com; @darbyslondon; Thu-Sat, Wed 10 pm, Sun 4 pm; closed Wed L closed Sun D, closed Mon & Tue.

Darwin Brasserie EC3 — £82 — 3 3 4
1 Sky Garden Walk   033 3772 0020   10–3D

The 36th-floor brasserie at the top of the City's Walkie-Talkie Tower may be the exception to the rule that restaurants with a "spectacular view" serve exorbitantly expensive menus of very ordinary grub. Yes, it's "fairly pricey", but consistent strong marks for food confirm reports that a meal here is "surprisingly good". / EC3E 8AF; skygarden.london/darwin; @sg_darwin; Sun-Thu 9.30 pm, Fri & Sat 10.30 pm.

Dastaan KT19 — £47 — 5 4 3
447 Kingston Rd   020 8786 8999   1–4A

"The best-value for money inside the M25" is not a ridiculous claim for Sanjay Gour and Nand Kishor's "crowded" (and some would say "boring") suburban curry house "set in an anonymous row of shops, just off an anonymous main road between Epsom and Kingston". The cooking (with some dishes "based on Mumbai street food") is nothing short of "terrific": "the flavours are so big that you may feel knocked out the next day!". ("I've eaten in most of the renowned Indian restaurants in London, and Dastaan's cooking matches or surpasses all of them…", "This was our second visit only because it is a 200 mile round trip! And as previously, we were absolutely delighted with the food and service. You would have to travel far and wide to match the quality of the cuisine here!"). Top Menu Tip – "quail and duck kebabs are exceptional" and the lamb chops are "a must". / KT19 0DB; dastaan.co.uk; @dastaan447; Tue-Sat 10.30 pm, Sun 9.30 pm; closed Tue-Fri L, closed Mon; booking weekdays only.

Daylesford Organic — £72 — 2 2 2
44b Pimlico Rd, SW1   020 7881 8060   6–2D
6-8 Blandford St, W1   020 3696 6500   2–1A
76-82 Sloane Avenue, SW3   awaiting tel   6–2C
208-212 Westbourne Grove, W11   020 7313 8050   7–1B

The food at the quartet of London cafés supplied by Lady Bamford's organic farm in the Cotswolds suffered a mauling from some reporters this year. The Daylesford brand does have some "huge fans", who praise its venues as "very pleasant for a good-quality snack". But critics – citing "long waits", "clueless staff" and "poor-quality, ropey ingredients" – feel they "may be a place to be seen but are overpriced and uninteresting".
/ www.daylesfordorganic.com; SRA-3 stars.

Dean Street Townhouse W1 — £74 — 2 3 4
69-71 Dean St   020 7434 1775   4–1D

"Great atmosphere in the heart of Soho" is the big draw at this all-day brasserie from the Soho House group, which provides "simple food cooked well and friendly, attentive staff" – a winning package that's particularly "perfect for breakfast" or "great for pre-theatre". / W1D 3SE; www.deanstreettownhouse.com; @deanstreettownhouse; Mon-Thu midnight, Fri & Sat 1 am, Sun 11 am; closed Sun D.

F S A

Dear Grace W12 NEW £48
195 Wood Lane 020 8187 1039 1–2B

"A great addition to White City", this vast new all-day operation caters for everything from big parties – it can accommodate 350 guests, feeding them "fabulous small plates and lovely wine" – to weekday working lunches (£15 for any large plate and a drink). On the site of the former Wellbourne brasserie, it's from the team behind Lost in Brixton and the Pergolas at Paddington and Olympia. Feedback is too limited for rating, but early reports are very positive. / W12 7FQ; www.deargracelondon.co.uk; @deargracelondon; Tue-Fri 11 pm, Mon 10 pm, Sat 6 pm; closed Sun.

Decimo WC1 £94 3 2 4
The Standard, 10 Argyle St 020 3981 8888 9–3C

"Trying very hard to be trendy and mostly succeeding" ("the views from the WC were a big hit in my party!") – Peter Sanchez-Iglesias's dramatic three-year-old occupies the high-ceilinged 10th-floor space of the über-funky Standard Hotel, with incredible views of St Pancras from its huge, floor-to-ceiling windows. (To enter, shoot up the side of the hotel in the red-pill-shaped, glass-sided lift). It's all very 1970s James Bond. "There are some really exceptional dishes" from a vibrant Spanish/Mexican menu (e.g. lobster with lime chilli, quail with mole glaze, even caviar tortilla). But while all reports rate it decently well, gripes about "silly prices and one or two disappointments" limit the overall verdict to good rather than outstanding. / WC1W 9JE; www.decimo.london; @decimo.london; Tue-Sat 10.30 pm; closed Tue-Thu L, closed Sun & Mon.

Dehesa W1 £66 2 2 2
25 Ganton Street 020 7494 4170 4–2B

"Delicious" Spanish and Italian tapas and "a great choice of wines by the glass" win plaudits for this "romantic candlelit restaurant", "tucked away conveniently behind Liberty just off Carnaby Street". However, since its fabulous debut 15 years ago, it is undeniably "less superb than it used to be", but "that's partly due to standing still while everyone else continues to press forwards". / W1F 9BP; www.saltyardgroup.co.uk/dehesa; @dehesarestaurant; Mon-Sat 11 pm, Sun 9 pm.

Delamina £49 4 3 3
56-58 Marylebone Lane, W1 020 3026 6810 3–1A
151 Commercial Street, E1 020 7078 0770 13–2B

"Exceptional Middle Eastern food" and "lovely staff" tick all the boxes at this modern duo in Shoreditch and Marylebone, from Tel Aviv-born cook Limor Chen and husband Amir. "It's hard to find interesting and well-priced venues in Marylebone, but Delamina manages both". It's a "small-plates, sharing concept and every dish is delicious", with a "beautiful combination of flavours" – "great with allergies too". / www.delaminaeast.co.uk; delaminakitchen.

The Delaunay WC2 £69 2 4 4
55 Aldwych 020 7499 8558 2–2D

"Calmer in tone than The Wolseley" (although still "tending to be noisy"): its "understatedly glamorous" sibling is even more in the "Austrian Grand Salon style" than the mothership. And being "well-located for the City and West End" (just off Aldwych), combined with "professional service" and "well-spaced tables", all foster its massive popularity for a "textbook business lunch", or the "archetypal City power breakfast". True to the group's culinary DNA, the food can seem "unimaginative". Viewed more positively, "the undemanding but reassuring menu" is "solid" and "reliable" and the specials of schnitzel, tarte flambée and sausages add to a "pleasing and cosseting" effect that "transports you to Mittel Europe". So, "even if it's never going to provide a top gastronomic experience, a meal at The Delaunay always feels special". Given the recent changes at The Wolseley Hospitality Group (as the business is now called), many reporters voice "trepidation" at the recent loss of the founders: "it's an example of Corbin & King at their best... whither now that they're no longer running the show?" That said, the ratings, here, actually improved on last year in our annual diners' poll. Top Menu Tip – "wonderful gateaux to go with good coffee" either after a meal or during the day. / WC2B 4BB; www.thedelaunay.com; @thedelaunay; Mon-Sat 10.30 pm, Sun 5.15 pm; closed Sun D.

Delfino W1 £61 3|3|2
121a Mount St   020 7499 1256   3–3B

This "consistently excellent" "family Italian restaurant" has knocked out "authentic pizza, pasta and secondi dishes" in Mount Street for more than 50 years – and all at decidedly un-Mayfair prices. It closed briefly for a make-over in summer 2022. / W1K 3NW; www.delfinomayfair.com; @Delfinomayfair; Mon-Sat 10.30 pm; closed Sun.

Delhi Grill N1 £33 3|2|3
21 Chapel Mkt   020 7278 8100   9–3D

This Punjabi 'dhaba' (roadside food stall) is a popular fixture in Islington's Chapel Market, winning praise for its light-hearted take on tasty Indian street food from fans (who have included veteran restaurant critic Fay Maschler). / N1 9EZ; www.delhigrill.com; @delhi_grill; Mon-Sat 10.30 pm, Sun 10 pm; cash only.

Les 2 Garcons N8 NEW £72 5|4|3
143b Crouch Hill   020 8347 9834   9–1C

"A great wallop of France at its best – superbe!". This Crouch Hill newcomer from a pair of industry veterans is "everyone's new favourite for good reasons" – "chef Robert Reid and his friend Jean-Christophe Slowik, who have worked at Michelin-starred restaurants in the past, have created a rural French bistro that is low on snobbery and pretence but has a genuine Gallic 'je ne sais quoi' that feels effortless. The food is delicious, the atmosphere is very pleasant and the worry is that it will soon become impossible to book here". / N8 9QH; www.les2garconsbistro.com; @les2garconsbistro; Tue-Sat 9.30 pm; closed Tue-Fri L, closed Sun & Mon.

Dhaba@49 W9 £35 3|3|2
49 Chippenham Road   020 3489 2424   7–1B

"Top butter chicken and a great selection of chaats" win a thumbs-up for this snazzily decorated Punjabi fixture in Maida Vale. / W9 2AH; @dhabaat49; Tue-Sat, Mon 10.30 pm, Sun 10 pm; closed Mon L.

Dim Sum Duck WC1 £24 5|2|2
124 King's Cross Road   020 7278 6018   9–3D

"Exactly what the name suggests" – "stunningly crafted dim sum and roast duck" – make this "minuscule" café, a short walk from King's Cross St Pancras, one of London's greatest cheap eats. "It's nothing to look at, but that doesn't matter at all as the array of different dumplings and cheung fun is truly fab, plus the prices are very reasonable". "You can't book and the queues can be long, so get here early or mid-late afternoon". / WC1W 9DS; dimsum-duck.business.site; @dimsumandduck; Mon-Sun 10 pm.

Din Tai Fung £57 2|2|2
5-6 Henrietta Street, WC2   020 3034 3888   5–3D
Centre Point, Tottenham Court Road, WC2   awaiting tel   5–1A

The London offshoots of a famous Taiwanese dumpling brand (in Covent Garden, Selfridges and, scheduled for late 2022 opening, a big 13,500 sq ft debut in Centre Point) are by most accounts "great fun", although "it's quite a different proposition to the Asian formula" – "more upmarket". There's plenty of enthusiasm for the "soup dumpling heaven" provided by the signature pleated dumplings (xiao long bao) – although be warned: they are "more expensive" than in Asia and "the bill can add up pretty fast". / www.dintaifung-uk.com.

F S A

The Dining Room, The Goring Hotel SW1 £113 3|3|4
15 Beeston Pl   020 7396 9000   2–4B

"Hooray for The Goring!" – this "enormously charming" and "quintessentially English" hotel, just behind Buck House, remains, for most reporters, one of London's most treasured bastions. Built by Otto Goring in 1910, Jeremy Goring is currently at the helm, and its unchanging style and popularity with royalty have done nothing to harm its following over the years. For a business occasion in particular, the "delightful" dining room complete with "old-style, classy, traditional fare" is ideal and "never fails to impress a first-timer"; and for "afternoon tea done to perfection" look no further than its "lovely and calming" lounges. "The pandemic seems to have hit them hard, though, including the loss of their Michelin star chef". To be honest, it always seemed a slightly strange idea that fancy haute cuisine was key to its success, so no immediate need for panic there. What is more concerning, though, is the decline in rating for what has always been a benchmark level of "discreet and professional" service: "it has sometimes been rather offhand lately – an unwelcome development they would do well to reverse…" / SW1W 0JW; www.thegoring.com; @thegoring; Mon-Sun 9.30 pm; closed Sat L; no shorts; booking max 6 may apply.

Dinings £101 5|4|2
22 Harcourt St, W1   020 7723 0666   9–4A
Walton House, Walton St, SW3   020 7723 0666   6–2C

"It feels like you're in Tokyo at this tiny place" in Marylebone ('Dinings Harcourt') – the two-floor original of this authentic duo, which increasingly now trade as separate entities: "just trust the chef to get you the best sushi at the counter". The odd reporter pronounces the Chelsea branch ('Dinings SW3') as "not as good, but still a strong contender", but actually, although W1 inspires more feedback, there's little to choose between them in terms of their ratings. One distinguishing feature – in summer you can eat outside in SW3, which has a small courtyard garden. / dinings.co.uk.

Dinner by Heston Blumenthal SW1 £152 2|2|1
Mandarin Oriental, 66 Knightsbridge   020 7201 3833   6–1D

"Mystified as to why this place is considered special in any way…" – too often the reaction at this Heston Blumenthal-group chamber off Knightsbridge. True, it does still have some loyal fans who "have never had a bad meal" from the menu of historically inspired dishes ("I can't agree that the meat fruit is getting boring!"); and who swoon at the "lovely view of Hyde Park". But even some who acknowledge its plus points feel that "what was once innovative and stylish is now populated almost exclusively by Instagram wielding tourists who have yet to realise London cuisine has moved on". And harsher critics encounter "one of the most disappointing meals ever": "no ambience and so much money!" ("the nitro ice-cream had no flavour and felt like a gimmick"). Inexplicably, this place continues to hold two Michelin stars. Actually, it's completely explicable when you realise that Michelin often act like slaves to celebrity… / SW1X 7LA; www.dinnerbyheston.com; @dinnerbyhb; Mon-Thu 9 pm, Fri-Sun 9.30 pm.

Dipna Anand Restaurant & Bar WC2 NEW £49 3|2|2
South Wing, Somerset House, Strand   020 7845 4646   2–2D

A "great location" in Somerset House provides a grand setting for this new central London offshoot from the venerable Brilliant, a leading light among the Indian restaurants of Southall – Dipna Anand is the niece of the founder. Early reports are all positive on the food front. / WC2W 1LA; dipnasomersethouse.co.uk; @dipnaatsomersethouse; Wed-Sat 10 pm, Sun 4 pm; closed Sun D, closed Mon & Tue.

FSA RATINGS: FROM 1 POOR — 5 EXCEPTIONAL

FSA

Dishoom £51 4|4|4
22 Kingly St, W1 020 7420 9322 4–2B
12 Upper St Martins Ln, WC2 020 7420 9320 5–3B
The Barkers Building, Derry Street, W8 awaiting tel 6–1A
Stable St, Granary Sq, N1 020 7420 9321 9–3C
Wood Wharf, 15 Water Street, E14 awaiting tel 12–1C **NEW**
7 Boundary St, E2 020 7420 9324 13–1B

"I have yet to find the person who does not absolutely love Dishoom!" – Shamil and Kavi Thakrar's "must-visit chain" remains our poll's most-commented-on group, on the strength of its "exceptional" homage to the Irani cafés of Bombay. "A sense of nostalgia for a vanished India and quirky colonial notices add to the fun" of its "cool", "evocative" branches, where "outstanding staff, even when very busy" (which is to say always) preside over "borderline hectic" conditions with great verve and efficiency. The "slightly different Indian food" ("with spice rather than heat") is "far better than it has any right to be" given the volumes it's served in… "superb"… "so consistent" and "extremely fairly priced" too. The "left field" breakfast menu is famous nowadays, and "awesome bacon and egg naan rolls" have "redefined what brekkie is all about" for many Londoners. Founded in 2010, they will hit six branches in London in 2022, with a big (355 covers) new Canary Wharf outlet, complete with a bar and terrace overlooking the docks. On the downside, bookings at all the outlets are restricted and "queues are half way down the street". "It's worth it though!!". Top Menu Tips – "Finally got to try the black dal… a big hug in a bowl" that's "to die for" and "Ruby Murray is a family favourite". And, with their burgeoning delivery business, "the fact you can now order the Bacon Naan for home consumption is a wonderful, wonderful thing". / www.dishoom.co.uk; dishoom.

Diwana Bhel-Poori House NW1 £31 3|2|1
121-123 Drummond St 020 7387 5556 9–4C
This canteen has served "delicious, great-value vegetarian thalis" and other South Indian specialities in the 'Little India' enclave behind Euston station for almost as long as the Queen has been on the throne. "Long may they reign their dosas over us!" / NW1 2HL; www.diwanabph.com; @diwanabhelpoorihouse; Mon-Sat 10 pm, Sun 9 pm; no Amex; may need 10+ to book.

Donostia W1 £59 4|3|3
10 Seymour Pl 020 3620 1845 2–2A
"What a fabulous restaurant!" – this tribute to the pintxo bars of San Sebastian (Donostia in Basque) maintains the highest of standards and is a "firm favourite" near Marble Arch, alongside its "sister across the road" (Lurra). / W1H 7ND; www.donostia.co.uk; @DonostiaW1; Thu & Fri, Tue, Wed, Sat 11 pm, Sun 9 pm; closed Tue, Wed, Sat & Sun L, closed Mon; booking max 8 may apply.

Double Standard WC1 £60 3|5|5
The Standard, 10 Argyle St 020 3981 8888 9–3C
Award-winning 1970s-tastic décor isn't the sole appeal of this groovy bar, "in a convenient location opposite St Pancras Station": "a great venue", and not just for those waiting for a train. Its "buzzy and trendy" style makes it a superb rendezvous (it's very 'in' as a meeting place for creative types), although you have to like the sometimes deafening retro playlist. On the menu, "surprisingly good, simple food", delivered by unusually "friendly" and professional staff. / WC1W 8EG; www.standardhotels.com/london/features/standard_london_isla; @isla.london; Mon-Sun 11 pm.

F S A

Dragon Castle SE17 £48 3|2|2
100 Walworth Rd   020 7277 3388   1–3C

"It was such a relief when Dragon Castle reopened" after a long post-Covid break – "it has long been a favourite, doing standard Cantonese dishes to a very high standard but also plenty of originals". It's a "huge, cavernous place with over-the-top Chinese décor", and proximity to the Elephant makes it "accessible from all parts of London". / SE17 1JL; www.dragoncastlelondon.com; @dragoncastle100; Mon-Sun 11 pm.

The Drapers Arms N1 £65 3|3|3
44 Barnsbury Street   020 7619 0348   9–3D

This incredibly popular, early Victorian Islington boozer has been transformed into "the perfect city gastropub" by licensee Nick Gibson. The "well-cooked hearty food, great service and excellent wine list" ensure that it's typically rammed. / N1 1ER; www.thedrapersarms.com; @thedrapersarms; Mon-Sat 10.30 pm, Sun 8.30 pm; no Amex.

The Drawing Room at The Dukes Hotel SW1 £67
35 Saint James's Place   020 7318 6574   3–4C

"Very peaceful… staff were lovely… we had an extra plate of sandwiches and I chose the mini set of Martini which were totally lush…" – this posh St James's hotel's top culinary attraction, according to our survey, is afternoon tea in its very comfortable drawing room or conservatory. / SW1S 1NY; www.dukeshotel.com; Mon-Sun 6 pm; closed Mon-Sun L.

Dropshot Coffee SW19 £22 3|4|4
281 Wimbledon Park Road   07445 673405   11–2B

This "great independent local coffee shop" on the road to the All England Club showcases an ever-changing list of coffees from different regions and roasteries, and serves "ace brunch food" all day (with tennis-themed names). Top Menu Tip – "the Break Point – eggs on muffins with ham and hollandaise is superb, with super-fresh deep-orange yolks". / SW19 6NW; dropshotcoffee.co.uk; @dropshotcoffeeldn; Mon-Fri 3 pm, Sat & Sun 4 pm; closed Mon-Sun D.

The Drunken Butler EC1 £158 3|4|4
20 Rosebery Avenue   020 7101 4020   10–1A

There's a host of no-choice, multi-course meals at this unusual Clerkenwell venture, where charismatic chef, Yuma Hashemi, showcases his Persian cuisine in a "fabulous room, set up like an affluent Tehran dining room c.1970". "The quality of the food is superb", and "the personal attention makes one feel as if eating at a friend's home – nothing commercial". There are "two mild flaws, though – 1) it's expensive for what it is; and 2) it's quite reliant on bread and rice". / EC1E 4SX; www.thedrunkenbutler.com; @thedrunkenbutler; Wed-Sun 11 pm; closed Wed-Sat L, closed Mon & Tue; booking online only.

The Duck & Rice W1 £75 3|3|3
90 Berwick St   020 3327 7888   4–2C

"A Chinese pub" – in Berwick Street, Soho – "that works!". This contemporary 'concept' successfully combines enjoyable food (including house Cantonese roast duck) with an "interesting drinks list" and characterful interior. Launched in 2015, by Alan Yau of Wagamama, Hakkasan, Yauatcha and Busaba Eathai fame, it's never caught fire in quite the same way as his other operations. / W1F 0QB; www.theduckandrice.com; @theduckandrice; Tue-Sat 11 pm, Sun 9 pm; closed Mon.

FSA RATINGS: FROM 1 POOR — 5 EXCEPTIONAL

F S A

Duck & Waffle EC2 — £97 — 2 2 3
110 Bishopsgate, Heron Tower   020 3640 7310   10–2D
Stunning 40th-floor views over London and 24/7 opening have drawn busy crowds to this perch at the top of the City's Heron Tower for 10 years now, and the signature "tasty duck and egg waffle" and other faux-rustic dishes go down well enough alongside a cocktail or two. / EC2N 4AY; www.duckandwaffle.com; @duckandwaffle; Mon-Wed 1.30 am, Thu-Sun midnight.

The Duck Truck E1 — £17 — 5 4 2
Bishops Square   07919 160271   13–2B
"Quackers about this place!" – a fixture of Spitalfields Market, this street food truck delivers "duck in a wrap and much, much more" from an "eclectic" and "mouthwatering" menu. And the duck comes with a very modest… bill (geddit?). / E1 6AN; www.theducktruck.com; @theducktruck; Mon-Fri 4 pm; closed Mon-Fri D, closed Sat & Sun.

Ducksoup W1 — £83 — 3 4 3
41 Dean St   020 7287 4599   5–2A
"A huge wine list packed with unfamiliar names" – all of them biodynamic or natural – "interesting, fairly priced, good-quality Mediterranean food" and a "guaranteed warm welcome" ensure this "fun place to eat always impresses". Now in its second decade, the "cool vibe" and funky atmosphere make it a pleasant throwback to the Soho of years past. / W1D 4PY; www.ducksoupsoho.co.uk; Wed-Sat, Tue 10.30 pm, Sun 5 pm; closed Tue L closed Sun D, closed Mon.

The Duke of Richmond E8 — £55 — 3 3 3
316 Queensbridge Road   020 7923 3990   14–1A
"The burgers and crab 'n' chip sarnies are great" at chef Tom Oldroyd's "brilliant local" with "charming staff" where Dalston meets Haggerston – "but be warned, you'll get messy!". ("I hope its sibling Oldroyd [in Islington, which closed under 2020 pandemic restrictions] returns as that was a perennial favourite, but until it does I'm happy to support the pub version!") / E8 3NH; www.thedukeofrichmond.com; @thedukeofrichmond; Mon-Thu 11 pm, Fri & Sat 9.30 pm, Sun 8 pm; closed Mon-Thu L.

The Duke of Sussex W4 — £62 — 3 3 3
75 South Pde   020 8742 8801   8–1A
A "great stalwart for years" – this spacious Victorian tavern by Acton Green Common is a "good local" with the unexpected feature of a "Spanish-inspired" selection of tapas and other dishes, alongside more standard British roasts on a Sunday. Look out for the charming rear dining room, with small garden. / W4 5LF; www.thedukeofsussex.co.uk; @metropubco; Mon-Wed 11 pm, Fri & Sat midnight, Thu 11 am, Sun 10 pm; closed Thu D.

Dulwich Lyceum SE21 — £54 — 3 4 4
7 Croxted Road   020 8670 5837   1–4D
"Like its sister restaurant Peckham Bazaar, this Dulwich three-year-old serves great food" cooked over a custom-built charcoal grill by chef-patron John Gionleka and his team, who take guests on a culinary exploration of the Balkans, Greece and eastern Med. / SE21 8SZ; www.dulwichlyceum.com; @dulwichlyceum; Tue-Sat 11 pm; closed Tue-Sat L, closed Sun & Mon.

Dumpling Shack x Fen Noodles E14 — £25 — 5 3
The Collective, 20 Crossharbour Plaza   no tel   12–2C
"The best chilli pork dumplings freshly cooked to order" are amongst the acclaimed spicy treats at this culinary Mecca on the Isle of Dogs: the in-house restaurant of an aparthotel, a short walk from Crossharbour DLR. Part of John & Yee Li's street food business in Spitalfields Market, a new outlet is also opening in the basement of their London Fields, Sichuan Fry, in August 2022 (see also). / E14 9YF; www.dumplingshack.co.uk; @dumplingshack; Wed-Sat 8.45 pm; closed Mon & Tue & Sun.

F S A

Dumplings' Legend W1   £30   3 2 2
16 Gerrard St   020 7494 1200   5–3A
This classic and efficient Chinatown operation is a popular choice for dim sum – especially for anyone "missing life in Hong Kong". The food is "all very tasty", if "nothing that really sets the world alight". / W1D 6JE; www.dumplingslegend.com; Mon-Thu 11 pm, Fri & Sat 3 am, Sun 10 pm.

Durbar W2   £43   3 3 2
24 Hereford Rd   020 7727 1947   7–1B
"The epitome of the local curry house", this "cosy" 65-year-old family-run tandoori off Westbourne Grove – one of London's oldest – serves "classic fare" that's "always delicious". / W2 4AA; www.durbartandoori.co.uk; closed Mon-Sat & Sun; booking evening only.

The Dusty Knuckle   £37   4 2 3
429 Green Lanes, N4   no tel   9–1D
Car Park, Abbot Street, E8   020 3903 7598   14–1A
"What a brilliant bakery!" – "the bread (especially the potato sourdough) is to die for"; "the pastries are also incredible" ("amazing sticky buns"), and "they serve a very decent filter coffee". "The sandwiches are massive and always filled with interesting and delicious things". Given that it's a social enterprise, providing job training and mentorship to at-risk young people, "this small chain (branches in Dalston and Haringey) deserves all the praise it gets". / www.thedustyknuckle.com; thedustyknuckle.

The Dysart Petersham TW10   £88   4 4 4
135 Petersham Road   020 8940 8005   1–4A
In its "somewhat obscure location" bordering Richmond Park, this spacious Arts & Crafts home has "a wonderfully relaxed ambience". It is an ideal showcase for Kenneth Culhane's "original and beautifully cooked meals" – some of the most culinarily ambitious around leafy Richmond, and presented with "immaculate service". It's "almost a surprising find"… except, with the help of the folks from Clermont-Ferrand, it's increasingly well-known. / TW10 7AA; www.thedysartpetersham.co.uk; @thedysartpetersham; Sat, Wed-Fri, Sun 8.30 pm; closed Wed-Fri, Sun L, closed Mon & Tue.

E Mono NW5   £23   4 3 2
285-287 Kentish Town Road   020 7485 9779   9–2B
The "exquisite kebabs" at this family-run Turk in Kentish Town (which takes its name from the original Victorian sign above the door) have "set the standard in north London for years". Don't be put off by the "limited menu and basic amenities (more like a local chippy)" – the food is "fresh, good quality and delicious", while "service is cheerful". / NW5 2JS; emonoturkishrestaurant.co.uk; Mon-Sun 11 pm; no booking.

E&O W11   £71   4 3 4
14 Blenheim Crescent   020 7229 5454   7–1A
"Still fab 20 years on" – Will Ricker's Notting Hill stalwart has proved amazingly enduring since its days as one of Madonna's fave raves: "it can be a bit hit and miss with its long-lasting Asian-fusion offering, but overall remains some of the tastiest food in Notting Hill" ("although they might change the menu occasionally"). There's a terrace with "excellent outdoor seating and heaters". / W11 1NN; www.eandolondon.com; @eandonotthill; Mon-Sat midnight, Sun 10 pm; booking max 6 may apply.

FSA

The Eagle EC1 £48   3 3 4
159 Farringdon Rd   020 7837 1353   10–1A

"The original and still the best gastropub" – this no-frills boozer "just keeps churning out sublime, flavoursome food packed with punchy rustic flavours". Set on an anonymous stretch of the busy Faringdon Road, it has never striven to go upmarket or cash in on its fame. "The Mediterranean menu changes on a daily basis and always features something interesting that you hadn't tried before". Many reporters have "never had a bad meal". Any complaints? "It's still too noisy and seating is pot luck, but the standard of cooking more than compensates". / EC1R 3AL; www.theeaglefarringdon.co.uk; @eaglefarringdon; Mon-Sat 10.30 pm, Sun 3.30 pm; closed Sun D; no Amex; no booking.

Eat Tokyo £38   3 2 1
16 Old Compton St, W1   020 7439 9887   5–2A
50 Red Lion St, WC1   020 7242 3490   2–1D
27 Catherine St, WC2   020 3489 1700   5–3D
17 Notting Hill Gate, W11   020 7792 9313   7–2B
169 King St, W6   020 8741 7916   8–2B
14 North End Rd, NW11   020 8209 0079   1–1B
628 Finchley Rd, NW11   020 3609 8886   1–1B

"Spartan surroundings…", "efficient service but can be stilted and without a smile…" yet "all is ultimately forgiven" at these "always busy" and "always reliable" Japanese canteens. "Given the price, you'd expect real mediocrity" and yet meals are almost invariably "acceptable and good quality (if somewhat formulaic)". Top Tip – "lovely bento boxes". (The 'G2' Golders Green branch specialises in Shabu Shabu – a variety of broths).
/ www.eattokyo.co.uk; eattokyoldn.

Eataly EC2 £52   2 2 3
135 Bishopsgate   07966 544965   10–2D

Entrepreneur Oscar Farinetti's glam food mall concept was a late arrival in London when it opened near Liverpool Street station in May 2021, given that he now has 42 scattered around the world. It offers a "fabulous selection of food and wine", alongside three restaurants (headed by the flagship Terra, where the dramatic centrepiece grill is apparently fired by wood shipped in from Calabria). Immediately very busy, the offerings include "super pizza", but, for a sceptical minority, "the whole place looks great but is merely a trap for wealthy, bored customers". / EC2E 3YD; www.eataly.co.uk; @eatalylondon; Mon-Sat 11 pm, Sun 10 pm.

Ekstedt at The Yard,
Great Scotland Yard Hotel SW1 £115   4 4 4
Great Scotland Yard   020 7925 4700   2–3C

"Really amazing use of the smoke and fire they cook with" ("there's practically no gas or electricity in the kitchen!") "produces lots of novel flavours" at star Swedish chef, Nicklas Ekstedt's Whitehall yearling, which well-travelled reporters say "lives up to the Stockholm original" with its "inspired Nordic cuisine" (matched with "a novel selection of wines"). And "the lovely staff are really engaged with what they serve you" at this dining room within the five-star Hyatt: arguably, the most interesting culinary arrival of the year. One gripe, though: "some rather mean portions". / SW1S 2HN; www.ekstedtattheyard.com; @ekstedtldn; Tue-Thu, Sat, Fri 10.30 pm; closed Tue-Thu, Sat, Fri L, closed Sun & Mon.

Ekte Nordic Kitchen EC4 £55 3|3|2
2-8 Bloomberg Arcade   020 3814 8330   10–3C
This "Nordic restaurant with classic and well-executed dishes from the region" is a more casual offering in the Bloomberg Arcade from Danish veteran City restaurateur Soren Jessen, of smart No 1 Lombard Street. There's a good choice of Danish smørrebrød – slices of rye bread with tasty toppings – and a matching selection of aquavit and Scandi gins. Although the odd reporter feels it's "rather let down by the austere ambience", it is "excellent for a quick work lunch". / EC4E 8AR; www.ektelondon.co.uk; @ektelondon; Mon-Sat 10.30 pm; closed Sun.

El Pastor £51 3|2|3
Brewer Street, W1   020 3092 4553   4–3C
7a Stoney Street, SE1   no tel   10–4C
"The tacos are tasty and the margaritas are fab" at this "fun and feisty" Mexican duo – part of the Hart Bros' empire (with the Borough Market original still being much more commented on than its Soho sibling, which opened in 2021 on the former site of Hix). "Sometimes the service is a little overwhelmed by how busy the place gets", and the "cheerful" ambience can be a bit "chaotic" as a result.

Ela & Dhani SW13 NEW £28 4|5|3
127 Church Road   020 8741 9583   11–1A
A trio of childhood friends who grew up together in the Punjab joined forces to launch their first venture (meaning cardamom and coriander in Sanskrit) in early 2022 in Barnes. The locals are rapturous: "loving this new Indian and the staff are so nice!" / SW13 9HR; www.eladhani.co.uk; @ela_and_dhani; Tue-Sun 10 pm; closed Tue-Sun L, closed Mon.

The Elder Press Café W6 £19 3|2|3
3 South Black Lion Lane   020 3887 4258   8–2B
If it wasn't for the A4 running 100m from the front door, this stylish café would have a "perfect location a short walk from the river at Hammersmith". Inside, the funky interior is almost "yoga studio-esque" in its level of zen, and does superb coffee, plus "super hot choc and buns" as well as some good-but-pricey light bites. / W6 9TJ; www.theelderpress.co.uk; Mon-Sun 5 pm; closed Mon-Sun D.

Eldr at Pantechnicon SW1 £79 3|3|4
19 Motcomb Street   020 7034 5422   6–1D
Limited but mostly positive feedback this year at this second-floor dining space, within the gobsmackingly lovely Belgravia Pantechnicon building. Despite the ambition of its Nordic menu (the name means 'fire' in old Norse), though, it is still not making many waves. Maybe it's because a peek up the staircase takes you out onto the gorgeous rooftop… / SW1S 8LB; www.pantechnicon.com; @_pantechnicon; Mon-Sat midnight, Sun 11 pm.

Elis E2 NEW
Town Hall Hotel, Patriot Square   awaiting tel   14–2B
On the site of The Corner Room, star chef Rafael Cagali is following the strategy adopted by former inhabitants of the main restaurant space with this large Bethnal Green hotel (Da Terra, see also) by opening a spin-off in these more humble quarters. From a 'Brazilian-Italian' menu, 'more rustic dishes' will feature than those at Da Terra – 'everything from my favourite street food to family meal celebration dishes that my grandma used to make'. / E2 9NF; @restaurant.elis; Mon-Sun midnight.

FSA

Elliot's £77 3 2 3
12 Stoney St, SE1   020 7403 7436   10–4C
121-123 Mare Street, E8   020 3302 5252   14–2B
This "fun little restaurant in Borough Market" has pioneered "very interesting natural wines" and wood-fire cooking for more than a decade, building a legion of fans in the process. "Have lost count of the number of times I've stopped by for a glass of wine and cheesy puffs", says one. "Sam [co-owner Samantha Lim] is the best host in London and the food matches the service in every way". A second branch opened on Mare Street in Hackney in summer 2021. / www.elliots.london; elliotslondon.

Elystan Street SW3 £103 3 2 3
43 Elystan Street   020 7628 5005   6–2C
Phil Howard – "in a former life, the chef at The Square, where he held two Michelin stars" – continues to deliver "sophisticated, precise and light" 'flexitarian' cuisine at his "quietly situated" Chelsea HQ, where he has been ensconced for the last six years now. It's rather "grown up" in style – "the atmosphere is very much of understated wellbeing" and the room "spacious". As at some other establishments, though, the pressures of the era dent its ratings this year: "post Covid, the previously first class service is not quite as slick as it was: still professional, but just missing a beat every now and then", and this can sometimes lead to a "lacklustre" overall impression. Many fans, though, still feel "you can't go wrong" here. Top Tip – "fair wine prices". / SW3 3NT; www.elystanstreet.com; @elystanstreet; Mon-Thu 2145 pm, Fri & Sat 10.30 pm, Sun 4 pm; closed Sun D.

Emilia's Crafted Pasta £51 3 4 3
12 George Street, Wood Wharf, E14   020 8176 1100   12–1C **NEW**
77 Alie Street, E1   020 3358 0317   10–2D
Unit C3 Ivory House, St Katharine Docks, E1   020 7481 2004   10–3D
The original – "a very friendly and very cosy little place with approximately 16 covers in St Katharine Docks" – is the most commented on of this small chain: "brilliant in its simplicity and delivery" of a straightforward pasta menu. Also with spin-offs near Aldgate and, more latterly, Canary Wharf. / www.emiliaspasta.com; emiliaspasta.

The Empress E9 £56 3 3 4
130 Lauriston Rd   020 8533 5123   14–2B
This well-known old tavern by Hackney's Victoria Park serves up "really good food" – and highly rated Sunday lunches – in "atmospheric" surroundings. "The new chef (Shannon Johnson, ex-Angela Hartnett's Murano) is a great refresher", with vegetarian dishes given equal billing on the menu. / E9 7LH; www.empresse9.co.uk; @the_empress_e9; Tue-Sat 10 pm, Mon 10.30 pm, Sun 9 pm; closed Mon L; no Amex.

Endo at The Rotunda W12 £285 5 5 5
The Helios, TV Centre,101 Wood Lane   020 3972 9000   1–2B
"Quite possibly the best meal of my life!" – Endo Kazutoshi delivers "magical experiences, time after time" in his "tiny but scenic restaurant in the old BBC Television Centre" and "there's no superior restaurant in London". "Endo blends theatre, passion and extraordinary ingredients" and diners "really appreciate his dedication" in creating an omakase ('leave it to the chef') meal that provides "an unparalleled quality of food served with personal flair". "More than a meal, it was an experience poured out of the heart and hands of Chef Endo… I will return… far more impressive than most 3 Michelin starred meals I have had". / W12 7FR; www.endoatrotunda.com; @kazutoshi.endo; Tue-Sat 11 pm; closed Tue, Wed L, closed Sun & Mon; booking online only.

Enoteca Turi SW1 £84 353
87 Pimlico Road 020 7730 3663 6–2D

Giuseppe & Pamela Turi's "phenomenal" stalwart was "a long-time favourite even before they moved from Putney to Pimlico" in 2015 (at an age when some couples would be considering retirement). "A place of calm refinement", they "rode out the pandemic with cheer and great service"; and by providing "precise northern Italian cooking with intense flavours". The special attraction, though, is Giuseppe's long term passion project: "one of the best Italian wine lists in London" offering a "to-die-for selection" that "starts at very reasonable price levels" (but "don't forget your wallet" if you want to do it full justice). / SW1W 8PH; www.enotecaturi.com; @enotecaturi; Mon-Sat 10 pm; closed Sun; no trainers; booking max 8 may apply.

The Enterprise SW3 £71 234
35 Walton St 020 7584 3148 6–2C

"Just an icon" in Chelsea's chichi Walton Street – this "pricey" but "lively and very nice upmarket gastropub" caters stylishly to a "mainly posh, middle-aged-plus clientele". / SW3 2HU; www.theenterprise.co.uk; @theenterprise35; Mon-Sat 10.30 pm, Sun 10 pm.

L'Escargot W1 £93 333
48 Greek Street 020 7439 7474 5–2A

London's oldest French restaurant (est 1927) has been beautifully maintained over the decades and is a charming relic of old Soho. It inspired diverging views this year though: recommended for top gastronomy by some but "rather average" or "a bit of a tourist trap" to others. A fair middle-ground report is as follows: "I have to admit that I had completely forgotten it existed, and it was actually very good. Seems impossible to imagine how well-regarded it was in its time, but still a perfectly decent place to go". / W1D 4EF; www.lescargot.co.uk; @lescargotsoho; Tue-Sat 10 pm, Sun 10.30 pm; closed Sun L, closed Mon.

Escocesa N16 £49 433
67 Stoke Newington Church Street 020 7812 9189 1–1C

"One of the very best restaurants in Stoke Newington" – this "crowded fish restaurant and oyster bar with rough and ready furnishings" serves "simple, fresh dishes in the style of tapas". (The owner, Glaswegian-born former record producer Stephen Lironi, is a fan of Spanish cuisine who learned that Scotland's best seafood was trucked to Spain – so he decided to 'hijack' some of it en route and serve it in London, alongside the pick of Spanish sherries, wine and produce). / N16 0AR; www.escocesa.co.uk; @escocesa_n16; Mon-Thu 10 pm, Fri & Sat 11 pm, Sun 9.30 pm; closed Fri L.

Estiatorio Milos SW1 £135 434
1 Regent St 020 7839 2080 4–4D

"Incredible, beautiful fish is displayed on ice and hosed down every five minutes for freshness" at this splendid St James's outpost of Costas Spiladis's glamorous Greek-based international chain. "Given the eye-watering prices", it's "a place for a special occasion", but if you're wallet is deep enough, it does deliver: "the food is memorably good", "service is silky smooth" and the interior design (complete with imported marble) is impressive (if, perhaps, "slightly cold"). / SW1Y 4NR; www.estiatoriomilos.com; @estiatoriomilos; Mon-Sat 11 pm, Sun 10 pm.

Evelyn's Table at The Blue Posts W1 £153 5 4 2
28 Rupert Street   07921 336010   4–3D

The Selby brothers' "very snug little basement venue for counter-top fine dining" shows "levels of skill and technique to compete with much better-known places that leave you with a far higher bill"; with cooking that's "consistently well-thought-out, imaginative and bold". "Ultimately there can be a clash between the expectation of enjoying fine cuisine and fine wines, while being perched on a stool with people brushing past", so "file this under 'one to watch' as they plan to build out the ambition even further". / W1W 6DJ; www.thebluposts.co.uk/evelyns-table; @evelynstable; Tue-Sat 11 pm; closed Tue-Sat L, closed Sun & Mon.

Everest Curry King SE13 £18 4 3 2
24 Loampit Hill   020 8691 2233   1–4D

"A reliable canteen for the local Sri Lankan community" – this popular Lewisham caff (with chiller cabinets showing off all the different options) offers "authentic South Indian and Sri Lankan cuisine for locals in the know" who appreciate its "very tasty dishes and excellent value". / SE13 7SW; Sun-Wed 11 pm, Thu-Sat 1 am.

Everest Inn SE3 £48 3 2 2
41 Montpelier Vale   020 8852 7872   1–4D

"A cut above your standard curry house", this Nepalese in Blackheath Village, overlooking the common, is a "decent destination in a culinary desert", offering "good cooking and very fair prices". / SE3 0TJ; www.everestinn.co.uk; @everestinn; Tue-Sun 10 pm; closed Tue-Fri L, closed Mon.

Facing Heaven E8 NEW £38
1a Bayford Street   no tel   14–2B

Owner Julian Denis previously ran the super-popular vegan Chinese Mao Chow just up the road. This new venture (named for the medium-hot pepper) is twice the size (although still only 28 seats) and promises 'an evolution' of the food there, incorporating flavours and techniques from Puerto Rican, Portuguese and American cuisines. No survey reports, but The Evening Standard's Jimi Famurewa found, in his May 2022 review, the vibe of a "dangerously raucous east London house party circa 2009" matched with food that needed "a little more finesse, and… enough confidence… that they don't reach for the chilli-and-umami hose at every juncture". As of August 2022, the restaurant's website shows no availability and says it's currently closed for a refurb that should have ended in July 2022? So change may be afoot. / E8 3SE; www.facing-heaven.com; @facing_heaven; Tue-Thu 9.30 pm, Fri & Sat 10 pm; closed Tue-Sat L, closed Sun & Mon; booking online only.

Fadiga W1 £36 4 4 3
71 Berwick Street   020 3609 5536   4–1C

This "casual pasta restaurant" and 'pastificio' in Soho conjures up the tastes of Emilia-Romagna "in a family environment – like your favourite grandma cooking you the Sunday dishes of a Bolognese family!". / W1W 8TB; www.fadiga.uk; @fadiga_ristorantebolognese; Tue-Thu 9.30 pm, Sat, Fri 10 pm, Sun 3 pm; closed Tue-Fri L closed Sun D, closed Mon.

Fair Shot Café W1
17 South Molton Street   020 7499 9007   3–2B

'Fighting for diversity in the workplace, one coffee at a time…' – Bianca Tavella's December 2021 newcomer is a café on one of Mayfair's more fashionable shopping streets that aims to address the UK's current 94% unemployment levels for young people with learning disabilities. Amen to that. And it delivers great vibes. But it's being forced to leave its current premises in January 2023, due to the South Molton Regeneration triangle: wishing them a successful crowdfund appeal for a new site! / W1W 5QT; fairshot.co.uk; @fairshotcafe; Mon-Sat 5 pm, Sun 4 pm; closed Mon-Sun D.

Fallow St James's SW1 £100 4|4|4
2 St James's Market   07785 937900   4–3B

"Love the vibey new location even though it's big" – in late 2021, Jack Croft and Will Murray moved from 10 Heddon Street (where their original 12 weeks residency lasted over a year) to this "stylish" new 150-cover site in St James's, incorporating a bar, terrace and chef's counter. One or two diners dismiss the new version as "nothing special", but most accounts are full-on raves for the sharing-styles plates, originating from the UK and their Esher smallholding: "this has to be future of restaurants – sensational food, sustainably sourced, creatively used… magic!" / SW1S 4RP; www.fallowrestaurant.com; @fallowrestaurant; Mon-Sun 10.30 pm; credit card deposit required to book.

La Famiglia SW10 £79 2|2|4
7 Langton Street   020 7351 0761   6–3B

This "old favourite" Tuscan may "live on its reputation" (stretching back to 1966) and the appeal of its superb garden, but on "weekend lunches half of Chelsea appears here" (the half that's not somewhere in the country…) taking the grandchildren for Sunday lunch. Fans say the food is "not the very best but good…", sceptics that "the only thing that isn't average is the price… still, it is one of the poshest SWs!" / SW10 0JL; www.lafamiglia.co.uk; @lafamiglia.sw10; Tue-Sat 10 pm, Sun 9.30 pm; closed Mon.

Farang N5 £49 4|4|3
72 Highbury Park   020 7226 1609   9–1D

"Brilliant Thai food" ("some of the best I've had outside Thailand, and properly spicy too") has won a loyal following for Sebby Holmes's former pop-up in Highbury. The menu has switched from tasting-only to offer à la carte, but the cooking is as uncompromising as ever. Top Tip – "the cook-at-home range sold in their 'larder' is great too". / N5 2XE; www.faranglondon.co.uk; @farangldn; Wed-Sat 9 pm; closed Mon & Tue & Sun; no Amex.

Fare EC1 £58 3|2|3
11 Old Street   020 3034 0736   13–1A

"A reliable spot for light Italian-style lunch or dinner" near Silicon Roundabout, with a strong drinks list courtesy of its co-founders: sommelier Michael Sager of Sager + Wilde and mixologist Marcis Dzelzainis. "The pizza dough is some of the best and the toppings are very different from your usual Italian", the pasta is home-made, and the grills are "just as good". / EC1E 9HL; farelondon.com; @fare_london; Mon-Sat 11 pm; closed Sun.

Farmacy W2 £71 4|3|4
74 Westbourne Grove   020 7221 0705   7–1B

A "delightful ever-changing menu of truly delicious and inventive vegan/vegetarian dishes" tickles the taste buds at Camilla Fayed's Bayswater venue, which is supplied by her Demeter-certified biodynamic farm in Kent. / W2 5SH; www.farmacylondon.com; @farmacyuk; Mon-Sun 10 pm.

The Farrier NW1 £54 3|2|4
Camden Market, Chalk Farm Road   020 8092 4100   9–2B

Cleverly converted from Victorian Grade II listed former stables into a faux-rustic gastroboozer, this Camden Town yearling has "a lovely atmosphere, looking out into buzzy Camden Market", and serves a "high-quality" menu of British comfort-food classics which are "a cut above your usual pub fare". There's also a hidden courtyard with a fire pit, and a good selection of locally brewed beers. / NW1 8AH; www.thefarriercamden.com; @thefarriercamden; Mon & Tue 7 pm, Wed & Thu 11 pm, Fri & Sat midnight, Sun 10 pm; payment – credit card only.

F S A

The Fat Badger TW10   £67   3 2 2
15-17 Hill Rise   01423 505681   1–4A
Not far from the Thames and Richmond High Street, the Gladwin family's fifth field-to-fork venture (with food and wines from their farm in Sussex) inspires the promising but mixed reviews that seem to be part of the DNA of their chain. Some excellent meals were enjoyed, but the odd disappointment sounds a warning note. / TW10 6UQ; www.thefatbadger-restaurant.com; @thefatbadger_resto; Mon-Sat 11 pm, Sun 5 pm.

Fatt Pundit   £57   4 3 2
77 Berwick Street, W1   020 7287 7900   4–1C
6 Maiden Lane, WC2   020 7836 8883   5–3D
"Absolutely delicious" Indo-Chinese dishes (inspired by the Hakka-influenced cuisine of Kolkata) makes it worth discovering these slightly offbeat eateries in Soho and Covent Garden: ("delectable chops, and it even converted me to liking okra!").

Fatto Pizza & Beer KX N1 NEW
Unit 1, 3 Pancras Square   020 3148 4900   9–3C
Since 2015, Fatto e Mano have taken Brighton by storm. This June 2022 newcomer is their first foray into the capital (well, if you leave out Croydon in 2020), occupying one of the glossy units near Google HQ in King's Cross, and serving, er, … / N1N; www.fattoamanopizza.com; @fattoamanopizza.

Fenchurch Restaurant, Sky Garden EC3   £106   3 3 4
20 Fenchurch St   033 3772 0020   10–3D
"Unbeatable views" from the 37th floor of the City's Walkie-Talkie building accompany chef Michael Carr's menus at this "high-end" operation from caterers Rhubarb. "The food varies from average to exceptional", but there "enough courses that succeed" to make dining here a worthwhile – even "romantic" – experience. / EC3M 3BY; skygarden.london/fenchurch-restaurant; @sg_skygarden; Fri & Sat 8.30 pm, Thu 9.30 pm, Sun 9 pm; closed Thu L, closed Mon & Tue & Wed; payment – credit card only; booking max 7 may apply.

FENN SW6   £61   5 4 3
194 Wandsworth Bridge Road   020 7371 9888   11–1B
"A top addition to West London's restaurant scene"; this quite basic, 30-seat sibling (plus terrace) to Hackney's Nest is "dreadful to get to" (unless you happen to live in Fulham near Wandsworth Bridge), but it more than repays the effort with "innovative and well-crafted food" that's "well-priced" plus "a great selection of wines", all served by a "passionate" front-of-house team. / SW6 2UF; fennrestaurant.co.uk; @fennfulham; Tue-Sat 9.30 pm, Sun 3.30 pm; closed Tue, Wed L closed Sun D, closed Mon.

Fez Mangal W11   £49   4 4 2
104 Ladbroke Grove   020 7229 3010   7–1A
"Tasty Turkish food" including "classic kebabs" combine with a "BYO policy and a mixed crowd to make for a fun and affordable meal out" at this Ladbroke Grove standby. For several years now it has been "full both at lunchtime and dinner". / W11 1PY; www.fezmangal.com; @fezmangal; Mon-Sun 11 pm; no Amex.

Fiend W10 £59 544
301 Portobello Road   020 3971 8404   7–1A

"Crazy food combinations that read so jarringly yet taste sensational", alongside "demonic cocktails" deserve to make a hell of a hit of Chris Denney's (ex 108 Garage) "dark and moody" yearling, just north of the Westway on the northerly section of the Portobello Road. You eat on the ground floor with its big open kitchen (with the option of a tasting menu as well as the à la carte), while in the basement there's a bar. Already something of an in-crowd hit amongst the fooderati, it deserves to be more widely known. / W10 5TD; www.fiend-portobello.com; @FIENDPORTOBELLO; Tue, Wed midnight, Thu-Sat 1 am; closed Tue, Wed L, closed Sun & Mon.

50 Kalò di Ciro Salvo WC2 £47 523
7 Northumberland Avenue   020 7930 9955   2–3C

"Properly Italian pizza" – "the best in London, possibly in the UK" – is hiding in plain sight in the heart of the West End, just off Trafalgar Square. Ciro Salvo is a third-generation pizza maestro based in Naples, and his London offshoot showcases his secret-formula high-hydration and long fermentation '50 Kalo' dough. "The dough is the fluffiest ever and every ingredient used is the best of the best, from olive taggiasche to Cetara anchovies to Piennolo pomodori. Incredible!". / WC2W 5BY; www.xn--50kal-yta.it/ciro__salvo.php; @50kalo; Mon-Sun 11 pm.

Firebird W1 NEW
29 Poland Street   020 3813 1430   3–1D

St Petersburg restaurateurs, Madina Kazhimova and Anna Dolgushina opened this 46-cover restaurant and biodynamic wine bar in summer 2022 newcomer too late for our annual diners' poll, on the Soho site that was previously Corazon (RIP). Greek chef, Nikos Kontongiannatos (formerly head chef at Caravan) delivers plates cooked over fire in a low-lit space that's all concrete and exposed brickwork. In her July 2022 review, The Guardian's Grace Dent was well-impressed: "The standard of cooking, matched with genuinely intriguing and appetising dishes, puts it right up there on my list of 2022's important openings". / W1W; @firebird.london; Mon-Sat 10 pm, Sun 6 pm.

Fischer's W1 £66 233
50 Marylebone High Street   020 7466 5501   2–1A

"Treat the winter blues with a schnitzel" at this Wolseley Group brasserie in Marylebone – a "smaller, more casual cousin of the Delaunay", whose "understated" but cosy interior "whisks you off into an ambience of Continental sophistication" and provides a "lively" backdrop to a meal. True to the culinary DNA of the group, the "Austrian-style food" is "somewhat mediocre", and given its inspiration "you need to be up-for some heavy dishes". Prices are "fair", though, and all in all, "it's a useful and reliable spot for lunch or a family meal". Top Tip – "they understand breakfast here!" / W1U 5HN; www.fischers.co.uk; @fischerslondon; Sun & Mon 9.30 pm, Tue-Sat 10 pm.

Fish Central EC1 £40 342
149-155 Central St   020 7253 4970   13–1A

"An institution" after more than 50 years, this "superior" Greek-Cypriot veteran "tucked away" in Clerkenwell, uses "Billingate's finest" to serve "really fresh fish at good prices". It's "always worth a visit, even when it gets too noisy for comfort". / EC1V 8AP; www.fishcentral.co.uk; @fishcentralrestaurant; Mon-Thu, Sat 10 pm, Fri 10.30 pm; closed Mon L, closed Sun.

fish! SE1 £75 323
Cathedral St   020 7407 3803   10–4C

This "evergreen, upmarket fish restaurant in bustling Borough Market" has been a fixture of the area surrounding this foodie hub for more than two decades, noted for its glass frontage and "top-quality fresh fish". It gets "busy", though, and can be "a bit chaotic and unpolished". / SE1 9AL; www.fishkitchen.co.uk; @fishboroughmarket; Sun-Wed 10 pm, Thu-Sat 11 pm.

Fishers SW6 £43 3 3 3
19 Fulham High Street   02073715555   11–1B
"Doing the basic stuff brilliantly" – this "excellent neighbourhood fish restaurant", on the north side of Putney Bridge, provides "fish 'n' chips as they should be served", and "in huge portions". Meanwhile, "the cosy interior adds to the fishy charm!" / SW6 3JH; www.fishersfishandchips.co.uk; Mon-Sun 11 pm.

Fishworks £79 3 3 2
7-9 Swallow St, W1   020 7734 5813   4–4C
89 Marylebone High St, W1   020 7935 9796   2–1A
2-4 Catherine Street, WC2   020 7240 4999   5–3D
"Lovely fresh fish", "cooked simply" and "at prices which should shame its neighbours", is the attractive offer from this trio of straightforward seafood brasseries in some of the pricier parts of town – Covent Garden, Marylebone and Swallow Street, just of Piccadilly. Top Tip – "there's a fishmonger's attached", so you can take some "high-quality fish" home with you. / www.fishworks.co.uk.

Fiume SW8 £76 2 2 3
Circus West Village, Sopwith Way   020 3904 9010   11–1C
The "best terrace in London" – on the south bank of the Thames near the newly redeveloped Battersea Power Station – provides "an amazing setting" for what should be a magnificent Italian restaurant. But it's hard to escape the feeling that restaurant group D&D London with their high-profile chef Francesco Mazzei have missed a trick, and that "far better food should be had at this price". / SW8 5BN; fiume-restaurant.co.uk; @Fiume.London; Mon-Sat 10 pm, Sun 4 pm; closed Sun D.

The Five Fields SW3 £193 5 5 3
8-9 Blacklands Ter   020 7838 1082   6–2D
"Set in a quiet little street off the King's Road", Taylor Bonnyman's "discreet and elegant" Chelsea townhouse HQ flies under the radar in terms of PR, but is one of the survey's Top 40 most-mentioned restaurants, thanks to its "exceptional" quality. "Top-class ingredients are beautifully treated by a first-class team" overseen by Taylor and head chef Marguerite Keogh to deliver "classically inspired British seasonal food" that's "refined and sophisticated, but never overwrought". Service is "slick" and "classy" but "always with a smile" and the "soothing crisp lines" of the "beautiful dining room" create an "intimate" and "welcoming" atmosphere. "A truly special place for a celebration", especially of a romantic nature. / SW3 2SP; www.fivefieldsrestaurant.com; @the5fields; Tue-Sat 10 pm; closed Tue, Wed L, closed Sun & Mon.

500 N19 £56 3 4 2
782 Holloway Rd   020 7272 3406   9–1C
"This gem of a restaurant" near Archway "doesn't look like much – tables are too close and it can be noisy" – but don't be put off: you'll find "excellent, inventive Italian food" and "always great service – I travel across London for a meal here". Milanese-born chef-patron Mario Mugli named it after the small but perfectly formed Fiat Cinquecento. / N19 3JH; www.500restaurant.co.uk; @500restaurant; Wed-Sat 10 pm, Sun 9 pm; closed Wed-Sat L, closed Mon & Tue.

500 Degrees SE24 £36 3 2 3
153a Dulwich Road   020 7274 8200   11–2D
This "dependable, family-friendly pizzeria" by Brockwell Park is "still good value and the same quality after many years", with "nice chewy crusts to the pizza and plenty of flavour". It has an offshoot in Herne Hill. / SE24; www.500degrees.co; @500degreeshernehill; Mon-Sat 11 pm, Sun 10 pm.

FKABAM (Black Axe Mangal) N1   £52   4 3 3
156 Canonbury Road   no tel   9–2D

"Love it!" – Lee Tiernan's "amazing" heavy-metal take on the Anatolian grill is back after a long lockdown break with a modified name (with a nod to Prince) and some new graffiti. It's tiny (30 covers), loud, and the funky flatbreads are "beautiful stuff". Top Tip – the current set menu is released via Instagram weekly to its 62k followers. / N1; www.blackaxemangal.com; @blackaxemangal; Wed-Fri 10.30 pm; closed Wed-Fri L, closed Mon & Tue, Sat & Sun; payment – credit card only; credit card deposit required to book.

The Flask N6   £52   2 3 4
77 Highgate West Hill   020 8348 7346   9–1B

"A classic venue for reliable pub grub after a walk across the Heath", this "atmospheric" Grade II listed gastroboozer, tucked away in its own backstreet behind Hampstead tube, boasts a "splendid courtyard", and gets "busy at weekends". / N6 6BU; www.theflaskhighgate.com; @itstheflask; Mon-Sat 10 pm, Sun 9 pm.

Flat Iron   £37   3 4 3
17 Beak St, W1   020 3019 2353   4–2B
42-44 James Street, W1   no tel   3–1A
17 Henrietta St, WC2   020 3019 4212   5–3C
9 Denmark St, WC2   no tel   5–1A
47-51 Caledonian Rd, N1   no tel   9–3D
112-116 Tooley Street, SE1   no tel   10–4D
41-45 The Cut, SE1   no tel   10–4A   **NEW**
Soho Wharf, Clink Street, SE1   no tel   10–3C
88-90 Commercial Street, E1   no tel   13–2C
77 Curtain Road, EC2   no tel   13–1B

"What they do – a limited repertoire – they certainly do well" at this "no-nonsense" steakhouse chain (which serves no starters or puds, just five or six mains and sides, plus "a tiny key they give you at beginning of meal to exchange for a delicious ice cream cornet to take with you as you go!"). It amounts to "amazing value for a good (ish) steak" – "tasty, not mind-blowing, but dependable and fairly priced, and elevated by the sides and sauces". On the site of a former Byron, the 10th branch opens in Waterloo in 2022. / www.flatironsteak.co.uk; flatironsteak.

Flat White W1   £12   3 3 2
17 Berwick St   020 7734 0370   4–2D

The original (back in 2005) and, say fans, still "best flat white in London" – this Antipodean-style indie in Soho's Berwick Street Market has launched imitators on every high street in Britain. / W1F 0PT; www.flatwhitesoho.co.uk; @flatwhitesoho; Mon-Sun 6 pm; payment – credit card only; no booking.

Flesh and Buns   £66   3 4 3
32 Berners Street, W1   020 3019 3492   3–1D
Bone Daddies, 41 Earlham Street, WC2   020 7632 9500   5–2C
1 Phillimore Gardens, W8   020 3019 3492   8–1D   **NEW**

"Very busy and bustling" – these "vibey" izakayas are part of Bone Daddies group, and provide an "inventive" mix of dishes from a wide-ranging menu: sushi, filled hirata buns, ceviche (not all branches) and a wide selection of other dishes. In addition to those in Fitzrovia and Covent Garden, they briefly added a Kensington site in 2022, but it is set to be converted to a Bone Daddies after just a few months. / www.fleshandbuns.com; fleshandbuns.

Flora Indica SW5   £55   3 2 3
242 Old Brompton Rd   020 7370 4450   6–2A

This "interesting" and unusual modern Indian in Earl's Court celebrates the Scottish botanists of the Victorian era who collected the flora of the subcontinent. There's a relatively short menu, but everything is "delicious" – "small portions, but they pack a fabulous punch of flavour". / SW5 0DE; www.flora-indica.com; @flora_indica; Mon-Sun 11 pm.

F S A

Flour & Grape SE1 £47 3 3 3
214 Bermondsey St   (020) 7407 4682   10–4D
This "noisy and bustling Bermondsey restaurant" is one of the new wave of pasta-only specialists, with "attentive staff" who serve "indulgent food" to happy guests. "The excellent pasta is well complemented by a great all-Italian wine list". There's also a gin bar in the basement. / SE1 3TQ; www.flourandgrape.com; @flourandgrape; Mon-Sun 10 pm; closed Mon L; booking max 6 may apply.

FM Mangal SE5 £49 3 3 2
54 Camberwell Church St   020 7701 6677   1–3C
"The chargrilled onions and flatbreads to start soon grab the attention" at this popular family-run Anatolian in Camberwell, founded across town in Islington more than 25 years ago. "The grilled lamb that follows is still as good as ever. Thankfully!". / SE5 8QZ; www.fmmangal.co.uk; @fm_mangal; Mon-Sun midnight; no Amex; no booking.

Foley's W1 £54 3 4 3
23 Foley Street   020 3137 1302   2–1B
Most (but not all) the diverse menu is of East Asian-inspiration at this 70-seater in Fitzrovia, complete with outdoor bar. The "excellent seafood" is worth a special mention – "some of the best calamari ever" – and it's "good value, too". / W1W 6DU; www.foleysrestaurant.co.uk; @foleysrestaurant; Mon-Sat 10 pm, Sun 9 pm.

Folie W1 £89 3 4 4
37 Golden Square   020 7600 6969   4–2C
With a menu inspired by the French Riviera, this spacious outfit in Golden Square "quickly became a firm favourite for business lunches", despite the unfortunate timing of its launch in late 2019. Parisian patron Guillaume Depoix's vision of the 'perfect Soho brasserie', it delivers "delicious French food done simply and well", with a "great clubby feeling, especially when the DJ is there at weekends". / W1W 9LB; folie.london; @folie_london; Mon-Thu 12.30 am, Fri & Sat 2 am; closed Sun.

Food House W1 £39
46 Gerrard Street   020 7287 2818   5–3B
In the late 1990s, Jonathan Meades in the Times regularly hailed the Harbour City – a previous Cantonese occupant of this site on Chinatown's main drag – as London's top choice for dim sum. Now this latest incumbent is receiving similar treatment on the back of an Eater article hailing it as "the trendiest restaurant in central London". According to The Observer's Jay Rayner, the new "very different" offering is "the grand, jumpy, thrilling, chilli and numbing peppercorn hullabaloo that those of us addicted to the Sichuan repertoire just adore". / W1W 5QH; Mon-Sat 11 pm, Sun 10 pm.

Fortnum & Mason,
The Diamond Jubilee Tea Salon W1 £86 3 3 4
181 Piccadilly   020 7734 8040   3–3D
"Perfect for foreigners with high expectations of afternoon tea" – this "sedate" chamber provides "everything you would expect" of the occasion. Staff are "so accommodating" and the spread is "outstanding every time": "the hot starters are delicious, the cakes plentiful and they keep arriving – take a little box home of the ones you can't eat". / W1A 1ER; www.fortnumandmason.com; @fortnums; Mon-Sat 7 pm, Sun 7.30 pm; no trainers.

FSA RATINGS: FROM 1 POOR — 5 EXCEPTIONAL

45 Jermyn St. SW1 £80 233
45 Jermyn Street   020 7205 4545   3–3D

Fortnum & Mason's "luxurious" and "cosseting" restaurant (with its own street entrance) makes "a top central destination at any time! – for breakfast, coffee, lunch, tea, dinner or for drinks" (as the bar does "superb cocktails"). "With its many booths, alcoves and corners, it's the ideal place to meet someone" (particularly on business), and "discreet staff will ensure your liaison goes swimmingly". Less kind reports feel "there's nothing to distinguish the inoffensive upmarket international food", but harsher critiques are absent. Top Menu Tip – "Be sure to try the caviar – served from a trolley". And, for breakfast, this is "an excellent alternative to the nearby Wolseley as it's much less frenetic" and available "with rare-breed eggs, caviar, winter or white truffles in season". / SW1S 6DN; www.45jermynst.com; @45jermynst; Mon-Sat 11 pm, Sun 6 pm; closed Sun D.

40 Maltby Street SE1 £62 332
40 Maltby St   020 7237 9247   10–4D

With its "carefully sourced and imaginatively prepared seasonal ingredients complemented by natural wines", this spartan venue in a Victorian railway arch behind London Bridge station has become a pilgrimage site for foodies in the past decade. Chef Steve Williams's menu is chalked up on a board each day, and there's no coddling of guests in what is still primarily a warehouse operated by the Gergovie biodynamic wine import business, who provide the in-house wines. A small minority feel the whole experience is "a bit overhyped", but there are no complaints about the quality of the food. / SE1 3PA; www.40maltbystreet.com; @40maltbystreet; Wed-Sat 10 pm; closed Wed-Fri L, closed Mon & Tue & Sun; no Amex; no booking.

Forza Win SE5 NEW
31 Camberwell Church Street   awaiting tel   1–3C

Having stormed Peckham, then closed during lockdown, Bash Redford and Michael Lavery have chosen Camberwell for the latest iteration of their Italian brand. The formula has become increasingly 'grown up' since it started in 2012 as a pop-up pizzeria in the Truman Brewery: its new guise will be that of a traditional Italian restaurant with primo, secundi, dolce, etc. / SE5 8TR; www.forzawin.com; @forzawin; Mon-Sun midnight.

Forza Wine SE15 £60 345
Floor 5, Rye Lane   020 7732 7500   1–4D

"Tremendous views over London" and sipping natural wines as you chill add to the heady experience of this "amazing rooftop restaurant and bar in the heart of Peckham Rye". Perched on the fifth floor of a co-working space, it is run by the team behind Peckham's Italian-focused Forza Win (no 'e', currently shifting sites). "It's a treat to work through the menu ('snacks' belies the culinary skills at work) while drinking a cocktail and admiring the sights". / SE15 4ST; www.forzawine.com; @forzawine; Sun-Thu 11.30 pm, Fri & Sat 12.30 am.

400 Rabbits £31 332
143 Evelina Road, SE15   020 7732 4115   1–4D
16a Ash Avenue, SE17   020 7703 1559   1–3C NEW
30-32 Westow St, SE19   020 8771 6249   1–4D
Brockwell Lido, Dulwich Road, SE24   020 7737 8183   11–2D
521 Norwood Road, SE27   020 8761 0872   1–4D

"Always fresh sourdough pizza" has helped build a strong local following for this hip southeast London group, with outlets in Crystal Palace, Nunhead, West Norwood, Herne Hill and Elephant & Castle. A new natural wine selection from specialist importer Les Caves de Pyrène is now available alongside the craft beers on tap. Top Tip – "make sure you leave room for the ice cream". / www.400rabbits.co.uk; 4hundredrabbits.

Four Regions TW9 £55 3|2|2
102-104 Kew Rd 020 8940 9044 1–4A
This "very solid local Chinese near Richmond" has plied its trade for more than 30 years, delivering "consistently good food with some great veggie choices" and "delicious dim sum". Named after China's four culinary regions, its menu covers the field from Cantonese seafood to spicy Sichuan dishes, and there are good-value set meal options. No wonder it's "often busy". / TW9 2PQ; www.fourregions.co.uk; Mon-Sat 10 pm, Sun 9 pm.

Four Seasons £67 4|1|1
11 Gerrard Street, W1 020 7287 0900 5–3A
12 Gerrard St, W1 020 7494 0870 5–3A
23 Wardour St, W1 020 7287 9995 5–3A
84 Queensway, W2 020 7229 4320 7–2C
"The roast duck is extraordinarily delicious and just melts in the mouth" (and the rest of the menu is worthy of exploration too) at these "squashed in" Cantonese pit stops in Bayswater and Chinatown, which waste little energy on interior design or customer service. (A new branch 'Chop Chop', is set to open in the basement of the Hippodrome casino, near Leicester Square, over summer 2022). / www.fs-restaurants.co.uk.

14 Hills EC3 £90 2|2|4
120 Fenchurch Street 020 3981 5222 10–3D
A 'forest in the sky' – 2,500 evergreens planted on the 14th floor of 120 Fenchurch Street by D&D London at a reputed cost of £5million – "brings something different to the usual City venue". It's a "buzzing room with good food to match" from a modern Anglo-French menu. It goes without saying that "you're paying for the views and the experience" – but it certainly makes for "a fun evening". / EC3E 5BA; www.danddlondon.com; @14hillsldn; Mon-Sat 10.30 pm, Sun 9.30 pm.

Fox & Grapes SW19 £62 3|2|2
9 Camp Rd 020 8619 1300 11–2A
This Georgian boozer on the edge of Wimbledon Common is "just what you want from a London 'village' gastropub" – "a reliable friendly local, with food that's a cut above the ordinary". / SW19 4UN; www.foxandgrapeswimbledon.co.uk; @foxandgrapeswimbledon; Wed-Sun 10.30 pm; closed Mon & Tue.

The Fox & Hounds SW11 £64 3|4|3
66-68 Latchmere Road 020 7924 5483 11–1C
"The perfect local" according to Battersea residents, who rate this old corner pub for its "well-kept beer, well-cooked food, and brilliant service every time". There's a "lovely hidden garden at the back" too. / SW11 2JU; www.thefoxandhoundspub.co.uk; @thefoxbattersea; Sun-Thu 9 pm, Fri & Sat 10 pm; closed Mon-Fri L.

The Fox and Pheasant SW10 £59 3|2|4
1 Billing Road 020 7352 2943 6–3B
A "superb atrium out the back", with a glass roof that opens completely, gives this self-styled 'country pub' in a cute corner of Chelsea (est. 1846) an edge over rivals. It's generally well-rated, but perhaps at its best for Sunday lunch. / SW10 9UJ; www.thefoxandpheasant.com; @thefoxandpheasantpub; Mon-Sat midnight, Sun 11 pm; closed Mon L.

Franco Manca £39 2 3 2
Branches throughout London

"A safe option each time, every time" – "they have got the pizza formula spot-on" at this stormingly good chain, which has grown remorselessly throughout recent times on the back of its "enjoyable" offering of "chewy" sourdough pizzas ("I go simple, but they have a good choice of interesting toppings"); plus "a small selection of beers and pluggable Italian wines". Perhaps some small competitors "do pizza better these days", but – "despite expansion" – these simply decorated, upbeat venues are "hard to improve on": "the food tastes fresh and unprocessed", "they turn around the orders quickly" and "are friendly to boot". And prices are "very competitive" too ("I am constantly amazed by how they can produce such a good product at such a low price"). "There are never leftovers here. You have to remind yourself just how far things have moved on occasionally... and these places do that". / www.francomanca.co.uk; francomancapizza.

Franco's SW1 £88 3 3 3
61 Jermyn St 020 7499 2211 3–3C

"An old classic that always feels fresh" – this spry 75-year-old Italian in St James's is "very consistent" and provides "a lovely, busy atmosphere" that's "suited to eating with clients or friends". That it's "a bit pricey" is a theme running through most reports on it, though ("very pleasant, but I have a strong sense that many – most? – diners are on expenses... lucky them!"; "...lovely for the deep-pocketed, with traditional fare that's well done, but at astronomical prices"). Top Tip – "they do a decent line in business breakfast". / SW1Y 6LX; www.francoslondon.com; @francoslondon; Mon-Sat 11 pm; closed Sun.

Frank's Canteen N5 £45 3 4 3
86 Highbury Park 020 7354 4830 9–1D

This Highbury operation started out as a catering company but has developed into a popular all-day café/restaurant serving highly rated modern European cooking, with evening meals on Thursday, Friday and Saturday. / N5 2XE; www.frankscanteen.com; @frankscanteen; Sun-Wed 4 pm, Thu-Sat 9.30 pm; closed Sun-Wed D; payment – credit card only; booking online only.

Franklins SE22 £61 3 3 3
157 Lordship Ln 020 8299 9598 1–4D

"A romantic neighbourhood favourite of longstanding" in East Dulwich, which has been serving "good modern European cooking with some unusual twists" for over 20 years now. / SE22 8HX; www.franklinsrestaurant.com; @franklinsse22; Mon-Sat midnight, Sun 10.30 pm; no Amex.

Frantoio SW10 £62 2 4 4
397 King's Rd 020 7352 4146 6–3B

"Enormous fun!" "Everyone is treated like a long-lost relative" at this "West London hangout", where charismatic host Bucci presides over a "wonderful local". "The food is perfectly OK without being special", and comes in "massive portions: never mind the quality, feel the width!" – which adds to its appeal as a firm family favourite. / SW10 0LR; frantoio.co.uk; @Frantonio_london; Mon-Sun 11 pm.

Frederick's N1 £66 3 4 4
106 Camden Passage 020 7359 2888 9–3D

The "cooking is as reliable as ever" at this calm and sprawling Islington institution – a fixture among the antiques shops of Camden Passage for more than half a century. Its modern European cuisine is "nothing wildly exciting, but assured and confident" and backed up by an "excellent wine list". Staff are "especially good to regulars" ("it's so nice to be recognised, welcomed and made to feel special"). And "when sitting in the quiet and civilised garden in the sunshine, it's hard to believe you're only moments from the fray of Upper Street". / N1 8EG; www.fredericks.co.uk; Tue-Fri 10.30, Sat 10.30 pm; closed Sun & Mon.

FSA

The French House W1 — £67 — 3 4 4
49 Dean Street 020 7437 2477 5–3A
"Another reincarnation for the slightly cramped room above 'The French'… and this is a good one!" – Neil Borthwick and his team produce *"simple and gutsy food, with big steaks, fresh fish, and tasty Gallic classics on a daily changing menu which will leave you full and pleased that you visit the old place"*: *"a London fixture of decades' standing"*. / W1W 5BG; www.frenchhousesoho.com; @FrenchHouseSoho; Mon-Sat 11 pm, Sun 10.30 pm.

Frenchie WC2 — £92 — 3 3 3
18 Henrietta Street 020 7836 4422 5–3C
"Paris in Covent Garden" is, say fans, found at this *"romantic"* small six-year-old – part of a group run by Gregory & Marie Merchand (the former nicknamed 'Frenchie' when he worked for Jamie Oliver at Fifteen). Some reporters, though, *"had high hopes but were disappointed"*: *"it was great but very overpriced and too fashionable…"* / WC2E 8QH; www.frenchiecoventgarden.com; @frenchiecoventgarden; Wed & Thu, Sun 9.30 pm, Fri & Sat 10.30 pm; closed Wed L, closed Mon & Tue.

Frog by Adam Handling WC2 — £208 — 4 4 3
35 Southampton Street 020 7199 8370 5–3D
"Outstanding showmanship" (*"food theatre for the TikTok generation"*) *"but matched with exceptional cooking running behind the gimmicks"* (*"dry ice, melting bubbles etc thrill but don't hide the perfect texture and a palate of savoury flavour combinations"*) has carved an impressive reputation for Adam Handling's acclaimed Covent Garden flagship. Despite its status as a foodie temple, staff are *"so relaxed and fun"* and the atmosphere generally is very *"informal"*, which fans feel *"makes the experience even better"*: *"you can really focus on the food"*. And with *"the kitchen being open, it allows you to see Adam leading his very disciplined brigade"*. On the downside, ratings dipped a little this year, with some diners questioning *"startling prices"*, or accusing the culinary pyrotechnics of allowing *"a triumph of style over substance"*. (*"The technical excellence is unquestionable, but really too much showing off… serving waffles with caviar and honey ought to be a capital offence!"*). Success came in other respects, though: it was finally – not before time – awarded a Michelin star. / WC2W 7HG; www.frogbyadamhandling.com; @Frogbyah; Wed-Sat, Tue 11 pm; closed Tue L, closed Sun & Mon.

La Fromagerie — £59 — 3 2 2
2-6 Moxon St, W1 020 7935 0341 3–1A
52 Lamb's Conduit St, WC1 020 7242 1044 2–1D
30 Highbury Park, N5 020 7359 7440 9–2D
"Lots of lovely cheese" is on the menu at this specialist trio in Bloomsbury, Marylebone and Highbury, complemented by a *"truly interesting and well-curated wine list"*. The *"delicious fondue and raclette go down well on a winter's day"*. / www.lafromagerie.co.uk.

The Frontline Club W2 — £49
13 Norfolk Pl 020 7479 8960 7–1D
There's an intriguing background to this quite smart venue near Paddington station, founded as a meeting place for international journos and snappers, and whose walls display iconic news photographs from around the world. Feedback has shrunk over the pandemic period, with the odd unsettled report, but it has in the past offered a useful dining option in this thin area, so we've included it but without a current rating. / W2 1QJ; www.frontlineclub.com; @frontlineclub; Fri, Mon-Thu 11 pm; closed Mon-Thu L, closed Sat & Sun; booking max 6 may apply.

FSA

Fumo WC2 £55 ३३३
37 St Martin's Lane 020 3778 0430 5–4C
"Don't go if you have a phobia of crowds" and it's a little "touristy", but this outpost of the San Carlo group by the Coliseum gets the thumbs-up: it's "buzzy and fun"; "the great small plates are "more than competent for a large, high turnover place"; and it has "a super location for pre-theatre meals". / WC2N 4JS; sancarlofumo.co.uk/restaurants/fumo-london; @sancarlorestaurants; Mon-Thu 11.30 pm, Fri & Sat midnight, Sun 10.30 pm.

Gallipoli Again N1 £49 ३४४
119 Upper Street 020 7226 8099 9–3D
"This old Upper Street favourite" (no longer with a nearby offshoot) wins high marks for its "well-grilled Turkish food" and "just brilliant, warm service". Jolly décor, with lots of "quiet corners", suits it to a variety of meals: from a budget celebration to lunch with the fam. / N1 1QP; gallipolicafe.co.uk.

Galvin at Windows, Park Lane London Hilton Hotel W1 £130 २३३
22 Park Ln 020 7208 4021 3–4A
"Stunningly located on the 28th floor of the Park Lane Hilton" – the Galvin Bros have run this well-known eyrie since 2006. Its "chief selling point is the panorama of London" of course, and a fair judgement currently is that: "the cooking is sound, well-executed and nicely presented, rather than stellar; but the view over Hyde Park and Buckingham Palace Gardens justify the steep prices and it's great place for a special occasion". Top Top – "the bar is worth a visit too, with an evening setting sun providing wonderful lighting", and you can take in the skyline there just for the price of a cocktail. / W1K 1BE; www.galvinatwindows.com; @galvinatwindows; Wed-Sat 9.30 pm, Sun 2.45 pm; closed Wed L closed Sun D, closed Mon & Tue; no trainers; booking max 5 may apply.

Galvin Bar & Grill WC1 NEW £88 ३४४
Kimpton Fitzroy, 1-8 Russell Square 020 7520 1800 2–1C
"The magnificent and historic, late-Victorian dining room makes for a truly stunning backdrop to any meal" at this "beautifully renovated" chamber: the main dining room of the monumental hotel (originally Hotel Russell) that dominates the north of Russell Square. Critics say the space is "the star of the show", feeling that the cuisine from the newly installed Galvin Brothers regime "fails to live up to it"; but taken overall, ratings for its "menu of British grill favourites" are good. Top Tip – "a very good family Sunday lunch option". / WC1W 5BE; galvinrestaurants.com/restaurant/galvin-bar-and-grill; @galvinbarandgrill; Tue-Sat 9.30 pm, Mon 10, Sun 3 pm; closed Sun & Mon D.

Galvin Bistrot & Bar E1 £65 ३२३
35 Bishops Square 020 7299 0404 13–2B
This "very reliable and enjoyable old-style bistrot" in Spitalfields is from "the same team as La Chapelle" (the Galvin brothers' deluxe flagship next door). Fans say that "means the food is top-notch for a bar" with a "well-prepared set menu that's great value", but ratings are capped by a minority of critics who feel it has "lost its magic since the revamp". Top Tip – "worth visiting for the Pilsner alone" – fresh unpasteurised Urquell delivered weekly and stored in copper tanks above the bar. / E1 6DY; galvinrestaurants.com; @galvinrestaurants; Tue-Sat 9.30 pm; closed Sun & Mon.

Galvin La Chapelle E1 £111 3 3 5
35 Spital Sq   020 7299 0400   13–2B

"One of the most pretty and impressive dining rooms in London" – an "amazing and beautifully lit" space often mistaken for a church, but in fact originally a late-Victorian girls' school – helps underpin the appeal of the Galvin Brothers' long-established destination, near Spitalfields Market. Although its ratings have come under pressure since Covid struck due to some uneven reports, this remains an "all-round treat", much nominated for both important business and romantic occasions thanks to its "well-spaced" interior; service that is "spot-on"; and "fantastic French cuisine", with numerous diners voting for it in our poll as their top gastronomic experience of the year. / E1 6DY; www.galvinlachapelle.com; @galvinrestaurants; Wed, Sun 9 pm, Thu-Sat 9.30 pm; closed Wed L, closed Mon & Tue; no trainers; booking max 8 may apply.

The Game Bird SW1 £123 3 4 4
16-18 St James's Place   020 7518 1234   3–4C

"A hidden gem in the heart of London" – this "discreet" dining room is tucked away in an Edwardian St James's five star, but well worth discovering nowadays as its "top-of-the-range", classic British cuisine is going from strength to strength, and its plush, traditional style is suited to many types of occasion including business and romance. In August 2021, Lisa Goodwin-Allen of Northcote in Lancashire (same ownership) was named as the new overseer from afar of the menu here. Perhaps she's behind the boost in ratings, although there's been no discernible revolution in its general culinary approach. / SW1S 1NJ; thestaffordlondon.com/the-game-bird; @thegamebirdlon; Mon-Fri 9 pm, Sun 5 pm, Sat 9 pm.

Ganapati SE15 £44 4 2 2
38 Holly Grove   020 7277 2928   1–4D

"A South London gem" – Claire Fisher's "authentic, fresh and delicious South Indian food" has been a "stalwart" of Peckham dining since 2004 (well before the area's gastro scene took off). It's a "lovely little restaurant", "if a bit cramped", especially if you "quite enjoy the fairly communal dining", and "its regularly changing menu still entices and surprises". Top Tip – "you must buy some jars of divine home-made pickles and chutneys to take home!". / SE15 5DF; www.ganapatirestaurant.com; @ganapati.peckham; Tue-Sat 10.30 pm, Sun 10 pm; closed Mon; no Amex.

Ganymede SW1 £88 4 4 3
139 Ebury Street   020 3971 0761   2–4A

"A surprisingly good replacement for the much loved Ebury St Wine Bar" (long RIP) – this new Belgravia venture "is a great find in an area devoid of good restaurants". Daniel Mertl is acclaimed as "a talented chef" producing a "superior" brasserie menu that's "all from the very top of the drawer". / SW1S 9QU; ganymedelondon.co.uk; @ganymedesw1; Mon-Sat 11 pm, Sun 6 pm.

The Garden Cafe at the Garden Museum SE1 £64 4 3 3
5 Lambeth Palace Rd   020 7401 8865   2–4D

The "fantastic food" is in a very different league to that of most museum cafés, in this attractive space off the gorgeous courtyard of Lambeth's Garden Museum, where former Padella chef, George Ryle, is responsible for "fresh and interesting cooking" with an Italian accent. But not all the typical norms have been neglected: there's also "delicious coffee and cakes". / SE1 7LB; www.gardenmuseum.org.uk; @gardenmuseumcafe; Mon, Wed & Thu, Sat & Sun 5 pm, Tue, Fri 9 pm; closed Mon, Wed & Thu, Sat & Sun D; no Amex; booking max 12 may apply.

Le Garrick WC2 £61 3|3|4
10-12 Garrick Street   020 7240 7649   5–3C

"The cramped basement is super-cute and atmospheric" ("its booths and candles making it one of the more romantic venues in town") at this "little piece of Paris in the heart of Covent Garden". With its "decent French provincial-style cooking" it is particularly tipped as a "very acceptable pre-theatre option". / WC2E 9BH; www.legarrick.co.uk; @le_garrick; Mon-Sat 11 pm; closed Sun.

The Garrison SE1 £77 3|3|3
99 Bermondsey Street   020 7089 9355   10–4D

A "stalwart of Bermondsey Street", this classy, green-tiled gastropub helped kick-start the area as a foodie destination with its launch 20 years ago. The team showed they still care with an "improved menu after lockdown". / SE1 3XB; www.thegarrison.co.uk; @thegarrisonse1; Mon-Thu 11 pm, Fri & Sat midnight, Sun 10.30 pm.

The Gate £58 3|3|3
22-24 Seymour Place, W1   020 7724 6656   2–2A
51 Queen Caroline St, W6   020 8748 6932   8–2C
370 St John St, EC1   020 7278 5483   9–3D

"Predictably good meat-free food that's worth a detour" has helped win a big fanclub for this small veggie chain, which vies with Mildreds as London's best multiple plant-based group. (The Gates are less well known than their rivals nowadays but score higher for food). In particular, there's high praise for "the original and best" location, which occupies a "lovely light-filled" space above a church, behind Hammersmith's Eventim Apollo (and with a 'secret garden' in summer). The St John's Wood spin-off closed this year, leaving two others near Sadlers Wells and in Seymour Village. If there's a gripe, it's the "somewhat unchanging menu", which has seemed more static of late. / thegaterestaurants.com; gaterestaurant.

The Gatehouse N6 £60 3|3|3
1 North Road   020 8340 8054   9–1B

"Surprisingly Spanish" – this "busy" former Wetherspoons in Highgate is taking the neighbourhood by storm with its very "decent" tapas. "Lovely Sunday lunches too" and they even have a small theatre upstairs! / N6 4BD; www.thegatehousen6.com; @thegatehousen6; Mon-Sat 10 pm, Sun 9 pm.

Gaucho £87 2|2|2
Branches throughout London

"Expensive but fun" is the upbeat take on this Argentinian steakhouse chain, where imported steaks are matched with an "excellent wine list" (including the largest selection of Argentinian wines outside the country). And the riverside branch in Richmond is a particular "go-to place for a celebration". On the downside, a worrying proportion of diners find it "overpriced" or plain "disappointing": "it's a good steak, but doesn't match the price tag". / www.gauchorestaurants.co.uk; gauchogroup; SRA-1 star.

Gauthier Soho W1 £120 3|3|3
21 Romilly St   020 7494 3111   5–3A

"If all vegan food was as good as this I'd convert… it's ceaselessly wonderful and served by brilliant staff in a fabulous setting" – that's the most upbeat view on Alexis Gauthier's "beautifully furnished and discreet townhouse smack in the middle of Soho", where you ring a doorbell to gain entry. Having been resolutely carnivorous on its launch in 2010, Alexis went vegan personally in 2016, and since June 2021 he has taken the restaurant meat-free as well. On the plus side, this is now one of the most ambitious and successful meat-free restaurants in town. But on the downside, practically none of his old meat-loving regulars like it so much now ("it was an old favourite, and I was interested to try the all-vegan menu, but it wasn't for us…"; "we so very much wanted to love this move to vegan cuisine from Gauthier Soho, but we were sadly disappointed…"; "excellent food, but I

mourn the loss of the non-vegan options…"). Still, even those "who are not totally convinced" say "there is no doubt that Gauthier manages to marry vegan cuisine with a high-end, gourmet experience more successfully than most". And "what is stunning is their wine flights, which are amazing!"
/ W1D 5AF; www.gauthiersoho.co.uk; @gauthierinsoho; Tue-Thu 10 pm, Fri & Sat 10.30 pm; closed Tue-Sat L, closed Sun & Mon; payment – credit card only; booking max 6 may apply.

Le Gavroche W1 £147 4 3 4
43 Upper Brook St   020 7408 0881   3–2A

"The pinnacle of traditional French cuisine" – "Michel Roux Jr's grand dame of London restaurants" is a cornerstone of "old-school brilliance". "Others may be more avant-garde, but if you want the classics, there's nowhere better" than this subterranean Mayfair venue, founded by his late father Albert and run by Michel since 1992. Under the former, it was the first UK restaurant with three Michelin stars, and has held two since 1993. "Some consider it old-fashioned" or even "dated"-looking (the décor is somewhat "akin to an old-style cruise ship of the 1980s"). But most reporters feel "it has what you want for a special night out": "classic Gallic cuisine of a kind that is hard to find even in France nowadays" delivered in a supremely cosseting setting ("the deep carpets, low hum of conversation and huge portraits of generations of Roux talent tell you you're in for a treat"). "Staff are knowledgeable and attentive, without being stuffy", although a decline in the service rating from its former formidable peak, perhaps reflects the fact that some diners feel "service is not as sharp of late – we miss Emanuel Landré!" (who relinquished the reins as GM to twins Sylvia & Ursula Perberschlager a couple of years ago). And, of course, there's no hiding that a meal here "costs an arm and a leg", particularly now that – due to post-Brexit staffing shortages – there is no longer the option of the much-mourned, marvellous-value set lunch (cancelled when the restaurant became dinner-only). Its food rating this year was more borderline, perhaps as a result. Still, "look up 'fine dining' in the dictionary and chances are a picture of Le Gavroche will appear before long"; and despite the ups and downs of recent times, the overall verdict is that it is "still keeping on top of its game". The fact that "Michel Roux regularly takes the time to speak with customers is an added bonus". Top Menu Tips – "The twice-baked cheese soufflé remains rightly famous as the stuff of many a fantasy last meal; and the epic cheese trolley really is a sight to behold". And, of course, the cellar is special here too: "a wonderfully deep wine list because of the establishment's longevity". / W1K 7QR; www.le-gavroche.co.uk; @le_gavroche_restauraunt; Tue-Sat 10 pm; closed Tue-Sat L, closed Sun & Mon; no shorts.

Gazette £64 2 2 3
79 Sherwood Ct, Chatfield Rd, SW11   020 7223 0999   11–1C
147 Upper Richmond Rd, SW15   020 8789 6996   11–2B
218 Trinity Road, SW17   020 8767 5810   11–2C **NEW**
17-18 Took's Court, EC4   020 7831 6664   10–2A **NEW**

This "buzzy" and "well-priced" modern Gallic quartet (Clapham, Putney and Wandsworth plus the City) keeps regulars happy with "interesting twists on the starters" and "some great weekly offers, eg 'Lobster Night'". One or two critics feel their performance is "half-hearted and disappointing", but on most accounts they are an "extremely likeable attempt to recreate a French bistro". / www.gazettebrasserie.co.uk.

GBR (The Great British Restaurant) at The Dukes Hotel SW1 £83 333
35 St James's Pl   020 7491 4840   3–4C

"Tucked away in Dukes Hotel, off St James's Street", this swish brasserie provides food that's "remarkably good and relatively inexpensive". "I have found it more or less empty at lunch-time, so peace and quiet reigns", but arguably "it deserves better support". Top Tips – "well-cooked breakfast" and "very reasonably priced set menus". / SW1A 1NY; www.dukeshotel.com; @gbr_london; Tue-Thu 9 pm, Fri & Sat 10 pm; closed Sun & Mon.

Gem N1 £45 443
265 Upper St   020 7359 0405   9–2D

"The name sums it up!" say fans of this busy spot near Angel serving "great Turkish grills with handmade relishes and sides" alongside "excellent" Greek and Kurdish dishes. Its 'Hidden Gem' basement can be booked for private parties. / N1 2UQ; www.gemrestaurant.org.uk; @gemrestaurantuk; Mon-Sat 11 pm; closed Sun; no Amex.

German Gymnasium N1 £70 123
1 King's Boulevard   020 7287 8000   9–3C

"The impressive building is the best part of the experience" at this D&D London operation, whose location – a Victorian former gym, immediately behind King's Cross station, could not make it handier as a rendezvous. Having opened in quite a promising vein in 2015, its ratings in recent times have started to match the "style-over-substance" performance too often discerned in the group's approach. Custom isn't a problem – it can be "so busy (and excessively noisy)". But service can be "perfunctory" ("they seem to think they do not have to try or otherwise expend any effort to retain customer loyalty") and although some fans do feel its "easygoing" menu of sausages, schnitzels, burgers and other brasserie fare are "great for your German fridge fix", too many find it "limited, unexciting and overpriced". Top Tips – most often recommended for business and/or breakfast. / N1C 4BU; www.germangymnasium.com; @thegermangym; Mon-Sat 10 pm, Sun 9 pm.

Giacomo's NW2 £48 342
428 Finchley Rd   020 7794 3603   1–1B

This traditional family-run "local Italian gem" in Child's Hill has provided "good home-cooked food, beautifully served" for more than two decades. / NW2 2HY; www.giacomos.co.uk; Tue-Sun 10.30 pm; closed Mon.

Giannino Mayfair W1 £119 243
8-10 Blenheim Street   020 8138 1196   3–2B

Few restaurants can boast the heritage of this Mayfair two-year-old: the first ever spin-off from a Milanese original of over 120 years' standing. It's still a case of promise unfulfilled, though, with reports that are very up and down, despite a general acknowledgement of "friendly service and a pleasant interior" (the latter very classical in style). "Eye-watering prices" are key to the ambivalence felt by diners, despite some dishes that are "clearly wonderful" – if you give it a go, perhaps try the set lunch, which is "exceptional value by comparison to other options here". / W1W 1LJ; gianninomayfair.com; @gianninomayfair; Mon-Sat 11.30 pm; closed Sun.

Ginger & White Hampstead NW3 £14 333
4a-5a, Perrins Ct   020 7431 9098   9–2A

This "ever-popular" haunt serves "excellent coffee", while "the food menu is perfectly acceptable", and includes a "really precise and delicious shakshuka". Any negatives? – "finding a spot can be a trial". / NW3 1QS; www.gingerandwhite.com; @gingerandwhitelondon; Mon-Fri 5.30 pm, Sat & Sun 6 pm; closed Mon-Sun D; no Amex; no booking.

Ginza Onodera SW1 £100   3|2|3
15 Bury St   020 7839 1101   3–3D
Some "outstanding fine Japanese cooking" is reported at this upmarket St James's basement, which has been through a number of names and owners in recent times, and re-opened in its current guise in Autumn 2021. It comprises a ground-floor bar, plus 70-seat subterranean dining space, incorporating three six-seat counters for teppanyaki, a robata chef's table, and a sushi counter. There is still the odd "disappointing" report, but the overall direction of travel here seems promising. / SW1S 6AL; www.ginza-stjames.com; @ginzastjames; Tue-Fri & Sat-Mon 10.30 pm.

Giulia W12 NEW £56   3|3|2
77 Askew Rd   020 8743 0572   8–1B
"Replacing the much-loved Adams Cafe" is no easy task, but this "new family-run Italian" in up-and-coming 'Askew Village' is "a local winner" on all accounts. "The small team provides a short, straightforward menu (pasta is homemade and delicious) and the brief wine list hits the right notes". / W12; Tue-Sat 10.30 pm, Sun 10 pm; closed Tue-Sun L, closed Mon.

Gloria EC2 £61   2|3|5
54-56 Great Eastern Street   no tel   13–1B
"It's such a lot of fun" (whether you eat "upstairs – think explosion in a china/flower shop; or downstairs – sexy booths") at the Big Mamma Group's "kitsch-but-in-a-great-way" Italian, which imports the brio of an imagined Amalfi coast, circa 1972, to this Shoreditch corner site. "You need to love a party" though – the filling cod-Italian cuisine is "not bad" but "doesn't match the buzz or the queues". / EC2E 3QR; www.bigmammagroup.com; @bigmamma.uk; Mon-Wed 10.45 pm, Thu-Sat 11 pm, Sun 10.30 pm.

La Goccia WC2 £62   3|2|4
Floral Court, off Floral Street   020 7305 7676   5–3C
The "gorgeous setting", in Covent Garden's newish Floral Court development and with an outside courtyard, is a highpoint at this venture from the family who own Richmond's well-known Petersham Nurseries: "perfect for a date". Although "expensive", it was complimented more often this year for its "lovely", simple Italian cuisine. / WC2W 9DJ; petershamnurseries.com/dine/la-goccia; @petershamnurseries; Tue, Wed 10 pm, Thu-Sat 11 pm, Sun 6 pm; closed Sun D, closed Mon.

Goddard & Gibbs E1 NEW £69
100 Shoreditch High St   020 7613 9802   13–1B
Occupying the former site of Hoi Polloi (RIP), this large, mid-2022 newcomer is part of the recently relaunched One Hundred Shoreditch hotel. Complete with Raw Bar, the menu focus is on fish, although with choices for non-pescatarians. An active PR campaign succeeded in dragging in both The Sunday Times's Marina O'Loughlin and The Guardian's Grace Dent, both of whom delivered a mixed verdict ("pleasurable rather than jaw-dropping…", "doing the very minimum it could to push out hundreds of covers a day, with few flourishes, scant innovation and often little flavour"). / E1 6JN; www.goddardandgibbs.com; @goddardandgibbs; Mon-Sun 11 pm.

Goddards At Greenwich SE10 £25   3|4|3
22 King William Walk   020 8305 9612   1–3D
"Pie 'n' mash is now fashionable" (as reported in GQ magazine) "and the grandkids love it". This "very friendly" outlet near Greenwich Park from the Goddard family – one of London's traditional pie-shop dynasties – is a good place to try the capital's original fast food, with some updates on the menu to offer more choice. / SE10 9HU; www.goddardsatgreenwich.co.uk; @goddardspies; Sun-Thu 7.30 pm, Fri & Sat 8 pm.

F S A

Gold W11 £71 2 2 4
95-97 Portobello Road   020 3146 0747   7–2B

"Youthful, hip and bursting at the seams", this "great W11 hang out" is a famous old pub once visited by Bill Clinton, now converted into a nightclubby setting by Nick House of Mahiki and Whisky Mist fame. The "tapas-style" food from ex-River Café chef Theo Hill "is hit and miss, with some great and some disappointing dishes" – "but that doesn't seem to bother the crowd, who are there mostly to drink, see and be seen" and soak up the "exciting", "Tel Aviv-style rustic ambience". It has a "beautiful courtyard" too, complete with palm trees and a glass ceiling. / W11 2QB; goldnottinghill.com; @goldnottinghill; Mon-Thu 12.30 am, Fri & Sat 1 am, Sun 11.30 pm.

Gold Mine W2 £45 3 2 2
102 Queensway   020 7792 8331   7–2C

"You'll likely find yourselves among Asian customers" at this classic Cantonese restaurant in Queensway. While perhaps "not the best Chinese food London has to offer", the cooking provides "the real thing", with roast duck the most recommended dish here. / W2 3RR; @goldmine.bayswater; Mon-Sun 11 pm.

Golden Dragon W1 £49 3 2 3
28-29 Gerrard St   020 7734 1073   5–3A

This "boisterous" stalwart is a prime choice on Chinatown's main drag – "the dim sum especially is a cut above all its rivals, but all the dishes are just done better here". / W1 6JW; www.gdlondon.co.uk; @goldendragon_uk; Mon, Wed-Sun 10 pm; closed Mon, Wed-Sun L, closed Tue.

Golden Hind W1 £49 3 2 2
73 Marylebone Ln   020 7486 3644   2–1A

"Great fish 'n' chips" is to be found at this Maylebone veteran – one of London's oldest chippies, given that it first opened in 1914. Your order can be steamed with olive oil and oregano and accompanied with mozzarella fritters and asparagus for those who want a change from the standard deep-fried option, and there's a mouth-watering selection of old-school English puds including spotted dick, rhubarb crumble and treacle syrup sponge, all served with custard or ice cream. / W1U 2PN; www.goldenhindrestaurant.com; Mon-Sat 10 pm; closed Sun.

Good Earth £75 3 3 2
233 Brompton Rd, SW3   020 7584 3658   6–2C
143-145 The Broadway, NW7   020 8959 7011   1–1B
11 Bellevue Rd, SW17   020 8682 9230   11–2C

"Several clicks above your average Chinese..." – this "very popular" family-owned chain with sites in Knightsbridge, Mill Hill, Wandsworth Common and Esher – remains a long-running success story. Purists might find the food too "safe" (and the menu "has changed little over the years"). Yet even one critic who has "yet to be convinced by the concept of a posh Chinese" feels "they give it a good go" here, and despite the "pretty punchy prices" most diners feel the experience is "well worth the extra money".
/ www.goodearthgroup.co.uk.

Goodman £95 3 3 2
24-26 Maddox St, W1   020 7499 3776   3–2C
3 South Quay, E14   020 7531 0300   12–1C
11 Old Jewry, EC2   020 7600 8220   10–2C

"Still the go-to New York-style steak house" – this Russian-owned chain has *"a distinct style from Hawksmoor" which it somewhat resembles; and though its fanbase is much smaller, it's held in equal regard by those who recommend it. Well located for expense accounters, its branches in Mayfair, the City and Canary Wharf are a "safe bet for good steak" and deliver a straightforward formula inspiring few grumbles. "The prices aren't dirt cheap, but those AAA steaks never were".* / www.goodmanrestaurants.com; goodman_london.

FSA RATINGS: FROM 1 POOR — 5 EXCEPTIONAL

Gordon Ramsay SW3 £210 332
68-69 Royal Hospital Rd   020 7352 4441   6–3D

Fans do rave over the "*beautiful cuisine from wonderful Matt Abé*", "*exceptional*" service and "*memorable*" all-round experience created by the f-word chef's original HQ. And there's little question that the classical-ish cuisine here is highly "*technically accomplished*", service "*friendly and well-informed*" ("*too much of it, if anything*") and the overall impression "*classy*". But it continues to struggle against diners' sky-high expectations, often inspired by Michelin's somewhat unfathomable continuation of its three-star rating promoting it as being at the very pinnacle of UK dining. A relatively small venue in deepest Chelsea, "*the dining room has the air of an art deco cruise ship, with its neutral tones and carpet*", all of which creates a setting that's "*tranquil*", but too "*cold*" or "*bland*" to some tastes. And when it comes to gastronomy, a typical critical report of the cuisine would be that it's "*not bad, some of it very good, but… frankly I was expecting outstanding… and it was a far cry from that… to the extent it was my biggest disappointment of the year*". It doesn't help that it's "*hugely expensive, which always puts on the dampers*". (Footnote – a number of reporters wish ex-maître d' Jean-Claude Breton well: "*thank you JC, enjoy your very well-deserved retirement!*") / SW3 4HP; www.gordonramsay.com; @Restaurantgordonramsay; Tue-Sat 11 pm; closed Sun & Mon; No jeans; booking max 9 may apply.

Gordon's Wine Bar WC2 £43 225
47 Villiers St   020 7930 1408   5–4D

"*Love it… I always feel like a spy when I drink there…*" – London's oldest wine bar (est. 1890), near Embankment tube, is worth a visit for its "*great interior*" alone, with ancient brick-lined vaults, but it also boasts one of the capital's biggest outside terraces. You no longer queue for the cold cuts, cheese and pies – they bring them to you with waiter service. The "*excellent selection of wines*" is by far the greater attraction. / WC2N 6NE; gordonswinebar.com; @gordonswinebar; Mon-Sat 11 pm, Sun 10 pm; no booking.

Gourmet Burger Kitchen £37 322
Branches throughout London

"*Quality burgers at a great price point*" make the capital's original posh burger chain "*a family favourite*" for many fans – "*the kids always want to go back*". Founded 22 years ago in Battersea's 'Nappy Valley' by a bunch of Kiwis, the group expanded rapidly and changed hands three times before hitting the buffers. Its fortunes appear to have stabilised since Birmingham-based 'chicken king' Ranjit Boparan bought it out of administration in 2020, although the 60-odd branches have been whittled down to 37 – half of them in London. / www.gbkinfo.com.

Goya SW1 £42 332
34 Lupus St   020 7976 5309   2–4C

"*This tapas bar/restaurant has been around forever*" – 30 years, to be precise, of serving solid Hispanic cuisine to a happy Pimlico clientele – "*but the standard is hard to beat*". "*The place is a delight. It doesn't rock, but it does everything else brilliantly!*". / SW1V 3EB; www.goyarestaurant.co.uk; Mon-Sat midnight, Sun 11.30 pm.

Granary Square Brasserie N1 £49 223
1 Granary Square   020 3940 1000   9–3C

This "*beautiful venue*" near King's Cross with "*lovely outside tables*" is part of Richard Caring's Ivy Collection and comes with similar pros and cons. It's "*lively and buzzy*", and a handy location makes it "*a fun place to meet friends*", but it takes flak for "*slow and unprofessional*" service and food that's "*the usual brasserie fare, but doesn't feel like it's cooked with love*" and "*isn't worth the price*". / N1N 4AB; www.granarysquarebrasserie.com; @granarysquarebrasserie; Mon-Sat midnight, Sun 11 pm; booking max 12 may apply.

F S A

Grand Trunk Road E18 £68 443
219 High Street 020 8505 1965 1–1D

"We are so lucky to have such a great restaurant on our doorstep!" – Rajesh Suri's (who managed Mayfair's Tamarind for 14 years) "exceptional local" is "a far cry from your usual Indian restaurant, so any extra expense is worth it" for the "delicious and unusual flavours, all well presented". "Glad I live in E18!" / E18 2PB; www.gtrrestaurant.co.uk; @grandtrunk_road; Tue-Sat 10.30 pm, Sun 8.30 pm; closed Tue-Thu L, closed Mon; no shorts.

Granger & Co £62 222
237-239 Pavilion Rd, SW1 020 3848 1060 6–2D
105 Marylebone High Street, W1 020 8079 7120 2–1A **NEW**
175 Westbourne Grove, W11 020 7229 9111 7–1B
Stanley Building, St Pancras Sq, N1 020 3058 2567 9–3C
The Buckley Building, 50 Sekforde St, EC1 020 7251 9032 10–1A

"Best brunch in London!" is an oft-repeated claim for Aussie celeb chef Bill Granger's chain of "pleasant light and airy" spaces, which its army of fans see as "perfect breakfast venues, with great food, strong coffee, and a buzzy atmosphere". The "varied" menu has the "Antipodean slant" you'd expect, but arguably "the food doesn't quite live up to its style" and "it pays to be adventurous with your ordering: be bold and try something new! – the safe options are very… safe". In August 2022, the group adds a fifth Marylebone site in what older readers will remember as 'Maison Sagne'.
/ grangerandco.com; grangerandco.

The Grazing Goat W1 £83 333
6 New Quebec St 020 7724 7243 2–2A

Promising 'layers of country pub' on its website, this popular pub/restaurant (also with rooms) is tucked away in a Marylebone townhouse. Part of the posh Cubitt House group, it offers "decent upmarket pub fare with reliable cooking and service" in a buzzing setting. / W1H 7RQ; www.thegrazinggoat.co.uk; @cubitthouse; Mon-Sat 9 pm, Sun 8 pm.

Great Nepalese NW1 £42 343
48 Eversholt St 020 7388 6737 9–3C

Time to kill near Euston station? Grab a bite at this "long standing, quality local" – a sweet-looking, little curry house (est 1982), still proudly displaying its Fay Maschler review from shortly after it opened. "It always delivers good dishes" – Nepalese specials are best – but prices are not as 'bargain basement' as its appearance might suggest. / NW1 1DA; www.great-nepalese.co.uk; Mon-Sat 10.30 pm; closed Sun.

Green Cottage NW3 £48 322
9 New College Pde 020 7722 5305 9–2A

"We keep coming and they keep feeding us" – this "longstanding, basic Chinese restaurant" in Swiss cottage "never lets you down", serving some of the "best roast duck outside Chinatown and Queensway". / NW3 5EP; Mon-Sun 11 pm; no Amex.

Greenberry Café NW1 £50 334
101 Regents Park Road 020 7483 3765 9–2B

"A favourite brunch venue" – this "lovely casual local café/restaurant" in Primrose Hill "offers all-day dining with plenty of choice from an eclectic menu". Top Tip – "winter lunch in one of their outdoor heated 'castaway shacks'". / NW1 8UR; greenberrycafe.co.uk; @greenberrycafe; Sun & Mon 3 pm, Tue-Sat 10 pm; closed Sun & Mon D.

The Grill at The Dorchester W1 £108 4 4 4
53 Park Lane   020 7629 8888   3–3A

This "stunning and beautiful dining room", off the hotel's main 'Promenade', inherited its Moorish décor from the 1930s and is currently riding high on the "wonderful dining experience" created by 27-year-old wunderkind chef, Tom Booton's cuisine: "a serious talent going right to the very top; and a humble and approachable guy whose restaurant reflects this ethos". Top Tip – "the set lunch is one of the capital's biggest bargains" and is great on a Sunday here. / W1K 1QA; www.dorchestercollection.com/en/london/the-dorchester; @thedorchester; Tue-Sat 10 pm, Sun 4 pm; closed Tue-Fri L closed Sun D, closed Mon; no trainers.

Grumbles SW1 £47 3 4 3
35 Churton St   020 7834 0149   2–4B

This "cosy, traditional and relaxed bistro" celebrates its 60th anniversary next year, and is proudly resistant to change: the wooden furnishings remain intact from the original £300 fit-out in 1964. It makes for "an unstuffy environment where you feel at home from the moment you walk in", and the food – solid, old-school British bistro fare – is "excellent" by the standards of "cheap 'n' cheerful" scoff. / SW1V 2LT; www.grumblesrestaurant.co.uk; @grumblesrestaurant; Mon-Sun 10 pm.

The Guildford Arms SE10 £56 3 3 3
55 Guildford Grove   020 8691 6293   1–3D

"'Cut-above' pub food" is served in this "beautiful Georgian tavern" in Greenwich, whose garden has been "transformed into a well-designed and extensive eating area" ("far nicer than the makeshift tents that often emerged in the pandemic"). / SE10 8JY; www.theguildfordarms.co.uk; @guildfordarms_; Tue-Thu 9 pm, Fri & Sat 9.30 pm, Sun 8.30 pm; closed Mon; payment – credit card only.

The Guinea Grill W1 £101 2 2 4
30 Bruton Pl   020 7409 1728   3–3B

"Proper man food!" is to be found at this "very old-school" Mayfair favourite – a dining room behind a well-known Young's pub in a cute central mews, which feels "like a different century" (est 1952). "If you like steak in a traditional environment", look no further: "there's an extensive menu including a mighty mixed grill, a variety of prime grass-fed steaks or tempting traditional pies". "Best of all, you can then go on for drinks in the attached pub!" No hiding, though, that its performance has taken a knock in these troubled times. While it's always been "a bit expensive (but completely unique)", some meals this year badly missed the mark due to service that was "nothing special" or poor preparation ("The Guinea used to be one of my favourite destinations for a sumptuous piece of charcoal-grilled beef, but the rib steak on my last visit was so tough it has hardly fit to eat").
BREAKING NEWS: *In July 2022, Oisin Rogers, who has managed the dining room here for the last 6 years, announced he is moving on to pastures new.* / W1J 6NL; www.theguinea.co.uk; @guineagrill; Mon-Sun 10 pm.

The Gun E14 £69 3 3 4
27 Coldharbour   020 7515 5222   12–1C

Directly across the Thames from the O2 – and a short drive from Canary Wharf – this Grade II listed tavern benefits from a superb waterside location, characterful old interior and large modern terrace. Nowadays run by Fuller's, it's not a foodie pub as it was a few years ago, but still wins praise for "great food, super cocktails and friendly staff". / E14 9NS; www.thegundocklands.com; @thegundocklands; Mon-Sat 9.30 pm, Sun 7 pm.

FSA

Gunpowder £52 4|3|3
20 Greek Street, W1 020 3813 7796 5–2A NEW
One Tower Bridge, 4 Crown Square, SE1 awaiting tel 10–4D
11 Whites Row, E1 020 7426 0542 13–2C
"Tops for combining punchy tastes and value": this Indian street-food trio –
in Spitalfields, near Tower Bridge, and – since late 2021 – now in Soho too –
offers a "distinct" and "modern spin" on Indian cuisine. Although the plates
are small, "it's amazing how they deliver such big flavours".
/ www.gunpowderlondon.com; gunpowder_london.

Gura Gura WC2 NEW
19 Slingsby Place no tel 5–3B
Set to be an October 2022 debut in Covent Garden's 'The Yards'
development – this new pan-Asian bar and kitchen concept will be a 110-
seater spread over two floors and offering a mix of sushi, sashimi, dim sum
and small plates. A walk-through wine tunnel will feature at the entrance.
/ WC2W 9DL; Mon-Wed 10 pm, Thu-Sat 10.30 pm.

Gustoso Ristorante & Enoteca SW1 £58 3|2|2
35 Willow Pl 020 7834 5778 2–4B
A "solid performer", this "reliable Italian occupies an area not over-blessed
with good places" – between Westminster Cathedral and Victoria station in
Pimlico. "Lovely wild boar ragu with pappardelle". / SW1P 1JH;
www.ristorantegustoso.co.uk; @gustoso_ristorante; Mon-Sat 9.30 pm; closed Sun.

Gymkhana W1 £84 5|3|3
42 Albemarle St 020 3011 5900 3–3C
The "standard-bearer for subcontinental food in London" – the Sethi family's
"exceptional" Mayfair destination nowadays ranks in the Top-20 most-
mentioned restaurants in our annual diners' poll, and is the highest-ranking
Indian. "An amazing selection of traditional dishes not found anywhere else"
delivers "top-quality flavours relying on taste, not heat" ("so delicious, I
couldn't stop eating!"), all in a "vibey" two-floor setting, with Indian-inspired
décor referencing Indian clubs and mansions. "Unbeatable... if you can get
in, that is..." / W1S 4JH; www.gymkhanalondon.com; @gymkhanalondon; Mon-Sun
10.30 pm; payment – credit card only.

Haché £47 4|3|3
95-97 High Holborn, WC1 020 7242 4580 2–1D
329-331 Fulham Rd, SW10 020 7823 3515 6–3B
24 Inverness St, NW1 020 7485 9100 9–3B
37 Bedford Hill, SW12 020 8772 9772 11–2C
153 Clapham High St, SW4 020 7738 8760 11–2D
147-149 Curtain Rd, EC2 020 7739 8396 13–1B
"Doing what they do very well" – "top burgers" are presented with a veneer
of Parisian sophistication at this seven-strong chain, popular not just for their
value but their "lovely" styling too. / www.hacheburgers.com.

Hackney Coterie E8 £46 3|4|3
230b Dalston Lane 020 7254 4101 14–1B
"Great value and unusual tasting menus, nice wines & lovely service" win all-
round applause for this yearling in a Hackney Downs warehouse from
Anthony Lyon (of Lyon's in Crouch End). Head chef Giuseppe Pepe (ex-Pidgin
and Marksman) is responsible for the seasonal, minimal-waste menu, and
his "food is beautifully presented and served". / E8 1LA; www.hackneycoterie.net;
@hackneycoterie; Wed & Thu 10 pm, Fri & Sat 10.30 pm; closed Wed & Thu L, closed
Mon & Tue & Sun.

F S A

Hakkasan £120 **3 1 2**
17 Bruton St, W1   020 7907 1888   3–2C
8 Hanway Pl, W1   020 7927 7000   5–1A
"Fantastic, modern Chinese food" has long driven this famous Asian phenomenon. Launched in 2001, it has gone from a big, "overly dark" and nightclubby basement ("horribly loud music") near Tottenham Court Road to spawn a very glam Mayfair offshoot; as well as 12 international spin-offs from NYC to Mumbai. "Eye-watering prices" and a mixed record when it comes to service, have always inspired jibes of "style over substance" here. But perhaps due to post-Covid challenges, such problems are in the foreground this year. Given that there have been blips before, they will probably get a grip. But it's hard at present to ignore the many former fans saying "these ageing stalwarts need a refresh" ("I used to love it, but I think the bill now is silly and unjustified and the service is half-hearted and surly").
/ www.hakkasan.com; hakkasanlondon; no trainers, no sportswear.

Halo Burger EC2 £19 **3 3 2**
105 Great Eastern Street   020 7490 0444   13–1B
For a meat-free burger, this tiny brand (the first vegan restaurant in Europe to use 'Beyond Meat' in its patties) is well worth a try if you need a bite near the Old Street roundabout, or are down Pop Brixton way. / EC2E 3JD; haloburger.co.uk; @haloburgeruk; Sun-Thu 10.30 pm, Fri & Sat 11 pm.

Ham NW6 £68 **4 4 3**
238 West End Lane   020 7813 0168   1–1B
"We are lucky to have this place on our doorstep!" – this *"cosy and informal"* West Hampstead five-year-old is an *"affordable luxury"* for its local fan club, where *"always-excellent bistro food"* is *"beautifully presented in sensible portions"*. Top Tip – *"the 6pm early-bird offer makes it amazing value for money, too"*. / NW6 1LG; www.hamwesthampstead.com; @Hamwhampstead; Tue-Sat 10 pm, Sun 3 pm; closed Sun D, closed Mon.

Ham Yard Restaurant,
Ham Yard Hotel W1 £66 **2 2 4**
1 Ham Yd   020 3642 1007   4–3D
"A quiet haven tucked away near Piccadilly Circus" – in summer, the outside courtyard is so peaceful it's hard to believe just how central you are. *"A lovely afternoon tea at sensible prices"* is the top culinary attraction here. At other times, the *"stylish"* setting is *"conducive to a relaxed meal"* but its *"bistro-style fare"* is a case of *"nothing to criticise, but with vastly better places in easy reach"*. / W1D 7DT;
www.firmdalehotels.com/hotels/london/ham-yard-hotel/ham-yard-bar-restaurant; @firmdale_hotels; Mon-Sat 11 pm, Sun 10.30 pm.

The Hampshire W6 £57 **3 4 3**
227 King Street   020 8748 3391   8–2B
Formerly 'The Hampshire Hog' – this stylish pub near Hammersmith Town Hall has been taken over and 'gone Indian' in recent times. Nipping in for a pint, little has changed, but food-wise it's more like a modern curry house. They are trying hard and it shows in the quality food and responsive service. And the big investment in their large, attractive garden to the rear really pays dividends in summer months. / W6 9JT; www.the-hampshire.com; @thehampshire; Mon-Fri midnight, Sat & Sun 11 pm.

Hankies £41 **3 2 2**
61 Upper Berkeley Street, W1   020 7958 3222   2–2A
67 Shaftesbury Avenue, W1   020 7871 6021   5–3A
Tapas based on Delhi street food is served in a roti at this Indian duo, with branches in Soho and in a smart hotel dining room near Marble Arch, for whom feedback remains limited but upbeat. (The Paddington branch has now closed). / www.hankies.london.

FSA

Hannah SE1 £122 3|3|2
Southbank Riverside, Belvedere Road   020 3802 0402   2–3D
This little-known "hidden Japanese gem" near the London Eye showcases the skills of chef-patron Daisuke Shimoyama, who spent six years as head chef at Umu in Mayfair before launching his own venture at this hotel in the former County Hall. His omakase "tasting menu is particularly impressive" and is matched by an interesting sake list selected by the chef, while budget options at lunchtime include a bento box. / SE1 7PB; www.hannahrestaurant.london; @hannah_japanese_restaurant; Wed 9 pm; closed Wed L, closed Mon & Tue, Thu-Sat & Sun; no trainers; credit card deposit required to book.

Hans' Bar & Grill SW1 £84 3|3|3
164 Pavilion Road   020 7730 7000   6–2D
On a most chichi little thoroughfare, this café/bar and all-day restaurant is part of nearby luxury boutique hotel 100 Cadogan Gardens. It charges Chelsea prices from breakfast on, but fans say it's a "perfect spot to have lunch when on a shopping expedition". / SW1S 0AW; www.hansbarandgrill.com; @hansbarandgrill; Mon-Sat 10 pm, Sun 7 pm.

Hare & Tortoise £43 3|3|2
11-13 The Brunswick, WC1   020 7278 9799   2–1D
373 Kensington High St, W14   020 7603 8887   8–1D
156 Chiswick High Rd, W4   020 8747 5966   8–2A
38 Haven Grn, W5   020 8810 7066   1–2A
296-298 Upper Richmond Rd, SW15   020 8394 7666   11–2B
90 New Bridge St, EC4   020 7651 0266   10–2A
The "mix of Asian food slightly adapted for all tastes" and offered at "really reasonable prices" makes this long-running chain "a family favourite". Founded at the Brunswick Centre in Bloomsbury 26 years ago, it now has branches in Ealing, Putney, Kensington and Chiswick, along with two delivery-only kitchens. Top Tip – "you can't beat the curry laksa".
/ www.hareandtortoise.co.uk.

Harrods Dining Hall SW1 £84 3|3|4
Harrods, 87-135 Brompton Road   no tel   6–1D
Worth it just for the gorgeous Edwardian tiling of this famous space: built to house the Harrods Food Hall's meat and fishmongers counters, and nowadays hosting London's swishest food court, with six outlets – Kama by Vineet; Kerridge's Fish & Chips; Pasta Evangelists; Caviar House & Prunier; as well as a grill and sushi bar. / SW1S 7XL; www.harrods.com/en-gb/restaurants; @harrodsfood; Tue-Sat 11 pm, Mon 9 pm, Sun 6 pm.

Harrods Social SW1 £78 3|3|3
87-135 Brompton Road   020 7225 6800   6–1D
"In the lower ground floor of Harrods opposite the wine department", this luxe brasserie from Jason Atherton's Social Group opened immediately after the pandemic. Unsurprisingly, prices are not bargain basement, but even those complaining about them rate the food as good, and the store at last has the comfortable, modern restaurant space it formerly lacked. Top Tip – very affordable set menu, but you must have booked ahead. / SW1S 7XL; www.harrods.com/en-gb/restaurants/harrods-social-by-jason-atherton; @harrodsfood; Tue-Sat 11 pm, Mon 9 pm, Sun 6 pm; closed Sun D.

Harry's Bar W1 £69 2️⃣2️⃣3️⃣
30-34 James Street   020 3971 9444   3–1A
Carrying the name of Richard Caring's famous Harry's Bar in Mayfair (which is still members only), this sub-brand spin-off near Selfridges aims to encapsulate classic La Dolce Vita-style glamour. All of the limited feedback acknowledges decent Italian cooking, but is riddled with quibbles feeding back to the level of expense ("good food but the tables are packed too tightly and we'll give it miss in future, as it did not have the right ambience for the price…"; "food was mediocre at the ridiculous price…"). / W1W 1EU; www.harrys-bar.co.uk; @harrysldn; Mon-Sun 11 pm.

Harwood Arms SW6 £81 3️⃣2️⃣3️⃣
Walham Grove   020 7386 1847   6–3A
"The best scotch eggs in London!" are a renowned attraction at this "lovely" boozer in the backstreets of deepest Fulham, whose food aristocracy backers include the Ledbury's Brett Graham, as well as game expert Mike Robinson. On the back of its "excellent and robust" cooking – particularly "perfect game" – it is again voted London's No. 1 pub in our annual diners' poll but, unsurprisingly "trying to get a table takes some planning: it's not a pub you can pop into if the mood takes you, especially when Chelsea are playing at home". It's also the case that service has been "a bit mixed" in recent times and that the cuisine – "though still pretty good, feels like it isn't quite at the standard it was when Sally Abé was in charge of the kitchen". / SW6 1QP; www.harwoodarms.com; @theharwoodarms; Mon-Thu, Sat 9.15 pm, Fri 9.15pm, Sun 8.15 pm; closed Mon-Thu L; credit card required to book.

Hashi SW20 £53 3️⃣3️⃣2️⃣
54 Durham Rd   020 8944 1888   11–2A
This "very good neighbourhood Japanese", one of the best in the Raynes Park enclave, earns plaudits year after year for its "excellent food and service". / SW20 0TW; @hashi_japanese_restaurant; Tue-Sat 10 pm, Sun 2.30 pm; closed Tue-Fri L closed Sun D, closed Mon; no Amex.

Hatched SW11 £79 4️⃣3️⃣2️⃣
189 Saint John's Hill   020 7738 0735   11–2C
This "buzzing local" brings "casual fine dining" to Battersea, with highly focused young chef Shane Marshall and his team striving to create an 'uncluttered' dining experience. That may sound like hard work, but "everything tastes good and portions are hearty". "Eat at the counter if you can for a great insight into how to inject maximum flavours into a dish". / SW11 1TH; www.hatchedsw11.com; @hatchedsw11; Tue-Sat 11 pm, Sun 1.30 pm; closed Tue-Thu L closed Sun D, closed Mon.

Haugen E20 £70 2️⃣2️⃣2️⃣
9 Endeavour Square   020 4568 1444   14–1D
Spectacular design and proximity to Westfield Stratford are not enough to win this Alpine-themed D&D London property much in the way of feedback. Such as we received is downbeat ("disappointing… Schnitzel done badly") and it's hard to demur from Grace Dent's damning assessment in her October 2021 review: a "huge, tourist-magnet restaurant"… "utterly hampered by someone's desperate need to make profit". / E20 1JN; www.haugen-restaurant.com; @haugenldn; Sun-Thu 9.45 pm, Fri & Sat 10.30 pm.

The Havelock Tavern W14 £59 3️⃣2️⃣4️⃣
57 Masbro Rd   020 7603 5374   8–1C
"Popular in the neighbourhood and very easy to recommend" – this blue-tiled Victorian tavern behind Olympia excels for "good, slightly pimped gastropub fare". Launched as a more foodie operation in 1996, it still draws fans from across west London and beyond. / W14 0LS; www.havelocktavern.com; @havelocktavern; Mon-Sat 9.30 pm, Sun 9 pm.

FSA

Hawker's Kitchen N1 £22 ५३२
64 Caledonian Road 020 8458 2064 9–3D

Mano Muthu worked at Euston's legendary Roti King for many years, and opened this simple shop-conversion caff, north of King's Cross, in mid 2021. The cooking here has more of a south Indian spin than its rival, with the inclusion of a selection of dosas, and fans (who include the Evening Standard's Jimi Famurewa) feel its "exceptional dishes potentially beat Roti King for the title of best rotis in London!" / N1 9DP; www.hawkerskitchen.com; @hawkers.kitchen; Mon-Sun 9.50 pm.

Hawksmoor £94 २२२
5a Air St, W1 020 7406 3980 4–4C
11 Langley St, WC2 020 7420 9390 5–2C
3 Yeoman's Row, SW3 020 7590 9290 6–2C
16 Winchester Walk, SE1 020 7234 9940 10–4C
Wood Wharf, 1 Water Street, E14 020 3988 0510 12–1C **NEW**
157 Commercial St, E1 020 7426 4850 13–2B
10-12 Basinghall St, EC2 020 7397 8120 10–2C

"Bloody good, succulent steaks", with "epic cocktails and wines", all served in "rather clubby", "classy" surroundings is a formula that's won fame and fortune for Huw Gott and Will Beckett's steakhouse phenomenon. "Many happy afternoons have been lost in these places!", which continue to be voted as London's "best steak chain by far", and "a go-to for business". "Everything is top-notch: the quality and cookery of the beef; the exemplary seafood (be it Salcombe crab on toast or their lobster); even down to their excellent sides of mac 'n' cheese, bone marrow or Caesar salad". However, a visit "is not exactly easy on the wallet". "It's verrrrrry expensive" (and "if you go with mates who like to chug back the wine, the bill will be massive!"). And ratings are coming under ever-more pressure due to "staff who seem unable to cope", or meals with "too many misses at too heavy a price to be a reliable bet". Last year, the team expanded to Manhattan and also opened a "stunning floating boat/barge" in the docks at Canary Wharf. Later in 2022, the group will also add a Liverpool branch to rival Manchester's; and a few months later make a Dublin debut on College Green too. "Are they losing some of their je-ne-sais-quoi as they get bigger and badder? There's a sneaking suspicion the lustre is being slightly lost." / www.thehawksmoor.com; SRA-3 stars.

Haya W11 £56 ३४३
184a Kensington Park Road 0203 995 4777 7–1B

This attractive modern Notting Hill café is inspired by visits to Tel Aviv, and the "energetic kitchen produces a small range of well thought-out dishes". Staff are "really friendly" too. / W11 2ES; haya.london; @haya.ldn; Mon-Sun 11.30 pm; payment – credit card only.

Haz £62 ३३२
10 Upper St Martin's Lane, WC2 no tel 5–3B **NEW**
9 Cutler St, E1 020 7929 7923 10–2D
14 Finsbury Square, EC2 020 7920 9944 13–2A
34 Foster Ln, EC2 020 7600 4172 10–2B
64 Bishopsgate, EC2 020 7628 4522 10–2D
6 Mincing Ln, EC3 020 7929 3173 10–3D

"Super-fresh" food, including "especially good starters and mezze", "friendly service" and "very good value for money" are the hallmarks of this "very good Turkish chain in the City". There's also a "large range of vegetarian dishes". The six branches are all heaving at lunchtime, but "St Paul's is the most spacious, in a great setting near the cathedral and much quieter too, especially at the weekends". / www.hazrestaurant.co.uk.

F S A

Heddon Yokocho W1 £29 3|2|3
8 Heddon Street   no tel   4–3B

This "wonderful Japanese noodle shop just off of Regent Street" is modelled on the 'yokocho' alleyways of old Tokyo, its retro 1970s theme lending itself well to pedestrianised Heddon Street. There's "great-tasting ramen with regular specials" and it "can be busy". Launched two years ago by the Japan Centre team, it also has branches in Panton Street, Soho, and Westfield Shepherd's Bush. / W1W 4BU; www.heddonyokocho.com; @ramenyokocho; Sun-Thu 10.30 pm, Fri & Sat 11 pm.

Hélène Darroze,
The Connaught Hotel W1 £174 2|3|2
Carlos Pl   020 3147 7200   3–3B

"The food is sublime"; "exceptional service" is "very friendly and interactive"; "… but WOW! the bill!!" – that's the headline story this year on this famous French chef's London outpost in this most blue-blooded of hotels. Despite numerous "exquisite" dishes featuring in reports, very many reporters feel "the costs verge on criminal" (and that "once you have seen the prices, it's difficult to get past them as the food just doesn't compensate for the full-blown attack on your wallet!!"). It doesn't help that the restaurant was recently elevated by Michelin to three stars, and that an "interesting but not amazing" experience can now seem well below par ("how this dining room has the tyre maker's top rating is beyond us"). And those seeking an old-school Mayfair environment should also look elsewhere: "the days of the Connaught of old are well and truly over", with "a conscious decision to move away from the previous old-style look" – a move dismissed by critics as "suburban lounge décor in what used used to be one of the handsomest dining rooms in London". / W1K 2AL; www.the-connaught.co.uk; @theconnaught; Tue-Sat 9.30 pm; closed Sun & Mon; no trainers.

Heliot Steak House WC2 £71 3|3|3
Cranbourn Street   020 7769 8844   5–3B

"To-die-for steaks" can be a surprise find in the restaurant overlooking the floor of London's biggest casino, on Leicester Square. It's a quirky space, in the circle of the former Hippodrome Theatre, and its USDA-imported meat and superior wines are something of a passion project for casino owner, Simon Thomas. / WC2H 7AJ; www.hippodromecasino.com; @hippodromecasino; Mon-Sat 1 am, Sun 11 pm; closed Mon-Fri L.

Helix (Searcys at The Gherkin) EC3 £86 3|3|5
30 St Mary Axe   0330 1070816   10–2D

"The food is as good as the view and worth a repeat-visit!", say fans of this iconic 40th-floor dining room, near the top floor of the Gherkin (run nowadays by the posh catering company, Searcys). "Great for a celebration and with reasonable prices (especially for London)", attractions include an "interesting and well-executed afternoon tea". / EC3E 8EP; searcysatthegherkin.co.uk/helix-restaurant; @searcysgherkin; Mon-Wed 10 pm, Fri & Sat 11 pm, Sun 6 pm; closed Sat L closed Sun D, closed Thu.

Hereford Road W2 £56 4|4|3
3 Hereford Rd   020 7727 1144   7–1B

St John alumnus chef Tom Pemberton "never disappoints" with his modern British cooking at the "small but not too noisy" Bayswater neighbourhood restaurant he opened in 2007, in a cleverly converted former butcher's shop. "Service is efficient, food is excellent and good value" and the "Sunday roasts are brilliant". / W2 4AB; www.herefordroad.org; Fri & Sat, Tue-Thu 10 pm, Sun 3.30 pm; closed Tue-Thu L closed Sun D, closed Mon.

FSA

Heritage SE21 £55 3|3|3
101 Rosedale Road   020 8761 4665   1–4D
This "impressive newcomer to the usually disappointing Dulwich food scene" arrived with a top pedigree for "high-class, high-taste" Indian cuisine under chef Dayashankar Sharma, a veteran of Tamarind, Zaika and Grand Trunk Road. The Guardian's Grace Dent was an early champion – "by rights it should become a south London classic" – but ratings are capped by one or two locals who feel it's "OK but not worth the hype". / SE21 8EZ; www.heritagedulwich.co.uk; @heritageindiandulwich; Tue-Sat 10.30 pm, Sun 9 pm; closed Tue-Fri L, closed Mon.

The Hero of Maida W9 £68 3|3|2
55 Shirland Rd   020 7266 9198   7–1C
This "great local Maida Vale gastropub" opened to considerable fanfare after an overhaul five years ago, and has now settled down with "a city-wide reputation for its Sunday lunches – you'll need to book well ahead". There's "a good selection of wine, beers and spirits", and it's "dog-friendly", too. / W9 2JD; theheromaidavale.co.uk; @theheroofmaida; Mon-Sat 11 pm, Sun 10 pm.

Hicce N1 £72 3|2|3
Coal Drops Yard   020 3869 8200   9–3C
"A stylish and trendy venue in stylish and trendy Coal Drops Yard" – Pip Lacey produces "an interesting menu of small plates" at this "lovely" venue, prominently situated within the development. There were some gripes this year about the "confusing wine list", and although everyone acknowledged some "superb" dishes, reservations remain about the value equation here ("great food, but the bill! For the size of the portions and overall amount of food and wine consumed it really felt steep!"). (Top Gear fans: Lacey now also has a side gig running the kitchen at Jeremy Clarkson's Diddly Squat Farm restaurant in the Cotswolds). / N1N 4AB; www.hicce.co.uk; @hiccelondon; Wed-Sat 11 pm, Sun 4 pm, Tue 10.30 pm; closed Tue L closed Sun D, closed Mon; payment – credit card only.

Above at Hide W1 £175 3|2|3
85 Piccadilly   020 3146 8666   3–4C
"There can be fewer better outlooks in London than the view over Green Park from the first-floor windows" of this beautifully appointed, modern Mayfair dining room. Overseen by Ollie Dabbous, the kitchen achieves "phenomenal flavour combinations and presentation" and "exceptional" overall results ("one of my best meals in London, maybe in life…"). And the "extraordinary wine list" is perhaps even more impressive: you can order any vintage from the acclaimed list sold by Hedonism Wines (who are under the same ownership), "or you can opt for the unusual and interesting wine pairings". But "any temptation to choose a nice bottle can be financially crippling!" – "when the final bill comes, it's a good job that you're already sitting down…". / W1W 8JB; www.hide.co.uk; @hide_restaurant; Mon-Sun 10 pm.

Hide Ground W1 £128 3|4|4
85 Piccadilly   020 3146 8666   3–4C
Fans say it's "nicer eating on the ground floor than being restricted to the much more expensive tasting menu upstairs" at this glossy landmark, opposite Green Park. Open from early morning, it's "an unusual but sophisticated haunt for breakfast in the heart of Mayfair". And, as with upstairs, "the availability of Hedonism Wines via a tablet, means the wine list has more toys than Hamleys!" / W1W; www.hide.co.uk; @hide_restaurant; Tue-Sun 9 pm; closed Tue L, closed Mon.

FSA RATINGS: FROM 1 POOR — 5 EXCEPTIONAL

F S A

High Road Brasserie W4 — £67 — 2️⃣2️⃣3️⃣
162-166 Chiswick High Rd   020 8742 7474   8–2A
The longstanding (est. 2006) Chiswick branch of Soho House seems to have been left behind as founder Nick Jones's empire spreads around the world. It occupies a prominent site on the busy High Road with a cute outside terrace, but generates precious little feedback these days – even by reporters who like its modern brasserie cooking. / W4 1PR; highroadbrasserie.co.uk; @highroadbrasserie; Sun-Wed 11 pm, Fri & Sat 1 am, Thu midnight; booking max 8 may apply.

High Timber EC4 — £66 — 3️⃣4️⃣3️⃣
8 High Timber Street   020 7248 1777   10–3B
This "high-grade hidden gem, just below the Millennium Bridge" – aka the Wobbly pedestrian bridge, directly opposite Tate Modern – is owned by a South African wine producer and "focuses on high-quality steaks and a Saffer-heavy wine list". If you're really interested, it's worth seeking out the "great off-menu wines". Top Tip – "the house biltong is delicious". / EC4V 3PA; www.hightimber.com; @hightimberrestaurant; Mon-Fri 10 pm; closed Sat & Sun.

Hispania EC3 — £79 — 3️⃣4️⃣4️⃣
72-74 Lombard Street   020 7621 0338   10–2C
This smart and expansive Hispanic spread over two floors in the heart of the City, opposite the Bank of England, scores well for its "classic tapas" and meat dishes, accompanied by a heavyweight wine list. / EC3V 9AY; www.hispanialondon.com; @hispanialondon; Mon-Fri 10 pm; closed Sat & Sun.

Hithe & Seek EC4 NEW — £41
60 Upper Thames Street   020 3988 0141   10–3B
"This low-key wine bar is an absolute gem", "hiding" in the new waterside Westin Hotel, "with a huge window looking across the Thames" to Tate Modern and Shakespeare's Globe theatre ("spending the evening watching the river drift by with a glass in hand is a really great way to end a tough week"). The interior has a contemporary Scandi look and the menu is put together by Jorge Colazo, ex-head chef at Aquavit. Feedback is too limited for a rating, but initial reports are upbeat, talking of "interesting wine and imaginative small plates". / EC4E 3AD; www.hitheandseek.com; @Hithe + Seek; Wed-Sat 11 pm; closed Wed-Sat L, closed Mon & Tue & Sun.

Holborn Dining Room WC1 — £83
252 High Holborn   020 3747 8633   2–1D
It's not been a vintage year for this grand British brasserie, known for its Pie Room, grills and charcuterie. Feedback has been very unsettled, with poor ratings across the board and reports of "stodgy and tasteless dishes", "breathtaking mark-ups", and "famous pies that were poorly cooked and really not worth the hype or the money". In June 2022, after the conclusion of our survey, the executive chef for the last eight years, Calum Franklin, moved on. Given that change seems to be afoot, we have left it unrated. / WC1V 7EN; www.holborndiningroom.com; @holborndiningroom; Mon-Fri 10 pm, Sat 10.30 pm, Sun 9.45 pm.

Holly Bush NW3 — £76 — 2️⃣2️⃣4️⃣
22 Holly Mount   020 7435 2892   9–1A
"A cosy gem" – this postcard-pretty Grade II listed Georgian tavern in a "lovely location" down a narrow street has been a must-visit in Hampstead village since Dr Johnson dropped in. It's an "expensive" place to eat by pub standards, but it's by no means a standard pub. "Go just for the real fire!". / NW3 6SG; www.hollybushhampstead.co.uk; @thehollybushpubhampstead; Mon-Thu 11 pm, Fri & Sat 10 pm, Sun 8 pm.

F S A

Holy Carrot SW1 NEW £56 344
Urban Retreat, 2-4 Hans Crescent   020 3897 0404   6–1D
"Every course can be eaten by a gluten-free vegan and yet your everyday carnivore will still enjoy the meal" at this new all-day vegan in a chichi 'Wellness & Beauty Salon' near Harrods. It receives nothing but praise: "this is what I call an outstanding vegan: imaginative food presented beautifully and they use NO sugar!" / SW1S 0LH; www.holycarrot.co.uk; @holycarrotrestaurant; Mon-Sat 10 pm, Sun 5 pm; closed Sun D.

Homeslice £54 433
50 James Street, W1   020 3034 0621   3–1A
13 Neal's Yd, WC2   020 7836 4604   5–2C
2 TV Centre, 101 Wood Ln White City, W12   020 3034 0381   1–2B
374-378 Old Street, EC1   020 3151 1121   13–1B
69-71 Queen Street, EC4   020 3034 0381   10–3C
"Still delivering on what it set out to do" – Alan and Mark Wogan's (yes, the late Terry's sons) hip pizza chain is the best-rated of the mid-sized groups, thanks to its *"huge and amazing pizzas with delicious and unusual toppings"* (*"now the choice is even easier with the 50/50 option!"*). Top Menu Tip – *"awesome vegan nduja pizza"* is amongst a growing number of plant-based options (and, from June 2022, they now have a fully meat-free site, in their 135-cover Shoreditch branch). / www.homeslicepizza.co.uk; homeslicedn.

Honest Burgers £37 322
Branches throughout London
"You get what it says on the tin" at this hugely popular, *"no frills"* (*"no starters and no puds"*) brand – the most commented-on burger multiple in our annual diners' poll – which is *"still consistently good, despite having turned into a massive chain"*. The *"top-quality meat and a good variety of specials"* (*"check out the latter for something a little different"*) are *"cooked to your liking from a basic menu"* and *"the wonderfully flavoured rosemary fries are a fab accompaniment"*. Having flirted with an all-vegan sub-brand in Leicester Square ('V Honest'), it was converted back to the core concept in June 2022. / www.honestburgers.co.uk.

Honey & Co WC1 £70
54 Lamb's Conduit Street   020 7388 6175   2–1D
After 10 years in which they helped establish modern Israeli cuisine as a new London staple, Sarit Packer and Itamar Srulovich (husband and wife) have relocated their much-loved venue from Warren Street to a much better Bloomsbury site that's double the size of the bijou original (the corner site that was formally Cigala, RIP). In its old home, fans were happy to be shoehorned in tighter than sardines for their "stellar" mezze-style inventions. Not everyone felt its performance always matched the hype, though, so we've left it unrated till after it's settled in here. But The Guardian's Grace Dent was impressed in a late July 2022 review, saying: "it's a little different now, perhaps more grown-up and formal, but the old loveliness is there in spades". / WC1W 3LW; www.honeyandco.co.uk; @honeyandcobloomsbury; Mon-Sat 10 pm; closed Sun.

F S A

Honey & Smoke W1 £69 4 2 2
216 Great Portland Street   020 7388 6175   2–1B

"Excellent Middle Eastern cooking, with some inventive dishes and excellent vegetarian options" continues to win applause for this grillhouse near Great Portland Street (sibling to Honey & Co). *"First-class natural ingredients are perfectly seasoned and prepared"*: *"in the wrong hands, these simple dishes could be bog-standard, but are lifted by excellent preparation (for instance, a simple tomato salad with a super, herby dressing)"*. *"Shame the restaurant is so Spartan, noisy and uncomfortable"*, though – *"it's not the place for a night out, but good for lunch or a quick bite"*. Top Menu Tip – the cheesecake, which Giles Coren from The Times says is *"the business… life-changing. Epochal. Aeonic"*. / W1W 5QW; honeyandco.co.uk/places/honey-smoke; @honeyandsmokerestaurant; Tue-Sat 10.30 pm; closed Sun & Mon.

Hood SW2 £58 4 4 2
67 Streatham Hill   020 3601 3320   11–2D

"We're very fortunate to have Hood nearby", say fans of this notably *"friendly"* Streaham local which tries harder than most neighbourhood places, with *"imaginative touches, such as foraged food"*. Produce is sourced as locally as possible, with a map on one wall pinpointing farms in the southern counties. / SW2 4TX; www.hoodrestaurants.com; @hoodstreatham; Wed-Sat 11 pm, Sun 3 pm; closed Sun D, closed Mon & Tue; booking online only.

Hoppers £52 4 3 3
49 Frith St, W1   no tel   5–2A
77 Wigmore Street, W1   020 3319 8110   3–1A
Unit 3, Building 4, Pancras Square, N1   020 3319 8125   9–3C

"Authentic flavours of Sri Lanka with superb, well-balanced spicing" won strong acclaim this year for JKS Restaurants' well-known, three-strong chain in Soho, Marylebone and King's Cross, where the eponymous 'hoppers' are coconut and rice flour pancakes with various fillings; highly rated for a *"superior tasting and reasonably priced"* bite. A fourth branch is on the cards for late 2022. Top Tip – *"it has a good range of options for vegans and vegetarians"*. / www.hopperslondon.com; hopperslondon.

Hot Stone N1 £90 4 4 3
9 Chapel Market   020 3302 8226   9–3D

"What a great place to enjoy wagyu steak… which, as its name indicates, is cooked on a hot stone at the table" – Padam Raj Rai's Islington ishiyaki is one of only a handful of UK restaurants selling certified Kobe beef, and also serves high-quality sushi and sashimi. Most reports are hymns of praise – occasional niggles relate to service that is occasionally *"hit or miss"*. Its former Fitzrovia sibling is now branded as Rai (see also). / N1 9EZ; www.hotstonelondon.com; @hotstonelondon; Mon-Thu 9 pm, Fri & Sat 9.30 pm, Sun 8 pm; closed Mon-Thu L.

Humble Chicken W1 £38 3 3 4
54 Frith Street   020 7434 2782   5–2A

"Super busy with good reason" – *"every part of a chicken is cooked to utter perfection married with moreish Japanese flavours"* at Angelo Sato's *"cool"* yearling in Soho: *"he's in front of you slaving away at the charcoal preparing yakitori skewers day after day"* and *"sitting at the bar you get a good view of the 'cogs' the delicious dishes have to go through to get to the counter in front of you"*. *"The prices are high for the portion sizes though"* and while fans *"warm to tendon and giblets"*, and feel *"there is something quite nice about the concept of using every part of a chicken"*, that doesn't float everyone's boat. / W1W 4SJ; www.humblechickenuk.com; @humblechicken_uk; Tue-Thu 10 pm, Fri & Sat 11 pm; closed Tue-Thu L, closed Sun & Mon.

FSA

Humble Grape £66 3 4 3
11-13 Theberton Street, N1 020 3887 9287 9–3D
2 Battersea Rise, SW11 020 3620 2202 11–2C
18-20 Mackenzie Walk, E14 020 3985 1330 12–1C
8 Devonshire Row, EC2 020 3887 9287 10–2D
1 Saint Bride's Passage, EC4 020 7583 0688 10–2A

"The whole package – great food, staff and incredible wines" – wins hymns of praise for James Dawson's wine shop/club/bar/kitchen combination that now has five branches across central London. The focus is on sustainable, small-scale independent producers, with many wines available by the glass. / www.humblegrape.co.uk; humblegrape.

Hunan SW1 £111 4 2 1
51 Pimlico Rd 020 7730 5712 6–2D

"Just say what you want and it keeps coming until you say 'stop!'" at this acclaimed, family-run veteran in Pimlico (founded in 1982), where, according to your preferences, Mr Peng orchestrates the ensuing "Chinese tapas-style" banquet. Many reporters "have been going for years, yet still find new dishes". And despite the odd concern this year about "staff turnover" and a slight "loss of touch", most are wowed "time after time" by the "amazing" results ("crazily good fun, if you go with an open mind"). "Talk to the owner about the wines too: he knows a lot and is very enthusiastic". / SW1W 8NE; www.hunanlondon.com; @hunanlondon; Mon-Sat 11 pm; closed Sun.

The Hunter's Moon SW3 £75 3 4 3
86 Fulham Road 07497 425819 6–2C

This "lively and friendly local" in South Ken rates well for its "high-quality menu complemented by daily specials". Opened three years ago by the Lunar Pub Company, it's "not somewhere for a quiet and romantic dinner, but the young local crowd make it a vibrant venue". / SW3 6HR; huntersmoonlondon.co.uk; @huntersmoonsw3; Mon & Tue, Thu 11 pm, Fri & Sat midnight, Sun 8.30 pm; closed Wed.

Huo SW10 £71 3 3 3
9 Park Walk 020 3696 9090 6–3B

"A new find" just off 'Chelsea Beach' – this yearling on the former site of Farm Girl offers "stylish pan-Asian catering to a stylish crowd". There's substance, too, with a "varied menu which means there's always something tasty to choose". Founder Michael Lim has worked a similar formula with success for many years at Uli in Notting Hill. / SW10 0AJ; huo.london; @huo.london; Mon-Sat midnight, Sun 11 pm.

Hush W1 £99 2 2 3
8 Lancashire Ct 020 7659 1500 3–2B

"An oasis away from the hustle and bustle of the West End" (and relatively "tourist-free"), with a "lovely quiet covered courtyard", this glitzy operation is pitched at those in the know – founding investors included Yegeny Lebedev, son of a Soviet spy, and our own 007, the late Roger Moore. "Easy to get to from Bond Street/Oxford Street/Regent Street", it's "perfect for business breakfast or lunch". But "this all comes at a price and it's one the food, whilst definitely pleasant, can struggle to fully justify". / W1S 1EY; www.hush.co.uk; @hushmayfair; Mon-Sat 10 pm; closed Sun; booking max 12 may apply.

FSA

Hutong, The Shard SE1 £119 2️⃣2️⃣3️⃣
31 St Thomas St   020 3011 1257   10–4C

"What an amazing place" – this Asian joint on the 33rd floor is never short of guests having a good time. However, "the prices are extremely steep"… just like the Shard's glass wall… which contributes to the mixed feelings it inspires. Business entertainers say it's "classy" ("I'm always willing to go… on someone else's budget!"), but even some fans feel that "even the stunning vista don't justify the bill". And others are more definite: "I'd rather eat at my local Chinese". / SE1 9RY; www.hutong.co.uk; @hutongshard; Mon-Sun midnight; no shorts.

Ibérica £64 2️⃣2️⃣2️⃣
Zig Zag Building, 70 Victoria St, SW1   020 7636 8650   2–4B
195 Great Portland St, W1   020 7636 8650   2–1B
12 Cabot Sq, E14   020 7636 8650   12–1C
89 Turnmill St, EC1   020 7636 8650   10–1A

For a "really enjoyable, reasonably authentic Tapas experience", all served in a "buzzing" environment, many would recommend this national chain's four London branches (in Victoria, Canary Wharf, Farringdon and Marylebone). "Uneven" service can make them "a bit hit 'n' miss" (especially in SW1) but one constant is "a particularly strong list of Spanish wines, many by the glass or carafe". / www.ibericarestaurants.com; ibericarestaurants.

Icco Pizza £19 3️⃣3️⃣2️⃣
46 Goodge St, W1   020 7580 9688   2–1C
21a Camden High Street, NW1   020 7380 0020   9–3B

"It's cheap 'n' very cheerful, but with great-quality authentic pizzas" at this basic Goodge Street spot ("worth foregoing a fancier meal for, as its thin-crust pizzas are so good!"). You'll find "very fast and friendly service", and that's it: "this place is all about the pizza and nothing else (unless you love Snapple drinks)". Opened in 1999, it now has a branch in Camden and delivery outlets in Wood Green, Colindale and Croydon. / www.icco.co.uk.

Ikeda W1 £92 4️⃣4️⃣2️⃣
30 Brook St   020 7629 2730   3–2B

The "superb Japanese food" at this little-known Mayfair veteran, now in its fifth decade, stands out in "an increasingly crowded market for Japanese gastronomy". Like many traditional restaurants in Tokyo or Kyoto, it is understated and unflashy to a fault. The sashimi and sushi are "moderately expensive, but then fish this good should be". Top Tip – "the Tekkadon Chirashi is simply delicious – sashimi of tuna, fatty tuna and seared tuna on a bed of rice". / W1K 5DJ; www.ikedarestaurant.com; Tue-Thu 9 pm, Mon, Fri 9.45 pm; closed Mon, Fri L, closed Sat & Sun.

Ikoyi SW1 £231 3️⃣2️⃣2️⃣
1 St James's Market   020 3583 4660   4–4D

"Flavours not experienced before" – "inventive haute cuisine takes on West African dishes using ingredients like plantain and sorghum" – continue to propel Iré Hassan-Odukale and Jeremy Chan's St James's trail-blazer to ever-greater heights of fame, as confirmed by the restaurant's further promotion by Michelin in January 2022. "With the second star comes the elevated price tag" however, and formerly stellar ratings here have sagged under the heightened expectations. Many "masterpieces" are still reported amongst meals, but a worrying new vein of bitter disappointments has also crept into diner commentary ("I was excited to try Ikoyi and discover its new approach, but hand on heart it was not worth the money…"; "we were angry and so disappointed, the food was really average, massively over-spiced and too hot"). Perhaps it's no coincidence that shortly after our diners' poll ended, Chan and Hassan-Odukale announced they were putting the original St

FSA

James's Market site on the market with a view to moving to an upgraded site (with options mooted including a move to the 180 Strand building). / SW1S 4AH; www.ikoyilondon.com; @ikoyi_london; Thu-Sat, Mon-Wed 8.45 pm; closed Mon-Wed L, closed Sun.

Imad's Syrian Kitchen W1 £26 333
Kingly Court, Kingly Street   07473 333631   4–2B

"A delight and an education": this "tiny restaurant with a tiny menu of Syrian food" – "hidden away on the second floor of Soho's Kingly Court" – is a "real favourite for its back story, for the quality of the dishes, and for the fact that you keep coming back". Chef Imad Alarnab fled Damascus in 2015, leaving behind his successful restaurant group, and cooked for fellow-refugees before making his comeback as a restaurateur in London two years ago. / W1W 5PW; imadssyriankitchen.co.uk; @imadssyriankitchen; Tue-Thu, Mon 8.30 pm, Fri & Sat 9.30 pm; closed Mon L, closed Sun.

Imperial China WC2 £55 322
25a Lisle St   020 7734 3388   5–3A

"Higher quality than the run-of-the-mill Chinatown stalwarts" – this big, "reliable" three-storey Cantonese (est. 1993) benefits from a cute, tucked-away location in a small courtyard, complete with fish pond, just north of Leicester Square. / WC2H 7BA; www.imperialchina-london.co.uk; @imperialchinalondon; Mon-Thu 11 pm, Fri & Sat 11.30 pm, Sun 10.30 pm.

Imperial Treasure SW1 £124 442
9-10 Waterloo Place   020 3011 1328   4–4D

"Some of the best Chinese cooking in London" is delivered at this West End three-year-old: the first London branch of a Singapore-based group with offshoots across mainland China. But even if the dishes are "divine", "you pay a serious premium" to dine here. And the atmosphere of this "beautiful" former banking hall, with "very smart" décor by the late Christian Liaigre, "can end up either too manic or funereal, with little in between". Top Menu Tip – the Peking duck is as "exceptional" as its price tag. / SW1S 4BE; www.imperialtreasure.com; @imperialtreasureuk; Mon-Sun 11 pm.

Inamo £45 333
134-136 Wardour St, W1   020 7851 7051   4–1D
11-14 Hanover Pl, WC2   020 7484 0500   5–2D

"So much fun for the kids!" – these "interactive, self-ordering 'Asian' feasts!" in Soho and Covent Garden feature funky projectors, so that the tabletop effectively operates as a touch-screen. "Placing an order here is really entertaining" and, though the food is not the main event, it's well-rated: "there's so much variety and their bottomless offers are amazing value". "The family always wants to go back…" / www.inamo-restaurant.com; W1: Mon - Thu 11.30pm, Fri & Sat midnight, Sun 10.30 pm – SW1: Mon - Thu 11pm, Fri & Sat 12.30pm, Sun 10.30pm.

India Club,
Strand Continental Hotel WC2 £29 323
143 Strand   020 7836 4880   2–2D

"Good scruffy fun with a side order of nostalgia" is to be had at this "hidden gem" in the Strand (a favourite with staff at the Indian High Commission opposite). "An almost anonymous doorway leads you up some stairs" where you "step back in time, not to a cheesy incarnation of the British Raj, but to the early days of independence". Founded in 1951 (Prime Minister Nehru was among the founding members), the 'club' is open to the public and serves food that can be (but is not invariably) "excellent" at a "great price", in an authentically "slightly chaotic atmosphere". It's been under siege for the past five years from a landlord itching to redevelop, but it's "an institution that deserves to survive, and an oasis of good value in central London". Top Tip – it's unlicensed – "pause for a drink in the bar downstairs before or after eating" or carry your pint to the table. / WC2R 1JA; www.theindiaclub.co.uk; @indiaclublondon; Mon-Sun 10.50pm; booking max 6 may apply.

Indian Moment SW11 £36 3 2 2
44 Battersea Rise   020 7223 6575 / 020 7223 1818   11–2C
This "smart, modern-style Indian" has established itself as a "really good-quality neighbourhood curry house" in its 20 years in Battersea. "Yes, it's a little cramped and can be noisy at its busiest times, but the food is always good and the fact it's BYOB helps keep the cost down" (£1.95 corkage fee). / SW11 1EE; www.indianmoment.co.uk; @indianmoment; Sun-Thu 11.30 pm, Fri & Sat midnight; closed Mon-Fri L.

Indian Ocean SW17 £31 3 3 3
214 Trinity Rd   020 8672 7740   11–2C
This "old-school curry house" near Wandsworth Common has for many years been a "reliable neighbourhood favourite", and fans say it "never fails" to produce the goods. / SW17 7HP; www.indianoceanrestaurant.com; Sun-Thu 11 pm, Fri & Sat 11.45 pm; closed Sun-Thu-Sat L.

Indian Rasoi N2 £35 3 3 2
7 Denmark Terrace   020 8883 9093   1–1B
This cute family-run Muswell Hill curry house with a small terrace for outdoor dining prides itself on its Mughal-inspired north Indian cuisine, which goes down well with a local clientele. / N2 9HG; www.indian-rasoi.co.uk; @indianrasoigeneva; Tue-Sun 10 pm; closed Mon; no Amex.

Indian Room SW12 £37 4 4 3
59 Bedford Hill   020 8675 8611   11–2D
"Very helpful staff" add to the appeal of this Balham High Street Indian, of over 15 years' standing. Whether it should be a perennial inclusion in TripAdvisor's top 10 London restaurants is debatable, but the (limited) feedback we receive says it's worth a visit. / SW12 9EZ; www.indianroom.co.uk; @indianroombalham; Sun-Thu 11 pm, Fri & Sat 11.30 pm; closed Mon-Fri L.

Indian Zing W6 £58 4 3 3
236 King St   020 8748 5959   8–2B
"Always fine flavours" with deft and "delicate spicing" delight disciples of this deceptively ordinary-looking "local Indian" near Ravenscourt Park, which, they claim, could "easily go head-to-head with any of London's most famous Indian restaurants". Perhaps that's over-egging it a little, but it's very consistently supported. (The late Michael Winner was an early fan when chef-owner Manoj Vasaikar opened here in 2005). / W6 0RS; www.indian-zing.co.uk; Mon-Sun 10 pm.

Indigo, One Aldwych WC2 £65 3 3 3
1 Aldwych   020 7300 0400   2–2D
This "well-situated" venue occupies an attractive mezzanine in a luxury hotel near Covent Garden that borrows buzz from the foyer below; and which makes a handy rendezvous for business or pleasure. Top Tip – "a most imaginative afternoon tea, and they cater automatically for those of us who are wheat and dairy free!" / WC2B 4BZ; www.onealdwych.com; @onealdwychhotel; Mon & Tue 10.30 am, Wed-Sat 9.30 pm, Sun 3 pm; closed Mon & Tue, Sun D.

INO W1
4 Newburgh Street   020 3701 6618   4–2B
There are still too few reports to give a rating to this Greek 'gastrobar' in Soho, but it looks promising, with a combination of interesting Greek wines (the name derives from the Ancient Greek word for wine); cocktails from the barrel; and charcoal-grilled plates – they even finish their spanakopita pies on the grill. It is from the team behind well-rated Opso and avant-garde Athens restaurant Funky Gourmet. / W1W; www.inogastrobar.com; @inogastobar; Mon-Sat 11 pm, Sun 5 pm; closed Sun D.

Ishtar W1 £70 3 3 3
10-12 Crawford St 020 7224 2446 2–1A
"Particularly tasty grilled meats and mezzes" are the highlights of the menu at this well-established Marylebone outfit, which has served "excellent Anatolian fare" for almost 20 years. "Service is friendly", and "there's evening entertainment too". / W1U 6AZ; www.ishtarrestaurant.com; @ishtarlondon; Sun-Thu 11 pm, Fri & Sat midnight.

Isibani SW1 NEW
9 Knightsbridge Green 07553 051171 6–1D
This July 2022 newcomer on Knightsbridge Green arrived well after our annual diners' poll had concluded so too late for rating. It's a debut from 26-year-old Nigerian-born London chef Victor Okunowo, a semi-finalist on BBC MasterChef The Professionals in 2020. The vibrantly decorated West African restaurant has a 22-seat fine-dining room, with more relaxed eating available on the first floor and 16-cover roof terrace. / SW1S 7QL; www.isibani.com; Mon-Thu midnight, Fri & Sat 2 am, Sun 11 pm.

Isla WC1 £62 3 5 4
The Standard Hotel, 10 Argyle Street 020 3981 8888 9–3C
Next to the Double Standard (see also), the hotel's book-lined lounge and restaurant (the books were inherited from St Pancras Library, previously on this site) shares the "buzzy atmosphere, convenient location, good value short menu" and impeccably cheerful and efficient service of its neighbour. In summer, it also has a superb, quiet covered terrace that feels a millions miles from WC1. / WC1W 8EG; www.islalondon.com; Mon-Sun 10.30 pm; closed Mon-Sun L.

Issho-Ni E2 £43 3 4 3
185 Bethnal Green Road 020 7366 0314 13–1D
Upbeat Bethnal Green izakaya, created four years ago by Claire Su (who converted the premises her parents ran as Noodle King). Praised for its "fresh sushi and interesting small plates", it's also known as a venue for cocktails and bottomless brunch. / E2 6AB; issho-ni.com; @isshoniuk; Tue-Thu 10.30 pm, Fri & Sat 11 pm; closed Sun & Mon.

Italiku W1 NEW £68 3 3 3
110 Great Portland Street 020 7323 1885 2–1B
"Modern Italian with a Japanese twist" – this late summer 2022 launch in Great Portland Street from Jean-Bernard Fernandez-Versini, founder of legendary Cannes pop-up Cosy Box, marries the two food cultures to good effect. Italian-born chef Ivan Simeoli says he's "not limited by tradition, but uses it as an inspiration" for a menu dominated by fish and seafood with plenty of raw options, while Italian Fassona and Japanese wagyu beef have cameo roles. / W1W 6PQ; italiku.co.uk; @italikulondon; Mon-Sat 10.30 pm; closed Sun.

Italian Greyhound W1 £57 2 2 3
62 Seymour Street 020 3826 7940 7–1D
Just off Edgware Road near Marble Arch, this attractive 80-seater yearling (with 20-seat outside terrace) serves a casual Italian menu, featuring pizza and pasta as well as some more substantial dishes. However, even those who feel the food is "good" say it can be "rather hit 'n' miss" and when full the interior becomes "noisy". / W1; theitaliangreyhound.co.uk; @greyhoundmarylebone; Wed-Sat 11 pm, Sun 7 pm; closed Mon & Tue.

FSA

The Ivy WC2 £97
1-5 West St   020 7836 4751   5–3B

"It's just so, so comforting… out-of-towners, especially those north of 50, always find it magical!" This "always buzzy" and still-famous Theatreland icon ('rolled out' by Richard Caring over the last ten years as a national chain) is, says fans, "still a wonderful experience". Such advocates often feel that "it never fails to impress" (even if the A-listers moved on a few years ago) and – for business occasions – appreciate the fact that "clients love it!" Even such boosterism often acknowledges, however, that "these days better food can be found elsewhere" ("it's not remotely going to challenge or educate your palate"). And, while it's long been accepted that "you don't come here for its comfort food", its ratings nowadays support harsher critics who feel that "it's just become an overworked cliché" – "the food is moving to the disappointing level of the chain… and service too". / WC2H 9NQ; www.the-ivy.co.uk; @theivywestst; Mon-Sat 11 pm, Sun 10.30 pm; no shorts; booking max 6 may apply.

The Ivy Asia £72
8-10 North Audley Street, W1   020 3751 4990   3–2A
201-203a King's Road, SW3   020 7486 6154   6–3C
20 New Change Passage, EC4   020 3971 2600   10–2B

"Great fun … despite lots of Instagram poseurs hanging around" – that's the most common view on Richard Caring's latest Ivy sub-brand: a mashup of "stunning" OTT interiors and a Pan-Asian menu which by-and-large totally avoids dishes from China to throw together Thai curries, wagyu beef and lots of fish and seafood (much of it presented as sushi or sashimi). Even fans would concede that "the food is secondary here – for entertainment value, this place has 'got it', but the menu is somehow lost in the mix". And there are those who discern "crazy levels of cultural appropriation (a floor-to-ceiling, fake banyan tree? Seriously?), stirred in with a menu that's less Asian-fusion than Asian-confusion, all creating a bit of a Caring-inspired mess". This year saw the addition of a Mayfair branch to the original one (in the shadow of St Paul's) and last year's opening in SW3 (where "very loud music can add to the already-high noise level"). / www.theivyasia.com.

The Ivy Café £65
96 Marylebone Ln, W1   020 3301 0400   2–1A
120 St John's Wood High St, NW8   020 3096 9444   9–3A
75 High St, SW19   020 3096 9333   11–2B
9 Hill Street, TW9   020 3146 7733   1–4A

"You know what you are getting" according to fans of this sub-brand, spin-off chain, whose 'café' branches are a cut below those trading as a 'brasserie'. They laud its "acceptable" cooking and say, "it's great to see how well the Ivy's formula has been rolled out with very atmospheric décor". Even fans of the "really nice buzz" inspired by these "costly surroundings" can find the food "pretty average" though. And harsher critics (of which there are many) say "what is the point of this expensive and dreadful group? They just demean memories of the original Ivy". Top Tip – "really reasonable for breakfast with decent portions in a pleasant atmosphere" (and you can book in advance for it, too). / ivycollection.com/our-restaurants.

The Ivy Grills & Brasseries £72
66 Victoria Street, SW1   020 3971 2404   2–4B
26-28 Broadwick St, W1   020 3301 1166   4–1C
1 Henrietta St, WC2   020 3301 0200   5–3D
197 King's Rd, SW3   020 3301 0300   6–3C
96 Kensington High St, W8   020 3301 0500   6–1A
One Tower Bridge, 1 Tower Bridge, SE1   020 3146 7722   10–4D
50 Canada Square, E14   020 3971 7111   12–1C **NEW**
Dashwood House, 69 Old Broad St, EC2   020 3146 7744   10–2D

"You wouldn't go for 'haute cuisine', but as a jolly place to eat comfort food in a spectacular setting, it is hard to beat" – that's the upbeat view, anyway,

on this now-"ubiquitous" brasserie chain. Eight years and 40 openings later, the spin-offs increasingly eclipse the Theatreland original (see also), whose Edwardian features provide the style-guide for its nationwide 'roll out'. "Even if the unchallenging food reaches no heights, there's a consistent buzz", which makes them a "posh", "fun" choice for a get-together, if not a particularly foodie one. This is particularly the case at the landmark London off-shoots: at 'Chelsea Garden' ("gorgeous greenery"); Kensington ("slick", with a "pretty glitzy crowd"); and on the Thames ("great views over Tower Bridge"). But while it's always been acknowledged that the mass offering is "a shadow of the mothership's" – with "average grub at not-so-average prices" – the feeling that the brand has become just "a chain that does not excite" is gaining ever-stronger currency. Service seems more "stretched" nowadays, and a sliding ambience rating is making the whole offering seem ever-more "overrated, for all its modern art and perky décor".
/ theivymarketgrill.com/menus.

Jamavar W1 £81 4|4|4
8 Mount Street 020 7499 1800 3–3B
"Real Indian cuisine" – "exquisite flavours from top-quality ingredients and stunning preparation" – have won a major reputation for this "top-class Indian", founded by Samyukta Nair, whose family own India's luxurious Leela Palace group. It occupies a "fantastic", tastefully decorated Mayfair site, near Berkeley Square: "quiet enough for conversation whilst busy enough to create a reassuring hum". / W1K 3NF; www.jamavarrestaurants.com; @JamavarLondon; Mon-Sat 10.30 pm, Sun 9.30 pm; no shorts.

Jashan N8 £42 3|2|2
19 Turnpike Ln 020 8340 9880 1–1C
This 32-year veteran curry house in Turnpike Lane is of the type that inspires "love" and devotion in its regulars. Post-pandemic, it emerged with a new format and menu and some fans regret the change: "the quality of food is generally back to its previously high, but the menu seems to have shortened, and service is now sometimes MIA". / N8 0EP; www.jashan.co.uk; Mon-Sat 10.30 pm, Sun 10 pm; closed Mon-Sun L; no Amex; may need 6+ to book.

Jean-Georges at The Connaught W1 £130 3|3|3
The Connaught, Carlos Place 020 7107 8861 3–3B
It's primarily as an afternoon tea haunt that this Mayfair base for the NYC star-chef attracts attention in our diners' poll, for its "excellent sandwiches and beautiful pastries that almost look too good to eat" ("staff always ask us if we would like more… we always do"). At other times, this plush conservatory serves a pretty conventional brasserie menu (with little hint of the south east Asian specialities that established JGV's Manhattan reputation), and on which one of the most popular items is, curiously, pizza.
/ W1W 2AL; www.the-connaught.co.uk/mayfair-restaurants/jean-georges; @theconnaught; Mon-Sun midnight.

Jeru W1 NEW £105 4|2|4
11 Berkeley Street 020 3988 0054 3–3C
"You have to like loud and vibey" if you visit celeb Aussie chef, Roy Ner's nightclubby newcomer in Mayfair, "beautifully decorated with large open kitchen and bars". Its launch wasn't smooth – with incidents of "comically bad service in the first week" – leading one or two critics to query: "is it the worst launch of the year?". But practically all reporters feel that "the Middle Eastern-style food certainly hits the spot" and there's a general sense that "once it beds in they may be able to work out their problems". / W1W 8DS; jeru.co.uk; @jerulondon; Tue, Wed 11.30 pm, Thu-Sat 12.30 am; closed Sun & Mon.

Jiji N1 £66 434
6g Esther Anne Place   020 7486 3929   9–3D
"In the gorgeous new location of Islington Square", this "fantastic" and unusual Israeli-Japanese newcomer is proving a promising addition to N1: "very buzzy, with cool vibes" and serving "small fusion plates" that are very "interesting". Even fans agree, however, that it's "very expensive… but definitely worth it… I'll be back!" / N1 1WL; jijirestaurants.com; @jijirestaurant; Tue-Sun 11 pm; closed Mon.

Jikoni W1 £76 333
21 Blandford Street   020 7034 1988   2–1A
Chef and food writer Ravinder Bhogal presents her "very original, beautifully prepared" take on East African Indian cuisine in a "homely" setting in Marylebone. The odd reporter accused it of being "hyped" but most reports do nothing but enthuse about the cooking's "inventive and surprising flavours". / W1U 3DJ; www.jikonilondon.com; @JikoniLondon; Wed-Sat 10 pm, Sun 3 pm; closed Wed-Fri L closed Sun D, closed Mon & Tue.

Jin Kichi NW3 £59 553
73 Heath St   020 7794 6158   9–1A
"Sit at the counter and you might almost think you were in Tokyo… until you step outside and walk back to town over Hampstead Heath" from this "favourite Japanese" – one of NW3's best claims to culinary fame. "A small place, it feels so down-to-earth and unassuming, and then blows you away with delicious sushi and yakitori grilled dishes, with even humbler items like seaweed salad made to perfection". We've rated it in accordance with its long-term trend, but – having closed for much of the last year – it reopens in summer 2022 almost doubled in size. Here's hoping they've kept the best facets of its former quaint and "most authentic" style. / NW3 6UG; www.jinkichi.com; Tue-Sat 10.30 pm, Sun 10 pm; closed Mon; payment – credit card only.

Jinjuu W1 £71 423
16 Kingly St   020 8181 8887   4–2B
"You can't go wrong" at this modern take on Korean cuisine off Carnaby Street. "The décor is quirky and the interior a little dark, but the food is the star" (especially since the departure of high-profile founder – Korean-American TV chef Judy Joo): and it's "tremendous value for money in Soho". / W1B 5PS; www.jinjuu.com; @jinjuusoho; Mon-Thu 10 pm, Fri & Sat 11 pm, Sun 7 pm.

Joanna's SE19 £59 334
56 Westow Hill   020 8670 4052   1–4D
"Popular in these parts for over 40 years", this bastion of Crystal Palace (est. 1978) has endured thanks to its "reliable" bistro fare and charming welcome, including to those with kids in tow. Great views of the London skyline too if you get the right table. / SE19 1RX; www.joannas.uk.com; @joannas_1978; Wed-Sat 10 pm, Sun 4 pm; closed Wed L closed Sun D, closed Mon & Tue.

Joe Allen WC2 £61 245
2 Burleigh St   020 7836 0651   5–3D
"Like a pair of comfy shoes that never let you down", this nostalgic Covent Garden sibling to an NYC Theatreland brasserie of the same name is "a go-to when we're in town" for its many fans ("I have been to many Michelin star establishments around the world but Joe Allen is my favourite restaurant"). It was moved – lock, stock and barrel – three years ago due to reconstruction on its original site: "the address has changed, but everything else is the same: thank god!". Even its fans concede that its unambitious staple menu "might not win prizes for the food" – it's a place for a bite post-show, not a foodie occasion (with its off-menu burger being its most celebrated culinary offering for those in-the-know). / WC2W 7PX; www.joeallen.co.uk; @joeallenlondon; Mon-Sat midnight, Sun 8 pm; closed Mon L.

F S A

Joe Public SW4   £16   3 3 2
4 The Pavement   020 7622 4676   11–2D
"Fab" California-style pizzas (bigger and fresher toppings, apparently) are all you can eat at this handy converted public convenience next to Clapham Common tube, apart from the breakfast butties served until 2pm. There's also red & white wine on tap, and own-label beers by the can. / SW4 7AA; www.joepublicpizza.com; @JOEPUBLICSW4; Sun-Wed 10 pm, Thu-Sat 11 pm; closed Mon-Fri L; no booking.

JOIA SW8 NEW
15th Floor, Battersea Power Stn, Circus Rd West   awaiting tel   11–1C
If you're of a certain age, your reading may have been punctuated since the 1980s with visuals in national newspapers of how a skyline bar/restaurant at the forever-about-to-be-redeveloped Battersea Power Station might look. Well, it's finally a reality! Portuguese chef Henrique Sá Pessoa will open these three distinct spaces – a 15th floor restaurant; a bar on the 14th floor; and a rooftop bar with infinity pool – as part of the new art'otel in the development. Sá Pessoa's existing interests include his two Michelin star Alma back home in his native Lisbon and acting as exec chef to art'otel Amsterdam. Authentic Portuguese and Catalonian cuisine is promised alongside other dishes of Iberian inspiration, with numerous items finished tableside for a bit of added glam. / SW8 5BN; artotellondonbattersea.com/joia; @joiabattersea; Mon-Sat midnight, Sun 11 pm.

Jones & Sons N16   £67   3 3 4
Stamford Works, 3 Gillett Street   020 7241 1211   14–1A
This industrial-style space in Dalston, with an 11-metre Carrara marble bar, serves a "great range of well-prepared and presented" modern British dishes – notably char-grilled steaks. The business celebrates its tenth anniversary this year, and moved to its current site in 2016 – a "cavernous place" that made it an ideal location for the Bafta-nominated film Boiling Point, shot in one take on the day before the first national lockdown in March 2020. / N16 8JH; www.jonesandsonsdalston.com; @jones.and.sons; Wed-Sat 10 pm, Sun 6 pm; closed Wed-Fri L, closed Mon & Tue; booking max 20 may apply.

The Jones Family Affair WC2 NEW   £67   4 3 4
40-42 William IV Street   020 3750 2121   2–2C
"An addition to the family!" – this new steakhouse from the eponymous clan is making a success of this big, well-located site off Trafalgar Square where a number of London's top restaurateurs have stumbled in the last decade, when it was Les Deux Salons, RIP. Its large interior is "beautiful"; and – "with superb meat, supplied by The Ginger Pig – it does one of the best steaks in London". And, leaving all that aside, it's just "great to have somewhere decent to eat so centrally". / WC2W 4DD; www.jonesfamilyaffair.co.uk; @jonesfamilyrestaurants; Tue-Sat midnight, Sun 7 pm; closed Mon.

The Jones Family Kitchen SW1   £53   4 4 4
7-8 Eccleston Yard   020 3929 6000   2–4B
"Superb with meat, especially the steaks: simply the most perfectly grilled ever…" – the Jones Family (formerly in Shoreditch) are making a good go of this steakhouse "oasis in busy Victoria" – a "fabulous, bright space with great art" (part of the stylish new Eccleston Yards project), where service "is delivered with a smile". "The ambience of its outdoor courtyard is very pleasant in summer" too. / SW1S 9AZ; www.jonesfamilykitchen.co.uk; @jonesfamilyrestaurants; Tue-Sat 11 pm, Sun 8 pm; closed Mon.

FSA RATINGS: FROM 1 POOR — 5 EXCEPTIONAL

José SE1 — £61 — 4 3 4
104 Bermondsey St   020 7403 4902   10–4D

"No wonder it remains popular after all these years" – José Pizarro's "tiny" Bermondsey bar "is always packed with a good vibe" thanks to its "short, perfectly executed tapas menu". It didn't score quite as highly this year, not because of harsh critiques, but just a sense that "while great and truly buzzing, it's not the old standard it once was". / SE1 3UB; www.josepizarro.com; @josepizarrorestaurants; Mon-Sat 10.30 pm, Sun 10 pm; no booking.

José Pizarro EC2 — £62 — 3 2 2
Broadgate Circle   020 7256 5333   13–2B

You find a "real taste of Spain" at this "small and friendly restaurant in Broadgate" from José Pizarro. Perhaps inevitably, the glossier surroundings here are a turn-off to those who know him via his revered Bermondsey original, for whom this "feels awfully like a franchise", but even so, all reports rate the food as good or better. / EC2M 2QS; www.josepizarro.com/jose-pizarro-broadgate; @josepizarrorestaurants; Mon-Fri 10.30 pm, Sat 9.45 pm; closed Sun.

José Pizarro at the RA W1 — £55 — 4 3 3
Royal Academy, Burlington Gardens, Piccadilly   020 7300 5912   3–3D

"I was expecting this to be a luke-warm franchise type of place, but the food was really exceptional!" – José P has confounded any sceptics with his takeover of this "relaxing oasis" within the famous Piccadilly art institution: "a fantastic addition to the dining scene in London" with "fabulous tapas", "served impeccably" in a "stunning" dining room where you eat "surrounded by art". / W1W 0BD; josepizarro.com/venues/jose-pizarro-royal-academy-arts; @josepizarrorestaurants; Tue-Sun 6 pm; closed Mon.

The Jugged Hare EC1 — £75 — 3 2 3
49 Chiswell Street   020 7614 0134   13–2A

"If you like game, this is the place for you" – a "lively" City gastropub with a focus on "fabulous British food" led by game in season, spit-roasted suckling pig and rare-breed meat. Handy for pre-show dining for visitors to the neighbouring Barbican arts centre, and "great-value Sunday lunches too". / EC1Y 4SA; www.thejuggedhare.com; @thejuggedhare; Mon-Sun 11 pm.

Julie's W11 — £92 — 2 3 4
135 Portland Rd   020 7229 8331   7–2A

After a four-year closure, "Julie's enjoyed a brief revival under head chef Shay Cooper, but sadly since his departure post-pandemic together with some key FoH staff" (to the Lanesborough) feedback has dropped off, with the odd "at best mediocre" report. Still, this remarkable, louche warren of subterranean rooms has been a romantic, if not a foodie destination since 1969: it's too early to write it off yet. / W11 4LW; www.juliesrestaurant.com; @juliesw11; Tue-Sat midnight; closed Sun & Mon.

Junsei W1 — £68 — 4 4 3
132 Seymour Place   020 7723 4058   7–1D

"Great chicken skewers" are the USP at this Japanese yearling in Marylebone which specialises in yakitori cooking – different cuts of meat "butchered and prepared in-house" so that not a scrap is wasted, and cooked on a robata grill. / W1W 1NS; junsei.co.uk; @junsei_uk; closed Mon-Sat & Sun.

Kaffeine — £17 — 2 5 3
15 Eastcastle St, W1   020 7580 6755   3–1D
66 Great Titchfield St, W1   020 7580 6755   3–1C

"They go the extra mile" at this Antipodean-style outfit whose "excellent" brews, including "the perfect espresso", ensure that is "always packed". Its two "convenient" sites in Fitzrovia make "a great escape not far from the Oxford Street chain experience", and they serve "decent food (especially by coffee shop standards)". / kaffeine.co.uk; kaffeinelondon.

Kahani SW1 £77 4 4 3
1 Wilbraham Place   020 7730 7634   6–2D

Ex-Tamarind exec chef, Peter Joseph's "real classic of an Indian" is tucked away in a tastefully decorated basement near Sloane Square (behind Cadogan Hall). Peter was raised in Tamil Nadu, and achieves "an exceptionally high standard" using British ingredients to create light, modern dishes with a focus on grills from the robata grill and tandoor. "Although it's a pricey curry, you certainly get some bang for your buck!" / SW1S 9AE; www.kahanilondon.com; @kahanilondon; Mon-Sat 10.30 pm, Sun 8 pm; closed Mon-Fri L.

Kai Mayfair W1 £125 3 3 3
65 South Audley St   020 7493 8988   3–3A

"A cut above any Chinese restaurant I have been to" – Bernard Yeoh's "attentive but not overbearing" Mayfair stalwart celebrates its 20th birthday in 2023 and continues to offer a luxurious mix of "absolutely fantastic contemporary Chinese cooking" (what Yeoh describes as 'liberated Nanyang cuisine') twinned with an impressive wine list (swelling with Premiers Crus from Bordeaux, Burgundy and beyond). Even those who say the food is "lovely" though, feel it comes at "eye-watering prices". / W1K 2QU; www.kaimayfair.co.uk; @kaimayfair; Mon-Sun 11 pm.

Kaifeng NW4 £74 3 3 2
51 Church Road   020 8203 7888   1–1B

This "consistently high-quality kosher Chinese" in Hendon has established a strong reputation across north London over more than 20 years. It is named after a Chinese city with a Jewish population dating back 1,000 years or more. / NW4 4DU; www.kaifeng.co.uk; Sun-Thu, Sat 10.30 pm; closed Sat L, closed Fri.

Kaki N1 £50 4 3 2
125 Caledonian Road   020 7278 6848   9–3D

"Prepare to numb your senses" at "one of the best Sichuan restaurants around" – this smartly modernised pub between King's Cross and Islington serves "red-hot and authentic cuisine by the canal on Caledonian Road". "Service is quick and friendly, the food delicious", and "the outside deck gives a lovely view over the canal in warm weather". Top Menu Tip – "the specials board is always worth a look – cumin lamb skewers, three treasures, pig intestine and twice-cooked pork belly are among the many stand-outs". / N1 9RG; www.thekaki.co.uk; @kaki_london; Sun-Thu 10 pm, Fri & Sat 11 pm.

Kalimera N8 £53 4 4 3
43 Topsfield Road   07446 981139   1–1C

"Tasty and reasonably priced plates of Mediterranean food" make this yearling from Télémaque Argyriou "a nice new addition to Crouch End". "How rarely do you get authentic Greek cuisine in London? Mostly you find Cypriot food (OK, but not at all the same thing) or tourist stuff. This is the real Greek in a London bistro style – wonderful!". (The ingredients are real, too – led by olives and oil from the patron's family farm in Greece). / N8 8PT; www.kalimera-streetfood.co.uk; @kalimeralondon; Tue-Sat 11 pm; closed Tue-Sat L, closed Sun & Mon.

Kanada-Ya £39 4 2 2
3 Panton St, SW1   020 7930 3511   5–4A
28 Foubert's Place, W1   020 3435 8155   4–1B **NEW**
64 St Giles High St, WC2   020 7240 0232   5–1B
35 Upper Street, N1   020 7288 2787   9–3D

The "very rich and extremely meaty pork broth" wins plenty of admirers for what some consider "London's top ramen". Founded by former cycle racer Kazuhiro Kanada in Kyushu 14 years ago, the small group now has four branches in the capital – Angel, Piccadilly, Covent Garden and Carnaby – and provide "food to savour on a chilly winter day". / www.kanada-ya.com; kanada_ya_ldn.

FSA

Kanishka W1 — £101 — 3 3 2
17-19 Maddox Street   020 3978 0978   4–2A

Atul Kochhar's "inventive" Northeastern Indian cuisine ("light and not too rich") continues to win a strong fanclub for this well regarded four-year-old in Mayfair. It would rate even higher, were it not for a few reporters for whom "it's sound all around but just not that next-level I'd expect at the price point". / W1W 2QH; kanishkarestaurant.co.uk; @kanishkamayfair; Mon-Sun 11 pm.

Kaosarn — £42 — 3 3 3
110 St Johns Hill, SW11   020 7223 7888   11–2C
181 Tooting High Street, SW17   020 8672 8811   11–2C
Brixton Village, Coldharbour Ln, SW9   020 7095 8922   11–2D

"Delicious Thai food" wins plaudits for this family-owned and run trio in Brixton, Battersea and Tooting, while the BYO policy keeps a lid on the bill. / www.kaosarnlondon.co.uk.

Kappacasein SE1 — £11 — 5 3 2
1 Stoney Street   no tel   10–4C

"Still simply the best cheese toastie after all these years" – perhaps "the best you'll ever find" – is to be treasured at the Borough Market stall of a Bermondsey dairy, which makes its cheese with organic cow's milk from Chiddingstone in Kent. / SE1 9AA; www.kappacasein.com; @kappacasein; Thu & Fri 3 pm, Sat 4 pm; closed Thu-Sat D, closed Mon-Wed & Sun; no booking.

Kasa & Kin W1 NEW — £46 — 3 4 3
52-53 Poland Street   020 7287 5400   4–1C

"A brightly coloured space" – this November 2021 newcomer (which translates to 'Home and Family' in Filipino) is run by the same crew as Romulo Café and gets a thumbs-up for "broadening the offer of Philippine cuisine in the UK" – "it's great to have an upscale option for contemporary Filipino food in the heart of Soho". One Filipino reporter feels that some dishes are too modified for local tastes, but agrees it's "fun, lively and with very acceptable food". Top Tip – "an array of sinful merienda/tea snacks in the adjoining bakery and patisserie counter". / W1W 7NQ; kasaandkin.co.uk; @kasaandkin; Mon-Wed 9 pm, Thu-Sat 10 pm, Sun 8 pm.

Kashmir SW15 — £49 — 3 3 2
18-20 Lacy Road   07477 533888   11–2B

"Proper and authentic regional food" gives this Kashmiri restaurant – apparently the first of its kind in Britain – a real point of difference in Putney. Regulars agree that it's "so good to try new dishes here, which are always delicious" – "served with ongoing geniality by the lovely owners", Rohit and Shweta Razdan, who ran restaurants in New Delhi and Singapore before moving to SW15. / SW15 1NL; www.kashmirrestaurants.co.uk; @kashmirrestuk; Mon, Wed & Thu 10.30 pm, Fri-Sun 11 pm; closed Mon, Wed-Fri L, closed Tue.

The Kati Roll Company W1 — £26 — 3 2 2
24 Poland Street   020 7287 4787   4–1C

A taste of Kolkata, via New York – these "Indian fast-food" joints in Soho and Bethnal Green serve buttery paratha flatbreads rolled around fillings originally grilled on skewers (kati means skewer), the street food from home that founder Payal Saha missed when she moved to Manhattan 21 years ago. / W1W 8QL; www.thekatirollcompany.com; @thekatirollcompany; Mon-Sun 11 pm.

FSA

Kazan SW1 £62 3 3 2
93-94 Wilton Rd   020 7233 7100   2–4B

"A Pimlico gem for so many years now, and even better than ever" – this "good-value" joint serving "good, honest Turkish food" celebrates its 21st anniversary this year. It's "heartening to see it so popular (deservedly so) since the latest lockdown ended", although it now operates on just one side of Wilton Road, having had two venues for years. / SW1V 1DW; www.kazan-restaurant.com; no Amex.

Kebab Queen WC2 £123 4 4 3
4 Mercer Walk   020 7439 9222   5–2C

"Real wow factor" inspires fans of this not-very-secret counter, in the basement of Kingly Court's Le Bab, which aims ' to push kebabs as far as they can go'. "The service experience – with food served by the chef onto the actual surface of the special heated counter directly in front of you" (no plates, you scoop it up in your fingers) – "brings a brilliant sense of fun to the whole meal". "But it's not at the expense of serious culinary intent": ex-Gavroche chef, Manu Canales creates "original food, with exceptional quality of ingredients and cooking". / WC2H 9FA; www.eatlebab.com; @eatlebab; Wed-Sat 11 pm; closed Mon & Tue & Sun.

Ken Lo's Memories SW1 £67 3 3 2
65-69 Ebury St   020 7730 7734   2–4B

"Still going strong after all these years" – although "long-since forgotten by the foodie fashionistas", the late Ken Lo's veteran Belgravian "still produces decent-quality, if perhaps westernised Chinese dishes, served with charm in comfortable surroundings". / SW1W 0NZ; www.memoriesofchina.co.uk; @kenlosmemoriesofchina; Wed-Sat, Tue, Sun 10.30 pm; closed Tue L, closed Mon.

Kennington Tandoori SE11 £56 3 4 3
313 Kennington Rd   020 7735 9247   1–3C

The closest thing to 'Parliament's official curry house' – frequented by prominent Westminster forkmen from Ken Clarke and John Prescott to David Cameron and BoJo – this Kennington institution is run by vascular surgeon Kowsar Hoque, whose father opened it in 1985. Fans say it's "difficult to go elsewhere when wanting an Indian dinner!" / SE11 4QE; www.kenningtontandoori.com; @Kennington tandoori; Mon-Sun 10.30 pm; closed Mon-Sun L; no Amex.

Kerridge's Bar & Grill WC2 £109 2 2 3
10 Northumberland Avenue   020 7321 3244   2–3C

"A little bit of Marlow on Embankment", say fans of TV-Tom's London HQ: a "smooth operation", which occupies a vast, atmospheric chamber within one of London's most glamorous five stars (well, if it's good enough for Ivanka…). The posh brasserie food, overseen by chef Nick Beardshaw, is "quite heavy and meaty" and fans say "while it's a bit pricey, you will have an enjoyable meal". On the downside, there's a disappointed minority for whom the atmosphere "is very hotel dining room" and who see this as "another disappointing experience from a TV-star branded establishment". / WC2W 5AE; www.kerridgesbarandgrill.co.uk; @kerridgesbandg; Mon-Sat 10.30 pm, Sun 9 pm.

Kerridge's Fish & Chips SW1 £115 3 3 5
Harrods, 87-135 Brompton Road   020 7225 6800   6–1D

"Expensive but amazing fish 'n' chips" and other "very tasty" seafood classics win nothing but praise for this year-old outlet, within Harrods Dining Halls (see also). "Most definitely go for the cockle popcorn and malted beer batter". / SW1S 7XL; www.harrods.com/en-gb/restaurants/kerridges-fish-chips; Tue-Sat 11 pm, Mon 9 pm, Sun 6 pm.

Khun Pakin Thai at The Salutation W6 £20 3️⃣3️⃣3️⃣
154 King Street   020 8748 3668   8–2C

A plug from Tom Parker Bowles in the Daily Mail did no harm at all to this Thai concession in an attractive old pub opposite the building site once known as 'Hammersmith Town Hall', where the cooking is a cut above that in a typical boozer. Top Tip – "if you get the chance, eat in the sun in the cute beer garden at the back: with some delish salt 'n' pepper squid, life is good!" / W6 0QU; www.salutationhammersmith.co.uk; Mon-Sat 11 pm, Sun 10.30 pm.

Kibou London SW11 £61 2️⃣2️⃣3️⃣
175-177 Northcote Road   020 7223 8551   11–2C

This "convenient neighbourhood Japanese" was a "welcome addition to Northcote Road" when it landed in Battersea's Nappy Valley in summer 2020 – vividly decorated and the first London branch of a popular Cheltenham-based group. Not all reporters are convinced, though, with gripes about "flustered service" or indifferent dishes weighing in the balance against those who continue to feel it's "good value". / SW11 6QF; kibou.co.uk; @kiboulondon; Tue-Sat 11 pm, Sun 10 pm; closed Mon.

Kiku W1 £70 4️⃣4️⃣2️⃣
17 Half Moon St   020 7499 4208   3–4B

This "classic Japanese stalwart" has offered an authentic taste of Tokyo in a Mayfair backstreet for 45 years – and is always "full of Japanese consular employees" from the nearby embassy. Top Tip – "go for the good-value lunchtime set menu". / W1J 7BE; www.kikurestaurant.co.uk; @kikumayfair; Mon-Sat 10.15 pm; closed Sun.

Kilig SE8 NEW
Deptford Arches, 2 Resolution Way   awaiting tel   1–3D

This July 2022 newcomer at Deptford Arches promises an interesting culinary mashup reflecting the founders' roots in the Philippines and Colombia. It opened too late for survey feedback, but The Evening Standard's Jimi Famurewa found it: "occasionally inspired and enormously likeable but also prone, here and there, to a kind of erratic overreach". / SE8 4NT; www.kiliglondon.co.uk; @kilig_ldn; Mon-Sat midnight, Sun 11 pm.

Kilis Kitchen N1 £51 3️⃣3️⃣3️⃣
4 Theberton Street   020 7226 5489   9–3D

This "excellent local" Turkish restaurant just off Islington's main drag offers a classic and extensive menu of "good food at a very reasonable price", served up in a "buzzy and friendly setting". / N1 0QX; www.kilis.co.uk; @kilis_kitchen; Sun-Thu 11 pm, Fri & Sat midnight.

Kiln W1 £50 5️⃣4️⃣4️⃣
58 Brewer Street   no tel   4–3C

"Exciting", "astonishingly good" and "incredible value" Thai-inspired BBQ fuels nothing but adulatory reviews for Ben Chapman's "incomparable" Soho destination ("we licked the plates clean and bemoaned the fact Manchester has nothing like this!"). This is "casual, bar-counter eating at its best", but the "buzzy, loud atmosphere is not conducive to a leisurely meal". Sitting upstairs "at the grill, watching the chefs cooking over the open flames is the highlight"; "downstairs is a bit grim and windowless" by comparison. "It's too good to be an occasional place, but the queues make it impossible for frequent visits" (and "with no booking, you have to chance it; and it can be a long queue, glaring at people to hurry up!"). Top Menu Tips – "the glass noodles, sausage, chicken glazing, larb squid and Cornish greens are exceptional". / W1F 9TL; www.kilnsoho.com; @kilnsoho; Mon-Sat 11 pm, Sun 9 pm.

FSA

Kin and Deum SE1 £47 4️⃣2️⃣3️⃣
2 Crucifix Lane   020 7357 7995   10–4D
"Extremely good" Thai food helps win a fair-sized fan club for this white-walled pub-conversion, near London Bridge. But *"when it's packed, it can be a bit noisy for a good conversation"*. / SE1 3JW; www.kindeum.com; @kindeum; Mon-Sun 10.30 pm.

Kindred W6 £44 3️⃣3️⃣3️⃣
Bradmore House, Queen Caroline Street   020 3146 1370   8–2C
Slap bang in the middle of Hammersmith Broadway, it's easy to ignore Grade II listed 'Bradmore House', nowadays a hip coworking club. The food (from a menu created by chef Andrew Clarke) doesn't aim for foodie fireworks, but is way better than you would expect just seconds from the tube platforms, as is the stylish and cosy basement location. / W6 9YE; www.wearekindred.com; @londonkindred; Tue, Wed 11 pm, Thu-Sat midnight, Mon 6 pm; closed Sun.

Kipferl N1 £54 3️⃣3️⃣3️⃣
20 Camden Passage   020 77041 555   9–3D
"Classic Austrian comfort food" is the order of the day at this Austrian-run all-day café, which opened in the City 20 years ago and moved to Islington's Camden Passage in 2011. The menu runs from *"great coffee and cakes"*, via *"delicious and decadent brunch"* to *"a choice of traditional main dishes, with very good veal in cream sauce or schnitzel and nice desserts"*. Commendably, there is little pandering to local tastes: everything is as close as possible to what you might eat in Vienna. / N1 8ED; www.kipferl.co.uk; @kipferl_london; Mon-Thu 10 pm, Fri & Sat 11 pm, Sun 7 pm.

Kiss the Hippo £27 3️⃣3️⃣2️⃣
51 Margaret Street, W1   no tel   3–1C
50 George Street, TW9   020 3887 2028   1–4A
"The coffee is the best!", according to fans of this *"zen"* Scandi-style café in Fitzrovia, from an ambitious ethical importer and roastery that has won a clutch of barista awards in the five years since it was founded (including Top Coffee House at the Harden's London Restaurant Awards 2021). The shop offers *"light snacks such as cinnamon rolls and cakes"* – and *"everything is good, not just the coffee"*. Their original venture, in Richmond, moved into a new address in summer 2022, and they also have kiosks in Shoreditch, King's Cross and Sloane Square. / kissthehippo.com; kissthehippo.

Kitchen Table W1 £330 4️⃣4️⃣4️⃣
70 Charlotte Street   020 7637 7770   2–1C
"Sublime on every level… if only it wasn't so expensive". James Knappett and Sandia Chang's 18-seater in Fitzrovia re-opened after a significant reformatting in July 2021 and *"it's both an exceptional meal and quite a show"* – *"the arrangement of the counter makes for a theatrical experience, with lots of opportunity to chat with the people cooking and running front of house"*, while the multi-course menu (each course focused on a single ingredient) is, all reports agree, utterly *"memorable"*. Practically all reports also mention the pricing though – *"OUCH!"*… *"it was amazing but the bill's crazy…"* / W1T 4QG; www.kitchentablelondon.co.uk; @kitchentable1; Tue-Sat 11 pm; closed Sun & Mon; booking online only.

FSA RATINGS: FROM 1️⃣ POOR — 5️⃣ EXCEPTIONAL

Kitchen W8 W8 £90 4 3 3
11-13 Abingdon Road   020 7937 0120   6–1A
"Polished cuisine" with a "creative mix of ingredients" – overseen from afar by star chef Phil Howard – elevates this "classic neighbourhood restaurant" off High Street Kensington into something "top class" and one of London's better-known foodie destinations. If criticism is made, it's typically that a diner "had heard great things, but was underwhelmed despite finding nothing obviously wrong". In a similar variable vein, service veers from "very pleasant" to "sometimes chaotic"; and the "well-spaced" dining room is "lovely" to some, too low-key for others. / W8 6AH; www.kitchenw8.com; @KitchenW8; Tue-Thu, Sun 9.30 pm, Fri & Sat 10 pm; closed Mon.

Kitty Fisher's W1 £76 3 3 4
10 Shepherd's Market   020 3302 1661   3–4B
This "very small, charming and romantic" venture in Shepherd Market was briefly the hottest ticket in town in the mid noughties (providing a much-PR'd date night for David & Samantha Cameron). Nowadays, those who remember the historic hype can find it "overrated" or "dependable rather than… wow!", but overall its food is well-rated. Top Menu Tip – Belted Galloway Wing Rib and "cosmic crispy potatoes!" / W1J 7QF; www.kittyfishers.com; @kittyfishers; Tue-Sat 9.30 pm; closed Sun & Mon.

Knife SW4 £73 4 4 3
160 Clapham Park Road   020 7627 6505   11–2D
"The best Sunday roasts… well cooked and hangover-busting!" are just one of the options for eating at this excellent, small brick-walled steakhouse on the Clapham/Brixton borders (a former winner of the Top Steaks category in the Harden's London Restaurant Awards). The menu has a good variety of choices, including beef sourced from farmers in the Lake District. / SW4 7DE; kniferestaurant.co.uk; @kniferestaurant; Wed-Sat 9.30 pm, Sun 4.30 pm; closed Wed-Sat L closed Sun D, closed Mon & Tue.

Koji SW6 £84 3 3 4
58 New King's Rd   020 7731 2520   11–1B
"A perfect place this side of town", say fans of this long-established pan-Asian – tucked away in Parson's Green – whose swish décor and diverse menu (sushi, sashimi tacos, udon noodles, wagyu steaks, kushiyaki skewers, wood-roasted fish…) can make it a good choice for a special celebration. But it doesn't attract the volume of feedback that it used to be. / SW6 4LS; www.koji.restaurant; @kojirestaurant; Tue, Wed 10.30 pm, Thu-Sat 11 pm; closed Tue-Sat L, closed Sun & Mon; payment – credit card only.

Kol W1 £124 4 4 4
9 Seymour Street   020 3829 6888   2–2A
"Ex-Noma pop-up chef, Santiago Lastra's sort-of fine dining Mexican successfully redefines street food at this warm and high-end dining room", just off Portman Square – "a welcome addition to Marylebone" that "deserves the hype" and which is emerging as one of London's more "exciting" destinations right now. "The open kitchen allows the man himself to be seen" and a meal "feels like an occasion", but one that's "earthy" and "fun". "The innovative use of British ingredients to recreate Mexican flavours is what makes this a really interesting culinary experience" – providing "twists on the genre which tantalise the palate" and deliver "immensely thoughtful and innovative" dishes with "deep savoury notes". "And the wine list is both unusual and worth taking a risk on too: some hidden gems from small producers and uncommon countries which complement the food well". "You are helped in your journey by a knowledgeable and unpretentious sommelier" and service generally is "excellent". "Always buzzy, tables are hard to come by". Top Tips – "the lobster taco is a real highlight and the mole something very special indeed", while there's "one of the finest vegan tasting menus in London". / W1W 7BA; kolrestaurant.com; @kol.restaurant; Tue-Sat midnight, Sun 2.30 pm; closed Tue L closed Sun D, closed Mon; payment – credit card only.

Kolamba W1 — £36 — 3 3 2
21 Kingly Street   020 3815 4201   4–2B

"Knock-out Sri Lankan small plates" at this Soho three-year-old deliver "bright and fiery dishes". There are "amazing veggie options", and it's "well-priced and authentic". / W1W 5QA; kolamba.co.uk; @kolamba.ldn; Mon-Sat 10 pm, Sun 9 pm.

Koya — £45 — 3 4 3
50 Frith St, W1   020 7434 4463   5–2A
10-12 Broadway Market Mews, E8   no tel   14–2B **NEW**
Bloomberg Arcade, Queen Victoria Street, EC2   no tel   10–3C

"Portions are perfect for the price and they don't 'cheap out' on the protein" at these "solid udon places" in Soho (est. 2010), a newer offshoot in the City's Bloomberg Arcade and now also with the opening of 'Koya Ko' in Hackney's Broadway Market (this last with a slightly different menu). "Very Japanese-chic, super-cosy and cute", their "staff are kind and helpful with answering questions about ingredients". Udon are more traditional and subtler than ubiquitous ramen, and arrive in Japan's famous light dashi stock. / www.koya.co.uk.

Koyn W1 **NEW**
38 Grosvenor Street   020 3376 0000   3–2B

On gracious Grosvenor Square – a Japanese-inspired izakaya-style from Mei Mei's Samyukta Nair; and her family's LSL Capital's fifth Mayfair venture; opening September 2022. The two-storey space is apparently inspired by 'enigmatic' Mount Fuji: 'On the round floor is MIDORI, the green room, representative of vegetative life on the snow-capped peak, and below is MAGMA, the charred room, representing an active, bubbling volcano'. Who'd have guessed! A broad spectrum of Japanese cuisine is trailed, featuring specialist dishes in their sushi bar and robata grill selections. / W1W 4QA; www.koynrestaurants.com; Tue-Sun midnight.

Kricket W1 — £52 — 5 4 4
12 Denman St   020 7734 5612   4–3C

As 10CC might have put it: "We don't like Kricket… we love it!". "Brilliant Indian sharing plates with an emphasis on taste, not heat" have bowled a hat-trick of successes for Rik Campbell and Will Bowlby since their street food pop-up went permanent in Soho, Brixton and White City. Their "interesting and flexible" small-plate menus are served in a "cool, vibey atmosphere", either eating at the counter or at tables – with more vibes next door in their speakeasy bar Soma for diners in Soho. / W1D 7HH; www.kricket.co.uk; @kricketlondon; Mon-Sat 10.30 pm; closed Sun.

Kudu SE15 — £60 — 4 4 4
119 Queen's Rd   020 3950 0226   1–4D

"A fun spot, with super food and surroundings" – Patrick Williams and Amy Corbin's (yes, that Corbin) Peckham venture has earned its place on London's foodie map with "quality" South African-influenced cooking and "personable" service. On warmer days, you can eat in the back garden. / SE15 2EZ; www.kuducollective.com; @kudu_restaurant; Thu-Sun 10 pm; closed Thu L, closed Mon & Tue & Wed.

Kudu Grill SE15 — £49 — 4 4 4
57 Nunhead Lane   020 3172 2450   1–4D

"A simply stunning South African braai restaurant" – Amy Corbin and Patrick Williams's "cosy and classy" yearling (opened in September 2021) delivers "some of the best food in a long time" to excited local reporters, "with confident, bold flavours" ("a special shout out to the delectable peri peri butter and monkey gland sauce"). "Superb service too (catered for the veggie and the vegan in our group without batting an eyelid, and without sacrificing flavour!)". / SE15; www.kuducollective.com; @kudugrill; Wed-Sat 10 pm, Sun 2.30 pm; closed Wed-Fri L closed Sun D, closed Mon & Tue.

F S A

Kutir SW3 £64 | 5 | 4 | 4 |
10 Lincoln Street   020 7581 1144   6–2D

"It's always a great pleasure to dine at this beautiful Chelsea townhouse with a lovely summer terrace upstairs!" Rohit Ghai's "inventive" cuisine is some of the best Indian food in London: "heavily spiced" and delivered by "impeccable staff" in a "bright, airy and compact dining room". / SW3 2TS; kutir.co.uk; @kutirchelsea; Tue-Sun 10 pm; closed Mon; no shorts; booking online only.

The Ladbroke Arms W11 £65 | 3 | 2 | 4 |
54 Ladbroke Road   020 7727 6648   7–2B

With its flower-bedecked exterior and "relaxed neighbourhood vibe", this Ladbroke Grove local is "certainly one of the better pubs" in the capital, serving "delicious food that's definitely more restaurant than pub grub" alongside "good beer". It's close to Holland Park, and attracts a good Sunday lunch crowd. / W11 3NW; www.ladbrokearms.com; @Ladbrokearms; Mon-Sat 9.30 pm, Sun 9 pm.

Lahore Kebab House E1 £35 | 5 | 2 | 2 |
2-10 Umberston St   020 7481 9737   12–1A

"Still the best authentic Pakistani grilled meat and curry" is to be had at this grunge-tastic Whitechapel legend of 50 years' standing, where "tastes are genuine" and prices "cheap as chips". Top Menu Tip – "love the lamb chops". / E1 1PY; www.lahore-kebabhouse.com.

Lahpet £59 | 3 | 4 | 3 |
21 Slingsby Place, WC2   020 3883 5629   5–3C
58 Bethnal Green Road, E1   020 3883 5629   13–1C

"Distinctive and exciting" flavours of Burma ("an under-represented cuisine in London") have now made their way from a stall near London Bridge, via a Hackney railway arch and a Shoreditch restaurant (still running) to the West End, in Covent Garden's newish 'The Yards' development, thanks to founders Dan Anton and Burmese chef Zaw Mahesh. Named after a salad of pickled tea leaves, Lahpet is "lively and noisy", and its food is "thrilling". Top Tip – "the luminescent ginger salad... so zingy and flavourful!" / lahpet.co.uk; lahpet.

Laksamania W1 £49 | 3 | 3 | 2 |
92 Newman Street   020 7637 9888   3–1D

"A topspot for Malaysian food", this three-year-old street-food specialist off Oxford Street serves "top-notch laksas", following both traditional recipes and chef Danny Tan's original variations. Service is overseen by the "friendly Aunties who run the front-of-house show". / W1W 3EZ; www.laksamania.co.uk; @laksamania; Mon, Wed & Thu 9 pm, Fri & Sat 9.30 pm, Sun 8 pm; closed Tue.

The Landmark, Winter Garden NW1 £88 | 2 | 3 | 5 |
222 Marylebone Rd   020 7631 8000   9–4A

"The most stunning venue, full of palm trees under a high glass roof", makes this eight-storey hotel atrium the perfect setting for brunch or an "excellent afternoon tea". "The pastries are wonderful" and there's a "fantastic choice of breakfast dishes" – but the real treat is the "superb ambience" created by one of London's most Insta-friendly spaces. / NW1 6JQ; www.landmarklondon.co.uk; @the_landmark_london; Mon-Sun 10 pm; no trainers; booking max 12 may apply.

FSA

The Lanesborough Grill SW1 £132
Hyde Park Corner   020 7259 5599   6–1D
The "stunning" atrium setting has always been a highlight of the light-filled dining room of this ultra-luxe hotel on Hyde Park Corner, which has been transformed this year. In April 2022, out went its haute-cuisine menu (and Michelin star) – in came this new posh brasserie offering (overseen by former Julie's chef, Shay Cooper), putting an emphasis on seasonal British produce (and with a number of dishes served tableside on gueridon trolleys). The change was sufficiently close to our annual diners' poll that it's more appropriate to leave a rating till next year. / SW1X 7TA; www.oetkercollection.com/hotels/the-lanesborough/restaurants-bars/restaurants/celeste; @the_lanesborough; no shorts.

Langan's Brasserie W1 £73   1 2 3
Stratton Street   020 7491 8822   3–3C
"Not the old Langans by any means" – the relaunch in late 2021 of this treasured old-faithful brasserie (est. 1976) near The Ritz has proved "a little mixed" to say the least, and a return to its A-list past now seems a very distant prospect. One or two fans do "love the entire experience" of this business favourite and its plutocratic comfort food. But more common are those whose "excitement turned to huge disappointment in the face of abysmal service and astronomical prices" for staple dishes, to the extent that some diners loathe the place: "arguably the most overrated restaurant in central London, made clear by all the Z-list celebrities I assume they get to dine for free…" – "should be rated zero zero zero!" / W1J 8LB; www.langansrestaurants.co.uk; @langansbrasserie; Mon-Sat 11 pm, Sun 9.30 pm.

(Palm Court)
The Langham W1 £98   2 3 4
1c Portland Place   020 7636 1000   2–1B
"Elegant silver and grey décor" helps set a refined tone in the plush lounge of this luxurious five star. Most reports of "very imaginative gateaux and sandwiches" suggest it lives up to its heritage (the ceremony of afternoon tea having, apparently, started here), but even fans can find the price tag "a little steep". / W1B 1JA; www.palm-court.co.uk; @langham_london; Mon-Sun 11 pm; no trainers.

Lao Cafe WC2 £39   3 3 2
60 Chandos Place   020 3740 4748   5–4C
This "modest but terrific" former pop-up near Trafalgar Square, from entrepreneurial Lao-Thai chef Saiphin Moore (of Rosa's Thai), is "well worth the visit" for "good-sized portions" of "authentic" Laotian food – a lesser-known Asian cuisine with meals revolving around the staple of sticky rice. / WC2N 4HG; laocafe.co.uk; @laocafelondon Follow; Mon-Sun 10 pm; may need 8+ to book.

Launceston Place W8 £102   4 3 3
1a Launceston Pl   020 7937 6912   6–1B
"A special place to dine in stylish and intimate rooms" – this "quirkily laid-out" townhouse (est. 1986) in a quiet Kensington backstreet "exudes gracious hospitality" and "never fails to delight", particularly as a "romantic" destination. Chef Ben Murphy joined in January 2017 and why Michelin have failed to award him a star is anyone's guess: his cuisine "is delicious with subtle flavour combinations and artistically presented plates" that all make up for a "memorable" occasion. (You would never know it was owned by D&D London – it stands head and shoulders over the rest of their portfolio nowadays.) / W8 5RL; www.launcestonplace-restaurant.co.uk; @launcestonplace; Wed-Sat 10 pm, Sun 9 pm; closed Mon & Tue.

FSA RATINGS: FROM 1 POOR — 5 EXCEPTIONAL

F S A

The Laundry SW9   £62   3 4 3
374 Coldharbour Lane   020 8103 9384   11–2D
This "impressive" three-year-old in Brixton is set in a handsome converted Victorian laundry. The first venture of Melanie Brown (a former chef and founder of the New Zealand and Australian Cellar wine businesses), it wins consistent ratings across the board for its "good food, great service and buzzy atmosphere". / SW9 8PL; thelaundrybrixton.com; @brixtonlaundry; Mon-Wed 11 pm, Thu-Sat midnight, Sun 9 pm; payment – credit card only.

Le Bab   £53   3 2 2
Top Floor, Kingly Court, W1   020 7439 9222   4–2B
4 Mercer Walk, WC2   020 7240 9781   5–2C
Circus West Village, Battersea Power Stn, SW11   no tel   11–1C **NEW**
408 Coldharbour Lane, SW9   07756 943372   11–2D **NEW**
Kingsland Locke, 130 Kingsland High St, E8   020 3877 0865   14–1A
231 Old Street, EC1   020 3456 7890   13–1A
"Intriguing twists on the kebab theme" (plus "good beer brewed on site" at the Kraft Dalston branch) continue to win consistently good ratings for this expanding chain, which in September 2022 adds a 20-seater in Brixton to its roster of locations. See also Kebab Queen. / https://www.eatlebab.com.

The Ledbury W11   £236   4 5 4
127 Ledbury Rd   020 7792 9090   7–1B
"Brett is indeed finally back!" at this Notting Hill luminary, which has often topped our annual diners' poll as London's top gastronomic destination, but which closed for the duration of the Covid pandemic. Virtually all feedback is ecstatic: "it's just so good to see it re-open!". "The dining room has had a thorough refresh" and the "slight reduction in the number of tables has significantly improved the ambience" ("you still feel you're in the same place, just with a more spacious feel"); and "service was top-notch even after just a couple of weeks of re-opening". When it comes to gastronomy, many fans feel that "while it didn't seem possible, if anything, Brett has raised his game even higher" since ditching the pre-pandemic à la carte menu format to focus on "a modern-style tasting menu", featuring 8 courses (and also at lunch with a cut-down option of 6 courses). A minority of reporters, though, are more cautious in their praise. The new "eye-watering level of prices" is the most widespread concern. But one or two deeper sceptics – while acknowledging "technically exquisite" or "knockout" cooking – think "it's not bad or disappointing, just not quite as good as it once was". So, as a result, The Ledbury food rating has not yet quite regained its customary level of 5/5. What's not in doubt, though, is that owner Nigel Platts-Martin's celebrated operation has survived its state of suspended animation to compete successfully once again at the highest level. / W11 2AQ; www.theledbury.com; Mon-Sat 9.45 pm; closed Mon-Thu L, closed Sun.

Legare SE1   £48   4 4 3
Cardamom Building, 31g Shad Thames   020 8063 7667   10–4D
"Top-top quality food" – from Matt Beardmore, formerly of Trullo – has established a glowing reputation for this small Italian on the South Bank near Tower Bridge. He opened it two years ago with ex-Barrafina manager Jay Patel, to immediate good reports – and "you can see why it has attracted all the hype". / SE1 2YB; legarelondon.com; @legarelondon; Wed-Sat, Tue 10 pm; closed Tue L, closed Sun & Mon.

F S A

Lemonia NW1 £60 233
89 Regent's Park Rd   020 7586 7454   9–3B
"Been going for 30+ years and still love it" – this *"shamelessly old-school Greek"* is a longstanding north London destination, and fans say it's *"such a nice change from the ubiquitous, pretentious, small-plates places"* in serving *"traditional taverna fayre that's perfectly decent, if not exciting"*. What people really go a bundle on though, is its *"lovely family-friendly atmosphere"*, as fostered by *"very approachable staff who have been there forever"* (but who *"can be slow at busy times"*). / NW1 8UY; www.lemonia.co.uk; Mon-Sat 10.30 pm, Sun 4 pm; closed Sun D; no Amex.

Leroy EC2 £69 333
18 Phipp Street   020 7739 4443   13–1B
It's hard to review this funky Shoreditch five-year-old without mentioning its star from the French tyre firm – the latter setting up expectations that are not always met. Many reports do give the highest praise to its creative small plates and well-curated selection of wines. But there's a disgruntled minority, who stumble on their feelings that it's over-egged. (*"I'm not a star chaser but I do want to have a good time, and somehow the whole experience felt a bit Spartan…"*; *"the food is indeed tasty, but is VERY overpriced. Is part of the problem that their Michelin star has pushed them into cramming as many tables in as possible?"*) / EC2E 4NP; www.leroyshoreditch.com; @leroyshoreditch; Mon-Sat 9.30 pm; closed Mon L, closed Sun; credit card deposit required to book.

Levan SE15 £60 332
3-4 Blenheim Grove   020 7732 2256   1–4D
"Innovative cooking, good cocktails and a relaxed, cool setting" draw the *"young hip crowd"* to this *"small Peckham restaurant"* from the team behind Salon in Brixton (RIP). All reports remain fundamentally upbeat, but a variety of gripes and some dishes *"not quite hitting the mark"* took its rating lower this year. / SE15 4QL; levanlondon.co.uk; @levanlondon; Tue-Sat 10 pm, Sun 3 pm; closed Sun D, closed Mon.

The Libertine EC3 NEW
The Royal Exchange   awaiting tel   10–2C
The vaults of The Royal Exchange are to become a posh Citified food court at the hands of the Incipio group, whose other operations include Pergola on the Wharf in Docklands and White City's Dear Grace. Open in October 2022, this is the business's seventh venue. / EC3E 3LR; Mon-Sat midnight, Sun 11 pm.

The Light House SW19 £65 333
75-77 Ridgway   020 8944 6338   11–2B
Celebrating its 25th year, *"this excellent, independent neighbourhood restaurant knocks out top-class Mediterranean dishes at no more than you'd pay in a nearby pub"* – in an *"imaginative"* culinary style that's *"not changed much over the years"*. It can seem pricey, or *"hit and miss"*, but there's also an argument that it's *"so underrated"*. / SW19 4ST; www.lighthousewimbledon.com; @lighthousewimbledon; Mon-Sat 10 pm, Sun 3.30 pm; closed Sun D.

The Lighterman N1 £58 222
3 Granary Square   020 3846 3400   9–3C
"A great location on the canal with lots of outdoor seating" – and with *"interesting views of the new developments around King's Cross"* – are the trump cards of this strikingly designed canalside gastropub on Granary Square. On the downside, the food is *"fairly standard pub fodder"* and it can just be *"too much, too busy, too noisy"*. / N1C 4BH; www.thelighterman.co.uk; @thelightermankx; Mon-Thu 11.30 pm, Fri & Sat midnight, Sun 10.30 pm.

FSA RATINGS: FROM 1 POOR — 5 EXCEPTIONAL

F S A

Lina Stores £47 4|3|3
13 Marylebone Lane, W1   020 3148 7503   3–1A NEW
51 Greek Street, W1   020 3929 0068   5–2A
20 Stable Street, N1   awaiting tel   9–3C
19 Bloomberg Arcade, EC4   020 3002 6034   10–3C NEW

"Beautiful fresh pasta, served from the heart by knowledgeable Italians" is the attractive offer at this small group, spun out of a famous veteran Soho deli (est. 1944) in the past five years under private equity outfit White Rabbit. The "food is good and good value, though limited and very focused on the pasta". There are now branches in King's Cross, the City's Bloomberg Arcade and most recently Marylebone; the farthest-flung is in Tokyo, while Clapham Old Town has been long promised. / www.linastores.co.uk; linastores.

Lino's NW6 NEW
6 Lonsdale Road   no tel   1–2B

Though well-received, the original Lino's near St Barts never properly got off the ground before Covid struck and closed during the pandemic. This September 2022 newcomer adds to the expanding Queen's Park scene, a two-floor site plus outside dining too. / NW6 6RD.

Lisboeta WC1 NEW £77 4|4|3
30 Charlotte Street   020 3830 9888   2–1C

"Nuno Mendes, London's most creative and friendly chef is back!" – partnering with MJMK Restaurants (who run Casa do Frango and Kol) – at this three-floor Fitzrovian in the thick of Charlotte Street, which "is set up for quick counter dining on the ground floor or longer meals upstairs". As usual, "his take on Portuguese food is outstanding", delivering "distinctive and gutsy flavours" with "flair". "The bill soon adds up", though, to the extent that one or two reporters find it "expensive and hyped". But the main complaint? – "the upstairs room can be painfully noisy". Top Menu Tip – 'abade de priscos' – the 'signature' custard pie pudding incorporating bacon.
/ WC1W 4AF; lisboeta.co.uk; @lisboeta.london; Tue-Sat 11.30 pm, Mon 11 pm, Sun 5 pm; closed Mon L closed Sun D.

Little Social W1 £77 4|3|3
5 Pollen Street   020 7870 3730   3–2C

"Opposite Jason Atherton's flagship in Pollen Street", its "high-class and intimate" younger sibling is in a more straightforward bistro style, and offers "simple food done exceptionally well". "Surroundings and service are warm" too, and "in summer you can eat outside on this pedestrianised street".
/ W1W 1NE; www.littlesocial.co.uk; @_littlesocial; Tue-Sat 9pm; closed Sun & Mon.

Little Taperia SW17 £53 3|3|3
143 Tooting High St   020 8682 3303   11–2C

"A local delight" in southwest London – "tasty, unusual tapas", "super-knowledgeable staff" and "buzzy, upbeat atmosphere add to the feeling that you're anywhere but Tooting High Street". "The prices are more like central London than SW17, but the quality's right up there to justify the premium". / SW17; www.thelittletaperia.co.uk; @thelittletaperia; Mon-Thu 11 pm, Fri & Sat midnight, Sun 10.30 pm; may need 6+ to book.

Llewelyn's SE24 £71 3|3|2
293-295 Railton Rd   020 7733 6676   11–2D

A "local favourite" opposite Herne Hill station for its "hearty and tasty European bistro food", "this restaurant goes from strength to strength. The cooking is inventive without being gimmicky and skilled without being over the top". It's "a lovely place", but "the room is strangely laid out", with a "cramped interior and hard surfaces, so it gets noisy" ("or you could say buzzy"). / SE24 0JP; www.llewelyns-restaurant.co.uk; @llewelynslondon; Tue-Thu 9 pm, Fri & Sat 9.30 pm, Sun 3.15 pm; closed Tue-Thu L closed Sun D, closed Mon; booking max 8 may apply.

FSA

La Lluna N10 £58 3 3 2
462 Muswell Hill Broadway   020 8442 2662   1–1B
This "wonderful local tapas bar with a buzzy vibe" in Muswell Hill wins strong ratings for its "surprisingly good food", served in a modern dining room with naked brick walls. A second branch (not listed) opened in Whetstone in summer 2021. / N10 1BS; www.lalluna.co.uk; @la_lluna_london; Mon-Thu 11 pm, Fri & Sat midnight, Sun 10 pm.

Locanda Locatelli W1 £103 2 3 2
Hyatt Regency, 8 Seymour St   020 7935 9088   2–2A
"Lovely to see Giorgio parading the floor and in the kitchen making sure everything is correct", say fans of his well-known, sophisticated and moodily "romantic" Italian, off Portman Square (run, with wife Plaxy, since 2002), for whom a visit is still "always a delight" with triumphant modern Italian cooking that's among London's best. Its ratings took a knock this year, though, from a number of former fans who said "it's not what it was" ("sorry, but we've had two or three disappointing meals here now").
/ W1H 7JZ; www.locandalocatelli.com; @locandalocatelli; Tue-Sat 11 pm, Sun 10 pm; closed Tue, Wed L, closed Mon; booking max 8 may apply.

London Shell Co. W2 £79 4 4 4
The Prince Regent, Sheldon Square   07818 666005   7–1C
"A cruise through Regent's Park to Camden Lock on the Grand Union canal is the perfect complement to five flavoursome fishy dishes, sluiced down with sommelier-advised wines" aboard the Prince Regent. Sister barge the Grand Duchess offers a similar seafood menu, permanently docked by Paddington station. Top Tip – "go as a group of four – smaller groups will end up sharing a table due to the limited space onboard". / W2 6EP; www.londonshellco.com; @londonshellco; Wed-Sat 9.30 pm, Sun 3 pm; closed Wed-Fri L closed Sun D, closed Mon & Tue.

London Stock SW18 £52 3 4 3
2 Bubbling Well Square, Ram Quarter   020 8075 3877   11–2B
"They're trying hard with the food here… perhaps too hard" – but that's about the worst anyone has to say about this 'relaxed, fine-dining concept', whose bare-brick walls are part of Wandsworth's 'Ram Quarter'. It's the first venture of Cordon-Bleu-trained Assem Abdel Hady and Andres Bernal, plus chef Sebastian Rast and presents an 8-course tasting menu 'drawing inspiration from the multicultural melting pot of the community in which it is based'. Even if "not every dish finds its mark, they are always beautifully presented" and some excellent overall meals are reported. Now entering its third year, it's yet really to make waves, but worth a try. / SW18 1UQ; londonstockrestaurant.co.uk; @ldnstockrestaurant; Wed-Sat 8 pm, Sun 3 pm; closed Sun D, closed Mon & Tue; payment – credit card only.

Long Chim W1 NEW
Horse & Dolphin Yard off Macclesfield Street   awaiting tel   5–3A
Chef David Thompson has built international renown for his Thai cuisine, although his previous London venture of over a decade ago – Nahm (long RIP), in Belgravia's swanky Halkin Hotel – never quite hit the mark (despite achieving a Michelin star). This Chinatown newcomer joins branches in Sydney, Perth and Dubai and incorporates a big basement, with a small ground-floor mezzanine and sizable exterior courtyard for outside dining. As you'd expect, this is a more down-to-earth formula than Belgravia's was, with a more casual, street-food-style menu. / W1W 5AZ; @longchim; Wed-Sat midnight, Sun 9 pm.

FSA RATINGS: FROM 1 POOR — 5 EXCEPTIONAL

The Lordship SE22 £42 3️⃣2️⃣2️⃣
211 Lordship Lane   020 8299 2068   1–4D

"This great local pub" in Dulwich excels for its "simple food – especially the pies". "It's always a big surprise to me that the Lordship isn't in Harden's. It's a huge room with lots of outdoor space, and very friendly, welcoming staff". / SE22 8HA; thelordshippub.co.uk; @lordshippub; Tue-Sat 10 pm, Mon 11 pm, Sun 9 pm; closed Mon L.

The Lore of the Land W1 £68 3️⃣3️⃣4️⃣
4 Conway Street   020 3927 4480   2–1B

This faux-rustic pub in deepest Fitzrovia from Guy Ritchie and David Beckham is "a class act", and serves some of the "best pub grub ever", including venison from Ritchie's Wiltshire estate. The pub has been around for almost 200 years and has previously been known as the Adams Arms and the Lukin. Two fires in the space of six months last year invited newspaper headlines about 'two smoking barrels'. / W1W 6BB; gritchiepubs.com; @loreofthelandpub; Tue, Wed 11 pm, Thu-Sat 11.30 pm, Sun 9 pm; closed Mon.

Lorne SW1 £71 5️⃣5️⃣3️⃣
76 Wilton Road   020 3327 0210   2–4B

"Fabulous Katie Exton and her team never disappoint" at her "lovely, small and intimate Pimlico restaurant", which "is coming into its own despite all the terrible setbacks when it opened" (including a flood closing it for months) and "hits a sweet spot of value and reliability". A major attraction is the "clean and well-executed modern European cuisine" – "with interesting ingredients and dishes on the right side of edgy" – but the rarer attraction is her "endearing" personal style and "enthusiastic gentle guidance to the right wine pairing" from the "supremely clever and wide-ranging wine list" she has assembled as "one of London's top sommeliers". Top Tip – "there is a great glassware selection too for a restaurant of its size, which is often overlooked in guides!" / SW1S 1DE; www.lornerestaurant.co.uk; @lorne_restaurant; Mon-Sat 9.30 pm; closed Mon L, closed Sun.

Louie WC2 £97 3️⃣2️⃣3️⃣
13-15 West Street   020 8057 6500   5–2B

Rihanna celebrated her birthday in February 2022 at this lavish Creole haunt next to The Ivy, in Covent Garden, where the former site of L'Atelier de Joël Robuchon nowadays combines a restaurant (ground floor), bar (first floor) and roof garden. Whether the tastes of New Orleans are faithfully replicated is a matter of some dispute – there is the odd take-down of "overpriced and under-seasoned dross", but most reports actually say its gumbo, Louisiana crab cakes and other eclectic dishes are "very good". / WC2W 9NE; www.louie-london.com; @louielondon_restaurant; Tue-Sat 10.30 pm; closed Tue, Fri L, closed Sun & Mon.

LPM W1 £116 5️⃣4️⃣4️⃣
54 Brook's Mews   020 7495 4774   3–2B

The Côte d'Azur comes to Mayfair at this glamorous, "super-slick" and "always busy" operation, tucked away near Claridges, which – since 2007 – has led the way with its "fantastic, light small plates": "not your typical French, heavy, creamy food" but heavenly dishes that "leave you feeling like you ate healthily". Even those rating it "outstanding all round" can find it "overpriced" – a better verdict would be "expensive but worth it". / W1K 4EG; www.lpmlondon.co.uk; @lpmlondon; Tue-Sat 10.30 pm, Sun 10 pm; closed Mon.

F S A

Luca EC1 £90 4 3 4
88 St John St   020 3859 3000   10–1A
"Subtle and original" cooking (from "the highest quality of ingredients", all of them British) wins high ratings at this "discreet, classic high-end Italian", which inhabits rambling and lovely premises north of Smithfield Market, complete with a beautiful rear conservatory. Other than being "a really special place", it bears no comparison to its sibling, The Clove Club. Top Tips – the Parmesan fries are a trademark; and it's "great for a business lunch". / EC1E 4EH; luca.restaurant; @luca.restaurant; Wed-Sat 11 pm; closed Mon & Tue & Sun.

Luce e Limoni WC1 £63 3 4 3
91-93 Gray's Inn Rd   020 7242 3382   10–1A
"Great food in a cosy, homely setting" – this Sicilian specialist on a stretch of the unlovely Gray's Inn Road "is a useful and reliable local restaurant in an area with limited options". Owner Fabrizio Zafarana "makes a real effort to get to know all his customers and will happily amend a dish to suit personal taste". / WC1X 8TX; www.luceelimoni.com; @restaurant_luce_e_limoni; Mon-Thu 10 pm, Fri & Sat 11 pm; closed Sat L, closed Sun.

Luciano's SE12 £58 3 4 3
131 Burnt Ash Road   020 8852 3186   1–4D
"Fabulous pizza and pasta (all made on site), friendly staff and an interesting wine list" add up to a "brilliant-value local Italian" in Lee – "a cut above neighbourhood standard". Named after Luciano Masiello, the one-time Charlton Athletic footballer and father of owner Enzo. / SE12; lucianoslondon.co.uk; @lucianoslondon; Mon-Sat 9.30 pm, Sun 8.30 pm; closed Mon-Fri L.

Lucio SW3 £98 3 3 2
257 Fulham Rd   020 7823 3007   6–3B
Celebrating its 20th anniversary this year, this family-run Italian on the Fulham Road is "everything you'd expect in an upmarket Chelsea restaurant" – although the service, led by host Lucio Altana and his sons Dario and Mirko, "is rather better than you might anticipate". / SW3 6HY; www.luciorestaurant.com; @luciorestaurant; Tue-Sat 10.30 pm, Sun 3 pm; closed Sun D, closed Mon.

Lucky & Joy E5 £46 4 3 4
95 Lower Clapton Road   07488 965966   14–1B
This "ridiculously low-key venue in Clapton" serves perhaps the best Chinese food in town that's prepared by Westerners – chef-owners Ellen Parr (ex-Rochelle Canteen and Moro) and Peter Kelly (ex-Morito). "It's a small menu so order everything!" / E5 0NP; luckyandjoy.co.uk; @luckyandjoyldn; closed Mon-Sat & Sun.

Lucky Cat W1 £84 2 2 2
10-13 Grosvenor Square   020 7107 0000   3–2A
This "loud" Gordon Ramsay-backed venue in Mayfair (on the former site of Maze, long RIP) aims to channel the glam 1930s drinking dens of the Far East and serves a hodgepodge of dishes: from sushi to steak; from salads to seafood. Dreary ratings overall support those who say there are "so many better places to get much better pan-Asian fare"… so it's just the time to start a roll-out then! with its first, much simpler spin-off – The Lucky Cat Noodle & Bar – taking over a Shoreditch site previously dedicated to chicken and waffles. / W1W 6JP; www.gordonramsayrestaurants.com/lucky-cat; @luckycatbygordonramsay; Mon-Wed midnight, Thu-Sat 3 am, Sun 11 pm.

FSA

Lume NW3 £87 3 3 2
38 Primrose Hill Road   020 7449 9556   9–2A

The "most charming front of house", led by "delightful owner Guiseppe" adds brio to this "passionate and cute little local", which occupies a quiet corner of Primrose Hill. "Good wines… it's also a wine shop" add to the gastronomic appeal of its "authentic" Sardinian/Sicilian gastronomia. / NW3 3AD; www.lume.london; @lumelondon; Tue-Sun 10 pm; closed Tue-Thu L, closed Mon.

Lupins SE1 £51 4 4 3
66 Union St   020 3908 5888   10–4B

This "awesome little spot" near London Bridge ("handy for Tate Modern") serves "fresh and really interesting" 'British tapas', including some "innovative vegetarian options". Five years after the launch, founders Lucy Pedder and Natasha Cooke have a second venue, Pomelo, at the Goods Way food market in King's Cross. / SE1 1TD; www.lupinslondon.com; @lupinslondon; Wed-Sat 10 pm; closed Wed L, closed Mon & Tue & Sun; payment – credit card only.

Lure NW5 £52 3 2 3
56 Chetwynd Rd   020 7267 0163   9–1B

"In some ways, an unremarkable eat-in experience but the fish is excellent" – this modern Dartmouth Park chippy is still recommended by locals for its "top-quality fish 'n' chips", but at times "its level of service can leave something to be desired". / NW5 1DJ; www.lurefishkitchen.co.uk; Wed-Sat 10 pm, Sun 9.30 pm; closed Wed-Fri L, closed Mon & Tue; booking weekends only.

Lurra W1 £67 4 3 3
9 Seymour Place   020 7724 4545   2–2A

"A simple, understated oasis of calm and deliciousness, just a stone's throw from the hullabaloo of Marble Arch" – this accomplished Basque venue in Seymour Village serves a *"concise but impressive menu"* of *"sublime Spanish food mixing tapas and some of the best meat and fish in London"*. In particular, *"the steaks are pretty amazing"*, with cuts from *"elderly dairy cows"* a particular feature. Top Menu Tips – as well as steak, the grilled turbot is *"perfectly cooked"*; and *"the cheesecake is, as everyone says, awe-inspiring… still thinking about it"*. / W1H 5BA; www.lurra.co.uk; Mon-Sat 10.30 pm, Sun 3.30 pm; closed Mon L closed Sun D.

Lutyens Grill, The Ned EC2 £106 3 2 4
27 Poultry   020 3828 2000   10–2C

"Is there a better business venue?" query fans of this plush steakhouse, which sits within a panelled corner of the vast former HQ of Midland Bank, next to the Bank of England. It's the prime dining option within the hotel accessible to those not blessed with membership of Soho House, featuring top-quality British and imported steak. / EC2E 8AJ; www.thened.com/restaurants/lutyens-grill; @thenedlondon; Mon-Sat midnight, Sun 4 pm; closed Sat L closed Sun D.

Lyle's E1 £97 5 4 3
The Tea Building, 56 Shoreditch High Street   020 3011 5911   13–1B

"Never failing to deliver extraordinary food" – James Lowe's famous (among foodies) canteen, at the foot of Shoreditch's well-known 'Tea Building, *"is so consistent in delivering seemingly simple, but actually quite intricate flavour combinations"*. These are offered as small plates at lunch and in the evening as a tasting menu. Originally he was inspired by a stint working at St John, but his own cuisine is nowadays something of a benchmark in its own right for modern seasonal British cooking, with *"a menu that changes all the time"*. / E1 6JJ; www.lyleslondon.com; @lyleslondon; Mon-Sat 11 pm; closed Sun.

FSA RATINGS: FROM **1** POOR — **5** EXCEPTIONAL

FSA

Lyon's N8 £57 4 4 3
1 Park Road   020 8350 8983   1–1C

"Big flavours and lots of spice" characterise the "inventive sharing plates of seafood" from the British Isles, prepared with influences from around the world, at this "lovely" (if "cramped" and "noisy") Crouch End three-year-old, where "there's always a great vibe and staff are super-friendly". Top Tip – "fabulous squid-ink bread and whipped butters". / N8 8TE; lyons-restaurant.com; @lyonsseafood; Tue-Sat 10 pm; closed Tue-Thu L, closed Sun & Mon.

M Restaurants £99 2 2 3
Zig Zag Building, Victoria St, SW1   020 3327 7776   2–4B
Newfoundland, E14   awaiting tel   12–1C **NEW**
2-3 Threadneedle Walk EC2   020 3327 7770   10–2C

Martin Williams's "customer-centric ethos" is on display at these slickly run and business-friendly 'Gastro Playgrounds', in the City, Victoria and – launching in August 2022 – in Canary Wharf, which deliver a mix of "amazing steaks", plus extensive wine (and the availability of memberships with access to the 'M Den Portal'). Its ratings were dented slightly this year though by one or two disappointing reports relating to "pedestrian dishes" and "awful mark-ups". / www.mrestaurants.co.uk; mrestaurants.

Ma Goa SW15 £43 3 3 3
242-244 Upper Richmond Rd   020 8780 1767   11–2B

The Kapoor family's "authentic Goan cuisine has been a stalwart in Putney for 30 years", at their well-known venue on the South Circular Road. Five years ago they implemented a complete make-over, modernising their offer in street-market style, with a new selection of "craft beers that are great accompaniments for the hot dishes". / SW15 6TG; www.magoaputney.co.uk; @magoalondon; Tue-Thu, Sun 9.30 pm, Fri & Sat 10.30 pm; closed Tue-Thu, Sun, Fri & Sat L, closed Mon.

Macellaio RC £68 2 2 3
39-45 Shaftesbury Avenue, W1   020 3727 6161   5–3A
6 Store Street, WC1   020 3848 7230   2–1C
84 Old Brompton Rd, SW7   020 7589 5834   6–2B
Arch 24, 229 Union St, SE1   07467 307682   10–4B
124 Northcote Rd, SW11   020 3848 4800   11–2C
38-40 Exmouth Market, EC1   020 3696 8220   10–1A

"Just the place to stuff yourself silly with beef!", say loyal fans of Roberto Costa's successful chain, where you choose your cut from "amazing meat displays to get the juices flowing": a formula that's brought expansion over the years to six locations across the capital, including on Shaftesbury Avenue (where it's branded 'Teatro del Carne'). Ratings sank this year, though, on a number of "disappointing" reports, with recurring themes including "quality meat undermined by poor cooking" and "high prices for wines considering their middling status". / www.macellaiorc.com.

Maddox Tavern W1 **NEW** £74
47 Maddox Street   020 3376 9922   3–2C

A very characterful Mayfair site – once a posh gentlemen's outfitters and more recently a branch of Browns – now hosts this July 2022 newcomer (which opened too late to be included in our annual diners' poll). Steaks feature prominently on a menu of 'elevated' British classics and there's also a seperate all-day 'tavern' selection. / W1W 2PG; www.maddoxtavern.com; @maddoxtavern; Mon-Thu midnight, Fri & Sat 12.30 am; closed Sun.

Made in Italy £56 3|2|2
249 King's Rd, SW3   020 7352 1880   6–3C
141 The Broadway, SW19   020 8540 4330   11–2B
"Rustic décor, friendly service and great pizza" win recommendations for this long-running duo, whose Chelsea branch boasts a heated roof terrace. They make their own fresh cheeses at a factory in Battersea, and their "burrata heart on a pizza is a creamy delight". / www.madeinitalygroup.co.uk; madeinitalylondon.

Magenta NW1 NEW £76 3|3|3
The Megaro Hotel, 23 Euston Road   0203 146 0222   9–3C
"Trying to be different", this new bar/restaurant in King's Cross is bang opposite the station, yet aims to defy its touristy location with natty décor and a northern Italian menu of some ambition. We've rated it on limited feedback which mentions some aspects that were "underwhelming" offset by others that were "very good"; and which imply it's worth a whirl if you are in the area. / NW1 2SD; www.magentarestaurant.co.uk; @magenta_kx; Tue-Sat 10 pm; closed Sun & Mon.

Maggie Jones's W8 £67 3|4|5
6 Old Court Pl   020 7937 6462   6–1A
Named after the pseudonym used by the late Princess Margaret for incognito dining, this cosseting 1970s-style brasserie provides a "cosy and romantic setting" for aristos or commoners in search of comforting Anglo-French classics, washed down with wine in magnum bottles whose consumption is measured by a dipstick. It's on top form these days, with improved ratings across the board. / W8 4PL; www.maggie-jones.co.uk; @maggiejonesrestaurant; Mon-Fri 9.30 pm, Sat & Sun 9.15 pm.

Maguro W9 £53 3|2|2
5 Lanark Pl   020 7289 4353   9–4A
This tiny Japanese near Little Venice is "well worth seeking out". "The food is served in a friendly manner and the sushi and sashimi is always very fresh". / W9 1BT; www.maguro-restaurant.com; @maguro.london; Mon-Sat 11 pm, Sun 10.30 pm; closed Mon-Sun L; no Amex.

The Maine Mayfair W1 £116 3|2|4
6 Medici Court, 20 Hanover Square   020 3432 2192   3–2C
"The burlesque show can come as a bit of a shock, but adds to the fun if somewhat tacky vibe" of this big, brash, American brasserie – all 350 covers of it, set over three floors of a grand Georgian townhouse in Mayfair. Fans feel "it's set to be a staple" aided by its enjoyable New England-style cuisine and glam, highly Instagrammable interior, but some reports do suggest that "while good, the food's nothing special and not cheap". Top Tip – recently they added a 100-cover foliage-filled terrace for lunch, dinner and drinks. / W1W 1JY; www.themainemayfair.com; @themainemayfair; closed Mon-Sat & Sun.

Maison Bertaux W1 £15 4|3|5
28 Greek St   020 7437 6007   5–2A
"Fight to get a seat and enjoy the best pâtisserie in town" at this "Soho institution" – founded by a Parisian exile in 1871 and frequented by generations of artists, revolutionaries and bohos. It's "eccentric to say the least", and not incidentally "one of the few pâtisseries still cooking on the premises – there are so few of these places left!". And while "still miles ahead of other French pâtisseries, they also offer a (very English) cream tea". "They do their utmost to squeeze you in (as it is always busy). I guess the ambience is a matter of taste but luxurious it isn't!" / W1D 5DQ; www.maisonbertaux.com; @maison_bertaux; Mon-Sun 6 pm; closed Mon-Sun D.

Maison François SW1 — £87 — 3 4 5
34 Duke Street St James's   020 3988 5777   3–3D

"Paris comes to St James's" at this "beautiful and buzzy" two-year-old, which has been one of the more impressive arrivals of recent years (it opened in autumn 2020). "Proper, well-executed French-brasserie food" (snails, crab salad, roast chicken, veal, steak and chips…) – "such a relief after all of the faddy nonsense dominating the London restaurant scene" – is delivered by "first-rate" staff throughout the day, from breakfast onwards. And together with the "amazing" high-ceilinged interior, the overall combination makes for a superb "all-round experience", if one "with prices to match the location". Top Tips – "the best dessert trolley in London!" and a "fun" basement wine bar called Frank's. / SW1S 6DF; maisonfrancois.london; @maisonfrancoislondon; Thu-Sat 1 am, Mon-Wed midnight, Sun 6 pm; closed Sun D.

Mallow SE1 — £56 — 4 2 3
1 Cathedral Street   020 7846 8785   10–4C

"A fantastic new addition from the Mildreds group" – this autumn 2021 newcomer makes "a good place to take people who are sceptical about meat-free food". It's "a pretty location with an excellent view of Borough Market" that's "full of atmosphere" and "it doesn't overly virtue-sell the plant-based experience: they just get on with making it excellent" with a "slightly more innovative approach to the seasonally changing menu" than in the main chain. "The wine list is limited, but they do have cocktails". / SE1 1TL; www.mallowlondon.com; @mallowlondon; Mon-Sat 11 pm, Sun 10 pm.

Mamma Dough — £51 — 4 3 2
40 Ladywell Road, SE13   020 8690 7550   1–4D
179 Queen's Rd, SE15   020 7635 3470   1–4D
76-78 Honor Oak Pk, SE23   020 8699 5196   1–4D
1 Station Road, SE25   020 8653 2537   1–4D
299 Kirkdale, SE26   020 8778 1234   1–4D
303-307 Balham High Road, SW17   020 3409 4671   11–2D
354 Coldharbour Ln, SW9   020 7095 1491   11–2D

"Tasty thin-crust dough – cooked well in the middle, so no soggy bottoms" – is the secret to the appeal of this seven-strong South London sourdough pizzeria group, where the emphasis is on local ingredients (including Shipton Mill flour and British-made buffalo mozzarella) washed down with locally brewed craft beers and juices from Kent. / www.mammadough.co.uk.

Mandarin Kitchen W2 — £68 — 4 3 2
14-16 Queensway   020 7727 9012   7–2C

"Who would order anything but the lobster noodles?" ("the best way to get the most out of a crustacean, and surprisingly good value!") at this "unbeatable Cantonese classic" in Queensway: a "chaotic, crowded and noisy", if "efficiently run" stalwart (est 1978) which sells more lobster than just about any other restaurant in the UK. If you do, there are other delicious seafood dishes to try (scallops, crab, razor clams…) and the Peking Duck's not bad either. / W2 3RX; www.mandarin.kitchen; @mandarinkitchenlondon; Mon-Sat 11.15 pm, Sun 23.

Mangal 1 E8 — £34 — 5 3 2
10 Arcola St   020 7275 8981   14–1A

"Succulent BBQ meat and great-value meze" have earned this Turkish grill in Dalston a major and well-earned reputation. For some, a meal here represents "the best value in London" – helped by a "liberal BYO policy that means you drink as well as your cellar allows". Top Tips: "the sweetbreads are sensational". And for an ambitious modern take on cooking over fire, head round the corner to Mangal 2, now run by owner Ali Dirik's sons Sertaç and Ferhat (see also). / E8 2DJ; www.mangal1.com; @mangal_ocakbasi; Sun-Wed midnight, Fri & Sat 1 am; closed Thu; cash only; no booking.

FSA

Mangal 2 N16 £80 4 4 2
4 Stoke Newington Rd   020 7254 7888   1–1C

"Mangal 2 has reinvented itself during the pandemic" with Ferhat and Sertaç Dirik (the sons of the founder), "transforming it from its previous incarnation as just another of one of the (good!) pile-'em-high Turkish restaurants on the Dalston/Stoke Newington strip into a totally new venue: still Turkish, but more small plates now than giant platters". All reports agree it's a successful switch, "standing on a solid par with the other good small-plates-and-wine joints around Hackney, while still doing something quite different". "The noisy room is a little Spartan, but the exciting and interesting food transports you" – "the Turkish influence is not that obvious" but the menu delivers "good ingredients very well cooked" (although "the wine list is a bit too natural, with no other conventional options"). / N16 8BH; www.mangal2.com; @mangal2restaurant; Mon-Sat 11 pm; closed Mon & Tue, Sat L, closed Sun.

Manicomio £86 2 2 3
85 Duke of York Square, SW3   020 7730 3366   6–2D
6 Gutter Lane, EC2   020 7726 5010   10–2B

This modern Italian "favourite" makes good use of its large and attractive terrace in Chelsea's peaceful Duke of York's Square, and has a big and loyal following as a result. Fans say the food is "interesting" too, but more sceptical diners feel that's debatable. It also has a twin in the City, which attracts much less comment. / www.manicomio.co.uk; manicomiorestaurant.

Manteca EC2 £50 5 2 4
49-51 Curtain Road   020 7033 6642   13–1B

"A fabulous range of super-tasty Italian small plates with some very memorable flavours (that pig skin ragu!!!!)" and incorporating "terrific homemade pasta" are making a smash hit of Chris Leach and David Carter's "absolutely rammed" venture, which relocated from Heddon Street to Shoreditch in October 2021. It wins nothing but praise and many nominations as "the top food experience of the last 12 months". "Enthusiastic" service can suffer under the weight of custom and – with its "deafening noise" – the setting does "slightly reek of (the former) PizzaExpress the site used to be" – but "given that it's exceptional, you'll get by... they can polish any rough edges later". / EC2E 3PT; mantecarestaurant.co.uk; @manteca_london; Mon-Sat 11 pm, Sun 5 pm; closed Sun D.

Manthan W1 £61 3 4 3
49 Maddox Street   020 7491 9191   3–2C

Rohit Ghai's "comfy and stylish" Mayfair yearling offers a homely menu inspired by the chef's Punjabi childhood. "Awesome" flavours from "the good variety of dishes" make it "a must-try" for fans. Sceptics, though – while acknowledging that "effort is put into both good food and service" – feel some results "lack punch" or "aren't quite at the top levels of food from the subcontinent in London". / W1W; manthanmayfair.co.uk; @manthanmayfair; Mon-Sun 10 pm.

Manuel's SE19 £60 4 5 3
129 Gipsy Hill   020 8670 1843   1–4D

Some of south east London's best Italian food is to be found at this attractive Gipsy Hill Sicilian, acclaimed for its "wonderful Mediterranean food, superb Sunday lunch... Live music events are always good fun (particularly the tribute acts!)". In summer the terrace comes into its own. / SE19 1QS; www.manuelsrestaurantandbar.com; @manuelsrestaurantgipsyhill; Tue-Sat 10.30 pm, Sun 9 pm; closed Mon.

FSA RATINGS: FROM 1 POOR — 5 EXCEPTIONAL

FSA

Manuka Kitchen SW6 £59 3|3|3
510 Fulham Rd   020 7731 0864   6–4A
This flexible and well-run New Zealand-inspired spot just off Parson's Green is an equally "dependable" option "for Chelsea pre-match brunches" and "candlelit dinners". / SW6 5NJ; manukakitchen.co.uk; @manukakitchen; Tue-Sat 11 pm, Mon 10 pm, Sun 4 pm; closed Mon L closed Sun D; booking max 8 may apply.

Manzi's W1
1 Bateman's Buildings   no tel   5–2A
This long-planned and long pandemic-delayed Soho seafood restaurant may be delayed still further by the management changes at Corbin & King, now renamed as The Wolseley Hospitality Group. It is envisaged as a 'fun and affordable' venue along the lines of stablemate Brasserie Zédel. But – in the absence of Jeremy King and Chris Corbin – who will now provide the vision for recreating the original Manzi's, which was, for decades, a treasured standby for theatregoers on the south corner of Chinatown? / W1W 3EN; Tue-Sat, Mon 11 pm.

Mar I Terra SE1 £54 4|4|3
14 Gambia St   020 7928 7628   10–4A
"Very good-quality" tapas and a "nice, buzzy" atmosphere greet guests at this converted small backstreet pub near the South Bank, one of the longer-established Hispanic specialists in town. It's a "favourite for a casual night out" and "conveniently located for the NT, Young Vic, Tate Mod and so on". / SE1 0XH; www.mariterra.net; Tue, Thu, Wed, Fri & Sat midnight; closed Wed, Fri & Sat L, closed Sun & Mon.

Marcella SE8 £46 3|4|3
165a Deptford High Street   020 3903 6561   1–3D
This hip five-year-old on Deptford High Street wins consistently high ratings for its simple and "authentic" Italian cooking, inspired by the great food writer Marcella Hazan. It is the younger sibling to Peckham star Artusi. / SE8 3NU; www.marcella.london; @marcelladeptford; Wed & Thu 10 pm, Fri & Sat 10.30 pm, Sun 4 pm; closed Sun D, closed Mon & Tue; may need 6+ to book.

Marcus, The Berkeley SW1 £172 3|3|3
Wilton Pl   020 7235 1200   6–1D
Marcus Wareing's Belgravia flagship keeps ploughing a steady course "at the level you would expect from a top Knightsbridge hotel", at this "well-spaced" venue which continues to be "run with expertise" despite a changeover of personnel this year (in January 2022, Mark and Shauna Froydenlund stepped down as chef-patrons, leaving head chef Craig Johnston and senior sous chef, Jack Hazell to take the reins). The modern French cuisine is "beautifully well-judged and thought out"; "service is wonderfully attentive and warm"; and "the wide range of wines provides interesting choices for any dish". There's the odd cavil that the food can be on the "rich" side, but the main objection here is the obvious: "the bill can get just a bit silly…" / SW1X 7RL; www.marcusrestaurant.com; @marcusbelgravia; Tue-Sat 10 pm; closed Sun & Mon; no trainers.

Mare Street Market E8 £53 3|2|4
117 Mare Street   020 3745 2470   14–2B
Funky chandeliers, plants and random artworks lend an eclectic and energetic vibe to the dining possibilities of this hiply transformed Hackney office block (nowadays a 10,000 square foot market), where you eat (the same menu) in either the 'Open Kitchen' or the 'Dining Room' (cosier, with a higher concentration of design pieces). An array of pizzas is a menu mainstay as is a selection of small plates and a few grills. It's not a foodie destination, but can be "good value". / E8 4RU; www.marestreetmarket.com; @marestreetmarket; Sun-Thu midnight, Fri & Sat 1 am.

Maremma SW2 £64   4 3 4
36 Brixton Water Lane   020 3186 4011   11–2D
This "brilliant local in Brixton" scores well for its "delicious, light food", taking inspiration from the Maremma, a region of coastal marshes in the south of Tuscany. "A lovely candlelit ambience" makes it "perfect for a fun date night". / SW2 1PE; www.maremmarestaurant.com; @maremma_restaurant; Wed-Sat 10 pm, Sun 4 pm; closed Wed & Thu L closed Sun D, closed Mon & Tue.

Margaux SW5 £74   4 4 3
152 Old Brompton Rd   020 7373 5753   6–2B
"Boeuf bourguignon was done to perfection" – typical of the "very solid French cooking of meat and fish courses" at this "reliable neighbourhood restaurant", on the well-heeled borders of Earl's Court and South Kensington. Top Tip – "it's best to eat upstairs". / SW5 0BE; www.barmargaux.co.uk; @barmargaux; Tue-Sat 10.45 pm; closed Tue L, closed Sun & Mon.

Margot WC2 £84   3 4 4
45 Great Queen Street   020 3409 4777   5–2D
"Suave" "classic, top-end Italian" in Covent Garden that's run by co-founder Nicolas Jaouën, who presides over "an elegant room, smooth service and capable cooking". It's "not cheap, but you leave feeling you have been looked after well". The "excellent list" numbers 350 wines. / WC2B 5AA; www.margotrestaurant.com; @margotldn_; Tue-Sat 9.30 pm; closed Sun & Mon.

Maria G's W14 NEW
Coe House, 1-4 Warwick Lane   020 3479 3772   8–2D
Retirement looks OK, judging by the glossy apartment buildings of the sprawling 'Riverstone Living' retirement complex in the former no-man's-land between the Tesco superstore on the A4 and Olympia. At the foot of one such building is this project overseen by Robin Gill – a neighbourhood Italian with a curt menu and a cute outside space. It opened too late for our annual diners' poll – hard to judge on initial reports whether it's more than a high-quality amenity for nearby residents. / W14 8FN; mariags.co.uk; @robin.gill.cook; Mon-Sat 10 pm, Sun 9 pm.

The Marksman E2 £75   3 3 3
254 Hackney Road   020 7739 7393   14–2A
The "short and desirable menu" of modern British dishes continues to win praise for this ambitious gastropub near Columbia Road Market, from former St John chefs Tom Harris and Jon Rotheram. A huge hit when it opened, it's adopted a lower profile over the years, but remains "just the place to take hard-to-impress young adult children". / E2 7SJ; www.marksmanpublichouse.com; @marksman_pub; Wed-Sat 10 pm, Sun 9 pm; closed Wed & Thu L, closed Mon & Tue.

Maroush £67   3 2 2
5 McNicol Drive, NW10   020 3941 3221   1–2A
38 Beauchamp Pl, SW3   020 7581 5434   6–1C
68 Edgware Rd, W2   020 7224 9339   7–1D
"Fun, reliable Lebanese cuisine served Beirut-style" – "shawarma and meze-type dishes at their best" – has built an empire over 40 years for Marouf and Houda Abouzaki's well-known chain (and its sister brand, 'Ranoush'). The pandemic brought branch closures, including of the original Edgware Road site, although Knightsbridge's Maroush II with its café-style ground floor (and including a sandwich wraps menu) is still going strong. And – showing the resilience for which the Lebanese are renowned – a large new "open plan" site opened in 2021 in distant Park Royal. / www.maroush.com.

F S A

Maru W1 £242 5 4 3
18 Shepherd Market   020 3637 7677   3–4B

This "minute restaurant" in Mayfair's Shepherd Market leapt "straight into the top tier of London's Japanese restaurants" when it opened in 2021, with its "top-class dishes centred around dry-aged fish". Taiji Maruyama, a third-generation sushi chef from Fukushima who has worked around the world, controls every aspect of the 20-course omakase (chef's choice) meal, from the crockery he made himself to the "food prepared in front of you", "expertly paired with sake, tea or wine". It's a "unique and intimate experience" – "very Tokyo" – and part of the new wave of tiny, ultra-focused Japanese operations in London, for those with deep enough pockets. / W1W 7QH; www.marulondon.com; @maru__london; Tue-Sat 11 pm; closed Tue-Sat L, closed Sun & Mon.

Marugame Udon £17 4 3 2
St Christopher's Place, W1   no tel   3–1B **NEW**
Unit 2.03 Entertainment Avenue, The O2, SE10   no tel   12–1D **NEW**
The Atrium Kitchen, Cabot Place, E14   no tel   12–1C **NEW**
114 Middlesex Street, E1   020 3148 2780   13–2B

"Decent noodles at rock-bottom prices" means these "new, authentic, incredibly reasonably priced Japanese canteens" are "always busy". An 800-strong global chain, it launched in London in July 2021 with a 100+ cover site just off Liverpool Street and is adding branches willy nilly, with the second half of 2022 seeing debuts in Oxford Circus, The Strand and Waterloo. "The food cannot be fresher from here: noodles are made on-site and tempura is fried just in front of you" and "they cater for both non-vegans and vegans". Finish your meal with "unlimited ice cream, which is unexpectedly delicious too". / marugame.co.uk; marugameuk.

Masala Zone £60 3 3 4
Selfridges, 400 Oxford Street, W1   020 7287 9966   3–1A
9 Marshall St, W1   020 7287 9966   4–2B
48 Floral St, WC2   020 7379 0101   5–2D
147 Earl's Court Rd, SW5   020 7373 0220   6–2A
75 Bishop's Bridge Rd, W2   020 7221 0055   7–1C
25 Parkway, NW1   020 7267 4422   9–3B

"I keep coming back for the reliably distinctive range of Indian dishes… when I'm pushed to try new things I rarely regret it" – the "always interesting menu" at these longstanding pioneers of street food and thalis delivers "very tasty grub in generous portions that's good value for money". It's run by MW Eats (the family company behind some of the capital's most prestigious subcontinental restaurants). / www.masalazone.com; masalazone.

Masalchi by Atul Kochhar HA9 **NEW** £42
2 Wembley Park Boulevard   01494 728126   1–1A

A world away from the Mayfair luxury that made his reputation, Atul Kochhar gets more 'down and dirty' with this new, glass-walled 120-seater in the shadow of Wembley Stadium with a budget street-food formula. So far, we've only had limited feedback, but it says the food is "very good" and in a December 2021 review, Jay Rayner of The Observer told readers to "expect uncompromising fire and depth". / HA9 0HP; masalchi.co.uk; @masalchi_wembley; Mon-Thu 10 pm, Fri & Sat 10.30 pm, Sun 9.30 pm.

Master Wei WC1 £32 4 2 2
13 Cosmo Place   020 7209 6888   2–1D

"Excellent Xi'an hand-pulled noodles" ("pasta-like noodles with chillies to make your eyes water") "at reasonable prices" ensure that chef-proprietor Wei Guirong's central London canteen, "tucked away in a narrow pedestrian street near Russell Square", is always "buzzing". It is a sibling to Xi'an Impression near Arsenal's Emirates Stadium. / WC1W 3AP; master-wei.com; @master.wei.3150; Sun-Thu 10 pm, Fri & Sat 10.30 pm.

FSA

Mathura SW1 £59 3 2 2
4 Greycoat Place   020 4549 1906   2–4C
"In an old Fire station near Victoria", Atul Kochhar's October 2021 newcomer is "a massive undertaking (with over 170 covers)". It inspires a wide range of reactions, none of them terrible, some of them rapturous, but many of them mixed. The "unusual" food has "amazing spicing, with a focus on fish", but some dishes can appear "too ordinary" or "needing a rethink" and even fans note they are "expensive". In a similar vein, the "friendly" service can be "iffy" in its efficiency; and "ambience can be lacking" despite the "stylish conversion". Still, it's an ambitious venture still finding its feet, and perhaps the fairest overall verdict at this stage is: "enjoyable rather than brilliant". / SW1S 1SB; mathura.co.uk; closed Mon-Sat & Sun.

Maya EC2 £67
81 Great Eastern Street   020 7550 1000   13–1B
With its "lovely setting on top of the Hoxton Hotel", this glam, loungey rooftop yearling (run by Soho House) is renowned mostly for its "fine selection of Tequilas and Mezcal". Reports are too scarce for a rating, but such as we have praise some "excellent modern Mexican dishes" too.
/ EC2E 3HU; thehoxton.com/london/shoreditch/maya-restaurant; @thehoxtonhotel; Mon-Sun 11 pm.

Mazi W8 £77 4 4 3
12-14 Hillgate St   020 7229 3794   7–2B
"The most delicious deconstructed Greek food" has earned this "buzzy" modern take on the taverna, tucked away near Notting Hill Gate station, an enviable reputation over the past 10 years. "I could just feast on their dip jars and the cheese pie". Top Tip – for the full Aegean summer atmosphere, "the outdoor courtyard is great". / W8 7SR; www.mazi.co.uk; @mazilondon; Mon-Sat midnight, Sun 11 pm.

The Meat & Wine Co Mayfair W1 NEW
17C Curzon Street   0203 988 6888   3–4B
This August 2022 newcomer in Mayfair is the steakhouse chain's twelfth internationally. South African Bradley Michael started the business 'down under' in Oz 35 years ago. Here, the focus is on Australian and British beef 'energised by Afro-centric flavours and cooking techniques'. / W1W 5HU; www.themeatandwineco.co.uk; @themeatandwineuk; Mon-Sun midnight.

MEATLiquor £46 4 2 2
37-38 Margaret Street, W1   020 7224 4239   3–1C
15-17 Brunswick Centre, WC1   no tel   2–1D NEW
17 Queensway, W2   020 7229 0172   7–2C
133b Upper St, N1   020 3711 0104   9–3D
14-15 Hoxton Market, N1   020 7739 8212   13–1B
37 Lordship Lane, SE22   020 3066 0008   1–4D
7 Dartmouth Rd, SE23   020 3026 1331   1–4D
74 Northcote Road, SW11   020 7228 4777   11–2C
13-19 Old Town, SW4   020 3026 8126   11–1D NEW
"Dead hippie sauce is a must" at these "very loud" operations, which "remain at the head of the gourmet burger pack" for many fans with "lots of options available". After 14 years of growth from a food van to a national chain with 10 venues in the capital, they "don't seem to have lost their way yet". "The dark and grungy ersatz New Orleans interior vibe" is of the love-it-or-hate-it variety. / meatliquor.com; meatgram.

FSA

Mediterraneo W11   £68   3|2|3
37 Kensington Park Rd   020 7792 3131   7–1A
"The real Italian deal, just off Portobello Road", this *"plain and simple"* trattoria has *"been going for ages and seems to be just as popular and noisy as ever"* — and *"always delivers solid good value"*. Founded 25 years ago, it has two sister restaurants in the same street, Essenza and Osteria Basilico. / W11 2EU; www.mediterraneo-restaurant.co.uk; Mon-Sun 10.30 pm; booking max 10 may apply.

Medlar SW10   £115   4|4|3
438 King's Rd   020 7349 1900   6–3B
"A class act that consistently punches above its weight": this low-key but high-quality Chelsea indie (opened in 2011) flies somewhat under the radar in terms of PR profile, but regularly ranks in the top 40 most-mentioned restaurants in our annual diners' poll. Joe Mercer Nairne's *"superior"* modern British cuisine is *"always a delight"*, often *"special"* and comes at a *"reasonable price"*. Service (overseen by co-owner David O'Connor) is *"likewise expert"* and it's *"well worth asking the sommelier to recommend something offbeat"*, as there are *"some unusual gems on the wine list"*. And while the interior is *"low key"*, the atmosphere is *"conducive to a wonderful evening"*. *"It's not clear why it lost its Michelin star"*: *"it should have regained it long ago"*. Top Tips — *"the tarte Tatin for two is to die for. Corkage of £10 at lunchtimes and £25 in the evenings is one of London's great bargains"*. / SW10 0LJ; www.medlarrestaurant.co.uk; @medlarchelsea; Mon-Sat 10.30 pm, Sun 9.30 pm.

Megan's   £50   2|2|3
Branches throughout London
With its inviting décor, this fast-expanding group has been a big *"winner"* since the pandemic, mushrooming to 18 sites, all of which have generally proved useful additions to their respective areas. But while *"it certainly looks the part, and the staff look after you well enough"*, the brunch-friendly fare can be hit 'n' miss, with reports ranging from *"surprisingly good"* to *"formulaic and really abysmal"*. Top Tip — *"always a top option for feeding the family"*. / megans.co.uk; megansrestaurants.

Mei Mei SE1   £70   3|3|2
Unit 52 Borough Market Kitchen, Jubilee Place   no tel   10–4C
"The tastes of Singapore" are still applauded at ex-Pidgin chef, Elizabeth Haigh's hawker-style stand (winner of Harden's Top Street Food in our September 2021 London Restaurant Awards), which sits amidst the clatter of the Market Kitchen area of Borough Market. But feedback was much more muted and a little more uneven this year, and it's hard not to conclude that the furore surrounding the cancelled launch of her recipe book hasn't taken some of the gloss off impressions here. / SE1 9AG; www.meimei.uk; @meimeilondon; Mon-Wed 4 pm, Thu & Fri 10.30 pm, Sat 11.30 pm; closed Mon-Wed D, closed Sun; payment — credit card only; no booking at lunch.

Mele e Pere W1   £54   2|3|2
46 Brewer Street   020 7096 2096   4–3C
"Simple Italian dishes", with everything freshly made in the kitchen, are on the menu at this ten-year-old independent in Soho, whose standout culinary feature is the range of house-made vermouths in the bar. Praise is pretty muted, though — and *"the room really lacks something despite good service"*. / W1F 9TF; www.meleepere.co.uk; @meleeperesoho; Mon & Tue, Sun 10 pm, Wed-Sat 11 pm; payment — credit card only; booking online only.

F S A

The Melusine E1 £78 4|3|3
Unit K, Ivory House, St. Katherine Dock   02077022976   10–3D
"Small and perfectly formed" two-year-old with a "wonderful waterside setting" in St Katharine Dock that serves "seafood that should appear on the end of Paul Whitehouse's rod – it's that fresh!". "On a sunny day with an outdoor table, it's the best" – the "fantastic shellfish" includes "the best langoustines ever and stellar scallops". Theodore Kyriakou, who set up both Livebait and The Real Greek back in the 1990s, is part of the founding team. / E1E 1AT; www.themelusine.co.uk; @themelusine_skd; Tue-Sat 10.30 pm, Sun 9.30 pm; closed Mon; cash only.

Meraki W1 £78 4|3|4
80-82 Gt Titchfield St   020 7305 7686   3–1C
This "slick operation" in Fitzrovia was created by restaurateurs Peter and Arjun Waney – of Zuma and Roka fame. It's not dissimilar to its pan-Asian stablemates: "buzzing, fun and loud, but with food that's very imaginative and well executed" – this time in a modern Greek idiom. They must be doing something right, as there are now branches in Mykonos, Riyadh and Porto Cervo on Sardinia's Costa Smeralda. / W1W 7QT; www.meraki-restaurant.com; @merakilondon; Tue-Thu 10.15 pm, Fri & Sat 10.45 pm; closed Sun & Mon.

Mercato Metropolitano SE1 £43 3|2|5
42 Newington Causeway   020 7403 0930   1–3C
"Very reasonably priced, good food and great fun" is all yours for the taking at this former paper factory near Elephant & Castle, converted to host more than 40 different food and drink pop-ups. "You just wander from one to another, then find a place to sit and eat in the common area", which includes London's biggest beer garden – "a great outdoor space". There are now three other MMs in London, following a concept launched in Italy (hence the name). / SE1 6DR; www.mercatometropolitano.com; @mercatometropolitano; Mon-Thu 11 pm, Fri & Sat midnight, Sun 10 pm.

The Mercer EC2 £79 3|3|3
34 Threadneedle St   020 7628 0001   10–2C
In a converted banking hall near the Bank of England, this well-established brasserie exists to serve a City clientele, from breakfast on. Opinions divide on whether it's a little "disappointing", like many in the Square Mile, or "perfect of its type and better than it needs to be". / EC2R 8AY; www.themercer.co.uk; @themercerrestaurant; Mon-Fri 9.30 pm; closed Sat & Sun.

Le Mercury N1 £38 2|2|2
140a Upper St   020 7354 4088   9–2D
This "fun, old-style bistro with dishes to match" has been one of the dining bargains of Islington's main drag for the best part of 40 years. It serves brunch from 10am as well as the standard Gallic brasserie menu for lunch and dinner. / N1 1QY; www.lemercury.co.uk; @lemercury; Mon-Thu midnight, Fri & Sat 1 am, Sun 11 pm.

Mere W1 £115 3|4|2
74 Charlotte Street   020 7268 6565   2–1B
"Service from David, Monica and the team is always excellent", say fans of their Fitzrovia basement where "everyone seems keen to make your visit a very memorable experience". TV star Monica's "top-quality cuisine strikes a great balance between classic and innovative" ("refined and packed with flavour but paradoxically, robust at the same time without being unsubtle") and "the wine list is extremely well-curated and has a wide ambit, as you might expect from David as a former Gavroche Sommelier". As with many top London restaurants this year, though, ratings dipped a fraction – the pressures of the times? – with more reports along the lines of "a very pleasant experience but slightly underwhelming". But while the proportion of

reporters saying they had their best meal of the year here has declined, more and more have taken it to their hearts as their "favourite" nomination. / W1W 4QH; www.mere-restaurant.com; @mererestaurant; Tue-Thu 9 pm, Fri & Sat 9.30 pm; closed Sun & Mon.

Meson don Felipe SE1 £48 334
53 The Cut   020 7928 3237   10–4A

"Top tapas in The Cut" – 'London's original tapas bar' still cuts it after 35 years, providing sterling pre- and post-show service to theatregoers visiting the nearby Young and Old Vic. The "very friendly, helpful owner" ensures there's a good atmosphere even when the joint is rammed. / SE1 8LF; www.mesondonfelipe.com; @mesondonfelipe; Mon-Sat 11 pm; closed Sun.

Meza Trinity Road SW17 £41 333
34 Trinity Rd   07722 111299   11–2C

This "lovely little café" was "the original Lebanese place in Tooting", and is known for its "great meze" and other Levantine plates, along with a warm welcome. The second branch in Mitcham Road has closed down. / SW17 7RE; www.mezarestaurant.com; @meza_res; Sun-Thu 11 pm, Fri & Sat 11.30 pm.

Michael Nadra £71 332
42 Gloucester Ave, NW1   020 7722 2800   9–3B NEW

Just by the Regent's Canal, Michael Nadra's high-quality French restaurant serves some of the "best food in the area" at the top of Regent's Park. On sunny days, it particularly benefits from its cute courtyard (regarding the interior, some diners feel it's "a shame that the odd layout can detract from its other qualities"). It used to have an (older) Chiswick sibling, but this has now closed: seemingly a victim of the pandemic. / www.restaurant-michaelnadra.co.uk.

Mien Tay £41 332
45 Fulham High St, SW6   020 7731 0670   11–1B
433 Lordship Lane, N22   020 3302 9530   1–1C
180 Lavender Hill, SW11   020 7350 0721   11–1C
122 Kingsland Rd, E2   020 7729 3074   14–2A

This quartet of family-run restaurants have won a big reputation for their southwest Vietnamese dishes, including pho and their famed goat with galangal. They started out 15 years ago in Shoreditch before heading across the river to Battersea. / mientay.co.uk.

Mike's Peckham SE15 £45 443
Unit 4.1, 133 Copeland Rd   020 7732 9012   1–4D

"Deliciously different pizza" comes by the slice in the "relaxed setting" of this yearling in a former grain warehouse (a former site of Forza Win). For all its "very basic" appearance, serious thought goes into the toppings, along with ingredients such as Sicilian datterini tomatoes, Calabrian tropea onions and Turkish figs. "The only problem is knowing when to stop ordering!" / SE15; mikespeckham.co.uk; @mikespeckham; Wed-Fri 10 pm, Sat 10.30 pm, Sun 5 pm; closed Sun D, closed Mon & Tue; payment – credit card only.

Mildreds £52 333
45 Lexington St, W1   020 7494 1634   4–2C
79 St Martin's Lane, WC2   020 8066 8393   5–3B NEW
200 Pentonville Rd, N1   020 7278 9422   9–3D
9 Jamestown Rd, NW1   020 7482 4200   9–3B
1 Dalston Square, E8   020 8017 1815   14–1A

Investment a few years ago turbo-charged this '100% plant-based' chain, whose stalwart original Soho branch (est 1988) suddenly spawned a handful of "airy" and "jolly" (somewhat "crammed") modern spin-offs across town. To this number, a new, two-floor Covent Garden branch opened its doors in

February 2022 with 120 covers. The expansion has gone well and its "earnest" and "flavourful" cooking is not just favoured by veggies: "I was taken not entirely voluntarily as a dedicated meat-eater but have changed my tune after dining here!" / mildredsrestaurants.

Milk SW12 £23 3|2|3
20 Bedford Hill   020 8772 9085   11–2C
"Be prepared to queue for the delicious and original brunches" at this Antipodean champion that has had devotees beating a path to Balham for 11 years (It's "achingly hip, which I'm emphatically not, but the food is so good I love it anyway"). / SW12 9RG; milklondonshop.uk/info; @milk.london; Mon-Fri 3.30 pm, Sat & Sun 4 pm; closed Mon-Sun D; no booking.

MiMi Mei Fair W1 £93 3|3|4
55 Curzon Street   020 3989 7777   3–3B
"Tucked away in a lovely Mayfair conversion", Samyukta Nair's (who studied in China) year-old Shanghai-inspired venture has suffered some tough press reviews (notably from Giles Coren in The Times) but generally pleases diners. OK, even many fans concede that it is "super-expensive", but "apart from the bill, everything else is amazing", including the superior dim sum (from an ex-Hakkasan, Chinese-Singaporean chef, Peter Ho) and "fabled Peking duck" (which you must pre-order). / W1W 8PG; mimimeifair.com; @mimimeifair; Mon-Sat 10.30 pm, Sun 10 pm.

Min Jiang, The Royal Garden Hotel W8 £100 4|3|5
2-24 Kensington High St   020 7361 1988   6–1A
"The most difficult restaurant in W8 to bag a table at" for good reason: the rooftop dining room of the 5-star Royal Garden Hotel combines "top Hong Kong-standard Chinese food" with "wonderful views over Kensington Gardens" – "the dim sum is excellent" and "I could cry with joy simply thinking about their Beijing duck", which is "one of the best in London". / W8 4PT; www.minjiang.co.uk; @minjianglondon; Mon-Sun 10.30 pm.

Mirch Masala SW17 £25 4|2|2
213 Upper Tooting Rd   020 8767 8638   11–2D
This Pakistani canteen is one of the stars of Tooting's 'curry corridor', and had a moment in the limelight when it was recommended a few years back by the area's most famous son, London mayor Sadiq Khan. / SW17 7TG; mirchmasala-takeaway.co.uk; @Dish No. 87 at Mirch Masala; Sun-Thu 11.30 pm, Fri & Sat 11.45 pm; cash only; no booking.

Miro Mayfair W1 NEW
15 Old Burlington Street   020 7183 9661   4–3A
From Cream Group (owners of Cirque le Soir, Restaurant Ours, Wild and The Windmill Soho), this July opening in Mayfair occupies the erstwhile 120-cover site of XO (RIP). Former Elystan Street head chef Toby Burrowes heads up an extravagant offering, which includes a £3,000 'sunken treasure' caviar platter; and a cocktail listed at £5,000 (a rare 1950s gin and a bottle of 1970 Dom Perignon BTW). All good PR. Opening in mid-July 2022, this new spot calls itself a 'clubstaurant' – not a term we feel needs encouragement. / W1W 2JR; www.miromayfair.com; @miromayfair; Wed-Sun 11 pm.

F S A

Miscusi £39 2️⃣2️⃣2️⃣
23 Slingsby Place, WC2   020 8089 8540   5–3B **NEW**
80 Upper Street, N1   020 8089 5847   9–3D **NEW**
One of Italy's recent hits, this sustainable fast-food pasta business with 12 branches arrived in Covent Garden in November 2021 (and quickly opened a second in Islington in June 2022). The limited feedback in our annual diners' poll was somewhat in tune with The Telegraph's William Sitwell (who was so disappointed he suggested the chain "be summoned to the foreign office and expelled"): "I was so excited based on all the social media around the place: food was average (as in something you'd make at home when you're in a rush)".

Miznon London W1 **NEW**
8-12 Broadwick Street   awaiting tel   4–1C
Tel Aviv, Paris, NYC... and now London – Soho (in July 2022) is the latest location for this eight-strong international chain, whose owner, Eyal Shani, is aiming for 150 locations once all is said and done. It's all about the filled pitas, with each branch's menu tailored to the locality. Soho's features an 'English Breakfast' option, alongside lots of fish and vegetarian possibilities. / W1W 8HN; @miznonlondon; Mon-Sat 11 pm, Sun 10 pm.

Los Mochis W8 £44 3️⃣3️⃣4️⃣
2 Farmer St   020 7727 7528   7–2B
This Mexican/Japanese hybrid in Notting Hill offers 'gangster tacos' served with Japanese elegance – and provides "the best fun dining out I have had in a long while", full of "exciting, flavour-packed mouthfuls". Finnish-born founder Markus Thesleff coined the label 'Baja Nihon' to cover a cuisine that does not exist elsewhere, and has taken over the site occupied by legendary fish 'n' chip restaurant Geales (RIP) for more than 50 years. Top Tip – "it's great for allergies – the entire menu is GF and you'd have no idea!" / W8; www.losmochis.co.uk; @osmochislondon; Mon-Sun midnight; closed Mon-Fri L; payment – credit card only.

Mon Plaisir Restaurant WC2 £69 2️⃣2️⃣4️⃣
19-21 Monmouth Street   020 7836 7243   5–2B
"Mon Plaisir felt like an old-fashioned time warp when I first started coming here in the 1980s, and it hasn't changed since!" – this sprawling bistro in Covent Garden is set in *"a French honeycomb of rooms"* and many of its devotees say it's *"still holding its own"* thanks to its *"delightful authenticity"* (*"serving French food – including proper snails and other bistro classics – in the French way"*) and its *"beguiling"* approach generally (*"a great place to look starry-eyed into your partner's eyes"*). Its ratings are sliding, though, due to numerous other long-term fans losing interest (*"I hadn't been in years and found average food, variable service and a tired impression generally"*: *"…a pity as it used to be so good!"*) / WC2H 9DD; www.monplaisir.co.uk; @monplaisiragram; Tue-Sat 9.30 pm; closed Sun & Mon.

Monmouth Coffee Company £7 3️⃣4️⃣3️⃣
27 Monmouth St, WC2   020 7232 3010   5–2B
2 Park St, SE1   020 7232 3010   12–2A
"Amazing coffee" – *"a wide selection from single estates that's carefully selected and optimally roasted"* – together with *"well-paired pastries and cakes as complements"* continue to make these *"lively and fun"*, artisanal brew stops *"a good morning 'perk me up'"*, and some of the most popular destinations in town. Staff are *"impressively calm and friendly"* too; *"worth queuing for"*. / www.monmouthcoffee.co.uk.

Morito £58 4|3|3
195 Hackney Road, E2   020 7613 0754   14–2A
32 Exmouth Mkt, EC1   020 7278 7007   10–1A
"The food is always a delight" at "the little brother of (and much cheaper than) Moro", nearby in Exmouth Market, which serves "excellent authentic tapas dishes washed down with delicious Spanish wine" or a "half-bottle of sherry". It's a notably "well run joint", with "staff who know their grub" and are "very welcoming without being fussy". Top Tip – "arrive early to nab one of their two outdoor tables on the paved street and imagine yourself in Spain as you watch life going by". / www.morito.co.uk; moritotapas.

Moro EC1 £77 3|3|2
34-36 Exmouth Mkt   020 7833 8336   10–1A
"Still going strong (after all these 25 years)… the only downside is that it can feel noisy when full" – that's long been the classic view on Sam and Sam Clark's "old favourite" on Exmouth Market, where an "interesting range of tasty", "Spanish/Moorish-influenced dishes" are provided alongside an "oenological tour of Spain" from the extensive Iberian wine list (which has an "exciting selection of wines by the glass"). Its ratings have been drifting south, however, over a period of years, due to the minority who "really want to like it, but find the food lacking punch" nowadays. Top Tip – "on a weekday, at lunchtimes, Moro sets up a stall in the street outside the restaurant, and sells tagine with couscous to take away: some of the best street food in the UK!" / EC1R 4QE; www.moro.co.uk; @restaurantmoro; Mon-Sun 10.30 pm; closed Mon L.

Morso NW8 £72 3|3|2
130 Boundary Road   020 7624 7412   9–3A
A "modern" take on an Italian local in Abbey Road, with a menu built around "delicious small plates and brilliant pasta" with "lots of great vegetarian options". It's "community-centred" and "very reliable", with "fantastic, helpful staff". A second branch in Kensal Rise closed down after two years in May 2022. / NW8 0RH; www.morsolondon.co.uk; @morsolondon; Tue-Sat 10.30 pm, Sun 9.30 pm; closed Mon.

Motcombs SW1 £65 2|3|4
26 Motcomb St   020 7235 6382   6–1D
All agree on the attractive style of this long-established (since 1982) and rather old-fashioned Belgravia stalwart, with nice pavement tables. Not everyone agrees on the value provided by its eclectic international menu (shepherds pie, seared tiger prawns, Dover sole, Belgravia burger…) but it is sometimes tipped for business. / SW1X 8JU; www.motcombs.co.uk; @motcombsrestaurant; Mon-Sun 11 pm.

Mr Bao SE15 £34 3|2|2
293 Rye Ln   020 7635 0325   1–4D
"A really good bet" in Peckham, serving "superb Taiwanese bao buns". It's "friendly, affordable and fun – so perfect for these challenging times". On the weekend it's "brunch heaven – kimchi pancakes and hash browns with ma po beans are really different and yummy". Daddy Bao in Tooting and Master Bao in Westfield Shepherd's Bush complete the family. / SE15 4UA; www.mrbao.co.uk; @mrbaouk; Mon-Sat 10.30 pm, Sun 9.30 pm; closed Mon-Wed L.

Mr Falafel W12 £9 5|4|2
15 Uxbridge Rd   07307 635548   8–1C
"Run by two chef brothers", this "tiny restaurant" is crammed into the north end of Shepherd's Bush Market and does a "brisk trade". Motto: 'We Speak Falafel Fluently' – you can order your wrap in the style of Syria, Iran, Lebanon or the owners' native Palestine. You get "absolutely fresh food, a warm welcome and the best prices in town!" / W12 8AH; Mon-Sun midnight.

Mr Ji W1 £15 3 3 2
72 Old Compton Street   020 7052 5770   4–2D
"Taiwanese chicken that's fun, fast and cheap" (plus other "great, dirty Asian bites"), has created a buzz around this tapas-inspired haunt in Soho. Founder Samuel Haim started out selling street food in Camden, and has now teamed up with Ta Ta Eatery's Ana Gonçalves and Zijun Meng, with a second site slated to open in Camden's Parkway in the latter half of 2022. / W1W 4UN; mrji.co.uk; @mrjirestaurant; Tue-Sat 10.30 pm, Sun 5.30 pm; closed Sun D, closed Mon; payment – credit card only; credit card deposit required to book.

Mr Todiwala's Petiscos IG9 £43 4 4 3
75 Queen's Road   020 8257 0816   1–1D
"Great atmosphere and something quite different!" – this "warm and welcoming" Buckhurst Hill operation mixes Goan and Portuguese influences. It's a partnership between Cyris & Pervin Todiwala and the Redman-Schaffer family from Woodford, delivering "great little dishes" ('petiscos') and "fantastic Portuguese wines from independent estates". / IG9 5BW; www.mrtodiwalaspetiscos.com; @mrtodiwalaspetiscos; closed Mon-Sat & Sun.

Munal Tandoori SW15 £34 3 4 2
393 Upper Richmond Road, Putney   020 8876 3083   11–2A
This "great-value local Indian" is a landmark on the South Circular near Putney which has built a sterling reputation over 32 years for its classic north Indian dishes supplemented by interesting Nepalese specialities such as momo steamed dumplings – all served in "huge portion sizes!". / SW15 5QL; www.munaltandoori.co.uk; @Munal Nepalese Restaurant (Official); Sun-Thu 10 pm, Fri & Sat 11 pm; closed Sun-Thu-Sat L.

Murano W1 £129 3 4 3
20-22 Queen St   020 7495 1127   3–3B
"Technically accomplished", Italian-inspired cuisine (which, at heart, is quite "classical") from Angela Hartnett, served "in a sophisticated-yet-relaxed setting, by outstanding-yet-unobtrusive staff" continues to inspire the many fans of her unflashy-yet-luxurious venue in Mayfair. But, while most diners applaud its overall performance, it has inspired a variety of gripes of late: the décor can be too "muted" for some tastes, and some repeat visitors have admitted to feeling "underwhelmed" of late by the odd "uninspiring" dish. On most accounts, though "the main difficulty here is answering the question: 'how many courses?'" (the options being a 3-course, 4-course, 5-course or 6-course meal). / W1J 5PP; www.muranolondon.com; @muranolondon; Mon-Sat 10 pm; closed Sun.

Muse SW1 £171 5 4 4
38 Groom Place   020 3301 2903   6–1D
"Tom Aikens gave us a night of culinary genius on a plate. Unforgettable" – his "original, informal and fun" two-year-old Belgravia HQ continues to deliver a "superlative" experience. The "incredible plates of food are full of little flavour bombs" and "whilst the menu inspiration of dishes tied to his life story risks getting a little passé if you're a regular, Tom does cook it well" ("it's great that he is often actually there in person"). There's "lovely trendy décor on both floors, and it's a fantastic experience on the ground floor stools slap bang in front of Tom and the chefs who are so friendly and engaging". Top Tip – perhaps reflecting Tom's health-conscious, ultramarathon leanings, "dietary intolerances are well catered for" and "vegetables prepared in interesting and exciting ways". / SW1S 7BA; www.musebytomaikens.co.uk; @musebytomaikens; Tue-Sat 11 pm; closed Tue, Wed L, closed Sun & Mon; booking online only.

F S A

Myrtle SW10 £84 5 4 3
1a Langton Street   020 7352 2411   6–3B
This "real gem of a restaurant" in a Chelsea townhouse is the work of Dublin-born chef Anna Haugh (who has worked for Phil Howard and Gordon Ramsay, among others). "Stunning Irish food" provides "course after course" tracing a route round the counties, and "all of them hit the mark". "The talent in the kitchen is matched by the warmth of the welcome and the efficiency of the service", all of which adds up to "one of the best and least expected openings in Chelsea of the past five years". Michelin don't even list it on their website, when they should be considering it for a star! / SW10 0JL; www.myrtlerestaurant.com; @myrtlerestaurant; Tue-Sat 10 pm; closed Sun & Mon.

Nandine SE5 £34 3 4 3
45 Camberwell Church Street   020 7703 3221   1–3C
"Kurdish delights in SE5!" – founder Pary Baban was forced to flee her home by Saddam Hussein's troops in 1989 and collected recipes on her travels. Now she shares them at her cafés in Camberwell and Peckham (Nandine means 'kitchen' in Kurdish), where you can "enjoy the great spicing and flavours" in a "lovely atmosphere". "Brunch is a particular highlight" – try Pary's "great shakshuka". / SE5 8TR; @nandineuk; Sun-Thu 10.30 pm, Fri & Sat 11 pm; closed Mon-Fri L.

The Narrow E14 £76 2 2 3
44 Narrow St   020 7592 7950   12–1B
"Great views" are by all accounts the main highlight of a meal at Gordo's Limehouse pub overlooking a bend in the river. But perhaps we expect too much of a chef happy to dish out a roasting to his peers: "I know a lot of people don't like it, but it did what it said on the tin – it's good pub food, and it's only if you anticipated more that you'll be disappointed". / E14 8DP; www.gordonramsayrestaurants.com/the-narrow; @thenarrowgordonramsay; Mon-Wed 11.30 pm, Thu-Sat midnight, Sun 10 pm.

Native at Browns W1 £78 5 4 4
Browns, 39 Brook Street   020 7549 5999   3–2B
"Everything on the menu is a triumph!" at Imogen Davis and Ivan Tisdall-Downes's "charming" yearling, in Mayfair's fashionable Browns store. "It has a cool vibe, having entered through the store" and the food can "far exceed expectations" – "wonderful, innovative dishes that will stick in the memory (for instance, the fudgy bone marrow crème brûlée, which got meatier as we got closer to the bone"). "It's not too expensive either, given the location". Top Tip – in summer, it has a 40-seat courtyard. / W1W 4JE; www.brownsfashion.com/uk/services/native-at-browns; @eatnative; Tue-Sat 9 pm; closed Sun & Mon.

Naughty Piglets SW2 £52 5 4 4
28 Brixton Water Ln   020 7274 7796   11–2D
Joe Sharratt and Margaux Aubry's informal French-inspired Brixton venue is a true leader of South London gastronomy, serving small sharing plates of "the best grub" and "most exciting wines" south of the river. "Margaux is a treasure – a Lyon-hearted wonder" who provides guests with expert guidance through the menu and excellent wine list. Foodie composer/impresario Andrew Lloyd Webber was such a fan that he invited the team to launch a spin-off at his 'The Other Place Theatre' in Victoria. / SW2 1PE; www.naughtypiglets.co.uk; @naughtypiglets; Fri & Sat, Tue-Thu 11 pm; closed Tue-Thu L, closed Sun & Mon; payment – credit card only.

Nautilus NW6 £38 322
27-29 Fortune Green Rd   020 7435 2532   1–1B
"Old-fashioned in the best way", this veteran West Hampstead chippy is known for "fantastic fresh fish 'n' delicious chips" – hailed as "the best in the NWs". "Matzo meal batter is light as a feather and not too greasy, and they can also do great grilled fish when you're on a health kick". The dining room remains "no-frills" despite a lockdown revamp and still "has a strip lighting aesthetic… but you don't come for the ambience". / NW6 1DU; @nautilusfishandchip; Mon-Sat 10 pm, Sun 9 pm; no Amex.

Nessa W1 NEW
1 Warwick Street   awaiting tel   4–3B
This 100-cover, autumn 2022 Soho newcomer is the work of Guy Ivesha (founder of Mortimer House) and has well-known chef Tom Cenci (whose CV includes Duck & Waffle) as executive chef. A casual bistro format is the aim, delivering a classic seasonal menu. It will sit on the ground floor of 1 Warwick, a sibling members' club to the original. / W1W 5LR; @nessasoho; Mon-Sun midnight.

NEST E9 £48 443
177 Morning Lane   020 8986 0065   14–1B
This "outstanding" four-year-old is an "engaging but cramped little venue" whose "absolute bargain of a menu" from co-owner Johnnie Crow (ex-Harwood Arms and Anglo), makes it "well worth the trip up to Hackney (booking essential!)". The meal is structured around one type of meat each month – chicken, game, wagyu – to minimise waste, and "service is personal, enthusiastic and charming". "You're unlikely to find much better value in town, with some truly stellar dishes given the mid-range price-point". / E9 6LH; www.nestfood.co.uk; @nest_food; Tue-Sat 10 pm, Sun 3 pm; closed Tue-Fri L closed Sun D, closed Mon.

Newens: The Original Maids of Honour TW9 £40 333
288 Kew Road   020 8940 2752   1–3A
"Very touristy of course, but also very atmospheric… and the afternoon teas are so good!" – This "very traditional tea rooms opposite Kew Gardens" is seemingly unchanged in many decades and offers a comforting slice of post-war life, having been built in mock-Tudor style in the late 1940s. "Famed for their 'maids of honour' pastries", "their tea is a simple classic affair of scones, jam, clotted cream, savoury pastries, pies, and aforementioned tarts". "It never fails to please and I just keep coming back after 40 years!" / TW9 3DU; theoriginalmaidsofhonour.co.uk; @theoriginalmaidsofhonour; Mon-Sun 6 pm.

Ngon W4 £28 322
195 Chiswick High Road   020 8994 9630   8–2A
"So much better than the chains" – this very no-frills canteen in the heart of Chiswick is worth remembering for its "simple but fresh" and vibrant Vietnamese dishes (bahn mi, salads, pho…) / W4 2DR; www.ngondeli.com; @ngondeli; Mon-Sat 8 pm, Sun 5 pm; closed Sun D.

The Ninth London W1 £105 543
22 Charlotte Street   020 3019 0880   2–1C
"They don't need to try too hard" at Jun Tanaka's "relaxed" but extremely accomplished Fitzrovia fixture. "Everything that's on the plate is there for a reason… a good reason!" – his "very high-quality" cuisine is "very well-balanced" and service is "charming". Top Menu Tips – "seared mackerel with pickles works well, beef cheeks is a signature, and turbot head is wonderful". BREAKING NEWS: In summer 2022, a fire closed the restaurant, with no reopening date set as of mid August 2022. / W1T 2NB; www.theninthlondon.com; @theninthlondon; Mon-Sat 9.30 pm; closed Sun.

FSA

No. Fifty Cheyne SW3 — £107 — 2 3 5
50 Cheyne Walk   020 7376 8787   6–3C

This gorgeous-looking brasserie in the heart of Old Chelsea is "always busy", with chef Iain Smith (a former associate of Jason Atherton) presiding over high-quality but rather pricey surf'n'turf grills and "Sunday roast to die for". Proprietor Jenny Greene, the theatre impresario who restored the Old Vic and owns Ronnie Scott's jazz club, upgraded the premises several years ago; it is now a licensed wedding venue with an upstairs bar and salon boasting impressive views over Albert Bridge. / SW3 5LR; www.fiftycheyne.com; @50cheyne; Wed-Sat midnight, Sun 6 pm; closed Wed & Thu L closed Sun D, closed Mon & Tue; payment – credit card only.

Noble Rot WC1 — £74 — 3 5 5
51 Lamb's Conduit St   020 7242 8963   2–1D

"Even the most jaded wine bore will find something new and special" at Mark Andrew and Daniel Keeling's "moody" watering hole in Bloomsbury – nowadays one of London's best-known destinations. Naturally the "expertly chosen and truly fascinating wine list" ("a top mix of classics and new wave/low intervention wines") is at the heart of its appeal, but its magic also owes much to its "fabulously knowledgeable staff" ("who really know their stuff and can make great recommendations to suit all price points"). A further major factor was the inspired choice six years ago of such splendidly apt premises: the "dark-lit" and charmingly mellow site that was for decades the forgotten-about, 1970s stalwart wine bar, 'Vats': "cosy and appealing with a lovely feel to it". And, while the "wine is always centre stage", the food is "surprisingly good" too – "on point with excellent ingredients". "Availability by the glass is fabulous" ("and by the bottle!"), but the "measures are small at 75 or 125ml" and – "be careful!" – prices of more exotic vintages can be "injurious to the bank account". But even those who feel "a visit quickly gets pricey given those tiny glasses" think it's "good for a treat". And for many aficionados "the fantastically diverse list encourages – nay insists! – that you blow your budget and reach for the stars!". Top Tip – "splendid set lunch". / WC1N 3NB; www.noblerot.co.uk; @noblerotsoho; Mon-Sat 9.30 pm; closed Sun.

Noble Rot Soho W1 — £59 — 3 4 4
2 Greek Street   020 7183 8190   5–2A

"After decades of being a Gay Hussar regular I now find myself at this fine replacement run by committed wine experts..." – this famous Soho address was resurrected in 2021 by Dan Keeling and Mark Andrew and fans are "happy to report standards just as high as at their original site in Holborn". Star of the show is the "gargantuan wine list" – "a treasure trove of interesting bins" (albeit "with some jaw-dropping prices") – "interpreted by knowledgeable and friendly staff", who help maintain the "charming and quirky" atmosphere of this "solid and comfortable" site (which, as its predecessor, opened in 1953). The "food is not as exceptional as the wine" but the "gutsy and value-led menu" of "good ingredients, served simply" is generally well-reviewed for its "delicious and unpretentious" qualities. Top Tip – "excellent-value set lunch". / W1W 4NB; noblerot.co.uk; @noblerotsoho; Mon-Sat 9.30 pm; closed Sun.

Nobu, Como Metropolitan Hotel W1 — £127 — 4 3 2
19 Old Park Ln   020 7447 4747   3–4A

"Definitely not as fashionable as it once was... the décor is now a bit old hat... but the food at this Nobu still has the edge" – the original London branch of Nobu Matsuhisa's famous international chain is "still the place to go if you like Japanese fusion-style cuisine", and "if you ignore the prices then the rest is simply wonderful!" Perhaps realising that they need to work harder now that the A-list crowd has moved on, service is often "spot on" too, nowadays. / W1K 1LB; www.noburestaurants.com; @nobuoldparklane; Sun-Wed 10 pm, Thu-Sat 10.30 pm.

FSA RATINGS: FROM 1 POOR — 5 EXCEPTIONAL

F S A

Nobu Portman Square W1 £104 3 3 4
22 Portman Square   020 3988 5888   2–1A

"More modern in style than its older Park Lane sister and far more trendy now" – this "large, dark and warmly" decorated venue, with outside terrace, beamed down into this latest outpost of the international chain in December 2020. But while "popular and packed", with Japanese-fusion cuisine that's often rated as "wonderful", it's "an expensive option compared with other Japanese venues" and "the food isn't quite as good as the original at The Met". / W1W 7BG; london-portman.nobuhotels.com; @nobulondonportman; Sun-Thu 10 pm, Fri & Sat 10.30 pm.

Nobu Shoreditch EC2 £127
10-50 Willow St   020 3818 3790   13–1B

With its big, high-ceilinged basement restaurant looking out onto a cool sunken garden – this style-conscious Shoreditch hotel (launched in 2017) never felt like it fully established itself fully prior to the pandemic. It closed from 2020 till June 2022, just after the conclusion of our survey, so our rating will have to wait till next year. / EC2E 4BH; www.london-shoreditch.nobuhotels.com; @nobulondonshoreditch; Sun-Wed 10.30 pm, Thu-Sat 11.30 pm; closed Sat & Sun L.

Noci N1 NEW £41 2 2 3
4-6 Islington Green   020 3937 5343   9–3D

"A welcome recent addition to Islington" – this March 2022 newcomer from Louis Korovilas serves a short, seasonal menu of pastas and a modern take on Italian street-food snacks. But while "it's a handy neighbourhood option for fresh pasta", the overall verdict is that "it doesn't quite compare to the likes of Padella or Bancone" (Korovilas used to work at the latter). / N1 2XA; www.nocirestaurant.co.uk; @nocipasta; Mon-Sat 11 pm, Sun 10 pm.

Noizé W1 £98 4 5 4
39 Whitfield St   020 7323 1310   2–1C

"A corner of France in London" – this "unassuming" but increasingly well-known Fitzrovia dining room "is brought to life by charming and attentive owner, Mathieu Germond and his team". The "relaxed atmosphere is helped by widely spaced tables and the menu brought to the table on a blackboard" which delivers "classic French dishes from top-class ingredients". The prime attraction, though, is the wine. "Matthieu has an encyclopaedic knowledge" and the "cracking list has something new to discover every time and at all price ranges". / W1W 2SF; www.noize-restaurant.co.uk; @noize_restaurant; Wed-Fri, Tue, Sat 10 pm; closed Tue, Sat L, closed Sun & Mon.

NoMad London WC2 £117 3 4 5
4 Bow Street   020 3906 1600   5–2D

A "simply brilliant addition to Covent Garden" – Grade II listed Bow Street Magistrates' Court, as was, is now the first London offshoot of Manhattan's hip NoMad hotel, with a dining room, 'The Atrium', that occupies a stunning indoors-outdoors glass-ceilinged space three storeys high. It's "great for breakfast (and lunch and dinner)", with exec chef Ashley Abodeely putting her NY/LA spin on the best seafood, meat and vegetables Britain can produce. "This is a really special dinner out... if you can stomach the prices", and while you're there you must slip into the Side Hustle, a bar occupying the old Bow Street police station, where Abodeely indulges a taste for tacos she developed while working in LA. "Special mention to the cocktails and very professional and friendly waiters". / WC2W 7AH; www.thenomadhotel.com/london; @thenomadhotel; Mon-Sat 10.30 pm, Sun 5 pm; closed Mon-Fri L closed Sun D.

FSA

Noor Jahan £52 4 4 2
2a Bina Gardens, SW5   020 7373 6522   6–2B
26 Sussex Place, W2   020 7402 2332   7–1D
This "ever-popular warhorse" has served "classic Indian food" in traditional curry house style to an appreciative audience on the Earl's Court-South Ken border for 60 years now. The "staff have been there forever and we love this happy and delicious place", say fans – it's "old-fashioned, but that's part of the appeal".

Nopi W1 £92 3 3 2
21-22 Warwick St   020 7494 9584   4–3B
"Unique food to die for" from a "very inventive Middle Eastern-inspired menu" inspires followers of Yotam Ottolenghi and the acclaimed Israeli chef's "bustling" Soho flagship: "each plate is heaven" and "you may discover some new wines" along the way. As is so often the case with his ventures, though, the pricing gives nothing away – "the food's great, but I didn't award full marks as it's not outstanding value for money". / W1B 5NE; ottolenghi.co.uk/restaurants; @ottolenghi; Mon-Sat 10.30 pm; closed Sun.

The Norfolk Arms WC1 £49 3 3 2
28 Leigh St   020 7388 3937   9–4C
"Superb tapas" are "served with a smile" in this deceptive Victorian pub in a sidestreet near King's Cross, that "still looks like a typical boozer". It's "very popular, justifiably, so booking ahead is required at busy times". / WC1H 9EP; www.norfolkarms.co.uk; Mon-Sat 11 pm; closed Sun; no Amex.

Norma W1 £84 4 4 4
8 Charlotte Street   0203 995 6224   2–1C
"The décor feels wonderfully indulgent without descending into kitsch" at the Stafford Hotel Group's "stylish" three-year-old. Something similar could be said about the "interesting spin on Sicilian cuisine" that's "excellently prepared and full of authentic flavour", and delivered in generous portions. "Staff are brilliant" too. Top Menu Tip – "a top choice for inventive and not-too-excessive pasta" or small plates (e.g. prawns, monkfish, burrata); "top it all off with first-rate tiramisu and rose-flavoured panna cotta". / W1W 2LS; www.normalondon.com; @norma_ldn; Mon-Sat 10.30 pm; closed Sun.

Normah's W2 £28 4 3 2
23-25 Queensway Market   07771 630828   7–2C
"The ambience might not be much (it is set inside a no-frills indoor market) but – oh boy! – the beef rending and mee goreng are deeeelicious" at this tiny, high-quality and exceptionally good-value Malaysian café in Bayswater, where Normah Abd Hamid has fulfilled a lifetime's ambition by sharing her brilliant home cooking with friends and strangers. / W2 4QP; www.normahs.co.uk; @normahs_place; Tue-Sat 9 pm; closed Tue-Sat L, closed Sun & Mon.

Normans Cafe N19 £25 4 4 4
167 Junction Road   no tel   9–1C
"Bringing the greasy spoon into the 21st century – Norman's hits the spot of traditional British food with top-notch ingredients at bargain prices". Chefs Elliot Kaye and Richard Hayes ditched jobs at Leroy and Lyle's in 2020 to open this Tufnell Park café, complete with gingham curtains and a classic photo of Bobby Moore holding aloft the Jules Rimet trophy – it is one of the few places on earth where you can have ham, two eggs and chips washed down by a negroni or a skin-contact wine. "The queues around the corner says it all. Get there early to secure a table!" / N19 5PZ; www.normanscafe.co.uk; @Normanscafelondon; Wed-Sun 3 pm; closed Wed-Sun D, closed Mon & Tue.

F S A

El Norte W1 NEW £108 3 3 3
19-20 Dover Street   020 3154 8182   3–3C

"Top-class Hispanic cuisine is served in an atmosphere of easy luxury" at this Mayfair yearling from Spanish twins Alberto and Arian Zandi – their third London restaurant following Zuaya and Como Garden in Kensington. *"Both taste and texture of the food are spot on"*, but even fans who say *"it really is a super restaurant"* can fret that *"prices are a bit out of control"* (but for the most part feel *"you get what you pay for"*). / W1W 4LP; el-norte.co.uk; @elnortelondon; Sun-Thu 12.30 am, Fri & Sat 1.30 am.

North China W3 £43 4 3 3
305 Uxbridge Rd   020 8992 9183   8–1A

The Lou family's West London fixture of almost 50 years' standing, was created by founder Hung Sun Lou (aka Chef Lou, now in his 80s) and more latterly has operated under his son Lawrence, the current owner, who virtually grew up in the restaurant. Lost on the outskirts of Acton, it provides northern Chinese cuisine of consistently *"high quality"*. / W3 9QU; www.northchina.co.uk; @northchinafood; Tue-Sun 10.30 pm; closed Mon.

North Sea Fish WC1 £51 3 3 2
7-8 Leigh St   020 7387 5892   9–4C

"Follow the black cabs and grab the battered goodies at this venerable chipper", say fans of this Bloomsbury fixture, run by the Beauchamp family since 1977. *"The place has been spruced up since my first visit decades ago, but it still could do with more sprucing up! But these are small criticisms and one doesn't go for the décor, but for what's on the plate"*. *"Friendly and well-informed service is a bonus, too"*. / WC1H 9EW; www.northseafishrestaurant.co.uk; @thenorthseafish; Mon-Sat 9.30 pm; closed Mon L, closed Sun.

The Northall, Corinthia Hotel WC2 £96 3 3 3
10a Northumberland Ave   020 7321 3100   2–3C

Despite its gracious, high-ceilinged interior, this luxury five-star's comfortable dining room – with its own dedicated entrance, near the Embankment – is sometimes overlooked by reporters. Those who make the trip, however, say the cuisine (overseen by executive chef, André Garrett) is *"good value"* (especially the set option) and that, in particular, it's *"a great lunch location"*. / WC2N 5AE; www.corinthia.com/london/restaurants-bars; @corinthialondon; Tue-Sat 11 pm, Mon 10.30 am, Sun 4 pm; closed Mon D.

Novikov (Asian restaurant) W1 £130 2 2 4
50a Berkeley Street   020 7399 4330   3–3C

"It feels like you're in a nightclub, and it's very expensive" at this oligarch playground in Mayfair, run by Arkady Novikov (who in past times boasted of his personal friendship with Vladimir Putin, but who more recently hoisted a 'Peace for Ukraine' flag on the restaurant website). For some folks the whole vibe is a complete turn off (*"this is what's wrong with London!"*), but for Eurotrash in party mood it's still just the job for nibbling on sushi, robata and other luxe bites. (There is also a grand Italian dining room to the rear, but it inspires practically no feedback this year). / W1J 8HA; www.novikovrestaurant.co.uk; @novikovrestaurant; Mon-Wed midnight, Thu-Sat 12.30 am, Sun 11 pm.

Numero Uno SW11 £63 2 3 2
139 Northcote Rd 020 7978 5837 11–2C

"White table clothes, Italian staff serving good, honest food. What's not to love" about this "old-style (this is a compliment) local that's been on Northcote Road for years". That's the upbeat view, anyway, but – while a majority of its Nappy Valley regulars still sing its praises – marks dipped this year amid the odd report that it is "losing its charm", with "tables far too close together" for comfort. Perhaps popularity has come at a cost. / SW11 6PX; www.numerounorestaurant.co.uk; @numerounoclapham?hl=en; Mon-Sun 11 pm; no Amex.

Nuovi Sapori SW6 £54 3 4 3
295 New King's Rd 020 7736 3363 11–1B

This "very friendly family-owned restaurant" near Parsons Green offers a small menu of "reliable Italian food", at "very good value for money". / SW6 4RE; www.nuovisaporilondon.co.uk; @nuovi_sapori_14; Mon-Sat 11 pm; closed Sun; booking max 6 may apply.

Nusr-Et Steakhouse SW1 £184 1 1 1
101 Knightsbridge 01821 687738 6–1D

"Suitable only for chavs and vulgarians" – social media hyperstar, Nusret Gökçe's "ludicrous" Knightsbridge outpost of his global steakhouse chain takes nothing but stiff flak in our annual diners' poll for its "grotesque" or even "filthy" pricing. Fair-minded reporters feel that "the steaks and dishes are good, however not at those prices! (which are much cheaper in Istanbul!"). Less forgiving ones say that "either Salt Bae is a pompous twat or just taking the piss out of morons with more money than sense!" (Whatever you feel, it's not a bad business model, posting £2m of profit in its first four months of operation.) / SW1S 7RN; www.nusr-et.com.tr/en/home.aspx; @nusr_et; Mon-Sat 1.30 am, Sun 12.30 am.

Nutshell WC2 £68 3 2 2
30 Saint Martin's Lane 020 3409 7926 5–4C

Mohammad and Marwa Paknejad's "sophisticated Iranian" in Theatreland serves a "short menu of very pretty, subtly flavoured dishes", from a modern open kitchen that uses fresh British ingredients along with Iranian spices. "The lightness of the cooking makes it perfect for a meal pre- or post-theatre". / WC2W 4ER; nutshelllondon.co.uk; @nutshelllondon; Tue-Sat 9.30 pm; closed Tue-Thu L, closed Sun & Mon.

O'ver £68 3 2 2
1 Norris Street, St James's Market, SW1 020 7930 9664 4–4D
44-46 Southwark Street, SE1 020 7378 9933 10–4B

"Pizza with imported sea water from Naples! What's not to like...?" ask fans of this studiedly authentic Neapolitan duo on Borough's main drag and in St James's Market. Portions are "generous", too. / www.overuk.com; over_uk.

Oak £67 3 2 4
243 Goldhawk Rd, W12 020 8741 7700 8–1B
137 Westbourne Park Rd, W2 020 7221 3355 7–1B

"Superb pizzas" and a "great local vibe" are the attractions at this smart pub conversion in "a trendy corner of Notting Hill" and its two offshoots (the Oak W12 off Ravenscourt Park and the Bird in Hand at Brook Green). "It's Roman-style pizza, with a thin, crispy base – not the chewy gooey style that is too popular". Top Tip – in W11, the upstairs lounge bar "is a gem for a pre- or post-dinner drink".

FSA

Obicà Mozzarella Bar, Pizza e Cucina £60 3|3|3
19-20 Poland St, W1   020 3327 7070   4–1C
1 West Wintergarden, 35 Bank St, E14   020 7719 1532   12–1C
Unit 4 5 - 7 Limeburners Lane,, EC4   020 3327 0984   10–2A
This international chain has three London representatives – in Soho, the City and Canary Wharf – and focuses on light Italian dishes (pizza, pasta and salads) showcasing the eponymous cheese from Campania alongside other Italian produce; plus a range of cocktails and wines. A good spot "for post-work drinks and nibbles". / obica.com; obicamozzarellabar; 10 pm - 11 pm; E14 Sat 8 pm; E14 & EC4 Closed Sun.

Oblix SE1 £107 2|2|4
Level 32, The Shard, 31 St. Thomas Street   020 7268 6700   10–4C
This all-day operation on the 32nd floor of the Shard celebrates its tenth anniversary this year, and still wows with its "amazing views" over London. The 'urban casual' menu from Rainer Becker (of Zuma and Roka) fits the (very expensive) bill without generating much excitement. It is divided in two, with Oblix East offering "excellent afternoon tea" and cocktails. / SE1 9RY; www.oblixrestaurant.com; @oblixrestaurant; Mon-Wed, Sat, Fri, Sun 11 pm, Thu midnight; booking max 6 may apply.

Odette's NW1 £82 3|2|2
130 Regents Park Road   020 7586 8569   9–3B
This classy north London institution in the heart of pretty Primrose Hill "never disappoints and is really good value" under renowned chef-patron Bryn Williams, who has been in charge for the last 15 of its 45 years, and whose family farm in Wales supplies the kitchen (including with "excellent, tender beef"). It's the venue of choice for locals with something to celebrate – while many from further afield just "love Sunday lunch at Odette's, sitting outside on a sunny day". / NW1 8XL; www.odettesprimrosehill.com; @odettesrestaurant; Wed-Sun 9.30 pm; closed Mon & Tue.

Off the Hook E1 NEW £21
27 Gauging Square, Vaughan Way   020 7709 0834   10–3D
"Sustainable, fresh, well-cooked with interesting Korean and Caribbean influences" – this avant-garde seafood operation in Wapping, from Dorset-based fish supplier Shaun Henderson and chef Neil Wager, opened in stages through 2022. The chippy came first – "but what fish 'n' chips!", with ten chip varieties, including 'extra-large smoked with togarashi and okono sauce' – followed by a full-service seafood restaurant and a 'butchery' specialising in dry-aged fish. Reports are too limited for a rating but initial feedback is very positive. / E1E 2AH; oth.fish; @offthehook.fish; Wed-Sat 10 pm; closed Mon & Tue & Sun.

Ognisko Restaurant SW7 £60 3|4|5
55 Prince's Gate, Exhibition Road   020 7589 0101   6–1C
"The magnificent interior of the entrance hall and dining room" of this characterful Polish émigré club in South Kensington (near the museums and Royal Albert Hall) creates a "lovely and airy" ambience boosted by its "warm and friendly" staff. And in recent years it has also added "a fabulous all-weather terrace" with "a marquee in the attractive garden" at the rear, where the atmosphere can be "incredible". The solid Polish fare is "good if not fantastic" but keenly priced and accompanied by a wide drinks list, including "fab homemade flavoured vodkas". Top Tip – support Ukraine by buying a 'Zelenskyy' – "a special (delicious) cocktail in the national colours". / SW7 2PG; www.ogniskorestaurant.co.uk; Mon-Sat 11.15 pm, Sun 10.30 pm; no trainers.

FSA RATINGS: FROM 1 POOR — 5 EXCEPTIONAL

Oka £57 3 3 2

Kingly Court, 1 Kingly Court, W1   020 7734 3556   4–2B
19 New Cavendish Street, W1   020 7486 4388   3–1A
251 King's Road, SW3   020 7349 8725   6–3C
71 Regents Park Rd, NW1   020 7483 2072   9–3B
88 Church Road, SW13   020 8741 8577   11–1A

These "busy and bustling fusion restaurants" offer a "wide choice" of East Asian dishes, headed by "Japanese-style favourites" – including various sushi or sashimi options and miso black cod – that are "competently and surprisingly well prepared". Israeli-born founder Ohad Kastro celebrates the 10th anniversary of the original launch in Primrose Hill this year; branches in Soho, Marylebone, Chelsea and Barnes have followed.
/ www.okarestaurant.co.uk.

Oklava EC2 £77 4 4 3

74 Luke St   020 7729 3032   13–1B

"Fabulous" Turkish-Cypriot cooking has won a major foodie reputation for Selin Kiazim's Shoreditch seven-year-old, aided by "genuine" service from business partner Laura Christie. It's a "lively" spot too (if "really noisy with chatter bouncing off the hard surfaces"). / EC2A 4PY; www.oklava.co.uk; @oklava_ldn; Wed-Sat, Tue 10 pm; closed Tue L, closed Sun & Mon; payment – credit card only; booking max 6 may apply.

Oliveto SW1 £71 3 2 2

49 Elizabeth Street   020 7730 0074   2–4A

"Great thin-crust pizzas" and other "simple but delicious" staples get a good reception at this Belgravia Italian from Sardinian Mauro Sanna's classy stable. It "does what it does very well": namely "good honest, earthy food" made with "fresh ingredients". The wine list majors on interesting bottles and magnums from Sardinia. / SW1W 9PP; www.olivorestaurants.com/oliveto; @olivorestaurants; Mon-Sun 10.30 pm.

Olivo SW1 £80 3 4 2

21 Eccleston Street   020 7730 2505   2–4B

"An old favourite", the 33-year-old original in Mauro Sanna's Belgravia mini-empire was "ground-breaking, as one of the first London Italian restaurants to serve simple 'peasant' dishes – in this case Sardinian. Now everyone does it! However, Olivo has never marketed itself at foodies, just well-heeled locals" – who are "never disappointed". It's "not cheap, but definitely not expensive compared with glitzier competitors" in the area. / SW1W 9LX; www.olivorestaurants.com; @olivorestaurants; Tue-Sun 10.30 pm; closed Sat & Sun L, closed Mon.

Olivocarne SW1 £87 3 3 2

61 Elizabeth St   020 7730 7997   2–4A

This "reliable Sardinian restaurant" is the meat specialist in Maura Sanna's Belgravia group, serving several cuts of beef along with 'porceddu' (slow-roasted suckling pig) and "some really good Italian and Sardinian wines". The décor is a modern take on Sardinian folk imagery, and there's a heated terrace where you can enjoy a Havana cigar from the in-house collection. / SW1W 9PP; www.olivorestaurants.com; @olivorestaurants; Tue-Fri, Sun 10.30 pm, Sat 11 pm; closed Mon.

Olivomare SW1 £82 3 3 2

10 Lower Belgrave St   020 7730 9022   2–4B

"This impressive neighbourhood restaurant" in Belgravia serves "wonderful seafood, Italian style". Opened in 2007, it is part of Sardinian-born Mauro Sanno's upmarket group in one of London's poshest enclaves. The interior design can seem a little "bleak" for some tastes: not an issue in summer at the outside tables. / SW1W 0LJ; www.olivorestaurants.com; @olivorestaurants; Tue-Sun 10.30 pm; closed Mon; booking max 10 may apply.

Olley's SE24 £39 3️⃣3️⃣3️⃣
65-69 Norwood Rd   020 8671 8259   11–2D

"Consistently excellent fish 'n' chips" have made their mark for more than 35 years at Harry Niazi's rustic spot by Brockwell Park, named after Oliver Twist (1837), in which Charles Dickens mentions a 'fried fish warehouse' – one of the earliest references to what became the national dish. / SE24 9AA; www.olleys.info; @olleysfishexperience; Tue-Sun 9.30 pm; closed Mon; no Amex.

Olympic Studios SW13 £57 2️⃣2️⃣3️⃣
117-123 Church Road   020 8912 5170   11–1A

"Barnes at brunch" is to be found at this "family-friendly" brasserie, on the ground floor of a complex created from legendary recording studios (The Beatles, The Rolling Stones, Ella Fitzgerald, Madonna, Prince… the list goes on) and which also incorporates an indie cinema and "very cool" members' bar. Fans say you get "decent food at reasonable prices" here at any time. Sceptics that "it has nice surroundings, but a limited and dull menu, which is pretty well executed, but just serves a purpose, nothing more". / SW13 9HL; www.olympiccinema.co.uk; @olympicstudios; Mon-Thu 10 pm, Fri & Sat 10.30 pm, Sun 9 pm; payment – credit card only.

Olympus Fish N3 £41 4️⃣4️⃣2️⃣
140-144 Ballards Ln   020 8371 8666   1–1B

"Always welcoming, always fresh fish and always wonderful chips" are the priorities at this modern family-run fish 'n' chips restaurant in Finchley (est. 2000). The fish can be fried or charcoal-grilled, and is backed up by a choice of Turkish mezze and side dishes. / N3 2PA; www.olympusrestaurant.co.uk; Mon-Sun 10 pm.

Ombra E2 £58 3️⃣4️⃣3️⃣
1 Vyner St   020 8981 5150   14–2B

This "fabulously located" Italian on the Hackney stretch of Regent's Canal has shades ('ombra' in Italian) of Venice, although head chef Mitshel Ibrahim hails from Milan, where his parents had an Ethiopian restaurant. "Terrific tastes are delivered by an obviously enthusiastic kitchen and serving team" – "if we didn't live 200 miles away this would be a regular haunt". Its lockdown project has turned into a permanent pasta factory next door. / E2 9DG; www.ombrabar.com; @ombrabar.restaurant; Mon, Thu-Sat 10 pm, Sun 5 pm; closed Mon L closed Sun D, closed Tue & Wed.

108 Brasserie W1 £73 3️⃣2️⃣3️⃣
108 Marylebone Ln   020 7969 3900   2–1A

This pavement brasserie, complete with outside seating in warmer months, is part of a well-situated hotel at the top of Marylebone Lane, near the High Street. The food is sometimes "variable", but can be "very good". / W1U 2QE; www.108brasserie.com; @108marylebonelane; Mon-Sat 11 pm, Sun 6 pm.

104 Restaurant W2 £102 4️⃣4️⃣4️⃣
104 Chepstow Road   020 3417 4744   7–1B

"Originally came here at the recommendation of a Michelin star chef – now it's our default treat". Richard Wilkins continues to win high ratings all round in reports on his Notting Hill 14-seater, praised for "generous portions of superb food" (with luxurious ingredients such as wagyu beef often a feature of the menu). / W2 5QS; www.104restaurant.com; @104restaurant; Wed-Sun 9.30 pm; closed Wed-Fri L, closed Mon & Tue.

101 Thai Kitchen W6 £45 3️⃣2️⃣2️⃣
352 King St   020 8746 6888   8–2B

"Whilst an unexciting-looking place, the food is consistently enjoyable" – both punchy Isaan dishes from the northwest and seafood from the south – at this "starkly decorated" canteen near Stamford Brook tube (often somewhat over-egged in fooderati 'best of' lists as a seminal cheap eat). / W6 0RX; www.101thaikitchen.uk; Mon-Sun 10.30 pm; no Amex.

116 at the Athenaeum W1 £68 2 4 3
Athenaeum Hotel, 116 Piccadilly   020 7499 3464   3–4B
The "wonderful afternoon tea" at this "luxury" hotel on Piccadilly hogs the limelight since the former Galvin at the Athenaeum dining room was rebranded during the pandemic. The lunch and dinner menus offer contemporary British cuisine from chef Ian Howard. Top Tip – the cream tea is a steal at £10 for homemade scones, Cornish clotted cream and strawberry jam plus a pot of tea. / W1; www.athenaeumhotel.com; @theathenaeum; Mon-Sat 10 pm, Sun 2.30 pm; closed Sun D.

1 Lombard Street EC3 £72 3 2 3
1 Lombard St   020 7929 6611   10–3C
"King of the City lunching scene" – Soren Jessen's "buzzing" stalwart in the very heart of the Square Mile, near Bank, continues to maintain its "consistent standards" and is "a decent if very 'City' restaurant". "Classic dishes" ("including some added when Mark Hix was still consultant chef") are served alongside "a well-chosen wine list" (and they do an "awesome breakfast" too). / EC3V 9AA; www.1lombardstreet.com; @1lombardstreet; Mon-Sat 11 pm; closed Sun; booking max 10 may apply.

123V W1 £57 3 2 3
Terrace & Lower Ground Floor at Fenwick, 63 New Bond Street   020 8132 9088   3–2B
"The basement of a department store doesn't lend itself to high ambience", but "half the fun of this place is the window shopping on the way in!" From Alexis Gauthier's "interesting all-vegan selection", the "amazingly crafted" sushi "looks amazing" and "is an engaging experience that comes close to 'the real thing' by look and taste". Fans say items like the vegan burgers "are also terrific", although there are also sceptics who find these other options "less convincing". But in summer, "any shortcomings are more than made up for by the brilliant outside location, with a large paved terrace abutting Bond street, where you could be in Cannes under the large umbrellas as you watch the fancy shopping bags and their owners wandering by". / W1W 1RQ; 123vegan.co.uk; @123vegan_w1; Mon-Sat 8 pm, Sun 5 pm; closed Sun D; payment – credit card only.

Only Food and Courses SW9 £66
Pop Brixton, 49 Brixton Station Road   07949 259067   11–1D
In one of Pop Brixton's hip containers, Robbie Lorraine's 6-course tasting menu aims to take guests on a nostalgia trip to the 80s and 90s and is almost as much about pop culture as it is about the food. On limited feedback, though, the latter is much more than an afterthought. STOP PRESS: in July 2022, Lorraine announced that he would be leading the kitchen at the new Boys Hall in Kent and there's no availability shown here till for the remainder of 2022, so its future direction seems up in the air. / SW9 8PQ; www.onlyfoodandcourses.co.uk; @onlyfoodandcourses; Thu-Sat 10.30 pm, Sun 4 pm; closed Sun D, closed Mon & Tue & Wed; booking online only.

Les 110 de Taillevent W1 £90 3 3 3
16 Cavendish Square   020 3141 6016   3–1B
Named for its "phenomenal wine list" – featuring 110 wines available by the glass using the Coravin wine storage system – this London outpost of a famous Parisian group offers a professional all-round formula, which also incorporates high-quality, modern French cuisine and "excellent service" (with particularly "superb sommelier knowledge"); all served in the "well-lit and welcoming" setting of a stylish dining room, looking onto Cavendish Square. On the downside, it can seem expensive; and "on a quiet night, atmosphere is lacking". / W1G 9DD; www.les-110-taillevent-london.com; @110london; Wed-Fri 2.30 pm, Tue, Sat midnight; closed Tue, Sat L closed Wed-Fri D, closed Sun & Mon; credit card deposit required to book.

Opera Tavern WC2 £58 2 2 3
23 Catherine Street   020 7836 3680   5–3D

This former pub in Covent Garden (part of Urban Pubs & Bars) serves "dependable tapas-style" Spanish and Italian small plates in an atmosphere that "feels both private and buzzing". Marks have dropped off in recent years, though, and those who remember it back in the day, when it really fizzed along, feel it's "lost its game". / WC2B 5JS; www.saltyardgroup.co.uk/opera-tavern; @operatavern; Mon-Sat 11 pm; closed Sun.

Opso W1 £93 3 2 3
10 Paddington St   020 7487 5088   2–1A

"Excellent modern Greek cuisine" (incorporating luxury non-traditional ingredients such as wagyu beef, English asparagus and truffle mayonnaise) is to be found on the menu at this Marylebone venue from the Athens-based Modern Greek Food Group. It has a funkier 'gastrobar' stablemate, Ino, off Carnaby Street. / W1U 5QL; www.opso.co.uk; @opso_london; Mon-Sat 10.15 pm, Sun 9.45 pm; closed Sun L.

The Orange SW1 £84 2 3 3
37 Pimlico Rd   020 7881 9844   6–2D

This "fun" rustic-chic pub/hotel/events space is a magnet for an "attractive crowd" on the Pimlico-Chelsea border, and serves a "varied range" of food, from wood-fired pizza in the bar to more formal meals in the dining room upstairs. / SW1W 8NE; www.theorange.co.uk; @theorangepublichouse; Mon-Sat 10 pm, Sun 9.30 pm.

Orange Pekoe SW13 £40 3 3 4
3 White Hart Ln   020 8876 6070   11–1A

"A neighbourhood treasure", this well-run tea shop near the river in Barnes serves "every kind of tea possible", plus "super cakes and sandwiches". It's "highly sought-after" for its afternoon teas – "you'll need to book for a cuppa and a slice of cake at busy times". More substantial meals for brunch/lunch can be "disappointing". / SW13 0PX; www.orangepekoeteas.com; @orangepekoeteas; Mon-Sun 5 pm; closed Mon-Sun D.

The Orange Tree N20 £66 3 3 3
7 Totteridge Village   020 8343 7031   1–1B

This 'country pub' in Totteridge village, on London's northern fringe, boasts a global menu which covers everything from oriental-inspired dishes to steaks from the grill, and wins a general thumbs-up from reporters. / N20 8NX; www.theorangetreetotteridge.co.uk; Tue-Sat 9 pm; closed Sun & Mon.

Orasay W11 £59 5 4 4
31 Kensington Park Road   020 7043 1400   7–1A

"Every dish screams eat me!" – "Jackson Boxer is delivering some seriously bold cooking" – in particular "incredibly delicious seafood" (but also "wonderful wood-fired meats") – at his Notting Hill three-year-old, named for the Hebridean island where he spent many childhood summers. Top Menu Tip – "the Mull scallop in vin jaune is a highlight amongst many, many brilliantly executed dishes". / W11 2EU; orasay.london; @orasay.london; Tue-Thu 10 pm, Fri & Sat 11 pm, Sun 3.30 pm; closed Tue-Thu L closed Sun D, closed Mon.

Oren E8 £64 4 3 2
89 Shacklewell Lane   020 7916 6114   14–1A

"I just love Oren's food", say the many fans of chef Oden Oren's simple 30-seater in Dalston, which catapulted into the front rank of new-wave Middle Eastern venues when it opened three years ago. The modern Israeli and eastern Med small plates, along with wines recommended by Zeren Wilson, "never disappoint". Top Tip – "pollock pastrami is really memorable". / E8 2EB; www.orenlondon.com; @orenlondon; Tue-Sat 11 pm; closed Tue-Fri L, closed Sun & Mon.

F S A

Orient London W1 £51   4 3 2
15 Wardour Street   020 7989 8880   5–3A
Near the gateway leading into Chinatown, this undistinguished looking Chinese venue is one of the better bets in the area: the food is "always tip top" and "less clichéd" than often is the case nearby. Seafood is tipped as is the "excellent dim sum". / W1W 6PH; www.orientlondon.com; @orientlondon; Sun-Thu 11.30 pm, Fri & Sat midnight.

Ormer Mayfair by Sofian,
Flemings Mayfair Hotel W1 £115   4 5 3
7-12 Half Moon Street   020 7016 5601   3–4B
"A choice of 6-course or 8-course tasting menus and a fantastic selection of wines" greets visitors to this 1930s-style, oak-panelled chamber in Mayfair, which scored uniformly high marks this year for Sofian Msetfi's accomplished, seasonal British cuisine. There are also vegetarian and vegan alternative menus (the latter of which requires 48 hours notice). / W1J 7BH; www.flemings-mayfair.co.uk/fine-dining-london/ormer-mayfair-restaurant; @ormer.mayfair; Mon-Fri 7 pm, Sat 5 pm; closed Sat D, closed Sun; no shorts.

Oro Di Napoli W5 £40   3 4 2
6 The Quadrant, Little Ealing Lane   020 3632 5580   1–3A
This Neapolitan pizzeria vies with nearby Santa Maria as "the pizza place of choice" in the local Ealing battle for supremacy. They also offer fried pizza for a different slant on the fast-food classic. / W5 4EE; www.lorodinapoli-ealing.com; @lorodinapoliealing; Mon-Sun 10 pm.

Orrery W1 £94   2 2 2
55 Marylebone High St   020 7616 8000   2–1A
Above Marylebone's Conran Shop, this "well-spaced", first-floor dining room has historically been a D&D London flagship thanks to its stylish interior, charming views over a churchyard, professional standards and – a relatively recent addition – a "lovely outdoor rooftop terrace". For the second year since the pandemic struck, though, its ratings remain well below their historical levels. Some do still report their best meal of the year here, praising "outstanding modern French cuisine"; but sceptics are "disappointed because it used to be so much better". It doesn't help that "the ambience of this long and thin chamber has always been slightly precarious" and, at worst, reports are of "mediocre food (relative to the price) served in a very underwhelming manner in a dead environment". One regular, though, thinks it's just a passing phase: "after being through something of a culinary slump, I had an excellent meal!" / W1U 5RB; www.orrery-restaurant.co.uk; @the_Orrery; Mon-Sat 10 pm, Sun 9 pm; booking max 8 may apply.

Oscar Wilde Lounge at Cafe Royal W1 £97   3 3 5
68 Regent St   020 7406 3333   4–4C
If you're ticking off London's luxe afternoon teas, that offered in the Café Royal's former Grill Room needs to be on your list. Its succession of cakes and savouries is well-reviewed, but of course the star of the show is the rococo room, designed in 1865: a story-book riot of mirrors and painted ceilings (which, for many decades back in the day, was one of the capital's great restaurant destinations). / W1B; www.hotelcaferoyal.com/oscarwildebar; @hotelcaferoyal; Tue-Sat midnight; closed Tue-Thu L, closed Sun & Mon.

Oslo Court NW8 £73   3 5 5
Charlbert Street   020 7722 8795   9–3A
"Let's do the time warp again (…and again, and again, and again, and…)" – this happy relic at the foot of a Regent's Park apartment block "hasn't changed in 30 years, and why should it?" Stuck in perpetuity in the mid-1970s (complete with salmon-pink décor; long-serving waiters from that era; and a menu that's not wittingly nostalgic, it just never changed) "it would take the hardest of hearts not to be moved to inexplicable joy by an occasional visit here". The "amazing staff really look after you", "you won't leave hungry", and the arrival of the dessert trolley provides a rapturous

climax to the occasion. They are also terrific with kids, who often dine here as part of large family groups incorporating relatives at least 70 years their senior. / NW8 7EN; www.oslocourtrestaurant.co.uk; Mon-Sat 11 pm; closed Sun; No jeans.

Osteria, Barbican Centre EC2 £53 3️⃣2️⃣2️⃣
Level 2 Silk Street 020 7588 3008 10–1B

It's pleasing that this monolithic arts centre boasts a respectable restaurant, in the form of this Searcy's-run operation, which is ideally situated for a meal around a performance, and uniformly well-rated. There are niggles though – even those who applaud "very decent Italian cuisine" can note "the odd lapse" in execution, or say the overall meal "lacked finesse". / EC2Y 8DS; osterialondon.co.uk; @SearcysLondon; Mon-Sat 7 pm; closed Sun.

Osteria Antica Bologna SW11 £67 3️⃣3️⃣2️⃣
23 Northcote Rd 020 7978 4771 11–2C

"Genuine Italian home cooking" has made this rustic, wood-panelled trattoria a "favourite place for family celebrations" for more than three decades in one of South London's top family zones, Clapham's 'Nappy Valley'. It's a useful reminder that there's more to la cucina Italiana than pizza and pasta, and "the wild boar is to die for!". / SW11 1NG; www.osteria.co.uk; @osteriaanticabologna; Tue-Fri 21.45 pm, Sat 10 pm, Sun 8.45 pm; closed Mon.

Osteria Basilico W11 £73 3️⃣3️⃣3️⃣
29 Kensington Park Rd 020 7727 9957 7–1A

"Friendly, neighbourhood Italian", now in its 31st year, that serves "good" if fairly standard food, and – following the lockdown puppy explosion – can appear to "welcome almost as many dogs as human customers". The only real problem is its popularity, which means it "can be a bit crowded as tables are very close to each other". If you can't squeeze in, its two younger siblings in the same street, Essenza and Mediterraneo, are worth a try. / W11 2EU; www.osteriabasilico.co.uk; Mon-Sun 10.30 pm; no booking, Sat L.

Osteria Tufo N4 £63 3️⃣4️⃣3️⃣
67 Fonthill Rd 020 7272 2911 9–1D

"Simple but delicious Italian food" and a "pretty, light and airy interior" are key ingredients at this good neighbourhood trattoria in Finsbury Park. The formula is topped off by "friendly proprietress Paola" (and, on occasion a "genuine opera-singing waiter") guaranteeing a "lively and fun atmosphere". Top Menu Tip – "leave room for the perfectly sized Cafe Tufo coffee with mascarpone". / N4 3HZ; www.osteriatufo.co.uk; @osteriatufo; Mon-Fri 10.30 pm, Sat 22.30 pm, Sun 8.30 pm; closed Mon-Fri L closed Sat D; no Amex.

Otto's WC1 £98 4️⃣4️⃣5️⃣
182 Gray's Inn Road 020 7713 0107 2–1D

"Unique and outstanding!" – "don't be fooled by the unprepossessing exterior" of Otto Tepasse's very "individual" venture, near Gray's Inn: "one of London's better restaurants". "Inside you find an eclectic, comfortable, old-fashioned interior" ("akin to the ambience of a country antique shop"), where le patron (much in evidence) and his "charming" team deliver "comforting and traditional, beautifully prepared French dishes", as part of an old-school and "romantic" experience that's "semi-theatrical in a very good way". "Their signature dish – ordered in advance – is Duck à la Presse": "quite a performance and possibly the richest three courses you'll ever eat" (safest "to be sampled only once in a lifetime!"). Other Top Menu Tips – "exceptional tournedos Rossini and steak tartare". / WC1X 8EW; www.ottos-restaurant.com; @ottos_restaurant; Wed-Fri, Tue, Sat 10 pm; closed Tue, Sat L, closed Sun & Mon.

Ottolenghi £71 4 3 2

28 Pavilion Road, SW1   020 3824 2818   6–2D **NEW**
63 Marylebone Lane, W1   020 3148 1040   2–1A
63 Ledbury Rd, W11   020 7727 1121   7–1B
287 Upper St, N1   020 7288 1454   9–2D
50 Artillery Pas, E1   020 7247 1999   10–2D

Still "a gold standard", with their "lovely, beautifully displayed food" – this small group of deli-cafés has expanded slowly since the first one opened in Notting Hill 21 years ago; the latest arrived in Pavilion Road, Chelsea, in January 2022. Hugely influential Israeli-born chef and writer Yotam Ottolenghi has transformed the way much of the world sees Middle Eastern cuisine – and vegetables. "I'm not a vegetarian, but I love eating the veg dishes here and I find I don't need to order any meat". (See also the chef's two grander restaurants, Nopi and Rovi). / www.ottolenghi.co.uk.

The OWO SW1

The Old War Office, 57 Whitehall Place   no tel   2–3C

Italian-Argentine megachef Mauro Colagreco, of Mirazur on the French Riviera, is the star gastronomic attraction of the late-2022 launch of the Raffles hotel and apartment complex, emerging from the Edwardian baroque shell of the Old War Office building opposite Whitehall Palace, owned since 2014 by the Hinduja Group. In all, there will be 11 restaurants and two bars on the sprawling site, with Colagreco responsible for 'a brasserie with a twist, a fine-dining restaurant and an avant-garde private chef's table'. / SW1S 2HB; www.theowo.london; @theowo.london; Sun-Thu 11 pm, Fri & Sat 11.30 pm.

Oxeye SW11 £169 5 4 4

14 New Union Square   020 8067 7532   11–1D

MasterChef: The Professionals winner, Sven-Hanson Britt has created something "super special" at this late 2021 newcomer, near the new American embassy in Nine Elms. "A Tardis-like journey takes you into such an intimate dining space" decked out with "dark industry-chic" décor. "Staff do a fantastic job of creating a welcoming atmosphere in a restaurant with only a few tables" and "having Sven the chef come out to tell you what each course is and the backstory of each dish is just brilliant!" The food is "sensational" too – "cooked with a lightness of touch which enables the flavours of excellent ingredients to sing" ("the only, minor, issue was that I couldn't eat all the food… just too much of it!"). "Well worth a trip south of the river (only a few minutes on the bus from Vauxhall station)!" / SW11 7AX; oxeyerestaurant.co.uk; @oxeyerestaurant; Wed-Sat 11 pm; closed Mon & Tue & Sun.

Oxo Tower, Restaurant SE1 £107 1 1 1

Barge House St   020 7803 3888   10–3A

"Great view… shame about the restaurant". This South Bank landmark provides "stunning views over the Thames to the lights of the City of London, bound to impress your date". But it remains "a pity that such an iconic location serves canteen-standard grub" that's "waayyyyyyy overpriced" ("the night would have been too expensive if it was free! But as it was we paid a hefty sum for a crushing disappointment"). / SE1 9PH; www.harveynichols.com/restaurant/the-oxo-tower; @oxo_tower; Mon-Sun 10 pm; booking max 10 may apply.

F S A

Oxo Tower, Brasserie SE1 £92 １１２
Barge House St   020 7803 3888   10–3A
Some do tip it as "a great place for a special occasion", but the slightly cheaper section of this Art Deco landmark is rated almost as poorly as the (more expensive) main dining room. Here, "very average food" is served in a space that's "incredibly noisy and crammed", leading to an experience that can seem "stale and poor"; and with a hefty price tag too. / SE1 9PH; www.oxotowerrestaurant.co.uk; @Oxo_tower; Mon-Sun 10 pm.

The Oystermen Seafood Kitchen & Bar WC2 £77 ３２２
32 Henrietta St   020 7240 4417   5–3D
"Lovely oysters and fab fresh fish generally" from a "daily changing blackboard of specials" fuel a meal at this successful joint which is "just like eating in a seaside restaurant". It's "a bit cramped and uncomfortable" for some tastes, but conversely "feels surprisingly intimate for Covent Garden". / WC2W 8NA; oystermen.co.uk; @theoystermen; Tue-Sat 10 pm, Sun 9 pm; closed Mon.

Ozone Coffee Roasters £45 ３４４
Emma Street, E2   020 7490 1039   14–2B
11 Leonard Street, EC2   020 7490 1039   13–1A
"A top choice for breakfast and coffee" – the Shoreditch and London Fields outlets of this 20-year veteran of the Antipodean speciality coffee scene have imported the chilled, high-quality approach of its branches back home in Auckland and New Plymouth. In E2, the galvanising aroma of roasting coffee wafts up from the beans being ground in the basement, adding to its superb hipster vibe. / ozonecoffee.co.uk.

P Franco E5 £57 ４３３
107 Lower Clapton Road   020 8533 4660   14–1B
This "too-cool-for-school" Clapton bar and bottle shop has long been a 'must-mention' by journalists creating roundups of East End foodie hot spots. It serves "interesting" low-intervention wines and "inventive small plates" whose "deft cooking and wonderful flavours is hidden by the simplicity of the menu". "The ambience is great too… if you're looking for a slightly tatty and bustling wine bar spilling out onto the pavement in a seedy shopping parade in Hackney". / E5 0NP; www.pfranco.co.uk; @pfranco_e5; Tue, Wed 9 pm, Thu-Sun 10 pm; closed Tue-Sun L, closed Mon; no Amex; no booking.

Pachamama £75 ２２３
18 Thayer Street, W1   020 7935 9393   3–1A
73 Great Eastern Street, EC2   020 7846 9595   13–1B
These "groovy Peruvian late-night bar/restaurants" make "a stylish and fun way to end a night out, with a multiplicity of delicious small dishes on the tasting menu". Best to go in a party mood: they can be "too noisy for conversation".

Padella £42 ４３３
6 Southwark St, SE1   no tel   10–4C
1 Phipp Street, EC2   no tel   13–2B
"Still some of the very best pasta in London at half the price of most places" continues to inspire rave reviews for these genius pit stops, where "pound for pound the great value for money is always good" ("and extends to the drinks"). "For an unplanned midweek supper there's nothing better", although at the mega-popular Borough Market original it can feel "like a conveyor belt" at busier times. At "the funky newish premises in Shoreditch" there's "rather more space than in SE1, with proper booking… what's not to like?". Top Menu Tip – "just go for the cacio e pepe… but everything else is good as well".

FSA

Pahli Hill Bandra Bhai W1 £83 3 2 2
79-81 Mortimer Street   020 8130 0101   3–1C
This contemporary two-year-old near Selfridges (on the former site of Gaylord, RIP) is the first London venture from New Delhi-based Azure Hospitality, and serves an "intriguing" menu inspired by the posh Mumbai suburb it is named after. The kitchen uses high-quality British produce, including some "interesting veggies", to produce cooking that's "full of enjoyable flavours". Meanwhile, down in 'Bandra Bhai', the basement 'smugglers den', you can find some "dangerously delicious cocktails!".
/ W1W 7SJ; palihill.co.uk; @palihilluk; Tue-Sat 10 pm, Sun 4 pm; closed Sun D, closed Mon.

Palace Lounge,
The Rubens at the Palace SW1
39 Buckingham Palace Rd   020 7834 6600   2–4B
"With window views of the back of Buckingham Palace and its comings and goings amidst refills of tea", this plush lounge can make a good stop-off for an afternoon treat. Feedback is limited, but praises "a lovely stack of sandwiches, pretty cakes and scones with fresh flavours". More substantial meals are available in the hotel's very comfortable and traditional dining room (The English Grill), complete with oil paintings and leather banquettes.
/ SW1W 0PS; www.rubenshotel.com; Sun-Wed 11 pm, Thu-Sat midnight; Jacket required.

Paladar SE1 £62 4 4 5
4-5 London Road   020 7186 5555   10–4A
"You go here to have an all-embracing 'good time'" if you pop down to this "quirky and fun" destination, near Elephant & Castle. "It specialises in Latin American recipes from across the continent" using "genuine ingredients" to produce "unusual and delicious dishes". "What also makes this restaurant stand out is the outstanding wine list and friendly and knowledgeable service": "they always make it feel that there is a big party on!" / SE1 6JZ; www.paladarlondon.com; @paladarlondon; Tue-Fri 9.30 pm, Mon 9 pm, Sat 10 pm, Sun 8 pm; closed Mon L; payment – credit card only.

The Palomar W1 £63 4 4 4
34 Rupert Street   020 7439 8777   4–3D
"In the teeth of ever-growing competition in the Middle Eastern/eastern Med bracket", this funky Tel Aviv-inspired grill on the edge of Chinatown continues to justify its reputation, serving "fantastic sharing plates" with "good robust flavours" in a "fun" and "buzzy" – if "rather crowded and very noisy" – setting. / W1D 6DN; www.thepalomar.co.uk; @PalomarSoho; Mon-Wed, Fri & Sat 11 pm, Thu 10 pm, Sun 9 pm.

Paradise W1 £60 4 3 3
61 Rupert Street   no tel   4–2D
"Top-quality Sri Lankan food" – full of "interesting flavours" – draws an appreciative crowd to this modern venue "in the heart of Soho", where the kitchen combines carefully sourced British produce with South Asian spicing. It's run by former Wasps rugby player Sam Jones, with consultant Zeren Wilson advising on the low-intervention wine list. / W1W 7PW; www.paradisesoho.com; @paradisesoho; Tue-Sat, Mon 11 pm; closed Mon L, closed Sun.

Paradise Hampstead NW3 £35 3 5 3
49 South End Rd   020 7794 6314   9–2A
This "wonderful and consistent Indian" has served generations of Hampstead locals for more than 50 years. Now run by the founder's son, its USP is the "very attentive service" – "we get a marvellous warm welcome each and every time". The food is "reliably tasty", too. Top Tips – "the lamb Ceylon and tarka dhal are to die for". / NW3 2QB; www.paradisehampstead.co.uk; Mon-Sun 11.30 pm.

Park Chinois W1 £143 3️⃣2️⃣4️⃣
17 Berkeley St 020 3327 8888 3–3C

Flamboyant décor and regular live entertainment aim to recreate the decadence of 1930s Shanghai at this showy Mayfair mandarin. As in previous years, it takes some flak for its pricing, but ratings for its luxurious cuisine (which includes Scottish Rib-Eye and imported Wagyu steaks, alongside Peking Duck, dim sum and more evidently Chinese dishes) were consistently good this year. / W1S 4NF; www.parkchinois.com; @parkchinois; Mon & Tue, Sun midnight, Wed & Thu 1 am, Fri & Sat 2 am; closed Mon-Fri L; No jeans.

Park Row W1 £105 2️⃣2️⃣4️⃣
77 Brewer Street 02037 453 431 4–3C

"A wonderful themed entrance, through a bookcase in a library and down dark, futuristic stairs" sets an appropriate scene at this Marvel-themed basement (in association with Warner Bros), just off Piccadilly Circus. "The décor of the restaurant itself, though, contains rather less fantasy… without the entrance you might not even guess the Marvel-connection… it feels more jazz-age New York or like an ocean liner". ("Contrary to my impression from the website, it is essentially one big room containing most of the different restaurants and bars, although the differences between them are subtle.") "The food is a mixed bag": some items are "excellent", but "despite the talented chef, other dishes are overpriced or subpar". Overall, though, leaving aside the cartoonish prices, everyone accepts that there is some serious culinary endeavour going on here. And such feedback that we have on the most expensive option (the exotic tasting menu in the separate 'Monarch Theatre' experience) says it's "exceptional". / W1W 9ZN; www.parkrowlondon.co.uk; @parkrowlondon; Tue, Wed 1 am, Thu-Sat 1, Sun 9 pm; closed Mon.

Parlour Kensal NW10 £66 4️⃣3️⃣4️⃣
5 Regent St 020 8969 2184 1–2B

Limited but upbeat feedback this year on this Kensal Rise fixture (akin to a gastropub) run by Jesse Dunford Wood, which opens from breakfast on (with a break in the afternoons). The place really comes into its own during brunch or Sunday lunch. Top Menu Tip – 'Cow Pie'. / NW10 5LG; www.parlourkensal.com; @parlouruk; Mon-Sun 10 pm.

Parrillan £121 3️⃣3️⃣3️⃣
Coal Drops Yard, N1 020 7018 3339 9–3C
Borough Yards, 4 Dirty Lane, SE1 no tel 10–4C **NEW**

"In an outdoor, but well-sheltered setting", the Hart Bros' outside-only terrace in Coal Drops Yard has won a good following: "dining outside on a sunny day is a highlight", and the tabletop 'parrilla' grills allow guests the fun of cooking their own meat, seafood and vegetables over coals. On the downside, though, "results can be very average at high prices" and "while it works as a novelty, having a proper chef to cook for you is generally a better option in a restaurant!" In May 2022 (too late for survey feedback), they opened a second Borough Yards location. Like its sibling, it too has an outside terrace (with 40 covers), also with grills. But, for the first time, you will not have to DIY here, there also being an indoor restaurant (with 60 covers) with a menu designed for sharing cooked for you in the open kitchen.

FSA

Parsons WC2 £65 4 4 3
39 Endell Street   020 3422 0221   5–2C

"If you can squeeze inside this tiny restaurant off Covent Garden (which has expanded out onto the pavement in recent years thankfully) you will be in for a real treat" and one "at a very fair price". Over its five years in operation, it's become one of London's top destinations for "spankingly fresh fish and seafood", "accurately cooked with brio in a small, bright space". "The unique gimmick here is that what's on the menu depends entirely on what they can get from the day boats in the morning and so could be anything. Dishes and prices are scrawled on the wall tiles with a reassuring lack of upselling; and wine comes from the ever-evolving selection at their sibling '10 Cases' over the road so you never have the same meal twice". "Lively and helpful" service completes the excellent offering. Top Menu Tips – "super oysters at £1 each" are a feature, "potted shrimp croquettes feature amongst the excellent-but-small selection of staples; and if you go in the winter you might be lucky enough to sample their legendary lobster mash". / WC2W 9BA; www.parsonslondon.co.uk; @parsons_london; Tue-Sat 10 pm; closed Sun & Mon.

Pascor W8 £61
221 Kensington High Street   020 7937 3003   8–1D

Perhaps because it's easy to ignore amongst the dross of Kensington High Street, this two-year-old venue focused on the eastern Med doesn't inspire much feedback, but such as we received is all positive. In June 2022, Tomar Amedi (former head chef of The Palomar) joined, and it is now billed as a 'Levantine Fire Kitchen'. Could be one to watch. / W8 6SG; www.pascor.co.uk; @pascor_restaurant; Mon-Sun 10 pm; closed Mon-Thu L.

Pastaio W1 £55 3 3 3
19 Ganton Street   020 3019 8680   4–2B

"A great place for a bowl of really well-executed pasta after a hard day's shopping or pre-theatre". "It's only a shame that this Soho pasta-café is almost the only place you can now experience Stevie Parle's lovely cooking". / W1W 7BU; www.pastaio.london; @pastaiolondon; Sun-Thu 10.30 pm, Fri & Sat 11 pm.

Pastan EC1 NEW £48 3 4 3
12-14 St John Street   020 7253 3333   10–1A

After successful pop-ups in Bristol and Notting Hill, this plant-based artisan pasta venture moved into its first permanent site in late 2021 (provocatively, perhaps, just off Smithfield meat market). Early reports are all positive – "I didn't even realise it was vegan!" / EC1E 4AY; pastan.co.uk; @pastanuk; Tue-Thu 9 pm, Fri & Sat 9.30 pm; closed Sun & Mon.

Patara £74 3 3 2
15 Greek St, W1   020 7437 1071   5–2A
7 Maddox St, W1   020 7499 6008   4–2A
181 Fulham Rd, SW3   020 7351 5692   6–2C
9 Beauchamp Pl, SW3   020 7581 8820   6–1C
82 Hampstead High St, NW3   020 7431 5902   9–2A
18 High St, SW19   020 3931 6157   11–2B

With its "authentic Thai food" (the mother restaurant is in Bangkok), this international group is still a "go-to Thai brand in the capital" for many reporters, especially if you want an experience "more up-market than at many of its competitors". Restaurateur Khun Patara Sila-On opened her first London branch in South Ken 33 years ago, and has added five more in central London, Hampstead and Wimbledon. / www.pataralondon.com; pataralondon.

Paternoster Chop House EC4 — £71 — 2 4 2
1 Warwick Court   020 7029 9400   10–2B

A dependable steak remains the menu highlight at this D&D London grill, but some regulars are "disappointed that it has moved location (from Paternoster Square to Ludgate Hill) and is no longer overlooking St Paul's". Oddly for a restaurant catering to City business diners, the previous venue became famous for hosting reality TV show 'First Dates'. / EC4M 7DX; www.paternosterchophouse.co.uk; @paternosterchophouse; Mon-Fri 10 pm, Sat 10.30 pm, Sun 4.30 pm; closed Sun D; booking max 12 may apply.

Patri — £47 — 3 3 2
139 Northfield Avenue, W13   020 3981 3388   1–3A
103 Hammersmith Grove, W6   020 8741 1088   8–1C

"Delhi-style street food" from an "extensive menu with different descriptions" has won a fan club for these "fun", "small" and basic cantinas in Ealing (x2) and on gracious Hammersmith Grove. Reviews this year however weren't quite as enthusiastic as in times past.

Patty and Bun — £44 — 3 2 2
18 Old Compton St, W1   020 7287 1818   5–2A
26 Kingly Street, W1   020 7287 9632   4–2A
54 James St, W1   020 7487 3188   3–1A
156 Portobello Road, W11   020 3951 9675   7–1B **NEW**
101 Wood Lane, W12   020 7223 0900   1–2B **NEW**
19 Borough High Street, SE1   020 7407 7994   10–4C
12 Northcote Road, SW11   020 7223 0900   11–2C **NEW**
20 Water Street, E14   no tel   12–1C **NEW**
2 Arthaus Building, 205 Richmond Road, E8   020 8525 8250   14–1B
22-23 Liverpool St, EC2   020 7621 1331   10–2D

"If you want your meal dripping down your chest, this is the place!" – "very consistent and superb-tasting burgers" again win a big thumbs-up for this expanding chain, which in 2022 adds branches in first Northcote Road, then Canary Wharf. Top Menu Tips – their classic 'Ari Gold' and 'Smokey Robinson' options are consistently great (cooked rare on request); vegetarian burgers get upvoted; and any "monthly specials are always worth a look" ("love the limited editions"); "decent sides too". / www.pattyandbun.co.uk; pattyandbun.

Pearl Liang W2 — £54 — 3 3 3
8 Sheldon Square   020 7289 7000   7–1C

With its "superior dim sum", this unusually spacious modern basement venue in Paddington Basin is often tipped as "better than the Chinatown options". From the main menu, the "great Cantonese cooking" comes in "generous portions", with pretty much "everything of an exemplary standard" – while service is "particularly accommodating and cheerful". / W2 6EZ; www.pearlliang.co.uk; @pearl_liang_restaurant; Mon-Sun 11 pm.

Peckham Bazaar SE15 — £61 — 4 3 3
119 Consort Rd   020 7732 2525   1–4D

"Boom! – of the school of cooking that says 'let's set fire to it and then drown it in olive oil'… wonderful!" – Albanian-born John Gionleka's Peckham pub conversion is based around a charcoal grill, as inspired by the cuisine of the former Ottoman Empire, stretching all the way from Croatia via the Balkans and Greece to Anatolia. The wine list covers much the same territory, with excursions into France and the Lebanon. / SE15 3RU; www.peckhambazaar.com; @peckhambazaar; Mon-Sat 11 pm, Sun 4 pm; closed Mon-Wed L closed Sun D.

F S A

Peckham Cellars SE15 — £59 — 4 4 3
125 Queens Road   020 7207 0124   1–4D
This "fantastic local wine bar is worth a trip" to Peckham, where it is a star of the foodie scene that has blossomed in recent years. An "informal" operation that "always has an interesting selection of food and unusual wines" – "the menu's not huge", but the modern European dishes are well thought-out, and "both food and wine represent very good value for what you're getting". (In 2023, they will launch a spin-off in Camberwell, called 'Little Cellars'.) / SE15 2ND; peckhamcellars.co.uk; @peckhamcellars; Tue-Sat 11 pm, Sun 3 pm; closed Tue-Thu L closed Sun D, closed Mon; credit card deposit required to book.

The Pelican W11 — £67 — 3 3 3
45 All Saints Rd   020 4537 2880   7–1B
This "newly opened pub with excellent food and vibe" is the latest iteration of a Notting Hill tavern built in 1872 and now tastefully buffed up. Jimi Famurewa of the Evening Standard gave chef Owen Kenworth a big thumbs-up for his "gutsy, sneakily creative food". It is also one of very few pubs to offer Pilates classes. / W11 1HE; thepelicanw11.com; @thepelican_w11; Mon-Sat midnight, Sun 10.30 pm; closed Mon-Thu L.

E Pellicci E2 — £22 — 3 5 4
332 Bethnal Green Rd   020 7739 4873   13–1D
"This top-notch Bethnal Green café" is "the place to go for London's best breakfast" – not just on account of the full English and bacon sarnies, but for the Art Deco wood panelling (Grade-II listed!) and the atmosphere created by four generations of the Pellicci family, who have run it since 1900. "What makes it different is the warm and funny staff", who draw "a happy mix of locals, tourists and everyone in between". Top Tip – "don't ask for anything gluten-free or they might laugh!" / E2 0AG; epellicci.has.restaurant; Mon-Sat 4 pm; closed Mon-Sat D, closed Sun; cash only; no booking.

The Pem SW1 — £98 — 4 4 2
Conrad London St. James, 22-28 Broadway   020 3301 8080   2–3C
Sally Abé has equalled the "superb" standard of British cooking that she achieved at the Harwood Arms at this Westminster yearling, named for a pioneering suffragette. But while the traditional hotel dining room she was imported to revivify is an "amazingly spacious and comfy space" – and benefits from "quietly super-efficient and knowledgeable staff" – it doesn't yet generate the volume of reports it perhaps deserves: "why was it empty? This deserves to be one of London's most popular restaurants!" / SW1S 0BH; thepemrestaurant.com; @thepemrestaurant; Tue, Sat, Wed-Fri 9.30 pm; closed Tue, Sat L, closed Sun & Mon.

Pentolina W14 — £61 — 4 4 4
71 Blythe Rd   020 3010 0091   8–1C
This "lovely local restaurant" run by an Italian couple in a quiet backwater near Brook Green is a popular choice for its "really delightful staff" and "excellent range of dishes". It's a small but light and airy space, with "tables outside in summer". / W14 0HP; www.pentolinarestaurant.co.uk; @pentolina_london; Tue-Sat 9.30 pm; closed Sun & Mon; no Amex.

Perilla N16 — £77 — 4 4 3
1-3 Green Lanes   020 7359 0779   1–1C
"Absolutely exceptional" modern European cuisine is created by chef Ben Marks (ex-Noma and The Square) at his former pop-up overlooking Newington Green. There's a "good-value tasting menu" (which incorporates a service charge), and an "excellent variety of dishes", making best use of relatively modest rather than 'luxury' ingredients. / N16 9BS; www.perilladining.co.uk; @perilladining; Fri & Sat, Tue-Thu 11 pm, Sun 6 pm; closed Tue-Thu L closed Sun D, closed Mon.

FSA RATINGS: FROM 1 POOR — 5 EXCEPTIONAL

FSA

The Perry Hill SE6 £53 3|4|4
78-80 Perry Hill 020 8699 3334 1–4D

A welcome 2021 relaunch after being closed for years – this roadhouse on the South Circular between Sydenham and Catford serves "generous" dishes that "elevate it beyond pub grub, but without pretending to be a gastropub". The food comes courtesy of Jamie Younger, who runs Peckham's Begging Bowl and was formerly at the Palmerston in East Dulwich; his "smoked and slow-cooked options are a triumph (red chicken, short ribs)". The "huge outdoor areas" make "weekend lunch en famille with toddlers a jolly affair" – a market sector enticed by a discount club for parents with young kids.
/ SE6 4EY; www.perryhillpub.co.uk; @perryhillpub; Mon-Sat 11 pm, Sun 10.30 pm.

Persian Palace W13 £32 3|4|2
143-145 Uxbridge Road 020 8840 4233 1–3A

"Consistently good food, huge portions and excellent value" win solid ratings for this Persian local in Ealing. There's a "great menu of traditional dishes including kebabs, kashk and ghormeh sabzi" – the classic Persian stew – while "the décor and ambience are authentic and make you feel like you're in another country". / W13 9AU; www.persianpalace.co.uk/ealing; @persianppalace; Mon-Thu 10.30 pm, Fri-Sun 11 pm.

The Petersham WC2 £102 2|2|3
Floral Court, off Floral St 020 7305 7676 5–3C

The undoubtedly "beautiful central London location" of this Covent Garden spin-off from the famous Richmond plant nursery makes it – for some reporters – "worth paying for the pricey food" in its two restaurants, especially if you have romance in mind. Plenty of others disagree, complaining of "disappointing" food in an operation that is "not even a decent shadow of the home port". / WC2W 9DJ; petershamnurseries.com; @petershamnurseries; Thu-Sat, Mon-Wed 9.30 pm; closed Sun; no trainers.

Petersham Nurseries Cafe TW10 £123 2|3|5
Church Lane (signposted 'St Peter's Church'), off Petersham Road
020 8940 5230 1–4A

"A stunning location – perfect for a summer's lunch" guarantees the appeal of this shabby-chic café, inside a garden centre amidst some of the plusher housing on the fringe of Richmond Park. When it comes to the ambitious cuisine, it's "always tempting and food is never disappointing… but when the bill arrives there's often a sense that it wasn't worth the final cost".
/ TW10 7AB; www.petershamnurseries.com; @petershamnurseriescafe; Tue, Wed, Sun 5 pm, Thu-Sat 11 pm; closed Tue, Wed, Sun D, closed Mon.

The Petersham Restaurant TW10 £80 2|2|3
Nightingale Lane 020 8003 3602 1–4A

"Excellent views over the meadows and Thames" make this dining room of a grand Richmond hotel (built in 1865) "a lovely place for a romantic dinner". Sunday lunch and afternoon tea are also popular choices. It's "a bit of a time-capsule", though, and even if prices have moved with the times, standards generally can be reminiscent of a former, less demanding, era.
/ TW10 6UZ; petershamhotel.co.uk/restaurant; @thepetershamhotel; Mon-Sun 9 pm.

Le Petit Beefbar SW3 NEW £179
27 Cale Street 020 4580 1219 6–2C

Riccardo Giradui's Chelsea newcomer is the first UK offshoot in a collection including branches in Mykonos, Dubai, Mirabel, and Monte-Carlo (the original). Giradui describes the concept as a 'temple of beef' with meat sourced globally. Too limited feedback for a review, but one seasoned reporter who lives locally notes: "There's no doubt you get a great steak here. Just expect to pay top dollar for it. The Monaco/Dubai connection drives the clientele, which is more Knightsbridge than Chelsea". / SW3 3QP; lepetit.beefbar.com; @lepetitbeefbar; Thu-Sat, Tue, Wed 10.30 pm, Sun 3 pm; closed Tue, Wed L closed Sun D, closed Mon.

FSA

Le Petit Citron W6 £56 333
98-100 Shepherds Bush Road   020 3019 1175   8–1C
"A nice and buzzy local bistro" that's attractively styled and "a good choice in the area" (a barren stretch of trafficky road, north of Brook Green). The formula is classically French, including a handy prix-fixe option. / W6 7PD; lepetitcitron.co.uk; @lepetitcitronw6; Mon-Sat 10 pm, Sun 4 pm; closed Sun D; payment – credit card only.

Petit Ma Cuisine TW9 £62 333
8 Station Approach   020 8332 1923   1–3A
This "very satisfying French throwback bistro" certainly looks the part, with its gingham tablecloths, Impressionist posters and tiled floor – and the menu of Gallic classics lives up to expectations: "we took French friends who thought it was fantastic!" Top Tip – "the prix-fixe lunch is super", and combines well with a visit to nearby Kew Gardens. / TW9 3QB; www.macuisinebistrot.co.uk; Tue-Sun 11.30 pm; closed Mon; no Amex.

Pétrus SW1 £144 221
1 Kinnerton St   020 7592 1609   6–1D
"Interesting and eclectic wine" continues to live up to the name of Gordon Ramsay's luxurious Belgravian (which is built around a large central wine cage), but its performance this year slipped well below its historic trend: no top meals of the year were reported and instead a big proportion of disappointments. It doesn't help that prices are "ridiculous" and that there's sometimes "no atmosphere". / SW1X 8EA; www.gordonramsayrestaurants.com; @petrusrestaurant; Wed-Sat 11 pm, Sun 6 pm; closed Sun D, closed Mon & Tue; no trainers.

Pham Sushi EC1 £49 333
159 Whitecross St   020 7251 6336   13–2A
"Handily close to the Barbican", this Japanese venue provides "quick and friendly service" and fans say the food is "always very, very good," too, from a "varied menu". Not all reports were as stellar this year, though. / EC1Y 8JL; www.phamsushi.com; @phamsushi; Mon-Fri 9 pm; closed Sat & Sun.

Phat Phuc SW3 £38 423
Chelsea Courtyard, 151 Sydney Street   020 7351 3843   6–3C
"Unique, authentic and to a high standard" – the tasty Vietnamese and Singaporean bowls at this noodle bar present some of the best eating value in expensive Chelsea. A South East Asian counterpart to the 'dirty burger', the name apparently means 'happy Buddha' – and you can buy the T-shirt or cap to prove you've eaten here. / SW3 6NT; www.phatphucnoodlebar.co.uk; @phat_phuc_noodle_bar; Mon-Sun 7 pm.

Phoenix Palace NW1 £64 322
5-9 Glentworth St   020 7486 3515   2–1A
"Always quick, always reliable" and "pretty authentic" – this vast and traditional Cantonese banqueting hall near Baker Street tube offers more than 300 different dishes on its eight menus – "so if you avoid the obvious, there are plenty of excellent choices". / NW1 5PG; www.phoenixpalace.co.uk; @thephoenixpalace; Mon-Sat 11.30 pm, Sun 10.30 pm.

Piazza Italiana EC2 £71 333
38 Threadneedle Street   020 7256 7223   10–2C
Occupying an impressive Edwardian banking hall in the heart of the City, this high-ceilinged space provides a large, classic Italian menu and – if you still have space – makes a feature of a sizeable cheeseboard, showcasing Italian cheeses. Reports are uniformly upbeat, including as a business choice (and, if Accounts are on your case, there's a good-value lunchtime set menu). / EC2E 8AY; www.piazzaitaliana.co.uk; @piazzaitalianauk; Mon-Wed 10 pm, Thu-Sat 11 pm; closed Sat L, closed Sun.

Pidgin E8
52 Wilton Way 020 7254 8311 14–1B £85 **4** **3** **2**

One of Hackney's better-known culinary destinations, this unassuming little spot wins high marks from everyone who reports on it for our annual diners' survey, on the basis of its "lovely tasting menu". On the downside, "the space is small so feels crammed" and – given all the excitement that's been whipped up over the years – the odd reporters find it "very good, but a mite underwhelming compared to the rave reviews". / E8 1BG; www.pidginlondon.com; @pidginlondon; Wed-Sun 11 pm; closed Wed-Fri L, closed Mon & Tue.

Pied à Terre W1
34 Charlotte St 020 7636 1178 2–1C £138 **4** **4** **4**

"Still impressive, reinventing itself and going strong!" – David Moore is the "warmest of hosts" and his exceptional Fitzrovian townhouse has been at the vanguard of London's dining scene for three decades now. "Many chefs pass through his patronage" – the current incumbent being Asimakis Chaniotis, whose "surprising" and "fabulously flavoursome" dishes include the option of one of London's foremost vegan tasting menus: "particularly impressive, imaginative and fun – even carnivores don't miss the meat!" It's not a huge site, but clever conversions over the years have created a "comfortable" and "lively" space (with a chef's table and bijoux private dining room on the upper floors). There were a couple of 'off' reports this year, of the "maybe-I-caught-it-on-a-bad-night" variety. But all-round raves remain the norm here: "I have been coming to this restaurant for over two decades and have never failed to be delighted!". Top Tip – "the vegan feast was a highlight of lockdown" and has continued as a home delivery option – "a wide range of delicious dishes, all with tantalisingly deep flavours". / W1T 2NH; www.pied-a-terre.co.uk; @PiedaTerreRestaurant; Thu-Sat, Tue, Wed 10 pm; closed Tue, Wed L, closed Sun & Mon; may need 8+ to book.

Pierre Victoire W1
5 Dean St 020 7287 4582 3–1D £55 **3** **2** **3**

Celebrating its quarter century this year, this Soho survivor of what was once a national chain is "bustling and busy, but you can't argue with really decent French bistro food at this price in central London" ("I was pleasantly surprised by the quality…" – "I don't know how they keep the prices so reasonable"). / W1D 3RQ; www.pierrevictoire.com/london/restaurant; Sun-Wed 11 pm, Thu-Sat 11.30 pm.

Pig & Butcher N1
80 Liverpool Road 020 7226 8304 9–3D £66 **3** **2** **3**

This "pretty decent gastropub" – "the best in Islington" by some reckoning – butchers its own meat for the table. Everyone agrees that the food is "high quality" – "even the snacks are great!" – but "it's a busy place and the service is a little chaotic". / N1 0QD; www.thepigandbutcher.co.uk; Mon-Sat 10 pm, Sun 9 pm.

The Pig's Head SW4 NEW
87 Rectory Grove 020 4568 5830 11–1D £77 **3** **3** **3**

"A great conversion of a big old pub in Clapham" – this November 2021 newcomer is the fourth site of the team behind Smokehouse, The Pig & Butcher and The Princess of Shoreditch. It's a "stylish and high-spec" renovation to create a buzzy attractive space over two levels. The main area is "a bit of a noisy barn" – "the mezzanine (with views to the kitchen) is the more interesting/quieter area foodwise". The menu has a sustainability focus ("the more 'unfashionable' meats: bone marrow, pig's head, mutton"), but at the overview it "serves up really well-cooked British pub dining". / SW4 0DR; www.thepigshead.com; @thepigshead; Mon-Fri 10 pm, Sat 10.30 pm, Sun 9 pm; closed Mon & Tue L; payment – credit card only; credit card deposit required to book.

FSA

Pique Nique SE1 £75 3 3 3
32 Tanner Street   020 7403 9549   10–4D

"One of the most oddly-located restaurants you can imagine", this "authentically French" outfit (sibling to Casse-Croûte on nearby Bermondsey Street) "looks like an ex-tennis clubhouse opposite a kids' playground". It's a "charming and delightful place", though, and the food is of "high quality" – sometimes "simply superb". / SE1 3LD; pique-nique.co.uk; @piquenique32; Mon-Sat 11 pm, Sun 5 pm; closed Sun D.

El Pirata W1 £54 2 3 3
5-6 Down St   020 7491 3810   3–4B

This old-school tapas bar tucked away in Mayfair boasts an "interesting wine list, attentive staff and fun atmosphere". There's a "good selection of dishes – nothing spectacular, but a pretty decent effort across hot and cold tapas". It's "not particularly cheap" by most standards, but in this part of London prices are often astronomical. The most famous pirate of modern times, Johnny Depp, has apparently swung by for a tapa or two. / W1J 7AQ; www.elpirata.co.uk; @elpiratamayfair; closed Mon-Sat & Sun.

Pivot by Mark Greenaway WC2 £96 4 4 3
3 Henrietta Street   020 3325 5275   5–3D

"Tucked away on the first floor of a Covent Garden townhouse", this late-2021 newcomer from top Scottish chef, Mark Greenaway, is "a great little venue" with a "beautiful setting overlooking Covent Garden piazza". "Pick the chef's counter and you'll be served by Mark himself: an engaging chef, but even if you can't sit at the counter, the restaurant seating has good views". The menu (including breakfast and a pre-theatre option) is versatile and "both delivers on taste and offers good value for the location". Top Menu Tip – beef and bone marrow pie. / WC2W 8LU; 3henrietta.com; @pivotbymarkgreenaway; Wed-Sat 11 pm, Sun 5 pm; closed Sun D, closed Mon & Tue.

Pizarro SE1 £66 4 4 3
194 Bermondsey St   020 7256 5333   10–4D

"A brilliant venue with its own distinct offer in a street not short of a restaurant or two" – José Pizarro's "buzzy", larger sibling to his nearby tapas bar is "not the place if you want a quiet night" but "consistently good" for its "excellent, authentic Spanish food" ("with lots of sharing options"). / SE1 3TQ; josepizarro.com/pizarro-restaurant-bermondsey; @josepizarrorestaurants; Mon-Sat 10.45 pm, Sun 5 pm; closed Sun D.

Pizza da Valter SW17 £49 4 3 3
7 Bellevue Road   020 8355 7032   11–2C

"Really good and very Italian pizza" emerges from the oven at this "somewhat basic" pizzeria in the "lovely surroundings" of Wandsworth Common's foodie Bellevue Parade, where neighbours include Chez Bruce. / SW17 7EG; www.pizzadavalter.co.uk; @pizzadavalter; Mon-Sun 11 pm.

Pizza East £59 3 3 3
310 Portobello Rd, W10   020 8969 4500   7–1A
56 Shoreditch High St, E1   020 7729 1888   13–1B

This "fun" Portobello pizzeria is "made by the excellent location" and has a less-commented-on twin in the equally funky post-industrial setting of Shoreditch's 'Tea Building'. Fans reckon it's "still the one to beat" for "great pizzas", nibbles and a small menu of dishes baked in the wood-fired oven, along with "one of the best Bloody Marys in town"; critics say the "food has lost a little sparkle from a couple of years ago". / www.pizzaeast.com.

Pizza Metro SW11 £56 3|2|2
64 Battersea Rise   020 7228 3812   11–2C
"Amazing pizza by the metre" has always been the offer at this Battersea Neapolitan that celebrates its 30th anniversary this year. The full 100 cm will set you back £65, and is the equivalent to four conventional circular pizzas. / SW11 1EQ; www.pizzametropizza.com; @pizzametropizza; Tue-Thu 10 pm, Fri, Sun 11.30 pm, Sat midnight; closed Tue-Fri L, closed Mon; no Amex.

Pizza Pilgrims £41 3|3|2
Branches throughout London
"Much better than the long-established, tired pizza chains!" – the Elliot brothers' growing group is the most-mentioned of London's more artisanal pizza multiples in our annual diners' poll, inspiring joy with their "authentic Neapolitan preparation, with quality ingredients" and featuring "yummy crusts and interesting flavour combinations". And you get "consistent quality irrespective of the branch visited" too, even if conditions can be "a little cramped and chaotic". / pizzapilgrims.co.uk; pizzapilgrims.

PizzaExpress £53 1|2|1
Branches throughout London
"They have lost the plot since their glory days" and it's increasingly unclear why we continue to review this "vibeless" high-street brand (est. 1965): nowadays solely recommendable as a kid-friendly emergency stand-by. For decades it was the gold standard of chain dining in the UK, but poor scores support those who feel "its decline has sadly continued" since, in 2021, its ownership passed to its bond holders. Recent developments include a new logo, bold new colours, pizza wraps 'to go' and a major curtailing of the cut-price deals for which the group had become notorious. And yet still ratings slide and even more positive reviews are often muted ("some of the new offerings are quite good…"; "nothing to complain about which shows improvement…"). However you cut it, what's undeniable is that, "there are so many hugely better pizzerias around". / www.pizzaexpress.co.uk.

Pizzeria Mozza W1 £48 4|2|3
Treehouse Hotel, 14-15 Langham Place   020 3988 4273   3–1C
"Brilliant pizza" from Netflix star, Nancy Silverton, justifies a trip to this bustling pit stop, at the foot of a hotel opposite Broadcasting House. As the FT's Tim Hayward so memorably put it in his October 2021 review: 'Goethe thought architecture was music, frozen; Silverton proves that meatballs are beatitude, minced'! / W1W 2QS; @staytreehouse; Wed-Sat 10 pm, Sun 6 pm; closed Mon & Tue.

Pizzeria Pappagone N4 £35 3|3|3
131 Stroud Green Rd   020 7263 2114   9–1D
This well-known Finsbury Park fixture celebrates its 25th anniversary this year, and is well established as a hub for north London's Italian community as well as locals drawn by its reliable "cheap and cheerful" Italian comfort food, led by pizza from the wood-fired stove. There's a bar in case you have to wait for a table, and bambini are made to feel welcome. / N4 3PX; www.pizzeriapappagone.co.uk; @pizzeriapappagone; Mon-Sun midnight.

Planque E8 £76 3|2|4
322 Acton Mews   020 7254 3414   14–2A
It helps to be a lover of funky offbeat wines, if you visit this 'Wine Drinkers' Clubhouse' (incorporating members' lounge, wine cellar, and retail store) in two so-now Haggerston railway arches, where much of the seating is at communal benches (achingly hip in every sense…). Its menu of creative small plates inspire reports that vary between highs and lows. / E8 4EA; www.planque.co.uk; @_planque_; Wed-Sat 11 pm, Sun 8.30 pm; closed Wed-Fri L, closed Mon & Tue; payment – credit card only; booking online only.

Plateau E14 £87   2 2 3
4th Floor, Canada Sq   020 7715 7100   12–1C
This "calm dining room" – with a "great vibe and nice vistas" – seems to have lost its former pre-eminence in the Canary Wharf dining scene, and no longer generates much feedback. Part of the D&D London empire, it is pitched at the expense-account trade. The "food is generally good, but has the odd misstep". / E14 5ER; www.plateau-restaurant.co.uk; @Plateaucanarywharf; Mon-Sat 11.30 pm; closed Sun.

Plaza Khao Gaeng WC1 NEW £36
Arcade Food Hall, 103-105 Oxford Street   no tel   5–1A
This mid-2022 newcomer is the flagship offering at JKS Restaurants' new Arcade Food Hall (see also) at Tottenham Court Road. It opened too late to general feedback in our annual diners' poll, but an early-doors report said its "very authentic impressive Thai food makes it a must-try", while The Evening Standard's Jimi Famurewa raved: it serves "food to quicken the pulse, dampen the brow and leave you gasping for more!" / WC1W 1DB; plazakhaogaeng.com; @plazakhaogaeng; Tue-Sat 10 pm, Sun 3 pm; closed Sun D, closed Mon.

The Plimsoll N4 £55   5 3 2
52 St Thomas's Road   no tel   9–1D
"The Dexter burgers are a cult classic by now" ("well-seasoned, crisp and juicy, with meat overflowing from the bun") and the "top choices of the young and trendy crowd" packed into Jamie Allan and Ed McIlroy's (aka 'Four Legs') new "loud and down-to-earth spot in Finsbury Park". But "don't overlook the other outstandingly great value dishes on the menu which are just as delicious", such as "a tasty cockle bouillabaisse or fresh lemon sole". They haven't wasted too much cash on their makeover of the knackered old boozer (fka 'The Auld Triangle') providing their new home – "a great spot for grabbing a pint", but "it seems not to have been redecorated since your great grandad called in on the way to the pre-premiership Arsenal game". / N4 2QW; @the.plimsoll; Mon-Fri 11 pm, Sat & Sun midnight; closed Mon-Fri L.

The Plough SW14 £61
42 Christ Church Rd   020 8755 7444   11–2A
This large 18th-century inn – a survivor from the era when East Sheen was a rural village – closed down in 2021 following a dispute between Fuller's and the landlord, to the dismay of locals. It reopened after a refurb last summer, and is likely to make a comeback given its great location near Richmond Park and gorgeous outside terrace. / SW14 7AF; www.plougheastsheen.co.uk; @PloughSheen; Mon-Thu 9.30 pm, Fri & Sat 10 pm, Sun 9 pm.

PLU NW8 £175   5 4 4
12 Blenheim Terrace   020 7624 7663   9–3A
"It is a complete mystery how the Michelin guide has failed to recognise Elliot Moss's wonderful food creations", say followers of his tiny but "opulent" three-year-old in St John's Wood, where the only option is an extended tasting menu. "The chef is a true artist who does everything himself: each phenomenal and fun dish looks too good to eat but the visuals are actually secondary to the insanely addictive deliciousness of the flavours" ("his foie gras dish leaves you desperate for 'just one more mouthful'… and I don't even like foie gras!") Fooderati insiders, Koffmann & Vines, also waxed lyrical over their meal here this year, proclaiming it 'a true gastronomic experience'. "May he go from strength to strength." / NW8 0EB; www.plurestaurant.co.uk; @PluRestaurant; Thu-Sat 10 pm; closed Thu-Sat L, closed Mon-Wed & Sun; credit card deposit required to book.

FSA

Plum Valley W1 £50 3|2|2
20 Gerrard St   020 7494 4366   5–3A
"Top dim sum" – "always well cooked and presented" – is the prime draw to this Gerrard Street Cantonese stalwart, which also benefits from an outdoor terrace. / W1D 6JQ; www.plumvalleylondon.com; @plumvalleyrestaurant; Mon-Sun 10 pm.

Pollen Street Social W1 £136 3|3|3
8-10 Pollen St   020 7290 7600   3–2C
"A restaurant I love to return to more than any other!" – Jason Atherton's "glamorous" and "lively" Mayfair HQ inspires dedication and adoration from its enthusiastic, large fan base: "exemplary cooking with imaginative touches" is the expected highlight and "it's great seeing Jason so calm and professional at the pass, which comes through in the staff". That said, ratings this year slipped due to a few more middling experiences: "I so wanted to like Pollen Street Social but it never quite reached the expected heights given the hype and prices!!" Top Tip – "a top spot for a business lunch or dinner". / W1S 1NQ; www.pollenstreetsocial.com; @pollen_street_social; Tue-Sat 9.30 pm, Sun 11 pm; closed Mon; booking max 6 may apply.

Le Pont de la Tour SE1 £96 2|2|2
36d Shad Thames   020 7403 8403   10–4D
"It's great to sit outside on a sunny day and see the beautiful London sights" – not least Tower Bridge of course – from the superb, Thames-side, heated terrace of this long-established D&D London destination on the South Bank. It can be "perfect for a quiet, professional meal", aided by an "amazingly wide wine list". In other respects, though, its atmosphere and classical Gallic cuisine are very "subdued" compared to yesteryear (when it was the famous flagship of Sir Terence Conran's restaurant empire). A fair summary? – "nice to eat by the river… not really worth the journey… food OK". / SE1 2YE; www.lepontdelatour.co.uk; @lepontdelatourldn; Mon-Sat 10 pm, Sun 9 pm; no trainers.

Popeyes E15 NEW £7 4|3|3
Westfield Stratford City, Montfichet Road   no tel   14–1D
"You get the best fried chicken, but practically nothing else" at this new Westfield Stratford outlet serving Louisiana-style fried chicken sandwiches: the first location of a big US fast-food chain that breezed into town in November 2021 and is aiming for 350 branches in no time flat. "There were huge queues even months after it was opened" and "The ambience is that of a food court", but fans (unexpectedly including The Times's Giles Coren) say "the chicken is worth it". / E15 1AZ; www.popeyesuk.com; @popeyesuk; Mon-Sat 10 pm, Sun 6 pm.

Popolo EC2 £56 5|3|2
26 Rivington Street   020 7729 4299   13–1B
"One of the best meals I had all year" – this "noisy, little spot in Shoreditch" showcases "simply great cooking" from kickboxer-turned-chef Jon Lawson, who prepares "awesome sharing-style Italian plates" with Spanish and North African touches. "Perfect for a date night if you want to impress, while still keeping it hip and intimate". The occasional duff note concerns the low-intervention wines: "interesting" to some, to others "expensive" or "an acquired taste". Top Tip – "grab a seat at the counter for the best ambience/experience". / EC2A 3DU; popoloshoreditch.com; @popoloshoreditch; Mon-Wed 10.30 pm, Thu-Sat 11 pm; closed Mon-Sat L, closed Sun; no booking.

FSA

Poppies £50 3|2|2
59 Old Compton St, W1   020 7482 2977   4–2D
30 Hawley Cr, NW1   020 7267 0440   9–2B
6-8 Hanbury St, E1   020 7247 0892   13–2C
You can "travel back in time" at this trio of deliberately retro chippies, with their "Formica tables and period posters creating a great atmosphere" – "the fish 'n' chips are excellent, too". Founder Pat 'Pops' Newland, an East Ender who started working at the age 11, was still a hands-on owner in his 80s when he died in April 2022.

Poppy's £36 3|2|4
129-131 Brackenbury Road, W6   020 8741 4928   8–1C
30 Greyhound Road, W6   020 7385 9264   8–2C
78 Glenthorne Road, W6   020 8748 2351   8–2C
"Good-value local Thai restaurants in Hammersmith that do reliable take-away too". BYO adds to the value of a trip, with the best branch – rammed with stuffed animals, foliage and bric-a-brac – on the site that was for yonks, The Brackenbury (long RIP), complete with cute outside terrace in summer.

Porte Noire N1 NEW £52
Unit A Gasholder 10, 1 Lewis Cubitt Square   020 7930 6211   9–3C
"Set inside one of the old gasholders behind Coal Drops Yard", Idris Elba's "beautiful" new Gastronomic Wine Bar & Shop opened in late 2021 on the periphery of this up-and-coming area, with a peaceful position and attractive outlook. Fans say it's "no gimmick restaurant, despite its Hollywood royalty backing, but a wine bar for grown-up people serious about their food and wine". More reports please! / N1N 4BY; www.portenoire.co.uk; @portenoirekx; Mon & Tue 9.30 pm, Wed-Sat 11.30 pm, Sun 4.30 pm; closed Sun D.

Il Portico W8 £73 3|3|3
277 Kensington High St   020 7602 6262   8–1D
This "old favourite" opposite the Design Museum, now in its sixth decade, is "always buzzing, with great Italian food and a sense that every patron is 'family'". It's family-run, too, with James Chiavarini having taken over from his father, Pino. "James has introduced some modernising touches but I love the feeling that you're in Italy when you walk in the door – there's nothing minimal or characterless about it". / W8 6NA; www.ilportico.co.uk; @ilportico.kensington; Mon-Sat 11 pm; closed Sun.

Portland W1 £97 4|5|3
113 Great Portland Street   020 7436 3261   2–1B
"Incredible cooking at very fair prices" matched with excellent wines has built a major following for Will Lander and Daniel Morgenthau's "homely and calm" Fitzrovia destination, with open kitchen on view. "Knowledgeable and classy service" adds considerably to the experience: "it feels like a treat, and yet also has a real neighbourhood feel to it too, which for food of this standard and this central can be rare". / W1W 6QQ; www.portlandrestaurant.co.uk; @portlandrestaurant; Tue-Sat 9.45 pm; closed Sun & Mon.

Portobello Ristorante Pizzeria W11 £70 3|3|3
7 Ladbroke Road   020 7221 1373   7–2B
"Always full for a good reason" – this "very friendly" and lively Notting Hill Italian has a large outside terrace and attractive covered area, and is one of the better, more affordable options in the 'hood (and they're "great with kids", too). Some regulars suggest that "the pizza is better than the rest of the menu". / W11 3PA; www.portobellolondon.co.uk; @portobello_ristorante_pizzeria; closed Mon-Sat & Sun.

Postbox SW13 NEW
201 Castelnau   07424 339379   11–1A
This July 2022 newcomer in north Barnes (just south of Hammersmith Bridge) is the work of Leo Noronha, who recently worked at Hoppers. Here, he and his family will present a short, seasonal menu focused on Portuguese-influenced Goan cuisine, with dishes marinated for 48 hours then cooked on a robata grill. / SW13 9ER; www.postboxrestaurantlondon.com; @postbox_ldn; Mon-Sun midnight.

Potli W6   £53   4 3 3
319-321 King St   020 8741 4328   8–2B
"Every dish tastes different with wonderful, rich depths of flavour" at this "interesting street-food-style" café on Hammersmith's 'restaurant row' near Ravenscourt Park: "both north and south India are covered" on a "great, regional menu", incorporating "delicious vegetarian options": "the wide range favours going with a big group, or ordering lots to have at home afterwards!" / W6 9NH; www.potli.co.uk; @potlirestaurant; Mon-Thu 10 pm, Fri & Sat 10.15 pm, Sun 8.45 pm.

La Poule au Pot SW1   £70   3 4 5
231 Ebury St   020 7730 7763   6–2D
"A candlelit supper for two here first is a surefire route to romance later!" according to fans of this "timeless" Gallic corner of Pimlico, which has "been a favourite for decades" (and which perennially nears the top of our list of London's most romantic destinations). With its "cosy and intimate" hidden nooks, the "warren-like" interior "oozes rural France", as do the "charming" and characterful waiters. Its "solid and traditional French bistro-style fare" is entirely in keeping: cassoulet, coq au vin, escargot, onion tart, steak frites, tarte Tatin, all washed down with "vin rouge from the large bottle" (with consumption measured by a dip-stick). "Why would you change anything about it?" Top Tip – in summer, the "good outside tables" come into their own. / SW1W 8UT; www.pouleaupot.co.uk; @lapouleaupotrestaurant; Mon-Sun 11 pm; no trainers.

Prawn on the Lawn N1   £68   5 3 2
292-294 St Paul's Rd   020 3302 8668   9–2D
"It's almost as good as eating on the beach" at this "very intimate" (as in "tables too close together") "small" restaurant on Highbury Corner, which serves "wonderful fresh fish and seafood". "The menu is on a blackboard because it changes every day" – depending on what is delivered fresh from Devon or Cornwall (where it has a sister establishment in Padstow). Perches are in high demand, so it pays to book ahead. / N1 2LH; prawnonthelawn.com; @prawnonthelawn; Wed-Sat 10 pm, Sun 5 pm; closed Sun D, closed Mon & Tue; no Amex.

Primeur N5   £61   3 4 3
116 Petherton Rd   020 7226 5271   1–1C
A "good local bistro with a short but punchy menu", set in a 1940s car showroom between Highbury and Stoke Newington. "The sort of place where you happily over-order because you want to try as many things as possible – and nothing disappoints." The same team are behind the nearby Westerns Laundry and Jolene bakery. / N5 2RT; www.primeurN5.co.uk; @menuprimeur; Tue-Sat 11 pm, Sun 20.30 pm; closed Tue-Fri L, closed Mon; booking max 7 may apply.

Princess of Shoreditch EC2 £75 5 3 3
76 Paul St 020 7729 9270 13–1B

"Superb food with a real eye for detail and quality" – Ruth Hansom's "outstanding modern cuisine" is really "going places" at this well-established gastroboozer, just off Great Eastern Street. The pleasant-enough dining area is quirkly located on the mezzanine, up a spiral staircase from the main bar: choose from either a five-course or eight-course tasting menu. / EC2A 4NE; www.theprincessofshoreditch.com; @princessofshoreditch; Mon-Sat 10 pm, Sun 8 pm; no Amex; booking D only.

The Princess Royal W2 NEW £82 3 3 3
7 Hereford Road 020 3096 6996 7–1B

It briefly traded as The Commander and then Pomona's (both RIP), but this attractive Notting Hill tavern (nowadays part of the upscale Cubitt House group) returned in February 2022 to being essentially the same pub it had been since the late 1800s. Despite punchy prices, reports are upbeat on its posh-for-a-pub menu, which includes a selection of oysters and dishes from the 'Raw Bar'. / W2 5AH; www.cubitthouse.co.uk/the-princess-royal; @cubitthouse; Mon-Sat 11.30 pm, Sun 11 pm.

The Princess Victoria W12 £52 3 3 3
217 Uxbridge Road 020 8749 4466 8–1B

This "beautifully restored, nearly 200-years-old gin palace" on the Uxbridge Road was named at its 1829 launch after the 10-year-old princess who went on to reign as Queen Victoria. These days it serves "really good pub food" – "I've never had a bad meal here" – and stocks 100 different gins at its dramatic horseshoe bar. Top Tip – "the pizza and gin-and-tonic lunch offer is a bargain (if a slippery slope)". / W12 9DH; www.princessvictoria.co.uk; @threecheerspubs; Mon-Thu 11 pm, Fri & Sat midnight, Sun 10.30 pm.

Prix Fixe W1 £47 3 2 2
39 Dean St 020 7734 5976 5–2A

"Affordable French bistro cooking", a "wide range of dishes" and "decent portion sizes" make this Gallic outfit (like its nearby stablemate Pierre Victoire) "just the thing for a Soho bite". It provides truly "exceptional value" for lunch and pre-theatre, but beware the price jump from 6pm, when it switches to an à la carte format. / W1D 4PU; www.prixfixe.net; @prixfixesoho; Mon & Tue, Sun 11 pm, Wed-Sat 11.30 pm.

The Promenade at The Dorchester W1 £157 3 4 4
The Dorchester Hotel, 53 Park Lane 020 7629 8888 3–3A

Afternoon tea in this "stunning" luxury hotel shows "England at its best", whether served in the Promenade (scheduled for a refurb) or the Orchid Room. It's a timeless experience, but one that moves with the times – they now serve what may be the poshest vegan afternoon tea in London. / W1K 1QA; www.dorchestercollection.com/en/london/the-dorchester/restaurant-bars/afternoon-tea; @thedorchester; Mon-Sun 10.30 pm; no shorts.

Provender E11 £45 3 4 2
17 High St 020 8530 3050 1–1D

This "real local gem" on Wanstead High Street serves "well-executed French bistro food which never disappoints" – and "at a fair price". Max Renzland, the veteran restaurateur who ran it for a decade stepped down in late 2021, with equally experienced Christophet Huber and Robin Tarver taking over the reins. / E11 2AA; www.provenderlondon.co.uk; @provenderwanstead; Tue-Thu 10 pm, Fri & Sat 11 pm, Sun 9 pm; closed Mon; booking max 10 may apply.

FSA

Prufrock Coffee EC1 — £15 — 3/2/2
23-25 Leather Ln   020 7242 0467   10–2A

"Great coffee" (and also stone-rolled and limited-edition tea) wins praise for this well-known brew stop near Hatton Garden, which also offers pastries, sarnies and other light bites. / EC1N 7TE; www.prufrockcoffee.com; @prufrockcoffee; Mon-Fri 4.30 pm, Sat & Sun 5 pm; closed Mon-Sun D; no Amex.

Punjab WC2 — £46 — 4/2/3
80 Neal St   020 7836 9787   5–2C

This veteran curry house to the north of Covent Garden has survived for 76 years by providing "fine-value and well-above-average cooking". Founded in 1946 and claiming to be the first north Indian restaurant in London, it is now owned and operated by the fourth generation of the same family and still sticks close to its gastronomic roots ("ate with a friend whose family come from the Punjab and he said the food was thoroughly authentic"). In recent years, "real effort has gone into the wine list, but the best wine to drink with curry remains…beer". / WC2H 9PA; www.punjab.co.uk; @punjabcoventgarden; Mon-Sat 11 pm, Sun 10 pm; booking max 8 may apply.

Pure Indian Cooking SW6 — £52 — 3/4/3
67 Fulham High Street   020 7736 2521   11–1B

"A real gem", serving "top-quality modern Indian cooking at sensible prices" on Fulham High Street near Putney Bridge. The "delicious, unusual food" comes courtesy of chef-owner Shilpa Dandekar, who trained with both India's Taj Group and Raymond Blanc. She and her husband Faheem Vanoo, who runs the front of house, have made a good impression on locals ("it's run by really nice people"). / SW6 3JJ; www.pureindiancooking.com; @pureindiancooking; Mon-Wed, Sat, Thu & Fri 11 pm, Sun 10.30 pm; closed Mon-Wed, Sat L.

Quaglino's SW1 — £93 — 2/3/4
16 Bury St   020 7930 6767   3–3D

As one of the late Sir Terence Conran's landmark openings, this big D&D London basement bar/brasserie in St James's was the talk of the town back in the 1990s, complete with racily dressed cigarette girl, and signature 'Q' ashtrays (a collectible selling for £70 online nowadays). Increasingly left to tourists and business-accounters, it still has fans for whom it's "exceptional all-round", but the proportion of disappointments over the years often hinders a more whole-hearted endorsement. / SW1Y 6AJ; www.quaglinos-restaurant.co.uk; @quaglinos; Mon-Thu midnight, Fri & Sat 1 am, Sun 7 pm; closed Mon-Fri L; no trainers.

The Quality Chop House EC1 — £92 — 4/4/4
88-94 Farringdon Rd   020 7278 1452   10–1A

"A London institution" since 1869, when it opened to feed the working classes of Clerkenwell – this 'Progressive Working Class Caterer' now attracts a more bourgeois crowd with "food cooked to melt-in-mouth perfection and informative, informal service. You feel that everyone loves their job". The menu still leans heavily on chops and steaks, leavened by good fish and vegetable options, and it's a "favourite place to show off to people" with its listed Victorian wooden booths and "very uncomfortable bench seats", softened by cushions. These days it is part of Will Lander and Daniel Morgenthau's Woodhead Group, alongside Portland and Clipstone, and has its own larder, daytime café and wine bar next door. / EC1R 3EA; thequalitychophouse.com; @qualitychop; Tue-Sat 10 pm, Sun 3.30 pm; closed Sun D, closed Mon.

Quartieri NW6 — £51 — 3/3/3
300 Kilburn High Road   020 7625 8822   1–2B

"Top Neapolitan pizza" (with a very wide range of choices and featuring ingredients shipped from Italy weekly) helps inspire fans of this casual, brick-walled Kilburn independent. / NW6 2DB; www.quartieri.co.uk; @quartierilondon; Mon-Sun 11 pm.

Queens of Mayfair W1 £37 3|4|4
17 Queen Street 020 7459 4617 3–3B

"A great change to the ghastly chains" – Victoria & Grace Sheppard's elegant, "friendly" café is tipped for its "terrific coffee", as well as a quiet bite or their 'bottomless brunch'. / W1W 5PH; www.queensofmayfair.com; @queensofmayfair; Mon-Fri 5.30 pm, Sat & Sun 6 pm; closed Mon-Sun D.

Le Querce SE23 £54 4|3|2
66-68 Brockley Rise 020 8690 3761 1–4D

The "great Italian/Sardinian food" at this family-run Brockley Rise trat is a regular treat for fans in this corner of SE London. Top Tip – leave room for the "delicious and unusual ice creams/sorbets" – including chilli, garlic and aubergine, if you're brave enough! / SE23 1LN; www.lequerce.co.uk; @le_querce; Wed-Sat 8 pm, Sun 4 pm; closed Wed-Sat L closed Sun D, closed Mon & Tue.

Quilon SW1 £86 5|4|2
41 Buckingham Gate 020 7821 1899 2–4B

"Superb, delicate and fragrant cuisine" from Kerala in southwest India, has been a top attraction for more than 20 years at this luxurious but muted hotel dining room in St James's, run by the luxury Taj Group (and still under founding chef Sriram Aylur). Seafood dishes are particularly good, and there's a tasting menu matched with beers. Top Tip – "weekend brunch is super value". / SW1E 6AF; www.quilon.co.uk; @thequilon; Wed & Thu, Sat & Sun 9 pm, Fri 9.30 pm; closed Mon & Tue.

Quo Vadis W1 £90 4|4|5
26-29 Dean St 020 7437 9585 4–1D

"Jeremy Lee continues to deliver seasonal excellence in elegant surroundings with an atmosphere to match" at the Hart Bros' "delightful" and "unfailing" bastion of old Soho (which also incorporates an eponymous members' club for the foodie in-crowd on the upper floors of this rambling property, whose blue plaque celebrates former tenant, Karl Marx). Lee's deft British cooking is "always thoughtful and cheering" and "the wonderful room is compact enough to ensure great service". / W1D 3LL; www.quovadissoho.co.uk; @quovadissoho; Tue-Sat 10 pm; closed Sun & Mon.

Rabbit SW3 £69 3|2|2
172 King's Rd 020 3750 0172 6–3C

This quirky, faux-rustic venture in Chelsea was the second in the Gladwin family's nowadays fast-growing farm-to-fork group. Its sustainable small-plates can be "very good", but there are also a few gripes in reports, including service that can be so-so and a feeling that "tables are too close together". / SW3 4UP; www.rabbit-restaurant.com; @rabbit_resto; Mon-Sat 10.30 pm, Sun 8 pm; closed Mon L.

Rabot 1745 SE1 £72 2|2|3
2-4 Bedale St 020 7378 8226 10–4C

"This Caribbean plantation-themed coffee shop" makes "amazing hot chocolate that scores highly in terms of VFC (Value For Calories!)". "The upstairs restaurant has a nice terrace overlooking Borough Market, which is a great space to enjoy drinks or dinner" (with chocolate cropping up at every possible juncture on the menu). / SE1 9AL; www.rabot1745.com; @rabot1745; Sun & Mon 4.30 pm, Wed-Sat 10 pm, Tue 5 pm; closed Mon & Tue, Sun D.

Radici N1 £70 2|2|2
30 Almeida St 020 7354 4777 9–3D

"Reliable pasta and pizza" and a setting that's "buzzy, not noisy, and not overcrowded" do win praise for this D&D London operation in the heart of Islington (on the site of Almeida, long RIP). But, especially given that renowned chef Francesco Mazzei is nominally in charge of the food here, enthusiasm seems rather muted. / N1 1AD; www.radici.uk; @radici_n1; Tue-Sat 10 pm, Sun 3.45 pm; closed Tue, Wed L closed Sun D, closed Mon.

Ragam W1 £35 4|2|2
57 Cleveland St   020 7636 9098   2–1B

This Keralan veteran near the Telecom Tower is "still producing good food after all this time" (almost 40 years), offering "super value" and "friendly service". The new interior "hasn't made it a looker, but there are so many great dishes on the menu, so who cares?" / W1T 4JN; www.ragamindian.co.uk; Mon-Thu 11 pm, Fri & Sat 11.30 pm; closed Sun.

RAI W1 NEW £112 4|4|3
3 Windmill Street   020 7419 0305   2–1C

"Melt-in-the-mouth Wagyu and exemplary sashimi" inspire rave reviews for Shrabaneswor Rai and chef Padam Raj Rai's Fitzrovia newcomer (previously a second branch of Hot Stone, which they also own). There's no à la carte – the format is one of a multi-course, omakase-style tasting menu and fans are "blown away by the quality of the food". / W1W; rairestaurant.com; @rai.restaurant; Wed-Sun 1 am.

Rambutan SE1 NEW
10 Stoney Street   no tel   10–4C

On the Borough Market site of a Konditor bakery, this 60-cover, two-floor spot will soon host the debut restaurant of Coventry-born Sri Lankan chef Cynthia Shanmugalingam. Opening in October 2022, it promises regularly changing menus featuring street food snacks and more substantial options. / SE1 9AD; www.rambutanlondon.com; @rambutan_ldn; Mon-Sun 7 pm.

Randall & Aubin W1 £83 4|4|5
14-16 Brewer St   020 7287 4447   4–2D

"A true Soho classic", with "the most fun front-of-house staff in London" and "fantastic fresh seafood" – served for the past quarter-century in a "lovely old butcher's shop" from 1911. "It isn't that romantic, but you can have the best times in this delightful spot", which is "great for pre-theatre or a post-matinee restorative". "When in need of a pick-me-up, one can't go wrong with huîtres and champers at R&A". / W1F 0SG; www.randallandaubin.com; @randallandaubin; Mon-Sat midnight, Sun 11 pm; booking L only.

Rangrez W6 £41 3|3|3
32 Fulham Palace Road   020 8563 7176   8–2C

Limited but good all-round feedback on this family-run Punjabi stalwart, which has long been a feature of the restaurant strip just to the south of Hammersmith's Eventim Apollo (and which sometimes only serves a restricted menu in the early evening during events there). It also has a branch in Ealing (not listed). / W6 9PH; www.rangrez.co.uk; Mon, Wed & Thu 10.30 pm, Fri-Sun 11 pm.

Rasa N16 £42 5|4|3
55 Stoke Newington Church St   020 7249 0344   1–1C

"It never fails to impress", chorus the many fans of Keralan-born Das Sreedharan's bright-pink Stokie fixture, which celebrates its 30th anniversary next year. Even if one can debate whether it's perhaps "not quite as good as it was at its peak", for some folks it's still "still the best South Indian vegetarian" in town, and no-one suggests other than that "the food here is delicious (and I'm not even a vegetarian!)" Over the years, it has spawned several spin-offs, but now operates only out of this single, original, venue (and for delivery). / N16 0AR; www.rasarestaurants.com; Sat & Sun 2.30 pm; closed Sat & Sun D, closed Mon-Thu & Fri.

Ravi Shankar NW1 £32 3|2|2
133-135 Drummond St   020 7388 6458   9–4C

"Really good and cheap veggie food" has established this fixture as a popular dining choice in the Little India street behind Euston station. The buffet lunch is even better value. / NW1 2HL; www.ravishankarbhelpoori.com; Mon-Sun 11 pm.

FSA

The Red Duck SW12 £44 4|2|2
1 Ramsden Road   020 8154 6838   11–2C

"Top-class Chinese food, served in canteen-style surroundings" has arrived in Balham with the pandemic-delayed opening of this first solo project from Chi San, former right-hand man to Alan Yau of Yauatcha and Hakkasan fame. The relatively short menu is filled with standard dishes from the Cantonese culinary canon, modernised through the use of high-quality produce, and there's an interesting selection of beers, wines and teas. / SW12 8QX; theredduck.co.uk; @_theredduck_; Tue-Sun 11 pm; closed Tue-Sun L, closed Mon.

Red Farm WC2 £88 3|2|3
9 Russell Street   020 3883 9093   5–3D

This modern pan-Asian in Covent Garden – an import from NYC – offers "playful dim sum", alongside other "cut-above" dishes. There are "relaxed long tables for groups or cosy red-checked spots for two diners", and the atmosphere is set by the "fun 90s playlist and friendly team". / WC2W 5HZ; redfarmldn.com; @redfarmldn; Mon-Thu 10 pm, Fri & Sat 10.30 pm, Sun 8.30 pm.

The Red Lion & Sun N6 £63 3|3|3
25 North Road   020 8340 1780   9–1B

"Top-notch" Highgate Village local that's arguably "the best gastropub in north London" currently – and perfect "for a late lunch after a walk on the heath". The menu stretches from a "generous Sunday roast" and "gastropub favourites" to "a great selection of seafood" and "Asian-accented dishes" – "all cooked with style and attention to flavour". "Great beer" too, but perhaps more notably an "excellent range of wines". / N6; www.theredlionandsun.com; @theredlionandsun; Mon-Sun 11 pm.

Regency Cafe SW1 £14 3|3|5
17-19 Regency Street   020 7821 6596   2–4C

"A Westminster institution loved by its regulars" – this "greasy spoon experience" occupies a site that's little changed since its opening in 1946, and continues to "plough its furrow regardless of modern fashion". "Fishy Fridays are a must" but, most vitally, it's "a great choice for a cheap breakfast, any time of the day". / SW1S 4BY; regencycafe.co.uk; Mon-Fri 7.15 pm, Sat 12 pm; closed Sat D, closed Sun.

Le Relais de Venise L'Entrecôte £58 3|2|3
120 Marylebone Ln, W1   020 7486 0878   2–1A
5 Throgmorton St, EC2   020 7638 6325   10–2C

"Formulaic… but it works a treat". These "jolly" French steakhouses thrive on their "excellent and simple" format. "There's just one choice on the menu, but it's brilliant": salad to start; then steak ("tender and delicious") with "their magic secret sauce" ("the start of addiction"), plus "piles of hot fries". (To follow there's "a wide selection of desserts.") "No wonder there's always a queue, but it's worth it, even though the inside is really crammed and can be chaos." With the closure of the Soho branch, the remaining outposts are in Marylebone and the City. Top Tip – "ideal for a business lunch". / www.relaisdevenise.com.

Republic W4 £49 4|4|3
301-303 Chiswick High Road   020 8154 2712   8–2A

"Really innovative Indian food" is making its mark at this newbie from Kuldeep Mattegunta and Mustaq Tappewale, who met while working at Kricket in Soho and have taken over the former premises in deepest Chiswick of much-lamented Hedone (RIP) – including the open kitchen ("sitting at the counter watching the food being cooked is fun"). "Unusual and superbly made dishes" put it "in a different league from most Indian restaurants." / W4 4HH; republicw4.com; @republic_chiswick; Mon-Sat 10 pm; closed Sun; booking online only.

The Residency W2 NEW
50 Westbourne Grove   no tel   7–1B

Regular DJs feature on the entertainment programme at this May 2022 newcomer in Bayswater (which opened too late for feedback in our annual diners' poll). Extensive wood panelling is the most eye-catching feature of the cosy interior, while the short dinner menu (earlier in the day there's one dedicated to brunch) looks more aimed at good-value sustenance than foodie fireworks. / W2 5SH; www.theresidencynottinghill.com; Sun-Thu 9.30 pm, Fri & Sat 10.30 pm.

Restaurant 1890
Savoy Hotel WC2 NEW   £144   3 4 4
Strand   020 7499 0124   5–3D

"A beautiful small and intimate newcomer" with gorgeous gold-hued décor, created by Gordon Ramsay in the bijou first-floor space above the Savoy Grill and overlooking the hotel entrance that some will remember as 'Upstairs' (long RIP). Chef James Sharp provides an accomplished nine-course tasting menu "well-prepared in classic Ramsay style" (and necessarily quite straightforward given the lack of kitchen facilities nearby) matched with "great attentive service from Sarah Rhone" and her team. The position, with many windows overlooking the entrance, provides many a talking point with the comings and goings down below. / WC2W 0EZ; www.gordonramsayrestaurants.com/restaurant-1890; @restaurant1890gordonramsay; Tue-Sat 11 pm; closed Tue-Sat L, closed Sun & Mon.

The Restaurant at The Capital SW3   £91   3 4 3
22-24 Basil Street   020 7591 1202   6–1D

A short walk from the back of Harrods, the bijou dining room of this luxury hotel changed its stripes a couple of years ago. Under chef Chris Prow, it now offers a much less formal dining style – with an all-day menu (majoring in dishes from the Josper grill) showcasing British cuisine – and an outside terrace in summer. Some regret the passing of the former incarnation, but overall ratings are good all round. / SW3 1AT; www.therestaurantatthecapitallondon.com; @thecapitalhotel; Mon-Sun 10 pm.

Restaurant St. Barts EC1 NEW
63 Bartholomew Close   no tel   10–2B

A new, even more ambitious venture from the team behind two of London's favourite neighbourhood restaurants, Nest in Hackney and Fulham's Fenn (Johnnie Crowe, Luke Wasserman and Toby Neill); the 15-course tasting menu (£120) from chef Kate Austen will focus on hyper-seasonal food. Opening September 2022, it's named after the church next door (St Bartholomew The Great), not the luxury island. / EC1E 7BG; www.restaurant-stbarts.co.uk; Wed-Sat 9.30 pm.

Reubens W1   £47   2 2 2
79 Baker St   020 7486 0035   2–1A

"One of very few places in town certified kosher" – this 50-year-old classic Jewish deli (with basement restaurant) in Baker Street is often tipped for its "excellent salt beef" and also lays claim to the title of longest-running kosher restaurant in Britain (although it has only operated on this site for about half of that time). Three years ago it was rescued from closure by restaurateur Lee Landau. / W1U 6RG; www.reubensrestaurant.co.uk; @reubens_restaurant; Sun-Thu 10 pm, Fri 2 pm; closed Fri D, closed Sat; no Amex.

FSA

Revolve EC2 NEW   £86
Unit G02 Broadgate ,100 Liverpool Street   020 3146 9603   13–2B
With a terrace overlooking Broadgate Circle, this May 2022 newcomer is an all-day, 115-cover operation that's part of the City's glossy, new 100 Liverpool Street building and serves a menu of French brasserie classics such as escargots, beef tartare, coq au vin…. The name hints at its guest chef series concept; some of the country's top culinary talents are promised as part of a programme to transform the offering each month via special dishes and ticketed events. / EC2E 2RH; www.revolve.london; @revolve.london; Mon-Wed 10 pm, Thu-Sat 10.30 pm; closed Sun.

Rhythm & Brews W4   £23   ③③④
22 Walpole Gardens   020 7998 3873   8–2A
"An absolute treasure to have on the doorstep" for Gunnersbury residents – this funky café south of Turnham Green dispenses excellent coffee and has an ace vinyl collection to rifle through and choose a tune. "The food is always delicious too, and imaginatively served. We love it!" / W4 4HA; rhythmandbrews.co.uk; Mon-Sat 6 pm, Sun 5 pm; closed Sun D.

The Rib Man E1   £14   ④④–
Brick Lane, Brick Lane Market   no tel   13–2C
"East London is where you get the best pork rolls in town" – courtesy of Mark Gevaux, a former butcher who has perfected the art of BBQ babyback ribs, from pigs reared outdoors in Norfolk and Suffolk, and his own famous 'Holy Fuck' sauces. Available only in Brick Lane Market on Sundays (they sell out early) and at West Ham home games. / E1 6HR; www.theribman.co.uk; @theribman; Sun 2 pm; closed Sun D, closed Mon-Fri & Sat; no booking.

Riccardo's SW3   £53   ③④③
126 Fulham Rd   020 7370 6656   6–3B
This "welcoming neighbourhood spot" on a Chelsea corner "won't win awards – but it won't let you down" with its "reliably tasty" Tuscan cooking. "The only downside is if you go late, the noise level is high." / SW3 6HU; www.riccardos.it; @riccardoslondon; Mon-Sun 11.30 pm.

Richoux W1 NEW   £56   ③④③
172 Piccadilly   020 3375 1000   3–3D
"Good to see Richoux return" on its old Mayfair site, and the new incarnation is "an improvement on the old chain" (which fell into administration in 2021). Its patisserie and all-day menu are still "excellent for a light meal or afternoon tea", but the cuisine generally (overseen by exMoor Hall chefs, Jamie Butler and Lewis Spencer) rises much above the workaday standards of its former format: "a simple French selection of dishes that's excellently executed", delivered by "friendly and charming service" and which provides very solid value too. / W1Y 9DD; www.richoux.co.uk; @RichouxUK; Tue-Sat 11 pm, Sun 5 pm; closed Sun D, closed Mon.

Rick Stein SW14   £85   ①②②
Tideway Yard, 125 Mortlake High St   020 8878 9462   11–1A
"The superb setting on the Thames by Barnes Bridge" provides appropriately "lovely views over the river" for this famous Cornish fish and seafood brand's London outpost. But while fans do applaud "fresh fish at its best", a huge proportion of sceptics discern a "tired" performance with "perfunctory" service and "uninteresting" food that can be plain "poor". / SW14 8SN; www.rickstein.com/eat-with-us/barnes; @ricksteinrestaurants; Mon-Sun 10 pm.

F S A

Riding House   £61   2 3 4
43-51 Great Titchfield St, W1   020 7927 0840   3–1C
Bernard Street, WC1   020 3829 8333   2–1D **NEW**

"Brilliant brekkie" has always been a star turn at this Fitzrovia haunt, whose attractions are heightened by its stylish setting and "friendly" staff. For more substantial meals, it can seem "competent, but not worth a detour". It celebrated 10 years in business by opening a sibling in a former branch of Carluccio's in Spring 2022 (no reports as yet). It's set within Bloomsbury's love-it-or-hate-it Brunswick Centre: a fine example of late-1960s modernist (brutalist?) architecture.

The Rising Sun NW7   £68   3 4 2
137 Marsh Ln   020 8959 1357   1–1B

This "busy, picturesque pub" – a Grade-II listed 16th-century building in Mill Hill – serves "delicious and beautifully presented Anglo-Italian grub". It's run by "energetic brothers" Luca and Matteo Delnevo, who have "developed a loyal and upmarket following". / NW7 4EY; www.therisingsunmillhill.com; @therisingsunmillhill; Tue-Sat 9.30 pm, Sun 8 pm; closed Tue, Wed L, closed Mon.

Ristorante Frescobaldi W1   £88   3 2 2
15 New Burlington Place   020 3693 3435   4–2A

The "superb Italian food and great wine list" are everything you would expect from its ownership, the Florentine Frescobaldi dynasty, bankers to English monarchs as far back as Edward I, who have been producing wine on their Tuscan estates since 1308. Needless to say, the opulent venue is "very expensive", but comes into its own in warm weather, with a "large outdoor terrace right in the heart of Mayfair that's perfect for spring and summer". / W1S 5HX; www.frescobaldi.london; @frescobaldi_london; Mon-Sat 11 pm; closed Sun.

Rita's Soho W1   £60   3 4 4
49 Lexington Street   no tel   4–2C

This well-travelled ten-year-old cult pop-up has been "a great addition to Soho" since it alighted in 2021 on the cute, quirky site formerly occupied by Aurora (RIP), opposite the venerable Andrew Edmunds on Lexington Street. Gabriel Price's highly rated cooking takes an American-inspired approach to the best of English ingredients, pleasing critics as disparate as Jimi Famurewa and Tom Parker Bowles, while Missy Flynn looks after the front of house and guarantees "so much fun". / W1W 9AP; www.ritasdining.com; @ritasdining; Tue, Wed, Fri, Thu, Sat midnight; closed Tue, Wed, Fri L, closed Sun & Mon.

The Ritz W1   £116   4 5 5
150 Piccadilly   020 7493 8181   3–4C

"A wow all-round that will live long in the memory" – this "dreamy" Louis XVI-style dining room is renowned for its "magical" décor (a rival for any Disney castle) and has long been a top choice for an 'expense-be-damned' celebration, particularly a romantic one. But, these days, many feel that "the mindblowing food can match it too!" While the classical cuisine has long been respected for its consistent quality, its current performance is notably "at the top of its game". "John Williams' masterful orchestration of his very fine kitchen, produces some of the best and most interesting food in London": "perfectly executed luxury dishes" with spoiling ingredients and "with sauces to die for". "The outstanding flavours will have you running out of superlatives and there is the added bonus of theatre via cooking at the table" ("the crêpes are pure visual and gustatory pleasure!!"). "Immaculate service" is "silky smooth" too and arguably "it is a mystery why Michelin award it only one star as there are many worse two and three star restaurants in the UK". It is mightily expensive, of course, but "sometimes it is worth forking out for a truly fantastic time". It is also – with its regular dinner dances and strictly enforced dress code – a bastion of how to celebrate in traditional fine style: "How marvellous to dine to the sounds of a live pianist or band, and in a dining room where everyone has been forced to dress properly. Tie-less slobs are still turned away!" and "not a pair of jeans or trainers in sight!" / W1J 9BR; www.theritzlondon.com; @theritzlondon; Mon-Sun 9.30 pm; Jacket & tie required.

The Ritz, Palm Court W1 £105 3 4 5
150 Piccadilly   020 7493 8181   3–4C

"You just can't beat the amazing old-world atmosphere, décor, service… and delicious afternoon tea" at this "world-beating" destination. "Yes it's a cliché, but it never fails to impress", "you feel like royalty for the afternoon" and "you won't need to eat in the evening afterwards". "You're either putting on The Ritz or just don't bother!" / W1J 9BR; www.theritzlondon.com; @theritzlondon; Mon-Sun 11 pm; Jacket & tie required.

Riva SW13 £79 3 4 2
169 Church Rd   020 8748 0434   11–1A

With the closure of Hammersmith Bridge, this Barnes stalwart of over 30 years' standing is no longer an easy Uber ride away for much of the fooderati (it's oft-cited by celeb chefs and the foodie in-crowd as a go-to Italian). Perhaps that's why feedback on it post-pandemic is very much more limited and more local than it was in times gone by. Devotees, though, still say it's an "old favourite", with "the same dependable Northern Italian cooking… What more can one ask?" / SW13 9HR; Tue-Sat 10 pm, Sun 9 pm; closed Mon.

The River Café W6 £132 3 2 3
Thames Wharf, Rainville Rd   020 7386 4200   8–2C

"Soldiering on with flair and confidence" – Ruth Rogers' world-famous café is "still the 'go-to' location for "exceptional quality", "ingredient-led", "expertly served" Italian cooking" ("even Italian winemakers are impressed by its authenticity and quality!") Stuck, "out-of-the-way", between a quiet Hammersmith backstreet and the Thames, a chic crowd (many of them regulars who live in the centre of town) cram themselves into this bright, unadorned room which started life as the staff canteen for Ruthie's late husband, Richard Rogers' architectural practice ("is it my imagination or are the tables getting even closer together nowadays?"). But, while practically "no one can doubt the quality of the food, even so the gobsmacking prices are hard to justify" and it is yet again voted the most overpriced restaurant in London in our annual diners' poll. As is now customary, comments mix awe at its virtues with frustration at the level of value: "I do love it, but I always get buyer's remorse afterwards" as "the pricing leaves a bitter taste after a fine meal"… "and yet we still go back…" Top Tips – 1) On a warm day, its location becomes a reliable attraction in itself: "it's enchanting sitting outside on the terrace beside the Thames". 2) When it comes to the menu, "it changes so much that it's pointless to pick out too many individual dishes but the fish and shellfish are cooked with great skill and attention to detail; and timeless favourites include the Ribollita and the Chocolate Nemesis". / W6 9HA; www.rivercafe.co.uk; @therivercafelondon; Mon-Sat 9.30 pm, Sun 3 pm; closed Sun D.

The River Restaurant, The Savoy WC2 £101 2 3 2
The Savoy, 91 The Strand   020 7499 0122   5–3D

In its heyday, this elegant room overlooking the Thames was one of London's key options for any kind of major occasion. But its relaunch and rebranding (from Kaspar's Seafood Bar & Grill, RIP) to its original identity, but now under Gordon Ramsay Holdings – in late 2021 inspired surprisingly limited survey feedback this year (and indeed few press reviews). It is sometimes recommended for the top fish and seafood that is its focus, but all-in-all reactions are muted and uneventful for what should be a top destination. / WC2R 0EU; www.gordonramsayrestaurants.com/river-restaurant; @riverrestaurantbygordonramsay; Mon-Sat midnight, Sun 10.30 pm; no trainers.

Riviera SW1 NEW
23 St James's St   020 7925 8988   3–4D

On the prime but quirky St James's site that was Sake No Hana (RIP), Arian and Alberto Zandi are to relaunch this 170-cover space in November 2022 (which also has a 35-cover terrace). This time, as the name hints, the culinary inspiration will be the luxurious lifestyle of the south of France.
/ SW1 1HA; Mon-Sun midnight.

Roast SE1   £76   2 2 4
Stoney St   0845 034 7300   10–4C

Occupying in part a glazed portico that was originally part of the Royal Opera House, the "bright, airy location overlooking Borough Market" and "adorable room" make this restaurant "a great place to take colleagues or clients". There's generally more muted enthusiasm for the "overpriced" retro-British menu – prawn cocktail, beef Wellington, knickerbocker glory.
/ SE1 1TL; www.roast-restaurant.com; @roast_restaurant; Tue-Fri, Mon, Sat 10 pm, Sun 6.30 pm; closed Sun L.

Rocca   £48   3 3 3
73 Old Brompton Rd, SW7   020 7225 3413   6–2B
75-79 Dulwich Village, SE21   020 8299 6333   1–4D

This duo of traditional local Italians are "perfectly good for a cheap 'n' cheerful meal", with pasta and pizza cooked to order and a "great atmosphere". Both branches have terraces for al fresco dining – both front and back in Dulwich Village; heated and covered in South Ken.
/ www.roccarestaurants.com.

Rochelle Canteen E2   £70   3 4 4
16 Playground Gardens   020 7729 5677   13–1C

"Delightful in every way" – this "hidden-away" venue occupies the bike sheds of a former school near Spitalfields, converted in 2006 by Melanie Arnold and Margot Henderson (wife of St John's Fergus). "Super relaxed" in style and with a "great outdoor space", it's in particular a "gorgeous setting" in summer, but, at any time of year, you can enjoy "robust British cooking with beautiful ingredients". (Its ICA branch was one of the more prominent victims of Covid, closing in September 2020.) / E2 7ES; www.arnoldandhenderson.com; @rochellecanteen; Sun-Wed 5 pm, Thu-Sat 10 pm; closed Thu-Sat L closed Sun-Wed D.

Rock & Rose   £61
270-272 Chiswick High Road, W4   020 4537 4566   8–2A NEW
106-108 Kew Rd, TW9   020 8948 8008   1–4A

'Food, Passion, Glamour' is the mantra of this funky neighbourhood bar/restaurant, owned by restaurateur Lorraine Angliss (of Annie's and Little Bird), who – having operated in Richmond for many years – opened a second site on Chiswick's main strip in Spring 2022.

Roji W1 NEW
56b South Molton Street   awaiting tel   3–2B

Tucked away in a Mayfair alleyway, this promising Japanese 10-seater opened in July 2022. Husband-and-wife team Tomoko Hasegawa and Tamas Naszai met at Tokimeite and are backed here by the owners of Chisou and Sushi Atelier. Japanese preparation is applied to top British ingredients to produce an omakase-style menu (which must be paid for on booking), which includes a sushi course and can be paired with a hand-picked selection of sake and wine. / W1W 5SH; ro-ji.co.uk; @ro_ji_ldn; Mon-Sat 11 pm, Sun 9 pm.

Roka £91 4 3 3
30 North Audley St, W1   020 7305 5644   3–2A
37 Charlotte St, W1   020 7580 6464   2–1C
Aldwych House, 71-91 Aldwych, WC2   020 7294 7636   2–2D
Unit 4, Park Pavilion, 40 Canada Sq, E14   020 7636 5228   12–1C

"Nailing it every time" – Arjun Waney and Rainer Becker's upscale Japanese-inspired operations endure on a deceptively simple formula of "great buzz… awesome food". Centre stage are the "expertly prepared" small plates – "a lovely combination of hot and cold Japanese-fusion dishes" featuring "gorgeous sushi, sashimi and robata" (from the centrally placed grill) – that are "pricey yet exceptional". As an offering, you could quibble that "it hasn't really evolved" in recent years, or you could say 'if it ain't broke, why fix it?' / www.rokarestaurant.com.

Roketsu W1 £285 5 4 3
12 New Quebec Street   020 3149 1227   2–2A

"A little bit of Kyoto in London" – Daisuke Hayashi's highly ambitious new 10-seater in Marylebone opened in early 2022, and is hailed in most reports as one of London's foremost Japanese restaurants. Sitting at the counter, is "like a trip to Japan" – you sample "a stunning 10-course tasting menu: a sublime experience with top-quality ingredients", where "every dish has a story… and it's wonderful". One or two reporters would only say it's only "good enough" at the "eye-watering prices", but even so Hayashi looks set to earn the renown here that he failed to garner during his short stint at Tokimeite. Wash down your meal with one of the 70 sakes assembled by former UMU sommelier, Ryosuke Mashio. / W1W 7RP; www.roketsu.co.uk; @roketsulondon; Tue-Sat 10 pm; closed Tue-Sat L, closed Sun & Mon.

Romulo Café W8 £63 3 4 3
343 Kensington High Street   020 3141 6390   8–1D

"Flying the flag for Philippine cuisine in the UK" – this "pioneering" Kensington fixture (owned by the grandchildren of a famous general) "was one of a handful of Filippino places when it opened" and its "consistently good" cooking and striking interior design has made it a good culinary ambassador, showcasing heirloom dishes from within the founding family. They also have three cafés under the same brand in the Philippines.
/ W8 6NW; www.romulocafe.co.uk; @romulocafelondon; Tue-Thu 9.30 pm, Fri-Sun 10.30 pm; closed Tue-Thu L, closed Mon.

Roof Garden at Pantechnicon SW1 £82 3 3 5
19 Motcomb St   020 7034 5426   6–1D

"Come rain or shine the rooftop is always buzzing" at this "simply super space" – a gorgeously decorated, 130-seat terrace on top of Belgravia's landmark Pantechnicon building, complete with retractable glass roof for rainy weather. Although some reporters say you only go for the great location, most accounts give it a thumbs-up all round, and "presenting something 'Nordic' and different" as its cuisine (from the kitchen at downstairs Eldr) goes down well (as do the "fab cocktails"…). / SW1X 8LB; www.pantechnicon.com/roof-garden; @_pantechnicon; Tue-Sat midnight, Sun 11 pm; closed Mon.

The Rosendale SE21 £56 3 3 3
65 Rosendale Rd   020 8761 9008   1–4D

This former coaching inn in West Dulwich is "a good pub for family gatherings", with its consistently well-rated food, "relaxed good service" and generous sense of space, both inside and in the garden and play area.
/ SE21 8EZ; www.therosendale.co.uk; @therosendalepub; Mon-Thu 11 pm, Fri & Sat midnight, Sun 10.30 pm; no Amex.

FSA

Rosmarino SW17 £43 3 4 4
23 Trinity Road   020 8244 0336   11–2C
"A stylish, family-run Italian" just a stone's throw from Tooting Bec: "an area in desperate need of a decent restaurant or three!" "Everyone always enjoys themselves and the food is really good"… "so popular that now they're expanding next door!" / SW17 7SD; Mon & Tue, Sun 9.30 pm, Wed-Sat 10 pm.

Rosslyn Coffee EC4 £8 5 4 3
78 Queen Victoria Street   no tel   10–3B
"The best coffee in the City of London" – not to mention "exceptional espresso-based drinks", "outstanding hot chocolate" and even yummy soft-serve ice cream – win rave reviews for James Hennebry and Mat Russell's artfully neutral brew-stops, founded in 2018 to 'combine the standards of an Australian Cafe with the warmth and community of an Irish Pub'. / EC4E 4SJ; Mon-Thu 10.30 pm, Fri-Sun 11 pm.

Roti Chai W1 £44 3 3 2
3 Portman Mews South   020 7408 0101   3–1A
"An interesting menu of Indian street-food" that is both "good value and delicious" has long been an attraction at this dependable spot near Selfridges. It's probably "best suited for lunch" to punctuate a day's shopping nearby (the evenings-only dining room is a little more formal, serving tandoor grills and regional specialities). / W1W 6AY; www.rotichai.com; @rotichai; Mon-Sat 9.45 pm, Sun 8.45 pm; booking D only.

Roti King £20 5 2 3
Ian Hamilton House, 40 Doric Way, NW1   020 7387 2518   9–3C
Battersea Power Station, SW8   awaiting tel   11–1C **NEW**
"Arrive early and expect to queue" at this "cramped basement" near Euston Station: an "absolute favourite" that's "100% worth the wait" thanks to its "really authentic Malaysian food" – "divine rotis", plus curries and noodle dishes that are "packed with flavour" and "so cheap". The sleek environs of the new Battersea Power Station development seem like the antithesis of the original's ethos, but a spin-off opened here in early 2022 in one of the railway arches adjacent to the old power station. / rotikinguk.

Rotunda Bar & Restaurant, Kings Place N1 £57 2 3 3
90 York Way   020 7014 2840   9–3C
Development after development is emerging around King's Cross, so it's easy to forget this early arrival, by Regent's Canal, at the foot of the Kings Place art centre. Run by top figures in 'the Murphia' (Green & Fortune's John Nugent alongside the building's owner Peter Millican) its top culinary attraction is beef sourced from its own dedicated Northumberland farm. In summer, enjoy the huge outside terrace by the water. / N1 9AG; www.rotundabarandrestaurant.co.uk; @rotundalondon; Mon-Wed 11 pm, Thu-Sat midnight, Sun 9 pm; closed Mon & Tue L.

ROVI W1 £89 3 2 3
59-65 Wells Street   020 3963 8270   3–1D
"I could become a vegetarian if I could cook like this!" – star chef Yotam Ottolenghi's Fitzrovia fixture is posher than his delis, and "while not a vegetarian restaurant, vegetables take centre stage". Set around a central bar, the clean-lined design of this 90-seater creates a "fresh and airy" atmosphere. Foodwise there's an emphasis on cooking over fire, but while most reports hail his "interesting and delectable dishes", ratings are dented by those who "wanted to love it, but while it was fine, didn't really feel the vibe, especially at the prices charged". Top Menu Tip – "the vegetarian shawarma with celeriac is next level". / W1W 3AE; www.ottolenghi.co.uk/rovi; @rovi_restaurant; Sun-Fri & Sat 10.30 pm.

FSA RATINGS: FROM 1 POOR — 5 EXCEPTIONAL

Rowley's SW1 — £85 — 3|2|3
113 Jermyn St   020 7930 2707   4–4D

"Steak. Chips. Wine. As much as you can eat. Luvverly." That's the formula at this straightforward St James's steakhouse, now in its fifth decade, which, fans say, manages to stay "traditional without being stuffy". It occupies the former site of Wall's butchers, of sausage fame since the 19th century. It was rated higher this year as it seemed to avoid the typical complaints about pricing often present in feedback. / SW1Y 6HJ; www.rowleys.co.uk; @rowleys_restaurant; Tue-Sat 11 pm; closed Sun & Mon.

Royal China — £65 — 3|1|2
24-26 Baker St, W1   020 7487 4688   2–1A
805 Fulham Rd, SW6   020 7731 0081   11–1B
30 Westferry Circus, E14   020 7719 0888   12–1B

"It can be very crowded so get there early" if you visit this well-known Cantonese chain: still a top choice for "very tasty dim sum". With the famous Queensway branch closing a couple of years ago, you now have to go to Baker Street, Canary Wharf or Fulham for your fix (although the latter is little commented on). "Whatever else keeps people coming back here, though, it's certainly not the service!" / www.royalchinagroup.co.uk.

Royal China Club W1 — £76 — 3|2|2
38-42 Baker Street   020 7486 3898   2–1A

"The cooking as always is wonderful" – "especially the great dim sum at lunchtime" – at the relatively smart Marylebone flagship of the well-known Royal China group. The ratings have slipped a little, but there are still plenty of fans who appreciate its "top authentic Cantonese food". / W1U 7AJ; www.royalchinagroup.co.uk/rccb.html; @royal_china_uk; Mon-Sun 9 pm; booking weekdays only.

Rudy's W1 — £34 — 3|3|3
80-82 Wardour St   020 7734 0195   4–2D

"Excellent value and decent pizzas" using ingredients imported from Naples win a solid thumbs up – if not quite full-on raves – from fans of this Mancunian import, on the Soho site recently vacated by Wahaca (which nowadays is expanding countrywide). A Birmingham branch is in the pipeline, and more locations around the capital are on the wishlist. / W1; www.rudyspizza.co.uk/soho; @wearerudyspizza; Sun-Thu 9 pm, Fri & Sat 10 pm.

Rudy's Vegan Diner — £42 — 3|3|2
206a Upper Street, N1   07547 832545   9–2D
729-731 Camden Stables Market, NW1   07384 342144   9–2B

"Delicious" plant-based versions of classic American comfort food – from burgers, seitan hot dogs and pastrami to milk-free shakes – cut the mustard at this pair of 'dirty vegan diners' in Camden Market and Islington. The Islington branch has a vegan butcher next door, touted as the world's first, with a concession in Selfridges. / rudysvegan.com; rudysDVD.

Rules WC2 — £83 — 3|4|5
35 Maiden Ln   020 7836 5314   5–3D

"It could so easily be a tacky tourist trap and is a bit pricey", but there remains a whole lot of love for this Dickensian landmark in Covent Garden (London's oldest restaurant to operate continuously on the same site – since 1798). The "beautiful" period dining room is "steeped in West End history and character" and the menu is "proper old-school" too – "no surprises, nothing extraordinary, but well-cooked and professionally served" grills, game, pies and puds. "And they do wonderful cocktails upstairs" too in the "splendid bar". Top Menu Tip – "well worth it for old favourites like steak 'n' kidney pudding followed by sponge pudding". / WC2E 7LB; www.rules.co.uk; @rules_restaurant; Mon-Sat 11.30 pm, Sun 5 pm; closed Sun D; no shorts.

FSA

The Rushmere SW19 NEW £47
89 Ridgway   020 8946 1652   11–2B
Formerly known as The Swan, this Wimbledon pub was extensively refurbished by the Metropolitan Pub Co, and reopened with a new name in March 2022. Too little feedback for a rating as yet, but one early-days visitor reported of "superior pub fare". / SW19 4SU; www.therushmeresw19.com; @RushmereSW19; Mon-Thu 11 pm, Fri & Sat midnight, Sun 10.30 pm.

Rye by the Water TW8 £50   3 2 2
Catherine Wheel Road   020 8560 9512   1–3A
This "charming waterside café/restaurant" headed by Ben Rand, former head chef at The Dairy in Clapham (RIP), is set in a new development in Brentford, where the Grand Union Canal connects with the Thames. "The food on the small menu is lovely", but it's a largely daytime-only operation, with occasional supper club evenings. / TW8 8BD; www.ryebythewater.com; @ryebythewater; Wed-Sun 3 pm; closed Wed-Sun D, closed Mon & Tue; no booking.

Sabor W1 £64   5 5 5
35 Heddon St   020 3319 8130   4–3A
"A little bit of San Sebastián in the heart of the West End" – "grab a seat at the counter and watch the magic unfold in front of you" at Nieves Barragan and José Etura's tapas bar (ground floor) and 'Asador' (first floor), an "all-time-favourite" which – despite the travails of the era – "just goes from strength to strength as one of the strongest Spanish restaurants in London". "Top-notch Iberian food is served with élan" – "heart and soul-filling, happy and warm, tear-inducing dishes" – and service is "so lovely and welcoming". "Limited bookings mean that there is always a queue to get in from when the doors open at lunch" and "the queue can be long". But "it's pleasing to hear that there are now bookable small tables upstairs", as many feel that "the Asador has got better now they have replaced the sharing benches with a proper arrangement". Top Tip – Asador means BBQ of a complete animal, and "if you crave suckling pig, this is the place!" / W1W 4BP; www.saborrestaurants.co.uk; @sabor_ldn; Wed-Sat 10.30 pm; closed Mon & Tue & Sun.

Sachi at Pantechnicon SW1 £80
19 Motcomb Street   020 7034 5425   6–1D
The luxurious mix of sushi plus meat and seafood grills has inspired too little feedback as yet to rate the large, barrel-vaulted lower-ground floor of this Belgravia food and retail emporium. But such as we have is all positive. / SW1X 8LB; www.pantechnicon.com/sachi; @_pantechnicon; Mon-Sat midnight, Sun 11 pm; closed Mon-Fri L.

Le Sacré-Coeur N1 £48   3 3 2
18 Theberton St   020 7354 2618   9–3D
This long-serving "no-nonsense bistro" just off Islington's main drag is a "hardy local stand-by at a very moderate price for those who like French bistro-style food and ambience". Top Tip – "escargots followed by steak frites for lunch at under £15 is an absolute steal". / N1 0QX; lesacrecoeurbistro.co.uk; @lesacrecoeurfrenchbistro; Sun & Mon 10 pm, Tue-Thu 10.30 pm, Fri & Sat 11 pm.

Sacro Cuore £43   4 2 2
10 Crouch End Hill, N8   020 8348 8487   1–1C
45 Chamberlayne Rd, NW10   020 8960 8558   1–2B
"Genuine Neapolitan pizza" is what they strive for at this 10-year-old Kensal Rise spot and its "compact" Crouch End spin-off – and it earns them higher marks for food than most competitors, year after year. / www.sacrocuore.co.uk; sacrocuorepizza.

FSA RATINGS: FROM 1 POOR — 5 EXCEPTIONAL

FSA

Sagar £41 3|2|2
37 Panton Street, SW1 020 3093 8463 5–4A **NEW**
17a Percy St, W1 020 7631 3319 3–1D
31 Catherine St, WC2 020 7836 6377 5–3D
157 King St, W6 020 8741 8563 8–2C
"Very tasty dosas" headline the "wide range of delicious, South Indian vegetarian dishes", "with many unusual choices" at this "unassuming-looking" small chain, whose most central branch is just off Leicester Square. "The food is good enough even to silence grumbling carnivores like me!" / www.sagarveg.co.uk.

Saigon Saigon W6 £48 2|3|2
313-317 King St 020 8748 6887 8–2B
Stalwart Vietnamese, complete with characterful, battered themey interior, that continues to thrive but somewhat divides opinion. To critics it's "what I would call watered-down Asian food" with flavours lacking bite, but its large local fan club remain delighted and "pleasantly surprised" by its "good value". / W6 9NH; www.saigon-saigon.co.uk; Sun & Mon 10 pm, Tue-Sat 11 pm.

Saint Jacques SW1 £80 3|3|3
5 St James's St 020 7930 2030 3–4D
"This beautiful and impressive dining room and outside terrace has a rich restaurant history" (most recently as Boulestin and L'Oranger), and its latest "pricey-but-good" incarnation is proving "a useful addition to St James's". "Solid and traditional" in style, it provides "accomplished French cooking and helpful service" in a luxurious interior that's "very stylish and relaxed". And come summer, "the courtyard is a destination" in itself. / SW1 1EF; www.saintjacquesrestaurant.com; @saintjacquesrestaurant; Mon-Fri 22, Sat 10 pm; closed Sat L, closed Sun.

St John Bread & Wine E1 £69 3|2|3
94-96 Commercial St 020 7251 0848 13–2C
"Move away from the ordinary and enjoy something special" at this "cracking venue" – an über-functional, white-walled Spitalfields canteen whose "great, innovative menu" of offbeat British dishes (such as chitterlings) is a stripped-down version of Trevor Gulliver and Fergus Henderson's world-famous Smithfield original. To some, it is even better: "I now prefer B&W to the mothership – it's more lively and wears the 'nose-to-tail' cloak a little more lightly". / E1 6LZ; www.stjohngroup.uk.com/spitalfields; @st.john.restaurant; Mon-Sun 9.30 pm.

St John Smithfield EC1 £82 4|4|3
26 St John St 020 7251 0848 10–1B
"Not for the faint hearted… you need to have some courage to eat at St John with its challenging menu and stark industrial aesthetic" (complete with "harsh acoustics"). But the "uncompromising ethos" of "nose-to-tail eating at its very best" is what's carved the international renown of Trevor Oliver and Fergus Henderson's ex-smokehouse near Smithfield Market. "No wonder many of the best chefs in the UK are alumni of this amazing kitchen": fans feel "this is the only place that treats every part of the animal with respect" and it remains an "all-time favourite" for very many diners ("been going for over 25 years, faultless food and personally I love the minimalism of the décor too"). Ratings did slip quite a bit this year, though, with one or two reports that "menus have been more routine of late, with execution below old standards". Perhaps the general strain of these post-Covid and post-Brexit times? / EC1M 4AY; stjohnrestaurant.com; @st.john.restaurant; Mon-Sat 10.30 pm, Sun 4 pm; closed Sun D.

FSA

St Johns N19 £60 3 4 5
91 Junction Rd 020 7272 1587 9–1C
"Still one of the best gastropubs in North London", this Archway tavern "bounced back" from the pandemic and "the food remains as interestingly reliable as ever". It's a "lovely place for a treat", especially under the "beautiful vaulted ceiling in the dining room" (originally built as a ballroom). / N19 5QU; www.stjohnstavern.com; @stjohnstavern; Tue-Sat 10 pm, Sun 6 pm; closed Tue-Thu L closed Sun D, closed Mon; no Amex; booking max 12 may apply.

St Moritz W1 £62 3 3 3
161 Wardour Street 020 7734 3324 4–1C
This retro-Swiss veteran in Soho which celebrates its half-century next year is "about the only place in London you can get real fondue", along with other classics of "authentic Swiss cuisine" (including rösti, spätzli and bratwurst) in appropriately chalet-style surroundings. The cooking is generally "excellent & generous" – so 'pröschtli' (cheers!) / W1F 8WJ; www.stmoritz-restaurant.co.uk; Mon-Sat 11.30 pm, Sun 10.30 pm.

Sakonis £34 3 2 2
127-129 Ealing Rd, HA0 020 8903 9601 1–1A
330 Uxbridge Road, HA5 020 8903 9601 1–1A
A "surprise find" for the uninitiated, this veggie Indian trio has actually grown out of a family-run Wembley stall set up in 1984. The food is "freshly prepared" and "full of flavours", with the Wembley and Kingsbury branches offering an unlimited buffet; Hatch End is à la carte only. / sakonis.co.uk; sakonis_uk.

Salaam Namaste WC1 £50 3 3 2
68 Millman Street 020 7405 3697 2–1D
Sabbir Karim's "reliably consistent" modern curry house near Great Ormond Street Hospital boasts an "extensive menu that goes well beyond the traditional Indian dishes"; offering "very good quality across the board". / WC1N 3EF; www.salaam-namaste.co.uk; Sun-Fri & Sat 11 pm; closed Sat L.

Sale e Pepe SW1 £83 3 5 3
9-15 Pavilion Road 020 7235 0098 6–1D
"Never lets you down… always fun… always noisy… always great food" – this "buzzy longstanding trattoria" (est. 1974), a short walk from the rear of Harrods, is "always a favourite" for a very loyal fan club, serving a long and traditional menu. "Ideal for date night" too. / SW1X 0HD; www.saleepepe.co.uk; @saleepepelondon; Mon-Sat 10.30 pm, Sun 10 pm.

Salloos SW1 £68 3 3 2
62-64 Kinnerton St 020 7235 4444 6–1D
Tucked away in a mews townhouse, this "dependable" Belgravia haunt has served upscale Pakistani cuisine to a wealthy crowd for 45 years. It particularly hits the spot for "meat-lovers" – "the lamb chops are seriously loveable" – while "the friendliness of the staff makes up for the rather boring Gulf and Russian clientele". / SW1X 8ER; www.salloos.co.uk; @salloos_restaurant; Mon-Sat 11 pm; closed Mon-Sat L, closed Sun; may need 5+ to book.

Le Salon Privé TW1 £58 3 3 3
43 Crown Rd 020 8892 0602 1–4A
A "classy" option deep in the 'burbs – chef-patron Gianluca di Monaco's (who worked under retired über-chef, Pierre Koffmann, for a time) "lovely little French spot" occupies a cute, if "understated" St Margaret's site long associated with gastronomy. For the odd sceptic, "sticking so strictly to the script of Gallic classics can seem a bit stifling in 2022", but for most customers that's exactly what makes it "a memorable place to visit". / TW1 3EJ; lesalonprive.net; @lesalon_prive; Tue-Sat 21.30 pm, Sun 4 pm; closed Sun D, closed Mon.

FSA RATINGS: FROM 1 POOR — 5 EXCEPTIONAL

F S A

Salt Yard £56 3 2 2
54 Goodge St, W1 020 7637 0657 2–1B
Westfield London, Ariel Way, W12 no tel 1–3B **NEW**
Winchester Walk, SE1 07585 338748 10–4C **NEW**
"A variety of excellent tapas" (mixing Spanish and Italian inspirations) and an appealing, *"buzzy"* (if sometimes *"loud"*) atmosphere created huge interest in the original Fitzrovia branch, when it opened back in 2005. But while still retaining a loyal fan club, it can seem overhyped nowadays (*"it's always listed as a go-to place, but there are much better tapas available elsewhere now"*). Having spawned various spin-offs (Dehesa, Opera Tavern, Ember Yard), since 2018 it's been part of Urban Pubs & Bars who have decided to roll it out: first to Westfield in Shepherd's Bush (which opened in July 2022) and coming soon to Borough Market if local planning objections can be overcome. / www.saltyardgroup.co.uk; saltyardgroup.

Saltie Girl W1 **NEW**
15 North Audley Street no tel 3–2A
A renowned Boston seafood chain is opening in Mayfair in late 2022; expect lobster rolls, oysters, 'seafood towers', chowder and very likely dishes from their established tinned seafood collection. / W1W 6WZ; @saltiegirl.london; Mon-Sat 9.30 pm, Sun 9 pm.

Salut N1 £72 3 4 4
412 Essex Road 020 3441 8808 9–3D
"A bit out of the way, on Islington's generally unlovely Essex Road", this *"small neighbourhood spot"* is worth discovering. *"The open kitchen gives it a lovely and buzzy vibe"*, as well as providing *"interesting"* and *"good value"* modern European cooking. *"It's open for Sunday lunch, but doesn't serve the ubiquitous roast."* / N1 3PJ; www.salut-london.co.uk; @salut.restaurant; Mon-Sat 10 pm; closed Mon-Thu L, closed Sun.

Sam's Café NW1 £27 3 3 3
40 Chalcot Road 020 7916 3736 9–3B
This artfully down-to-earth, all-day (and most evenings) café, run by Primrose Hill locals actor Sam Frears and writer Andrew O'Hagan, is *"the best place to start the day"*, with *"delightful staff delivering decent coffee and lovely food"*. The fortnightly supper club provides *"simple but tasty food"* and the opportunity to *"meet unknown neighbours in a friendly environment"*. Artists are invited to display their work on the walls; broadcaster and writer Andrew Marr exhibited a selection of his abstract drawings. / NW1 8LS; www.samscafeprimrosehill.com; @samscafeprimrosehill; Mon & Tue, Thu-Sun 10 pm, Wed 5 pm; closed Wed D.

Sams Riverside W6 £78 4 4 5
1 Crisp Walk 020 8237 1020 8–2C
"A superb position by the river" helps set the scene at this *"outstanding, modern and really well designed"* independent venue by Hammersmith Bridge – part of the revamped Riverside Studios complex – which has *"a very buzzy atmosphere inside and lovely terrace outside"*. *"Sam is a great host"* (some regulars recall his Sam's Brasserie in Chiswick) and inspires *"prompt and caring"* service from his staff who give a *"lovely welcome"*. *"Very well-sourced seafood"* is the highlight of a luxurious brasserie menu that *"if not quite exceptional, is very good"*. *"It's a place of real quality and a genuine alternative to the River Café down the towpath if they're full or your budget doesn't quite stretch that far"*. / W6 9DN; samsriverside.co.uk; @samsriversidew6; Mon-Sat 10 pm, Sun 4 pm; closed Sun D.

FSA RATINGS: FROM 1 POOR — 5 EXCEPTIONAL

F S A

Sambal Shiok N7 £45 3 2 2
171 Holloway Road   020 7619 9888   9–2D
"The food is simply wonderful, from fiery laksas to cool and piquant gado-gado" at this *"buzzy, crowded, hawker-style stall"* on the Holloway Road, presided over by Kuala Lumpur-born Mandy Lin and her team. *"One of London's increasing number of properly good Malaysian restaurants."*
/ N7 8LX; www.sambalshiok.co.uk; @sambalshiok; Tue-Thu 9 pm, Fri & Sat 10 pm; closed Tue L, closed Sun & Mon; payment – credit card only; booking online only.

San Carlo SW1 £78 3 3 4
2 Regent Street Saint James's   020 3778 0768   4–4D
This *"sophisticated Italian restaurant"* north of Pall Mall, from Sicilian-born Carlo Distefano's national group, inspires relatively limited feedback despite (because of?) its heart-of-the-West-End location. It's consistently well-rated, though – fans say it *"can always be relied on for business and social meals"*.
/ SW1S 4AU; sancarlo.co.uk/restaurants/san-carlo-london; @sancarlorestaurants; Tue-Sun 11 pm, Mon 10 pm.

San Carlo Cicchetti £66 3 3 3
215 Piccadilly, W1   020 7494 9435   4–4C
30 Wellington St, WC2   020 7240 6339   5–3D
6 Hans Road, SW3   020 7846 7145   6–1D **NEW**
These *"slick and professional"* Italians (offshoots of the national San Carlo chain) are *"buzzy and convenient sorts of places, where you can enjoy an upbeat bite without hanging around too long"*. They serve *"an extensive menu of small Venetian sharing plates"*: *"at best they're excellent"* and almost invariably a meal is *"good fun"*. The best known outlet is steps from Piccadilly Circus – *"it might look like a tourist trap in its prime location but it's a reliable and smartly decorated venue"*. / www.sancarlocicchetti.co.uk.

San Pietro W8 £52 3 2 3
7 Stratford Road   020 7938 1805   6–1A
"Really excellent Italian local" that occupies a smart, if tightly packed, two-floor site in an off-the-beaten-track Kensington backwater. It's a *"cheerful place"* with lovely fresh fish, *"beautifully displayed packed in ice"*. / W8 6RF; www.san-pietro.co.uk; @Sanpietro7; Mon-Sun 10 pm.

Santa Maria £45 3 3 3
160 New Cavendish St, W1   020 7436 9963   2–1B
92-94 Waterford Road, SW6   020 7384 2844   6–4A
11 Bond Street, W5   020 8579 1462   1–3A
189 Upper Street, N1   020 7288 7400   9–2D **NEW**
"Pizza of similar quality to those you'd find in a Naples basement" (with *"authentic slow fermentation of the dough"*) inspire followers of this growing, twelve-year-old group, which they say is *"second-to-none for texture and flavour"*. But the relocated original site in Ealing is *"cramped"* and seems *"really dull"* compared to the old one: *"the pizza remains good, but it's lost the sense that you were part of something special and secret"*. (In recent times, they've also added an Islington branch and one in Brentford – not listed – that's part of a car showroom!) / www.santamariapizzeria.com.

Santa Maria del Sur SW8 £58 3 3 2
129 Queenstown Rd   020 7622 2088   11–1C
"Tremendous steaks" are to be found at this *"friendly"* Argentinian steakhouse that has made itself at home in Battersea for almost 15 years – *"worth the trip south of the river!"* / SW8 3RH; www.santamariadelsur.co.uk; @stamariadelsur; Mon-Sun 10 pm.

FSA

Santini SW1 £111 2 3 3
29 Ebury St   020 7730 4094   2–4B
This "time-capsule" version of the classic Belgravia Italian restaurant attracted the likes of Frank Sinatra in its 1980s heyday. These days it is run by Laura Santini, daughter of the founder, Gino – and the food is by all accounts "undeniably delicious". Even fans, though, can find it "outrageously expensive". / SW1W 0NZ; www.santinirestaurant.com; @santinirestaurant; Mon-Sat 10.30 pm; closed Sat L, closed Sun.

Santo Mare W1 £90 3 3 3
87-89 George Street   020 7486 0377   2–1A
"You feel like you're in Italy as soon as you step in the door" of this chichi seafood specialist in Marylebone – "a tank of live lobsters and beautifully presented fresh fish on a bed of crushed ice give you the flavour of the specialities". The restaurant is supplied by fresh fish flown in from the Tyrrhenian sea, where the dynamic young owner Andrea Reitano has a twin restaurant in Porto Cervo, Sardinia. Top Menu Tips – "great fritto misto – and pasta with lobster, or langoustines, also delight". / W1W 8AQ; www.santomare.com/london-restaurant; @santomare; Mon-Sun 11 pm.

Santo Remedio £66 3 2 2
152 Tooley Street, SE1   020 7403 3021   10–4D
55 Great Eastern Street, EC2   020 7403 3021   13–1B
Edson and Natalie Diaz-Fuentes's authentic cuisine – washed down with delicious margaritas – wins consistently high ratings, if from a small fan club, for their Bermondsey restaurant. No feedback on their newer cafe in Shoreditch – a return to the area where they began their career in the capital seven years ago.

Santore EC1 £56 3 2 2
59-61 Exmouth Mkt   020 7812 1488   10–1A
This "very authentic Italian local" has been filling happy bellies in Exmouth Market for more than 20 years, with Neapolitan pizzas, pastas and other dishes – "nothing too refined, but plenty of choice and not expensive". The only complaint: "some options are just too big and hearty". / EC1R 4QL; www.santorerestaurant.london; @santorerestaurant_ldn; Sun-Thu 10 pm, Fri & Sat 11 pm.

Sarap Filipino Bistro W1 NEW £41 3 3 3
10 Heddon Street   020 3488 9769   4–3B
"Amongst the surging number of Filipino places, this is one to recommend!" – Ferdinand 'Budgie' Montoya brings his "upscale and creative Filipino food" to Mayfair's Heddon Street in this new venture, which follows his Sarap try-outs in Dalston, Soho and Brixton. The dishes are "original and delicious" although it's perhaps no surprise that they come at "eye-watering prices, if you've ever been to the Philippines" (and Filipino diners don't always rate the cuisine as highly as non-natives). Top Tip – "memorable crispy stuffed pig's trotter!" / W1W 4BX; saraplondon.com; @sarap_london; Tue, Fri & Sat 11 pm, Wed & Thu 10.30 pm, Sun 4 pm; closed Tue L closed Sun D, closed Mon.

Saravanaa Bhavan HA0 £50 3 3 2
531-533 High Rd   020 8900 8526   1–1A
A "massive range of dosas" and other "very authentic, traditional South Asian options" ensure that this Chennai-based vegetarian chain's London branches are "very popular with the local Asian community". It's "not fancy", but there are "lots of dishes that don't make it on to many English Indian menus". Founded in 1981, the chain now operates in 23 countries. Founder P Rajagopal was imprisoned for the murder of an employee whose wife he wanted to marry, and died behind bars four years ago. / HA0 2DJ; saravanabhavanlondon.com; Sun-Thu 10.30 pm, Fri & Sat 11 pm.

FSA RATINGS: FROM 1 POOR — 5 EXCEPTIONAL

Sartoria W1
20 Savile Row   020 7534 7000   4–3A   **£92**   3 4 3

This swish "old-fashioned Italian" with "very smooth and welcoming staff" has "real style" befitting its environs alongside the bespoke tailors of Savile Row (for which it is named). Owned by D&D London, the kitchen nowadays is run by distinguished Calabrian-born chef Francesco Mazzei. Prices have never been bargain basement here, but most reporters reckon the expense is "worth it for the excellent cooking using top-class ingredients" and the "divine selection of Italian wines". / W1S 3PR; www.sartoria-restaurant.co.uk; @sartoriarestaurant; Mon-Sat 10 pm; closed Sun.

The Savoy Hotel, Savoy Grill WC2
Strand   020 7592 1600   5–3D   **£147**   2 2 3

In Thatcher's day, this was London's power dining scene par excellence, and this "luxurious, opulent and dark" panelled chamber, just off the hotel foyer, remains "a fabulous room", especially in which to do business. Run by Gordon Ramsay since 2003, it has ploughed a safe-if-unexciting culinary course in recent times, focused on classics such as Beef Wellington and Lobster Thermidor, with results being consistently decent, if unexceptional. But reports this year took a dive due to concerns about the very poor level of value. Even a positive account hailing "outstanding Arnold Bennett soufflé starters and a superb all-round experience" noted that "the eye-watering bill makes it one just for a special occasion". For more sceptical souls, "the food is fine, but certainly not worth the price tag put on it". In particular, critical wine buffs feel the "list is borderline robbery, with incomprehensible mark-ups that seem extreme even for the capital… and unfortunately there aren't as many oligarchs around now daft enough to pay such prices!" / WC2R 0EU; www.gordonramsayrestaurants.com/savoy-grill; @savoygrillgordonramsay; Mon-Sat midnight, Sun 11.30 pm.

The Savoy Hotel, Thames Foyer WC2
The Savoy, The Strand   020 7420 2111   5–3D   **£112**   2 3 4

The "typically English afternoon tea", "beautifully presented by polished staff" in the elegant foyer of this landmark hotel, is "everything you want it to be" – "and the little extras, such as the pianist, make it a real treat". "I've had a lot of afternoon teas and this one is second to none!" / WC2W 0ER; www.thesavoylondon.com/restaurant/thames-foyer-restaurant; @TheSavoyLondon; Mon-Sat midnight, Sun 11.30 pm.

Scalini SW3
1-3 Walton St   020 7225 2301   6–2C   **£93**   3 4 3

"Classic" old-school trattoria (down to the photo gallery of visiting celebs), five minutes from Harrods, that's "bonkers expensive", but keeps its well-heeled crowd powerfully happy. "Portions are huge (they assume you're starving)" and it's "good fun, reliably noisy and… well… Italian" – a formula that has served it well for 35 years, and brought spin-offs in Cannes and across the Middle East in recent years. / SW3 2JD; www.scalinilondon.co.uk; @scaliniuk; Mon-Sun 11.30 pm; no shorts.

The Scarsdale W8
23a Edwardes Sq   020 7937 1811   8–1D   **£59**   3 3 5

In one of London's prettiest squares, this "lively" pub classic has the dubious honour of being Piers Morgan's local – he claims to have met the then-actress Meghan Markle here on the day she later met Prince Harry. (TV crime buffs will also remember it from the late-70s series The Professionals). The scoff's mostly unreformed pub grub, but good value. / W8 6HE; www.scarsdaletavern.co.uk; @scarsdalew8; Mon-Sat 11 pm, Sun 10.30 pm.

FSA

Schnitzel Forever N16 £47 3 | 2 | 2
119 Stoke Newington Church Street   020 7419 0022   1–1C

The humble schnitzel – a flattened cut of meat or fish, even cheese or mushrooms, covered in breadcrumbs and fried – is rescued from semi-oblivion and celebrated at this black-and-white-tiled Stoke Newington newbie that started life in 2020 as a delivery-only business that managed to achieve "remarkably crisp and fresh" results. There was not enough feedback for a rating this year, but longstanding schnitzel aficionado Jay Rayner was an instant convert, declaring it "the cornerstone of a blossoming high street chain with many outposts across the country. It just doesn't quite know it yet." / N16 0UD; www.schnitzelforever.co.uk; @schnitzel_forever; Mon, Wed & Thu, Sat 10 pm, Fri 10.30 pm, Sun 9.30 pm; closed Tue.

Scott's W1 £99 4 | 4 | 4
20 Mount St   020 7495 7309   3–3A

"Eternally elegant" – this "discreet and yet see-and-be-seen" Mayfair A-lister (007's preferred lunch spot) "always feels like a special occasion" ("people spotting here becomes a game"), and its mix of "glamour" with "very fine seafood and effective service", helps to put it in London's Top-5 most-mentioned restaurants in our annual diners' poll (and it's only narrowly beaten by its stablemate J Sheekey in nominations for the capital's best fish). "The menu is both familiar and innovative, with frequent new dishes and specials in addition to the classic fish and fruits de mer it is famous for" (of the former, for example, "top Dover sole"). "It is even more expensive than it ever was, but somehow one never minds the bill because the food and service seem to justify every penny." And while it has "an upmarket and lovely interior", if you can nab one of the pavement tables "sitting outside on Mount Street and watching the world go by adds to the ambience". / W1K 2HE; www.scotts-restaurant.com; @scottsmayfair; Mon-Sat 1 am, Sun 12.30 am; booking max 6 may apply.

Scott's on the River TW9
Whittaker Avenue   no tel   1–4A

Not content with pimping 'The Ivy', Richard Caring is now setting about knocking off copies of the famous Mayfair seafood veteran, starting with this two-floor opening on the Richmond riverside. Finally, after months of wrangling, the planning objections of the original architect for the site have been overcome and it debuts in Autumn 2022. Open seven days a week, we are promised 'the finest fish and shellfish alongside a variety of meat and seasonal game, in an atmosphere exuding urbane sophistication'. The lower floor will have a crustacea and Champagne bar and the upstairs bar will host DJs every Thursday to Saturday. Hmmm... the latter doesn't sound at all like Scott's Mayfair – couldn't he have called it 'The Ivy Seafood', rather than knackering a second great name? Top Tip – a 32-cover terrace promises splendid al fresco dining. / TW9 1EH; caprice-holdings.co.uk; Sun-Thu 12.30 am, Fri & Sat 1.30 am.

Scully SW1 £91 3 | 3 | 2
4 St James's Market   020 3911 6840   4–4D

"Wildly different and by-and-large exceptional" – Ramuel Scully's "brilliantly creative food" delivers "subtly spiced, multiply layered, classy and novel tastes" at his St James's Market five-year-old. "For those close to the open kitchen, it's almost like a chef's table" and the "kitchen brigade and front-of-house team deliver an experience that is at the same time other-worldly and disarmingly intimate". Even its strongest fans can feel the trip is "let down by the interior", however, and ratings more generally were undercut this year by those who found it pricey or felt there were "too many odd combinations". / SW1S 4QU; www.scullyrestaurant.com; @scully_chef; Tue, Wed, Sat, Thu & Fri 9.30 pm; closed Tue, Wed, Sat L, closed Sun & Mon; booking online only.

Sea Containers, Mondrian London SE1 £78 2 2 3
20 Upper Ground   020 3747 1000   10–3A

"It feels like a place to see and be seen, which can account for the expense, but fun and with good river views…" – not a bad overview of this "buzzy" dining room, designed by Tom Dixon, near Blackfriars Bridge. (A harsher view is that it's "a typically over-priced hotel joint, trying to be smarter than it really is".) Top Tip – "super weekend brunch, lots of choice, and the bar is good too". / SE1 9PD; www.seacontainerslondon.com; @seacontainersldn; Sun-Wed 11 pm, Thu & Fri 6.30 pm; closed Sun L, closed Sat.

The Sea, The Sea £70 5 4 4
174 Pavilion Road, SW3   020 7824 8090   6–2D
337 Acton Mews, E8   020 7824 8090   14–2A

"Extraordinary food served with commitment" in a "cutting-edge omakase" format makes the new Haggerston branch of this seafood duo one of the most exciting culinary arrivals of the year. "In a very stylishly decorated railway arch venue", it is focused on a 12-seat chef's table overseen by chef Leandro Carreira: "a beautiful sea-like resin counter", where the "very skilled and friendly chefs are centre stage in front of diners, preparing the food as you watch". "This is perfect fish cooking with innovation in each course, where you can fully differentiate the taste of each fish"; and with "dishes that are Noma-like in their execution and quality". (Our meal ran: "sea urchin with almond milk, savoury custard with jus, fabulous churrasco of tuna belly, monkfish with leek, roasted fennel seed ice cream and Portuguese sponge cake and caviar.) And while the focus is on E8 this year, the original SW3 branch in a quiet mews near Sloane Street still wins favourable mention for "wonderfully fresh fish excellently prepared".
/ www.theseathesea.net; theseathesea_.

Seabird at The Hoxton, Southwark SE1 £82 3 2 5
The Hoxton, 40 Blackfriars Road   020 7903 3000   10–4A

"Fabulous views", "delicious seafood"… "it ticks every box" according to fans of this 14th-floor rooftop: part of a Southwark hotel, which sets a glam tone. Ratings have softened a little since it opened a couple of years ago, however, with mounting concern that the height of the prices is starting to match that of the venue! / SE1 8NY; thehoxton.com/london/southwark/hotels; @thehoxtonhotel; Sun-Thu midnight, Fri & Sat 1 am.

The Seafood Bar W1 NEW £101 4 4 4
77 Dean Street   020 4525 0733   4–1D

"No frills or pretension – just generous platters of great seafood" in a "variety of options (raw and roasted)" help make the De Visscher family's new import from Amsterdam into "a great addition to Soho". "Unless you have a serious appetite, the plates may serve two or even three with a bowl of fries, making the evening a steal." And "it's not a place to worry about table manners – just grab one of their complimentary bibs and your claw crackers and have at it!" / W1W 3SH; www.theseafoodbar.com; @theseafoodbar; Sun-Thu 10 pm, Fri & Sat 10.30 pm.

Seafresh SW1 £59 3 3 2
80-81 Wilton Rd   020 7828 0747   2–4B

"Great fish" and "friendly staff" attract a steady crowd of regulars to this veteran Pimlico fish specialist, run by the same family since 1961. It's been modernised in relatively recent times, and serves classic fish 'n' chips alongside more elevated seafood options, including octopus, lobster and Dover sole meunière. / SW1V 1DL; www.seafresh-dining.com; Mon-Sun 10.30 pm.

FSA

Searcys St Pancras Grand NW1 £77 2 3 4
Upper Concourse   020 7870 9900   9–3C

"Better than anything the Gare du Nord can offer (although perhaps that's not saying much!)" – this "beautiful" operation overlooking the Eurostar tracks comprises a "comfortable and well-spaced", large interior with a stylish concourse bar (Europe's longest, apparently) whose seating runs along the platforms from on high (the latter closing in summer 2022 for a major upgrade and a new focus on its extensive Champagne range of bottles and magnums). The brasserie fare (served seven days a week from breakfast) is sometimes criticised for being "unimaginative", but one or two reports felt it had "stepped up a gear" this year, with recommendations as a business or romantic rendezvous; or for its luxurious afternoon tea. It's certainly "convenient" (and, in the bar, "you can't beat it for a view of the trains"). / NW1 2QP; stpancrasbysearcys.co.uk; @searcystpancras; Mon-Sat 10.30 pm, Sun 10 pm.

The Sea Shell NW1 £57 3 3 2
49-51 Lisson Grove   020 7224 9000   9–4A

"Really good fish 'n' chips, big portions, always tasty"; the not-so-secret recipe for this legendary family-owned chippy's century – and more – of success. There are multiple cooking choices for the "lovely fish", which can be grilled or fried with panko, matzo-meal and gluten-free options and is served with 'bottomless' chips. Despite its heritage, though, it's been through various owners and refurbs over the decades – the interior is fine, but don't go expecting quirky period charm. / NW1 6UH; www.seashellrestaurant.co.uk; @seashellrestaurant; Tue-Sat 10.30 pm, Sun 7 pm; closed Tue, Wed L, closed Mon.

SeaSons W1 £123 2 2 2
6-10 Bruton Street   020 3725 7700   3–2C

In the former Mayfair home of The Square (RIP), it's hard to know quite what to make of this high-end fish and seafood venture, which opened in late 2021 (and which, according to its website, is soon to open in Miami and New York). This basement site has always seemed a bit "corporate", and it still does, although visiting jazz singers can sometimes inject a sense of brio. Meanwhile, the luxurious, sustainable seafood menu (which curiously also incorporates black truffle or lobster pizza to share, and a few random meat options) inspires a range of opinions: from "very good" to "such a disappointment". / W1W 6PU; seasonsdream.com; @seasons_bistrot; Tue-Sat 1 am; closed Sun & Mon.

Sessions Arts Club EC1 £60 3 3 5
24 Clerkenwell Green   020 3793 4025   10–1A

"Believe the gushy reviews!" This "stunning" dining room – part of "a glorious Georgian building" in Clerkenwell which features in Dickens's 'Oliver Twist' – is London's highest profile opening of the year and "worth the hype!": "it's a restaurant that has everything!". "From the moment you start looking for the inconspicuous entrance, to the concierge and the lift, then the big reveal into the dining room upstairs: it's the perfect place to surprise someone". And "what an interior!" – like "a faded palazzo" – "there's something about the high ceilings and the ambient lighting and the rugs on the floor that makes it the ultimate in shabby chic glamour". Chef Florence Knight "can somehow combine ingredients that appear unpromising and end up with the most delicious, adventurous and unusual dishes": "delectable small plates for sharing, with some meat but mainly fishy/veggie options". "It's just a shame it's almost impossible to get a table now… it's so hot!" Top Menu Tip – "the smoked eel and potato sandwich is unmissable, crisp outside and meltingly smoky and fishy within". / EC1E 0NA; sessionsartsclub.com; @sessionsartsclub; Wed-Sat, Tue 10 pm; closed Tue L, closed Sun & Mon; payment – credit card only.

Seven Park Place SW1 — £170 — 3 3 3
7-8 Park Pl 020 7316 1621 3–4C

"In a part of Mayfair heaving with Michelin stars, William Drabble and his team (operating out of a townhouse hotel) continue to knock it out of the park", providing a "wonderful and very extravagant time". "William is always in the kitchen where he belongs, not in the TV studios" and some fans feel he "doesn't get all the plaudits he deserves" for his "exceptional cuisine, with big bold flavours. Nothing is done only for effect, as every ingredient on a plate serves a purpose. The tasting menu delivers upon this, course after course. Combine all that with knowledgeable and approachable staff and this really is a place to rave about". / SW1A 1LS; www.stjameshotelandclub.com; @stjameshotelandclub; Tue-Sat 10 pm; closed Sun & Mon; no trainers.

7 Saints W11 — £64 — 3 4 4
7 All Saints Road 020 7460 8566 7–1B

"What a find!" – this *"intimate"* spot on a *"beautiful cosy corner"* off Portobello Road boasts a *"small but perfectly formed menu"* of *"exciting food"*. Owner James Gummer (ex-maître d' at The Wolseley) leads the front of house, looking after guests so well that *"it feels as if you're in New York"*. / W11 1HA; 7saints.co.uk; @7saintsrestaurant; Tue-Sat 10 pm; closed Tue-Fri L, closed Sun & Mon.

Sexy Fish W1 — £103 — 1 1 3
1-4 Berkeley Sq 020 3764 2000 3–3B

"So loud" in every aspect – Richard Caring's prominently sited seafood scene is an orgy of ostentatious styling, luxe seafood and sushi, and a crowd that's Mayfair's answer to 'Love Island'. The kind view is that it's *"fun and full of life"* (*"they made our daughter feel very special for her 15th birthday"*). The majority view is that *"service is sloppy and prices absolutely outrageous"*. / W1J 6BR; www.sexyfish.com; @sexyfishlondon; Sun-Wed 1 am, Thu-Sat 2 am; booking max 6 may apply.

Shackfuyu W1 — £49 — 3 2 2
14a Old Compton St 020 3019 3492 5–2A

This *"tasty"* and fun Soho side project from the Bone Daddies group sounds like a post-modern Japanese joke – a western take on a Japanese take on western cuisine! It started out as a pop-up, but proved popular enough to stick around on a permanent basis, serving hits from Korean fried wings and tuna tacos to kinako French toast with soft-serve ice cream. / W1W 4TJ; bonedaddies.com/shack-fuyu; @shackfuyu; Mon-Sat 10 pm, Sun 9 pm; no booking.

Shahi Pakwaan N2 — £36 — 3 3 2
25 Aylmer Parade, Aylmer Road 020 8341 1111 1–1B

"A local gem", this *"high-quality"* five-year-old takes its cue from the royal cuisine of Hyderabad in south-central India, and attracts regulars from beyond its East Finchley neighbourhood. / N2 0PE; www.shahipakwaan.co.uk; @Shahi Pakwaan; Mon-Sat 11 pm; closed Sun.

The Shed W8 — £66 — 3 4 4
122 Palace Gardens Ter 020 7229 4024 7–2B

"A bit of an oddball" – this *"quirky little place with a fun atmosphere"* off Notting Hill serves a selection of creative dishes using sustainably sourced produce that's foraged or from the Gladwin family's farm in Sussex and is one of their better-rated venues. The Gladwins have now opened six restaurants under their 'Local & Wild' brand across west and central London, with more expected to follow. / W8 4RT; www.theshed-restaurant.com; @theshed_resto; Tue-Sat, Mon 11.30 pm; closed Mon L, closed Sun.

FSA

J Sheekey WC2 £88 3 3 4
28-34 St Martin's Ct   020 7240 2565   5–3B

"Tucked away in a side alley in the centre of Theatreland", this "old school" veteran (est. 1896) regained its No. 1 slot in this year' poll, both as London's most-mentioned destination; and also for providing the capital's best fish and seafood. "All the classics are perfectly prepared" ("the freshest shellfish, unforgettable dressed crab, oysters and huge portions of Dover sole, washed down with a chilled bottle of Chablis… perfection"). And, they are served in a "quirky and atmospheric" series of picture-lined rooms, whose nooks and "intimate booths" further buoy its traditional appeal. Post-Covid, meals here did not always seem as sure-footed as in the past, with staffing often diagnosed as a problem. But recovering ratings this year suggest more of a return to the "classy" form that's typically the norm here. "It's pricey, but Sheekey's still keeps its spot as one of the capital's greats!" / WC2N 4AL; www.j-sheekey.co.uk; @jsheekeyldn; Mon-Sat 11.30 pm, Sun 10.30 pm; booking max 6 may apply.

J Sheekey Atlantic Bar WC2 £88 4 3 4
28-32 St Martin's Ct   020 7240 2565   5–3B

A semi-independent addition to the original venue next door, its "reliably fresh fish" and glam, casual styling make this American-style seafood bar "a great post-theatre favourite". There are no specific gripes about food or service, but "the pricing seems to be approaching the level of the main restaurant, taking away some of its raison d'être". / WC2N 4AL; www.j-sheekey.co.uk; @sheekeys; Mon-Sat 11.30 pm, Sun 10.30 pm; booking max 3 may apply.

Shikumen, Dorsett Hotel W12 £70 4 2 3
58 Shepherd's Bush Grn   020 8749 9978   8–1C

"One of the best Chinese restaurants in London" is where you might least expect it – in a modern hotel overlooking one side of Shepherd's Bush Green. Better still, it occupies a "smart, spacious room, so has a calm atmosphere with reasonable noise levels". The menu comprises "great-quality Cantonese plus other regions", including "consistently superior dim sum – all well and freshly cooked, with some unusual items alongside old favourites". / W12 5AA; www.shikumen.co.uk; @shikumen.w12; Mon-Sun 11 pm.

Shilpa W6 £36 3 2 2
206 King St   020 8741 3127   8–2B

Ignore the "very downmarket ambience" – "authentic dishes" and "good value" are the cornerstones of this "first-class", "cheap 'n' cheerful" South Indian café on Hammersmith's main drag. / W6 0RA; shilpahammersmith.co.uk; @shilpa-indian-restaurant; Sun-Wed 11 pm, Thu-Sat midnight.

Shoryu Ramen £59 3 3 2
9 Regent St, SW1   no tel   4–4D
3 Denman St, W1   no tel   4–3C
5 Kingly Ct, W1   no tel   4–2B
35 Great Queen Street, WC2   no tel   5–1D
190 Kensington High Street, W8   no tel   8–1D **NEW**
45 Great Eastern Street, EC2   no tel   13–1B
Broadgate Circle, EC2   no tel   13–2B

"Genuine Japanese-style ramen and dumplings" from Japan Centre owner Tak Tokumine hit the spot with "generous portions, excellent flavours" and "very good service" at his expanding group based in the West End. There are now seven venues in London, plus Ichiba food hall in Westfield Shepherd's Bush and offshoots in Oxford and Manchester. The summer 2022 launch of a branch in Kensington High Street was expected to be the first of several under a new franchising arrangement.

The Sichuan EC1 £45 4 3 2
14 City Road   020 7588 5489   13–2A
This "cracking Sichuanese restaurant on the unglamorous and busy City Road" (near the Honourable Artillery Company) is "not for the chilli-hater!" "Go for the authentic and freshly cooked regional specialities" from chef Zhang Xiao Zhong, whose grandfather was personal chef to Sichuan-born Deng Xiaoping, Chairman Mao's successor as China's leader. / EC1Y 2AA; www.thesichuan.co.uk; Mon-Sun 11 pm.

Sichuan Folk E1 £52 4 3 2
32 Hanbury St   020 7247 4735   13–2C
This "tiny place near Truman's old brewery" serves an "excellent and authentic take on Sichuan cuisine, in a calm atmosphere, away from the agitation of Brick Lane". Top Tip – "'numb and spicy' dumplings live up to their name". / E1 6QR; www.sichuan-folk.co.uk; @sichuanfolklondon; Sun-Thu 10.30 pm, Fri & Sat 10.45 pm; no Amex; booking online only.

Sichuan Fry E8 NEW
2 Westgate Street   no tel   14–2B
Above a new branch of Dumpling Shack in the basement, John and Yee Li's ground-floor operation in London Fields will host this new outlet based on spicy burgers ('The Sichuan', 'The Vegan' and 'The Hot and Mala Mapo') in potato rolls plus 'shake shake' fries, as road-tested over a couple of years at Spitalfields Market. / E8 3RN; Mon-Sun midnight.

Signor Sassi SW1 £70 3 3 3
14 Knightsbridge Green   020 7584 2277   6–1D
Near Harrods, this Italian of 35 years' standing is recently part of the San Carlo brand, but fits well into the glamorous, traditional mould of that Manchester-based group. "The food can be excellent, but is also erratic at times." / SW1X 7QL; www.signorsassi.co.uk; @sancarlorestaurants; Mon-Sun 11 pm.

Silk Road SE5 £26 5 2 2
49 Camberwell Church St   020 7703 4832   1–3C
"Basic room, basic service… but man, the food is good!!" – and "incredible value" – at this Camberwell canteen, which is renowned as one of the capital's better cheap eats. It knocks out "fiery but tasty" dishes from Xinjiang in China's northwest, home of the Muslim Uighurs. / SE5 8TR; silkroadlondon.has.restaurant; Mon-Sun 11 pm; closed Mon-Sun L; cash only; no booking.

Silo E9 £61 4 4 3
The White Building, White Post Lane   020 8533 3331   14–1C
Very limited feedback (but all of it upbeat) for Douglas McMaster's more-eco-than-eco, zero-waste project, above Crate in Hackney Wick's canalside White Building, which – in its drive for 'quality through purity' and 'a more primitive diet… born from clean farming' serves a menu of wacky, meat-free small plates and very off-piste wines. / E9 5EN; silolondon.com; @silolondon; Wed-Sat 11 pm; closed Wed-Fri L, closed Mon & Tue & Sun.

The Silver Birch W4 £77 3 4 3
142 Chiswick High Road   020 8159 7176   8–2A
This "fantastic independent neighbourhood restaurant" in Chiswick serves an "adventurous" modern European menu of "delicious and unusual dishes". Approaching its second birthday, it's the first solo project from well-travelled American-born Kimberley Hernandez, previously head chef at XU and Kym's, and is more ambitious than most such locals – "still finding its feet, but with so much potential". / W4 1PU; silverbirchchiswick.co.uk; @silverbirchchiswick; Wed-Sun 9.30 pm; closed Mon & Tue.

Simpson's in the Strand WC2 £93   2 3 4
100 Strand   020 7420 2111   5–3D

"The roast beef commands attention!" – carved at the trolley in this famous grill room near The Savoy, serving "quintessentially British cooking in very generous portions". Its performance has been very inconsistent in recent times and it was closed for an extended period over Covid, making it hard to recommend unequivocally, other than as a 'slam dunk' for entertaining foreigners on business. / WC2R 0EW; www.simpsonsinthestrand.co.uk; @simpsons1828; closed Mon-Sat & Sun; no trainers.

Simpson's Tavern EC3 £50   2 3 5
38 1/2 Ball Ct, Cornhill   020 7626 9985   10–2C

This "unique" institution – a traditional City chophouse founded in 1757 – is "the sort of place cooking the kind of food that doesn't exist any more… except it does here!". Guests seated in 19th-century oak-panelled stalls feast on full English breakfasts and grills or pies for lunch followed by the signature stewed cheese pudding (there is no evening or weekend service). "My father took me there 65 years ago – it's hardly changed, but there's no longer an open fire!" / EC3V 9DR; www.simpsonstavern.co.uk; @simpsonstavern; Mon-Fri 3.30 pm; closed Mon-Fri D, closed Sat & Sun.

Singapore Garden NW6 £56   4 2 2
83a Fairfax Rd   020 7624 8233   9–2A

"Always good, always reliable, always full… which is unfortunate if you want a table last minute" – this Singaporean/Malaysian "old favourite" in a shopping parade near Swiss Cottage is sought out by hungry regulars, "as it has been for decades" (fans include Giles Coren, restaurant critic of The Times). Service is "fast", but it can also be a little "rushed and unsmiling". / NW6 4DY; www.singaporegarden.co.uk; @singapore_garden; Mon-Thu 10.30 pm, Fri & Sat 11 pm, Sun 10 pm; closed Mon-Thu L.

Singburi Royal Thai Café E11 £26   4 4 3
593 Leytonstone High Rd   020 8281 4801   1–1D

This "vibrant" shopfront Thai in Leytonstone is "full of fun" and fans say they could "eat here every night of the week" thanks to its excellent dishes and the BYO policy which helps keep prices down. / E11 4PA; @Singburi_e11; Tue-Sat 11 pm, Sun 10 pm; closed Mon; cash only.

Six by Nico £64   3 3 3
33-41 Charlotte Street, W1   020 7580 8143   2–1C
6 Chancellor Passage, E14   020 3912 3334   12–1C

"Such amazing value for a six-course, themed, tasting menu" that changes every six weeks – that's the USP of Nico Simeone's national chain, which, over five years, has grown from its Glasgow base to number nine in total (with London having two: in Fitzrovia and Canary Wharf). Of course it's "slightly gimmicky", but on the whole it's "a good effort at a budget experience": "you get what you pay for, and while not all dishes hit the mark, and service can be a bit hit 'n' miss (particularly at busy times), it is innovative, has a great buzz and is a lot of fun". / www.sixbynico.co.uk; sixbynico.

Six Portland Road W11 £80   3 4 2
6 Portland Road   020 7229 3130   7–2A

"Low-key but capable of great cooking" – Jesse Dunford Wood's "friendly neighbourhood spot" does sterling service for Holland Park, serving a "short but well-curated menu" for lunch and dinner, seven days a week, alongside an "awesome wine list", in an "understated setting that makes clear that the food is the main attraction". With just 36 seats, it can get a little loud with larger groups. / W11 4LA; www.sixportlandroad.com; @SixPortlandRoad; Mon-Sun 10 pm.

F S A

The Six Restaurant & Bar KT8 £60 3|3|3
2 Lion Gate   020 8016 6630   1–4A

A couple of excellent reports suggest it's worth considering this old pub reinvented as a hotel and restaurant (a couple of years ago), between the maze of Hampton Court Palace and Bushy Park. The refit is very attractive and the menu of superior gastropub fare is well-rated. / KT8 9DD; www.thesixrestaurant.co.uk; @kingsarmshamptoncourt; Mon-Sun 9 pm.

Skal Nordic Dining N1 £37 4|4|3
149 Upper Street   07308 031151   9–2D

This "small" Swedish restaurant in Islington serves "amazing", "absolutely delicious" meals based around Nordic 'husmanskost', meaning home cooking. It took over the Grade-II listed premises vacated by fellow-Scandi Rök (RIP) three years ago, making for an easy transition for locals with a taste for the north. / N1 1RA; www.skalnordicdining.co.uk; @skalnordic; Tue-Fri 11 pm; closed Mon, Sat & Sun.

Sketch,
Lecture Room at Library W1 £223 3|4|5
9 Conduit St   020 7659 4500   4–2A

"In an utterly fairytale setting full of glamour, you can't help but feel a sense of occasion" on the "unbelievably OTT" top floor of this grand Mayfair palazzo: "from the entrance to the fine-dining experience, it makes for a fabulous date night!" But its "pocket-bursting prices" are a source of widespread complaint, and one or two reporters feel that its elevation by Michelin to its highest echelons was misjudged ("three stars! REALLY? Nowhere near"). While converts are "over the moon due to the stunning reality" of the "joyful intricacy of the cuisine" from a "wacky but delightful" menu designed (from afar) by Gallic superstar Pierre Gagnaire, others discern "a confusing medley of French fiddliness that feels rather outdated". Service is "faultless" on most accounts, if "in the breathless French-formal style". Top Tip – "best to go for lunch if you want value for money". / W1S 2XG; sketch.london; @sketchlondon; Fri & Sat, Wed & Thu 9 pm; closed Wed & Thu L, closed Mon & Tue & Sun; no trainers; booking max 6 may apply.

Sketch,
Gallery W1 £98 3|3|4
9 Conduit St   020 7659 4500   4–2A

You pay top dollar to eat quite literally inside an art installation in this room within Mourad Mazouz's idiosyncratic Mayfair venue, where artist Yinka Shonibare's pan-African vision replaced the former lurid pink-walled David Shrigley showcase in spring 2022. It makes for "great artefacts to look at", while the food – either a lavish all-day 'afternoon tea' or dinner – is "very, very good". "But my word it's expensive" – even "unbelie overpriced" – is a repeated lament even from very enthusiastic reporters. / W1S 2XG; sketch.london; @sketchlondon; Sun-Thu 10 pm, Fri & Sat 11 pm.

Skewd Kitchen EN4 £64 3|3|3
12 Cockfosters Parade   020 8449 7771   1–1C

This "really buzzy upmarket Turkish restaurant" puts a modern slant on the traditional Anatolian grill. It makes a "great local addition" to Cockfosters, and celebrates its tenth year in 2023. / EN4 0BX; www.skewd.com; @skewdkitchen; Mon-Thu, Sat, Fri 11 pm, Sun 10 pm; closed Mon-Thu L.

FSA RATINGS: FROM POOR —— 5 EXCEPTIONAL

F S A

Skylon, South Bank Centre SE1 £78 2 2 3
Belvedere Rd 020 7654 7800 2–3D

"Great views over the Thames" and a vast interior (it was built as 'The People's Palace' – the destination restaurant originally at the heart of the Brutalist South Bank arts centre), make this D&D London operation "good for both business and social" dining. The cuisine has often seemed like an afterthought here, but was mostly well-rated this year. / SE1 8XX; www.skylon-restaurant.co.uk; @skylonrestaurant; Mon-Sat 9 pm, Sun 5 pm; closed Sun D; no trainers.

Smith & Wollensky WC2 £109 2 2 3
The Adelphi Building, 1-11 John Adam St 020 7321 6007 5–4D

Fans proclaim "excellent steaks" (including imported prime, dry-aged USDA fillets) and "not a fault to find" at this plush steakhouse off the Strand; the first international branch of the famous NYC chain. Its pricing, though, has often struck Londoners as "totally out of order", leading to poor ratings across the board. / WC2N 6HT; www.smithandwollensky.co.uk; @sandwollensky; Mon-Thu 11.30 pm, Fri & Sat midnight, Sun 10 pm; closed Mon L.

Smith's Wapping E1 £76 4 3 3
22 Wapping High St 020 7488 3456 12–1A

"Stunning views of Tower Bridge and brilliant seafood" are twin highlights at this popular destination (sibling to a similar veteran, in Ongar), which is "right on the river" in Wapping. "It's a bit out of the way, but well worth going off the beaten track for". "As for the décor, who doesn't love a restaurant with white tablecloths and smartly presented staff?" / E1W 1NJ; www.smithsrestaurants.com; @Smithsofwapping; Mon-Sat 10 pm, Sun 9 pm; no trainers.

Smiths of Smithfield, Top Floor EC1 £81 2 3 3
67-77 Charterhouse St 020 7251 7950 10–1A

The City views are splendid at this rooftop venue, in the fine Grade II-listed former Smithfield market warehouse – converted into a multi-floor destination in the 1990s, of which this is the flagship dining option. Though it can seem a little 'City' in its approach, fans feel it's "still a solid choice for lunch". But not everyone's wild about the new menu ("just say no to small plate hell – this should have remained a steak restaurant!") / EC1M 6HJ; www.smithsofsmithfield.co.uk; @Thisissmiths; Mon-Fri 9.30 pm, Sat 9 pm, Sun 3 pm; closed Sun D; booking max 10 may apply.

Smoke & Salt SW17 £52 5 4 3
115 Tooting High St no tel 11–2C

"Fine food in a casual setting" wins exceptional ratings for this former pop-up that is contributing to Tooting's rising reputation as a gastronomic destination. Remi Williams and Aaron Webster celebrate the ancient preserving techniques of salting, smoking and curing with "a menu of universally delicious sharing plates", served in a "bustling, vibrant atmosphere". / SW17; www.smokeandsalt.com; @smokeandsaltldn; Tue-Sat 10 pm; closed Sun & Mon; payment – credit card only.

Smokehouse Islington N1 £63 3 3 3
63-69 Canonbury Rd 020 7354 1144 9–2D

"Quality meat and good value" have carved a fine reputation for this Canonbury gastropub (part of Noble Inns), which is entering its 10th year in 2023. Whole carcasses are butchered on-site, fish is delivered daily, and it's a beer-lovers dream, with 20 on tap and 60 bottled. / N1 2RG; www.smokehouseislington.co.uk; @smokehousen1; Mon-Sat 10.30 pm, Sun 10 pm; closed Mon-Thu L.

F S A

Smokestak E1 £51 **5****3**4
35 Sclater Street   020 3873 1733   13–1C
"The hint is in the name" at David Carter's "funky" Brick Lane venue, whose moody interior is inspired by southern US grill houses. Alongside the fingerlickin' smoked meats and pickled chillies, there are "some surprise hits – who knew that chargrilled cabbage is totally delicious?". "The dining room can be a bit smoky" – but that's why you should never BBQ indoors at home! / E1 6LB; www.smokestak.co.uk; @smokestakuk; Mon-Sat 11 pm, Sun 10 pm.

Smoking Goat E1 £57 **4**3**3**
64 Shoreditch High Street   no tel   13–1B
"Just superb flavours… and those chicken wings are to die for!" – Ben Chapman's "sensational" Thai has it all: "the Shoreditch location, the vibe, and the plates of fresh and inventive dishes". It "can be cramped" but folks "travel across town just to eat here". / E1 6JJ; www.smokinggoatbar.com; @smokinggoatbar; Mon-Sat 11 pm, Sun 10 pm.

Socca W1 NEW
41 South Audley Street   020 3376 0000   3–3A
Set to open in the second half of 2022, on a Mayfair site that was formerly a branch of Richoux – this collaboration between Claude Bosi and Samyukta Nair will 'pay homage to the coastal towns of Cannes, Marseille and Nice, with an emphasis on French-Italian style dishes and wines'. It will all be more homespun than Bosi's Bibendum, apparently, with rustic options like rabbit with garlic cited as typical of the fairly traditional fare. / W1W 2PS; soccabistro.com; Mon-Sun 7 pm.

Social Eating House W1 £104 **3**3**3**
58-59 Poland St   020 7993 3251   4–1C
With its "sexy and atmospheric interior" and accomplished cuisine, the 10-year-old Soho branch of Jason Atherton's 'Social' brand is a venue recommended both for business meals and for "secret assignations" – kick off the occasion in his speakeasy 'The Blind Pig', which is hidden upstairs. / W1F 7NR; www.socialeatinghouse.com; @socialeathouse; Tue-Sat 10 pm; closed Sun & Mon.

Soffice London SW15 NEW £44 **3**4**3**
236 Upper Richmond Road   020 3859 4335   11–2B
"Wonderful and authentic Sicilian food" – in particular, "incredible fresh pasta" – can be found at this "deli/restaurant, newly opened in Putney". It calls itself a 'gastro-bakery', so all sorts of Sicilian nibbles are available alongside the "unusual pasta". "Staff are friendly and welcoming", and "the ambience is lively". / SW15 6TG; www.sofficelondon.com; @soffice_london; Mon-Sun 11 pm.

Soif SW11 £64 **3**22
27 Battersea Rise   020 7223 1112   11–2C
This rustic French spot on Battersea Rise is operated by the pioneer importer of organic and biodynamic wines, Les Caves de Pyrène, and, although its mix of small plates and offbeat vintages no longer seems as original as once it did, it's consistently well-rated. / SW11 1HG; www.soif.co; @soif_sw11; Wed-Sat, Tue 11 pm, Sun 5 pm; closed Tue L closed Sun D, closed Mon.

SOLA W1 £104 5 3 2
64 Dean Street 020 7734 8428 5–2A

"One of London's finest gastronomic experiences" – Victor Garvey's "slightly unorthodox" Californian in Soho ('SO'ho via 'LA') had its late-2019 debut slightly stymied by Covid, but is nowadays "consistently serving some of the most interesting food in London, using exceptional produce"; and with "brilliant ideas and concepts in each dish". Staff are "chatty" – "overly so" for one or two diners, but "passionate and knowledgeable" to others – while the setting is "lacking atmosphere" or cleanly designed according to your taste. Dishes inspiring comment have included "amazing extra-large langoustines", "superb tuna and caviar" and a "delicious grapefruit dessert". / W1W 4QQ; solasoho.com; @solasoho; Wed-Sat 11 pm; closed Mon & Tue & Sun.

Sollip SE1 NEW £98 5 4 3
8 Melior Street 020 7378 1742 10–4C

"Truly an epic fusion of Asian and French cooking techniques, flavours and produce" justify the trip to husband-and-wife Woongchul Park and Comee Ki's French/Korean passion project, in the grungy streets surrounding London Bridge and Guy's Hospital (winner of the Top Gastronomic category at Harden's London Restaurant Awards 2021). The "austere" interior can seem "clinical", but fans feel that "every part is beautiful and considered like the food itself". "You have to try the Insta-famous daikon tarte Tatin, but something even as humble as a cassoulet is raised to life-enriching memorableness here". / SE1 3QQ; www.sollip.co.uk; @sollip_restaurant; Tue-Thu 11 pm, Fri & Sat 11.30 pm; closed Tue-Sat L, closed Sun & Mon; payment – credit card only.

Som Saa E1 £55 5 3 3
43a Commercial St 020 7324 7790 13–2C

"Better than any Thai food I had in Thailand… and with a cool Shoreditch vibe" – this former factory near Spitalfields Market offers dishes with an "intensity and complexity of flavours that's second to none" – the "real Thai tastes (spicy, hot, sour, sweet and sharp) are tongue tingling!" "The front of the restaurant is more light and airy. The back gives a kitchen view but is dark"; "the team are relaxed, friendly and informative about the dishes (an essential point, as many options do require explanation for those not 'au fait' with Thai cuisine)". / E1 6BD; www.somsaa.com; @somsaa_london; Mon-Wed 10 pm, Thu-Sat 10.30 pm, Sun 9 pm; closed Mon & Tue L.

Sông Quê E2 £42 3 3 2
134 Kingsland Rd 020 7613 3222 14–2A

"Great pho" and other Vietnamese crowd-pleasers is the attraction at this well-known "cheap and cheerful" canteen on the 'Pho Mile' stretch of Shoreditch's Kingsland Road. / E2 8DY; www.songque.co.uk; @songquecafe; Mon-Sat 11 pm, Sun 10.30 pm; no Amex.

Sorella SW4 £66 4 3 2
148 Clapham Manor Street 020 7720 4662 11–1D

"The neighbourhood Italian restaurant that you always wanted to have" is now chef Robin Gill's Clapham flagship following the closure of near-neighbour Dairy (RIP). It's "noisy and buzzy" in the proper Italian manner, and the cooking is "interesting and delicious", with highlights including "arancini to die for". / SW4 6BX; www.sorellarestaurant.co.uk; @sorellaclapham; Wed-Sat 10 pm, Sun 3 pm; closed Wed L closed Sun D, closed Mon & Tue; no Amex.

Soutine NW8 £65 | 2 4 4
60 St John's Wood High Street 020 3926 8448 9–3A

"Oh là là – looking 100 years old and dripping with charm" this "slick and relaxing" brasserie in St John's Wood is proving "another instant Corbin & King classic": "the décor is delightful and service is warm and graceful under pressure". True to the form, the "food could be more ambitious", but "for a family meal this lovely place is hard to beat". (With the founders recently sacked, "will the new regime ruin everything?"). / NW8 7SH; soutine.co.uk; @soutinestjohn; Mon-Sat 10 pm, Sun 9 pm.

The Spaniard's Inn NW3 £42 | 2 2 4
Spaniards Rd, Hampstead Heath 020 8731 8406 9–1A

This ancient (circa 1585) wood-panelled inn at the top of of Hampstead Heath is drenched in historical and literary associations: Dick Turpin's father was the landlord, Byron, Dickens and Bram Stoker all drank here, and Keats reputedly composed his Ode to a Nightingale in what is now a walled beer garden. But if you're just after Sunday lunch, its leafy location and affordable scoff mean it's "always popular and well attended". / NW3 7JJ; www.thespaniardshampstead.co.uk; @thespaniardsinn; Mon-Sat 11 pm, Sun 10.30 pm.

Sparrow SE13 £55 | 4 3 4
Rennell Street 020 8318 6941 1–4D

"Don't be misled by the nondescript exterior" at this little local restaurant in Lewisham – "this is a serious kitchen, producing delectable and innovative small sharing plates". Husband-and-wife chef team Terry Blake and Yohini Nandakumar bring together their combined European and Asian heritages to create an unusual and ever-changing menu – which is always well received. / SE13 7HD; sparrowlondon.co.uk; @sparrow.london; Wed-Sat 10 pm, Sun 3 pm; closed Wed & Thu L closed Sun D, closed Mon & Tue.

Sparrow Italia W1 NEW
1 - 3 Avery Row awaiting tel 3–2B

Hot on the heels of a debut in LA, this US Italian restaurant concept is set to launch on this 190-cover site in Mayfair in late 2022, which will incorporate a ground floor bar, first floor dining room and terrace, and cigar lounge. It will offer an Italian/Mediterranean menu including pizza and pasta. More branches are planned both in the capital and back home in the US of A. / W1W 4AJ; Mon-Sun midnight.

Speedboat Bar W1 NEW
30 Rupert Street awaiting tel 4–3D

Named to be reminiscent of the canals of Bangkok's Chinatown, JKS Restaurants and chef Luke Farrell launch their second Thai concept together (the first was at the Arcade Food Hall) in September 2022 in Soho, to offer curries plus 'fast and furious wok cookery with roasted meats and zingy seafood salads', using UK-grown Thai herbs from Farrell's Forest nursery. / W1W 6DL; @speedboatbar; Mon-Sun midnight.

Spring Restaurant WC2 £116 | 3 3 4
New Wing, Lancaster Place 020 3011 0115 2–2D

"One of the prettiest chambers in London" – Skye Gyngell's "wonderful, light and airy venue" has a "lovely and calming vibe" and makes "beautiful use of the Somerset House dining room". Her "assured and imaginative" modern cuisine makes it a major favourite, although it was much less often recommended this year for hitting the peaks of gastronomy. Top Menu Tip – "the ethics, creativity, utility and value for money of the 'Scratch Menu' are brilliant!" ("delicious reimagined 'leftovers' served from a no-choice menu between 17.30 and 18.30"). / WC2R 1LA; www.springrestaurant.co.uk; @spring_ldn; Wed-Sat 9.30 pm; closed Sat L, closed Mon & Tue & Sun; credit card required to book.

F S A

St Martin's House WC2 NEW £70
4a Upper St Martin's Lane   020 7836 7591   5–3B

Styling itself as 'Your new home in Covent Garden' – this new all-day British brasserie in London's Theatreland opened in spring 2022 (just before our survey) in the prominent and convenient site formerly occupied by Tredwell's (RIP). In limited initial feedback, reports are of highs and lows – it seems safest to leave a rating till next year. / WC2W 9NY; www.stmartinshouselondon.co.uk; @stmartinshouselondon; Sun-Thu 11 pm, Fri & Sat 1 am.

Stanley's SW3 £93   3|2|3
151 Sydney Street   020 7352 7664   6–3C

Just off the King's Road, this two-year-old courtyard bar and restaurant (with outside booths) is a "lovely" venue in partnership with the nearby Chelsea Gardener. The straightforward British seasonal food is consistently well-rated, but no-one suggests it's going to set the earth on fire. / SW3 6NT; www.stanleyschelsea.co.uk; @stanleys_chelsea_; Mon-Sat 11.30 pm, Sun 7.30 pm.

Stem & Glory £44   3|3|2
60 Bartholomew Close, EC1   020 3969 9392   10–2B
100 Liverpool Street, EC2   07970 646 779   10–2D NEW

"A vegan delight", say fans of this meat-free three-year-old near Barts Hospital: a crowdfunded spin-off from an acclaimed Cambridge venture. Results can be uneven ("maybe I chose badly…"; "some of the food missed but more was a hit…"), but they must be doing something right as a new Broadgate branch launches in September 2022. / www.stemandglory.uk; stemandglory.

Steven Edwards Bingham Riverhouse TW10 £80   4|2|4
61-63 Petersham Road   020 8940 0902   1–4A

"Lovely views of the Thames" and "fabulous food" combine to make this Richmond boutique hotel dining room "difficult to beat". The "exceptional tasting menu you can adapt to as many courses as you want" – from highly rated chef Steven Edwards (who owns etch in Brighton) – can be enjoyed "at a window table overlooking the river", "on the terrace or in a garden dome". / TW10 6UT; www.binghamriverhouse.com; @binghamriverhouse; Fri & Sat 08 pm, Thu 8 pm, Sun 1.30 pm; closed Thu L closed Sun D, closed Mon & Tue & Wed; no trainers.

Sticks'n'Sushi £66   3|2|2
3 Sir Simon Milton Sq, Victoria St, SW1   020 3141 8810   2–4B
40 Beak Street, W1   020 3141 8191   4–2C
11 Henrietta St, WC2   020 3141 8810   5–3D
113-115 King's Road, SW3   020 3141 8181   6–3C
1 Nelson Road, SE10   020 3141 8220   1–3D
58 Wimbledon Hill Rd, SW19   020 3141 8800   11–2B
1 Crossrail Place, E14   020 3141 8230   12–1C

The "surprisingly delicious and wide-ranging menu" combines sushi with yakitori skewers (the so-called 'sticks') at this extremely popular Japanese-inspired group, whose "bustling" branches betray the Scandi style of their Copenhagen-based owners. It's "a perfect choice if not everyone wants sushi" (even if it's "expensive and portions are a bit on the small side"). A tenth branch is promised in late 2022 in Westfield W12. / www.sticksnsushi.com; sticksnsushi.

Sticky Mango SE1 £61   3|2|2
33 Coin Street   020 7928 4554   10–4A

"Not out of the ordinary, but what it does it does well" – chef Peter Lloyd's transformation of the revered South Bank French restaurant RSJ (RIP) into a "Malaysian-style" venue over three storeys disappointed former regulars, but has become a "firm favourite" with a new crowd for its "imaginative food, friendly service and a buzzy celebratory atmosphere". / SE1 9NR; www.stickymango.co.uk; @stickymangoldn; Tue-Sun, Mon 10.30 pm; closed Mon L.

F S A

Story SE1 £272 3|3|3
199 Tooley St   020 7183 2117   10–4D

"Love the edible candle that drips into the best sourdough bread you have ever tasted…" – Tom Sellers *"isn't frightened of including strong flavours and rich, unctuous sauces"* at his acclaimed foodie hotspot in *"a slightly cultural/culinary desert"* near Tower Bridge. *"Dishes are served by all the staff including the chefs as the 'story' is told"* over ten courses – *"a great range of tastes and textures keeps you guessing"* and there are some *"unusual wine pairings"*. *"The quirky approach can be annoying"* but most reporters feel *"the whole experience is phenomenal"*. But, even those who rate it as *"exceptional all round"* can still feel it is becoming significantly *"overpriced"*; and ratings were also undercut this year by one or two *"gruesomely unbalanced"* or *"unsubstantial"* meals. In January 2023, the restaurant will close for several months as a new storey is added to the building. BREAKING NEWS – also in 2023, Sellers will open a new restaurant in Mayfair, near The Ritz: at '1 Hotel Mayfair' which promises 'eco-conscious luxury and contemporary design'. / SE1 2UE; www.restaurantstory.co.uk; @rest_story; Thu-Sun 8.30 pm; closed Mon & Tue & Wed; no shorts.

Straker's W10 NEW
91 Golborne Road   07502 300962   7–1A

Thomas Straker spent lockdown becoming an Instagram star uploading cooking videos. His debut restaurant was going to be 'Acre' in Queen's Park, but his plan had an upgrade and name change to this 40-seater in Notting Hill. His aim is for it to be an 'epic neighbourhood restaurant' with 'east London wine bar vibes'; and a local-sourcing ethos designed to 'really ensure each ingredient has its moment in the spotlight'. / W10 5NL; www.strakers.london; @strakers_london; Mon-Sat 10 pm, Sun 9 pm.

Street Burger £47 2|2|2
13-14 Maiden Lane, WC2   020 7592 1214   5–3D
24 Charing Cross Road, WC2   020 7592 1361   5–4B
222 Kensington High Street, W8   020 7592 1612   8–1D
341 Upper Street, N1   020 7592 1355   9–3D
Entertainment District, The O2, SE10   020 7352 2512   12–1D
26 Cowcross Street, EC1   020 7592 1376   10–1A NEW
One New Change, EC4   020 7592 1217   10–2B

In looks they are often *"almost indistinguishable from the Byron that was replaced"*, and Gordon Ramsay's expanding chain (which has snapped up many of its rival's former sites) does have fans who say it's *"better than expected"* for *"a decent burger"*. On the flipside, though, there are almost an equal number of sceptics who feel *"it trades on the Ramsay name with cooking that's below par"*: *"we went not long after this branch had opened hoping for a reliable burger like we used to get there when it was Byron… never have we eaten one so awful"*. Still, the roll-out continues with a recent addition near Farringdon station.
/ www.gordonramsayrestaurants.com/street-burger; gordonramsaystreetburger.

Sucre London W1 £80 3|4|4
47b Great Marlborough Street   020 3988 3329   4–1B

Everyone *"loves the décor"* of this import from Buenos Aires, overseen by star Latino chef, Fernando Trocca: the glamorous makeover of a 300-year-old Soho building that once housed the London College of Music, complete with chandeliers, open kitchen and fire pit! Staff are *"convivial"* too and *"the downstairs bar (Abajo) really helps round off an evening"*. The vibrant South American food? Marina O'Loughlin in The Sunday Times was not impressed, but some diners had their *"best meal of the year"* here, and even a reporter who found it *"ever so slightly underwhelming"* said *"but it feels like it could really gain traction!"* / W1W 7HS; www.sucrerestaurant.com; @sucre.london; Mon-Sat 1 am, Sun midnight.

SUDU NW6 NEW
30 Salusbury Road   020 7624 3829   1–2B

Fatizah and Irqam Shawal (whose parents opened the venerable Satay House in 1973) are set to open this Malaysian style 'kopitiam' (a kind of South East Asian coffee shop) in ever-more happening Queen's Park late in 2022. Many of the fave rave dishes from Satay House will feature on the menu here. / NW6 6NL; @sudu.ldn; Mon-Sun midnight.

Sukho Fine Thai Cuisine SW6   £52   4 5 2
855 Fulham Rd   020 7371 7600   11–1B

"Delicious Thai food, served with charm" has won a very loyal local following and something of a wider reputation for this long-established café-style venture in a Fulham shop conversion. Arguably "tables are too close together", but most feel "even if it's cramped, it's still worth it". / SW6 5HJ; www.sukhogroups.com; @sukho_thairestaurant_fulhamsw6; Mon-Sat 10.30 pm, Sun 9.30pm.

Sumak N8   £44   3 4 2
141 Tottenham Lane   020 8341 6261   1–1C

"A favourite Turkish spot" – this well-run Crouch End local offers a "reliably delicious range of vegetarian, meat and fish dishes", and "treats regulars as old friends, eating at a 'home from home'". It's "not as cheap as the majority of Turkish/Kurdish restaurants in nearby Green Lanes, but the standard is higher and well worth the extra pound or two". / N8 9BJ; sumakrestaurants.com; @sumakrestaurant; Mon-Thu 11.30 pm, Fri & Sat midnight, Sun 11 pm.

Sumi W11   £94   4 5 4
157 Westbourne Grove   020 4524 0880   7–1B

Endo Kazutoshi's "cute little local" on the edge of Notting Hill – the more casual spin-off from White City's exceptional Endo at Rotunda – "punches above its weight". Named after the sushi master's mother, it offers a taste of his artful creations at much more approachable prices, and "a wonderful and delicious take on traditional Japanese food". In September 2022, it reopens having expanded (from 45 to 60 covers) and with a new chef: Christian Onia. / W11 2RS; www.sushisumi.com; @sumilondon; Tue-Sat 10 pm, Sun 5 pm; closed Sun D, closed Mon; booking online only.

The Summerhouse W9   £73   3 3 5
60 Blomfield Rd   020 7286 6752   9–4A

"Ducks and houseboats drift slowly by" at this tranquil spot that's all decked out in a white-and-blue nautical theme in Little Venice, which has a "perfect location right on Regent's Canal". But while nobody questions the "views and great vibe", there's a minority "who wanted to like the place, but wish the food was more consistent". For most folks though, "what is not to like about this buzzing restaurant right on the canal serving lovely fresh fish?" / W9 2PA; www.thesummerhouse.co; Mon-Sat 11 pm, Sun 10.30 pm; no Amex.

Sunday in Brooklyn W2   £72   3 3 4
98 Westbourne Grove   020 7630 1060   7–1B

This Notting Hill yearling, an offshoot of a modish Williamsburg original, hits the spot for lovers of NY-style comfort nosh. Most of it is "delicious" – "OK, not the most sophisticated, but hey – it's American brunch", and "sometimes they're trying a bit too hard to be hip", but ratings are good across the board. / W2 5RU; sundayinbk.co.uk; @sundayinbrooklyn_ldn; Mon & Tue 4.30 pm, Wed & Thu 10 pm, Fri & Sat 11 pm, Sun 9 pm; closed Mon & Tue D; payment – credit card only.

F S A

Supa Ya Ramen E8
499 Kingsland Road   no tel   14–1A

Luke Findlay launched his first 15-cover restaurant on Hackney Road in March 2020, only to close just a few days later due to the first lockdown. This Dalston 20-seater with open kitchen is the hard-fought-for sequel and opened in September 2021. Feedback in our annual diners' poll remains surprisingly limited given the rave-review delivered on opening by The Evening Standard's Jimi Famurewa: "a verve, simplicity and slurpable magic that feels, thrillingly, like the future". / E8 4AU; supayaramen.myshopify.com/products/bubble-booking; @supa_ya_ramen; Tue-Sat 10 pm, Sun 4 pm; closed Tue-Fri L closed Sun D, closed Mon.

Supawan N1   £54   5 4 3
38 Caledonian Road   020 7278 2888   9–3D

"By day a florist, by night an exceptional Thai restaurant" – Wichet Khongphoon's "refined and authentic" spot in King's Cross is "one of the best Thai eateries in town" and certainly the most unusual – "it always feels celebratory to eat among the colourful blooms". The "high-quality and interesting food is not your western-style menu", but reflects Wichet's upbringing on Phuket in southern Thailand. / N1 9DT; www.supawan.co.uk; @supawan_thaifood; Mon-Sat 11 pm, Sun 10.30 pm.

Super Tuscan E1   £65   4 3 3
8a Artillery Passage   020 7247 8717   13–2B

"So tiny you could miss it" – this "authentic Italian" is a "very cosy and friendly" spot of a type rare for somewhere near the City (it's in the warren of streets around Spitalfields). "Impeccable" dishes are served with "minimal fuss" – "joyous!". / E1 7LJ; www.supertuscan.co.uk; @enoteca_super_tuscan; Mon-Fri 9 pm; closed Sat & Sun.

Sushi Atelier W1   £61   4 4 3
114 Great Portland Street   020 7636 4455   2–1B

This contemporary Japanese outfit near Oxford Circus from the Chisou group is – according to its biggest fans – "simply outstanding" ("the head chef gave us personal advice and even created tailor-made sushi for us"… "sublime"). Not everyone would go quite as far, but all reports rate the food here as good or better. / W1W 6PH; www.sushiatelier.co.uk; @sushiatelierlondon; Tue-Sat 11 pm; closed Sun & Mon.

Sushi Bar Makoto W4   £38   4 3 1
57 Turnham Green Terrace   020 8987 3180   8–2A

"Very consistent and reliable sushi" wins a loyal local following for this no-frills, family-run pit stop, a short walk from Turnham Green tube. / W4 1RP; www.sushibarmakoto.co.uk; @sushi_makoto; Mon-Sat 10 pm, Sun 9 pm.

Sushi Masa NW2   £47   3 3 2
33b Walm Lane   020 8459 2971   1–1A

"The best food in Willesden Green" is arguably a double-edged compliment, but should do nothing to detract from this accomplished Japanese, acclaimed by locals for its "super-fresh, true-tasting sushi" and other "exquisitely prepared dishes". As with its long-time predecessor on this site (Sushi Say, long RIP), what is potentially a "dull" space is enlivened by the "charming" service. / NW2 5SH; Mon-Sat 10 pm; closed Sun.

Sushi Murasaki W9   £56   4 4 2
12 Lauderdale Road   020 3417 8130   7–1C

"Exceptional", "really high-quality, fresh sashimi and moreish sushi" make this "on-point Japanese neighbourhood spot" a "regular favourite of Maida Vale locals". It also serves "good-value lunchtime bento boxes". / W9 1LU; sushi-murasaki.co.uk; @sushimurasakiuk; Mon-Sat 11 pm, Sun 10.30 pm.

F S A

Sushi on Jones N1 £56
Goods Way, 11 Goods Way   020 3179 2800   9–3C
This NYC sushi sensation, with its 45-minute, 12-course omakase formula, created barely a ripple of interest in our annual diners' survey. It could be the poor timing of the pandemic relative to its March 2020 debut, or it could be the rather peripheral location, near Google HQ on the edge of King's Cross's Pancras Square development. / N1N 4PW; www.sushionjones.com; @sushionjones; Wed-Sun 10 pm; closed Wed-Sun L, closed Mon & Tue.

Sushi Revolution SW9 £31   3 3 2
240 Ferndale Road   020 4537 4331   11–1D
Local reporters are full of praise for this Brixton newbie from Aidan Bryan and Tom Blackshaw, which has a perch in the swanky conversion of the old Bon Marché department store (now the HQ of Squire & Partners architectural practice). It doesn't generate huge amounts of feedback, but fans say "the menu's varied and the sushi's as good as it gets". / SW9 8FR; www.sushirevolution.co.uk; @sushirevolution; Mon-Sun 10 pm; payment – credit card only.

Sushi Show £22   3 3 2
28 Camden Passage, N1   020 7354 1329   9–3D
136 Bethnal Green Road, E2   020 7613 1926   13–1C
Kaz Tateishi's "conscientious and consistent" (and therefore very Japanese) sushi shop with eat-in seats is tucked away in Islington's cute Camden Passage. A meal here (or taken away in a box) "always feels like money well spent". There is now a second outlet in Shoreditch. / www.sushishowlondon.com; @sushi_show_london.

Sushisamba £116   2 2 3
Opera Terrace, 35 The Market, WC2   020 3053 0000   5–3D
Heron Tower, 110 Bishopsgate, EC2   020 3640 7330   10–2D
"Views are to die for" on the "glitzy" 38th floor of the Heron Tower, which – with its swish bar, outside terrace and vibrant dining space is "still a great place to see and be seen!" With "imaginative" and luxurious Japanese/South American fusion cuisine, the City branch of this US-based group should have it all, but enjoyment is blunted by the "exorbitant bill" and "service that seems like it's 'dialled in'". The Covent Garden location, on the first floor of the market itself and with a large outside terrace overlooking the back of the Royal Opera House, also occupies a prime London site: feedback is more limited, but similar in tone. / sushisamba.com; @SUSHISAMBA.

Sussex W1 £52   3 4 3
63-64 Frith Street   020 3923 7770   5–2A
"Creative food, interested staff and a pleasant space" (formerly Arbutus, RIP) have made this 'farm-to-fork' venue from the prolific Gladwin family "a great addition to Soho". Launched in 2019, it's their only outpost in the West End but they now have six London restaurants stretching from 'The Shed' in Notting Hill to 'The Fat Badger' in Richmond – this is the best-rated of the bunch. / W1W 3JW; www.sussex-restaurant.com; @sussex_resto; Tue-Sat 10.30 pm; closed Sun & Mon.

Suzi Tros W8 £66   3 3 3
18 Hillgate Street   020 7221 2223   7–2B
"Delicious food served in a relaxed and, at times, noisy ambience" earns consistent praise for this Notting HIll three-year-old which focuses on the cuisine of Thessalonica and northern Greece. It's a "more casual" spin-off from Adrien Carre and Christina Mouratoglou's Mazi nearby, and is named after a classic Greek film that has come to symbolise the good life and eating well. / W8 7SR; www.suzitros.com; @suzitros; Tue-Sat 11 pm; closed Sun & Mon.

F S A

The Swan W4 £64 3 4 4
1 Evershed Walk, 119 Acton Ln   020 8994 8262   8–1A

With "one of West London's top pub gardens", this "great local" – on the Acton-Chiswick border – with a green-tiled Art Deco facade excels for its "delicious food and welcoming service" under the direction of "a proper landlady". There's also a "charming nook-filled room" for "Sunday lunch gatherings in the winter". / W4 5HH; www.theswanchiswick.co.uk; @theswanchiswick; Mon-Thu 10 pm, Fri & Sat 10.30 pm, Sun 9.30 pm; closed Mon-Fri L.

The Swan at the Globe SE1 £70 2 2 4
21 New Globe Walk   020 7928 9444   10–3B

The "amazing setting" – part of Shakespeare's Globe with "spectacular views" over the Thames – is the USP of this venue. There's an "excellent range of cakes, sandwiches and teas" (including the oddly named 'Mr Falstaff's' savoury afternoon tea… forgetting Sir John's knighthood). But more generally, while the food's fine, "it's not a serious challenger for the title of restaurant rather than gastropub". / SE1 9DT; www.swanlondon.co.uk; @swanglobe; Mon-Sat 9.30 pm, Sun 9.45 pm.

Sweet Thursday N1 £48 3 3 2
95 Southgate Rd   020 7226 1727   14–1A

This handy De Beauvoir Town pizzeria and bottle shop majors on "delicious" Neapolitan-style pizzas, backed up with a range of 'pizza sandwiches' and 'no-dough starters' by Portuguese superchef Nuno Mendes (of Chiltern Firehouse and Lisboeta fame). / N1 3JS; www.sweetthursday.co.uk; @sweetthursdaypizza; Mon-Thu 10 pm, Fri & Sat 10.30 pm, Sun 9 pm.

Sweetings EC4 £89 3 2 4
39 Queen Victoria St   020 7248 3062   10–3B

"Sitting cheek by jowl at a counter that dates from the 19th century… bliss!" – this "City legend amongst fish restaurants" is "such a haven of bygone days, which gives it its special ambience and devoted following". Founded in the 1830s, and on its current site since the 1920s, it's "still serving sensational oysters (washed down with a pewter tankard of Black Velvet) after all these years" alongside "very traditional fish cooked simply and well" (e.g. "divine whitebait"). "It's a bit pricey and you can't book but otherwise excellent." / EC4N 4SA; sweetingsrestaurant.co.uk; @#Sweetingslondon; Mon-Fri 3 pm; closed Mon-Fri D, closed Sat & Sun; booking lunch only.

Sycamore Vino Cucina, Middle Eight Hotel WC2 £66 3 2 2
Middle Eight Hotel, 66 Great Queen Street   020 7309 9300   5–1D

This "stylish" two-year-old in Covent Garden, "puts a different, modern spin on the usual Italian type offerings". Service is only "good in parts", though, and that it can feel compromised by being "too near the hotel lobby" (or "too integral to the lively bar of the hip hotel it's part of") is a repeat complaint. / WC2W 5BX; www.middleeight.com; @middle_eight_hotel; Mon-Fri 11 pm, Sat 10 pm, Sun 5 pm; closed Sun D.

Ta Ke Sushi W5 £34 4 3 2
3-4 Grosvenor Parade   020 8075 8877   1–3A

"A top Japanese restaurant in an area full of Japanese restaurants" – this "very reasonably priced" Ealing two-year-old serves "a wide-ranging menu covering every avenue – ramen, maki, sashimi, donburi – delivering all with panache and a friendly smile". "Reminds me of Japan… by the looks of the large number of Japanese customers, they think so too!" / W5 3NN; takesushiealing.co.uk; Sun, Mon-Wed 10 pm, Thu-Sat 10.30 pm.

F S A

Tab X Tab W2 — £31 — 4|4|3
Westbourne House, 14-16 Westbourne Grove   020 7792 3445   7–1B
"Incredible coffee" (roasted by Kiss the Hippo) is the star turn at Mathew and Charmain Tabtabai's four-year-old Bayswater venture. They do a "great breakfast", too, with "excellent scrambled eggs" – and a range of cocktails for later in the day. / W2 4UJ; tabxtab.com; @tabxtablondon; Wed & Thu, Sun 4 pm, Sat, Fri 5 pm; closed Wed & Thu, Sat & Sun, Fri D, closed Mon & Tue; payment – credit card only; booking online only.

Table Du Marche N2 — £59 — 3|3|2
111 High Road   020 8883 5750   1–1B
Happy habitués of this "reasonably priced French bistro" in East Finchley applaud its "good-quality" cuisine and a properly Gallic atmosphere around the marble-topped bar. Top Tip – "the lunch menu at £15 to £19 is extremely good value". / N2 8AG; tabledumarchelondon.co.uk; @tabledumarche; Mon-Sat 11 pm, Sun 10 pm.

Tacos Padre SE1 — £38 — 3|3|4
Borough Market Kitchen, Winchester Walk   07582 636186   10–4C
This "small" Borough Market taqueria is the brainchild of Nick Fitzgerald, who worked at Pujol (one of Mexico's most famous restaurants before coming to London), starting as a pop-up in 2017 and going permanent here in 2019. "It's a great location with a lovely atmosphere" and all reports rate the food as good or better. / SE1 5AG; www.tacospadre.com; @tacospadre; Fri, Thu 10 pm, Sun, Mon-Wed 3 pm, Sat 11.30 pm; closed Sun, Mon-Wed D.

Taka Marylebone W1 — £99 — 2|2|3
109 Marylebone High Street   020 3637 4466   2–1A
Views diverged this year on this modern Marylebone Japanese – an exponent of 'Shun' (meaning 'food should only be eaten when it is at its best and at the height of its season'). Fans say it's a "lovely" place offering "novel and delicious" flavours from its wide-ranging, funky menu ('rock and rolls', 'plant-based power', 'raw to the core', 'robata'…) – sceptics say that it's "overpriced, with miniscule portions". / W1W 4RX; takalondon.com; @takarestaurants; Fri & Sat 10.30 pm, Tue-Thu 10 pm; closed Tue-Thu L, closed Sun & Mon.

Takahashi SW19 — £57 — 5|5|3
228 Merton Road   020 8540 3041   11–2B
"Like a work of art!" – the "beautifully presented, elegant, superior-quality food and delightful service" at this tiny and "minimalist" Japanese restaurant in the unlikely surroundings of a parade of shops near South Wimbledon tube are a match for anything in the West End. Taka, a former Nobu chef, and his wife Yuko have consistently earned our highest possible food ratings since opening seven years ago. / SW19 1EQ; www.takahashi-restaurant.co.uk; @takahashi_wimbledon; Wed-Sat 10.30 pm, Sun 7.30 pm; closed Wed-Sun L, closed Mon & Tue.

Tamarind W1 — £81 — 5|4|3
20 Queen St   020 7629 3561   3–3B
"An absolutely fabulous place", this pioneer of upscale Indian food for almost 30 years (and the first in the world to bag a Michelin star) is flying high again after a major refurb doubled the size of its Mayfair premises a couple of years ago. "Despite newcomers" taking curry to new levels, fans say "this remains the best Indian food" – "the brilliant taster menu is exceptional and demonstrates the skill and versatility of the kitchen" (now run by Karunesh Khanna, formerly head chef of Amaya). / W1J 5PR; www.tamarindrestaurant.com; @tamarindofmayfair; Mon-Sat 10.15 pm, Sun 9.15 pm; no trainers.

F S A

Tamarind Kitchen W1 £62 4 4 4
167-169 Wardour St   020 7287 4243   4–1C

This "sparky version of its parent Tamarind" in a "busy part of Soho" knocks out "delicious twists on quintessential Delhi street food" in a "large, stylish and comfortable dining room". "Jovial staff" add to the "very special" package. / W1W 8WR; tamarindkitchen.co.uk; @tamarindkitchenlondon; Tue, Mon, Wed-Sat 10.30 pm, Sun 9.30 pm; closed Mon, Wed-Sat L.

The Tamil Prince N1 NEW
115 Hemingford Road   07988 750721   9–2D

The people behind Tamila in Hackney, chef Prince Durairaj and Glen Leeson (both ex-Roti King), took over the former Cuckoo pub in the middle of Barnsbury to launch this June 2022 newcomer: a South Asian restaurant, mixing small and large plates, accompanied by cocktails. In his early doors review, the Evening Standard's Jimi Famurewa found dishes inspiring "plate-licking, wanton lust". / N1 1BZ; www.thetamilprince.com; @the_tamil_prince; Tue-Sat 11 pm, Sun 10.30 pm; closed Mon.

Tamp Coffee W4 £27 3 4 3
1 Devonshire Road   no tel   8–2A

"Wonderful coffee and great pastries" are served at this rustic Chiswick spot, inspired by the cultural coffee shops where artists and politicos gather in Rio. All the baked goods – empanadas, croissants and pasteis de nata – are made daily on the premises, and they have begun to roast their own Brazilian coffee beans. / W4; www.tampcoffee.co.uk; @tampcoffee; Mon-Fri 3.30 pm, Sat & Sun 4 pm; closed Mon-Sun D; no booking.

Tandoor Chop House WC2 £61 3 3 3
8 Adelaide Street   020 3096 0359   5–4C

"Buzzy" Anglo-Indian hybrid in a "perfect central location" just off Trafalgar Square that serves "tapas-sized selections of delicious Indian food to share"; there's "not a huge choice", but there are "plenty of vegetarian options". An offshoot in Notting Hill is no longer in operation. / WC2N 4HW; tandoorchophouse.com; @tandoorchop; Mon-Thu 11 pm, Fri & Sat 11.30 pm, Sun 10 pm; booking max 6 may apply.

Tapas Brindisa £64 3 2 2
46 Broadwick St, W1   020 7534 1690   4–2B
7-9 Exhibition Rd, SW7   020 7590 0008   6–2C
18-20 Southwark St, SE1   020 7357 8880   10–4C
Battersea Power Station, SW11   020 8016 8888   11–1C NEW
Hotham House, 1 Heron Square, TW9   020 8103 8888   1–4A NEW

"Delicious tapas with a view of the River Thames" from "a large open terrace" is going down a storm at the instantly popular, new Richmond branch of the well-known chain (occupying the prominent site that was formerly Jackson & Rye, RIP). Backed by the firm of wholesalers of the same name, the group has steadily grown from its Borough Market origins over the last 10 years, and fans feel "it's exactly what you would expect from a place run by Spanish produce importers". On the downside, though, there is a school of thought that "while the food's done decently, it's serviceable but unexciting". / www.brindisakitchens.com; brindisaspanishfoods.

Taqueria £42 4 4 3
141-145 Westbourne Grove, W11   020 7229 4734   7–1B
8-10 Exmouth Market, EC1   020 3897 9609   10–1A NEW

With its "shortish menu of delicious small plates of tacos, fajitas and quesadillas" plus "lots of tequila and five flavours of margarita cocktails", this Notting Hill original and its Exmouth Market spin-off serve "some of the best Mexican food in London" – both "authentic" and "good value". A veteran of the capital's taco scene, it started out with a stall in Portobello Road before moving into permanent premises 18 years ago. / taqueria.co.uk; taqueriauk.

FSA RATINGS: FROM 1 POOR — 5 EXCEPTIONAL

F S A

Taro £36 3 | 3 | 2
1 Churton Street, SW1   020 7734 5826   2–4B **NEW**
61 Brewer Street, W1   020 7734 5826   4–3C
356 Regents Park Road, N3   020 7734 5826   1–1B **NEW**
414 Kennington Road, SE11   020 7735 7772   1–3C
193 Balham High Road, SW12   020 8675 5187   11–2C
76 High Street, E17   020 7734 5826   1–1D **NEW**

"It's easy to walk past" these "unassuming" Japanese canteens, but "don't go on in!" There's a "great choice on the menu of both cooked plates and sushi"; "the food is always delicious" and prices are keen for a cuisine that can be very expensive. After two decades in Soho, the group has now pushed into Balham, Kennington and Finchley, with Pimlico and Walthamstow scheduled for late 2022. / tarorestaurants.uk; tarorestaurants.

Tas Pide SE1 £40 3 | 3 | 3
20-22 New Globe Walk   020 7928 3300   10–3B

"Good food at reasonable prices" is just what's called for at this "great spot" adjacent to Shakespeare's Globe theatre on the South Bank. An offshoot of the well-known Turkish mezze chain, it is decked out in cosy Anatolian style and specialises in stuffed 'pide' flatbreads. / SE1 9DR; www.tasrestaurants.co.uk; @tasrestaurantuk; Sun & Mon 10.30 pm, Tue-Sat 11.30 pm.

Tatale SE1
The Africa Centre, 66 Great Suffolk Street   020 8004 6436   10–4B

African cuisine has come a long way in London since Calabash – the capital's first African restaurant in the basement of the former Africa Centre in Covent Garden – opened in 1964. On the site of the new Africa Centre, in a repurposed Southwark office block, this Summer 2022 50-seater is run by Ghanaian-British restaurateur Akwasi Brenya-Mensa. Named after a form of plantain pancake, it aims to reflect the spirit of busy African roadside 'chop bars'. On the menu: omo tuo nkatenkwan sesame (mashed rice with groundnut, peanut soup); and buttermilk chicken burger topped with shito chilli, citrus yogurt and basil oil. / SE1 0BL; www.tataleandco.com; @tataleandco; Tue-Thu 10 pm, Fri & Sat 11 pm, Sun 4 pm.

Tattu London WC2 £111 2 | 3 | 3
The Now Building Rooftop, Denmark Street   020 3778 1985   5–1A

This scene-y Chinese operation from a Manchester-based chain is the signature restaurant of Oxford Street's 'The Now Building' (newly opened near Centre Point, featuring giant digital video screens). It's an Instagrammer's dream, but reports are mixed on the culinary front: the "food looks sensational", but is "overpriced" by a number of accounts and – although it may well find its market – foodies are likely to see it as an "example of how money and pretentions can go a long way". / WC2W 8LH; tattu.co.uk; @tattulondon; Mon-Sun 10.30 pm; closed Mon-Wed L.

Tavernaki W11 £29 3 | 2 | 2
222 Portobello Road   07510 627752   7–1A

A "delightful neighbourhood Greek restaurant, where real Greeks eat!" opened two years ago in Portobello by chef Harris Mavropoulos, with a straightforward menu of classic taverna dishes. It's a cosy place, with a downstairs bar, 'Mykonos'. / W11 1LJ; www.tavernakiportobello.co.uk; @tavernaki.portobello; Mon-Sun 11 pm.

Tavolino SE1 £52 2 | 1 | 3
Unit 1, 2 More London Place   020 8194 1037   10–4D

"Because of the fabulous view of the Tower of London and the river", this modern Italian (with large outside terrace) in the More London development by City Hall will attract custom come what may. Even those who consider it "overpriced" however, say the food's "OK" and fans say it has it all: "really good pizzas", "excellent pasta" and "a wonderful location thrown in". / SE1 2JP; www.tavolino.co.uk; @tavolinokitchen; Mon-Wed 9 pm, Thu-Sat 10 pm, Sun 8 pm.

FSA

Tayyabs E1 £34 **4**|**1**|**2**
83 Fieldgate St   020 7247 6400   10–2D
"You come to eat, not dine" at this "loud and popular" 500-seater, which "lives up to its reputation as the go-to curry house in (well, near to) Brick Lane". Top Menu Tip – "the lamb chops are meatilicious and the dry meat curry is rich and very tasty"; BYO. / E1 1JU; www.tayyabs.co.uk; @1tayyabs; Mon-Sun 11.30 pm.

Tea House Theatre SE11 **3**|**3**|**4**
139 Vauxhall Rd   awaiting tel   11–1D
'Where there's tea there's hope' is the philosophical underpinning of this "quirky café", which occupies a converted pub by Vauxhall Pleasure Gardens, and "does amazing breakfasts" and "unusual teas", plus yummy buns. "They are a tea house though, so there is no coffee available!!" / SE11 5HL; Mon-Sun midnight.

The Telegraph SW15 £51 **3**|**4**|**4**
Telegraph Road, Putney Heath   020 8194 2808   11–2A
Billing itself as "a country pub in London", this beautifully located hostelry on leafy Putney Heath is "much nicer since the change in ownership and refurb," having been purchased by Chester-based Brunning & Price a couple of years ago. "Food and beer are consistently good, with a choice of spacious indoor or attractive outdoor settings", the latter in the big beer garden. (For history buffs, the "wonderful site" itself was originally an optical telegraph station linking London to Portsmouth during the Napoleonic wars).
/ SW15 3TU; www.brunningandprice.co.uk/telegraph; @telegraphputneyheath; Mon-Thu 11.30 pm, Fri & Sat midnight, Sun 10 pm.

temper £54 **3**|**2**|**4**
25 Broadwick Street, W1   020 3879 3834   4–1C
5 Mercers Walk, WC2   020 3004 6669   5–2C
78 Great Eastern Street, EC2   020 3879 3834   13–1B **NEW**
Angel Court, EC2   020 3004 6984   10–2C
"Sitting at the counter with all of its theatre is amazing" at Neil Rankin's "noisy, buzzy and fun" outlets, whose "really cool (well, hot) feature are the 'fire pit' cooking stations", from which they offer "a great mix of meat dishes" (including rare-breed steaks), plus fish options. There were some "off days" reported this year, though: in particular, service has sometimes been "under pressure" or even "shambolic". / temperrestaurant.com; temperlondon.

The 10 Cases WC2 £77 **3**|**4**|**3**
16 Endell St   020 7836 6801   5–2C
"Cramped, buzzy, with a great wine list" to accompany "innovative and reliable food" – it's no surprise that this "very different" 'bistrot à vin' a couple of minutes' walk from the Opera House is such a Covent Garden "favourite". They only order ten cases of any wine (hence the name), which means you'll always find something "interesting" to drink – and "the head sommelier is wonderful!" / WC2H 9BD; www.10cases.co.uk; @The 10 Cases; Mon-Thu 10 pm, Fri & Sat 11 pm; closed Sun.

10 Greek Street W1 £69 **4**|**3**|**3**
10 Greek St   020 7734 4677   5–2A
"As good as ever" – this modern and understated Soho wine bar favourite provides "good food, if in rather cramped and noisy surroundings". A key feature is its handwritten 'Black Book' which lists the fine wines available each day. / W1D 4DH; www.10greekstreet.com; @10greekstreet; Tue-Sat 10.30 pm; closed Sun & Mon; No jeans; booking L only.

Tendido Cero SW5 £61 444
174 Old Brompton Road   020 7370 3685   6–2B

"Innovative and exquisite tapas" and "excellent (if pricey) Spanish wines" have long attracted Hispanophiles to this bar, directly opposite its older sibling, Cambio de Tercio. "Lighting and service are top-notch", too. The only complaint is that "the buzzy ambience can change quickly to unpleasantly loud when there are too many groups in". / SW5 0BA; www.cambiodetercio.co.uk; @cambiodetergiogroup; Tue-Sat 11.30 pm, Sun, Mon 11 pm.

Tendril EC1 £56 433
102 Bunhill Road   07842 797541   4–2C

"Wow. Who would believe it? A vegan restaurant that's amazing" – Rishim Sachdeva (ex-Fat Duck and Chiltern Firehouse) was a 'hard-core carnivore' until he challenged himself to see if he could create plant-based dishes that would satisfy himself as both a meat-eater and a chef. The answer was 'yes', the experiment changed his life, and he has spent three years doing pop-ups and residencies – most recently at a handy site just off Regent Street – while crowdfunding to raise capital for a permanent site. He has also gained a body of fans who have "visited several times for the unusual combinations and elevated vegan plates", which represent "superb value for money". Note – technically, Tendril is "mostly vegan", with cheese making an occasional guest appearance. / EC1E 8ND; www.tendrilkitchen.co.uk; @tendril_kitchen; Wed & Thu 10 pm, Fri & Sat 10.30 pm; closed Wed & Thu L, closed Mon & Tue & Sun.

The Tent (at the End of the Universe) W1 NEW
17 Little Portland Street   awaiting tel   3–1C

Initially launched as part of an invite-only private members' club, John Javier's small (34-cover) August 2022 newcomer in Fitzrovia is his first venture featuring Middle Eastern cuisine, zhushed up with – for instance – Asian seasonings, plus funky cocktails and wines. Expect Bedouin-style décor, DJs and live music. / W1W 8BP; Mon-Sun midnight.

Terra Rossa N1 £61 333
139 Upper Street   020 7226 2244   9–3D

"An absolute hidden gem" – this "unassuming Italian in the heart of Angel", close to the Almeida Theatre, is a "perfect neighbourhood spot", serving "generous portions of fantastic rustic food" and "well-selected wines" that make a meal "like being on holiday". It takes its name from the red earth of the Salento peninsula, the 'heel' of Puglia. / N1 1QP; terrarossa-restaurant.co.uk; @terrarossa.london; Mon-Sat 10.30 pm, Sun 9.30 pm.

Thali SW5 £49 333
166 Old Brompton Rd   020 7373 2626   6–2B

"Well worth seeking out on South Ken's 'Curry Corner'" – this "family-run restaurant with Bollywood paraphernalia on the walls" certainly "punches above its weight", with "a good selection of north-Indian dishes" and especially "delicious starters". / SW5 0BA; @thali_london; Mon-Sat midnight; closed Mon-Sat L, closed Sun.

Theo Randall
InterContinental London Park Lane W1 £81 542
1 Hamilton Place   020 7318 8747   3–4A

"In spite of many renovations it is still difficult to get away from the 'hotel dining room' feel" at this windowless and "bland" chamber, off the foyer of a large 1970s hotel on Hyde Park Corner. "Theo Randall's cooking does make up for it", though, and – in contrast to many top London destinations this year – ratings are going from strength to strength for its "fabulous Italian dining experience using stunning produce". In particular, Theo's series of "interesting, themed, regional menus are tremendous and very good value"; while "friendly and attentive" staff bring some conviviality to the "calm" space. Top Tip – "the set-price lunch menu may be the best-value lunch in the whole of London". / W1J 7QY; www.theorandall.com; @theo.randall; Tue-Sat 10 pm, Mon 10.30 , Sun 11 am; closed Sun & Mon D.

Theo's SE5 £39 3 3 2
2 Grove Ln 020 3026 4224 1–3C

"Excellent, well-charred sourdough bases with interesting toppings" are knocked out at these "buzzy neighbourhood pizza indies", with locations in Camberwell and Elephant & Castle. "In the Franco Manca vein", it's "just as good as it was when it opened". / SE5; www.theospizzeria.com; @theospizzeria; Tue-Thu 10.30 pm, Sun & Mon 10 pm, Fri & Sat 11 pm; no Amex; may need 6+ to book.

34 Mayfair W1 £117 2 3 3
34 Grosvenor Sq 020 3350 3434 3–3A

"You need deep pockets" to have a good time at this luxurious, rather conventional-looking American-style grill near the old US Embassy in Mayfair, from Richard Caring's Caprice group – but those who do say it "never disappoints"… "couldn't have asked for more (apart from a smaller bill!!)" / W1K 2HD; www.34-restaurant.co.uk; @34mayfair; Mon-Sun 11 pm; closed Sat & Sun L.

The Thomas Cubitt Pub Belgravia SW1 £75 2 2 3
44 Elizabeth St 020 7730 6060 2–4A

This "posh and busy pub with a lovely buzz throughout" was named after the master builder who developed surrounding Belgravia in the Georgian era. It's "fab for people-watching" in smart Elizabeth Street, while "the food is good without wowing". / SW1W 9PA; www.thethomascubitt.co.uk; @thethomascubitt; Mon-Sat 10 pm, Sun 9.30 pm.

Three Uncles £34 5 3 3
Unit 199 Hawley Wharf, NW1 07597 602281 9–2B
Unit 19&20, Brixton Village, SW9 020 3592 5374 11–2D **NEW**
12 Devonshire Row, EC2 020 7375 3573 10–2D

"Excellent Cantonese roast meats on rice" ("the Hainan chicken rice fills your heart with the warmth of a hug and a blanket from childhood!") at prices that represent "very good value for money" inspire the highest praise for these Cantonese operations, near Liverpool Street and "tucked away" in Camden Town's Hawley Wharf. The brainchild of Hong-Kong-raised pals, Pui Sing, Cheong Yew and Mo Kwok, they opened a new branch in March 2022 in Brixton Market (praised by The Evening Standard's Jimi Famurewa for its "cooking of immense focus, skill and real endorphin-spiking intensity").

Tila SE8 £48
14 Deptford Broadway 020 8692 8803 1–3D

On limited (but positive) feedback, this casual two-year-old bar/restaurant is worth knowing about, particularly in the thinly-served environs of Deptford. Many dishes are cooked over fire, and come with some eastern-Med influences. / SE8 4PA; www.tiladeptford.com; @tila.deptford; Wed-Fri 11 pm, Sat 10 pm, Sun 5 pm; closed Wed-Fri L closed Sun D, closed Mon & Tue.

TING SE1 £95 2 3 4
Level 35, 31 St Thomas St 020 7234 8108 10–4C

"Fantastic views" are the universally acknowledged highpoint of a visit to this swish Asian / British restaurant on the Shard's 35th floor. It is most often recommended for its "great twist on a traditional afternoon tea" (including an "exceptional vegan tea") – for more substantial meals, it is too often "not worth the price you pay for uninspiring dishes". / SE1 9RY; www.ting-shangri-la.com; @tinglondon; Mon-Sun 10.15 pm; no trainers; credit card required to book.

FSA

Tish NW3 £90   3 3 4
196 Haverstock Hill   020 7431 3828   9–2A

"Excellent modern kosher food in a beautiful setting" wins solid praise for this Belsize Park brasserie with a large and attractive outdoor terrace. The menu's European dishes include family favourites handed down to the owner, David Levin, by his Hungarian-Jewish mother and grandmother. / NW3 2AG; www.tish.london; @tish_london; Sun-Thu midnight; closed Fri & Sat.

Toff's N10 £51   4 3 2
38 Muswell Hill Broadway   020 8883 8656   1–1B

"Top-quality fish" has kept this Muswell Hill chippy high on the list of North London favourites for more than five decades, with two generations of the Greek-Cypriot Georgiou family maintaining the legacy left by the original 'Toff', Andreas Ttofalli. / N10 3RT; www.toffsfish.co.uk; @toffsfish; Mon-Sat 10 pm; closed Sun.

Tofu Vegan £22   4 3 2
105 Upper Street, N1   020 7916 3304   9–3D
28 North End Road, NW11   no tel   1–1B **NEW**

"Wonderfully yummy plant-based food with no compromise on flavour" – "and so much more interesting than the standard Chinese offering" too – has made a big hit of this Islington yearling, whose mix of Sichuan, Cantonese and other influences make it "one of the best places ever!" It's already on to branch number two, which opened in April 2022 – "a brilliant addition to Golders Green, all vegan and very tasty!"

TOKii W1 £94
The Prince Akatoki Hotel,
50 Great Cumberland Place   020 7724 0486   2–1A

Within the first international branch of a Japan-based group of five-star luxury hotels, this dining room near Marble Arch serves a non-traditional menu, focused on sushi, sashimi, seafood and meat cooked on the robata grill. Reports are too thin for a rating, but the odd exceptional meal is reported here. Top Tip – to give it a go, look out for their extremely keenly priced set menus. / W1W 7FD; www.tokii.co.uk; @tokiilondon; Mon-Sun 10 pm.

Tokimeite W1 £96
23 Conduit St   020 3826 4411   3–2C

Too limited feedback for a rating on this Mayfair Japanese centred around an open kitchen, which – in its six years of operation – has never seemed quite to fulfil its potential. Nowadays owned by famous food importers Atariya and supplied by Zen-Noh (Japan's agricultural cooperative), it should be an undisputed champion of Nipponese cuisine, but is still sometimes accused of being "incredibly expensive for what it delivers". / W1S 2XS; www.tokimeite.com; Tue-Sat 10.30 pm; closed Sun & Mon.

Toklas WC2 £70   4 2 3
1 Surrey Street   020 3930 8592   2–2D

"A sparse interior in a Brutalist building" off the Strand "disguises a fantastic place to enjoy excellent food" at this new arrival from the founders of the art fair, Frieze: "a big, classy concrete space", complete with "a massive terrace that looks like a brilliant draw once the weather turns summery". "British seasonal dishes" are done to a high standard, although service is "a bit hit 'n' miss". / WC2W 2ND; www.toklaslondon.com; @toklas_london; Tue-Sat 11 pm; closed Tue L, closed Sun & Mon.

Tokyo Sukiyaki-Tei & Bar SW3
85 Sloane Avenue   020 3583 3797   6–2C
Just off Sloane Avenue, this 'Japanese Wagyu Specialist' features a number of interesting, offbeat dishes on its menu, including Wagyu & truffle sushi; Wagyu shabu-shabu and yakiniku with Wagyu, ox tongue and Kobe beef (although there's also lots for fish-lovers too). Feedback is too limited for a rating. / SW3 3DX; www.tokyosukiyakitei.com; @tokyosukiyakitei; closed Mon-Sat & Sun; no shorts.

Tommi's Burger Joint   £36   3 3 2
30 Thayer St, W1   020 7224 3828   3–1A
37 Berwick Street, W1   020 7494 9086   4–2D
The "Scandi bro-burger" consistently "hits the spot" at this Marylebone and Soho duo from Icelander Tómas Tómasson, who has 41 years in the burger business and a mini empire that stretches from his native Reykjavik to Copenhagen, Berlin, London and Oxford. Fun fact: Tómasson became the oldest first-time member of the Althing (Iceland's parliament) in its 1,000-year history when he won election at the age of 72 last year.
/ www.burgerjoint.co.uk; burgerjointuk.

Tomoe SW15   £42   4 4 2
292 Upper Richmond Road   020 3730 7884   11–2B
This "very popular" Japanese nook in Putney wins strong local support for its authentic sushi and other classics – with cooking, produce and service of a standard that belies its (authentically) downbeat appearance. / SW15; www.tomoe-london.co.uk; @tomoe.london; Wed & Thu 9 pm, Fri & Sat 9.30 pm; closed Mon & Tue & Sun.

Tonkotsu   £47   2 2 2
Branches throughout London
This "slurpy Japanese noodles" outfit has grown from a 2011 pop-up to a fledgling national chain (14 branches in London, plus Brighton and Brum). These days it "feels formulaic, but the ramen does the business – the tonkotsu (pork broth, from which the place gets its name) is satisfyingly porky and the chilli chicken has a spicy hum". Critics are not so sure, pointing to "very disappointing noodles" and "drab stock".
/ www.tonkotsu.co.uk; tonkotsulondon.

Tosa W6   £39   3 4 2
332 King St   020 8748 0002   8–2B
"Down-to-earth," small Japanese, a short walk from Stamford Brook tube, that's "a perfect local": "service is patient and thoughtful" and the "menu covers all the bases (sushi, sashimi, tempura, etc) in good style but with the real winners coming from the robata grill" ("succulent morsels that help the beer go down… grilled mackerel is stunning"). / W6 0RR; www.tosa.uk; @tosa_hammersmith; Wed-Sun 11.30 pm; closed Mon & Tue.

Toulouse Lautrec SE11   £68   3 4 3
140 Newington Butts   020 7582 6800   1–3C
Complete with regular jazz in its upstairs club, this Gallic brasserie near Kennington's Imperial War Museum is one of the brighter sparks in this thin area, and open all day (most days the hours are noon till midnight).
/ SE11 4RN; www.toulouselautrec.co.uk; @tlvenue; Mon-Sat midnight, Sun 10.30 pm.

F S A

Townsend @ Whitechapel Gallery E1 £46 3 3 3
77-82 Whitechapel High St   020 7539 3303   10–2D

This "excellent gallery restaurant" has proved "a great addition to the Whitechapel area", with "well-cooked small plates of British food on an ever-changing menu". Chef Nick Gilkinson is making a speciality of this type of venue – he was previously at the Garden Museum in Lambeth. Here, he is joined by Joe Fox, ex-head chef at Petersham Nurseries. (The name refers to the gallery's architect, Charles Harrison Townsend.) / E1; www.whitechapelgallery.org/townsend; @whitechapelgallery; Tue, Sun 6 pm, Wed-Sat 11 pm; closed Tue & Sun D, closed Mon.

Tozi SW1 £61 3 2 3
8 Gillingham St   020 7769 9771   2–4B

"The place I return to over and over again" – this popular Pimlico spot in a hotel near Victoria station excels for its modern Venetian cicchetti ("Italian small/sharing plates") and "demon cocktails". Top Tip – "the airy room comes out best at lunchtime". / SW1V 1HN; www.tozirestaurant.co.uk; @tozirestaurant; Tue-Sat 9.30 pm; closed Sun & Mon.

Trattoria Raffaele SE26 £32 3 3 2
94 Sydenham Road   020 8778 6262   1–4D

"All ages have a great time in true Italian style" at this Sydenham fixture, a "family-owned trattoria with a devoted following of regulars" who come for the classic, fresh-cooked pasta and pizzas. / SE26 5JX; www.trattoriaraffaele.com; Tue-Sat 10 pm, Sun 4 pm; closed Tue-Sat L closed Sun D, closed Mon.

Trinity SW4 £113 5 4 3
4 The Polygon   020 7622 1199   11–2D

"You would pay a fortune to eat here if it was in Mayfair" – "Adam Byatt's excellent flagship" near Clapham Common is "so much more than a neighbourhood local" and "perfect for a fancy meal, especially if you live in south London!" Often inviting comparisons with nearby Chez Bruce, with ratings tracking its rival's closely, it is never quite as high in our ranking of London's Top 40 most-mentioned destinations (and has taken a little more flak for "high prices" of late). "Tastefully decorated" – the fact that it's "not pretentious, with just the right amount of friendliness from the staff" is key to its "pleasant" appeal, as, of course, is the "top-class food and wines". Top Tip – a large outside terrace is a relatively recent addition. / SW4 0JG; www.trinityrestaurant.co.uk; @Trinityclapham; Mon-Sun 8 pm.

Trinity Upstairs SW4 £64 3 3 3
4 The Polygon   020 3745 7227   11–2D

Upstairs from Adam Byatt's classy Clapham flagship Trinity, is "a casual space with big windows letting in plenty of light". It's frequented by locals in the know, who reckon that "Adam shoots and scores on a formula of tapas-themed sharing plates and accessible wine list". A mild dip in ratings this year backs up those who feel it's "slightly slipped from previous peaks", but no-one questions that it delivers "delicious, albeit simple food" and it's still very much "the local place to go if you can get a booking for a Sunday lunch". / SW4 0JG; www.trinity-upstairs.co.uk; @trinityclapham; Tue-Sat 8.30 pm, Sun 4 pm; closed Tue-Sat L closed Sun D, closed Mon.

Trishna W1 — £74 — 5 4 3
15-17 Blandford St   020 7935 5624   2–1A

"Absolutely flawless…", "exceptional and memorable…", "consistently superb" – the superlatives just keep coming for JKS Restaurants' original venture, which scores just as highly as its sibling, Gymkhana, even if the latter is much better known nowadays. It's a cosy and "upscale" experience, set in quirky U-shaped premises, off Marylebone High Street, and enlivened by "discreet and friendly" staff. Top Menu Tips – "don't leave without trying the lamb chops"; "mushroom biryani is a standout"; and "crazy as it may sound for a mere piece of bread, the duck keema naan is a real highlight."
/ W1U 3DG; www.trishnalondon.com; @trishnalondon; Mon-Sat 10.15 pm, Sun 9.45 pm; closed Mon & Tue L.

Trivet SE1 — £142 — 3 3 3
36 Snowsfields   020 3141 8670   10–4C

Since its opening in late 2019, this Bermondsey three-year-old from Fat Duck alumni Jonny Lake (chef) and Isa Bal (sommelier) has burnished a formidable reputation as one of the more interesting culinary arrivals of recent years. Jonny's cuisine is "superb and delicate" and "if the food is outstanding, then the wine list is outstanding-er!" – "an incredible and esoteric range" with "a focus on Georgia, Turkey and Armenia". And it's a "comfortable" space too where, for once, "you can hear yourself think". It would score higher were there not a less wowed minority of reporters who either found the overall approach "excessively serious", or who were "not convinced by the menu combinations despite having high hopes". / SE1 3SU; trivetrestaurant.co.uk; @trivetrestaurant; Wed-Sat, Tue 11 pm; closed Tue L, closed Sun & Mon.

La Trompette W4 — £101 — 4 3 2
5-7 Devonshire Rd   020 8747 1836   8–2A

"Still worth the schlep across town", says an E18-based fan of this "elegant corner of Chiswick" – "a brilliant, upscale neighbourhood restaurant" in a quiet backwater off the high street, which fans say is "pretty much on a level with its sibling Chez Bruce"; and which regularly features in the Top 40 most-mentioned restaurants in our annual diners' poll. Like its famous Wandsworth Common stablemate, its culinary attractions include modern British cuisine that's "up to date, with ingredients centre stage," "complemented by a very fine wine list," and with "a very good cheese selection". But whereas reports this year often match the flawless pattern established over two decades ("just effortlessly excellent…"; "we have been regulars for a decade…never disappoints…"; "post-lockdown it continues to shine…"), there is also a growing minority concern that "while the food is still very good, the service has slipped", with quite a few accounts of a "haphazard and brusque" experience. "Maybe it's just because of these difficult times…" / W4 2EU; www.latrompette.co.uk; @latrompettechiswick; Wed & Thu 9 pm, Fri & Sat 10 pm, Sun 3 pm; closed Sun D, closed Mon & Tue.

Trullo N1 — £78 — 3 3 3
300-302 St Paul's Rd   020 7226 2733   9–2D

"It's so good to have on my doorstep" – Tim Sidiatan and Jordan Frieda's "teeming local favourite" is "precisely the type of neighbourhood spot everyone wants to have": "a relaxed, chic atmosphere makes for a stress-free, no-frills meal out that just feels special" ("choose downstairs for romance"). "Italian-inspired open-fire cooking is a focus, with frequently changing fish and meat dishes," but "it's worth a visit for the pasta alone". And it all comes at "sensible prices". Top Tip – "mouthwatering ragu!"
/ N1 2LH; www.trullorestaurant.com; Mon-Sat 10.30 pm, Sun 9.30 pm; no Amex.

FSA

Tsunami SW4 £57 4 3 2
5-7 Voltaire Rd   020 7978 1610   11–1D
"Excellent modern Japanese food with a twist" has given this Clapham local a cutting-edge vibe that has barely faltered since its launch in 2001 by a trio of ex-Nobu chefs. Top Menu Tips – "perfect black cod (gin dara) and the best scallops ever: presented flaming in a sea shell with enoki mushrooms in a creamy chilli sauce with the crunch of tobiko. Sublime!" / SW4 6DQ; www.tsunamirestaurant.co.uk; @tsunami_restaurants; Sun-Thu 9.30 pm, Fri & Sat 10.30 pm; closed Mon-Fri L; no Amex.

Turnips with Tomas Lidakevicius SE1 £120 4 3 3
43 Borough Market, Off Bedale Street   020 7357 8356   10–4C
Tomas Lidakevicius produces "very innovative dishes using seasonal produce" at this zeitgeisty venture, attached to a greengrocer's stall in Borough Market, where a pop-up quickly went permanent in 2021. You book either for the sharing plates or full (£90) tasting menu experience – in either case "the place feels like being in a market stall to create an evening to remember; and it's close to the Thames for a nice walk home". / SE1 9AH; www.turnipsboroughmarket.com/restaurant; @turnipsborough; Wed-Sat 11.30 pm; closed Mon & Tue & Sun.

12:51 by chef James Cochran N1 £54 3 2 3
107 Upper Street   07934 202269   9–3D
"When the food is good it can be amazing" at former Ledbury chef James Cochran's Islington venue, which fans say "deserves to be better known" for his "fantastic tasting menu at sensible prices" (including "interesting" ingredients such as mutton and goat that reference the chef's part-Caribbean heritage). Even some fans can acknowledge one or two "samey" results, though, and grades slipped a fraction this year due a few disappointments. Perhaps any unevenness is due to distraction from other projects: in June 2022 he opened Valderrama's – a 90s-themed sports bar a short walk along Upper Street featuring the buttermilk fried chicken he developed for his Around The Cluck lockdown project. / N1 1QN; www.1251.co.uk; @1251_twelve_fifty_one; Tue-Sat 11 pm, Sun 8 pm; closed Tue-Thu L, closed Mon; payment – credit card only; booking online only.

28 Church Row NW3 £57 4 4 3
28 Church Row   020 7993 2062   9–2A
Serving "the best tapas in Hampstead" – this "wonderful little hideaway" serves "simply exceptional vegetable plates" as well as "great fish and meat", with Italian as well as Spanish dishes on the menu. In the gracious approach to St John-at-Hampstead – it's "a brilliant conversion: they really got the ghost out of this basement", ensuring a "fun visit every time". / NW3 6UP; www.28churchrow.com; @28churchrow; Mon-Sat 10.30 pm, Sun 9.30 pm; closed Mon-Thu L.

28-50 £80 2 2 2
15-17 Marylebone Lane, W1   020 7486 7922   3–1A
4 Great Portland Street, W1   020 7420 0630   3–1C **NEW**
300 King's Road, SW3   020 7349 9818   6–3C
96 Draycott Ave, SW3   020 7581 5208   6–2C
An "impressive wine list" is the undoubted highlight of this small group, with branches in the West End and Chelsea – the newest branch is a 120-cover site near Oxford Circus. No-one has terrible things to say about its food selection, though, which is judged "passable…", "OK…", "…tasty if a little pricey".

FSA

24 The Oval SW9 £50 343
24 Clapham Road 020 7735 6111 11–1D

'Old-fashioned, modern British cooking' is the promise at this "very enjoyable" bistro near Oval tube – sister restaurant to Clapham's Knife and with a menu that similarly makes a feature of both top steaks and Sunday lunch. / SW9 0JG; www.24theoval.co.uk; @24theoval; Wed-Sat 9.30 pm, Sun 4.30 pm; closed Wed-Sat L closed Sun D, closed Mon & Tue.

Twist Connubio W1 £69 332
42 Crawford St 020 7723 3377 2–1A

"Fantastic food and professional service" combine at this Marylebone tapas bar, where Amalfi-born chef Eduardo Tuccillo creates a 'connubio' or marriage of Mediterranean flavours, drawing broadly on Spain for the meat dishes and his native Italy for vegetables. If choosing is tricky, there is a range of tasting menus to ease ordering. / W1H 1JW; www.twistconnubio.com; @twistconnubio; Sun-Wed-Sat 11 pm; closed Sun-Wed L.

Two Brothers N3 £38 322
297-303 Regent's Park Rd 020 8346 0469 1–1B

"Excellent fish" and "friendly and helpful" staff ensure that this smart and well-run chippy remains a Finchley favourite after more than a quarter of a century. "Been eating here for years – it's always good!" / N3 1DP; www.twobrothers.co.uk; Tue-Sun 10 pm; closed Mon.

222 Veggie Vegan W14 £45 332
222 North End Rd 020 7381 2322 8–2D

"Excellent food and service" earns the thumbs-up for this small, 100% vegan café, just north of the gyratory joining Fulham's North End Road with the Lillie Road. Their version of a 'burger' is made with asparagus and petits pois, served on house gluten-free bread. / W14 9NU; www.222vegan.com; @222vegancuisine; Tue-Sun 9 pm; closed Mon.

2 Veneti W1 £54 322
10 Wigmore Street 020 7637 0789 3–1B

This "honest Italian" near Wigmore Hall is "one of the few places in London where you can eat cuisine of the Veneto region"; "the dishes are simply prepared with high-quality ingredients," and there's a good wine list to match. It's not wildly fashionable, but "always provides an enjoyable meal served by professional staff in a relaxed ambience". / W1U 2RD; www.2veneti.com; @2veneti; Mon-Fri 9.45 pm, Sat 10.30 pm; closed Sat L, closed Sun.

Uli W11 £73 344
5 Ladbroke Road 020 3141 5878 7–2B

A "wonderful local with delicious Thai/China/Singapore-inspired Asian food" that's now in its second incarnation – a stripped-wood and pastel-shades venue in Ladbroke Grove, having moved from All Saints Road, where it opened in 1997. "Great service under owner Michael Lim's watchful eyes." "There is a large outdoor covered terrace at the front, warm in winter and cool in summer". BREAKING NEWS: in late 2022 a new branch will open in Seymour Village. / W11 3PA; www.ulilondon.com; @ulilondon; Mon-Sat midnight, Sun 11 pm.

Umu W1 £153 443
14-16 Bruton Pl 020 7499 8881 3–2C

The "amazing" Kyoto-style kaiseki menu is a longstanding fixture of this low-key stalwart, in a quiet Mayfair mews (which was sold out of administration in 2020 after the collapse of the M.A.R.C. group). But, under executive chef, Ryo Kamatsu, it also offers a luxurious à la carte ranging from caviar to British game to sushi created from the finest Cornish fish. Predictably, there are complaints of "small portions at exquisite prices", but this remains one of London's most notable addresses for Japanese cuisine. / W1J 6LX; www.umurestaurant.com; @umurestaurant; Tue-Sat 10 pm; closed Sun & Mon; no shorts; booking max 10 may apply.

FSA RATINGS: FROM 1 POOR — 5 EXCEPTIONAL

Unwined SW17 £33   3 4 2
21-23 Tooting High Street   020 3583 9136   11–2C

Laura Aitkin & Kiki Evans's "quirky" wine bar in Tooting Market is "worth a visit for a fun evening" spent with an "eclectic wine list and food menu" – the latter from a succession of guest chefs ("go for the unusual wines based on themes e.g. myths"). The pair have a second wine bar in a shipping container by Waterloo station. / SW17 0SN; unwinedbars.co.uk; @UnwinedSW17; Wed-Sat 11 pm; closed Wed L, closed Mon & Tue & Sun; booking online only.

Upstairs at The George W1 £80
55 Great Portland Street   no tel   2–1B

The upstairs dining room of this 18th-century pub close to Oxford Circus has reopened under a dream team of owners JKS (the group behind Gymkhana, Bao, Arcade Food Hall etc) chef James Knappett of Kitchen Table and publican Dominic Jacobs of the Running Horse. The same formula has been an uneven success at The Cadogan Arms, but early feedback here is more encouraging. / W1W 7LQ; thegeorge.london; @thegeorgepublichouse; Wed-Sat 10 pm, Sun 6 pm; closed Mon & Tue.

Le Vacherin W4 £71   4 4 3
76-77 South Parade   020 8742 2121   8–1A

"Authentic bourgeois French cuisine" is on the menu at this *"old-fashioned"* but *"superbly run"* Gallic fixture with a *"lovely atmosphere"* by Acton Green. *"Classic and reliable but with real flair"*, locals consider themselves *"lucky to have this in W4"*, while plenty of regulars from further afield appreciate the *"very good value for a full-service French restaurant"*. / W4 5LF; www.levacherin.com; @le_vacherin; Mon-Sat 10.30 pm, Sun 9 pm.

Vardo SW3 £72   2 2 3
9 Duke of York Square   020 7101 1199   6–2D

With its *"great location"* and *"lovely outside tables"* on Duke of York Square, together with the bold contemporary architecture of its circular premises (complete with roof garden), this three-year-old – named after the traditional Romany horse-drawn wagon – has much going for it. Fans would say this includes its diverse menu (similar to its Caravan group siblings) which *"ranges from tasty Levantine dishes to delicious pizzas, so giving great variety for families to enjoy"*. But ratings are undercut by complaints of *"disappointing food"* and a feeling that *"they need to do something about the service"*. / SW3 4LY; vardorestaurant.co.uk; @vardorestaurant; Mon & Tue, Sun 10 pm, Wed & Thu 11 pm, Fri & Sat midnight.

Vasco & Piero's Pavilion W1 £72   4 5 4
11 D'Arblay Street   020 7437 8774   4–1C

"Welcome back!" Every cloud has a silver lining and *"having been unceremoniously evicted from its longtime Poland Street location during Covid"*, this *"delightful"* Soho veteran has *"found a new, better site just round the corner"* (it's actually the second time the restaurant, founded in 1971, has had to move). *"Traditional, Tuscan food as it is meant to taste, with a wine list to match"* are served by the *"superb"* staff in a *"most convivial"* setting. *"They are good at remembering their customers"* and *"it's a great place to have a conversation, as they play no music"*. / W1W 8DT; www.vascosfood.com; Tue-Sat 10 pm; closed Sat L, closed Sun & Mon.

Veeraswamy W1 £94   4 4 4
Victory Hs, 99-101 Regent St   020 7734 1401   4–4B

Approaching its centenary, London's oldest Indian, near Piccadilly Circus, continues to thrive as part of the high-quality group that also owns Chutney Mary. It may be an *"old favourite"* for many fans of decades' standing, but the *"relaxing"* interior is modern and without any 'heritage' appeal. *"Service is friendly and professional – not pushy, but there when you want them"* – and the cooking has *"sublime flavours and fragrances"*. / W1B 4RS; www.veeraswamy.com; @veeraswamy.london; Mon-Sat 10.30 pm, Sun 10 pm; closed Mon L; booking max 12 may apply.

F S A

Vermuteria N1 £56
38-39 Coal Drops Yard   020 3479 1777   9–3C

The vintage styling – that of a classic European café – is at odds with ever-more über-sleek Coal Drops Yard. Reports on Anthony Demetre's all-day operation (named for the vermouth which is a feature of its drink offering) are still few, but suggest its well-sourced tapas, charcuterie and more substantial fare (including steak) can make it a handy refuge, from breakfast onwards (for which there's a dedicated selection). / N1N 4AB; vermuteria.cc; @vermuteria_london; Sun-Wed 10 pm, Thu-Sat 11 pm.

Via Emilia N1 £48   3 3 2
37a Hoxton Square   020 7613 0508   13–1B

"Exemplary small-plates and pasta" is the focus at this small Hoxton showcase for the marvellous cuisine of Emilia-Romagna (think Bologna, Modena, Parma, etc). The dishes are even named in the local dialect. / N1 6NN; www.via-emilia.com; @viaemilia.restaurant; Mon-Sat 11 pm, Sun 10.30 pm.

Il Vicolo SW1 £67   3 3 2
3-4 Crown Passage   020 7839 3960   3–4D

"A real 'find' amongst the big beasts", tucked away in a St James's alleyway, "this small family-run Italian is welcoming and good value" – "intimate when quiet, a nice buzz when fuller". They are "clearly passionate about their ingredients", and offer "absolutely delightful service". / SW1Y 6PP; www.ilvicolorestaurant.co.uk; @ilvicolo.restaurant; Mon-Sat 10 pm; closed Sun.

The Victoria SW14 £60   3 3 3
10 West Temple Sheen   020 8876 4238   11–2A

Close to Richmond Park's Sheen Gate, this sprawling and "very friendly local pub" serves "outstanding food" from TV chef and owner Paul Merrett. A refurbished Victorian tavern, it has six boutique bedrooms, a large garden and a conservatory where family Sunday lunches are a big feature. / SW14 7RT; victoriasheen.co.uk; @thevictoriasheen; Wed-Sun 10.30 pm; closed Mon & Tue; no Amex.

Viet Food W1 £41   3 2 3
34-36 Wardour St   020 7494 4555   5–3A

"Delicious" Vietnamese street-food classics and original creations from the founder, ex-Hakkasan chef Jeff Tan, draw a bustling crowd to this two-storey warehouse-style venue in Chinatown, which is "perfect pre- or post-theatre". It now has a sibling in South Ken, Go Viet. Top Menu Tip – "the green garlic sauce is a must". / W1D 6QT; www.vietnamfood.co.uk; @vietfoodlondon; Sun-Thu 10.30 pm, Fri & Sat 11 pm.

Viet Garden N1 £34   3 3 2
207 Liverpool Rd   020 7700 6040   9–3D

This "reliable" family-run Vietnamese in Islington welcomes a steady crowd, and "almost everyone eating here is local". It has "a friendly atmosphere created by people who love their native cuisine". Top Menu Tip – "the pork kho is deeply savoury, warming and comforting on cold winter nights". / N1 1LX; www.vietgarden.co.uk; @vietgardenuk; Sun-Thu 11 pm, Fri & Sat 11.30 pm; closed Mon-Fri L; no Amex.

Vijay NW6 £38   4 4 1
49 Willesden Ln   020 7328 1087   1–1B

"Proper Indian food, proper paper napkins" – this Kilburn institution, which claims to have been Britain's first South Indian restaurant when it opened in 1964, remains "exactly as it was when the great Michael Winner recommended it back in 1990-something. 'Historic', said the old boy, and it still is". "Unfortunately you have to eat in drab surroundings" – which is a tactful way of putting it – but fans (who apparently include luminaries ranging from Diana Ross and Harrison Ford to the Indian cricket team), reckon it's worth it for the "top-notch" food and "really polite and

professional" service. It caters equally for "meat-eaters, vegetarians and vegans". Top Tip – you may be tempted to eat in the more salubrious quarters of your own home, but the nosh is "so much better fresh than take-away". / NW6 7RF; www.vijayrestaurant.co.uk; @vijayindiauk; Sun-Thu 10.45 pm, Fri & Sat 11.45 pm; no booking.

Villa Bianca NW3 £71 2 2 3
1 Perrins Ct   020 7435 3131   9–2A

"Classic old-school Italian" in a "lovely setting in Hampstead", with white linen and walls living up to its name. Even some who consider it "an old favourite" acknowledge that the experience is "hit 'n' miss", with sometimes "snooty service" but it still draws an enthusiastic crowd: "my business days are over, but judging by the other diners there must be plenty of business going on!" / NW3 1QS; villabiancagroup.com/villabianca; @villabiancanw3; Tue-Sat 11.30 pm, Sun 10.30 pm; closed Mon.

Villa Di Geggiano W4 £87 3 4 4
66-68 Chiswick High Road   020 3384 9442   8–2B

"A little piece of super-smooth Chiantishire dropped into W4" – this "spacious and comfortable" venue on a trafficky highway between Chiswick and Hammersmith makes "an amazing neighbourhood restaurant – very lucky locals!". Named after the 500-year-old Tuscan estate that owns it and supplies organic wines for the list, it "isn't cheap but the food is generally excellent" and "presentation and service are impeccable". / W4 1SY; www.villadigeggiano.co.uk; @villa_di_geggiano_london; Tue-Fri 10.30 pm, Sun 9 pm; closed Mon & Sat.

The Vincent Rooms, Westminster Kingsway College SW1 £45 3 2 3
76 Vincent Sq   020 7802 8391   2–4C

"Top-quality food from third-year students at ridiculously low prices" is the term-time offer at this Vincent Square venue operated by Westminster Kingsway College. "Service by first-years can be very random but is always entertaining!" Choose between the formal Escoffier Room and the more relaxed brasserie. Top Tip – "excellent sourdough bread also at knockdown prices for sale in the foyer". / SW1P 2PD; www.thevincentrooms.co.uk; @thevincentrooms; Mon, Fri 3 pm, Tue-Thu 9 pm; closed Mon & Fri D, closed Sat & Sun; no Amex.

Vinoteca £63 2 2 2
18 Devonshire Rd, W4   020 3701 8822   8–2A
One Pancras Sq, N1   020 3793 7210   9–3C
Borough Yards, Stoney Street, SE1   020 3376 3000   10–4C NEW
7 St John St, EC1   020 7253 8786   10–1B
Bloomberg Arcade, Queen Victoria Street, EC2   awaiting tel   10–3C

"It's wonderful being able to choose so many wines by the glass" from the "eclectic list" at these popular modern wine bars, liked for their approachable contemporary style. "Obviously the liquid refreshment is the main point here", but the "simple" cooking can be "more assured than you might expect", if from a "limited menu". A new branch opened in late 2021 at Borough Yards in SE1, while in late 2022 its oldest site, on Seymour Place in Marylebone, shut up shop. Other particularly notable branches include the one right by King's Cross station (with a convenient and excellent terrace) and Chiswick. / www.vinoteca.co.uk.

FSA

Vivat Bacchus £72 3 3 3
4 Hay's Ln, SE1   020 7234 0891   10–4C
47 Farringdon St, EC4   020 7353 2648   10–2A
This duo of venues in Farringdon and London Bridge have some of the capital's best collections of South African wine, alongside a selection of 'Old World' vintages. To soak them up, there's a miscellaneous assortment of dishes majoring in steaks, with some Saffa-inspired garnishes, and SA-style dried meats providing the most exotic options. Save space for the cheese, chosen in a walk-in room. / www.vivatbacchus.co.uk.

Volta do Mar WC2 £66 4 4 3
13-15 Tavistock Street   020 3034 0028   5–3D
An "always good", culinarily interesting Covent Garden three-year-old, from Salt Yard founder Simon Mullins and his Portuguese wife Isabel Almeida Da Silva. Named after the 'return from the sea': it serves a menu not just from Portugal but from the territories it traded with or colonised, from Brazil in the west via parts of Africa to Goa, Macau and Nagasaki in the east. / WC2W 7PS; voltadomar.co.uk; @voltadomar_ldn; Thu-Sat, Tue, Wed 10.30 pm; closed Tue, Wed L, closed Sun & Mon.

VQ £55 2 2 3
St Giles Hotel, 111a Gt Russell St, WC1   020 7636 5888   5–1A
325 Fulham Rd, SW10   020 7376 7224   6–3B
9 Aldgate High St, EC3   020 3301 7224   10–2D
"Don't think high end, but these local 24-hour cafés are reliable and pleasant for a plain meal at any hour of the night or day", but particularly come into their own in the wee hours. In fact, only the well-known Chelsea original and the Aldgate spin-off (in a hotel) are open 24/7: opening hours in Bloomsbury are more selective. (Aldgate also has a standalone bar with a 24-hour alcohol licence). / www.vingtquatre.co.uk; vqrestaurants.

Wagamama £51 2 2 2
Branches throughout London
"You know what you'll get" at this Japanese-inspired chain, which celebrated its 30th birthday last year: "quick, tasty noodles with something for everyone", all at a "relatively cheap" price. True, it can seem merely "fine" or "unexciting in every sense" and ("anyone wanting spice might need to look elsewhere)". But, in particular, it's "a solid family bet" – "very child-friendly" and "kids love it". (Now with over 150 branches in the UK, in May 2022 they launched a new London flagship at Marble Arch, complete with outside seating by Hyde Park and a new cocktail menu). / www.wagamama.com; SRA-3 stars.

Wahaca £46 2 3 3
Branches throughout London
"A fun, cheerful Mexican atmosphere" and "enjoyable, fresh tasting" street food dishes can still make "an excellent standby" of this stalwart chain, which has 10 sites in London nowadays. "Even if nothing on the menu is going to wow, its consistent quality and value are reassuring", with ratings and popularity starting to regain their historic high standing since a majority stake was sold to Nando's owner, Dick Enthoven, a couple of years ago. / www.wahaca.com; wahaca; SRA-3 stars.

The Wallace,
The Wallace Collection W1 £45 2 2 5
Hertford Hs, Manchester Sq   020 7563 9505   3–1A
The "fabulous atrium" of the famous Wallace Collection, just north of Oxford Street, makes "a perfect setting for a lovely tea" – which is also "very good value compared with many places providing afternoon tea in London". The lunch offering is not nearly as enticing. / W1U 3BN; www.peytonandbyrne.co.uk; @peytonandbyrne; Mon-Sun 4 pm; closed Mon-Sun D; no Amex; booking max 10 may apply.

FSA RATINGS: FROM 1 POOR — 5 EXCEPTIONAL

The Walmer Castle W11   £45
58 Ledbury Rd   020 4580 1196   7–1B
A perpetual hit with the minted ne'er-do-wells of Notting Hill, this chichi old boozer changed hands in early 2022. Previously a plaything of Guy Ritchie and David Beckham, its new owner is posh nightclub owner, Piers Adam, owner of Prince Harry's old favourite, Mahiki. Nowadays billed as 'in collaboration with The Craigellachie Hotel' (also owned by Adam), the website promises that 'The Walmer brings the essence of Speyside to London' although – cue cynical laughter – this apparently includes such Caledonian specialities as Crispy Monkfish Tacos, Truffled Lobster Macaroni, and Salmon Ceviche. Whether the trustafarians who cram the place will notice anything other than the fun new refurb and more single malts at the bar is debatable. / W11 2AJ; www.walmercastlenottinghill.co.uk; @walmercastle_nottinghill; Mon-Thu 11.30 pm, Fri & Sat midnight, Sun 10.30 pm; closed Mon & Tue L.

Walter's SE21   £67   3 3 4
84 Park Hall Road   020 8014 8548   1–4D
Off the beaten track, in a shopping parade near Dulwich College, this "very traditional brasserie" *was opened a year ago by* "the guys behind The Oystermen, seafood royalty of Covent Garden", *in a surprise move that avoided the danger of being typecast. It has* "a very strong vibe of a good neighbourhood restaurant serving solid local fare" *– prawn cocktail, lamb, ox cheek –* "it's not food to blow your socks off, but it's not intended to". / SE21 8SW; waltersdulwich.co.uk; @waltersdulwich; Wed-Sat 11 pm, Sun 6 pm; closed Mon & Tue.

The Water House Project E2   £152   4 3 4
1 Corbridge Crescent   07841 804119   14–2B
"A really exceptional experience... a real find... a fantastic night out" *– Gabriel Waterhouse inspires acclaim for his relocated Bethnal Green supper club, whose gracious permanent home occupies a high-ceilinged space in Cambridge Heath. Every night, there's* "a one-sitting, 9-course tasting menu with low-intervention wine" *(or non-alcoholic pairings) delivering* "some really innovative dishes". *Ratings would be even higher, were it not for one or two reports along the lines of* "love the new menu, but too many foams…" / E2 9DS; www.thewaterhouseproject.com; @thewaterhouseproject; Wed-Sat 11 pm; closed Wed-Sat L, closed Mon & Tue & Sun.

The Wells Tavern NW3   £69   3 4 3
30 Well Walk   020 7794 3785   9–1A
"Possibly the best overall eating experience in NW3" *– this characterful Georgian tavern in Hampstead (run for two decades by Beth Coventry, sister of the veteran restaurant critic Fay Maschler) is a great all-rounder. The* "consistent food is excellent for a local pub", "the setting is delightful" *(choose from three different dining rooms) and* "it's a friendly place that combines well with a walk on the Heath". / NW3 1BX; thewellshampstead.london; @thewellshampstead; Mon-Sat 10 pm, Sun 9.30 pm; no Amex.

West 4th SW6   £52   3 2 2
175 New King's Road   020 8161 1776   11–1B
This Parson's Green yearling is a tribute to the Canadian West Coast, and is named after the Vancouver street where founders Livia Boumeester and Louisa Stevenson-Hamilton hung out when they lived there. "Don't expect stars; do expect earthy comfort food." *Poutine – the chips, cheese curds and gravy combo that is Canada's gift to a hungry world – is on the menu, along with* "the best mac 'n' cheese around". / SW6 4SW; www.west4thlondon.co.uk; @west4thkitchen; Tue-Thu 10 pm, Fri & Sat 11 pm, Sun 4 pm; closed Sun D, closed Mon; payment – credit card only.

Westerns Laundry N5 £68 3 3 4
34 Drayton Park 020 7700 3700 9–2D

"Beautifully prepared fish-centric tapas and a super-cool setting" make this "fab Holloway Road local" small-plates venue "a perfect place to impress your out-of-towner mates… or even those that live in London!" There's a "small but interesting list" of "brilliant orange and other low-intervention wines". Top Tip – "leave space for the rum baba – you'll need to share". / N5 1PB; www.westernslaundry.com; @westernslaundry; Tue-Sat 10.30 pm, Sun 9 pm; closed Tue-Fri L, closed Mon.

The Wet Fish Café NW6 £53 3 3 3
242 West End Lane 020 7443 9222 1–1B

"A top local that's still going strong". This "cut above" West Hampstead fixture, set in the conversion of a 1930s fishmongers (and still selling retail) has a large fan club fostered by its "quirky and passionate" approach. The top draw is the "short selection of well-priced, very fresh fish", but it's "everything a true café should be," too (serving all day). "It might score even higher if the menu offered more choice." / NW6 1LG; www.thewetfishcafe.co.uk; @thewetfishcafe; Mon-Sun 11 pm; booking evening only.

The Wigmore, The Langham W1 £63 4 4 4
15 Langham Place, Regent Street 020 7965 0198 2–1B

Michel Roux Junior has reimagined the British pub as only a French master chef could at this fine hostelry near Oxford Circus – a partnership with the neighbouring Langham Hotel, who carved the pub out of some under-used space. "Simple British dishes are presented as you have never tasted them before" ("shepherd's pie and Scotch eggs were particularly memorable, but everything was delightful") and its "great buzzy ambience" helps make it an excellent West End meeting place. / W1W 3DE; www.the-wigmore.co.uk; @wigmorelondon; Tue-Sat 11 pm; closed Sun & Mon.

Wild Heart W1 £39
20 Warwick Street 020 7292 6100 4–3B

"Great name… even better food" say fans of this casual, Japanese-inspired dining experience within a Soho hotel, whose all-day dining possibilities (breakfast, lunch, dinner, and afternoon tea…) were conceived by star chef Garry Hollihead. Too limited feedback as yet, though, for a full rating of its mix of poke bowls, salads, sliders and main plates, complemented by an oriental cocktail list and sake menu. / W1W 5NF; www.sanctumsoho.com/restaurant; @karmasanctumldn; Mon & Tue 11, Wed-Sat 10 pm, Sun 11.30; closed Mon & Tue, Sun D.

Wild Honey St James SW1 £96 3 3 3
Sofitel, 8 Pall Mall 020 7389 7820 2–3C

"Perfect, joyous French cooking with pitch-perfect flavours" inspires fans of Anthony Demetre's well-regarded venture, which he moved here from Mayfair pre-Covid. The very "spacious" and "tasteful" dining room and its superb position – just off Trafalgar Square, but away from the madding crowds – makes it an excellent business choice (or pre/post-theatre). In terms of value, many diners tip any set options here over the à la carte. / SW1S 5NG; www.wildhoneystjames.co.uk; @wildhoneystjames; Wed-Sat 9.30 pm, Tue 2.30 pm; closed Tue D, closed Sun & Mon.

Wild Tavern SW3 £111 2 3 3
2 Elystan Street   020 8191 9885   6–2C

"Hopping Chelsea local" (overlooking Chelsea Green), whose owners George Bukhov-Weinstein and Ilya Demichev also play a part in other casual luxury brands such as Beast and Burger & Lobster. Here, a vaguely Alpine interior hosts an offering whose menu incorporates a raw bar and pastas, plus prime steaks and fish grills sold by the 100g. Results are generally good, but whether they represent fair value is debated ("such an exceptional bill should not be presented to anyone with a weak heart…") / SW3 3NS; www.wildtavern.co.uk; @wildtavern; Mon-Sat 10 pm, Sun 9.30 pm.

Wiltons SW1 £108 3 3 3
55 Jermyn St   020 7629 9955   3–3C

"Like a London club but with infinitely better food" – this "very civilised" St James's veteran (London's oldest restaurant, established in 1742, but not on this site) is "a real throwback to another era" ("it's probably not the place to attract 'influencers', whoever or whatever they are!"). The menu (which majors in fish and seafood) is "as traditional as one can expect (as is the clientele)" – you are served "classic food, classically executed and classically served" and at its best results are "simply exceptional". "Service is old-school professional" although, perhaps due to the strains of Covid, did not enjoy its customary 5/5 rating this year. Even so, Wiltons remains "a great place for meeting on business" and its pricing is such that it's best to let the corporate credit card take the strain whenever possible. Top Menu Tips – "the Dover sole is still the best in the capital" and "their lobster thermidor is rich and everything you want in an indulgent food item". Game is excellent in season and they do a "magnificent bone-in rib served from the trolley". / SW1Y 6LX; www.wiltons.co.uk; @wiltons1742; Mon-Sat 10.30 pm; closed Sat L, closed Sun.

The Windmill W1 £60 3 2 3
6-8 Mill St   020 7491 8050   4–2A

"Great home-made pies (in five flavours) and mash to go with a pint of Young's bitter – what's not to like?" about this "traditional pub" just off Regent Street, from the same stable as the Guinea Grill. There's a newish (est. 2020) upstairs restaurant and terrace which is more what you might expect in Mayfair, white tablecloths and all. / W1S 2AZ; www.windmillmayfair.co.uk; @windmill_pub; Mon-Sat 11 pm, Sun 6 pm.

The Wine Library EC3 £48 2 2 4
43 Trinity Sq   020 7481 0415   10–3D

This 19th-century vaulted wine cellar near Tower Hill offers "an amazing and enjoyable selection of wines to buy and then open and drink right there" (at off-licence prices plus £9.50 corkage). "Service is 'fetch your own'", and platters of buffet-style "finger food" – charcuterie, French cheeses, and more – contribute to an "always agreeable visit". / EC3N 4DJ; www.winelibrary.co.uk; Tue-Fri 8 pm, Mon 6 pm, Sat 5.30 pm; closed Sat D, closed Sun.

The Wolseley W1 £77 1 2 4
160 Piccadilly   020 7499 6996   3–3C

"The sheer style of the room" helps create an "unbeatable buzz" at this "very classy and smartly located" Continental Grand Café by The Ritz, which has, for nearly 20 years, established itself as London's premier venue for a "reliably impressive" business occasion; but also as "the absolute go-to for a totally unrivalled breakfast" ("a cliché, but really it is the best place to enjoy eggs Benedict in London"). And "afternoon tea is excellent too, with a good choice of sandwiches and cakes." Established by Christopher Corbin and Jeremy King in 2003 in an erstwhile Edwardian car showroom (which provided the restaurant's name), it has perennially been "the permanent buzz not the average food that's created the magic of the place". The "simple comfort fare at West End prices" has often rated poorly next to the "sparkling" atmosphere and "star-studded people watching" carefully cultivated by its well-connected founders. So "whether the place will survive *the recent departure of those same founders remains to be seen". A shareholder battle post-Covid saw Corbin & King edged out by their financial backers, the Thai Minor group, and many reporters fear "a ravens-leaving-the-tower moment" ("fingers crossed they don't let the money-men spoil this…"; "it's wait-and-see time…"; "if they ruin it, we will revolt…"). The schism happened in April 2022, immediately prior to our survey, and ratings this year are significantly down across the board. It could be that Brexit-induced staffing shortages bear some of the blame, but already some reporters fear the reason is clear: "it's lost its soul now Jeremy and Chris have been ousted".* / W1J 9EB; www.thewolseley.com; @thewolseley; Mon-Sat 11 pm, Sun 10 pm.

Wong Kei W1 £32 3|1|1
41-43 Wardour St 020 7437 8408 5–3A

"Tasty mountains of food" served with *"no frills"* make this Cantonese landmark one of London's most enduring low-budget eats. *"Yes, it's basic"* and the *"super-quick"* service *"no longer has the 'rudeness' of the 1990s"* that had its own masochistic entertainment value. But many reporters note that *"they are still visiting after decades, so something works"*: *"it's great cheap food"*. *"The ambience is tired with token Chinese decoration … wouldn't have it any other way!"* / W1D 6PY; Mon-Sat 11.30 pm, Sun 10.30 pm; cash only.

Wright Brothers £71 3|2|3
56 Old Brompton Rd, SW7 020 7581 0131 6–2B
11 Stoney St, SE1 020 7403 9554 10–4C
26 Circus Road West, SW8 020 7324 7734 11–1C

"The best oysters and crustacea in a bustling market-facing venue" is how many restaurant-goers think of this *"buzzy and packed"* small group, whose SE1 branch at Borough Market is better known than its Battersea Power Station sibling. *"Order from the blackboard for the freshest catch."* *"You come for the seafood, not the sparkling repartee"* and service *"can get a bit frazzled"*. (We have continued to list the South Kensington outlet, but as we go to press it is 'temporarily closed' due to staff shortages). / thewrightbrothers.co.uk; WrightBrosLTD.

Wulf & Lamb £53 3|2|2
243 Pavilion Road, SW1 020 3948 5999 6–2D
66 Chiltern Street, W1 020 8194 0000 2–1A

Plant-based versions of comfort-food classics such as black-bean burgers and *"interesting mac'n'cashew cheese"* are menu highlights at this pair of meat-free cafés, out to prove that vegan dining has graduated from shabby to chic. Its menu of plant-based borrowings from cuisines around the world impresses even the occasional carnivore – *"I forget I'm not vegan!"* / www.wulfandlamb.com.

Wun's W1 £61 3|2|3
24 Greek Street 020 8017 9888 5–2A

A *"very good"* modern take on classic Cantonese cuisine from Z He and Alex Peffly (of Bun House) is presented in an atmospheric *"neon-lit underground parlour in Soho, with the menus on newspapers, giving a gentlemen's club/opium den vibe"*. / W1W 4DZ; tearoom.bar; @wunstearoom; Tue-Fri midnight; closed Tue-Fri L, closed Mon, Sat & Sun; booking online only.

Xi'an Impression N7 £37 3|2|1
117 Benwell Rd 020 3441 0191 9–2D

"Cheap and authentic": *"the noodles are so unctuous and delicious"* at this canteen opposite the Emirates stadium – *"and it's BYO to boot"*. For Gooners, the *"excellent food tastes even better if Arsenal win"*. / N7; www.xianimpression.co.uk; @Xianimpression; Mon-Sun 10 pm; no booking.

FSA

Yama Momo SE22 020 8299 1007 1–4D £64 3 2 2
72 Lordship Ln
This "great local Japanese" in East Dulwich is the "small, younger brother of Tsunami in Clapham", and attracts a "buzzing crowd of local regulars" with its "good sushi and sashimi, crisp tempura, and sizzling hot plates of steak, chicken and fish". Service is "cheerful if occasionally haphazard". / SE22 8HF; www.yamamomo.co.uk; @yamamomo_eastdulwich; Mon-Thu 10 pm, Fri & Sat 10.30 pm, Sun 9.30 pm; closed Mon-Thu L.

Yard Sale Pizza £43 4 4 2
54 Blackstock Road, N4   020 7226 2651   9–1D
46 Westow Hill, SE19   020 8670 6386   1–4D
39 Lordship Lane, SE22   020 8693 5215   1–4D
393 Brockley Road, SE4   020 8692 8800   1–4D **NEW**
63 Bedford Hill, SW12   020 8772 1100   11–2C
622 High Road Leytonstone, E11   020 8539 5333   1–1D
15 Hoe Street, E17   020 8509 0888   1–1D
184 Hackney Road, E2   020 7739 1095   14–2A
105 Lower Clapton Rd, E5   020 3602 9090   14–1B
"Such good pizza in very decent sizes for the price" earns this (south) east London chain some of the highest ratings for pizza in the capital and they're "consistently quick" too. The latest addition to the group is a branch in Crofton Park. / yardsalepizza.com; yardsalepizza.

Yashin £109 4 3 3
117-119 Old Brompton Rd, SW7   020 7373 3990   6–2B
1a Argyll Rd, W8   020 7938 1536   6–1A
Flying under the radar, as they have for over a decade now, Yasuhiro Mineno's and Shinya Ikeda's offbeat duo – a two-floor site in a Kensington backstreet (est. 2010), and the newer 'Ocean House' spin-off (est. 2013, in the quirky former Brompton Library) – never inspire a huge volume of feedback, perhaps because they are by no means cheap. The owners have fine CVs though and all reports continue to say the sushi here can be exceptional. / yashinsushi.com.

Yauatcha £104 3 2 2
Broadwick House, 15-17 Broadwick St, W1   020 7494 8888   4–1C
Broadgate Circle, EC2   020 3817 9888   13–2B
"Exquisite" dim sum – in particular "addictive cheung fun and venison puffs" – have won fame for these Hakkasan spin-offs, which are quite different in nature. The original site occupies a "blingy, dark, rammed-full Soho basement" (and you can also eat in the ground-floor tea room); while the Broadgate spin-off is vast by comparison and much more swish and corporate, with large outside terraces for cocktails. Both outlets share the shortcomings of Hakkasan, though: they can be "sooooooo pricey", and service can be "slow" or "entitled". Top Tip – their "cakes are incredible; small and perfectly formed!" / www.yauatcha.com.

The Yellow House SE16 020 7231 8777 12–2A £52 3 4 3
126 Lower Rd
"A true local gem to be cherished in a downbeat area for restaurants" – this endearing local near Surrey Quays station wins applause for its "small and friendly team" and "always amazing" wood-fired pizza and other fare. "I could not be more relieved that these guys survived the pandemic!" / SE16 2UE; www.theyellowhouse.eu; @theyellowhouserestaurant; Wed & Thu 9.30 pm, Fri & Sat 10 pm, Sun 6.30 pm; closed Wed-Sun L, closed Mon & Tue.

Yuca W1 NEW
10 - 11 Lancashire Court 020 7518 9388 3–2B

The duo behind Brazilian-Japanese spot Mano, Alexis Colletta and Romain Fargette, are opening another Mayfair fusion haunt in the neighbourhood in summer 2022. This one will be Japanese-Mexican, sited where Mews of Mayfair (RIP) was, and will feature a 300-cover restaurant and a club in the basement. / W1W 1EY.

Zafferano SW1 £96 4 3 3
15 Lowndes St 020 7235 5800 6–1D

A short stroll from Knightsbridge, this Belgravia stalwart seems increasingly forgotten about, certainly compared with its mid-'90s glory days when it was the talk of the town. Its fans, though, continue to regard it as a "fantastic premium Italian", with a capable wine list and deftly realised pasta and other classic dishes. / SW1X 9EY; zafferanorestaurant.com; @zafferanorestaurant; Mon-Sun 10 pm.

Zaffrani N1 £48 2 2 2
47 Cross St 020 7226 5522 9–3D

This "handy local Indian restaurant" near the Almeida Theatre in Islington is rather smarter than the average curry house, and has a wide choice of fish and seafood dishes in addition to the standard meat and veg range. / N1 2BB; www.zaffrani.co.uk; @zaffrani_restaurant; Mon-Sun 10.30 pm; closed Mon-Sun L.

Zahter W1 £89 3 2 3
30-32 Foubert's Place 07775 156768 4–1B

"An impressive addition to the Carnaby Street scene" – this modern Eastern-Med newcomer from Turkish chef Esra Muslu is decorated in an informal café style that's deceptive given the high quality of the cuisine. The open kitchen and counter on the ground floor "give you so much to talk about (I just love watching the flames in the oven)" and "the food can be as light or heavy as you wish" according to which small plates you go for. "Love it"… but it can be "ridiculously noisy", "staff don't always seem to know what they're doing" and the small dishes come at chunky prices. / W1W 7PS; zahter.co.uk; @zahterlondon; Tue-Thu 11.30 pm, Fri & Sat 12.30 am; closed Sun & Mon.

Zaibatsu SE10 £41 3 3 2
96 Trafalgar Rd 020 8858 9317 1–3D

"Rough and ready, cramped, but charming" – this unassuming Japanese BYO on the edge of Greenwich is "mostly known for perfectly decent sushi at reasonable prices", along with some less commented-on pan-Asian dishes. / SE10 9UW; www.zaibatsufusion.co.uk; Tue-Sat 11 pm, Sun 9 pm; closed Mon; cash only.

Zaika of Kensington W8 £67 3 4 4
1 Kensington High Street 020 7795 6533 6–1A

The "beautiful dining room" ("an old bank building") hosts a menu inspired by the historic royal cuisine of Lucknow, at this smart restaurant near Kensington Gardens. It "never seems to make it into the 'top' lists", unlike its highly rated stablemate Tamarind in Mayfair, "but the modern cooking never disappoints and is of the highest quality". / W8 5NP; www.zaikaofkensington.com; @zaikaofkensington; Mon-Sat 10.15 pm, Sun 9.15pm; closed Sun & Mon L; no trainers; credit card required to book.

Zephyr W11 NEW
100 Portobello Road 020 4599 1177 7–2B

In Notting HIll, this summer 2022 newcomer from Pachamama Group occupies a sizable 3,000 sq ft site. A restaurant and late-night cocktail bar, it aims to apply the bold flavours of Asian cuisine to a Greek-inspired formula… that's a new one on us. / W11 2QD; www.zephyr.london/book-a-table; Mon-Sun midnight.

FSA

Zheng SW3 £69   3 3 2
4 Sydney St   020 7352 9890   6–2C

"Really interesting Malay/Chinese combo" cuisine sets this smart, if low key, Chelsea venue apart, minimally decked out with painted black walls. Spun off from an original in Oxford, it is named after the Chinese admiral who explored South East Asia 600 years ago. "Staff are very friendly and helpful" in navigating the menu, with its collision of Chinese, Malay and Indian food cultures. / SW3 6PP; www.zhengchelsea.co.uk; Mon, Wed-Sun 11 pm; closed Mon, Wed-Fri L, closed Tue; no shorts.

Zia Lucia £52   4 2 2
61 Blythe Road, W14   020 7371 4096   8–1C
Boxpark Wembley, 18 Olympic Way, HA9   020 3744 4427   1–1A
61 Stoke Newington High Street, N16   020 8616 8690   1–1C **NEW**
157 Holloway Road, N7   020 7700 3708   9–2D
65 Balham High Road, SW12   020 3093 0946   11–2C
356 Old York Road, SW18   020 3971 0829   11–2B
12a Piazza Walk, E1   020 7702 2525   10–2D

"Love the different pizza-base options such as charcoal and gluten-free" (there's also wholemeal and 'traditional') at these popular pizza pit stops, where the dough is fermented for 48 hours then cooked in purpose-built gas and wood ovens. Two branches were added in 2022: in Stoke Newington in April and in Canary Wharf in summer. / zialucia.com; zialuciapizza.

Ziani's SW3 £66   3 3 3
45 Radnor Walk   020 7351 5297   6–3C

This diminutive but "highly enjoyable" Venetian trattoria off Chelsea's King's Road (named in honour of the Doge who laid out Venice's Piazza San Marco) is "really popular with the locals" for its "great buzz", led by the "loud and funny waiters". Founder Roberto Colussi died five years ago, but it has carried on in the way he intended, and will celebrate its 40th anniversary next year. / SW3 4BP; www.ziani.co.uk; Mon-Sun 10 pm.

Zoilo W1 £84   3 3 3
9 Duke St   020 7486 9699   3–1A

Grilled beef, both Argentine and British, is the star of the show at Argentinian chef-patron Diego Jacquet's comfortable modern outfit near the Wallace Collection – and, after more than a decade, it "hasn't lost the quality", while the "service is always good and friendly". Oenophiles enjoy the range of Argentinian wines, while the prix fixe lunch is a steal. / W1U 3EG; www.zoilo.co.uk; @zoilolondon; Tue-Sat 10 pm; closed Tue, Wed L, closed Sun & Mon.

Zuma SW7 £105   4 3 5
5 Raphael St   020 7584 1010   6–1C

The crowd (especially in the bar) can be "bling personified", but Rainer Becker and Arjun Waney's glitzily glam scene, a short walk from Harrods, delivers way more than "a fun cocktail", serving luxurious Japanese-fusion dishes that are "just heaven". For fine food with a pulse, this remains "one of the best dining experiences in London". Top Menu Tips – "outstanding Wagyu tartare, crispy langoustines and seared tuna salads, and melt-in-the-mouth otoro sushi". / SW7 1DL; www.zumarestaurant.com; @Zumalondonofficial; Mon-Sat 11 pm, Sun 10.30 pm; booking max 8 may apply.

AREA OVERVIEWS

AREA OVERVIEWS | CENTRAL

CENTRAL

Soho, Covent Garden & Bloomsbury
(Parts of W1, all WC2 and WC1)

£200+	Frog by Adam Handling	*British, Modern*	4 4 3
£180+	Aulis London	*British, Modern*	4 4 4
£150+	Evelyn's Table	*British, Modern*	5 4 2
£140+	The Savoy Hotel, Savoy Grill	*British, Traditional*	2 2 3
	Restaurant 1890	*French*	3 4 4
£130+	Bustronome	*British, Modern*	2 3 4
£120+	Gauthier Soho	*Vegan*	3 3 3
	Kebab Queen	*Turkish*	4 4 3
£110+	NoMad London	*American*	3 4 5
	Spring Restaurant	*British, Modern*	3 3 4
	Sushisamba	*Fusion*	2 2 3
	Thames Foyer, Savoy	*Afternoon tea*	2 3 4
	Tattu London	*Chinese*	2 3 3
£100+	SOLA	*American*	5 3 2
	Kerridge's Bar & Grill	*British, Modern*	2 2 3
	Park Row	"	2 2 4
	Social Eating House	"	3 3 3
	River Rest', Savoy	*Fish & seafood*	2 3 2
	The Seafood Bar	"	4 4 4
	The Petersham	*Italian*	2 2 3
	Smith & Wollensky	*Steaks & grills*	2 2 3
	Yauatcha	*Chinese*	3 2 2
£90+	Christopher's	*American*	2 2 3
	Clos Maggiore	*British, Modern*	3 3 5
	The Ivy	"	2 2 3
	The Northall	"	3 3 3
	Pivot by Mark Greenaway	"	4 4 3
	Quo Vadis	"	4 4 5
	Simpson's in the Strand	*British, Traditional*	2 3 4
	L'Escargot	*French*	3 3 3
	Frenchie	"	3 3 3
	Louie	"	3 2 3
	Otto's	"	4 4 5
	Nopi	*Mediterranean*	3 3 2
	Decimo	*Spanish*	3 2 4
	Hawksmoor	*Steaks & grills*	2 2 2
	Oscar Wilde Lounge	*Afternoon tea*	3 3 5
	aqua kyoto	*Japanese*	3 3 4
	Roka, Aldwych House	"	4 3 3
£80+	Balthazar	*British, Modern*	1 2 3
	Bob Bob Ricard	"	2 4 5

FSA Ratings: from 1 (Poor) to 5 (Exceptional)

CENTRAL | **AREA OVERVIEWS**

	Name	Cuisine	Ratings
	Ducksoup	"	3 4 3
	Galvin Bar & Grill	"	3 4 4
	Holborn Dining Room	British, Traditional	- - -
	Rules	"	3 4 5
	Randall & Aubin	Fish & seafood	4 4 5
	J Sheekey	"	3 3 4
	J Sheekey Atlantic Bar	"	4 3 4
	Folie	French	3 4 4
	Margot	Italian	3 4 4
	Dalloway Terrace	Afternoon tea	2 3 4
	Cecconi's Pizza Bar	Pizza	2 2 4
	Sucre London	Argentinian	3 4 4
	Zahter	Turkish	3 2 3
	Red Farm	Chinese	3 2 3
£70+	Big Easy	American	2 2 3
	Dean Street Townhouse	British, Modern	2 3 4
	Heliot Steak House	"	3 3 3
	The Ivy Market Grill	"	2 2 3
	Noble Rot	"	3 5 5
	St Martin's House	"	- - -
	The Ivy Soho Brasserie	British, Traditional	2 2 3
	Fishworks	Fish & seafood	3 3 2
	The Oystermen	"	3 2 2
	The 10 Cases	International	3 4 3
	Café Murano Pastificio	Italian	2 2 2
	Da Mario	"	2 3 2
	Vasco & Piero's	"	4 5 4
	Toklas	Mediterranean	4 2 3
	Lisboeta	Portuguese	4 4 3
	Barrafina	Spanish	5 4 4
	Cakes and Bubbles	Pâtisserie	3 4 3
	Burger & Lobster	Burgers, etc	3 3 3
	Ceviche Soho	Peruvian	3 2 3
	The Barbary	North African	4 3 4
	The Duck & Rice	Chinese	3 3 3
	Chotto Matte	Japanese	4 4 4
	Jinjuu	Korean	4 2 3
	Patara Soho	Thai	3 3 2
£60+	Paradise	Sri Lankan	4 3 3
	Joe Allen	American	2 4 5
	Andrew Edmunds	British, Modern	3 4 5
	Cora Pearl	"	3 3 4
	Double Standard	"	3 5 5
	The French House	"	3 4 4
	Ham Yard	"	2 2 4
	Indigo, One Aldwych	"	3 3 3
	Isla	"	3 5 4
	The Jones Family Affair	"	4 3 4
	Riding House Bloomsbury	"	2 3 4
	10 Greek Street	"	4 3 3
	The Delaunay	East & Cent. European	2 4 4
	Parsons	Fish & seafood	4 4 3
	Blanchette	French	3 4 3
	Brasserie Blanc	"	2 2 2

AREA OVERVIEWS | CENTRAL

	Le Garrick	"	3 3 4
	Mon Plaisir Restaurant	"	2 2 4
	Bocca di Lupo	Italian	4 3 3
	Dehesa	"	2 2 2
	La Goccia	"	3 2 4
	Luce e Limoni	"	3 4 3
	Obicà	"	3 3 3
	San Carlo Cicchetti	"	3 3 3
	Sycamore Vino Cucina	"	3 2 2
	Volta do Mar	Portuguese	4 4 3
	Tapas Brindisa Soho	Spanish	3 2 2
	Il Teatro della Carne	Steaks & grills	2 2 3
	St Moritz	Swiss	3 3 3
	L'Antica Pizzeria da Michele	Pizza	5 3 2
	Rita's Soho	Mexican	3 4 4
	The Palomar	Middle Eastern	4 4 4
	Berenjak	Persian	4 4 4
	Nutshell	"	3 2 2
	Haz	Turkish	3 3 2
	Four Seasons	Chinese	4 1 1
	Wun's	"	3 2 3
	Masala Zone	Indian	3 3 4
	Tamarind Kitchen	"	4 4 4
	Tandoor Chop House	"	3 3 3
	Flesh and Buns	Japanese	3 4 3
	Sticks'n'Sushi	"	3 2 2
£50+	Hoppers	Sri Lankan	4 3 3
	The Black Book	British, Modern	3 4 4
	Café Deco	"	3 2 2
	Noble Rot Soho	"	3 4 4
	Sussex	"	3 4 3
	VQ, St Giles Hotel	"	2 2 3
	Cork & Bottle	British, Traditional	2 4 4
	Cigalon	French	3 3 3
	Pierre Victoire	"	3 2 3
	Boulevard	International	2 3 3
	La Fromagerie Bloomsbury	"	3 2 2
	Ave Mario	Italian	3 3 4
	Bancone	"	4 4 3
	Ciao Bella	"	3 4 5
	Fumo	"	3 3 3
	Mele e Pere	"	2 3 2
	Pastaio	"	3 3 3
	Opera Tavern	Spanish	2 2 3
	Blacklock	Steaks & grills	3 4 3
	Mildreds	Vegetarian	3 3 3
	North Sea Fish	Fish & chips	3 3 2
	Poppies	"	3 2 2
	Homeslice	Pizza	4 3 3
	temper Covent Garden	"	3 2 4
	temper Soho	BBQ	3 2 4
	El Pastor Soho	Mexican	3 2 3
	Le Bab	Middle Eastern	3 2 2
	Lahpet	Burmese	3 4 3
	Barshu	Chinese	5 2 2

FSA Ratings: from 1 (Poor) to 5 (Exceptional)

CENTRAL | **AREA OVERVIEWS**

	Fatt Pundit	"	4 3 2
	Imperial China	"	3 2 2
	Orient London	"	4 3 2
	Plum Valley	"	3 2 2
	Din Tai Fung	Chinese, Dim sum	2 2 2
	Cinnamon Bazaar	Indian	4 4 4
	Dishoom	"	4 4 4
	Fatt Pundit	"	4 3 2
	Gunpowder Soho	"	4 3 3
	Kricket	"	5 4 4
	Salaam Namaste	"	3 3 2
	Oka, Kingly Court	Japanese	3 3 2
	Shoryu Ramen	"	3 3 2
	Kiln	Thai	5 4 4
£40+	The Norfolk Arms	British, Modern	3 3 2
	Brasserie Zédel	French	1 4 5
	Chez Antoinette	"	3 4 3
	Prix Fixe	"	3 2 2
	Gordon's Wine Bar	International	2 2 5
	Casa Tua	Italian	4 2 3
	Lina Stores	"	4 3 3
	Haché	Burgers, etc	4 3 3
	MEATliquor	"	4 2 2
	Patty and Bun Soho	"	3 2 2
	Street Burger	"	2 2 2
	50 Kalò di Ciro Salvo	Pizza	5 2 3
	Chick 'n' Sours	Chicken	4 3 3
	The Barbary Next Door	North African	4 2 2
	Bubala Soho	Middle Eastern	4 4 3
	Golden Dragon	Chinese	3 2 3
	Kasa & Kin	Filipino	3 4 3
	Hankies	Indian	3 2 2
	Punjab	"	4 2 3
	Sagar	"	3 2 2
	Dipna Anand	Indian, Southern	3 2 2
	Bone Daddies	Japanese	3 3 3
	Koya-Bar	"	3 4 3
	Shackfuyu	"	3 2 2
	Bibimbap Soho	Korean	3 3 2
	Hare & Tortoise	Pan-Asian	3 3 2
	Inamo	"	3 3 3
	Cay Tre	Vietnamese	3 3 2
	Viet Food	"	3 2 3
£35+	Kolamba	Sri Lankan	3 3 2
	Bar Italia	Italian	2 4 5
	Fadiga	"	4 4 3
	Miscusi	"	2 2 2
	Flat Iron	Steaks & grills	3 4 3
	Tommi's Burger Joint	Burgers, etc	3 3 2
	Food House	Chinese	- - -
	Baozi Inn	Chinese, Dim sum	3 2 2
	Eat Tokyo	Japanese	3 2 1
	Humble Chicken	"	3 3 4
	Kanada-Ya	"	4 2 2

AREA OVERVIEWS | CENTRAL

	Name	Cuisine	Rating
	Taro	"	3 3 2
	Wild Heart	"	– – –
	C&R Café	Malaysian	3 2 2
	Lao Cafe	Thai	3 3 2
	Plaza Khao Gaeng	"	– – –
	Bao Soho	Taiwanese	3 4 4
£30+	Café in the Crypt	British, Traditional	2 2 4
	Rudy's	Pizza	3 3 3
	Coqfighter	Chicken	4 3 2
	Master Wei	Chinese	4 2 2
	Wong Kei	"	3 1 1
	Dumplings' Legend	Chinese, Dim sum	3 2 2
£25+	Imad's Syrian Kitchen	Syrian	3 3 3
	India Club	Indian	3 2 3
	The Kati Roll Company	"	3 2 2
	Heddon Yokocho	Japanese	3 2 3
£20+	Bageriet	Sandwiches, cakes, etc	4 2 2
	Dim Sum Duck	Chinese, Dim sum	5 2 2
£15+	Mr Ji	Fusion	3 3 2
	Maison Bertaux	Afternoon tea	4 3 5
	Bun House	Chinese	4 3 3
	Dai Chi	Japanese	– – –
£10+	Flat White	Sandwiches, cakes, etc	3 3 2
£5+	Monmouth Coffee Company	Sandwiches, cakes, etc	3 4 3

Mayfair & St James's (Parts of W1 and SW1)

	Name	Cuisine	Rating
£380+	The Araki	Japanese	5 4 3
£240+	Maru	Japanese	5 4 3
£230+	Ikoyi	International	3 2 2
£220+	Alain Ducasse	French	2 3 2
	Sketch, Lecture Rm	"	3 4 5
£190+	Amethyst	British, Modern	– – –
£170+	Above at Hide	British, Modern	3 2 3
	Hélène Darroze	French	2 3 2
	Seven Park Place	"	3 3 3
£150+	The Connaught Grill	British, Modern	– – –
	The Promenade	Afternoon tea	3 4 4
	Umu	Japanese	4 4 3

FSA Ratings: from 1 (Poor) to 5 (Exceptional)

CENTRAL | **AREA OVERVIEWS**

£140+	Le Gavroche	French	4 3 4
	Park Chinois	Chinese	3 2 4

£130+	Pollen Street Social	British, Modern	3 3 3
	Estiatorio Milos	Fish & seafood	4 3 4
	Le Comptoir Robuchon	French	3 4 3
	Galvin at Windows	"	2 3 3
	Cut	Steaks & grills	3 3 3
	Cubé	Japanese	4 4 2
	Jean-Georges	Pan-Asian	3 3 3
	Novikov (Asian restaurant)	"	2 2 4

£120+	Hide Ground	British, Modern	3 4 4
	The Game Bird	British, Traditional	3 4 4
	SeaSons	Fish & seafood	2 2 2
	Il Borro	Italian	3 3 3
	Murano	"	3 4 3
	Hakkasan Mayfair	Chinese	3 1 2
	Kai Mayfair	"	3 3 3
	Nobu	Japanese	4 3 2

£110+	Corrigan's Mayfair	British, Modern	3 4 3
	The Maine Mayfair	"	3 2 4
	Ormer	"	4 5 3
	The Ritz	British, Traditional	4 5 5
	Bar des Prés	French	3 4 4
	LPM	"	5 4 4
	Giannino Mayfair	Italian	2 4 3
	34 Mayfair	Steaks & grills	2 3 3
	Coya	Peruvian	3 3 3
	RAI	Japanese	4 4 3

£100+	Colony Grill Room	American	3 4 4
	The Grill at The Dorchester	British, Modern	4 4 4
	Wiltons	British, Traditional	3 3 3
	Sexy Fish	Fish & seafood	1 1 3
	Bocconcino Restaurant	Italian	2 2 2
	El Norte	Spanish	3 3 3
	The Guinea Grill	Steaks & grills	2 2 4
	Claridges Foyer	Afternoon tea	3 4 4
	The Ritz, Palm Court	"	3 4 5
	Jeru	Middle Eastern	4 2 4
	China Tang	Chinese	2 3 3
	Kanishka	Indian	3 3 2
	Ginza Onodera	Japanese	3 2 3

£90+	Charlie's at Brown's	British, Modern	4 5 5
	Hush	"	2 2 3
	Quaglino's	"	2 3 4
	Wild Honey St James	"	3 3 3
	Bentley's	Fish & seafood	4 4 3
	Scott's	"	4 4 4
	Sketch, Gallery	French	3 3 4
	Amazonico	International	3 3 4
	Scully	"	3 3 2
	Chucs Dover Street	Italian	2 2 3

267

AREA OVERVIEWS | CENTRAL

	Sartoria	"	3 4 3
	Aquavit	Scandinavian	2 3 2
	Goodman	Steaks & grills	3 3 2
	Hawksmoor	"	2 2 2
	MiMi Mei Fair	Chinese	3 3 4
	Benares	Indian	4 4 4
	BiBi	"	5 5 4
	Chutney Mary	"	4 3 4
	Veeraswamy	"	4 4 4
	Ikeda	Japanese	4 4 2
	Roka	"	4 3 3
	Tokimeite	"	– – –
£80+	Apricity	British, Modern	2 4 3
	45 Jermyn St.	"	2 3 3
	GBR, Dukes Hotel	British, Traditional	3 3 3
	Boudin Blanc	French	3 3 4
	Maison François	"	3 4 5
	Saint Jacques	"	3 3 3
	Cecconi's	Italian	2 2 4
	Franco's	"	3 3 3
	Ristorante Frescobaldi	"	3 2 2
	Theo Randall	"	5 4 2
	Rowley's	Steaks & grills	3 2 3
	Drawing Room (Browns)	Afternoon tea	3 4 4
	Diamond Jub (F&M)	"	3 3 4
	Gymkhana	Indian	5 3 3
	Jamavar	"	4 4 4
	Tamarind	"	5 4 3
	Lucky Cat	Pan-Asian	2 2 2
£70+	The American Bar	American	2 3 5
	The Avenue	"	3 3 3
	Kitty Fisher's	British, Modern	3 3 4
	Langan's Brasserie	"	1 2 3
	Little Social	"	4 3 3
	Maddox Tavern	"	– – –
	Native at Browns	"	5 4 4
	The Wolseley	"	1 2 4
	Fishworks	Fish & seafood	3 3 2
	Café Murano	Italian	2 2 2
	San Carlo	"	3 3 4
	Burger & Lobster	Burgers, etc	3 3 3
	Bombay Bustle	Indian	5 4 4
	Chisou	Japanese	3 2 2
	Kiku	"	4 4 2
	The Ivy Asia Mayfair	Pan-Asian	2 3 4
	Patara Mayfair	Thai	3 3 2
£60+	Bellamy's	British, Modern	3 5 4
	116 at the Athenaeum	"	2 4 3
	The Windmill	British, Traditional	3 2 3
	Al Duca	Italian	3 2 2
	Il Vicolo	"	3 3 2
	Sabor	Spanish	5 5 5
	Drawing Room, Dukes	Afternoon tea	– – –

FSA Ratings: from 1 (Poor) to 5 (Exceptional)

CENTRAL | AREA OVERVIEWS

	Delfino	Pizza	3 3 2
	O'ver	"	3 2 2
	Manthan	Indian	3 4 3
£50+	123V	Vegan	3 2 3
	José Pizarro at the RA	Spanish	4 3 3
	El Pirata	"	2 3 3
	Richoux	Sandwiches, cakes, etc	3 4 3
	Shoryu Ramen	Japanese	3 3 2
£40+	Sarap Filipino Bistro	Filipino	3 3 3
	Chourangi	Indian	4 3 3
£35+	Queens of Mayfair	British, Modern	3 4 4

Fitzrovia & Marylebone (Part of W1)

£330+	Kitchen Table	British, Modern	4 4 4
£280+	Roketsu	Japanese	5 4 3
£140+	Akoko	West African	4 4 4
£130+	Pied à Terre	French	4 4 4
£120+	Beast	Steaks & grills	2 2 2
	Kol	Mexican	4 4 4
	Hakkasan	Chinese	3 1 2
£110+	Mere	East & Cent. European	3 4 2
	Ampéli	Greek	3 4 3
£100+	The Chiltern Firehouse	American	2 2 5
	The Berners Tavern	British, Modern	2 2 5
	The Ninth London	"	5 4 3
	Locanda Locatelli	Italian	2 3 2
	Arros QD	Spanish	2 2 2
	Dinings	Japanese	5 4 2
	Nobu Portman Square	"	3 3 4
£90+	Portland	British, Modern	4 5 3
	28-50 Oxford Circus	"	2 2 2
	Santo Mare	Fish & seafood	3 3 3
	Noizé	French	4 5 4
	Les 110 de Taillevent	"	3 3 3
	Orrery	"	2 2 2
	Opso	Greek	3 2 3
	Palm Court, The Langham	Afternoon tea	2 3 4
	Cavita	Mexican	- - -
	Roka	Japanese	4 3 3
	Taka Marylebone	"	2 2 3
	TOKii	"	- - -

AREA OVERVIEWS | CENTRAL

£80+			
	Clipstone	British, Modern	4 3 2
	The Grazing Goat	"	3 3 3
	Upstairs at The George	"	- - -
	Clarette	French	3 3 3
	La Brasseria Milanese	Italian	3 3 3
	Norma	"	4 4 4
	ROVI	Mediterranean	3 2 3
	Zoilo	Argentinian	3 3 3
	The Bright Courtyard	Chinese	3 2 2
	Pahli Hill Bandra Bhai	Indian	3 2 2
£70+			
	Brasserie of Light	British, Modern	2 2 5
	108 Brasserie	"	3 2 3
	Fishworks Marylebone	Fish & seafood	3 3 2
	Chotto Matte	Fusion	4 4 4
	Meraki	Greek	4 3 4
	Carousel	International	4 3 2
	Caffè Caldesi	Italian	3 2 2
	Blandford Comptoir	Mediterranean	3 3 3
	Ottolenghi	"	4 3 2
	Burger & Lobster	Burgers, etc	3 3 3
	Daylesford Organic	Sandwiches, cakes, etc	2 2 2
	Pachamama	Peruvian	2 2 3
	Honey & Co	Middle Eastern	- - -
	Ishtar	Turkish	3 3 3
	Royal China Club	Chinese	3 2 2
	Jikoni	Indian	3 3 3
	Trishna	"	5 4 3
£60+			
	Granger & Co	Australian	2 2 2
	The Ivy Café	British, Modern	1 2 2
	The Lore of the Land	"	3 3 4
	The Wigmore, The Langham	British, Traditional	4 4 4
	Fischer's	East & Cent. European	2 3 3
	Twist Connubio	Fusion	3 3 2
	Six by Nico	International	3 3 3
	Briciole	Italian	3 3 2
	Harry's Bar	"	2 2 3
	Riding House Café	Mediterranean	2 3 4
	Ibérica	Spanish	2 2 2
	Lurra	"	4 3 3
	Honey & Smoke	Middle Eastern	4 2 2
	Royal China	Chinese	3 1 2
	Masala Zone at Selfridges	Indian	3 3 4
	Italiku	Fusion	3 3 3
	Flesh and Buns Fitzrovia	Japanese	3 4 3
	Junsei	"	4 4 3
	Sushi Atelier	"	4 4 3
£50+			
	Hoppers	Sri Lankan	4 3 3
	Wulf & Lamb	Vegan	3 2 2
	Caravan	British, Modern	2 2 2
	La Fromagerie Café	International	3 2 2
	Circolo Popolare	Italian	3 3 5
	Italian Greyhound	"	2 2 3
	2 Veneti	"	3 2 2

FSA Ratings: from 1 (Poor) to 5 (Exceptional)

CENTRAL | **AREA OVERVIEWS**

	Name	Cuisine	Ratings
	Donostia	*Spanish*	4 3 3
	Salt Yard	"	3 2 2
	Relais de Venise	*Steaks & grills*	3 2 3
	The Gate	*Vegetarian*	3 3 3
	Homeslice	*Pizza*	4 3 3
	Oka	*Pan-Asian*	3 3 2
	Foley's	*Thai*	3 4 3
£40+	The Wallace	*French*	2 2 5
	Lina Stores	*Italian*	4 3 3
	MEATLiquor	*Burgers, etc*	4 2 2
	Patty and Bun	"	3 2 2
	Golden Hind	*Fish & chips*	3 2 2
	Pizzeria Mozza	*Pizza*	4 2 3
	Santa Maria	"	3 3 3
	Reubens	*Kosher*	2 2 2
	Delamina	*Middle Eastern*	4 3 3
	Hankies Marble Arch	*Indian*	3 2 2
	Roti Chai	"	3 3 2
	Sagar	"	3 2 2
	Bone Daddies	*Japanese*	3 3 3
	Laksamania	*Malaysian*	3 3 2
£35+	Cin Cin	*Italian*	3 4 4
	Flat Iron Marylebone	*Steaks & grills*	3 4 3
	Tommi's Burger Joint	*Burgers, etc*	3 3 2
	Ragam	*Indian*	4 2 2
	Bao Fitzrovia	*Taiwanese*	3 4 4
	CoCoRo	*Japanese*	4 3 2
£25+	Kiss the Hippo	*Sandwiches, cakes, etc*	3 3 2
£15+	Icco Pizza	*Italian*	3 3 2
	Kaffeine (Eastcastle Street)	*Sandwiches, cakes, etc*	2 5 3
	Marugame Udon	*Japanese*	4 3 2
£10+	Boxcar Baker & Deli	*Sandwiches, cakes, etc*	3 3 3

Belgravia, Pimlico, Victoria & Westminster (SW1, except St James's)

	Name	Cuisine	Ratings
£240+	The Aubrey	*Japanese*	3 4 3
£180+	Nusr-Et Steakhouse	*Steaks & grills*	1 1 1
£170+	Marcus, The Berkeley	*British, Modern*	3 3 3
	Muse	"	5 4 4
£150+	Dinner	*British, Traditional*	2 2 1
£140+	Pétrus	*French*	2 2 1
£130+	The Lanesborough Grill	*British, Modern*	– – –
	The Collins Room	*Afternoon tea*	3 3 4

AREA OVERVIEWS | CENTRAL

£120+	Imperial Treasure	*Chinese*	4 4 2
£110+	Goring Dining Rm	*British, Traditional*	3 3 4
	Kerridge's Fish & Chips	*Fish & seafood*	3 3 5
	Santini	*Italian*	2 3 3
	Ekstedt at The Yard	*Scandinavian*	4 4 4
	A Wong	*Chinese*	5 5 3
	Hunan	*"*	4 2 1
£100+	Fallow St James's	*British, Modern*	4 4 4
	Crystal Moon Lounge	*Afternoon tea*	3 4 4
£90+	The Pem	*British, Modern*	4 4 2
	Chucs	*Italian*	2 2 3
	Zafferano	*"*	4 3 3
	Al Mare	*Mediterranean*	3 3 3
	Cedric Grolet	*Pâtisserie*	3 4 4
	M Restaurant	*Steaks & grills*	2 2 3
£80+	Ganymede	*British, Modern*	4 4 3
	Hans' Bar & Grill	*"*	3 3 3
	The Orange	*"*	2 3 3
	Olivomare	*Fish & seafood*	3 3 2
	Harrods Dining Hall	*International*	3 3 4
	Enoteca Turi	*Italian*	3 5 3
	Olivo	*"*	3 4 2
	Olivocarne	*"*	3 3 2
	Sale e Pepe	*"*	3 5 3
	Roof Garden	*Scandinavian*	3 3 5
	Boisdale of Belgravia	*Scottish*	2 2 3
	Amaya	*Indian*	5 3 4
	Quilon	*Indian, Southern*	5 4 2
	Sachi at Pantechnicon	*Japanese*	– – –
£70+	Alfred Tennyson	*British, Modern*	2 2 3
	Blue Boar Pub	*"*	3 2 2
	Daylesford Organic	*"*	2 2 2
	The Ivy Victoria	*"*	2 2 3
	Lorne	*"*	5 5 3
	Thomas Cubitt	*"*	2 2 3
	La Poule au Pot	*French*	3 4 5
	Harrods Social	*International*	3 3 3
	Caraffini	*Italian*	3 4 3
	Signor Sassi	*"*	3 3 3
	Eldr at Pantechnicon	*Scandinavian*	3 3 4
	Burger & Lobster	*Burgers, etc*	3 3 3
	Oliveto	*Pizza*	3 2 2
	Ottolenghi	*Middle Eastern*	4 3 2
	The Cinnamon Club	*Indian*	4 3 4
	Kahani	*"*	4 4 3
£60+	Granger & Co	*Australian*	2 2 2
	Colbert	*French*	2 3 3
	Motcombs	*International*	2 3 4
	Tozi	*Italian*	3 2 3
	Ibérica, Zig Zag Building	*Spanish*	2 2 2

FSA Ratings: from 1 (Poor) to 5 (Exceptional)

CENTRAL | **AREA OVERVIEWS**

	Kazan	Turkish	3 3 2
	Ken Lo's Memories	"	3 3 2
	Sticks'n'Sushi	Japanese	3 2 2
	Salloos	Pakistani	3 3 2
£50+	Holy Carrot	Vegan	3 4 4
	The Jones Family Kitchen	British, Modern	4 4 4
	Gustoso	Italian	3 2 2
	Wulf & Lamb	Vegetarian	3 2 2
	Seafresh	Fish & chips	3 3 2
	Cyprus Mangal	Turkish	3 2 2
	Mathura	Indian	3 2 2
£40+	Vincent Rooms	British, Modern	3 2 3
	Chez Antoinette	French	3 4 3
	Grumbles	International	3 4 3
	Goya	Spanish	3 3 2
	Sagar	Indian	3 2 2
	Bone Daddies, Nova	Japanese	3 3 3
£35+	Kanada-Ya	Japanese	4 2 2
	Taro	"	3 3 2
£25+	Bleecker Burger	Burgers, etc	4 2 2
	Aloo Tama	Indian	4 4 3
£20+	Café Kitsuné	Japanese	3 3 4
£10+	Regency Cafe	British, Traditional	3 3 5

AREA OVERVIEWS | WEST

WEST

Chelsea, South Kensington, Kensington, Earl's Court & Fulham (SW3, SW5, SW6, SW7, SW10 & W8)

£210+	Gordon Ramsay	*French*	3 3 2
£190+	The Five Fields	*British, Modern*	5 5 3
	Bibendum	*French*	4 3 4
£170+	Le Petit Beefbar	*Steaks & grills*	– – –
£110+	Medlar	*British, Modern*	4 4 3
	Wild Tavern	*Italian*	2 3 3
£100+	Elystan Street	*British, Modern*	3 2 3
	Launceston Place	"	4 3 3
	No. Fifty Cheyne	"	2 3 5
	Min Jiang	*Chinese*	4 3 5
	Dinings	*Japanese*	5 4 2
	Yashin Ocean House	"	4 3 3
	Zuma	"	4 3 5
£90+	Bluebird	*British, Modern*	2 1 4
	Clarke's	"	4 4 3
	Kitchen W8	"	4 3 3
	Stanley's	"	3 2 3
	28-50 Chelsea	"	2 2 2
	Restaurant, Capital Hotel	*British, Traditional*	3 4 3
	Le Colombier	*French*	2 4 4
	Chucs	*Italian*	2 2 3
	Lucio	"	3 3 2
	Scalini	"	3 4 3
	Hawksmoor Knightsbridge	*Steaks & grills*	2 2 2
£80+	Harwood Arms	*British, Modern*	3 2 3
	Bibendum Oyster Bar	*Fish & seafood*	4 3 4
	Myrtle	*Irish*	5 4 3
	Daphne's	*Italian*	2 2 3
	Manicomio Chelsea	"	2 2 3
	Cambio de Tercio	*Spanish*	5 4 4
	Bombay Brasserie	*Indian*	3 3 3
	Akira at Japan House	*Japanese*	3 3 2
	Koji	"	3 3 4
£70+	Big Easy	*American*	2 2 3
	Daylesford Organic	*British, Modern*	2 2 2
	The Enterprise	"	2 3 4
	The Hunter's Moon	"	3 4 3
	The Ivy Chelsea Garden	"	2 2 3
	The Sea, The Sea	*Fish & seafood*	5 4 4
	Wright Brothers	"	3 2 3
	Margaux	*French*	4 4 3
	Mazi	*Greek*	4 4 3

FSA Ratings: from **1** (Poor) to **5** (Exceptional)

WEST | **AREA OVERVIEWS**

	Name	Cuisine	F	S	A
	Vardo	International	2	2	3
	La Famiglia	Italian	2	2	4
	Il Portico	"	3	3	3
	Chicama	Peruvian	3	3	3
	Alexandrie	Egyptian	3	3	3
	Good Earth	Chinese	3	3	2
	Chisou	Japanese	3	2	2
	Huo	Pan-Asian	3	3	3
	The Ivy Asia	"	2	3	4
	Patara	Thai	3	3	2
£60+	The Abingdon	British, Modern	3	3	3
	Brinkley's	"	2	2	3
	Brook House	"	3	3	3
	The Cadogan Arms	"	2	2	3
	FENN	"	5	4	3
	Rabbit	"	3	2	2
	The Shed	"	3	4	4
	Maggie Jones's	British, Traditional	3	4	5
	Suzi Tros	Greek	3	3	3
	Cicchetti Knightsbridge	Italian	3	3	3
	Frantoio	"	2	4	4
	Ziani's	"	3	3	3
	Pascor	Mediterranean	–	–	–
	Ognisko Restaurant	Polish	3	4	5
	Tapas Brindisa	Spanish	3	2	2
	Tendido Cero	"	4	4	4
	Macellaio RC	Steaks & grills	2	2	3
	Maroush	Lebanese	3	2	2
	Royal China	Chinese	3	1	2
	Romulo Café	Filipino	3	4	3
	Kutir	Indian	5	4	4
	Masala Zone	"	3	3	4
	Zaika of Kensington	"	3	4	4
	Flesh and Buns	Japanese	3	4	3
	Sticks'n'Sushi	"	3	2	2
	Zheng	Malaysian	3	3	2
£50+	West 4th	Canadian	3	2	2
	The Fox and Pheasant	British, Modern	3	2	4
	Manuka Kitchen	"	3	3	3
	VQ	"	2	2	3
	The Scarsdale	International	3	3	5
	Chelsea Cellar	Italian	3	4	4
	Made in Italy	"	3	2	2
	Nuovi Sapori	"	3	4	3
	Riccardo's	"	3	4	3
	San Pietro	"	3	2	3
	The Atlas	Mediterranean	3	2	3
	Daquise	Polish	2	2	3
	Cocotte	Chicken	3	4	3
	Dishoom	Indian	4	4	4
	Flora Indica	"	3	2	3
	Noor Jahan	"	4	4	2
	Pure Indian Cooking	"	3	4	3
	Oka	Japanese	3	3	2

AREA OVERVIEWS | WEST

	Name	Cuisine	Ratings
	Shoryu Ramen	"	3 3 2
	Sukho Fine Thai Cuisine	Thai	4 5 2
£40+	Churchill Arms	British, Traditional	3 2 3
	Los Mochis	Fusion	3 3 4
	Aglio e Olio	Italian	3 2 2
	Da Mario	"	2 3 3
	Haché	Steaks & grills	4 3 3
	Street Burger	Burgers, etc	2 2 2
	Fishers	Fish & chips	3 3 3
	Cinquecento	Pizza	2 2 3
	Rocca	"	3 3 3
	Santa Maria	"	3 3 3
	Ceru	Middle Eastern	3 2 2
	Best Mangal	Turkish	4 4 2
	Chakra	Indian	3 2 3
	Thali	"	3 3 3
	Addie's Thai Café	Thai	3 2 2
	Mien Tay	Vietnamese	3 3 2
£35+	Phat Phuc	Vietnamese	4 2 3
£25+	Big Fernand	Burgers, etc	4 4 2

Notting Hill, Holland Park, Bayswater, North Kensington & Maida Vale (W2, W9, W10, W11)

	Name	Cuisine	Ratings
£230+	The Ledbury	British, Modern	4 5 4
£220+	Core by Clare Smyth	British, Modern	5 5 4
£110+	Caractère	Mediterranean	4 5 4
£100+	104 Restaurant	British, Modern	4 4 4
£90+	Julie's	British, Modern	2 3 4
	Chucs Westbourne Grove	Italian	2 2 3
	Sumi	Japanese	4 5 4
£80+	The Princess Royal	British, Modern	3 3 3
	Six Portland Road	"	3 4 2
	La Brasseria	Italian	3 3 3
£70+	Sunday in Brooklyn	American	3 3 4
	Daylesford Organic	British, Modern	2 2 2
	Gold	"	2 2 4
	London Shell Co.	Fish & seafood	4 4 4
	The Summerhouse	"	3 3 5
	The Cow	Irish	3 2 3
	Assaggi	Italian	3 4 3
	Osteria Basilico	"	3 3 3
	Portobello	"	3 3 3
	Ottolenghi	Mediterranean	4 3 2
	Farmacy	Vegetarian	4 3 4

FSA Ratings: from 1 (Poor) to 5 (Exceptional)

WEST | **AREA OVERVIEWS**

	E&O	*Pan-Asian*	4 3 4
	Uli	"	3 4 4
£60+	Granger & Co	*Australian*	2 2 2
	The Hero of Maida	*British, Modern*	3 3 2
	The Ladbroke Arms	"	3 2 4
	The Pelican	"	3 3 3
	7 Saints	"	3 4 4
	Buvette	*French*	2 2 3
	Mediterraneo	*Italian*	3 2 3
	The Oak W2	"	3 2 4
	Maroush	*Lebanese*	3 2 2
	Four Seasons	*Chinese*	4 1 1
	Mandarin Kitchen	"	4 3 2
	Bombay Palace	*Indian*	5 4 3
	Masala Zone	"	3 3 4
£50+	Fiend	*British, Modern*	5 4 4
	Orasay	"	5 4 4
	The Cheese Barge	*British, Traditional*	2 3 3
	Hereford Road	"	4 4 3
	Cepages	*French*	4 3 4
	Haya	*Mediterranean*	3 4 3
	Pizza East Portobello	*Pizza*	3 3 3
	Cocotte	*Chicken*	3 4 3
	Pearl Liang	*Chinese*	3 3 3
	Noor Jahan	*Indian*	4 4 2
	Maguro	*Japanese*	3 2 2
	Sushi Murasaki	"	4 4 2
£40+	The Frontline Club	*British, Modern*	– – –
	The Walmer Castle	*Scottish*	– – –
	MEATliquor	*Burgers, etc*	4 2 2
	Patty and Bun Portobello	"	3 2 2
	Cinquecento	*Pizza*	2 2 3
	Taqueria	*Mexican*	4 4 3
	Ceru	*Middle Eastern*	3 2 2
	Fez Mangal	*Turkish*	4 4 2
	Gold Mine	*Chinese*	3 2 2
	Durbar	*Indian*	3 3 2
£35+	Dhaba@49	*Indian*	3 3 2
	Eat Tokyo	*Japanese*	3 2 1
£30+	Tab X Tab	*International*	4 4 3
£25+	Tavernaki	*Greek*	3 2 2
	Normah's	*Malaysian*	4 3 2
£20+	Books for Cooks	*International*	3 4 4

AREA OVERVIEWS | WEST

Hammersmith, Shepherd's Bush, Olympia, Chiswick, Brentford & Ealing
(W4, W5, W6, W12, W13, W14, TW8)

£280+	Endo at The Rotunda	*Japanese*	5 5 5
£130+	The River Café	*Italian*	3 2 3
£100+	La Trompette	*French*	4 3 2
£80+	Villa Di Geggiano	*Italian*	3 4 4
£70+	Sams Riverside	*British, Modern*	4 4 5
	The Silver Birch	"	3 4 3
	Le Vacherin	*French*	4 4 3
	Shikumen, Dorsett Hotel	*Chinese*	4 2 3
£60+	The Anglesea Arms	*British, Modern*	4 4 4
	The Broadcaster	"	3 3 3
	City Barge	"	2 2 3
	The Duke of Sussex	"	3 3 3
	High Road Brasserie	"	2 2 3
	Rock & Rose	"	– – –
	Vinoteca	"	2 2 2
	Brasserie Blanc	*French*	2 2 2
	Annie's	*International*	3 3 4
	L'Amorosa	*Italian*	4 4 4
	Cibo	"	4 4 3
	The Oak W12	"	3 2 4
	Pentolina	"	4 4 4
	The Swan	*Mediterranean*	3 4 4
£50+	Brackenbury Wine Rooms	*British, Modern*	2 3 3
	The Crabtree	"	3 3 4
	The Havelock Tavern	"	3 2 4
	The Princess Victoria	"	3 3 3
	Le Petit Citron	*French*	3 3 3
	Giulia	*Italian*	3 3 2
	The Carpenter's Arms	*Mediterranean*	3 3 3
	Salt Yard	*Spanish*	3 2 2
	The Gate	*Vegetarian*	3 3 3
	The Bird in Hand	*Pizza*	4 4 4
	Homeslice	"	4 3 3
	Zia Lucia	"	4 2 2
	The Hampshire	*Indian*	3 4 3
	Indian Zing	"	4 3 3
	Potli	"	4 3 3
£40+	222 Veggie Vegan	*Vegan*	3 3 2
	Dear Grace	*British, Modern*	– – –
	Kindred	"	3 3 3
	Patty and Bun	*Burgers, etc*	3 2 2
	Oro Di Napoli	*Pizza*	3 4 2
	Santa Maria	"	3 3 3
	Angie's Little Food Shop	*Sandwiches, cakes, etc*	2 4 2

WEST | **AREA OVERVIEWS**

	Best Mangal	Turkish		4 4 2
	North China	Chinese		4 3 3
	Copper Chimney	Indian		3 3 3
	Patri	"		3 3 2
	Rangrez	"		3 3 3
	Republic	"		4 4 3
	Sagar	"		3 2 2
	Hare & Tortoise	Pan-Asian		3 3 2
	101 Thai Kitchen	Thai		3 2 2
	Saigon Saigon	Vietnamese		2 3 2
£35+	Base Face Pizza	Pizza		3 4 3
	Chateau	Lebanese		3 4 2
	Shilpa	Indian, Southern		3 2 2
	Eat Tokyo	Japanese		3 2 1
	Sushi Bar Makoto	"		4 3 1
	Tosa	"		3 4 2
	Poppy's Thai Eatery 3	Thai		3 2 4
£30+	Avanti	Mediterranean		3 3 2
	Persian Palace	Persian		3 4 2
	Ta Ke Sushi	Japanese		4 3 2
£25+	Bleecker Burger	Burgers, etc		4 2 2
	Tamp Coffee	Sandwiches, cakes, etc		3 4 3
	Ngon	Vietnamese		3 2 2
£20+	Rhythm & Brews	Sandwiches, cakes, etc		3 3 4
	Khun Pakin Thai	Thai		3 3 3
£15+	The Elder Press Café	British, Modern		3 2 3
£5+	Mr Falafel	Middle Eastern		5 4 2

AREA OVERVIEWS | NORTH

NORTH

Hampstead, West Hampstead, St John's Wood, Regent's Park, Kilburn & Camden Town (NW postcodes)

£170+	PLU	*French*	5 4 4
£90+	Chucs	*Italian*	2 2 3
	Tish	*Kosher*	3 3 4
£80+	Booking Office 1869	*British, Modern*	3 3 5
	Landmark (Winter Gdn)	"	2 3 5
	Odette's	"	3 2 2
	Lume	*Italian*	3 3 2
	Carmel	*Mediterranean*	5 4 4
£70+	Searcys St Pancras Grand	*British, Modern*	2 3 4
	Holly Bush	*British, Traditional*	2 2 4
	L'Aventure	*French*	4 4 4
	Michael Nadra	"	3 3 2
	Oslo Court	"	3 5 5
	Bull & Last	*International*	3 3 3
	La Collina	*Italian*	3 2 3
	Magenta	"	3 3 3
	Morso	"	3 3 2
	Villa Bianca	"	2 2 3
	Good Earth	*Chinese*	3 3 2
	Kaifeng	"	3 3 2
	Patara	*Thai*	3 3 2
£60+	Bradley's	*British, Modern*	2 2 2
	The Clifton	"	3 4 4
	Ham	"	4 4 3
	The Ivy Café	"	1 2 2
	Parlour Kensal	"	4 3 4
	The Wells Tavern	"	3 4 3
	Lemonia	*Greek*	2 3 3
	Soutine	*International*	2 4 4
	Anima e Cuore	*Italian*	4 2 2
	The Rising Sun	"	3 4 2
	L'Antica Pizzeria da Michele	*Pizza*	5 3 2
	Cinder	*BBQ*	2 2 2
	Chameleon	*Israeli*	3 3 4
	Maroush Park Royal	*Lebanese*	3 2 2
	Skewd Kitchen	*Turkish*	3 3 3
	Phoenix Palace	*Chinese*	3 2 2
	Masala Zone	*Indian*	3 3 4
£50+	The Wet Fish Café	*British, Modern*	3 3 3
	The Farrier	*British, Traditional*	3 2 4
	Lure	*Fish & seafood*	3 2 3
	Greenberry Café	*Fusion*	3 3 4
	L'Artista	*Italian*	2 4 3
	Calici	"	3 2 2

FSA Ratings: from **1** (Poor) to **5** (Exceptional)

NORTH | **AREA OVERVIEWS**

	Quartieri	"	3 3 3
	28 Church Row	Spanish	4 4 3
	Mildreds	Vegetarian	3 3 3
	Poppies Camden	Fish & chips	3 2 2
	The Sea Shell	"	3 3 2
	Zia Lucia	Pizza	4 2 2
	Cocotte	Chicken	3 4 3
	Crocker's Folly	Lebanese	4 3 4
	Bonoo	Indian	3 3 3
	Saravanaa Bhavan	"	3 3 2
	Jin Kichi	Japanese	5 5 3
	Oka	"	3 3 2
	Singapore Garden	Malaysian	4 2 2
£40+	Rudy's Vegan Diner	Vegan	3 3 2
	Authentique Epicerie & Bar	French	3 3 3
	The Spaniard's Inn	International	2 2 4
	Giacomo's	Italian	3 4 2
	Haché	Steaks & grills	4 3 3
	Sacro Cuore	Pizza	4 2 2
	Green Cottage	Chinese	3 2 2
	Great Nepalese	Indian	3 4 3
	Masalchi by Atul Kochhar	"	– – –
	Sushi Masa	Japanese	3 3 2
	Bang Bang Oriental	Pan-Asian	3 2 2
£35+	Nautilus	Fish & chips	3 2 2
	Paradise Hampstead	Indian	3 5 3
	Vijay	"	4 4 1
	Asakusa	Japanese	4 3 2
	Eat Tokyo G2 (Shabu-Shabu)	"	3 2 1
£30+	Ali Baba	Egyptian	3 2 2
	Balady	Middle Eastern	4 2 1
	Three Uncles	Chinese	5 3 3
	Diwana Bhel-Poori House	Indian	3 2 1
	Ravi Shankar	"	3 2 2
	Sakonis	"	3 2 2
	Anjanaas	Indian, Southern	3 2 2
£25+	Sam's Café	British, Traditional	3 3 3
	Chutneys	Indian	3 3 2
£20+	E Mono	Turkish	4 3 2
	Tofu Vegan	Chinese	4 3 2
	Roti King	Malaysian	5 2 3
£15+	Icco Pizza	Pizza	3 3 2
£10+	Ginger & White Hampstead	Sandwiches, cakes, etc	3 3 3

AREA OVERVIEWS | NORTH

Hoxton, Islington, Highgate, Crouch End, Stoke Newington, Finsbury Park, Muswell Hill & Finchley (N postcodes)

£120+	Parrillan	Spanish	3 3 3
£90+	Hot Stone	Japanese	4 4 3
£80+	Coal Office	Mediterranean	4 3 4
	Mangal 2	Turkish	4 4 2
£70+	Hicce	British, Modern	3 2 3
	Perilla	"	4 4 3
	Les 2 Garcons	French	5 4 3
	German Gymnasium	German	1 2 3
	Salut	International	3 4 4
	Radici	Italian	2 2 2
	Trullo	"	3 3 3
	Ottolenghi	Mediterranean	4 3 2
	Barrafina	Spanish	5 4 4
	Casa Pastór & Plaza Pastór	Mexican	3 2 2
£60+	Granger & Co	Australian	2 2 2
	The Bull	British, Modern	3 3 3
	The Clarence Tavern	"	3 4 3
	The Drapers Arms	"	3 3 3
	Frederick's	"	3 4 4
	Humble Grape	"	3 4 3
	Pig & Butcher	"	3 2 3
	The Red Lion & Sun	"	3 3 3
	Westerns Laundry	"	3 3 4
	St Johns	British, Traditional	3 4 5
	Prawn on the Lawn	Fish & seafood	5 3 2
	Jiji	Fusion	4 3 4
	The Orange Tree	International	3 3 3
	Primeur	"	3 4 3
	Osteria Tufo	Italian	3 4 3
	Terra Rossa	"	3 3 3
	Vinoteca	Mediterranean	2 2 2
	Bar Esteban	Spanish	3 3 3
	Camino King's Cross	"	2 3 2
	The Gatehouse	"	3 3 3
	Smokehouse Islington	Steaks & grills	3 3 3
£50+	Caravan King's Cross	British, Modern	2 2 2
	The Lighterman	"	2 2 2
	The Plimsoll	"	5 3 2
	Porte Noire	"	– – –
	Rotunda	"	2 3 3
	12:51 by chef James Cochran	"	3 2 3
	Kipferl	East & Cent. European	3 3 3
	Lyon's	Fish & seafood	4 4 3
	Bellanger	French	2 2 2
	Table Du Marche	"	3 3 2
	Kalimera	Greek	4 4 3
	Banners	International	2 3 3

FSA Ratings: from 1 (Poor) to 5 (Exceptional)

NORTH | **AREA OVERVIEWS**

	FKABAM (Black Axe Mangal)	"	4 3 3
	The Flask	"	2 3 4
	La Fromagerie	"	3 2 2
	Citro	Italian	4 3 2
	500	"	3 4 2
	La Lluna	Spanish	3 3 2
	Vermuteria	"	– – –
	Mildreds	Vegetarian	3 3 3
	Toff's	Fish & chips	4 3 2
	Zia Lucia	Pizza	4 2 2
	Cocotte	Chicken	3 4 3
	Arabica KX	Middle Eastern	3 4 2
	Kilis Kitchen	Turkish	3 3 3
	Kaki	Chinese	4 3 2
	Dishoom	Indian	4 4 4
	Hoppers	"	4 3 3
	Sushi on Jones	Japanese	– – –
	Supawan	Thai	5 4 3
£40+	Rudy's Vegan Diner	Vegan	3 3 2
	Chriskitch	British, Modern	3 3 3
	Frank's Canteen	"	3 4 3
	Granary Square Brasserie	"	2 2 3
	Schnitzel Forever	East & Cent. European	3 2 2
	Caravel	French	3 3 4
	Le Sacré-Coeur	"	3 3 2
	Attimi	Italian	3 3 3
	Lina Stores	"	4 3 3
	Noci	"	2 2 3
	Via Emilia	"	3 3 2
	Escocesa	Spanish	4 3 3
	MEATLiquor Islington	Burgers, etc	4 2 2
	Street Burger	"	2 2 2
	Olympus Fish	Fish & chips	4 4 2
	Sacro Cuore	Pizza	4 2 2
	Santa Maria	"	3 3 3
	Sweet Thursday	"	3 3 2
	Yard Sale Pizza	"	4 4 2
	Chuku's	West African	4 4 3
	Gallipoli Again	Turkish	3 4 4
	Gem	"	4 4 3
	Sumak	"	3 4 2
	Jashan	Indian	3 2 2
	Zaffrani	"	2 2 2
	Rasa	Indian, Southern	5 4 3
	Sambal Shiok	Malaysian	3 2 2
	Farang	Thai	4 4 3
	Mien Tay	Vietnamese	3 3 2
£35+	Two Brothers	Fish & seafood	3 2 2
	Le Mercury	French	2 2 2
	Miscusi	Italian	2 2 2
	Pizzeria Pappagone	"	3 3 3
	Skal Nordic Dining	Scandinavian	4 4 3
	Flat Iron	Steaks & grills	3 4 3
	The Dusty Knuckle	Sandwiches, cakes, etc	4 2 3

AREA OVERVIEWS | NORTH

	Xi'an Impression	Chinese	3 2 1
	Indian Rasoi	Indian	3 3 2
	Shahi Pakwaan	"	3 3 2
	Kanada-Ya	Japanese	4 2 2
	Taro	"	3 3 2
	Bund	Pan-Asian	3 3 3
	Cafe Bao	Taiwanese	3 4 4
£30+	Che Cosa	Italian	3 3 2
	Afghan Kitchen	Afghani	3 2 2
	Delhi Grill	Indian	3 2 3
	Viet Garden	Vietnamese	3 3 2
£25+	Big Jo Bakery	British, Modern	3 3 3
	Normans Cafe	"	4 4 4
£20+	Tofu Vegan	Chinese	4 3 2
	Sushi Show	Japanese	3 3 2
	Hawker's Kitchen	Malaysian	5 3 2

284 FSA Ratings: from **1** (Poor) to **5** (Exceptional)

SOUTH | **AREA OVERVIEWS**

SOUTH

South Bank (SE1)

£270+	Story	*British, Modern*	3 3 3
£140+	Trivet	*British, Modern*	3 3 3
£120+	Turnips	*International*	4 3 3
	Parrillan	*Spanish*	3 3 3
	Hannah	*Japanese*	3 3 2
£110+	Aqua Shard	*British, Modern*	2 2 3
	Hutong, The Shard	*Chinese*	2 2 3
£100+	Oblix	*British, Modern*	2 2 4
	Oxo Tower, Restaurant	"	1 1 1
£90+	Oxo Tower, Brasserie	*British, Modern*	1 1 2
	TING	"	2 3 4
	Le Pont de la Tour	*French*	2 2 2
	Sollip	"	5 4 3
	Hawksmoor	*Steaks & grills*	2 2 2
£80+	Butlers Wharf Chop House	*British, Traditional*	2 2 3
	Seabird	*Fish & seafood*	3 2 5
	La Barca	*Italian*	3 3 3
£70+	Elliot's	*British, Modern*	3 2 3
	The Garrison	"	3 3 3
	The Ivy Tower Bridge	"	2 2 3
	Sea Containers	"	2 2 3
	Skylon, South Bank Centre	"	2 2 3
	The Swan at the Globe	"	2 2 4
	Roast	*British, Traditional*	2 2 4
	Applebee's Fish	*Fish & seafood*	3 3 3
	fish!	"	3 2 3
	Wright Brothers	"	3 2 3
	Vivat Bacchus	*International*	3 3 3
	Cafe Murano	*Italian*	2 2 2
	Barrafina	*Spanish*	5 4 4
	The Coal Shed	*Steaks & grills*	3 3 3
	Pique Nique	*Chicken*	3 3 3
	Rabot 1745	*Caribbean*	2 2 3
	Mei Mei	*Malaysian*	3 3 2
£60+	The Anchor & Hope	*British, Modern*	3 3 3
	40 Maltby Street	"	3 3 2
	Garden Cafe	"	4 3 3
	Vinoteca Borough	"	2 2 2
	Brasserie Blanc	*French*	2 2 2
	Casse-Croute	"	4 4 4
	Macellaio RC	*Italian*	2 2 3
	José	*Spanish*	4 3 4
	Pizarro	"	4 4 3

AREA OVERVIEWS | SOUTH

	Name	Cuisine	Rating
	Tapas Brindisa	"	3 2 2
	O'ver	Pizza	3 2 2
	Santo Remedio	Mexican	3 2 2
	Paladar	South American	4 4 5
	Antillean	Caribbean	3 2 3
	Bala Baya	Middle Eastern	3 3 3
	Sticky Mango	Pan-Asian	3 2 2
£50+	Bermondsey Larder	British, Modern	4 4 3
	Boiler & Co	"	5 4 3
	Caravan Bankside	"	2 2 2
	Lupins	"	4 4 3
	BOB's Lobster	Fish & seafood	3 4 2
	Tavolino	Italian	2 1 3
	Bar Douro	Portuguese	4 4 4
	Casa do Frango	"	4 2 3
	Andanza	Spanish	4 3 3
	Mar I Terra	"	4 4 3
	Salt Yard	"	3 2 2
	Mallow	Vegetarian	4 2 3
	El Pastór	Mexican	3 2 3
	Arabica Bar and Kitchen	Lebanese	3 4 2
	Gunpowder	Indian	4 3 3
	Champor-Champor	Thai	4 3 3
£40+	Flour & Grape	Italian	3 3 3
	Legare	"	4 4 3
	Mercato Metropolitano	"	3 2 5
	Padella	"	4 3 3
	Meson don Felipe	Spanish	3 3 4
	Patty and Bun	Burgers, etc	3 2 2
	Tas Pide	Turkish	3 3 3
	Kin and Deum	Thai	4 2 3
£35+	Flat Iron, The Cut	Steaks & grills	3 4 3
	Tacos Padre	Mexican	3 3 4
	Baozi Inn	Chinese	3 2 2
	Bao Borough	Taiwanese	3 4 4
£10+	Kappacasein	Sandwiches, cakes, etc	5 3 2
£5+	Monmouth Coffee Company	Sandwiches, cakes, etc	3 4 3

Greenwich, Lewisham, Dulwich & Blackheath
(All SE postcodes, except SE1)

	Name	Cuisine	Rating
£80+	Copper & Ink	British, Modern	4 3 3
£70+	Coal Rooms	British, Modern	4 3 3
	Llewelyn's	"	3 3 2
£60+	The Alma	British, Modern	3 3 4
	Bobo Social	"	3 3 3
	The Camberwell Arms	"	4 4 4

FSA Ratings: from **1** (Poor) to **5** (Exceptional)

SOUTH | **AREA OVERVIEWS**

	The Crooked Well	"	3 3 3
	Franklins	"	3 3 3
	Levan	"	3 3 2
	Walter's	"	3 3 4
	Toulouse Lautrec	French	3 4 3
	Peckham Bazaar	Greek	4 3 3
	Forza Wine	Italian	3 4 5
	Manuel's	"	4 5 3
	Kudu	South African	4 4 4
	Sticks'n'Sushi	Japanese	3 2 2
	Yama Momo	"	3 2 2
£50+	The Guildford Arms	British, Modern	3 3 3
	Peckham Cellars	"	4 4 3
	The Perry Hill	"	3 4 4
	The Rosendale	"	3 3 3
	Sparrow	"	4 3 4
	Joanna's	International	3 3 4
	The Yellow House	"	3 4 3
	Artusi	Italian	4 3 3
	Luciano's	"	3 4 3
	Le Querce	"	4 3 2
	Dulwich Lyceum	Mediterranean	3 4 4
	Mamma Dough	Pizza	4 3 2
	Babur	Indian	5 5 3
	Heritage	"	3 3 3
	Kennington Tandoori	"	3 4 3
	The Begging Bowl	Thai	4 4 3
£40+	The Lordship	British, Modern	3 2 2
	Tila	"	– – –
	Brookmill	International	3 3 3
	Marcella	Italian	3 4 3
	MEATliquor ED	Burgers, etc	4 2 2
	Street Burger	"	2 2 2
	Mike's Peckham	Pizza	4 4 3
	Rocca	"	3 3 3
	Yard Sale Pizza	"	4 4 2
	Kudu Grill	South African	4 4 4
	FM Mangal	Turkish	3 3 2
	Dragon Castle	Chinese	3 2 2
	Everest Inn	Indian	3 2 2
	Ganapati	"	4 2 2
	Bone Daddies	Japanese	3 3 3
	Zaibatsu	"	3 3 2
£35+	Olley's	Fish & chips	3 3 3
	500 Degrees	Pizza	3 2 3
	Theo's	"	3 3 2
	Taro	Japanese	3 3 2
£30+	Trattoria Raffaele	Italian	3 3 2
	400 Rabbits	Pizza	3 3 2
	Nandine	Middle Eastern	3 4 3
	Mr Bao	Taiwanese	3 2 2

AREA OVERVIEWS | SOUTH

£25+	Goddards At Greenwich	British, Traditional	3️⃣4️⃣3️⃣
	Silk Road	Chinese	5️⃣2️⃣2️⃣
£15+	Everest Curry King	Sri Lankan	4️⃣3️⃣2️⃣
	La Chingada	Mexican	4️⃣3️⃣2️⃣
	Marugame Udon	Japanese	4️⃣3️⃣2️⃣

Battersea, Brixton, Clapham, Wandsworth Barnes, Putney & Wimbledon
(All SW postcodes south of the river)

£160+	Oxeye	British, Modern	5️⃣4️⃣4️⃣
£110+	Trinity	British, Modern	5️⃣4️⃣3️⃣
£100+	Chez Bruce	British, Modern	5️⃣4️⃣3️⃣
£80+	Black Radish	British, Modern	4️⃣5️⃣3️⃣
	Rick Stein	Fish & seafood	1️⃣2️⃣2️⃣
	Darby's	Irish	3️⃣3️⃣4️⃣
£70+	The Crossing	British, Modern	3️⃣2️⃣3️⃣
	Hatched	"	4️⃣3️⃣2️⃣
	The Pig's Head	"	3️⃣3️⃣3️⃣
	Wright Brothers	Fish & seafood	3️⃣2️⃣3️⃣
	Fiume	Italian	2️⃣2️⃣3️⃣
	Riva	"	3️⃣4️⃣2️⃣
	Knife	Steaks & grills	4️⃣4️⃣3️⃣
	Good Earth	Chinese	3️⃣3️⃣2️⃣
	Patara	Thai	3️⃣3️⃣2️⃣
£60+	The Laundry	Australian	3️⃣4️⃣3️⃣
	Bistro Union	British, Modern	3️⃣4️⃣2️⃣
	The Black Lamb	"	– – –
	Brunswick House Café	"	3️⃣2️⃣5️⃣
	Church Road	"	3️⃣4️⃣3️⃣
	Humble Grape	"	3️⃣4️⃣3️⃣
	The Ivy Café	"	1️⃣2️⃣2️⃣
	Only Food and Courses	"	– – –
	Trinity Upstairs	"	3️⃣3️⃣3️⃣
	The Victoria	"	3️⃣3️⃣3️⃣
	Fox & Grapes	British, Traditional	3️⃣2️⃣2️⃣
	The Plough	"	– – –
	Gazette	French	2️⃣2️⃣3️⃣
	Soif	"	3️⃣2️⃣2️⃣
	Brinkley's Kitchen	International	2️⃣2️⃣3️⃣
	The Light House	"	3️⃣3️⃣3️⃣
	Artisans of Sardinia	Italian	3️⃣4️⃣3️⃣
	Maremma	"	4️⃣3️⃣4️⃣
	Numero Uno	"	2️⃣3️⃣2️⃣
	Osteria Antica Bologna	"	3️⃣3️⃣2️⃣
	Sorella	"	4️⃣3️⃣2️⃣
	The Fox & Hounds	Mediterranean	3️⃣4️⃣3️⃣
	Tapas Brindisa	Spanish	3️⃣2️⃣2️⃣

FSA Ratings: from 1️⃣ (Poor) to 5️⃣ (Exceptional)

SOUTH | **AREA OVERVIEWS**

	Macellaio RC	*Steaks & grills*	2️⃣2️⃣3️⃣
	Cinnamon Kitchen Battersea	*Indian*	3️⃣3️⃣3️⃣
	Kibou London	*Japanese*	2️⃣2️⃣3️⃣
	Sticks'n'Sushi	"	3️⃣2️⃣2️⃣
£50+	The Brown Dog	*British, Modern*	3️⃣2️⃣3️⃣
	Coppa Club Putney	"	2️⃣3️⃣4️⃣
	Hood	"	4️⃣4️⃣2️⃣
	London Stock	"	3️⃣4️⃣3️⃣
	Olympic Studios	"	2️⃣2️⃣3️⃣
	The Telegraph	"	3️⃣4️⃣4️⃣
	24 The Oval	"	3️⃣4️⃣3️⃣
	Canton Arms	*British, Traditional*	3️⃣3️⃣4️⃣
	Smoke & Salt	"	5️⃣4️⃣3️⃣
	Augustine Kitchen	*French*	4️⃣4️⃣3️⃣
	Cent Anni	*Italian*	3️⃣2️⃣2️⃣
	Made in Italy	"	3️⃣2️⃣2️⃣
	Pizza Metro	"	3️⃣2️⃣2️⃣
	Boqueria	*Spanish*	3️⃣3️⃣2️⃣
	Little Taperia	"	3️⃣3️⃣3️⃣
	Naughty Piglets	*Steaks & grills*	5️⃣4️⃣4️⃣
	Mamma Dough	*Pizza*	4️⃣3️⃣2️⃣
	Zia Lucia	"	4️⃣2️⃣2️⃣
	Santa Maria del Sur	*Argentinian*	3️⃣3️⃣2️⃣
	Le Bab	*Middle Eastern*	3️⃣2️⃣2️⃣
	Chook Chook	*Indian*	4️⃣3️⃣3️⃣
	Hashi	*Japanese*	3️⃣3️⃣2️⃣
	Oka	"	3️⃣3️⃣2️⃣
	Takahashi	"	5️⃣5️⃣3️⃣
	Tsunami	"	4️⃣3️⃣2️⃣
£40+	The Rushmere	*British, Modern*	– – –
	Danclair's	*International*	– – –
	Rosmarino	*Italian*	3️⃣4️⃣4️⃣
	Soffice London	"	3️⃣4️⃣3️⃣
	Black Bear Burger	*Burgers, etc*	4️⃣3️⃣2️⃣
	Haché	"	4️⃣3️⃣3️⃣
	MEATliquor	"	4️⃣2️⃣2️⃣
	Patty and Bun	"	3️⃣2️⃣2️⃣
	Bravi Ragazzi	*Pizza*	4️⃣2️⃣2️⃣
	Pizza da Valter	"	4️⃣3️⃣3️⃣
	Yard Sale Pizza	"	4️⃣4️⃣2️⃣
	Orange Pekoe	*Sandwiches, cakes, etc*	3️⃣3️⃣4️⃣
	Chishuru	*West African*	3️⃣3️⃣2️⃣
	Meza Trinity Road	*Lebanese*	3️⃣3️⃣3️⃣
	The Red Duck	*Chinese*	4️⃣2️⃣2️⃣
	Black Salt	*Indian*	5️⃣3️⃣2️⃣
	Kashmir	"	3️⃣3️⃣2️⃣
	Ma Goa	"	3️⃣3️⃣3️⃣
	Bone Daddies	*Japanese*	3️⃣3️⃣3️⃣
	Tomoe	"	4️⃣4️⃣2️⃣
	Hare & Tortoise	*Pan-Asian*	3️⃣3️⃣2️⃣
	Kaosarn	*Thai*	3️⃣3️⃣3️⃣
	Mien Tay	*Vietnamese*	3️⃣3️⃣2️⃣

AREA OVERVIEWS | SOUTH

£35+	BabaBoom	Middle Eastern	3 3 2
	Indian Moment	Indian	3 2 2
	Indian Room	Indian	4 4 3
	Taro	Japanese	3 3 2
	Awesome Thai	Thai	3 3 2
	Daddy Bao	Taiwanese	4 3 3
£30+	Amrutha	Vegan	4 5 2
	Unwined	Mediterranean	3 4 2
	Three Uncles	Chinese	5 3 3
	Indian Ocean	Indian	3 3 3
	Munal Tandoori	"	3 4 2
	Sushi Revolution	Japanese	3 3 2
	Cher Thai	Thai	4 4 3
£25+	Ela & Dhani	Indian	4 5 3
	Mirch Masala	Pakistani	4 2 2
£20+	Dropshot Coffee	British, Modern	3 4 4
	Milk	Sandwiches, cakes, etc	3 2 3
	Roti King	Malaysian	5 2 3
£15+	Joe Public	Pizza	3 3 2

Outer western suburbs
Kew, Richmond, Twickenham, Teddington

£120+	Petersham Nurseries Cafe	British, Modern	2 3 5
£80+	The Dysart Petersham	British, Modern	4 4 4
	The Petersham Restaurant	"	2 2 3
	Steven Edwards	"	4 2 4
£70+	Bacco	Italian	3 3 2
£60+	The Fat Badger	British, Modern	3 2 2
	The Ivy Café	"	1 2 2
	Six Restaurant	British, Traditional	3 3 3
	Petit Ma Cuisine	French	3 3 3
	A Cena	Italian	3 3 3
	Tapas Brindisa Richmond	Spanish	3 2 2
	Rock & Rose	Pan-Asian	– – –
£50+	Black Dog Beer House	British, Modern	4 4 3
	Rye by the Water	"	3 2 2
	Le Salon Privé	French	3 3 3
	Four Regions	Chinese	3 2 2
£40+	Newens	Afternoon tea	3 3 3
	Dastaan	Indian	5 4 3
£25+	Kiss the Hippo	Sandwiches, cakes, etc	3 3 2

FSA Ratings: from 1 (Poor) to 5 (Exceptional)

EAST | **AREA OVERVIEWS**

EAST

Smithfield & Farringdon (EC1)

£200+	The Clove Club	*British, Modern*	4️⃣4️⃣3️⃣
£150+	The Drunken Butler	*French*	3️⃣4️⃣4️⃣
£130+	Club Gascon	*French*	4️⃣3️⃣3️⃣
£100+	Anglo	*British, Modern*	5️⃣4️⃣2️⃣
£90+	The Quality Chop House	*British, Traditional*	4️⃣4️⃣4️⃣
	Luca	*Italian*	4️⃣3️⃣4️⃣
£80+	St John Smithfield	*British, Traditional*	4️⃣4️⃣3️⃣
	Smiths (Top Floor)	*Steaks & grills*	2️⃣3️⃣3️⃣
£70+	The Jugged Hare	*British, Modern*	3️⃣2️⃣3️⃣
	Daffodil Mulligan	*Irish*	3️⃣4️⃣3️⃣
	Moro	*Spanish*	3️⃣3️⃣2️⃣
£60+	Granger & Co	*Australian*	2️⃣2️⃣2️⃣
	The Coach	*British, Modern*	2️⃣3️⃣3️⃣
	Sessions Arts Club	"	3️⃣3️⃣5️⃣
	Vinoteca	"	2️⃣2️⃣2️⃣
	Bleeding Heart Bistro	*French*	3️⃣3️⃣4️⃣
	Apulia	*Italian*	3️⃣2️⃣2️⃣
	Macellaio RC	"	2️⃣2️⃣3️⃣
	Ibérica	*Spanish*	2️⃣2️⃣2️⃣
	Berber & Q Shawarma Bar	*Middle Eastern*	5️⃣4️⃣4️⃣
£50+	Tendril	*Vegan*	4️⃣3️⃣3️⃣
	Caravan	*British, Modern*	2️⃣2️⃣2️⃣
	The Clerk & Well	"	– – –
	Café du Marché	*French*	3️⃣4️⃣5️⃣
	Santore	*Italian*	3️⃣2️⃣2️⃣
	Fare	*Mediterranean*	3️⃣2️⃣3️⃣
	Morito	*Spanish*	4️⃣3️⃣3️⃣
	The Gate	*Vegetarian*	3️⃣3️⃣3️⃣
	Homeslice by Symplicity	*Pizza*	4️⃣3️⃣3️⃣
	Le Bab	*Middle Eastern*	3️⃣2️⃣2️⃣
£40+	Stem & Glory	*Vegan*	3️⃣3️⃣2️⃣
	Fish Central	*Fish & seafood*	3️⃣4️⃣2️⃣
	Trattoria Brutto	*Italian*	3️⃣4️⃣5️⃣
	Pastan	"	3️⃣4️⃣3️⃣
	The Eagle	*Mediterranean*	3️⃣3️⃣4️⃣
	Black Bear Burger	*Burgers, etc*	4️⃣3️⃣2️⃣
	Street Burger	"	2️⃣2️⃣2️⃣
	Taqueria	*Mexican*	4️⃣4️⃣3️⃣
	The Sichuan	*Chinese*	4️⃣3️⃣2️⃣
	Bone Daddies, The Bower	*Japanese*	3️⃣3️⃣3️⃣
	Pham Sushi	"	3️⃣3️⃣3️⃣
	Cây Tre	*Vietnamese*	3️⃣3️⃣2️⃣

AREA OVERVIEWS | EAST

£30+	Balady	Middle Eastern	4 2 1
£15+	Prufrock Coffee	Sandwiches, cakes, etc	3 2 2
£10+	Daddy Donkey	Mexican	4 3 2

The City (EC2, EC3, EC4)

£140+	La Dame de Pic	French	4 4 3
£120+	Nobu Shoreditch	Japanese	– – –
£110+	Angler, South Place Hotel	Fish & seafood	3 3 4
	Coya	Peruvian	3 3 3
	Sushisamba	Japanese	2 2 3
£100+	City Social	British, Modern	3 3 4
	Fenchurch, Sky Garden	"	3 3 4
	Aviary	Steaks & grills	2 3 4
	Lutyens Grill, The Ned	"	3 2 4
	Yauatcha City	Chinese	3 2 2
£90+	Duck & Waffle	British, Modern	2 2 3
	14 Hills	"	2 2 4
	Coq d'Argent	French	2 2 3
	Goodman City	Steaks & grills	3 3 2
	Hawksmoor Guildhall	"	2 2 2
	M Restaurant	"	2 2 3
£80+	Bread Street Kitchen	British, Modern	2 3 3
	Darwin Brasserie	"	3 3 4
	Helix	"	3 3 5
	Sweetings	Fish & seafood	3 2 4
	Bob Bob Ricard City	French	2 4 5
	Cecconi's, The Ned	International	2 2 4
	Revolve	"	– – –
	Manicomio City	Italian	2 2 3
£70+	The Ivy City Garden	British, Modern	2 2 3
	The Mercer	"	3 3 3
	1 Lombard Street	"	3 2 3
	Princess of Shoreditch	"	5 3 3
	Paternoster Chop House	British, Traditional	2 4 2
	Cabotte	French	3 5 4
	Vivat Bacchus	International	3 3 3
	Piazza Italiana	Italian	3 3 3
	Bibo by Dani García	Spanish	2 2 3
	Hispania	"	3 4 4
	Burger & Lobster	Burgers, etc	3 3 3
	Pachamama East	Peruvian	2 2 3
	Oklava	Turkish	4 4 3
	Brigadiers	Indian	5 4 4
	The Ivy Asia	Pan-Asian	2 3 4

FSA Ratings: from 1 (Poor) to 5 (Exceptional)

EAST | **AREA OVERVIEWS**

£60+			
	High Timber	*British, Modern*	3️⃣4️⃣3️⃣
	Humble Grape	"	3️⃣4️⃣3️⃣
	Leroy	"	3️⃣3️⃣3️⃣
	Vinoteca City	"	2️⃣2️⃣2️⃣
	Brasserie Blanc	*French*	2️⃣2️⃣2️⃣
	Gazette	"	2️⃣2️⃣3️⃣
	Caravaggio	*Italian*	2️⃣3️⃣2️⃣
	Gloria	"	2️⃣3️⃣5️⃣
	Obicà	"	3️⃣3️⃣3️⃣
	Camino Shoreditch	*Spanish*	2️⃣3️⃣2️⃣
	José Pizarro	"	3️⃣2️⃣2️⃣
	Maya	*Mexican*	– – –
	Santo Remedio Café	"	3️⃣2️⃣2️⃣
	Haz	*Turkish*	3️⃣3️⃣2️⃣
	Cinnamon Kitchen	*Indian*	3️⃣3️⃣3️⃣

£50+			
	The Anthologist	*British, Modern*	2️⃣2️⃣3️⃣
	Caravan	"	2️⃣2️⃣2️⃣
	Coppa Club Tower Bridge	"	2️⃣3️⃣4️⃣
	VQ	"	2️⃣2️⃣3️⃣
	Simpson's Tavern	*British, Traditional*	2️⃣3️⃣5️⃣
	Eataly	*Italian*	2️⃣2️⃣3️⃣
	Manteca	"	5️⃣2️⃣4️⃣
	Osteria, Barbican Centre	"	3️⃣2️⃣2️⃣
	Popolo	"	5️⃣3️⃣2️⃣
	Casa do Frango	*Portuguese*	4️⃣2️⃣3️⃣
	Ekte Nordic Kitchen	*Scandinavian*	3️⃣3️⃣2️⃣
	Blacklock	*Steaks & grills*	3️⃣4️⃣3️⃣
	Relais de Venise	"	3️⃣2️⃣3️⃣
	temper Shoreditch	"	3️⃣2️⃣4️⃣
	Homeslice	*Pizza*	4️⃣3️⃣3️⃣
	temper City	*BBQ*	3️⃣2️⃣4️⃣
	Shoryu Ramen	*Japanese*	3️⃣3️⃣2️⃣

£40+			
	Stem & Glory Broadgate	*Vegan*	3️⃣3️⃣2️⃣
	Hithe & Seek	*British, Modern*	– – –
	The Wine Library	*International*	2️⃣2️⃣4️⃣
	Lina Stores	*Italian*	4️⃣3️⃣3️⃣
	Padella Shoreditch	"	4️⃣3️⃣3️⃣
	Haché	*Burgers, etc*	4️⃣3️⃣3️⃣
	Patty and Bun	"	3️⃣2️⃣2️⃣
	Street Burger	"	2️⃣2️⃣2️⃣
	Ozone Coffee Roasters	*Sandwiches, cakes, etc*	3️⃣4️⃣4️⃣
	Koya	*Japanese*	3️⃣4️⃣3️⃣
	Hare & Tortoise	*Pan-Asian*	3️⃣3️⃣2️⃣

£35+	Flat Iron	*Steaks & grills*	3️⃣4️⃣3️⃣

£30+	Three Uncles	*Chinese*	5️⃣3️⃣3️⃣

£25+	Bleecker Burger	*Burgers, etc*	4️⃣2️⃣2️⃣

£20+	Cincinnati Chilibomb	*American*	3️⃣4️⃣2️⃣

£15+	Halo Burger	*Burgers, etc*	3️⃣3️⃣2️⃣

AREA OVERVIEWS | EAST

| £5+ | Rosslyn Coffee | *Sandwiches, cakes, etc* | 5 4 3 |

East End & Docklands (All E postcodes)

£220+	Da Terra	*Fusion*	5 4 4
£150+	The Water House Project	*British, Modern*	4 3 4
£110+	Galvin La Chapelle	*French*	3 3 5

£90+	Brat at Climpson's Arch	*British, Modern*	4 3 3
	Lyle's	"	5 4 3
	Cornerstone	*Fish & seafood*	5 5 4
	Goodman	*Steaks & grills*	3 3 2
	Hawksmoor	"	2 2 2
	M Restaurant	"	2 2 3
	Roka	*Japanese*	4 3 3

£80+	Brat	*British, Modern*	4 3 3
	Bright	"	4 4 3
	Pidgin	"	4 3 2
	Plateau	*French*	2 2 3
	Cecconi's Shoreditch	*Italian*	2 2 4

£70+	Big Easy	*American*	2 2 3
	Elliot's	*British, Modern*	3 2 3
	The Ivy in the Park	"	2 2 3
	The Narrow	"	2 2 3
	Rochelle Canteen	"	3 4 4
	Smith's Wapping	"	4 3 3
	The Marksman	*British, Traditional*	3 3 3
	Behind	*Fish & seafood*	5 5 4
	The Melusine	"	4 3 3
	The Sea, The Sea	"	5 4 4
	Planque	*French*	3 2 4
	Casa Fofó	*International*	5 4 3
	Canto Corvino	*Italian*	2 2 3
	Brawn	*Mediterranean*	– – –
	Ottolenghi	"	4 3 2
	Haugen	*Swiss*	2 2 2
	Burger & Lobster	*Burgers, etc*	3 3 3

£60+	Allegra	*British, Modern*	3 3 3
	The Gun	"	3 3 4
	Humble Grape	"	3 4 3
	Jones & Sons	"	3 3 4
	Silo	"	4 4 3
	St John Bread & Wine	*British, Traditional*	3 2 3
	Goddard & Gibbs	*Fish & seafood*	– – –
	The Boundary	*French*	– – –
	Chez Elles	"	3 3 3
	Galvin Bistrot & Bar	"	3 2 3
	Angelina	*Fusion*	4 2 3
	Six by Nico	*International*	3 3 3

FSA Ratings: from 1 (Poor) to 5 (Exceptional)

EAST | **AREA OVERVIEWS**

	Obicà	*Italian*	3️⃣3️⃣3️⃣
	Super Tuscan	"	4️⃣3️⃣3️⃣
	Oren	*Mediterranean*	4️⃣3️⃣2️⃣
	Boisdale of Canary Wharf	*Scottish*	3️⃣2️⃣4️⃣
	Ibérica	*Spanish*	2️⃣2️⃣2️⃣
	Berber & Q	*Middle Eastern*	5️⃣4️⃣4️⃣
	Haz	*Turkish*	3️⃣3️⃣2️⃣
	Royal China	*Chinese*	3️⃣1️⃣2️⃣
	Café Spice Namaste	*Indian*	5️⃣4️⃣4️⃣
	Grand Trunk Road	"	4️⃣4️⃣3️⃣
	Sticks'n'Sushi	*Japanese*	3️⃣2️⃣2️⃣
£50+	Cafe Cecilia	*British, Modern*	2️⃣2️⃣3️⃣
	Caravan	"	2️⃣2️⃣2️⃣
	The Culpeper	"	3️⃣3️⃣3️⃣
	The Duke of Richmond	"	3️⃣3️⃣3️⃣
	The Empress	"	3️⃣3️⃣4️⃣
	Mare Street Market	"	3️⃣2️⃣4️⃣
	P Franco	"	4️⃣3️⃣3️⃣
	Il Bordello	*Italian*	3️⃣2️⃣3️⃣
	Emilia's Crafted Pasta	"	3️⃣4️⃣3️⃣
	Ombra	"	3️⃣4️⃣3️⃣
	Morito	*Spanish*	4️⃣3️⃣3️⃣
	Mildreds	*Vegetarian*	3️⃣3️⃣3️⃣
	Burger & Beyond	*Burgers, etc*	4️⃣3️⃣2️⃣
	Ark Fish	*Fish & chips*	3️⃣3️⃣2️⃣
	Poppies	"	3️⃣2️⃣2️⃣
	Pizza East	*Pizza*	3️⃣3️⃣3️⃣
	Zia Lucia Aldgate	"	4️⃣2️⃣2️⃣
	Smokestak	*BBQ*	5️⃣3️⃣4️⃣
	Le Bab at Kraft Dalston	*Middle Eastern*	3️⃣2️⃣2️⃣
	Lahpet	*Burmese*	3️⃣4️⃣3️⃣
	Sichuan Folk	*Chinese*	4️⃣3️⃣2️⃣
	Dishoom	*Indian*	4️⃣4️⃣4️⃣
	Gunpowder	"	4️⃣3️⃣3️⃣
	Smoking Goat	*Thai*	4️⃣3️⃣3️⃣
	Som Saa	"	5️⃣3️⃣3️⃣
£40+	Hackney Coterie	*British, Modern*	3️⃣4️⃣3️⃣
	NEST	"	4️⃣4️⃣3️⃣
	Townsend	"	3️⃣3️⃣3️⃣
	Provender	*French*	3️⃣4️⃣2️⃣
	Mr Todiwala's Petiscos	*Portuguese*	4️⃣4️⃣3️⃣
	Black Bear Burger	*Burgers, etc*	4️⃣3️⃣2️⃣
	Patty and Bun	"	3️⃣2️⃣2️⃣
	Yard Sale Pizza	*Pizza*	4️⃣4️⃣2️⃣
	Ozone Coffee Roasters	*Sandwiches, cakes, etc*	3️⃣4️⃣4️⃣
	Chick 'n' Sours	*Chicken*	4️⃣3️⃣3️⃣
	Acme Fire Cult	*BBQ*	– – –
	Andina Spitalfields	*Peruvian*	2️⃣1️⃣3️⃣
	Bubala	*Middle Eastern*	4️⃣4️⃣3️⃣
	Delamina East	"	4️⃣3️⃣3️⃣
	Lucky & Joy	*Chinese*	4️⃣3️⃣4️⃣
	Issho-Ni	*Japanese*	3️⃣4️⃣3️⃣
	Koya Ko	"	3️⃣4️⃣3️⃣
	Mien Tay	*Vietnamese*	3️⃣3️⃣2️⃣

AREA OVERVIEWS | EAST

	Name	Cuisine	Ratings
	Sông Quê	"	3 3 2
£35+	Flat Iron	Steaks & grills	3 4 3
	Crate Brewery and Pizzeria	Pizza	3 2 3
	The Dusty Knuckle	Sandwiches, cakes, etc	4 2 3
	Facing Heaven	Chinese	– – –
	Taro	Japanese	3 3 2
	Lahore Kebab House	Pakistani	5 2 2
	Bao Noodle Shop	Taiwanese	3 4 4
£30+	Alter	Vegan	4 3 2
	Mangal 1	Turkish	5 3 2
	Tayyabs	Pakistani	4 1 2
£25+	Bleecker Burger	Burgers, etc	4 2 2
	Dumpling Shack	Chinese	5 3 1
	Singburi Royal Thai Café	Thai	4 4 3
£20+	Off the Hook	Fish & seafood	– – –
	E Pellicci	Italian	3 5 4
	Attawa	Indian	3 3 2
	Sushi Show	Japanese	3 3 2
£15+	The Duck Truck	Burgers, etc	5 4 2
	Marugame Udon	Japanese	4 3 2
£10+	Brick Lane Beigel Bake	Sandwiches, cakes, etc	4 2 1
	The Rib Man	Burgers, etc	4 4 –
	Popeyes	Chicken	4 3 3

FSA Ratings: from **1** (Poor) to **5** (Exceptional)

MAP 1 – LONDON OVERVIEW

MAP I – LONDON OVERVIEW

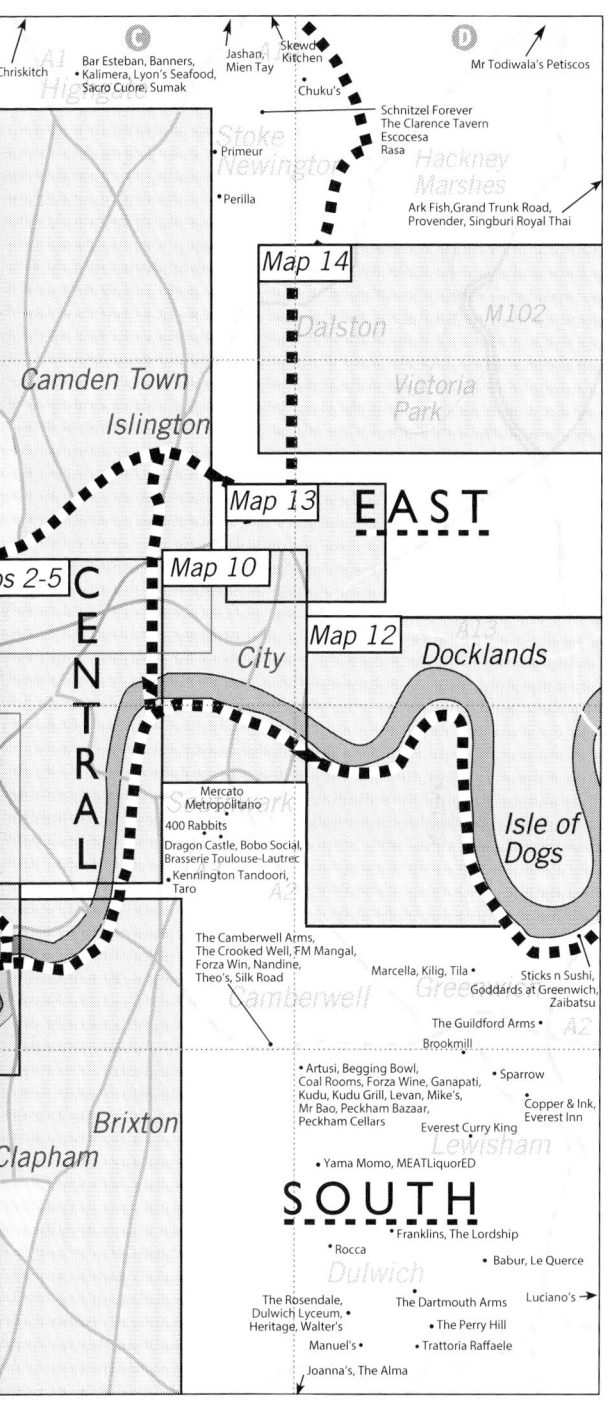

MAP 2 – WEST END OVERVIEW

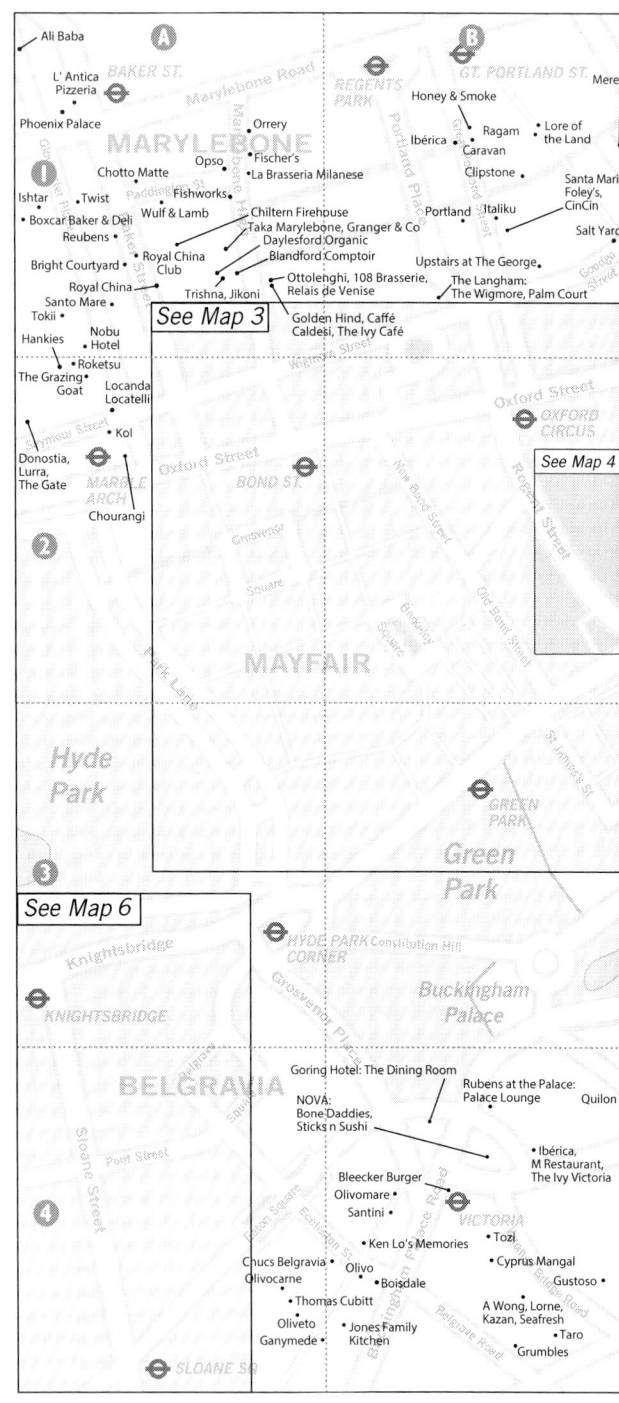

MAP 2 – WEST END OVERVIEW

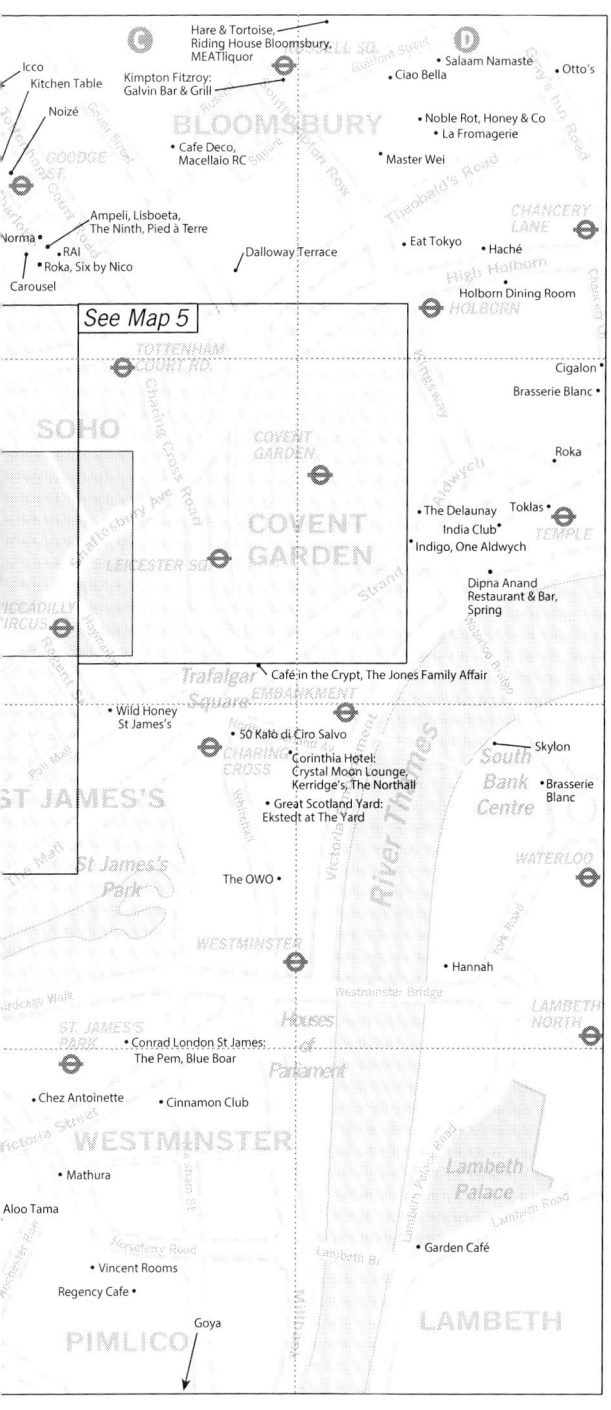

MAP 3 — MAYFAIR, ST. JAMES'S & WEST SOHO

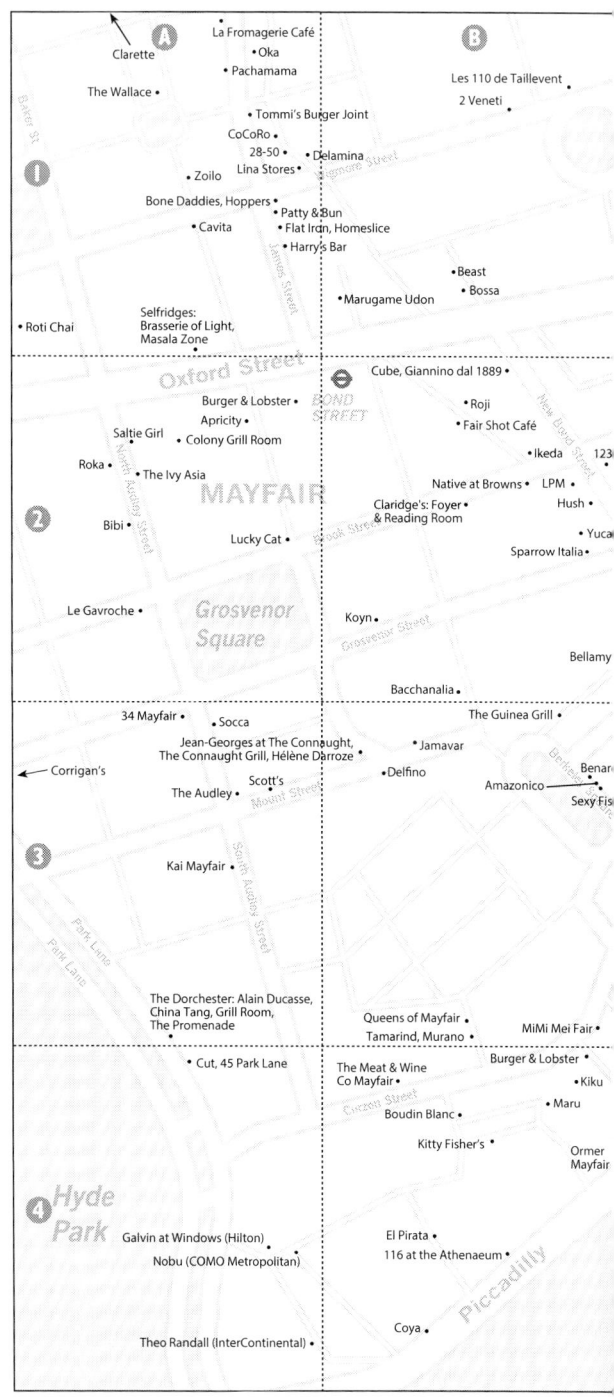

MAP 3 – MAYFAIR, ST. JAMES'S & WEST SOHO

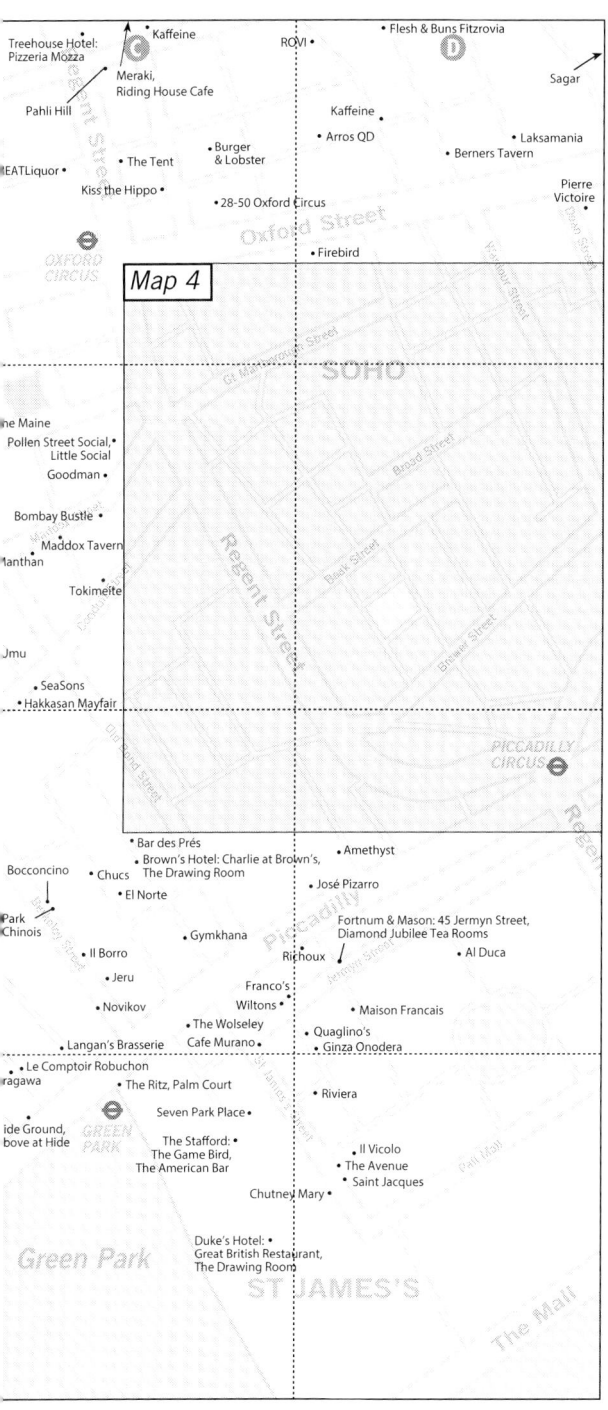

MAP 4 – WEST SOHO & PICCADILLY

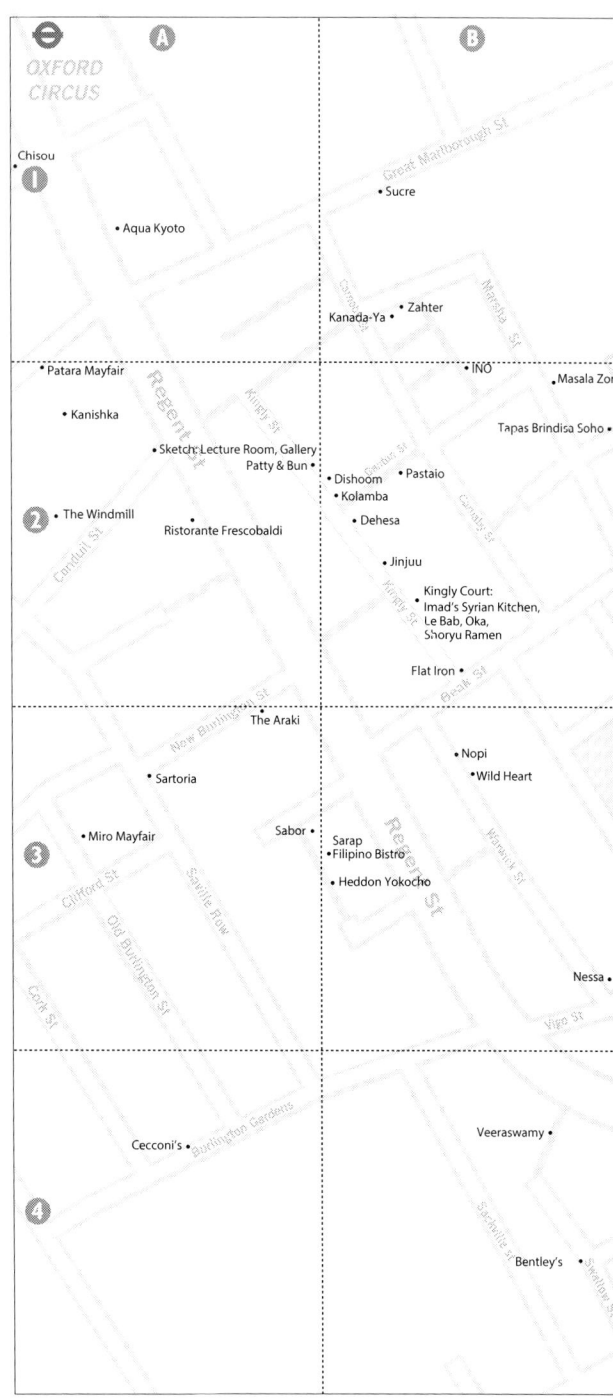

MAP 4 – WEST SOHO & PICCADILLY

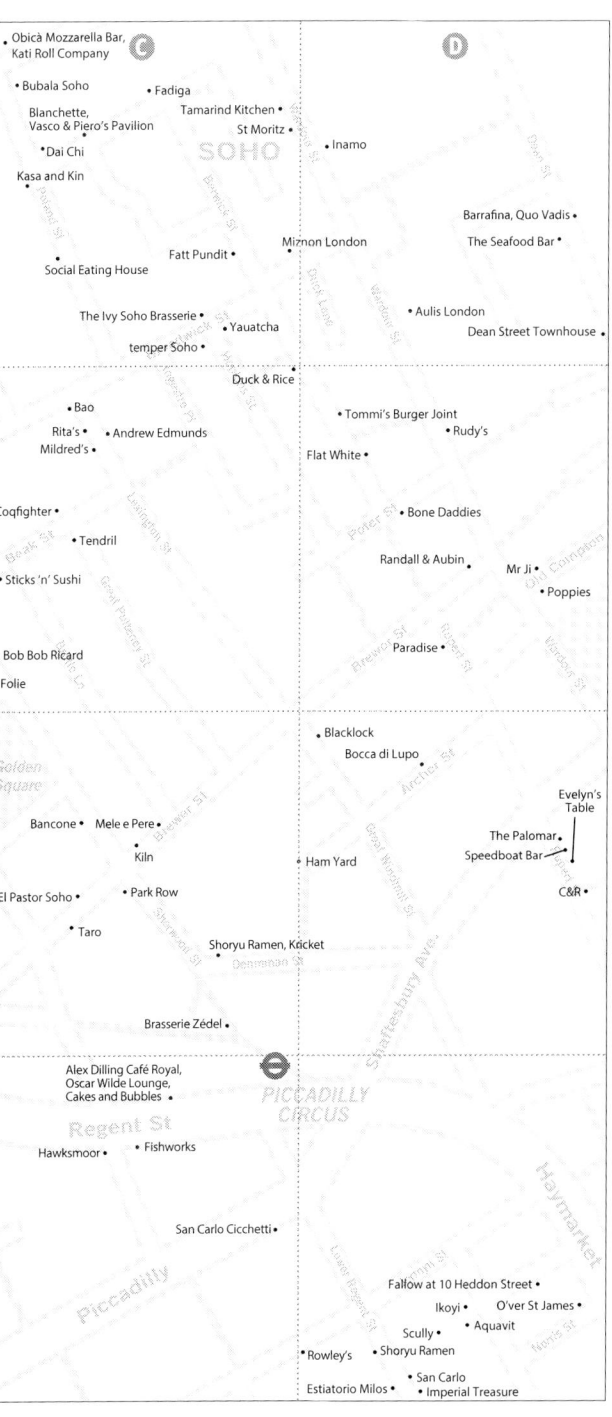

MAP 5 – EAST SOHO, CHINATOWN & COVENT GARDEN

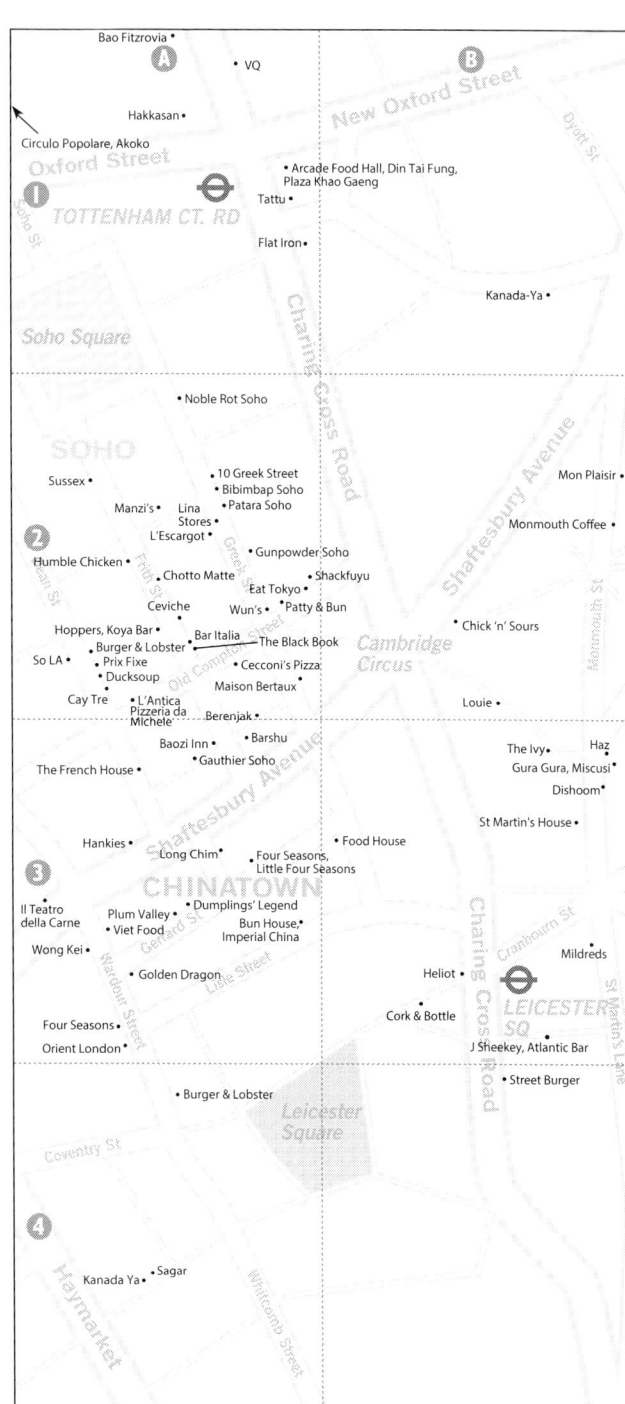

MAP 5 – EAST SOHO, CHINATOWN & COVENT GARDEN

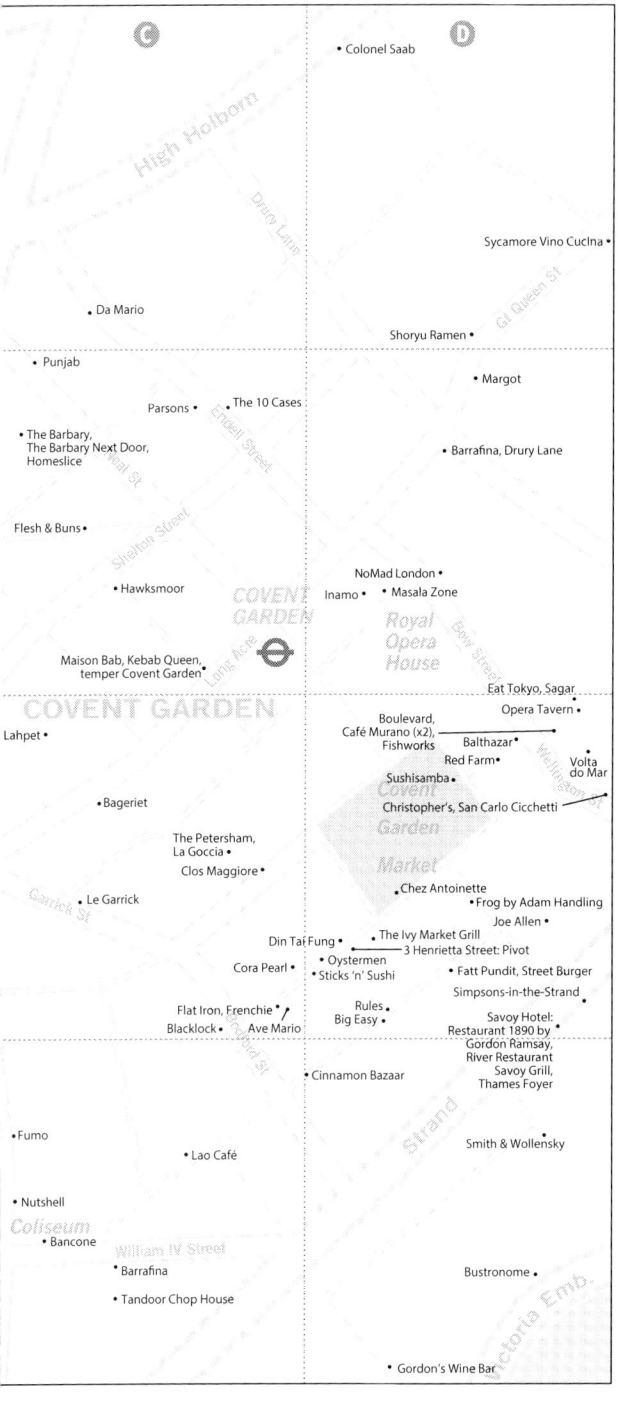

MAP 6 – KNIGHTSBRIDGE, CHELSEA & SOUTH KENSINGTON

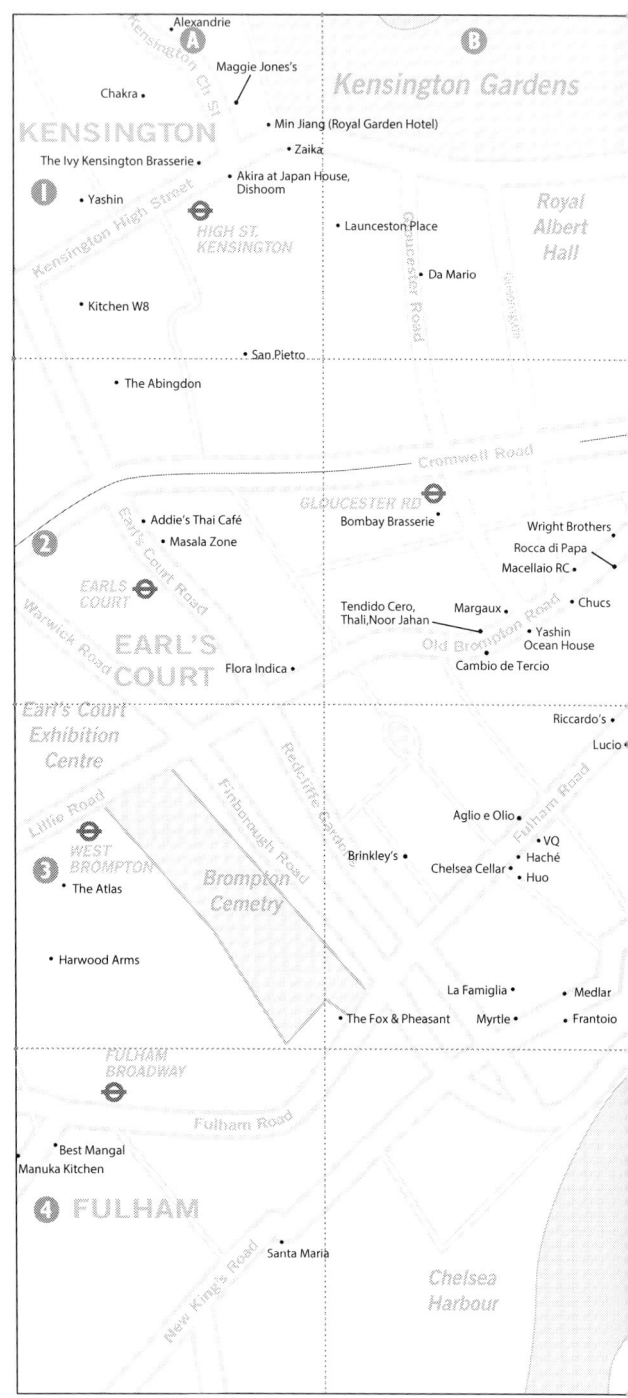

MAP 6 – KNIGHTSBRIDGE, CHELSEA & SOUTH KENSINGTON

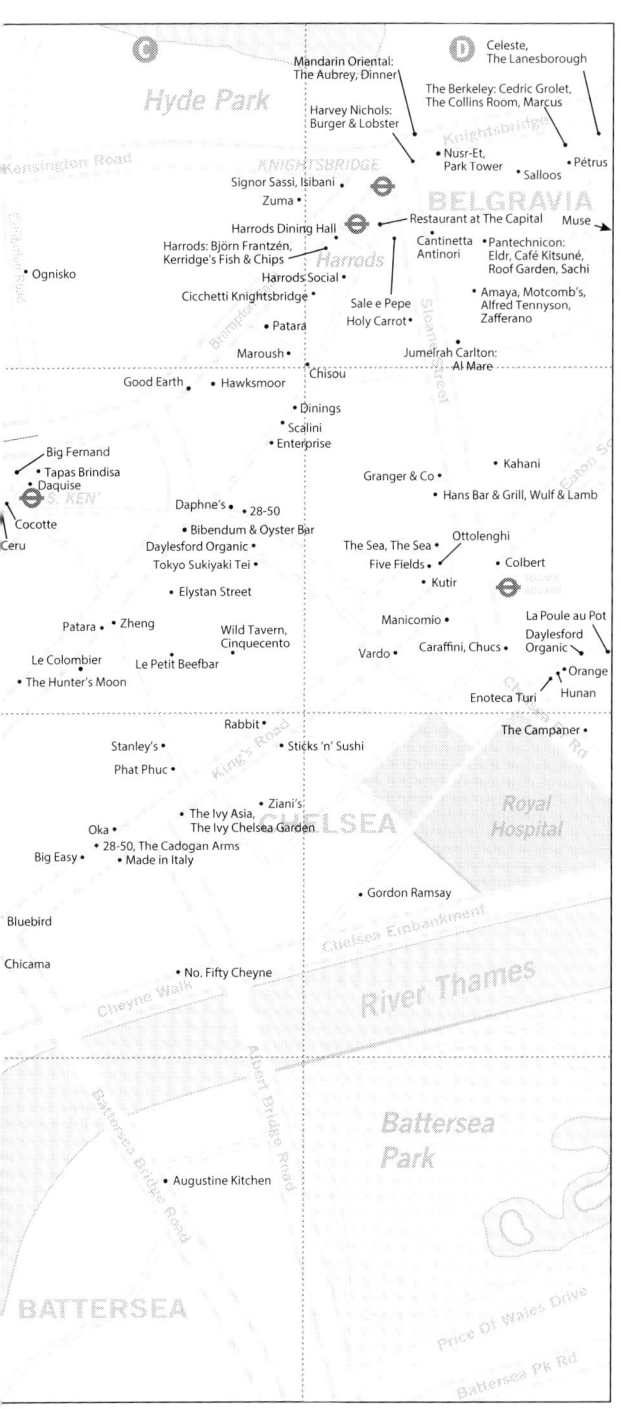

MAP 7 – NOTTING HILL & BAYSWATER

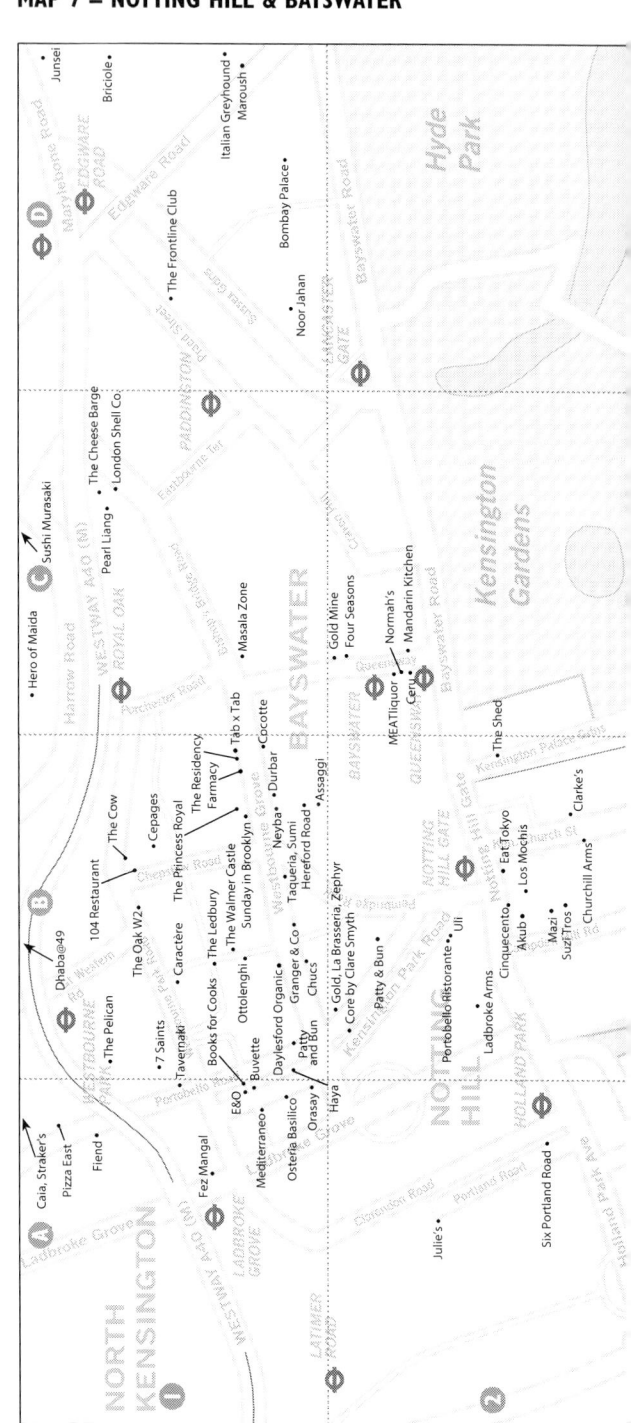

MAP 8 – HAMMERSMITH & CHISWICK

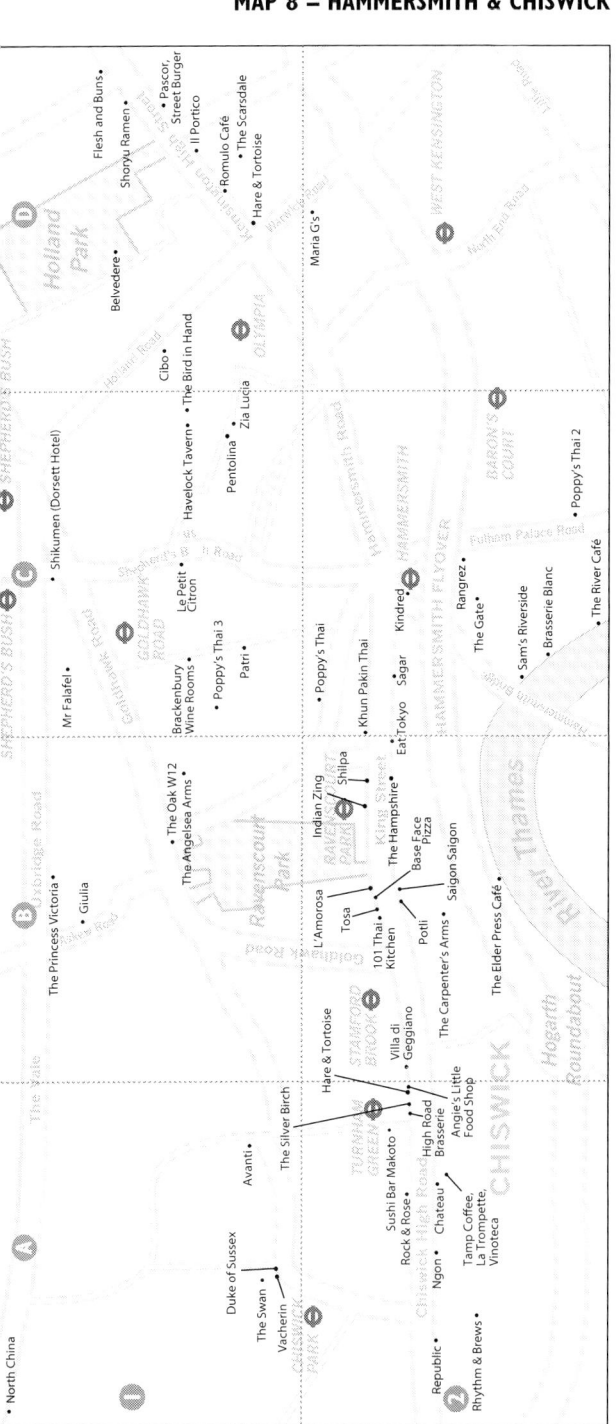

MAP 9 – HAMPSTEAD, CAMDEN TOWN & ISLINGTON

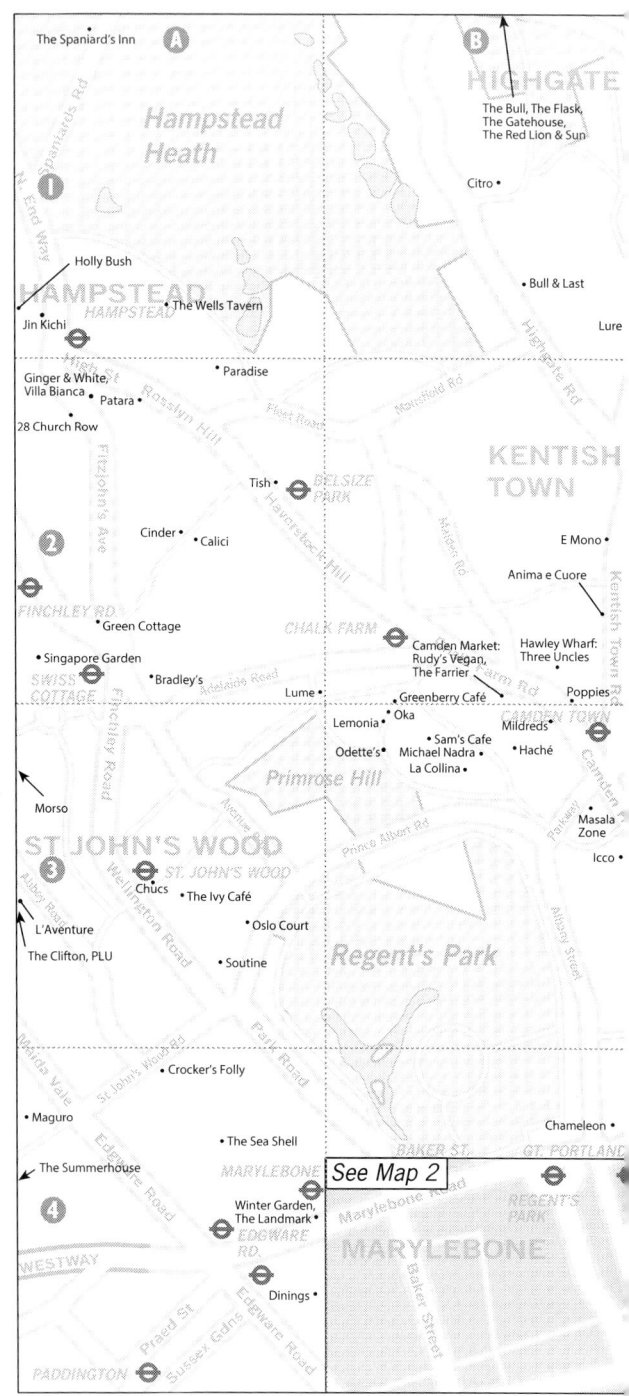

MAP 9 – HAMPSTEAD, CAMDEN TOWN & ISLINGTON

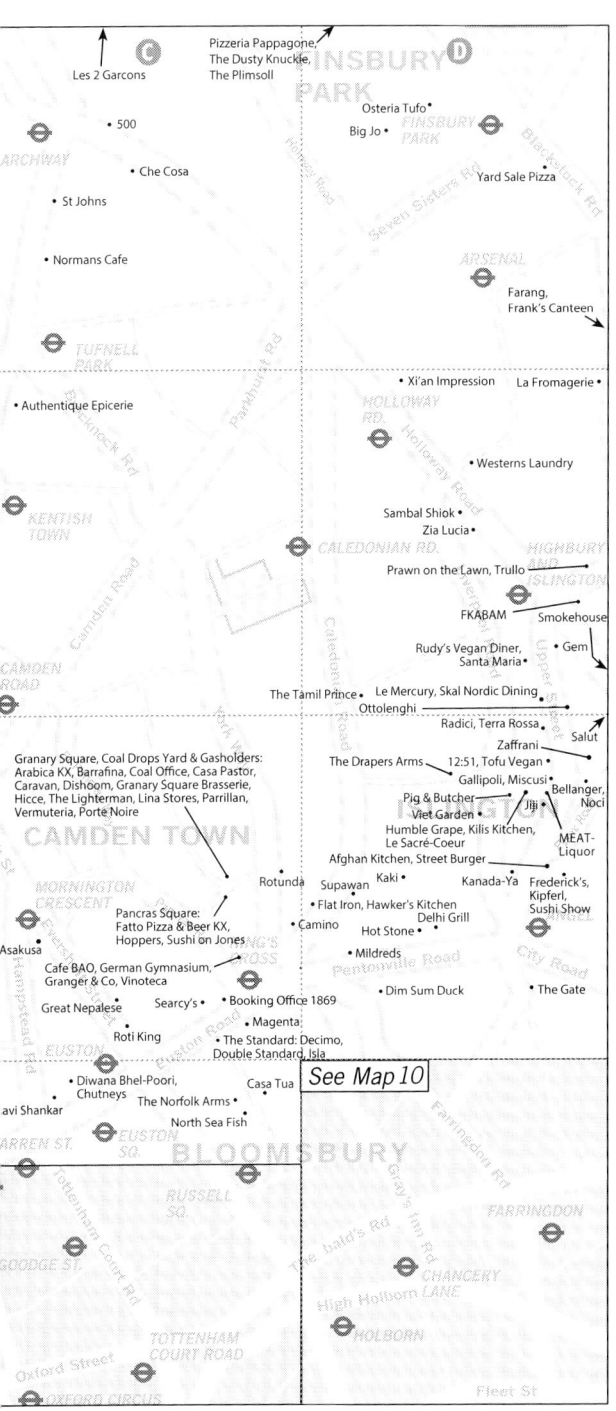

MAP 10 – THE CITY

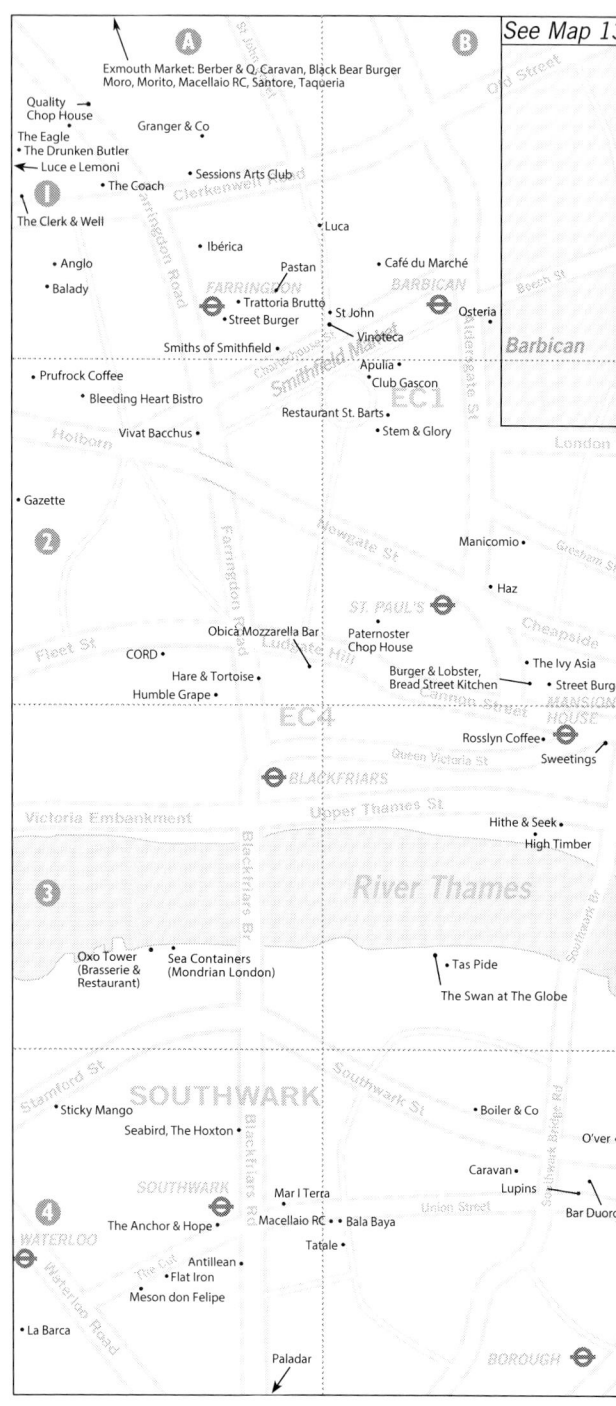

MAP 10 – THE CITY

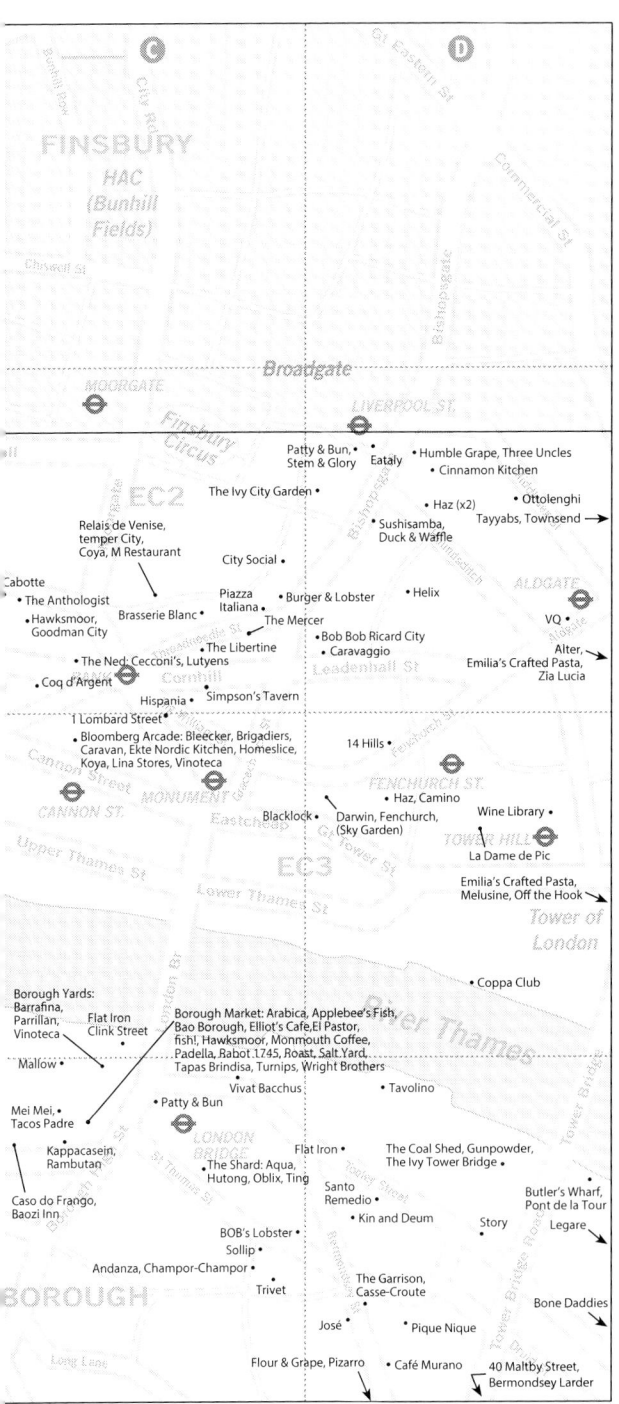

MAP 11 – SOUTH LONDON (& FULHAM)

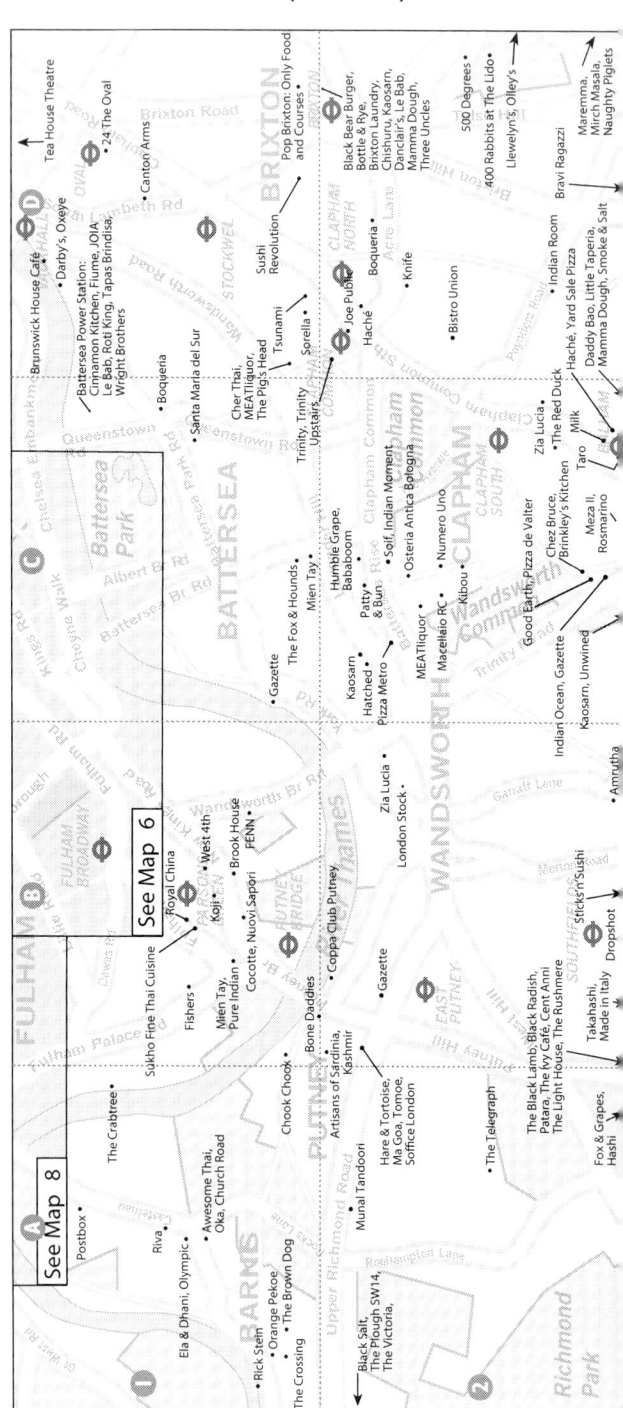

MAP 12 – EAST END & DOCKLANDS

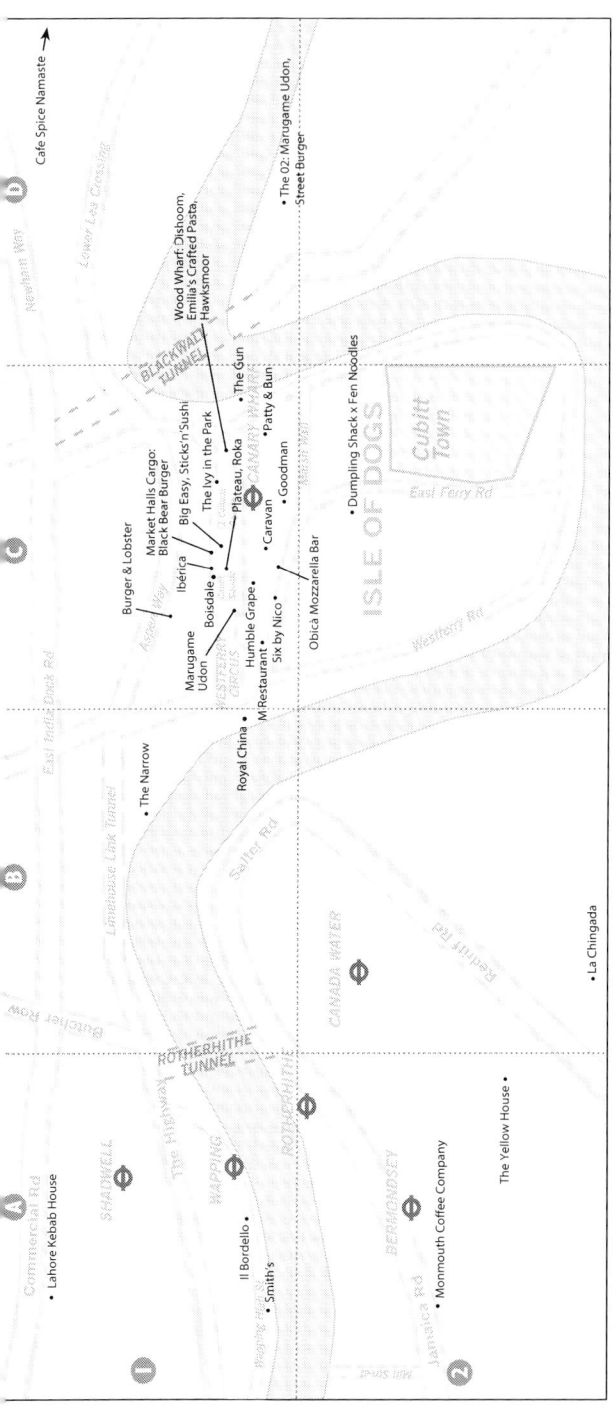

MAP 13 – SHOREDITCH & BETHNAL GREEN

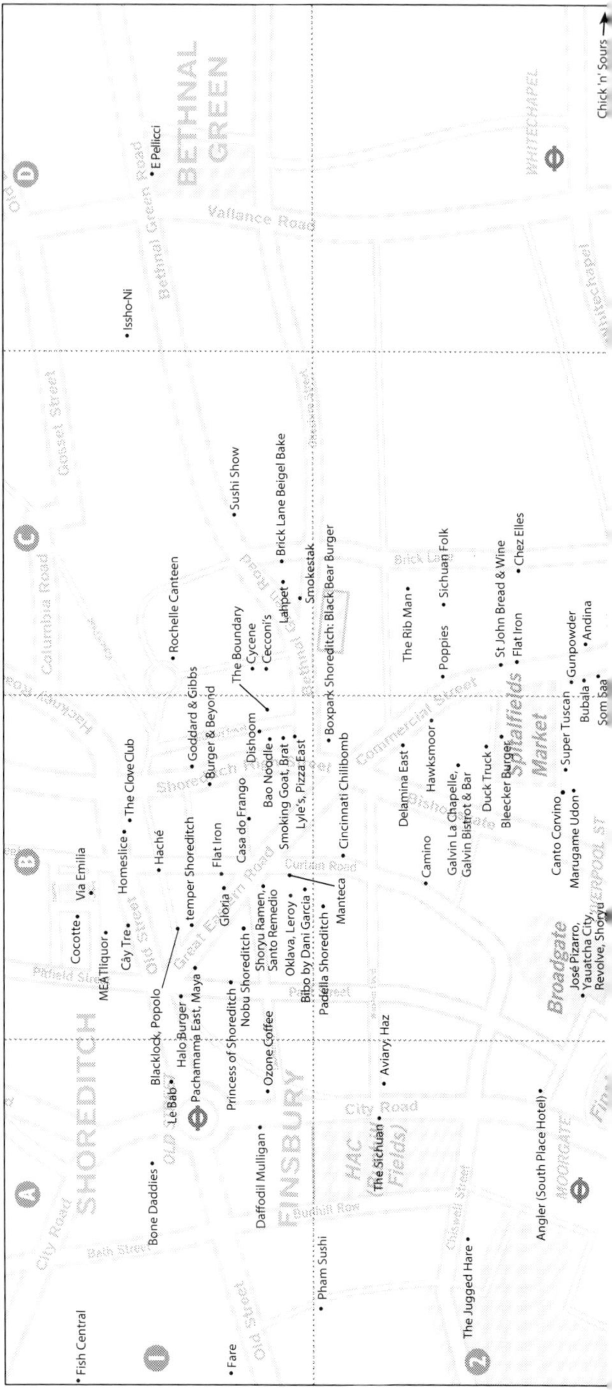

MAP 14 – EAST LONDON

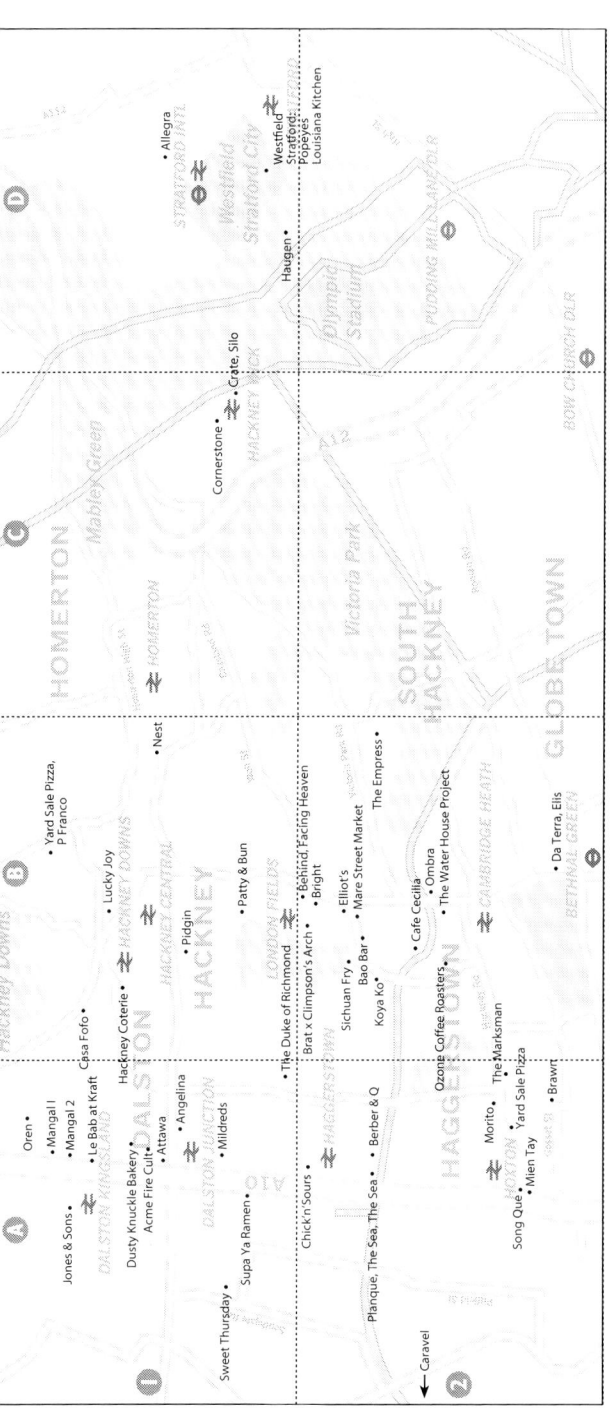